Separation of Powers

Understanding Constitutional Principles

Separation of Powers
Documents and Commentary

Edited by Katy J. Harriger

CQ PRESS

A Division of Congressional Quarterly Inc.
Washington, D.C.

CQ Press
1255 22nd Street, N.W., Suite 400
Washington, D.C. 20037

202-729-1900; toll-free: 1-866-4CQ-PRESS (1-866-427-7737)

www.cqpress.com

♾ The paper used in this publication meets the minimum requirements of the American National Standard for Information Sciences—Permanence of Paper for Printed Library Materials, ANSI Z39.48-1992.

Cover design by Gary Gore

Interior design by Auburn Associates

Printed and bound in the United States of America

07 06 05 04 03   5 4 3 2 1

Library of Congress Cataloging-in-Publication Data

Separation of powers : documents and commentary / edited by Katy J. Harriger.
    p. cm. — (Understanding constitutional principles)
Includes bibliographical references and index.
  ISBN 1-56802-727-3 (hardcover : alk. paper)
  1. Separation of powers—United States.   2. United States—Politics and government—20th century.   I. Harriger, Katy J. (Katy Jean)   II. Series.
  JK305.S465 2003
  320.473′04—dc21
                                        2002156710

Contents

List of Documents

Section IV   Supreme Court Responses to Boundary Struggles

Preface

When students of law think of the Constitution, they are probably more likely to think about the Bill of Rights and controversies over such "hot button" issues as free speech, abortion, and affirmative action than they are to consider the structure of the U.S. government. The latter they likely find less interesting, or they assume that issues concerning the separation of powers are settled. To make either of these assumptions, however, is to overlook the most important aspects of constitutionalism and the fascinating historical and contemporary political conflicts that are profoundly important to the U.S. experiment in self-government.

The founding generation's writings reveal that the Constitution's framers believed that a properly structured government was the linchpin for protecting individual liberty. They viewed the separation of powers—dividing responsibility among separate but interdependent branches of government—as the best way to avoid the concentration of power that had led in the past to abuse and the deprivation of liberty. Schooled in the classics and familiar with the writings of Montesquieu and John Locke, the framers sought to avoid the vices of monarchy and the weaknesses of previous attempts at self-government. As James Madison notes in *Federalist* No. 51, they did so by dispersing power and arming each branch with the "necessary constitutional means, and personal motives, to resist encroachments of the others." In arguing against the necessity of a Bill of Rights before ratification of the Constitution, Alexander Hamilton contended in *Federalist* No. 84 that the Constitution itself protected liberty through such safeguards as the limitation on the suspension of the writ of habeas corpus and through the very structure of government. Although few people today would agree with Hamilton's view on the Bill of Rights, most should take seriously his argument that the structure of government is the most important means by which liberty is protected: Citizens and residents of the United States have depended on an independent Supreme Court and democratically elected executives and legislatures to uphold and defend their rights. At times these institutions have failed in this endeavor, but usually, when one branch has overreached in a manner that threatened liberty, one or both of the other branches have acted to rein it in.

Such institutional cooperation and conflict tell the story of U.S. constitutionalism and what it means to live in a system of separated powers. All too frequently, the version of separation of powers taught in schools is a dry one of the three branches—the legislative, executive, and judicial—each with its own duties—to make the law, enforce the law, and interpret the law, respectively. Omitted from the story are the dynamism and complexity of the separation of powers in practice. The chapters and documents contained herein bring this process to life. It is difficult, if not impossible, to understand the separation of powers by examining each branch in isolation: Studying Congress alone will never present an adequate picture of how law is made, nor will a similar study of executive power elucidate the nature of the presidency in a system of separated powers. Likewise, solely focusing on the Supreme Court provides only an incomplete picture of the political process of constitutional interpretation.

Chapters one and two of *Separation of Powers* introduce historical and theoretical frameworks for understanding how the framers of the Constitution devised the U.S. system of separated powers and how it has evolved. Chapters three through five focus on the core powers of each branch of government, revealing their flux and evolution in response to events and the individuals occupying federal offices. Chapters six through twelve address a number of separation of powers issues and demonstrate the extent to which the constitutional structure invites struggle over the boundaries between the branches. Institutional battles over war making, foreign affairs, impeachment, executive privilege, and other issues are central to the separation of powers and the constitutional development of the United States.

The primary documents presented here provide further context for understanding these issues. They include excerpts from philosophers who shaped the thinking of the framers, the writings of some of the major figures of the founding generation, and congressional, presidential, and judicial responses to the boundary struggles discussed in the chapters.

The editor of a volume such as this one always owes much to many. In particular I would like to thank the authors of the essays—political scientists, historians, lawyers, and political practitioners—who share a passion for understanding and explaining the separation of powers in all of its dynamism and complexity. I am especially grateful to John Dinan, my colleague at Wake Forest University, and Christopher Anzalone, acquisitions editor at CQ Press, who helped identify and locate documents, and to Robin Surratt, project editor at CQ Press, who edited the essays and documents. Finally, I am grateful for the longtime mentorship of the late Harold Seidman, who spent his life studying the intricacies of governance in the U.S. system and who taught me that institutions matter.

Katy J. Harriger

Contributors

About the Editor

Katy J. Harriger is professor of political science at Wake Forest University. She is the author of *The Special Prosecutor in American Politics* (2000) and *Independent Justice: The Federal Special Prosecutor in American Politics* (1992) and has published articles and essays on a variety of topics, including American constitutional law, the independent counsel, and government ethics.

About the Contributors

Richard A. Baker has directed the U.S. Senate Historical Office since its creation in 1975. He is the author of *Conservation Politics: The Senate Career of Clinton P. Anderson* (1985), *The Senate of the United States* (1988), and numerous articles on congressional history. Baker also coedited *First among Equals: Outstanding Senate Leaders of the Twentieth Century* (1991).

Neal Devins is Goodrich Professor of Law and professor of government at the College of William and Mary Marshall-Wythe School of Law. He is the author of *Shaping Constitutional Values: Elected Government, the Supreme Court, and the Abortion Dispute* (1996), coauthor of *Political Dynamics of Constitutional Law* (1992), and coeditor of *Redefining Equality* (1998) and *Federal Abortion Politics* (1995). He is also the series editor for *Constitutional Conflicts*.

John Dinan is associate professor of political science at Wake Forest University. He is the author of *Keeping the People's Liberties: Legislators, Citizens, and Judges as Guardians of Rights* (1998) and has published several articles on federalism, state constitutionalism, and U.S. political development.

Louis Fisher is a senior specialist in separation of powers with the Congressional Research Service of the Library of Congress. His many books include *The Constitution between Friends* (1978), *Constitutional Dialogues* (1988), *Political Dynamics of Constitutional Law* (1995), *Constitutional Conflicts between Congress and the President* (1997), *The Politics of Shared Power* (1998), *Congressional Abdication on War and Spending* (2000), and *American Constitutional Law* (2003). He is coeditor of the *Encyclopedia of the American Presidency* (1994).

Michael J. Gerhardt is Arthur B. Hanson Professor of Law at the College of William and Mary Marshall-Wythe School of Law. He is the author of *The Federal Appointments Process* (2000) and *The Federal Impeachment Process: A Constitutional and Historical Analysis* (2000). He is also the coauthor of the second edition of *Constitutional Theory: Arguments and Perspectives* (2000) and has published more than fifty law review articles on constitutional law.

Mark A. Graber is professor of government and politics at the University of Maryland, College Park, and adjunct professor at the University of Maryland School of Law. He is the author of *Rethinking Abortion: Equal Choice, the Constitution, and Reproductive Politics* (1996), *Transforming Free Speech: The Ambiguous Legacy of Civil Libertarianism* (1991), and *Dred Scott and the Problem of Constitutional Evil* (forthcoming). He has published more than two dozen articles on U.S. political development, political theory, and constitutionalism.

Nancy Kassop is professor of political science and international relations at the State University of New York at New Paltz. Her publications include "Expansion and Contraction: Clinton's Impact on the Scope of Presidential Power," in *The Presidency and the Law: The Clinton Legacy,* edited by David Gray Adler and Michael A. Genovese (2002); "The White House Counsel's Office," coauthored with Karen Hult and MaryAnne Borrelli, in *White House World: Transitions, Organization and Office Operations,* edited by Martha Joynt Kumar and Terry Sullivan (forthcoming 2003); "The Clinton Impeach-

ment: Untangling the Web of Conflicting Considerations," *Presidential Studies Quarterly* 30, no. 4 (December 2001); and "The Courts and the Political Branches: Interpretation, Accommodation and Autonomy," in *Politics and Constitutionalism: The Louis Fisher Connection,* edited by Robert J. Spitzer (2000).

William E. Leuchtenburg is professor emeritus of history at the University of North Carolina at Chapel Hill. He is the author or editor of several books, including *In the Shadow of FDR: From Harry Truman to George W. Bush* (2001), *The FDR Years* (1995), and *The Supreme Court Reborn: The Constitutional Revolution in the Age of Roosevelt* (1995).

Harold C. Relyea is a specialist in national government with the Congressional Research Service (CRS) of the Library of Congress. Since joining CRS in 1971, he has produced a number of major studies for Congress, including analyses of the office and powers of the president, executive branch organization and management, congressional oversight, and various aspects of government information policy and practice. His publications include *Silencing Science: National Security Controls and Scientific Communication* (1994), *Federal Information Policies in the 1990s* (1996), and *The Executive Office of the President* (1997).

Thomas O. Sargentich is professor of law and co-director of the Program on Law and Government at the American University Washington College of Law. He was the editor of *An Administrative Law Anthology* (1994), is coediting *Major Acts of Congress* (forthcoming), and has written numerous articles on the separation of powers and checks and balances, the adminis- trative process, and topics in constitutional law.

Keith E. Whittington is associate professor of politics at Princeton University. He is the au- thor of *Constitutional Construction: Divided Powers and Constitutional Meanings* (1999), *Constitutional Interpretation: Textual Mean- ing, Original Intent, and Judicial Review* (1999), and articles on U.S. constitutional theory and development, federalism, and the presidency.

Separation of Powers

Lame duck president John Adams signing judicial commissions for forty-two fellow Federalists on his last night in office. Although the Senate had previously confirmed these "midnight appointments," four justices of the peace—including William Marbury—did not receive their commissions when Adams's outgoing secretary of state (and incoming chief justice of the United States), John Marshall, failed to deliver them. James Madison, newly elected president Thomas Jefferson's secretary of state, refused to deliver the commissions, leading Marbury to ask the Supreme Court to force him to do so. The decision in Marbury v. Madison *(1803) emphatically established the principle of federal judicial review and the Court's power to declare acts of Congress unconstitutional. Despite the Marshall Court's assertion of this power, it was rarely exercised until the twentieth century, when judicial review became integral in settling separation of powers disputes among the three branches of government.* Source: National Geographic Society

CHAPTER ONE

The Separation of Powers at the Founding

KEITH E. WHITTINGTON

The concept of the separation of powers emerged at the founding of the United States based on theory and practice. It was, however, only partially developed. Although the purpose of separating powers within government was clear to the founding generation, the most appropriate manner in which to do it was not. In an extraordinary flurry of constitutional experimentation in the years during and immediately after the revolution, Americans tested various political arrangements and practices. Some of these experiments were short-lived and quickly abandoned, others found greater favor and proved more enduring, but all were subject to constant tinkering, adjustment, and further development over time. The founders left a great deal to be worked out by those who had to operate within the constitutional framework that they had designed.

In the early days of the Republic, the idea of the separation of powers was still a fairly recent one in the history of political thought. The development of such a doctrine required an appropriate categorization of government powers and the belief that those powers should be allocated. The basic distinction among the legislative, executive, and judicial powers of government was not always so fundamental. In medieval conceptions of law, for example, all government officials were understood to be concerned with the clarification and application of the natural law. The modern idea of a legislative, or law*making*, power required the secularization of government and political authority and a shift away from thinking of government as primarily concerned with resolving disputes. Moreover, in a time in which all government powers were often consolidated in the hands of a single official—a monarch—abstracting the things government did into such categories as legislative or executive was by no means obvious.

Developments in Europe

Political struggles in Britain pushed forward the development of notions of the separation of powers. Building on classical political thought, Britain was long understood to have a mixed, or balanced, constitution, one embodying elements of monarchy, aristocracy, and democracy. These elements also happened to be embodied in separate institutions: the king, the House of Lords, and the House of Commons. As tensions and eventually war developed between Parliament, or more specifically the

Commons, and the king, the groundwork was laid for making functional distinctions between those competing institutions. Given that few wished to abandon the monarchy altogether, the key issue became finding the proper role for a monarch within an increasingly parliamentarian system.[1]

As the seventeenth century progressed, the proper relationship between king and Parliament came increasingly to be one of executive and legislature. In 1643, for example, a supporter of Parliament, Philip Hunton, distinguished a "legislative" from a "Gubernative or Executive" power. The former was centrally defined as "the power of making new Lawes," though Hunton also included Parliament's traditional power to raise taxes since the power to make law and raise taxes "have such a neernesse, that they cannot be divided."[2] Thirteen years later, in the widely circulated *Excellencie of a Free State*, which was still read in revolutionary America, Marchamont Nedham argued that it was a grave error to permit "the Legislative and Executive Powers of a State, to rest in one and the same hands and persons."[3] The legislative power, "the Power of making, altering, or repealing Laws," was properly located in a representative assembly which could respond to "matters of grievance . . . such are obvious to the people, who best know where the shooe pinches them."[4] The executive power "is derived from the other" and involves "the administration of Government, in the Execution of those Laws," always "accountable to the peoples Assemblies."[5] A few decades later, the philosopher John Locke observed that in all "well-framed Governments" the "Legislative and Executive Power are in distinct hands."[6] Those powers must be kept separate

so that the people "shall be govern'd by *declared Laws,* or else their Peace, Quiet, and Property will still be at the same uncertainty, as it was in the state of Nature."[7]

The British learned the benefits of separating legislative and executive power through bitter experience, and their initial efforts to articulate the distinction between these two kinds of political power had immediate political purposes. King Charles I, responding to his parliamentary challengers in 1642, described the Commons as "an excellent conserver of liberty, but never intended for any share in government." Even if it were to absorb all the powers of government to itself, it would still be obliged to establish "some close committee" to administer the government since the Commons was "incapable of transacting affairs of state with the necessary secrecie and expedition."[8] After seven years of civil war, Charles was impeached and executed by Parliament. The operation of the Long Parliament gave even parliamentary supporters pause, however. Even as Charles was meeting his end, the lawyer John Sadler wrote, "[I]f Lawmakers be judges, of those that break their Laws; they seem to be Judge in their own cause: which our Law, and Nature it self, so much avoideth and abhorreth, so it seemeth also to forbid, both the Lawmaker and the Judge to Execute."[9] Sadler was among the first to clearly distinguish the judicial as a third function of government. The poet and pamphleteer John Milton, among others, later admitted that even a legislative government would need a small council "for the carrying on some particular affairs with more secrecy and expedition."[10] Locke likewise observed that a legislative assembly "is usually too numerous; and so too slow, for the dispatch requisite to Execution."[11]

He further fleshed out the executive power by recognizing the need for executive discretion since "it is impossible to foresee, and so by laws provide for, all Accidents and Necessities, that may concern the publick" and other things for "which the Law can by no means provide," ultimately including, Locke thought, international relations.[12]

Although the idea of the separation of powers had been previously developed, no one was more influential in formalizing and popularizing it than Montesquieu, the French nobleman and intellectual. Montesquieu gave canonical form to the concept in his 1748 political masterpiece, *The Spirit of the Laws*. In a chapter on the "constitution of England," he states plainly, "All would be lost if the same man or the same body of principal men, either of the nobles, or of the people, exercised these three powers: that of making the laws, that of executing public resolutions, and that of judging the crimes or the disputes of individuals."[13] He clearly distinguished the principle of separation of powers from classical concerns, with a balanced government that would represent each of the major divisions of society in a separate political institution, or from modern concerns, with a democratic government that preserves liberty by making governors accountable to the people. He concluded that the relatively democratic Italian republics still "provide less liberty than in our monarchies" because these "three powers are united."[14] In addition to identifying these three basic powers and calling for their institutional separation, Montesquieu also urged the adoption of checks and balances. If liberty is to be preserved, "power must check power by the arrangement of things."[15] In particular, "[i]f the executive

power does not have the right to check the enterprises of the legislative body, the latter will be despotic, for it will wipe out all the other powers."[16] A veto power over legislation would allow the executive "to defend himself" and force the branches of government either "to move in concert" or not move at all.[17] At the same time, however, the legislature must have the right and the means "to examine the manner in which the laws it has made have been executed."[18] A good constitution cannot allow "the raising of public funds without the consent of the legislature" or else the "executive power will become the legislator on the most important point of legislation"; the executive must be made dependent on the legislature.[19] Similarly, the raising, funding, and demobilization of armies must be controlled by the legislature, though their direction must be controlled by the executive, "as its concern is more with action than with deliberation."[20]

It is difficult to know how much influence a writer actually has on political events. Just as Montesquieu and other writers drew lessons from the British experience, so the Americans drew on their own experience with British political and legal institutions to reach many of the same conclusions. On the eve of the American Revolution, the prominent Virginia patriot Patrick Henry declared he could only be guided by "the lamp of experience," and at the federal Constitutional Convention of 1787 John Dickinson, a respected Philadelphia attorney, echoed Henry in warning his colleagues that "experience must be our only guide."[21] At the same time, the "spirit" of political theorists such as Montesquieu "permeated the debates" of the revolutionary and founding eras even when they were not explicitly cited.[22] The thoughts, words, and names of these writers were often employed by partisans seeking to explain, justify, and win support for their political and constitutional positions. Montesquieu was, in fact, the most cited author in public debates in America during the last decades of the eighteenth century.[23]

The Colonial Experience

Although European writers gave shape to American ideas about constitutionalism, the details of constitutional arrangements remained in a constant state of development in the late eighteenth century. As historian Jack Rakove has noted, there were "no simple formulas to determine the exact form the new government should take. . . . [A] wide number of solutions could be made compatible with the first principles of republicanism."[24] The drafting of the U.S. Constitution at Philadelphia came near the end of the flurry of constitution making that was launched with the American Revolution. Of course, the original federal constitution, the Articles of Confederation, had been adopted in 1778. By the time the Constitution was ratified in 1788, the original thirteen states had adopted fifteen constitutions. Eight more state constitutions would be drafted and adopted during the subsequent decade, including those for the two new states of Kentucky and Tennessee.[25] As James Madison observed, these early state constitutions often "carry strong marks of the haste, and still stronger of the inexperience, under which they were framed," but they still provided useful lessons to the founders of the federal constitution "the sense in which [the principle of separation of powers] has hitherto been understood in America."[26]

The British colonies in North America had constitutional experience even before their revolutionary declarations of independence. One constitutional historian argues, "Very probably the decisive step in the development of the American variety of constitutions was made when the crown granted charters to certain individuals under which they were to be allowed to plant colonies in the new world." These charters served as "instruments of government beyond the power of the companies, the proprietors, or the colonists to alter" and were supplemented by locally generated constitutional documents.[27] Connecticut and Rhode Island continued to operate under their colonial charters until well into the nineteenth century. In short, British constitutional traditions were imported into the colonies, and among these imports was a form of separation of powers. The governors were often the king's appointed representatives in the colonies, but they found their power repeatedly challenged and eroded by elected colonial assemblies that asserted the right to act as legislatures, including the power to control the public purse. One of many points of tension between the governors and the assemblies was the organization of colonial courts. Although assemblies eventually won the right to participate in the creation of new courts, governors continued to insist that judges only served at the pleasure of the Crown rather than for fixed terms or during good behavior as the assemblies wanted.[28]

The colonial experience had important implications for American thinking about constitutionalism in general and the separation of powers in particular. At the most basic level, Americans inherited a set of constitutional, political, and legal ideas and institutions from

Britain, including constitutional thinking about the proper division between legislative and executive powers that emerged from the turbulent seventeenth century. The colonists were, importantly, children of the parliamentary revolution in Britain and held to some of those ideals even after the British themselves had moved on.[29] The added context of being colonists in an empire had particular consequences for American thinking about the separation of powers, however.[30] Since the governor was the imperial arm in the colony, and as such was bestowed with royal prerogatives greater than those enjoyed by the king in Britain, the Americans gained a robust distrust of gubernatorial power and an appreciation for politically restraining the executive. At the same time, however, many of the colonial grievances that built up in the years leading to the revolution were directed at the Parliament. A central struggle of these years was the degree of local autonomy to be enjoyed by the North American colonies. Parliamentary authority in Britain had grown enormously over the course of the eighteenth century, and thus it was Parliament that took action in the prerevolutionary years to reassert British dominion over the colonies and displace the colonial assemblies. Parliament was the target of revolutionary cries of "no taxation without representation" when it claimed the authority, against the colonial assemblies, to pass such legislation as the 1765 Stamp Act. In the colonists' eyes, "the Commons had become part of the ministerial conspiracy against liberty; the lower house now was the enemy of the people, not their protector."[31] The colonial experience made evident to Americans that legislatures could also be abusive and thus required constitutional checks against them.

The First American Constitutions

For most of the colonies, the adoption of a state constitution was part and parcel of declaring independence from Britain. The Pennsylvania provincial congress's call for the election of delegates to the first state constitutional convention reminded voters, "Your liberty, safety, happiness, and everything that posterity will hold dear to them, to the end of time, will depend upon their deliberations."[32] The proper separation of powers was widely regarded as central to that task. Many of the early state constitutions declared, as did the Virginia Constitution of 1776, "The legislative, executive, and judiciary departments shall be separate and distinct, so that neither exercise the powers properly belonging to the other: nor shall any person exercise the powers of more than one of them at the same time."[33] Indeed, one of the many complaints made against the proposed U.S. Constitution was that it did not include such an explicit statement of the principle in its text. Madison responded to such complaints by emphasizing that the principle of separation of powers was embodied in the constitutional design, and that an effective structure of checks and balances was far more important to maintaining such a separation than the mere "parchment barrier" of a declaration of principle.[34] Even so, popular opinion on the issue was such that an amendment making that principle explicit was nearly included as part of the Bill of Rights.[35]

The Articles of Confederation had created a federal Congress but no independent executive or judiciary. Rather, executive and judicial officials were directly appointed and controlled by the federal legislature. Congress first attempted to perform executive functions through legislative committees but later appointed boards, before finally creating departments headed by single executives in an effort to improve performance.[36] Gen. George Washington repeatedly complained about the "Delay, the Waste, and unpunishable Neglect of Duty" resulting from the reliance on multimember committees to organize and supply the Revolutionary War effort.[37] Washington's aide, Alexander Hamilton, was among those who pressed for the creation of executive departments, calling for "a Minister of War, a Minister for foreign Affairs, a minister for Finance and a Minister of marine. There is always more decision, more dispatch, more secrecy, more responsibility where single men, than when bodies are concerned." Congress had simply "kept the power too much into their own hands and have meddled too much with details of every sort" in attempting "to play the executive."[38] John Jay's experience as ambassador to Spain and secretary of foreign affairs had convinced him that the three powers of government "should be forever separated," for in Congress "so much time is spent in deliberation, that the season for action often passes by before they decide on what should be done."[39] Such sentiments were commonplace and fed the desire for constitutional reform that would not only give new power to the national government but would restructure the government so that it could more effectively meet the responsibilities it already had.

Similar lessons were being learned at the state level in the years during and immediately following the revolution. The states did not generally attempt to eliminate the executive and judiciary, but rather sought to enhance the power and authority of the legislature. One anonymous Philadelphia writer set the tone, observing, "The executive power is ever restless, ambitious, and ever grasping at encrease of power."[40] The reconstituted governor of Virginia was to be, according to Thomas Jefferson, "solely executive," an "Administrator" without independent legislative or policymaking powers, including that of declaring war.[41] In most states, governors were given no power to veto legislation. They were to be elected, with short terms, subject to legislative impeachment and removal, and often with constitutional limits on the number of consecutive terms that an individual could hold the office. Fearful of the type of power the royal governors had gained by handing out offices, titles, and honors, the drafters of the revolutionary constitutions generally shifted the power of appointing executive and judicial officials either to the legislature alone or to the legislature and executive acting together. They also prohibited legislators from holding other government offices. Colonial judges had been subject to appointment and removal by the governor, so the new constitutions sharply limited gubernatorial control of the judiciary. A primary concern with keeping judicial power accountable, however, left few constitutional barriers against legislative tampering with the courts. The ability of citizens to petition legislatures to redress even their private grievances also tended to blur the distinction between the legislative and judicial power, allowing the legislature to intervene in lawsuits and even overturn judicial rulings.[42] Early constitutions also created small elected executive councils to advise the governor and, in some cases, exercise a veto over his actions.

The initial thrust of American constitution making at the state and national levels was toward legislative dominance, with somewhat indistinct separations between the legislative and the other spheres of government. Nonetheless, it was well recognized that effective constitutional limits needed to be placed on even electorally accountable legislatures. As the colonial governments collapsed during the revolution, "provincial congresses" initially assumed political power. Understood to be emergency conventions rather than ordinary legislatures, the conventions drafted initial state constitutions while simultaneously operating the government and conducting the war. The operation of these conventions provoked stern warnings from local political leaders and the press about the dangers of too much power being exercised by "the same person, or persons."[43]

The principle of separation of powers had initially encouraged the American states to eliminate the gubernatorial veto over legislation, insisting "that the persons appointed to hold the executive power, have no share or negative in the legislature."[44] In a pure separation of powers, a governor who held the executive power could not also participate in the legislative process through the veto power. The difficult problem of restraining legislative power, however, suggested the need for the introduction of checks and balances. Constitutional checks could be created only by compromising the rigid separation of powers. The executive officer, for example, could be given a veto over legislation in order to help restrain the legislature and prevent it from encroaching on the proper duties of the executive branch. John Adams argued that "without this Weapon of Defence [the governor] will be run down

like a Hare before the Hunters."[45] In 1780 Massachusetts adopted a constitution that influentially included a limited gubernatorial veto, giving the governor a period of time in which to exercise the veto and allowing the legislature an opportunity to override the veto with a two-thirds vote. The other states gradually adopted this model for an executive veto as, of course, did the framers of the U.S. Constitution.[46]

The Constitution of the United States

The movement to write a new federal constitution was motivated as much by unhappiness with the performance of the state legislatures as with that of the Congress under the Articles of Confederation. Nonetheless, devising a system for the separation of powers was a basic aspect of the task of those who gathered in Philadelphia in the summer of 1787 for the Constitutional Convention. Indeed, the initial proposals for a new constitution introduced at the convention called for a separation of government powers, and on the second day of deliberations the convention resolved "that a national governt ought to be established consisting of a supreme Legislative Executive & Judiciary," a notion that set the guidelines for subsequent debate.[47] Actually keeping the powers separate, however, proved vexing.

During the Philadelphia deliberations, for example, James Madison observed that "[I]n all the states these [state judiciaries] are more or less dependt on the Legislatures," becoming the "willing instruments of the wicked & arbitrary plans of their [legislative] masters."[48] He thought the state executives were hardly better. The "Executives of the States are in general little more than Cyphers; the legislature omnipotent." Overall, "[e]xperience had proved a tendency in our governments to throw all power into the Legislative vortex."[49] Madison later repeated this warning when advocating the ratification of the Constitution. The document had to guard above all "against the enterprising ambition" of the legislature, which in a republic would be "inspired by a supposed influence over the people with an intrepid confidence in its own strength." In a democracy, the "legislative department is everywhere extending the sphere of its activity" against the "more feeble" branches of government.[50] It was crucial, therefore, "to provide some practical security for each, against the invasion of the others."[51]

The founders gave more attention to the problem of securing the independence of the executive than to specifying executive powers. The convention delegates quickly resolved that the executive should have "power to carry into effect the national laws, to appoint to offices in cases not otherwise provided for, and to execute such other powers not Legislative nor Judiciary in their nature as may from time to time be delegated by the national Legislature."[52] The delegates, however, had difficulty agreeing on whether the executive power should be held by one person or a council. James Wilson of Pennsylvania was perhaps most important in pushing for a single executive armed with a veto and elected directly by the people—the model of the relatively powerful New York governorship. A single executive was more capable of "energy dispatch and responsibility" and thus would be more effective and more virtuous in executing laws and appointing officers than would an executive council.[53] Ultimately,

provisions for senatorial consent to appointments and treaties weakened some of the effects of lodging so much power in one person. A veto power was essential for "[w]ithout such a self-defense the Legislature can at any moment sink it [the executive] into non-existence."[54] Wilson would have preferred an absolute veto, but a qualified veto allowing for the possibility of congressional override balanced the risks of legislative usurpation and executive obstruction.

The delegates' most vexing problem was creating the system of selecting the executive. The dominant mode in the states was through legislative appointment. Some delegates thought state governments should have some role in selecting the national executive, but Wilson and others argued "in favor of an appointment by the people" to insure that the executive would be independent of the legislature and in order to "produce more confidence among the people in the first magistrate."[55] The inventive compromise in the form of the electoral college set the presidency on an independent political foundation and soon allowed holders of the office to assert their own authority as representatives of the people.

The courts posed fewer difficulties than the other branches did for the convention delegates. Madison observed that the judiciary and the executive "expounded & applied" the laws, but the executive exercised greater discretion in conducting its duties and had greater responsibility for "the collective interest & security."[56] There was less to be feared from the judicial power, so it provoked less controversy. The judicial power itself was readily understood, and the delegates generally accepted that judges should not be dependent on others for retaining their offices or salaries. Those delegates such as Madison, who favored a strong national government, likewise favored an extensive national judiciary, for a "Government without a proper Executive & Judiciary would be a mere trunk of a body, without arms or legs to act or move."[57] Others favored relying on state courts to enforce federal laws, despite (or perhaps because of) state judges' relative lack of independence from state legislatures. The convention compromised by leaving the creation of federal trial courts to Congress. Although the judiciary was initially given jurisdiction over impeachments, delegates feared that the power would tend to draw judges into politics and "intrigues."[58]

The delegates defeated a proposal favored by Madison and others to unite the judiciary with the executive in a council of revision that would have a general veto power over legislation. On the one hand, including judges in such a council was seen as giving the judiciary some defensive check against legislative encroachment. On the other hand, the council might be understood to give judges a role in "framing the laws" and thereby subvert their independence when later "exercising the function of expositers" of the law.[59] Anticipating the power of judicial review, Luther Martin of Maryland argued that judges were not qualified to evaluate the general wisdom of legislation, but "as to the Constitutionality of laws, that point will come before the Judges in their proper official character. In this character they have a negative on the laws."[60] The founders quite self-consciously empowered the state and federal courts to review the constitutionality of state legislation, regarding such a power as essential to the goals of constitutional reform.[61]

The document that emerged from the Philadelphia convention adhered to the by-then common American model of distributing government powers across three separate branches. The Constitution of the United States recognized a basic functional distinction among legislative, executive, and judicial powers, and it prohibited one person from holding more than one office simultaneously, to prevent individuals from exercising more than one of those powers. At the same time, however, the founders had learned to distrust "parchment barriers" between the branches and were particularly concerned with arming the executive and judiciary with effective checks against the encroachments of the legislature. They also sought to create a general balance among the three branches in order to prevent individual branches from becoming too powerful, while still allowing the government as a whole to perform effectively.

"In the Course of Practice"

The initial separation of powers and the supplementary checks and balances created tensions within the constitutional structure. As Madison admitted, some of these tensions were inherent in juggling multiple political values and goals. Moreover, constitutional draftsmanship was simply an imperfect art:

> Experience has instructed us that no skill in the science of government has yet been able to discriminate and define, with sufficient certainty, its three great provinces—the legislative, executive, and judiciary; or even the privileges and powers of the different legislative branches. Questions daily occur in the course of practice which prove the obscurity which reigns in these subjects, and which puzzle the greatest adepts in political science. . . . All new laws, though penned with the greatest technical

skill and passed on the fullest and most mature deliberation, are considered as more or less obscure and equivocal, until their meaning be liquidated and ascertained by a series of particular discussions and adjudications.[62]

Disputes over the implications of the constitutional structure arose almost immediately after the new government was organized under its authority. Some resolutions formed lasting constructs that established the effective meaning of the text. Others, however, resulted only in temporary settlements that prefigured debates destined to recur in varying forms throughout U.S. history.

Among these early disputes was how to remove executive branch officials from office. Impeachment is the only mechanism that the Constitution provides for removing appointed officials against their will. The impeachment power, however, was clearly not designed for routine removals. Substantively, impeachment and removal can only be justified by the commission of "high crimes and misdemeanors." Procedurally, impeachments are difficult to accomplish and time-consuming. The Constitution states explicitly that federal judges hold office "during good behavior," which was understood to be a life term. The Constitution clearly assumes the existence of appointed executive branch officials, but it is silent about their term of office, though the founders did not seem to contemplate their holding office for life. The absence of an explicit removal power would appear to have been an oversight, so it was widely assumed that a removal power must be implicit in the text—but where? Who held the power to remove executive officers and under what circumstances?

Two months into the first session of the First Congress, the House of Representatives heard a proposal to create three executive departments—foreign affairs, treasury, and war. Madison moved for the establishment of these three departments, headed by a secretary "who shall be appointed by the President, by and with the advice of the Senate; and to be removable by the President."[63] There were quick objections to Madison's provision for presidential removal, which forced what became an elaborate constitutional debate on the removal power. The first possibility raised was that there was no implicit removal power; impeachment was the only constitutional option for removing officials. As James Jackson of Georgia pointed out, the Constitution placed in the House of Representatives the sole power of impeachment, and "if the House had the power of removal by the Constitution, they could not give it out of their hands; because every power recognized by the constitution must remain where it was placed by that instrument."[64] There was relatively little support for this position on the floor of the House, however.

Others understood Madison's proposal as simply making explicit where the Constitution had already placed the removal power. John Vining of Delaware, among others, instead argued that "there were no negative words in the constitution to preclude the President from the exercise of this power; but there was a strong presumption that he was invested with it: because it was declared, that all executive power should be vested in him, except in cases where it is otherwise qualified," such as the requirement that the Senate advise and consent to presidential appointments.[65] In this reading, there was an implicit but inherent presidential power of unilateral removal, though it might be "prudent to make a legislative declaration of the sentiments of Congress on this point" to remove all doubts.[66]

A third position held that "the power which appointed should remove."[67] The Senate had an essential role in the appointments process, which "would be rendered almost nugatory if the President had the power of removal."[68] If the removal power were to parallel the appointment power, then officers could not be removed by the president without the consent of the Senate. Just as the president could not undo a treaty ratified by the Senate, it was said, so the president could not undo an appointment confirmed by the Senate.[69]

In response, Madison sketched out yet another possibility. "Congress may establish offices by law; therefore, most certainly, it is in the discretion of the Legislature to say upon what terms the office shall be held, either during good behavior or during pleasure. Under this construction, the principles of the constitution would be reconcilable in every part."[70] In this reading, there was no implicit constitutional power of removal to be discovered. Instead, Congress held the power to fill this gap in the constitutional design legislatively, in keeping with its constitutional authority "To make all Laws which shall be necessary and proper for carrying into Execution . . . Powers vested by this Constitution in the Government of the United States." Madison later endorsed the idea of an inherent presidential authority of removal that Congress could not modify, but others insisted that the removal power was a matter of legislative discretion and not "executive in its nature."[71]

This congressional debate lasted for days. The representatives developed their arguments in great detail and marshaled every variety of evidence and consideration. On the one side stood those who thought the Senate had a share of the "executive" removal power. On the other side stood those who thought the president alone should exercise this authority, though some thought the power was inherent in the presidency and others thought the power needed to be delegated to the chief executive by statute. The majority favored presidential removal, but no majority existed for any single theory of the removal power. Representatives eventually (and narrowly) passed a bill that included language implying an inherent presidential removal authority, but there was no consensus behind that view.[72]

During this era of gentlemanly politics, removals were not made lightly, but uncertainty over who possessed removal power remained, with lingering consequences. As political parties were established and partisan conflict became routine, executive appointments and removals took on new significance. By the mid-nineteenth century, legislators had a personal stake in most appointments, and the control of executive offices was a source of party power. Newly elected presidents were expected to clean house and fill the executive branch with their own partisans. The early rise of senatorial privilege, in which fellow senators and presidents were expected to defer to the appointment preferences of individual senators regarding offices based in their own states, reflected the pragmatic accommodations made in relation to this shared power.

Appointment politics have often been a source of conflict between the president and the Senate, and the removal power has been a related point of tension. President Andrew

Johnson's impeachment resulted from his attempt to remove Secretary of War Edwin Stanton, whom he inherited from Abraham Lincoln, in defiance of a congressional statute attempting to stay dismissals of executive officials. Later in the nineteenth century, civil service reform and the creation of independent regulatory commissions limited the circumstances under which presidents could remove certain officials. Similarly and more recently, the statute allowing independent counsels stated that they would not serve at the pleasure of the president but rather could only be removed from office for cause. Such statutory innovations would not be possible if the removal power were an inherent feature of the executive authority vested in the president by the Constitution.

Such boundary disputes between the various branches of government arose in numerous contexts in the early Republic and continue to do so. Even such basic issues as how Congress should address the president—"His Highness the President"?—and whether the president should physically appear in Congress and speak directly with legislators required debate and decision. Early presidents struggled with any number of issues: whether Congress was entitled to see all documents produced in the executive branch or whether some information was privileged; whether the Senate had to be asked for its "advice" during treaty negotiations or whether its "consent" could simply be acquired in the form of ratification after a treaty had been signed; whether the executive could spend more public funds than Congress had appropriated to meet contingencies or whether the executive was obliged to always seek legislative approval before drawing from the public purse. Fewer but still significant disagreements surrounding the courts likewise arose. Working out the judiciary's place within the separation of powers became particularly pressing once the supporters of Thomas Jefferson swept the elections of 1800 only to face a federal judiciary filled with their political opponents. Administration officials and supporters were soon faced with deciding important issues, including what behavior might justify the impeachment of a judge; whether judicial offices could be abolished and the judiciary reorganized without violating judicial independence; whether the federal courts could issue commands to the president as to how laws should be executed, and whether judges should be active in electoral politics; and, of course, whether courts had the power to ignore laws that were thought to violate the Constitution.

Conclusion

Some basic principles of U.S. governance had been settled prior to the drafting of the Constitution. The abstract ideal of the separation of powers had received wide praise. State and previous national constitutions tended to organize government into three basic units, though the legislative branch tended to be predominant. It was a well-known political maxim that no single individual or group of individuals should occupy more than one of these three seats of power, but it was also recognized that some overlapping powers would be necessary to check against subversion of the constitutional design or the abuse of political power. The details of how to balance the three branches against one another or what powers belonged in the legislative, executive, or judicial sphere were still subject to disagreement. The delegates who helped draft the Constitution worked out some of those details. Many others remained for those who followed.

Notes

1. Scott Gordon, *Controlling the State: Constitutionalism from Ancient Athens to Today* (New York: Oxford University Press, 1999), 223–283.
2. W. B. Gwyn, *The Meaning of the Separation of Powers: An Analysis of the Doctrine from Its Origins to the Adoption of the United States Constitution* (New Orleans: Tulane University Press, 1965), 31.
3. Ibid., appendix p. 131.
4. Ibid., appendix p. 131 and p. 31.
5. Ibid., appendix p. 131 and p. 32.
6. John Locke, *Two Treatises of Government*, ed. Peter Laslett (New York: Cambridge University Press, 1988), Second Treatise, sec. 159.
7. Ibid., sec. 136.
8. Gwyn, *Meaning of the Separation of Powers*, 32.
9. M. J. C. Vile, *Constitutionalism and the Separation of Powers*, 2d ed. (Indianapolis: Liberty Fund, 1998), 50.
10. Gwyn, *Meaning of the Separation of Powers*, 32.
11. Locke, *Second Treatise of Government*, sec. 160.
12. Ibid., sec. 159.
13. Charles Louis de Secondat Montesquieu, *The Spirit of the Laws*, ed. Anne Cohler, Basia Miller, and Harold Stone (New York: Cambridge University Press, 1989), 157.
14. Ibid.
15. Ibid., 155.
16. Ibid., 162.
17. Ibid., 164.
18. Ibid., 162.
19. Ibid., 164.
20. Ibid., 165.
21. H. Trevor Colbourn, *The Lamp of Experience: Whig History and the Intellectual Origins of the American Revolution* (New York: W. W. Norton, 1974), viii; Forrest McDonald, *Novus Ordo Seclorum: The Intellectual Origins of the Constitution* (Lawrence: University Press of Kansas, 1985), 7.
22. McDonald, *Novus Ordo Seclorum*, 7.
23. Donald S. Lutz, "The Relative Influence of European Writers on Late Eighteenth-Century American Political Thought," *American Political Science Review* 78 (1984): 192–195.
24. Jack N. Rakove, *Original Meanings: Politics and Ideas in the Making of the Constitution* (New York: Vintage, 1996), 19.
25. G. Alan Tarr, *Understanding State Constitutions* (Princeton, N.J.: Princeton University Press, 1998), 61.
26. James Madison, *Federalist* No. 47, in Alexander Hamilton, James Madison, and John Jay, *The Federalist Papers,* ed. Clinton Rossiter (New York: New American Library, 1961), 307–308.
27. Benjamin F. Wright Jr., "The Early History of Written Constitutions in America," in *Essays in History and Political Theory in Honor of Charles Howard McIlwain,* ed. Carl Wittke (Cambridge, Mass.: Harvard University Press, 1936), 346.
28. Alfred H. Kelly, Winfred A. Harbison, and Herman Belz, *The American Constitution: Its Origins and Development,* 7th ed. (New York: W. W. Norton, 1991), 1:1–40.
29. Louis Hartz, *The Founding of New Societies* (New York: Harcourt, Brace and World, 1964); Bernard Bailyn, *The Ideological Origins of the American Revolution* (Cambridge, Mass.: Harvard University Press, 1967); John Phillip Reid, *Constitutional History of the American Revolution* (Madison: University of Wisconsin Press, 1987–1993).
30. Jack P. Greene, *Peripheries and Center: Constitutional Development in the Extended Polities of the British Empire and the United States, 1607–1788* (Athens: University of Georgia Press, 1986).
31. Marc W. Kruman, *Between Authority and Liberty: State Constitution Making in Revolutionary America* (Chapel Hill: University of North Carolina Press, 1997), 9.
32. Ibid., 17.
33. Ibid., 110.
34. James Madison, *Federalist* No. 48, in *Federalist Papers,* 308.
35. David E. Kyvig, *Explicit and Authentic Acts: Amending the U.S. Constitution, 1776–1995* (Lawrence: University Press of Kansas, 1996), 104.

36. Charles C. Thach Jr., *The Creation of the American Presidency: A Study in Constitutional History* (Baltimore: Johns Hopkins University Press, 1923).

37. Louis Fisher, "The Efficiency Side of Separated Powers," *Journal of American Studies* 5 (1971): 116.

38. Ibid., 118.

39. Ibid., 120, 121.

40. Gordon S. Wood, *The Creation of the American Republic, 1776–1787* (New York: W. W. Norton, 1972), 135.

41. Ibid., 136, 137.

42. Edward S. Corwin, "The Progress of Constitutional History between the Declaration of Independence and the Meeting of the Philadelphia Convention," *American Historical Review* 30 (1925): 511–536.

43. Kruman, *Between Authority and Liberty,* 113.

44. Ibid., 123.

45. Ibid., 125.

46. John A. Farlie, "The Veto Power of the State Governor," *American Political Science Review* 11 (1917): 473–493.

47. James Madison, *Notes of Debates in the Federal Convention of 1787* (New York: W. W. Norton, 1987), 36.

48. Ibid., 305.

49. Ibid., 312.

50. Madison, *Federalist* No. 48, 309.

51. Ibid., 308.

52. Madison, *Notes of Debates in the Federal Convention of 1787,* 47.

53. Ibid., 46.

54. Ibid., 61.

55. Ibid., 49, 50.

56. Ibid., 311.

57. Ibid., 72.

58. Ibid., 315.

59. Ibid., 338.

60. Ibid., 340.

61. Rakove, *Original Meanings,* 171–180.

62. James Madison, *Federalist* No. 37, in *Federalist Papers,* 228–229.

63. *Annals of Congress,* 1st Cong., 1st sess., 1789, 1:385.

64. Ibid., 1:389.

65. Ibid., 1:388.

66. Ibid.

67. Ibid., 1:389.

68. Ibid., 1:388.

69. Ibid., 1:397.

70. Ibid., 1:389.

71. Ibid., 1:490.

72. David P. Currie, *The Constitution in Congress: The Federalist Period, 1789–1801* (Chicago: University of Chicago Press, 1997), 36–41.

CHAPTER TWO

The Separation of Powers in the Modern Context

KATY J. HARRIGER

The founders and the first few Congresses under the new Constitution did not settle the meaning of the separation of powers doctrine. Rather, as Keith Whittington notes, the first interpreters of the doctrine engaged in "constitutional experimentation," and the institutional arrangements were subject to "constant tinkering, adjustment, and further development."[1] The doctrine of the separation of powers is an evolving one that has maintained certain basic principles from its inception but has also adapted as the United States has grown and changed. Examination of the doctrine in its twentieth- and twenty-first-century contexts reveals several key elements important to a contemporary understanding of it. First, changes in the major institutions of the U.S. government were of significant import in shaping the larger separation of powers doctrine and influencing the way in which politics is practiced in the United States. Second, the doctrine has been constantly contested, with disagreement among institutional actors, political parties, and political and legal scholars about how best to interpret and implement it. Third, the nature of this contest is evident in the decisions of the Supreme Court, which has been quite active in the last several decades in attempting to define the boundaries of each government institution's powers. The separation of powers in practice and the separation of powers in legal theory have not always coincided, a reminder that in understanding constitutional interpretations, it is important to look not only at the Supreme Court's opinions on the subject but to examine the behavior of other institutional actors as well.

Evolving Institutions and Power Shifts

The primary institutions of U.S. government—the legislative, executive, and judicial branches—have changed since the early days of the Republic. Additionally, the relationships among the branches have also changed as power has shifted in response to institutional developments and larger social and political forces.

Several significant constitutional changes have affected the legislative branch since the founding. The Civil War amendments—particularly the Fourteenth and Fifteenth Amendments—gave Congress an additional source of lawmaking authority vis-à-vis state governments. The Seventeenth Amendment made senators subject to popular election rather than to election by state legislatures as had been established in the 1787 Constitution. During the nineteenth century Congress was the dominant institution in the U.S. government, which is what the framers had planned. Between the nineteenth and twentieth centuries, however, its institutional powers shifted significantly. A number of factors contributed to an ebbing of congressional power in relation to the executive and the judiciary: the increased demand and authority for national action in the post–Civil War period (following adoption of the Fourteenth Amendment in 1878 and the Fifteenth Amendment in 1880) and during the New Deal (in the 1930s and 1940s), the emergence of the United States as an actor on the world stage after World Wars I and II, and the authority exerted by the Supreme Court through its increased exercise of judicial review in the latter part of the twentieth century. In a larger, more complex, and more nationalized politics, Congress found the need to delegate more of its authority to executive and independent regulatory agencies. The president's ability to act quickly preempted its foreign affairs and war powers. Some observers assert that in the age of the constant media campaign, Congress has found it preferable to abdicate much of its constitutional authority in politically difficult situations or to use its authority irresponsibly,[2] knowing that the Supreme Court will rectify its failings.[3]

The modern presidency is far different from the one that operated for much of the first century of the Republic. As Congress's star has fallen, the executive's has risen, advantaged by its ability to act with secrecy and dispatch and to monopolize public attention in the image-driven age of television. Discussion of the modern presidency requires consideration of the oc-cupant of the office in roles far beyond those granted in Article 2 of the Constitution, including those as manager of the economy, chief of party, and at one point the so-called leader of the free world.[4] The constitutional powers of commander in chief, chief diplomat, and nominator of judges and cabinet officers have been enhanced by foreign and domestic opportunities that present themselves in the modern political context. This shift in power to the presidency has not come without a struggle or the recognition by Congress that it has lost ground to the executive. Periodic efforts by Congress to regain some authorities, such as the War Powers Resolution, the Budget and Impoundment Control Act, and the Ethics in Government Act, all passed in the 1970s, have demonstrated what James Madison hoped for in defending the constitutional checks and balances scheme in 1787—that "ambition would be made to check ambition,"[5] and the branches would be ever vigilant to efforts by the others to usurp their power. Although the struggle continues, at the start of the twenty-first century the president is clearly stronger and the Congress clearly weaker, which was not the case in the first American century.

The Supreme Court and the federal judiciary more generally have gained more power since their inception. The principle of judicial review was established in *Marbury v. Madison* (1803), but it was not much exercised until the twentieth century, as government grew and the Fourteenth Amendment invited federal challenges to state action. Between 1803 and 1910, the Court found only 35 acts of Congress to be unconstitutional. From 1910 until 1998, 117 acts of Congress were overturned through judicial review.[6] The Court's decisions have checked presidential power as well as legislative power at the national and state levels. Although it is now apparent that the Court rarely has "the last word" and is unlikely in the long run to prevail in an interpretation of the Constitution that the White House, Congress, and the public disagree with,[7] in the short-term the Court can have, and has had, a significant impact on the branches and the interplay of power between them. For example, its unanimous decision in *United States v. Nixon* (1974) sealed the fate of President Richard Nixon and made it more likely that under pressure from Congress he would resign rather than be impeached. Its 4-3 opinion in *Bush v. Gore* (2000) decided who would succeed Bill Clinton as president.

The dimensions of the separation of powers doctrine cannot be fully understood without examining the three branches of government in relation to each other. Rarely does one branch exercise its power free of the influence of at least one of the other two. While basic agreement exists that each branch should be relatively independent of the others in exercising its duties, the history of the separation of powers doctrine demonstrates that the boundaries of executive, legislative, and judicial power are not static. Rather, they shift over time with the workings of the political process.

Formalism v. Functionalism

Among contemporary scholars of the separation of powers there are two primary and competing theories of how the doctrine should be understood and interpreted. These concepts—formalism and functionalism—find their way into decisions by the Supreme Court, critiques

of Court opinions, arguments about how the Court should exercise its power, and policy justifications by members of Congress and sitting administrations.

Formalism argues that the powers of each branch are exclusive to it unless the Constitution specifically says otherwise. Thus, while the lawmaking power belongs almost exclusively to Congress, the president does have a constitutionally granted role in the lawmaking process through the veto power. While the judicial power is almost exclusively that of the federal courts, Congress exercises judicial power in the impeachment process. Formalists conclude that exclusivity is assumed in the text, which means that judges, when interpreting the Constitution, should be bound by the notion of a distinct separation between the three branches and should not permit legislative experiments that blur these lines. They should proceed with the understanding that the "structural provisions establish a set of rules that must be followed whatever the consequences."[8] Defenders of the formalist approach argue that it should be followed because it is in line with what the framers of the Constitution intended as structural limits on governmental actions in order to assure individual liberty, it is consistent with a notion of a written constitution that should only be changed through amendment, and it is the best way "of imposing discipline in government."[9]

Functionalism assumes that in practice it is impossible to sharply distinguish between the powers of the three branches and is inappropriate to do so other than to acknowledge the basic division into three governmental functions. Functionalists focus on what they consider to be the interdependence, rather than independence, of the branches, and they note the way in which the system of checks and balances promotes that interdependence. The key to effective and responsive government is maintaining a "proper balance" between the three branches, not attempting to rigidly demarcate the powers of each. Thus, when courts seek to interpret the separation of powers doctrine, "structural disputes should be resolved not in terms of fixed rules but rather in light of an evolving standard designed to advance the ultimate purposes of a system of separated powers."[10] Defenders of functionalism contend that experience and the realities of the complex modern administrative state require a functionalist approach.[11] As demands for federal government action to regulate the economy increased during the Depression, for example, Congress was forced to delegate some of its lawmaking authority to the executive and independent regulatory commissions. The rules and regulations needed were too specialized and complex to be produced by the generalists sitting in Congress. Thus, functionalists argue for a pragmatic or flexible approach to the separation of powers, insuring that each branch is not hampered in its ability to carry out its core function but encouraging judicial deference to the other branches in resolving the power struggles in the gray areas.

Critics of formalism argue that this approach is unworkable in politics because the "exclusivity postulate"[12] ignores the realities of complex modern government and the institutional means available to the branches to compromise, bargain, negotiate, and settle boundary struggles without staking out rigid formulations of their powers. Other critics have objected to what they see as the bias to-

ward executive power in modern formalist thought. For example, William Haltom argues that formalism "results in enforcing separation for the sake of separation, exacerbating democratic deadlock, and encouraging growth of powers in the least defined of the three categories, the executive branch. By treating any overlap as a violation of the principle, [formalists] augmented executive powers, thereby threatening the tyranny the separation was designed to avoid."[13] Finally, critics have suggested that the use of formalism by the Supreme Court is deceptive, because it implies that judges are not exercising real power but instead are simply applying the textual requirements of the Constitution. Since in reality, critics say, judges are always making choices about how to interpret the text, their value judgments and political preferences are driving these decisions as well, but they are hiding their power behind the screen of formalism.[14]

Critics of functionalism complain most generally about the "nebulous" and "indeterminate" nature of functionalism. If the powers of the three branches are not clearly demarcated by the constitutional text, does this not invite value judgments by judges when attempting to determine the boundaries between branches and whether a balance among them is being maintained? The approach either gives judges too much leeway or lends too much deference to the legislative branch to transform U.S. government.[15] Critics go on to say that although the values of efficiency and expediency underlie functionalism, neither of these values was of primary importance to the framers of the Constitution. Rather, they valued deliberative decision making, checks and balances that forced such deliberation, limited government in order to ensure liberty, and accountability for those exercising governmental authority.[16]

In the contemporary debate about the separation of powers, those favoring increasing executive power have tended to argue from a formalist position, and those favoring congressional power to legislate and regulate have tended to favor a functionalist approach. Political rhetoric tends to follow suit. Presidents justify actions and defend executive prerogative with formalist arguments, while members of Congress more often resort to the language of functionalism when justifying their actions. The Supreme Court, which has increasingly been called upon to resolve interbranch disputes, has not adopted either approach.

The Supreme Court and the Structure of Government

Throughout its history, the Supreme Court has been drawn into struggles between Congress and the executive and between the federal government and the states. *Marbury v. Madison* was at its root an epic struggle between two political parties—one in decline, the other ascendant—over the meaning of judicial power, the power of the president, and the legitimacy of previous congressional action. *McCulloch v. Maryland* (1819) was about the extent of legislative power and the balance of power between the federal government and the states. The central battle, over the legitimacy of a national bank, would pit Congress against a president disinclined to accede to the Supreme Court's views on the constitutionality of the bank.

At the beginning of the twentieth century, with the rise of the administrative state and the creation of new federal agencies with regula-

tory power of significant proportions, the Court was called upon again to help define the boundaries of the branches' powers and those of the federal government vis-à-vis the states. That none of these cases provided "the final answer" on the separation of powers and federalism is clear by the political history of the times. After initially resisting the New Deal with a formalist approach to how government should operate, the Court accepted the new administrative state and ushered in a long period of functionalist deference to the other branches' determinations of how the policy process should operate. It supported a broad reading of Congress's interstate commerce power, allowed for vast delegations of power to independent and executive-controlled agencies, and avoided interfering with the expansion of presidential powers in foreign affairs and war making.

The Supreme Court has always been a player in deciding the separation of powers, sometimes asserting itself, sometimes deferring to the other branches, but always playing a role in interpreting the doctrine's meaning. What is new is the increasing number of cases coming before the Court in which it is addressed and the positions argued in the Court's opinions. Since *United States v. Nixon,* the Court has decided a number of significant cases involving separation of powers. Some of these are already considered among the most important (and in some instances landmark) cases of the late twentieth century:

- *Buckley v. Valeo* (1976), finding unconstitutional Congress's attempt to control the appointment of some officers of the Federal Election Commission

- *Nixon v. Administrator of General Services* (1977), finding that Congress may pass legislation limiting presidents' control of their papers after they leave office
- *INS v. Chadha* (1983), striking down the legislative veto
- *Bowsher v. Synar* (1986), finding key portions of the Gramm-Rudman-Hollings Act to be unconstitutional
- *Morrison v. Olson* (1988), upholding the independent counsel provisions of the Ethics in Government Act
- *Mistretta v. United States* (1989), upholding judicial participation in the Federal Sentencing Commission
- *Clinton v. City of New York* (1998), striking down the line item veto[17]

Having once all but abandoned any real attempt at articulating a theory of federalism based on state sovereignty, the Court has returned in recent years to structural argument in cases involving Congress's regulatory powers. In cases challenging Congress's power to regulate action taken by state governments, the Court has sided with claims that such regulations are unconstitutional infringements on state autonomy. Perhaps most significant here is a string of cases beginning with *National League of Cities v. Usery* (1976), which found federal law regulating the wages and hours of state employees to be an infringement of the Tenth Amendment provision that the "powers not delegated to the United States by the Constitution, nor prohibited by it to the States, are reserved to the States respectively, or to the people." The Court reversed that opinion in *Garcia v. San Antonio Metropolitan Transit Authority* (1985), but renewed its Tenth Amend-

ment jurisprudence in the 1990s with decisions in *New York v. United States* (1992), *United States v. Lopez* (1995), and *Printz v. United States* (1997). Perhaps even more significant, the Court turned to the arcane area of Eleventh Amendment law, which restricts federal judicial power by forbidding citizens of one state from suing another state in federal court. In *Seminole Tribe of Florida v. Florida* (1996), *Alden v. Maine* (1999), and *College Savings Bank v. Florida Prepaid Postsecondary Education Expense Board* (1999), the Court revived the notion of state sovereign immunity, freeing states from federal laws that allow citizens to sue state entities. In these cases the Court signaled a desire to reign in Congress's regulatory powers and revealed disagreement among the justices about the structure of the federal system.

Whereas most twentieth-century separation of powers jurisprudence had tended to be functionalist in approach, emphasizing the flexibility of the separation of powers doctrine and its adaptability to changing circumstances, several of the most important of the Court's opinions in the 1980s revealed a new formalism in argument, emphasizing a more rigid allocation of powers and a stricter reading of the constitutional provisions in question.[18] While the concepts of formalism and functionalism are usually applied to separation of powers issues, they are also an appropriate construct for the federalism debate. A formalist interpretation of the Tenth Amendment would find it a positive barrier to federal action, because the approach imagines the line between state and federal power to be clear. A functionalist or flexible approach would find protection of the states in the political process—often called the process model of federalism[19]—and the Tenth Amendment to be a "truism."

The Court's recent decisions are substantially more formalist in both these areas of the law than at any other time since the post–New Deal Court. On the other hand, one cannot conclude with absolute certainty that the Court has now adopted formalism as its only approach to structural questions. The presidency of Ronald Reagan was a period of heightened debate about constitutional interpretation generally and the extent of executive powers specifically. The Reagan administration challenged Court interpretations of the law in a number of areas, including school prayer, abortion, and executive control of administrative agencies. The administration also challenged on two fronts the very role the federal courts had played in policymaking during the previous several decades. It did so through the appointment of judges who shared the values of the administration and through the presentation of its positions in court cases in which the government was involved.[20] These efforts were aided by conservative scholars who had been writing about the threat to executive power posed by the numerous efforts of Congress to reign it in following the Vietnam War and Watergate.[21]

Lawyers in the Reagan Department of Justice asserted themselves by refusing to defend before the Court statutes that they considered to be intrusions on executive power on the grounds that they violated the separation of powers. In addition, Attorney General Edwin Meese publicly challenged the long-held notion that independent regulatory commissions were constitutional, arguing instead that executive power could only be exercised by those directly accountable to the president.[22] The Court had previously upheld

such agencies in the landmark *Humphrey's Executor v. United States* (1935), which found that the limitations on presidential removal of federal trade commissioners were constitutional since these officers were not carrying out purely executive functions.

The legislative veto is a devise requiring congressional approval of regulations drafted by the executive in carrying out responsibilities delegated to it by Congress. It had been a source of controversy for many years before the Court found it to be unconstitutional in *Chadha*. The practice had its supporters and opponents and was a subject of considerable debate among legal scholars. Both sides of the debate tended to view the use of the legislative veto as a "powerful policymaking instrument" and "a powerful instrument of congressional control" over executive branch administration of the law.[23] At the same time that lines were being drawn in this debate, interbranch conflict on a whole host of issues intensified. According to Jessica Korn, the legislative veto landed in court as "a direct result of the inter-branch hostility that arose between the Republicans in the executive branch and the Democrats in Congress in the early 1970s."[24]

In the *Chadha* decision, seven of the justices agreed that the legislative veto was unconstitutional, an opinion that invalidated some two hundred legislative provisions passed during the preceding five decades. The Court majority argued that the Constitution clearly sets out the roles of the legislative and executive branches in the passage of legislation. The requirements that both houses of Congress approve a bill and that it be presented to the president for approval or veto—Article 1, sections 1 and 7—were viewed by the Court as the only constitutional means for making legislation. Finding that the legislative veto was a legislative act and that it did not go through this process, the Court concluded that the practice was unconstitutional.[25] By adopting the argument that all legislative actions must follow this process, the Court implied that all legislative vetoes, which by definition do not involve presentment to the president, are unconstitutional. The argument and the language used by the majority in this decision reflect the formalistic approach to the separation of powers, emphasizing clearly delineated procedures for lawmaking and rejecting arguments that the veto was a necessary adaptation to the realities of modern government. Chief Justice Warren Burger wrote,

> The Constitution sought to divide the delegated powers of the new federal government into three defined categories, legislative, executive, and judicial, to assure, as nearly as possible, that each Branch . . . would confine itself to its assigned responsibility. The hydraulic pressure inherent within each of the separate branches to exceed the outer limits of its power, even to accomplish desirable objectives, must be resisted.[26]

The *Chadha* decision was greeted by its supporters and detractors alike as "a major victory for the executive branch" and "the court's most important separation-of-powers ruling since the White House tapes case of the Watergate era." Some observers considered it among the "most important such decisions in history." The ruling was considered to have "dramatically altered the balance of power between Congress and the executive branch."[27]

The Reagan administration considered *Chadha* of great precedential value as it continued to advance its view of executive powers and assert executive prerogatives in other areas. In 1985 Congress adopted the Balanced Budget and Emergency Deficit Control Act, also known as the Gramm-Rudman-Hollings Act. In the early years of the Reagan administration, the federal deficit had ballooned as the result of tax cuts, military spending increases, and an inability to cut domestic spending. The 1985 act was a response to that deficit and an effort to force (or at least appear to force) fiscal discipline on a federal government in which political agendas called for lower taxes and increased spending. During the debate over Gramm-Rudman-Hollings, a number of members of Congress expressed concerns about the constitutionality of the act's mechanisms, particularly the provision for automatic cuts to be enforced by the comptroller general, the head of the General Accounting Office, a part of the legislative branch. Unwilling to give the president the power to make the cuts, Congress had come up with a compromise solution. Agencies within each branch, the Congressional Budget Office, and the executive branch's Office of Management and Budget were charged with identifying where cuts should occur. The comptroller general would be given the power to direct that they be carried out.[28]

In *Bowsher v. Synar,* the Court struck down the automatic cut provisions with the same formalistic argument used in *Chadha*. Writing for the majority, Chief Justice Burger argued that the comptroller general, as a legislative officer removable by Congress, could not exercise executive functions. The Court believed that the automatic cuts constituted execution of the laws and thus could not be carried out by a legislative officer.[29]

Court watchers interpreted the decision as a further endorsement of executive power because the justices adopted the more formalist and far-reaching argument. Laurence Tribe noted the Court's "distressing tendency to side with the President in resolving controversies over the separation of powers" and warned that "the appointment of even one additional Justice inclined to defer to the President would take us a giant stride closer to the reality of an imperial presidency."[30]

That the Reagan administration interpreted *Bowsher* as helpful in their attack on independent agencies is revealed in their response to the controversy over the constitutionality of the independent counsel statute, a post-Watergate arrangement that provided for independent investigation and prosecution of high-level executive branch officials by a judicially appointed attorney. During reauthorization hearings for the provisions in 1982 and 1987, the Department of Justice took the position that the arrangement violated the separation of powers doctrine because it gave executive powers of law enforcement to an officer not controllable by the president.[31] Because of the perceived public and congressional bipartisan support for the arrangement, Reagan signed the reauthorization bills into law, but on the occasion of his 1987 signing he noted the continued opposition of his administration to the provision, arguing that an officer with law enforcement powers "must be subject to executive branch appointment, review, and removal. There is no other constitutionally permissible alternative." Reagan justified his signing of an "unconstitutional" bill based on the need for public confidence in ongoing investigations, including the Iran-contra affair, and noted his administration's continued compliance with the law despite "constitutional misgivings." "Even

as the constitutional issues grew more clear, aided by the pronouncements of the Supreme Court in *Chadha* in 1983 and *Bowsher* in 1986," Reagan said, "we took extraordinary measures to protect against constitutional challenge the work of the more recently appointed independent counsel by offering each of them appointments in the Department of Justice."[32]

Given the Court's formal leanings in its rulings on *Chadha* and *Bowsher*, the Reagan administration was hopeful that the majority of the justices would take the same approach toward *Morrison v. Olson*. In the Court's decision upholding the independent counsel statute, however, only one justice, Antonin Scalia, dissented. In legitimizing the creation of an independent office exercising executive power, the Court made clear its continued support for the *Humphrey's Executor* precedent. In fact, the Court extended the reach of that case, eschewing its distinction heretofore between "purely executive officers" and those exercising "quasi-judicial" or "quasi-legislative" powers. Instead, the Court argued that the test of legitimacy for restrictions on the president's ability to remove officers should depend on the extent to which the removal provisions "interfere with the President's exercise of the 'executive' power and his constitutionally appointed duty to 'take care that the laws be faithfully executed' under Article II." Chief Justice William Rehnquist wrote, "The real question is whether the removal restrictions are of such a nature that they impede the President's ability to perform his constitutional duty." While the independent counsel in *Morrison* did exercise some discretion in carrying out her law enforcement duties under the act, the Court could not see "how the President's need to control the exercise of that discretion is so central to the functioning of the Executive Branch as to require as a matter of constitutional law the counsel be terminable at will by the President."[33]

Given the Court's record, many commentators were surprised by the size of the majority that upheld the independent counsel statute. As one commentator noted, with some cynicism,

> The Supreme Court likes and uses both formalism and functionalism, but does not give much guidance about what triggers one mode of analysis and justification over another in particular cases. This is a familiar, if unsatisfactory, position in constitutional law: two lines of cases using two kinds of analysis leading in different directions to different results, with the Court in the position to pick and choose, but with no evident principled basis with which to pick and choose.[34]

The Court's rejection of formalism seemed to be complete with *Mistretta v. United States,* which upheld the validity of the U.S. Sentencing Commission. In this case, the role of federal judges on the commission was challenged as a violation of Article 3, which gives only judicial power to the federal courts, not the power to make rules governing sentences. Judges on the commission had the authority to establish binding criminal sentencing guidelines. Opponents contended that this provision was an unconstitutional delegation of legislative power to members of the judiciary. In rejecting this argument, the Court adopted, even more clearly than it had in *Morrison,* a flexible approach to the separation of powers. It recognized that the commission arrangement was "an unusual hybrid" but found nothing in the Constitution that prohibited Congress "from calling upon the accumulated wisdom and experience of the Judicial Branch in creating pol-

icy on a matter uniquely within the ken of judges."[35] The only argument on the Court seemed to be between Justice Scalia, who again wrote a lone dissent, and the rest of the Court.

Conclusion

In the 1980s the Supreme Court's jurisprudence concerning the separation of powers was interpreted as a signal of its adoption of a formalist approach that would change the distribution of powers between the branches of government and affect the construction of the modern administrative state. The Court's functionalist approach to *Morrison* and *Mistretta* at the end of the 1980s, however, made clear that formalism had not been embraced by a majority of the Court. Perhaps some members of the Court were influenced in their analysis of the separation of powers by whether the judiciary is given a role in the disputed arrangement. In several of the Court's decisions, including *Morrison,* the judiciary was implicated in the debate. When it was, the Court appears to have been "reminded" of the value of a flexible approach to the separation of powers. Perhaps this lies in the value of knowing thyself and, thus, believing that ambiguous grants of power are not dangerous in the hands of the "least dangerous branch." Such a view may underlie the *Morrison* Court's willingness to accept duties that were not clearly "judicial" under the independent counsel arrangement, minimizing the threat that such an exercise of power might pose to individuals or to the executive.

The Court's *Mistretta* decision is a case in point. While the Court admits that the sentencing commission is "an unusual hybrid in structure and authority," its opinion suggests that the "intractable dilemma" of sentence disparity justifies the delegation of legislative power to the judiciary because it is so well suited to resolving this difficult problem. This faith in the judiciary may have also affected the Court's decision in *Morrison*.

The debate about the modern meaning of the separation of powers reveals that constitutional interpretation is a political process involving not only the Supreme Court but the other institutional actors in U.S. politics as well. The boundaries between the branches of government, the meaning of the separation of powers doctrine itself, and the rules that should govern how judges apply the doctrine have been contested throughout U.S. history. Examination of the doctrine today is the study of this debate and its application to U.S. domestic political conflicts.

Notes

1. Keith Whittington, "The Separation of Powers at the Founding," in *Separation of Powers: Commentary and Documents,* ed. Katy J. Harriger (Washington, D.C.: CQ Press, 2003), 1.
2. Louis Fisher, *Congressional Abdication on War and Spending* (College Station: Texas A & M University Press, 2000).
3. Neal Devins, "Congress as Culprit: How Lawmakers Spurred on the Court's Anti-Congress Crusade," *Duke Law Journal* 51 (2001): 435.
4. Clinton Rossiter, *The American Presidency* (Baltimore: Johns Hopkins University Press, 1987).
5. James Madison, Alexander Hamilton, and John Jay, *The Federalist Papers,* ed. Isaac Kramnick (New York: Penguin Books, 1987), 319.
6. David M. O'Brien, *Constitutional Law and Politics: Struggles for Power and Governmental Accountability,* 4th ed. (New York: W. W. Norton, 2000), 36.
7. Louis Fisher, *Constitutional Dialogue: Interpretation as Political Process* (Princeton, N.J.: Princeton University Press, 1988).
8. Thomas W. Merrill, "The Constitutional Principle of Separation of Powers," *Supreme Court Review* (1991): 230.
9. Geoffrey P. Miller, "Independent Agencies," *Supreme Court Review* (1986): 54–56.
10. Merrill, "Constitutional Principle," 231.
11. Peter L. Strauss, "The Place of Agencies in Government: Separation of Powers and the Fourth Branch," *Columbia Law Review* 84 (1984): 573.
12. Merrill, "Constitutional Principle," 234.
13. William Haltom, "Separating Powers: Dialectical Sense and Positive Nonsense," in *Judging the Constitution,* ed. Michael W. McCann and Gerald L. Houseman (Glenview, Ill.: Scott, Foresman, 1989), 127–153.
14. Ibid.
15. Merrill, "Constitutional Principle," 234.
16. Miller, "Independent Agencies," 54–55.
17. Nadine Cohadas, "Courts Play Larger Role as Inter-Branch Referee," *Congressional Quarterly Weekly Report,* January 7, 1989, 13–15.
18. Peter Strauss, "Formal and Functional Approaches to Separation of Powers Questions—A Foolish Inconsistency?" *Cornell Law Review* 72 (1987).
19. Herbert Wechsler, "The Political Safeguards of Federalism: The Role of the States in the Composition and Selection of the National Government," *Columbia Law Review* 54 (1954): 543; Jesse Choper, *Judicial Review and the National Political Process* (Chicago: University of Chicago Press, 1980).
20. Lincoln Caplan, *The Tenth Justice: The Solicitor General and the Rule of Law* (New York: Knopf, 1987); Cornell W. Clayton, *The Politics of Justice: The Attorney General and the Making of Legal Policy* (Armonk, N.Y.: M. E. Sharpe, 1992).
21. For a discussion of Congress's activities in this regard, see James Sundquist, *The Decline and Resurgence of Congress* (Washington, D.C.: Brookings Institution, 1981). For representative essays of the criticisms of these developments, see L. Gordon Crovitz and Jeremy Rabkin, eds., *The Fettered Presidency* (Washington, D.C.: American Enterprise Institute, 1989).
22. Caplan, *Tenth Justice,* 119.
23. Jessica Korn, *The Power of Separation: American Constitutionalism and the Myth of the Leg-*

islative Veto (Princeton, N.J.: Princeton University Press, 1996), 28–30.

24. Ibid., 30.

25. *INS v. Chadha,* 462 U.S. 919 (1983).

26. Ibid., 951.

27. "Supreme Court Invalidates Legislative Veto," *Congressional Quarterly Almanac, 1983* (Washington, D.C.: Congressional Quarterly, 1984), 565–566.

28. "Constitutionality of Automatic Cuts Challenged," *Congressional Quarterly Almanac, 1985* (Washington, D.C.: Congressional Quarterly, 1986), 461.

29. *Bowsher v. Synar,* 478 U.S. 714 (1986).

30. Laurence H. Tribe, *God Save This Honorable Court: How the Choice of Supreme Court Justices Shapes Our History* (New York: Random House, 1985), 118–119.

31. U.S. House Committee on the Judiciary, *Amendment of the Special Prosecutor Provisions of Title 28: Hearings before the Subcommittee on Administrative Law and Governmental Relations,* 97th Cong., 2d sess., 1982; U.S. Senate Committee on Governmental Affairs, *Independent Counsel Reauthorization Act of 1987,* 100th Cong., 1st sess., 1987, S. Rept. 100-123.

32. "Statement on Signing the Independent Counsel Reauthorization Act of 1987, December 15, 1987," *Public Papers of the Presidents: Ronald Reagan* (Washington, D.C.: Government Printing Office, 1989), 2:1524.

33. *Morrison v. Olson,* 487 U.S. 654, 685–693 (1988).

34. Gary Goodpaster, "Rules of the Game: Comments on Three Views of the Independent Prosecutor Case," *American University Law Review* 38 (Winter 1989): 393.

35. *Mistretta v. United States* 488 U.S. 361 (1989).

CHAPTER THREE

The Lawmaking Power

RICHARD A. BAKER

The first sentence in the Constitution unambiguously confers on Congress "All legislative powers herein granted." Yet, in making the nation's laws, Congress operates in an uneasy and often acrimonious alliance with the executive and judicial branches. Each branch has its own answer to the question "What is the law?" This struggle, implicit in 1789, intensified in the 1830s and blossomed following the Civil War, as the federal government participated more broadly in the nation's economic development. By the 1880s the Supreme Court had come to devote nearly half its caseload to an interpretation of congressional statutes. At the beginning of the twentieth century, new international responsibilities shifted the balance of influence from Congress, which spoke with many voices, to the presidency, which spoke with one. In the years following World War II, as the role of government in American life expanded exponentially, Congress experienced a resurgence of strength in its relationship vis-à-vis the executive. It pursued its legislative responsibilities with renewed vigor, armed with greatly enhanced professional staffs and resources and under greater pressures from the executive and judicial branches.

Extent and Limits

Eighteen clauses in Article 1, section 8, of the Constitution spell out the primary legislative powers of Congress. Among them are the authority to provide for the nation's defense by organizing military and naval forces, to declare war, to regulate commerce among the individual states, to tax, to borrow and coin money, to establish post offices, and to promote the arts and sciences through a system of patent and copyright protections. This section also contains an important qualifier. In its final clause, it confers on Congress the authority to "make all laws which shall be necessary and proper for carrying into Execution the foregoing Powers, and all other Powers vested by this Constitution in the Government of the United States."

The language of this section reflects fundamental questions about the very nature of the Constitution. Is it, as Thomas Jefferson and James Madison believed, a compact among states that is designed to safeguard their sovereignty within a framework of national interest, or is it, as Alexander Hamilton and the emerging Federalist Party thought, a broad grant of responsibility to the federal government to address what it believes to be fundamental national concerns? Hamilton argued that Congress, in taxing and spending, could go beyond the Constitution's direct grants of legislative power so long as its legislative acts promoted the country's general welfare. He illustrated his concept of implied powers by explaining that the power to provide for the nation's defense flows from the constitutionally expressed powers to raise an army and navy and to declare war. "If the end be clearly comprehended within any of the specified powers [and] if the measure has an obvious relation to that end, and is not forbidden by any particular provision of the constitution—it may safely be deemed to come within the compass of the national authority."[1]

James Madison read the Constitution more literally, believing, for example, that the document's general welfare clause allowed Congress to raise and appropriate money only to carry out the other enumerated powers of the Constitution. As he explains in *Federalist* No. 45, "The powers delegated by the proposed constitution to the federal government, are few and defined. Those which are to remain in the state governments are numerous and indefinite."[2] Disagreements over interpretation, such as those of Hamilton and Madison, gave birth to the nation's political party system, a development wholly unanticipated in the Constitution.

Although the Constitution grants all legislative powers to Congress, it also places significant limits on the way in which Congress may exercise those powers. Perhaps the most important among these limitations is the division of Congress into two chambers, with the requirement that all legislation be passed by both bodies in identical language. (In most other nations with bicameral legislatures, it is possible for the lower house to prevail in passing legislation over the objections of the upper house.) The Congress under the Articles of Confederation (1781–1789) had consisted of only one chamber and had severely restricted powers. It lacked the fundamental ability to raise taxes or to regulate commerce among the states and with other nations. In granting these and other vital powers to the Congress convened under the Constitution, the framers created the checking mechanism of a two-chambered legislature with each house elected by a significantly different constituency. Citizens entitled to vote for members of their state legislatures were also allowed to elect members of the House of Representatives, while the state legislatures had the responsibility of electing their state's two U.S. senators. This system prevailed until 1913, when the Seventeenth Amendment provided for the direct popular election of senators.

The president's authority to veto legislation also serves as a formidable check on congressional lawmaking powers. To overcome a veto and secure final enactment, both houses must pass the vetoed measure by supermajorities of two-thirds of those members voting. For the first seventy-five years of the Republic, presidents rarely used their veto power. In more recent decades, however, they have wielded it as a policy weapon. President Franklin Delano Roosevelt issued 372 vetoes during his twelve years in office; Ronald Reagan came closer to the modern average, with 39 during eight years in office.

Another major source of congressional limitations appears in Article 1, section 9, of the Constitution, directly following the section 8 catalog of enumerated powers. Section 9 contains six clauses denying Congress authority to make laws in specific areas. They include suspension of the writ of habeas corpus (except in times of national emergency); enactment of bills of attainder (imposing capital punishment on grounds such as treason or felony without proper judicial proceedings) or ex post facto statutes (criminalizing an act that was not illegal at the time of its commission); imposition of "direct taxes" (unless the burden of those taxes is allocated in proportion to the general population) and taxes on items being exported; and passage of laws that give preference to the ports of one state over those of another.

The First Congress, convened in New York City on March 4, 1789, devised a package of constitutional amendments designed to protect individual rights. Those protections restrict the lawmaking prerogatives of Congress as well as actions by the executive and judicial branches. Only the First Amendment specifically singles out Congress, limiting its power to make laws "prohibiting the free exercise [of religion], . . . or abridging the freedom of speech, or of the press; or the right of the people peacefully to assemble, and to petition the Government for a redress of grievances."

Evolution of the Lawmaking Power

Suspicion and innate rivalry developed quickly between the two houses of Congress shortly after they first convened. These sentiments confirmed the belief James Madison expresses in *Federalist* No. 51 about the wisdom of creating a bicameral legislature, rendering its chambers "by different modes of election and different principles of action, as little connected with each other, as the nature of their common

functions, and their common dependence on society will admit."[3]

Both houses took their constitutional powers very seriously. When Indian warriors inflicted a major defeat on an expedition of U.S. military forces, the House of Representatives launched an investigation in 1792 that became the precedent for subsequent congressional inquiries. This proceeding established the basic premise that Congress cannot legislate effectively without means to acquire necessary information. For its part, the Senate actively exercised its power to advise and consent regarding presidential nominations by rejecting a candidate for customs collector in its first months of existence. Members went further, in 1795, by refusing to confirm President George Washington's nominee as chief justice of the United States because that candidate had publicly attacked the Senate's handling of the controversial Jay's Treaty with Great Britain.

The year 1800 brought in an era of major changes in congressional operations. That year the government moved to the permanent capital, Washington, D.C., after residing from 1789 to 1790 in New York City and for a decade in Philadelphia. Within months of settling into rustic temporary quarters in the Senate wing of the unfinished Capitol, the Supreme Court rendered its decision in *Marbury v. Madison* (1803). For the first time, the high court specifically exercised a power that was only implied in the Constitution—the power to invalidate laws of Congress. Although decades would pass before the Court would strike down another statute as inconsistent with the Constitution, members of both houses well remembered this judicial assertion of limitations on their lawmaking powers.

As political parties took root in the institutional operations of Congress, members who allied with Thomas Jefferson's expanding Democratic-Republican Party decided in 1804 to push for the removal of a Federalist Supreme Court justice. Earlier that year, Congress had removed a lower court federal judge because of actions that suggested his insanity. Thus emboldened, the Republican-controlled House of Representatives impeached Justice Samuel Chase on politically based charges of biased and inflammatory conduct on the bench, but the Senate—in a major victory for the independence of the judiciary—decided by a narrow margin to leave Chase in office.

In 1819 the Supreme Court contributed greatly to the expansion of Congress's lawmaking powers with its pivotal decision in *McCulloch v. Maryland* (1819). Writing for the Court, Chief Justice John Marshall set forth the doctrine of incidental implied powers. In a tremendous boost for the primacy of federal sovereignty over state sovereignty, the Court ruled that the state of Maryland could not tax a federal branch bank. The Court thereby accepted Congress's practice of passing laws outside the immediate authority of its enumerated powers to include those indirectly helpful to implementing those purposes. Congress could create a national bank, as Marshall declared in *McCulloch,* to manage the functions implicit in the enumerated purposes: "Let the end be legitimate, let it be within the scope of the constitution, and all means which are appropriate, which are plainly adapted to that end, which are not prohibited, but consist with the letter and spirit of the constitution, are constitutional."[4] Once past this milestone, a wide range of permissible legislative action lay on the horizon. The principle of incidental implied powers introduced significant flexibility and choice to the lawmaking process.

Until 1820 the House of Representatives proved to be a more active arena for creative legislative activity than the Senate. Previously, the Senate had tended to serve, as some framers had anticipated, as a "council of revision," tempering and modifying the legislative work of the House. This relationship changed significantly as Congress began to debate allowing slavery to expand into the nation's territories. In the House, where membership is reapportioned every ten years according to shifts in population, the majority of members increasingly came from the Northeast and Midwest. In the Senate—with each state represented equally irrespective of its population and with an equal number of slave states and free states—the South enjoyed parity with the North. New states admitted to the Union under the provisions of the 1820 Missouri Compromise—which barred slavery north of specially established boundaries—would enter in pairs composed of one slave state and one free state to maintain sectional parity. This ensured that future debate and major decisions on this issue would take place in the Senate chamber, with the disposition of the House clearly established. Important separation of powers struggles played out in the Senate's ornate theater-like setting during the decades leading to the Civil War.

A fundamental challenge to the lawmaking powers of Congress arose in the late 1820s, when legislators from South Carolina revived a theory Thomas Jefferson and James Madison had articulated thirty years earlier: a state could "nullify" federal laws it considered to be unconstitutional, and in the face of federal force it could secede from the Union. South Carolina senator John C. Calhoun emerged as the principal proponent of this view, as his state adopted an ordinance nullifying a tariff that it believed discriminatory, thus banning collection of duties within the state. In response, President Andrew Jackson mobilized federal troops and threatened (privately) to hang Calhoun, who had recently resigned as Jackson's vice president to move to the Senate.

State nullification triggered a major debate in the Senate about the nature of the Union: Was it merely a compact among sovereign states that could decide for themselves which federal laws they wished to obey or a nation with collective interests beyond those of individual states? Responding to legislation to override South Carolina's nullification ordinance, Calhoun charged, "Congress has assumed, without any warrant from the Constitution, the right of exercising this most important power [imposing duties on imports], and has so exercised it as to impose a ruinous burden on the labor and capital of the State, by which her resources are exhausted, the enjoyments of her citizens curtailed, the means of education contracted, and her interests essentially and injuriously affected."[5] Although an 1833 legislative compromise resolved this crisis, the underlying issue remained before Congress until the Civil War settled it by force of arms.

Another constitutional crisis arose in 1833, as Congress and the president struggled to shape their constitutional roles. President Jackson believed that the Bank of the United States, a federally chartered private financial institution, was unconstitutional and unfairly benefited the commercial classes of the Northeast.

Jackson's veto of legislation to renew the bank's charter triggered a confrontation in which the Senate censured the president for his refusal to turn over executive branch documents related to the bank. Although the Senate lacked constitutional authority for this action, it highlighted issues involving the right of Congress to full information and the right of the president to keep separate counsel. This confrontation sharpened political divisions and spawned the Whig Party to stand against the Jacksonian Democratic Party. Although the pressure of slavery-related issues eventually splintered the Whigs in the 1850s, that party helped define the lawmaking process of that era and led to the establishment of the modern political party system.

Massachusetts Whig senator Daniel Webster, one of the great legislative statesmen of the antebellum era, committed political suicide in 1850 by supporting a series of compromise proposals over slavery that were designed to preserve the Union. One of these agreements provided for the return of fugitive slaves to their masters. His support of the measure outraged antislavery constituents in Webster's native New England and destroyed his political base. Nevertheless, the delicately fashioned package of legislative agreements that constituted the Compromise of 1850 demonstrated that the lawmaking power of Congress remained vital against hurricane-force political opposition.

Two events in the mid-1850s ultimately destroyed this legislative compromise. The first was the Kansas-Nebraska Act of 1854, which repealed the limits on slavery in the territories established under the 1820 Missouri Compromise and allowed residents of the territories to determine whether their area would enter the Union as a slave state or a free state. This statute immediately turned the territories into political battlegrounds and millions of previously indifferent free-state Americans into abolitionists.

Three years later, the Supreme Court's decision in *Dred Scott v. Sandford* (1857) added much new fuel to this spreading conflagration. For only the second time in its history, the high court invalidated a congressional statute. Declaring the Missouri Compromise unconstitutional on the grounds that Congress lacked authority to exclude slavery from the territories, the *Scott* decision held—in the words of Chief Justice Roger Taney—that blacks were not citizens and therefore had no rights under the Constitution "which the white man was bound to respect."[6] The Court's ruling intensified sectional conflict, hastened the march to civil war, and foreshadowed the Court's role as a formidable competitor with Congress in the lawmaking process.

In the cautiously optimistic afterglow of the Compromise of 1850, Congress had appropriated funds to expand the Capitol, providing large new chambers for both houses. By early 1859 the House and Senate had settled into their new quarters. Within two years, these quarters seemed even more spacious as representatives of the newly formed Confederate States of America withdrew and civil war began.

Civil War, Reconstruction, and the Early Twentieth Century

Late in 1861 Radical Republicans in Congress, moved by frustration over corruption, inefficiency, and incompetence in executive branch management of military operations, established the Joint Committee on the Conduct of the War. Members of this powerful panel visited generals on the battlefield and directly involved themselves in overseeing military activities. Ultimately, the committee expanded the war's objectives beyond preservation of the Union to include the abolition of slavery. While its critics viewed the joint committee as a troublesome inquisitor and an abuse of congressional lawmaking powers, its members publicized enemy atrocities and the need for firmer political direction of the military effort.

At the end of the war, Radical Republicans took aim at President Andrew Johnson's lenient policies toward readmission of the defeated Confederate states and established a joint committee to oversee Reconstruction. That committee was instrumental in encouraging both houses to pass the Tenure of Office Act of 1867. Directed at the president's decision to replace Secretary of War Edwin Stanton, who was closely allied with the Radical Republicans, this act put into formal legislative language a position that had engaged members of Congress from the institution's earliest days: Was the advice and consent of the Senate required to remove officials whom the Senate had confirmed? Citing Johnson's violation of this statute in removing Stanton without Senate approval, the House of Representatives, for the first time, impeached a president. Johnson remained in office only because the Senate, by a one-vote margin, decided as it had in the 1805 trial of Justice Chase that constitutional checks should not be employed for political purposes against the other branches.[7]

In 1866 Congress addressed the festering issue of the separation of powers by drafting a constitutional amendment that was ratified in 1868 as the Fourteenth Amendment. During Reconstruction, the struggle between Congress and President Johnson reached new heights over the issue of civil rights for freed slaves. Johnson vetoed the Civil Rights Act of 1866 because he believed that Congress lacked the power to enact a law protecting these rights. According to the president's interpretation of the Constitution, that power resided with the states. Congress overrode Johnson's veto, but to remove any ambiguity about its own power to protect civil rights, it placed in section 1 of the Fourteenth Amendment the requirement that "No State shall make or enforce any law which shall abridge the privileges and immunities of citizens of the United States; nor shall any state deprive any person of life, liberty, or property without due process of law; [or] deny to any person within its jurisdiction the equal protection of the laws." This sentence, the subject of extensive and conflicting judicial interpretation, ultimately reinforced the lawmaking powers of Congress over those of the individual states.

As the nation rapidly industrialized after the war, Congress passed an increasing volume of legislation related to the economic and social issues associated with this expansion. The statutes that had an impact on the activities of large corporations set the stage for judicial challenges in lower federal courts and in the Supreme Court. By 1882 nearly half of the Supreme Court's caseload involved the interpretation of congressional laws. While during the nation's first century the high court had overturned only twenty-one acts of Congress as inconsistent with the Constitution or other federal laws, it invalidated almost twice that

number over the next forty years, beginning in 1889.

The Civil War had forced Congress to reassess its revenue-raising role. For much of the nation's early history, the federal government relied on two major sources of revenue: excise taxes on the consumption of commodities and customs duties. During the emergency conditions of the Civil War, the House and Senate raised urgently needed revenue by passing several direct income tax measures. Although Congress repealed that legislation in 1872, after the emergency had subsided, it enacted a new income tax in 1894. A year later, in *Pollock v. Farmers' Loan and Trust Co.,* the Supreme Court declared the tax unconstitutional on the ground that it was a direct tax rather than an equally apportioned one as the Constitution required. Finally, in 1909, Congress passed and sent to the states the Sixteenth Amendment, which gave the national legislature the right to "lay and collect taxes on incomes, from whatever source derived, without apportionment among the several States." Soon after the Sixteenth Amendment was ratified, in 1913, Congress enacted the first permanent income tax. Because of exemptions for all but the highest earners of income, until World War I this new law affected very few Americans.

To meet the country's sizeable revenue needs during World War I, Congress structured federal tax laws to generate 60 percent of the nation's revenues. In 1926 the Senate and House established the Joint Committee on Internal Revenue Taxation to study executive branch operations related to administering the tax system and to recommend improvements. That committee quickly became a valued source of technical and policy expertise to both houses of Congress and a model for the future introduction of professional staff in Congress.

The growing complexity of American life at the turn of the twentieth century placed a premium on specialized expertise in lawmaking. Without professional staff of its own, Congress had little choice but to delegate authority over technical matters, under broad guidelines, to executive agencies, boards, or commissions. Such delegation had begun at the state level after the Civil War as various legislatures created commissions to regulate railroad rates. It moved to the national stage in 1887, when Congress established the Interstate Commerce Commission to set rates for commercial traffic between states.

The twentieth century marked a new era in relations between Congress and the presidency. For much of the previous century, the legislative had been the dominant branch of the national government, with notable exceptions during the Jefferson, Jackson, and Lincoln administrations. As the nation gained international stature in the wake of the Spanish-American War of 1898, however, presidents began to consolidate the resources available to them. Two strong executives, Theodore Roosevelt and Woodrow Wilson, pushed Congress to enact reforms against the abuses flowing from the rapid expansion of industrial capitalism. Roosevelt's success as a political leader grew from his ability to mediate effectively between Capitol Hill's old guard preservers of the industrial order and its progressive reformers.

Wilson won the White House for the Democrats in 1912 because of a split in the Republican ranks. He realized that he needed to be an activist "legislator-in-chief" to advance his am-

bitious program of tariff, banking, and antitrust reform before the Republicans had the opportunity to regroup. Wilson met regularly with congressional committee chairs and revived the practice, dormant since 1801, of personally delivering his annual message to a joint session of Congress. Despite Wilson's best intentions, his rigid personality and ongoing animosities between the legislative and executive branches soon ended his effectiveness in Congress. When the Republicans regained control of both houses in 1919, Wilson took his campaign for ratification of the Treaty of Versailles over the heads of the legislators to the American people. This move led to the collapse of his health and the defeat of the treaty.

In the 1920s Congress enjoyed a brief resurgence as the dominant branch of government. The times and the issues cast the presidents of that era in roles far less active than those Roosevelt and Wilson had pursued. During the decade, Congress reformed the federal budget and accounting systems and modernized operations of the federal judiciary, including funding for a Supreme Court building. In 1935 the Court moved from its "temporary" quarters in the Capitol to its current facility.

In assessing the nation's experience in World War I, Congress resumed its investigative responsibilities with a vigor reminiscent of its joint probes during the Civil War and Reconstruction. The Supreme Court's ruling in *McGrain v. Daugherty* (1927) firmly established the right of Congress to conduct full-scale investigations, reasoning that "a legislative body cannot legislate wisely or effectively in the absence of information respecting the conditions which the legislation is intended to affect or change."[8]

*The New Deal through
Post–World War II*

The stock market crash of 1929 and the Great Depression placed intense strains on relations between Congress and the other two branches of government. After the Supreme Court struck down laws central to Franklin Roosevelt's New Deal, the president and his allies in Congress searched for ways to rein in the high court. With the reluctant support of congressional leaders, Roosevelt decided to seek legislation to expand the Court's membership so that he could appoint jurists sympathetic to his programs. In a bitter fight through the spring and summer of 1937, Congress ultimately rejected the president's Court-packing plan. In this action, legislators placed a higher value on maintaining the independence and integrity of a separate branch of government than on short-term political considerations, which had been the case in the Chase and Johnson impeachment acquittals. Pressure for change in the Court's structure also lessened significantly as older justices departed and were replaced by members more sympathetic to the goals of the New Deal.

The New Deal and World War II enhanced the powers of the executive over the legislature. In times of national emergency, Congress tends to follow the broad outlines set by the executive. When the emergency passes, however, Congress customarily moves to reassert its coequal status. This tension was particularly evident in the final years of World War II. In 1944 President Roosevelt ignored the strong objections of his party's congressional leaders and vetoed a tax bill. Disgusted by the chief executive's heavy-handedness, the Senate Demo-

cratic majority leader, Alben Barkley of Kentucky, charged that the president, by his actions, had made a "calculated and deliberate assault on the legislative integrity of every member of Congress."[9] In a dramatic gesture, Barkley resigned his leadership post; his party colleagues immediately reelected him in a show of congressional defiance at Roosevelt's dictatorial attitude.

With the war ended and former senator Harry Truman in the White House, Congress passed the single most significant piece of congressional reform legislation in the institution's history—the Legislative Reorganization Act of 1946. This statute reduced the number of committees in each house, modernized committee procedures, and allowed members of Congress and congressional committees to hire professional staffs. This last provision soon reduced congressional dependence on the executive branch and outside interest groups for timely and unbiased information. The staff available to review executive branch proposals and operations included such legislative branch agencies as the Congressional Budget Office, the General Accounting Office, and the Congressional Research Service, which greatly accelerated the pace of and expanded the dimensions of Congress's lawmaking abilities.

The executive and judicial branches continued to challenge the scope of congressional lawmaking powers through the half-century that followed World War II. From the late 1930s to the mid 1950s, the Supreme Court, under Chief Justice Earl Warren, had shifted from a posture of restraint to one of activism. In the 1950s and early 1960s Congress fell under the anti-activist influence of a conservative coalition of southern Democrats and western Republicans. Under the Warren Court, policy disputes over civil rights, school prayer, and legislative apportionment became major constitutional struggles. In the process, the Court assumed a substantively legislative role in addressing the nation's social problems. From Congress came discussion of such retaliatory actions as impeaching justices, limiting the Court's jurisdiction, and sanctioning judicial salaries.

The mid-1960s witnessed a remarkable outpouring of pent-up domestic policy legislation under the heading of the Great Society. In foreign affairs, Congress facilitated the nation's escalating military involvement in Southeast Asia, passing the 1964 Gulf of Tonkin Resolution by votes of 416-0 in the House and 88-2 in the Senate. Congress's action allowed President Lyndon Johnson to take "all necessary steps" to protect U.S. forces in Vietnam. Although Johnson later referred to passage of the resolution as the equivalent of a congressional declaration of war, key legislators countered that the president had misrepresented the Gulf of Tonkin incident to gain congressional support that might otherwise have been withheld. By 1970, as legislators prepared to repeal the resolution, President Richard Nixon unilaterally widened the war with an invasion of Cambodia. Moving to reassert congressional prerogatives, both houses adopted restrictions on the use of U.S. ground forces in Cambodia. Finally, in 1973, Congress passed the War Powers Resolution, limiting the president's power to commit American troops without congressional approval. Implementation of this resolution continues to be controversial, as the executive branch chafes at this attempt by Congress to reestablish its constitutional

power to declare war, thus challenging the usurpation of that power by presidents acting constitutionally as commanders in chief.

A year after adopting the War Powers Resolution, Congress imposed greater legislative control over government spending. The Congressional Budget and Impoundment Control Act of 1974 curtailed the president's ability to "impound" congressionally appropriated funds as a means of killing programs the executive could not block in the normal legislative process. Throughout most of U.S. history, presidents have occasionally refrained from spending appropriated funds, primarily for routine administrative reasons acceptable to Congress. In 1973, however, President Nixon declared that he planned to impound funds when their expenditure might increase prices or taxes. This assertion, aimed at wiping out or crippling entire programs (including one funded at $9 billion), infuriated congressional members, who took it as a major constitutional challenge. The 1974 Congressional Budget and Impoundment Control Act created House and Senate budget committees and established a mechanism to ensure that Congress managed its annual appropriations process in an expeditious manner.

The 1980s and 1990s brought the Supreme Court into two more fundamental lawmaking disputes between the legislative and executive branches—the delegation of legislative authority to executive agencies and control over appropriations. In *INS v. Chadha* (1983), the Supreme Court invalidated, in a single stroke, provisions of 200 laws. (The Court itself had only overturned 115 statutes since its inception.) From its earliest days, Congress had employed shortcuts to the otherwise inherently time-consuming process of making laws. Beginning in the 1930s, as its workload grew under the emergency conditions of the Great Depression, Congress began to assign specific legislative powers to the executive branch. In *Chadha*, the Court ruled that this procedure violated the principle of bicameralism and the constitutional requirement that all acts of Congress be presented to the president for approval. Critics of the decision argued that the Court took an excessively formalistic view of the lawmaking process, ignoring the many informal shortcuts that had evolved over the centuries.

In a move reminiscent of President Nixon's early 1970s efforts to expand his executive prerogatives to impound appropriated funds, President Bill Clinton in the early 1990s sought to increase executive powers over Congress through the use of the line-item veto. In 1996 a Republican Congress gave the Democratic president the tool that he believed he needed in the form of the Line-Item Veto Act. This statute expanded the executive's constitutional power to veto laws passed by Congress by giving the president the option of discarding specific, line-item, provisions within an appropriations act instead of the traditional choice of vetoing the entire measure or allowing it to pass. If Congress objected to one or more of these vetoes, it had the option, under its customary lawmaking powers, of enacting a statute of disapproval.

The line-item veto had first appeared in the 1860s, and today more than forty states have adopted some form of the device. Those who advocated its implementation at the national level argued that it would allow the president to curb "runaway" spending and "pork-barrel" projects inserted in legislation by influential members of Congress. Opponents countered that the measure would profoundly alter the balance between the legislative and executive branches, improperly providing lawmaking authority to the president. Such a fundamental restructuring of governmental powers could take place, they argued, only through an amendment to the Constitution. In *Clinton v. City of New York* (1998), the Supreme Court declared the Line-Item Veto Act of 1996 unconstitutional.

Conclusion

Congress has constantly struggled to define and preserve its lawmaking powers, just as it has worked to buttress the constitutional viability of the executive and judicial branches. The framers of the Constitution could not possibly have imagined what tests those powers would face over a period of more than two centuries. No one in the eighteenth century openly envisioned a nation that would grow to span the North American continent and rise to world power status. Yet mindful of James Madison's counsel that "ambition must be made to counteract ambition,"[10] the framers would have admired the ongoing struggle between the houses of Congress and the executive and judicial branches, as they contend for responsibility in determining the nation's laws. Presidents continue to covet war power authority and control over appropriations just as the Supreme Court aggressively continues its challenge of Congress's lawmaking authority through the process of judicial review. In recent decades, the reality of "divided government"— in which one party controls the White House and the other is in the majority in at least one house of Congress—has greatly added to the complexity of the process.

A strengthened but embattled Congress, a presidency nourishing "imperial" ambitions, and a Supreme Court savoring the evolving concept of "judicial sovereignty"[11] guarantee that the lawmaking process will continue to be one charged with drama, frustration, and a constant struggle to meet the unprecedented challenges of a rapidly diversifying society.

Notes

1. "Opinion of the Constitutionality of an Act to Establish a Bank, February 23, 1791," in *The Papers of Alexander Hamilton,* ed. Harold C. Syrett (New York: Columbia University Press, 1961–1987), 8:107.
2. Alexander Hamilton, John Jay, and James Madison, *The Federalist: A Collection,* ed. George W. Carey and James McClellan (Indianapolis: Liberty Fund, 2001), 241.
3. Ibid., 269.
4. *McCulloch v. Maryland,* 17 U.S. 421 (1819).
5. *Register of Debates in Congress,* 22d Cong., 2d sess., 1833, 520–521.
6. Don E. Fehrenbacher, *The Dred Scott Case: Its Significance in American Law and Politics* (New York: Oxford University Press, 1978), 360–362; *Dred Scott v. Sandford,* 60 U.S. 407 (1857).
7. Congress repealed the Tenure of Office Act in 1887, and the Supreme Court in *Myers v. United States,* 272 U.S. 52 (1926) upheld the authority of the president to control the tenure of executive officials by ruling unconstitutional a statute allowing the Senate to approve the removal of postmasters. Subsequent high court decisions—*Humphrey's Executor v. United States,* 295 U.S. 602 (1935), *Bowsher v. Synar,* 478 U.S. 714 (1986), and *Morrison v. Olson,* 487 U.S. 654 (1988)—have reinforced the president's exclusive authority to remove officers who perform executive functions.
8. *McGrain v. Daugherty,* 273 U.S. 175 (1927).
9. *Congressional Record,* 78th Cong., 2d sess., 1944, 90:1964–1966.
10. *The Federalist,* No. 51, 268.
11. The distinction between judicial supremacy and judicial sovereignty is made in Larry D. Kramer, "We the Court," *Harvard Law Review* 115 (November 2001): 13.

CHAPTER FOUR

The Evolution of Presidential Power

WILLIAM E. LEUCHTENBURG

The founders had a difficult time deciding what kind of institution they wanted the presidency to be. Having denounced the tyranny of George III, they eyed warily any attempt to impose a homebred monarch on the new republic. In the aftermath of the American Revolution, the Articles of Confederation and state constitutions provided for a weak executive, a plural executive, or no executive at all. These experiments, however, resulted in ineffectual governance. Furthermore, a rural uprising in western Massachusetts led the fearful elite to conclude that firmer leadership would be necessary to preserve social order. Conservative New Yorker John Jay, observing the deleterious consequences of weak government, went so far as to ask, "Shall we have a king?"[1]

The framers of the Constitution vested the presidency with so much power that the fiery Virginian Patrick Henry complained that the document was a "squint toward monarchy."[2] Article 2 states unequivocally, "The executive Power shall be vested in a President of the United States of America." This article also authorizes the president to appoint ambassadors, Supreme Court justices, and other high-ranking federal officials; provides the president a prominent role in foreign affairs, including the treaty-making responsibility; designates the president as commander in chief of the armed forces; authorizes the president to grant pardons and to summon Congress into special session; and allows for indefinite reelection, a provision that excited fears that, like a royal head of state, a president of the United States could have life tenure. The president is also instructed to "take Care that the Laws be faithfully executed," a simple statement with formidable implications.

A number of presidents have contended that the combination of the "take Care" and "executive Power" clauses justifies the assumption that the office of the presidency has "inherent power" beyond the considerable allotment enumerated or implied in the Constitution. In its most presumptuous formulation, this "residuum" of power has been likened to the prerogative once claimed by the Crown. The framers knew well political philosopher John Locke's articulation of this prerogative: "Power to act according to discretion for the publick Good, without the prescription of the Law, and sometimes even against it."[3] Other branches of government have looked askance at this claim to executive prerogative, but it has not been easy to cabin presidential power by confining it to the text of the Constitution.

From their experience as colonists under the British Crown, and from their reading of Locke and the French philosopher Montesquieu, however, the framers had concluded that it was unwise for all power to be concentrated in a single branch of government. Consequently, in keeping with the principle of separation of powers, they created two countervailing branches of government: Congress and the federal judiciary. They endowed Congress, in particular, with a number of ways to check the president, especially through power of the purse. Though treaties can be negotiated by the president, they must be ratified by the Senate. Also, although the president appoints federal officials, including Supreme Court justices, Congress must confirm them. The president has the right to veto bills passed by Congress, but by a two-thirds vote Congress can override a presidential veto. Deliberately, the framers created overlapping responsibilities and pitted one branch against another. As James Madison wrote in *Federalist* No. 51, "Ambition must be made to counteract ambition."[4] Presidents, however, retain a vast realm of authority, but the full power of the office has come to depend less on phrasings of the Constitution than on the vision and temperament of particular incumbents.

The Early Presidency

Early presidents had a considerably more circumscribed view of the office than their twentieth-century successors. George Washington provided a model of restraint, epitomized by his refusal to serve more than two terms, a disavowal of ambition creating a precedent that would last for one hundred forty years. Marcus Cunliffe speculates, "If he had felt too much like a king, or an angry party chieftain bent on revenge, and had determined to offer himself again for election in 1800—as a few desperate Federalists urged him to do—what chaos might not have befallen America?"[5] In the early years of the Republic, chief executives were reluctant even to use their power to veto legislation unless they thought a measure was patently unconstitutional. John Adams and Thomas Jefferson never used it. Within half a century, self-effacement had degenerated into the sorry spectacle of Franklin Pierce and James Buchanan being swept aside by the riptide of events moving the country inexorably toward civil war.

In the generation after the Civil War, the institution of the presidency seemed alarmingly feeble. Nothing showed the dominance of Congress in this age of legislative supremacy as well as the impeachment by the House of Representatives of President Andrew Johnson, who was spared removal from office only because his enemies fell a single vote shy of the required two-thirds of the Senate. Massachusetts Republican senator George Frisbie Hoar later recalled that in this era of Chester Arthur and Benjamin Harrison, his "most eminent" colleagues "would have received as a personal affront a private message from the White House expressing a desire that they should adopt any course in the discharge of their legislative duties that they did not approve. If they visited the White House, it was to give, not to receive, advice."[6] In *Congressional Government*, the young scholar Woodrow Wilson summed up much of the experience of the first century of the executive when he wrote that the presidency was "too silent and inactive, too little like a premiership and too much like a super-intendency."[7]

There appear to be two conspicuous exceptions to Wilson's generalization: Andrew Jackson and Abraham Lincoln. A tribune of the people, Jackson waged war on the Second Bank of the United States, vetoed legislation for internal improvements, and defied the Supreme Court. His opponents called Old Hickory "King Andrew." Lincoln reasoned that the tandem of the commander in chief clause and the take care clause permitted him to act wholly on his own authority in raising an army against the Confederacy, issuing the Emancipation Proclamation, and suspending the writ of habeas corpus. Lincoln, said Lord Bryce, "wielded more authority than any single Englishman has done since Oliver Cromwell."[8] According to E. S. Corwin, Jackson's performance, however, was "more bark than bite."[9] He used his powers not to expand the national government but to rein in those who would enlarge it. A president, Jackson believed, should be limited to one term. Lincoln acted as he did only because he had little alternative in the midst of the greatest crisis in U.S. history. As befitted a former Whig, he thought a president should defer to Congress. Jackson and Lincoln would have been shocked by the twentieth-century conception of the president.

Yet, as Corwin states, "the history of the presidency is the history of aggrandizement,"[10] and even reticent presidents have contributed to the growth of the office. George Washington established the right of a chief executive to remove federal officials at will, even on caprice, without seeking congressional approval. Also ignoring Congress, he issued the Neutrality Proclamation and expelled a French diplomat who had an ar-

dent following in Congress. Washington took advantage of his powers as commander in chief to call out troops to put down the Whiskey Rebellion, though he had no congressional authority to do so. He set an important precedent by asserting a claim to executive privilege in refusing a request from the House of Representatives for papers pertinent to the negotiation of Jay's Treaty, which angry critics charged had surrendered American trading rights to the British. During Washington's presidency, there emerged two institutions nowhere mentioned in the Constitution—political parties and the cabinet. The rise of parties made it possible for the people to have greater influence in the choice of presidents and gave chief executives an important new role: party leader.

At times, Washington's successors also acted resolutely. Thomas Jefferson broadly interpreted the Constitution in negotiating the Louisiana Purchase and in bypassing Congress to send a naval squadron on a secret mission to rout the Barbary pirates. James Monroe single-mindedly asserted the doctrine bearing his name that warned against European meddling in the Western Hemisphere, and James K. Polk was so militant about the Mexican War that it was called "Mister Polk's War." The White House was not altogether dormant even in the post–Civil War era of presidential eclipse. On slim statutory authority, Rutherford B. Hayes and Grover Cleveland, reluctant though they were to extend the reach of the federal government, undertook a number of forays, including using troops to break strikes. Still, the last president of the nineteenth century, William McKinley, counted a White House staff of only six, and at 4 P.M. each day left his desk to take a nap.

The Expanding Presidency

The modern, leviathan presidency begins with McKinley's successor, Theodore Roosevelt. "My view," he states in his autobiography, "was that every executive officer . . . was a steward of the people. . . . I declined to adopt the view that what was imperatively necessary for the Nation could not be done by the President unless he could find some specific authorization to do it."[11] Promising the American people a "square deal," he assailed the trusts; he became the first chief executive to intervene forcefully on behalf of labor, by compelling mine owners to accept arbitration of a costly strike. Viewing his office as a "bully pulpit," Roosevelt promoted conservation and other personal causes. To call the nation's attention to problems and to generate new solutions, he created national commissions of experts, a practice later adopted wholesale by Herbert Hoover.

The first president after the Spanish-American War catapulted the United States to prominence as a world power. Roosevelt declared an African expression as his motto, "Speak softly and carry a big stick!" An unapologetic imperialist, he added to the Monroe Doctrine the Roosevelt corollary: the obligation of the United States to punish "chronic wrongdoing" in Latin America. He pushed through his scheme to dig the Panama Canal with little regard for the sovereignty of other nations. On leaving the White House, he boasted to an English friend, Sir George Otto Trevelyan, "I have used every ounce of power there was in the office and I have not cared a rap for the criticisms of those who spoke of my 'usurpation.' "[12]

During Roosevelt's administration, one of his admirers, Woodrow Wilson, who had viewed the presidency as infirm not many years before, declared that the president "is the only national voice in affairs. Let him once win the admiration and confidence of the country, and no other single force can withstand him. . . . The President is at liberty both in law and in conscience, to be as big a man as he can."[13] As chief executive, Wilson revived a practice abandoned a century before of addressing Congress in person. (Jefferson had jettisoned the rite because he thought it smacked of the king's speech from the throne.) Like a British prime minister with a balky House of Commons, Wilson kept Congress in session for more than a year and a half in order to drive through his New Freedom legislation, including the Federal Reserve Act and an income tax.

During his administration, Wilson became the most prestigious world leader of his time. In response to Germany's resumption of unrestricted submarine warfare, he sought congressional authority to arm U.S. merchant vessels, and when he failed to get it, he acted on his own. Soon thereafter, he took the momentous step of leading the nation into World War I by asking Congress to recognize that a state of war already existed because of German actions. During the war, Wilson supervised so far-reaching a regimentation of the economy that it was called war socialism. Afterward, he sailed to Europe to take an active part in drafting the Treaty of Versailles. When Wilson returned home, he worked himself into a collapse while touring the country, proselytizing on behalf of the League of Nations. For Roosevelt and Wilson, foreign affairs and national security were the engines that propelled the expanded presidency.

Neither Roosevelt nor Wilson, however, explored all the possibilities of the twentieth-

century presidency. Roosevelt did not fully develop his conception of the New Nationalism,
with its large role for the federal government,
or his stewardship theory of the presidency
until after he had left the White House. While
in office, he made thunderous proclamations,
but they were often bluff and bluster. Wilson
made significant strides in economic policy, but
he did so not to promote a managerial state
but a market economy in which small busi-
nesspeople would have greater opportunities.

Not until 1933, when Franklin Delano Roosevelt entered the White House, did the modern presidency fully emerge. In his first inaugural address, Roosevelt alerted the nation that
if necessary in order to cope with the Great Depression, he would seek emergency powers as
great as if the country were being invaded.
During the First Hundred Days of 1933 he
sponsored measures to mobilize industry and
agriculture to an extent unprecedented in
peacetime, and during the Second Hundred
Days of 1935 he put the United States on the
road to the welfare state. As Democratic Party
leader, he fostered "the FDR coalition," which
centered on lower-income voters, who have
been the core of the party since. So popular
was Roosevelt that in 1940 he dared to defy
George Washington's taboo by running for,
and winning, a third term. In 1944 he won a
fourth term.

When Roosevelt reached out to the American people with his radio addresses so informal
and intimate that they were called "fireside
chats," and when he initiated freewheeling
press conferences, he encouraged a multitude
of citizens who had never regarded the government in Washington as accessible to write
to him. One of the members of his "brain

trust" of advisors summed up what Roosevelt
wrought: "No monarch . . . unless it may have
been Elizabeth or her magnificent Tudor father,
or maybe Alexander or Augustus Caesar, can
have given quite that sense of serene presiding,
of gathering up into himself, of really representing, a whole people."[14]

Few chief executives have devoted so much
attention to the structure of the federal government, especially to the immense bureaucracy that has evolved since George Washington's day. Ostensibly a part of the Roosevelt
administration, it was often autonomous and
regarded interest groups or congressional blocs
as its clients. Roosevelt formed a committee to
study the structure of the federal government
in order to gain control of it and to reconfigure
it. The committee reported back with a particularly harsh view of the independent regulatory agencies, describing them collectively as a
"fourth branch" created by Congress that was
not answerable to the president and that
drained executive power. Roosevelt's attempt
to achieve the fundamental reorganization his
committee recommended met with defeat in
Congress, but in 1939 he could claim credit for
one particularly important innovation—the
Executive Office of the President.

Roosevelt also exercised formidable power
in foreign affairs. From the moment he took
office, he looked for ways to combat the rise of
Nazi Germany, and after World War II began
he brushed past constitutional and statutory
restraints to speed aid to the Allies. In 1940, in
contravention of two acts of Congress, he negotiated a deal to supply U.S. destroyers to the
beleaguered British. After the bombing of Pearl
Harbor, he plotted global military and naval
strategy in guiding the country to victory over

the Berlin-Rome-Tokyo axis, mobilized the U.S. economy, created the Pentagon, sped the construction of the atomic bomb, and built the framework of the United Nations. Every poll of historians ranks Roosevelt as the greatest twentieth-century president, but he also arouses complaints of having accumulated too much power and of not always using it wisely.

Harry Truman, Roosevelt's successor, changed the institution of the presidency in more ways than is usually acknowledged. His tenure brought the unification of the armed services under a new Department of Defense and the creation of the Central Intelligence Agency (CIA), the Atomic Energy Commission, and the Council of Economic Advisers. Without seeking congressional approval, Truman plunged the country into the Korean War. Drawing upon his constitutional authority as commander in chief, he struck the most dramatic blow for civilian control of the military by dismissing the highly popular but headstrong Gen. Douglas MacArthur for insubordination. Truman also not only set up the President's Committee on Civil Rights, a move that incurred the wrath of the Southern bloc in Congress, but issued an executive order accelerating desegregation of the armed forces. Another edict placed thousands of federal employees under a loyalty program intended to weed out communists. In addition, he undertook a series of initiatives in foreign policy: the Marshall Plan, the Berlin airlift, NATO, and, of course, the Truman Doctrine, which established the policy of containing communism.

Every post–World War II president has contributed in some fashion to the expansion of the presidency, if only to a modest degree. Dwight Eisenhower was repelled by grandiose conceptions of the office, but he covertly authorized the CIA to meddle in Iran and Guatemala, and he sent U-2 reconnaissance planes into Soviet air space. Without seeking congressional advice, John F. Kennedy brought the country to the brink of nuclear war over Soviet missiles in Cuba. Gerald Ford employed the presidential pardon on behalf of Richard Nixon, and Jimmy Carter granted blanket amnesty to Vietnam-era draft dodgers. Carter also used personal diplomacy in getting Israel and Egypt to draft a peace treaty at Camp David, and as commander in chief he sent helicopters to the Iranian desert in a failed mission to rescue Americans held hostage after the Iranian Revolution. Ronald Reagan railed against elephantine government, but did not hesitate to break the air traffic controllers' strike or to send troops to Grenada and Lebanon. Drawing upon the presidential reservoir of powers, George Bush assembled a global coalition against the Iraqi invasion of Kuwait; Bill Clinton defined the policy of the armed services toward homosexuality and intervened in Somalia and Haiti; and George W. Bush created a far-reaching national security apparatus in the war against terrorism.

Two of the postwar chief executives caused such consternation over their excesses that critics warned of an "imperial presidency." Lyndon Johnson turned his gargantuan energy to advantage by persuading Congress to enact long-overdue social legislation, including Medicare, and by launching the War on Poverty, but he also aroused alarm by his conduct in other areas. Only months after winning election on a peace platform, Johnson escalated the war in Vietnam, which would cost many thousands of lives. Richard Nixon earned praise when he signed such measures as the one creating the Environmental Protection Agency, but he elicited strong condemnation for his willful actions in further expanding the war in Southeast Asia and by "impounding" millions of dollars legitimately appropriated by Congress for social programs. He met his downfall when he abused the public trust by taking part in the vast conspiracy to cover up a series of "dirty tricks" against his rivals in the Watergate scandal.

Attempts to Constrain Presidential Power

This expansion of presidential authority has not gone unchallenged. Time and again, Congress has crushed the aspirations of presidents by denying them legislation that they have sought, refusing to appropriate money for their favorite programs, or rejecting one or more of their nominees to high office. In the aftermath of World War I, the Senate bitterly disappointed President Wilson by refusing to approve U.S. membership in the League of Nations. As Hitler and Mussolini conspired to devour their neighbors, Congress tied Franklin Roosevelt's hands by legislating U.S. neutrality. Not long after Roosevelt's death, Congress ensured that there would never be another four-term president by sending to the states for ratification the Twenty-second Amendment, limiting presidents to two terms. Congress has twice used the ultimate power over a president: In 1868 it impeached and nearly removed Andrew Johnson from office, and in 1998 the House impeached Bill Clinton, though he, too, survived the attempt to expel him. In 1974 the House had begun impeachment proceedings against Nixon that would have resulted in his ouster if he had not resigned.

Presidents have also run into trouble with the federal judiciary. In the landmark *Marbury v. Madison* (1803), the Supreme Court claimed the right to monitor presidential behavior.[15] Chief executives from Jefferson to Lincoln to Theodore Roosevelt have denounced the alleged arrogance of the federal courts. In the 1930s the Court's determination to strike down Franklin Roosevelt's New Deal led to a constitutional crisis. During Roosevelt's first term, the justices invalidated the National Industrial Recovery Act and the Agricultural Adjustment Act, the foundations of his program to lift the country out of the Great Depression,[16] and deprived him of the power to remove officials of independent regulatory commissions.[17] The Court relented only after Roosevelt threatened it with drastic legislation to add as many as six justices of his choice. During the Korean War, President Truman claimed that his powers as chief executive and commander in chief entitled him to order the seizure of steel mills to maintain production needed for the war, although Congress had prescribed a different course of action. The Supreme Court held him to the letter of the law.[18]

Nixon thought that he had shaped the Court to his liking when he was able to appoint four justices, including Chief Justice Warren Burger. During the Watergate controversy, Nixon claimed the inherent power to exercise total control of presidential papers, but the Court, in an opinion written by Burger, unanimously denied that there was absolute executive privilege. The Court instead determined that the ultimate authority to determine what papers should be made available lay with the judiciary, not with the executive branch. When papers were required for a criminal prosecution, the president, like any other citizen, had to obey subpoenas.[19] The Court's decision compelling Nixon to surrender incriminating documents sealed his fate.

Some chief executives, however, found ways to elude the restraints the other branches sought to impose, especially in the conduct of foreign affairs. To get around the power of the Senate to reject treaties, presidents have resorted to executive agreements, which do not require ratification. Franklin Roosevelt employed this device in signing the Atlantic Charter in 1941 and in negotiating the Yalta agreement in 1945. The Constitution assigns exclusive power to Congress to declare war, but presidents have often rendered that power meaningless by actions that have made war inescapable. In retaliation, Congress has enacted laws to forestall presidents from engaging in reckless adventures abroad, but to little avail. Reagan flouted the provisions of a congressional statute in conniving to sell arms to Iran in order to arm and fund Nicaraguan contras with the proceeds. Although Reagan took note of the War Powers Resolution of 1973 by consulting with congressional leaders when he ordered the 1986 bombing of Libya, he did so only after the bombers had taken off. The Supreme Court, too, has had trouble disciplining presidents. It has handed down rulings denouncing violations of civil liberties by the executive branch in wartime, but only after conflict has ended.[20]

In considering the relationship among the three branches, there is a more important consideration—that far from being eternally locked in combat, they frequently support one another. In World War I Congress delegated to Wilson an astonishing range of powers, including seizing and operating the railroad, telegraph, and telephone systems. During the Great Depression, Congress was so willing to cooperate with Franklin Roosevelt that the Supreme Court reprimanded it for surrendering some of its lawmaking authority to the executive. The Senate legitimated Lyndon Johnson's venture in Vietnam by adopting the Gulf of Tonkin Resolution, and after the September 11, 2001, attacks on the United States, both houses of Congress rallied behind President George W. Bush.

The Supreme Court has sustained presidential actions far more than it has denied them. The executive has benefited in numerous cases involving the separation of powers doctrine. The Court has held that only the president may exercise the veto power and the appointing power.[21] In turn, presidents have come to the aid of the judiciary, as Eisenhower did in sending airborne troops to Little Rock, Arkansas, to back federal court rulings desegregating the city's public schools.

Some Court decisions that were severe blows to presidential powers have simultaneously contained rulings sustaining executive claims. In *Youngstown Sheet and Tube Co. v. Sawyer,* the steel mill seizure case that set back Truman, three of the justices accepted the administration's bold assertion of the right to ignore an act of Congress, and four confined the limitations on executive power to the specific features of the case. In *United States v. Nixon,* a devastating blow to Nixon's desire to remain in office, the Court formally recognized the claim of executive privilege, which, it said, "is fundamental to the operation of Government and inextricably rooted in the separation of powers under the Constitution."[22]

Never has the Supreme Court set aside the action of a president in the role of commander in chief. In 1863 the Court validated Lincoln's blockade of Confederate ports after the firing on Fort Sumter, although he imposed it without authorization from Congress. In a crisis, the Court said, the president has to act "without waiting for any special legislative authority."[23] On several occasions a century later the Court dismissed challenges to the constitutionality of the Vietnam conflict despite the fact that it was waged without a formal declaration of war by Congress.[24]

The most extravagant expression of judicial sanction for the virtually limitless powers of a president in foreign affairs came in 1936, at the time that the Court was striking down Franklin Roosevelt's domestic programs. In *United States v. Curtiss-Wright Export Corp.,* Justice George Sutherland declared that the power to make foreign policy is a "very delicate, plenary and exclusive power of the President as the sole organ of the federal government in the field of international relations—a power which does not require as a basis for its exercise an act of Congress." Sutherland even asserted that a president's prerogatives in this realm predates the Constitution, having been inherited from the Crown.[25]

The response of the federal government in the 1960s to discrimination against racial minorities illustrates that the separation of powers can be consonant with effective government. In a moving address shortly after the assassination of John Kennedy, Lyndon Johnson asked Congress to approve a bill ending racial discrimination as a memorial to the slain president. Following months of intense debate, bipartisan coalitions in both houses of the legislative branch approved the Civil Rights Act of 1964, which mandated change in the nation's practices with regard to race, and also, as a consequence of an amendment, to gender. In accordance with his duty under the Constitution to "take Care that the Laws be faithfully executed," Johnson then saw to it that the act was vigorously enforced. When the constitutionality of the law was challenged, the Supreme Court ruled that it was a valid exercise of the commerce power.[26] All three branches had contributed to this highly significant accomplishment.

Conclusion

The expansion of presidential power has not destroyed the system of checks and balances, but it has at times put it under strain. In an age requiring instant responses to intercontinental missiles with nuclear warheads, Congress is unlikely to ever regain the war-making power, attenuated as it was. The evolution of presidential authority has not been one in which the executive has simply overpowered the judicial and legislative branches. Within the past generation, the Supreme Court brought Nixon to heel, and, more recently, Congress initiated impeachment proceedings against President Clinton. Such conflicts are inevitable, and, quite often, healthy, for it is vital that each branch retain its integrity.

Yet, as the Supreme Court states in *United States v. Nixon* the "separate powers were not intended to operate with absolute independence."[27] Disputes grab the headlines, but the collaboration among the three branches is more important. The U.S. government could not function if there were no common ground. By vigilantly guarding their own constitutional rights, each of the three branches preserves the principle of separation of powers. Not infrequently, however, it is by breaking through these boundaries and negotiating agreements that the federal government best serves the nation.

Notes

1. James T. Patterson, "The Rise of Presidential Power before World War II," *Law and Contemporary Problems* 40 (spring 1976): 40.

2. Marcus Cunliffe, *The American Heritage History of the Presidency* (New York: American Heritage, 1968), 13.

3. John Locke, *Second Treatise of Civil Government*, ed. Charles L. Sherman (New York: D. Appleton-Century, 1937), 109.

4. Alexander Hamilton, James Madison, and John Jay, *The Federalist Papers*, ed. Roy P. Fairfield, 2d ed. (Baltimore: The Johns Hopkins University Press, 1981), 160.

5. Marcus Cunliffe, *The Presidency*, 3d ed. (Boston: Houghton Mifflin, 1987), 60.

6. George Frisbie Hoar, *Autobiography of Seventy Years* (New York: Scribners, 1903), 2:46.

7. Woodrow Wilson, *Congressional Government: A Study in American Politics* (Boston: Houghton Mifflin, 1885), 45.

8. Quoted in Arthur M. Schlesinger Jr., *The Imperial Presidency* (Boston: Houghton Mifflin, 1973), 59.

9. E. S. Corwin, *The President: Office and Powers, 1787–1948*, 4th rev. ed. (New York: New York University Press, 1957), 311.

10. Ibid., 29–30.

11. Theodore Roosevelt, *Autobiography* (New York: Scribners, 1913), 357.

12. Joseph B. Bishop, *Theodore Roosevelt and His Time Shown in His Own Letters* (New York: Scribners, 1920), 2:94.

13. Woodrow Wilson, *Constitutional Government in the United States* (New York: Columbia University Press, 1908), 68–73.

14. R. G. Tugwell, "The Experimental Roosevelt," *Political Quarterly* (July 1950): 262.

15. 1 Cranch 137 (1803).

16. *A. L. A. Schechter Poultry Corp. v. United States,* 295 U.S. 495 (1935); *United States v. Butler,* 297 U.S. 1 (1936).

17. *Humphrey's Executor v. United States,* 295 U.S. 602 (1935).

18. *Youngstown Sheet and Tube Co. v. Sawyer,* 343 U.S. 579 (1952).

19. *United States v. Nixon,* 418 U.S. 683 (1974).

20. *Ex parte Milligan,* 4 Wallace 2 (1866); *Duncan v. Kahanamoku,* 327 U.S. 304 (1946).

21. *INS v. Chadha,* 462 U.S. 919 (1983); *Buckley v. Valeo,* 424 U.S. 1 (1976). See also *Bowsher v. Synar,* 478 U.S. 714 (1986).

22. *United States v. Nixon,* 708.

23. *Prize Cases,* 2 Black 635 (1863).

24. *Massachusetts v. Laird,* 400 U.S. 886 (1970); *Holtzman v. Schlesinger,* 414 U.S. 1304 (1973).

25. *United States v. Curtiss-Wright Export Corp.,* 299 U.S. 304, 320 (1936).

26. *Heart of Atlanta Hotel v. United States,* 379 U.S. 241 (1964); *Katzenbach v. McClung,* 379 U.S. 294 (1964).

27. *United States v. Nixon,* 707.

CHAPTER FIVE

The Law and Politics of Judicial Review

MARK A. GRABER

Judicial review is a legal and a political practice. Judicial rulings on the constitutionality of government acts are based (or expected to be based) on distinctive forms of legal reasoning. These differ significantly from the more pragmatic forms of reasoning that guide legislative, executive, and other political decisions. The political decisions government officials make are constrained by what justices have declared or are thought likely to declare constitutional. At the same time, what happens in the rest of the political universe constrains the legal arguments justices use to reach their decisions. Justices typically hold views similar to those of the elected officials responsible for staffing the Supreme Court, and they may be reluctant to challenge very strong political majorities in those rare instances where judicial preferences sharply diverge from the preferences of most other political actors. Recognizing judicial review as a political practice does not deny that judicial review is also a legal practice and a practice that must be justified. What must be justified is the actual practice, not the theory of the practice.

The Practice of Judicial Review

Judicial review refers to the power of justices to determine in the context of an ordinary lawsuit whether a government law, regulation, or action is constitutional. The Supreme Court of the United States in *United States v. Eichman* (1990) exercised the power of judicial review when declaring that Shawn Eichmann could not be convicted for burning a flag. The federal statute banning flag burning, the judicial majority concluded, violated the First Amendment. The Supreme Court of Wisconsin in *In re Booth* (1854) exercised the power of judicial review when declaring that Sherman Booth was entitled to a writ of habeas corpus. Booth could not be convicted of violating the Fugitive Slave Act of 1850, the justices concluded, because the Constitution did not vest the national government with the power to pass that law. The Supreme Court in *Youngstown Sheet and Tube Co. v. Sawyer* (1952) exercised the power of judicial review when ordering President Harry Truman to return to their owners the steel mills seized by the government during the

Korean War. The Constitution, a 6-3 judicial majority ruled, did not give the president the power to expropriate private property in the absence of statutory authority from Congress.

Judicial review as practiced in the United States differs from analogous practices in other countries.[1] All courts in the United States may declare laws unconstitutional, but only in the context of an actual lawsuit. Some European countries permit only specialized courts to resolve constitutional issues. A local trial court in the United States is permitted and expected to decide whether evidence in a criminal case was collected in a manner consistent with the Fourth Amendment. Local trial courts in many European countries abjure such decisions. Instead, they seek rulings by special constitutional tribunals whenever a constitutional issue arises. The constitutions of other European countries entitle elected officials under certain conditions to have courts determine whether legislative proposals pass constitutional muster before those proposals became law, a practice known as abstract judicial review. Courts in the United States may make constitutional decisions only after a bill becomes a law, and only after persons claim they have been injured by the operation of that law.

Judicial review involves, but is not identical to, constitutional interpretation. Before determining whether a government action is unconstitutional, the justices must first determine the extent to which the Constitution authorizes judicial review in the case before the court. The Constitution in some instances may vest some other governing institution with the power to determine whether particular government actions are constitutional. The Supreme Court has historically recognized a number of so-called political questions or constitutional issues that courts are not authorized to adjudicate. One example is (Walter) *Nixon v. United States* (1993), in which the Court ruled that the Senate had the constitutional power to determine the proper procedures during the impeachment trial of a federal judge. The Constitution in other instances may require justices to give some weight to constitutional judgments made by other governing officials. James Bradley Thayer famously maintained that justices should declare unconstitutional only government actions no reasonable person would think constitutional.[2] A justice of this view might uphold a prosecution for burning the flag, even though the justice believed the statute outlawing that conduct was probably unconstitutional. Difficult questions of constitutional interpretation, according to this theory of judicial review, are best left to elected officials.

The consequences of judicial decisions declaring laws unconstitutional are subject to political and jurisprudential dispute. Some commentators think judicial decisions on constitutional issues should affect only the rights of the parties involved in the lawsuit. Abraham Lincoln famously declared that when the Supreme Court in *Dred Scott v. Sandford* (1856) asserted that Congress had no power to ban slavery in any U.S. territory, the only legal consequence of that decision was that Dred Scott remained a slave.[3] The decision, Lincoln insisted, did not determine the rights of any other persons then being held as slaves or limit in any way the constitutional authority of Congress to ban slavery in any U.S. territory. Other constitutional commentators view judicial decisions on constitutional issues as binding all government actors. Stephen Douglas, in his debates with Lincoln, declared that once the Supreme Court in *Scott* asserted that Congress could not ban slavery in the territories, all federal and state officials had to accept that assertion as the authoritative exposition of the Constitution.[4] Supreme Court decisions, in his view, resolve lawsuits and determine the meaning of the Constitution.

Some contemporary scholars distinguish between judicial powers by using "judicial review" to refer to the power of courts to determine the constitutionality of government actions when deciding the rights of parties to a lawsuit and "judicial supremacy" to refer to the power of courts to determine what constitutional provisions mean. This terminology is not, however, universal. Justices and legal scholars during the first century of constitutional life did not speak of either judicial review or judicial supremacy. The expression "judicial review" was coined in the twentieth century.[5] The contemporary distinction between judicial review and judicial supremacy is largely confined to the academy. Justices speak now only of judicial review, even when referring to what many scholars consider judicial supremacy. One must typically determine from the broader context whether a justice or commentator thinks the judicial power to declare laws unconstitutional is the power to decide constitutional issues in the context of a particular lawsuit or the power to determine what the constitution means.

Legal Foundations and Justifications

The Constitution of the United States provides the legal foundations for judicial review and all other powers of national institutions in the country. The legal argument for judicial review, and all other legal arguments, involves the interpretation of a legal text. Legal arguments examine such sources as the actual words of the legal text, the original understanding of the text, the general principles underlying that text, and past interpretations of that text. Whether Congress is constitutionally authorized to pass laws including the phrase "under God" in the Pledge of Allegiance depends on the plain meaning of the words used in the First Amendment, the original meaning of the First Amendment, the general principles that best explain why Americans ratified the First Amendment, and previous interpretations of the First Amendment.

The process of interpreting the Constitution or a constitutional provision is hardly mechanical. As demonstrated by the bitter controversy over the 2002 judicial decision declaring unconstitutional the federal statute that added the phrase "under God" to the Pledge of Allegiance, Americans dispute what counts as a legal argument (Does constitutional language have any meaning other than what the provisions were intended to mean?), the appropriate weight to give different kinds of legal arguments (Do arguments from historical practice outweigh arguments from general principles?), and the proper application of an accepted legal argument (Did the persons responsible for the constitution intend to ban ceremonial references to deities?).

Legal arguments may incorporate (but are not identical to) moral or policy arguments. Many justices and leading scholars believe that when interpreting such provisions as the equal protection clause, justices should consider the broad philosophical issues associated with equality. Legal arguments, however, subordinate moral claims to interpretive claims. The moral argument against segregated schools ends with the demonstration that Jim Crow education violates fundamental human rights. A justice may rely on the premise that segregated schools violate fundamental human rights only if that premise helps the justice determine the best meaning of the phrase "equal protection of the laws" in the Fourteenth Amendment. Differences in judicial voting patterns often reflect differences in judicial beliefs about the morality and expedience of the underlying policy.[6] Still, legal practice ensures that the range of alternatives justices choose from is different and typically far more constrained than the policy alternatives open to other governmental actors. Justices who make decisions about the national economy by interpreting the phrase "Congress shall have Power To . . . regulate Commerce . . . among the several States" have historically behaved differently from other political actors who are charged with making nonlegal decisions about the national economy. Supreme Court justices do not second-guess decisions about the prime interest rate in large part because they have no legal power to do so.

The legal justification for judicial review in the United States relies on such legal sources as the language of Articles 3 and 6 of the Constitution, the original understanding of the framers of the Constitution, the more general understanding that written constitutional limits on government are best enforced by the judiciary, and two hundred years of legal precedents supporting the judicial power to declare laws unconstitutional. Article 3 declares that "(t)he Judicial Power shall extend to all Cases . . . arising under this Constitution." The phrase "arising under this constitution" suggests that justices are expected to adjudicate claims that a state or federal law is unconstitutional. Article 6 declares that "[t]his Constitution . . . shall be the supreme Law of the Land; and the Judges in every State shall be bound thereby, any Thing in the Constitution or Laws of any State to the Contrary notwithstanding." If state judges must declare state laws unconstitutional that conflict with the Constitution, then federal judges who hear appeals from state courts must also have the power to declare state laws unconstitutional.

History provides additional legal support for judicial review.[7] The evidence, while sketchy, suggests that the persons responsible for the Constitution believed that judges should have the power to declare laws unconstitutional. Judicial review was not discussed at length during the framing and ratification debates, but prominent delegates at the Constitutional Convention in 1787 assumed that courts would have some power to declare laws unconstitutional. Those Federalists and Anti-Federalists who considered judicial power during the ratification debates agreed that courts would have the power to declare state and federal laws unconstitutional.[8] Many persons think judicial review is implied from the decision to place written constitutional limits on government power. If the Constitution is fundamental law and courts are organs of the law, then courts have an obligation to decide in favor of the more fundamental law when fundamental law conflicts with ordinary law. The Constitution, as higher law, trumps statutes passed by legislatures that exist only by virtue of the Constitution.

The strongest legal foundation for the judicial power to declare laws unconstitutional is the historic judicial claim that courts have the power to declare laws unconstitutional. This assertion is not a tautology. The United States is a common law country. Previous judicial decisions in common law countries are important sources of law. When a court in a common law country declares that existing law protects the right to burn a flag, that decision creates a precedent, providing an additional legal reason for a subsequent court to conclude that existing law protects the right to burn a flag. The crucial plurality opinion in *Planned Parenthood v. Casey* (1992) asserted that an important legal reason for interpreting the Constitution as protecting abortion rights was that past Supreme Court decisions had interpreted the Constitution as protecting abortion rights. When courts interpret the Constitution as vesting the judiciary with the power to declare laws unconstitutional, these precedents provide additional legal reasons for supporting the judicial power to declare laws unconstitutional.

Precedent explains the legal significance of *Marbury v. Madison* (1803), the first case in which the Supreme Court explicitly declared a law unconstitutional and defended judicial review at length. The actual law declared unconstitutional was forgettable and forgotten. The justices interpreted (or probably misinterpreted)[9] a provision in the Judiciary Act of 1789 as authorizing the Court to adjudicate a case that the justices then interpreted (or, again probably misinterpreted)[10] the Constitution as mandating be first adjudicated by some other court. Far more important was the lengthy justification in *Marbury* given for the judicial power to declare laws unconstitutional. Chief Justice John Marshall's opinion for the court

declared that the power of judicial review was inherent in the notion of a written constitution that specifically limited the power of elected officials, implied by the judicial oath to obey the constitution, and necessary to prevent legislative violations of clear constitutional provisions.[11] Even for those who found and find Marshall's logic less than compelling, *Marbury* clearly established a legal precedent for judicial review. That precedent has been reaffirmed for almost two hundred years. Every Supreme Court opinion that considers judicial power defends the judicial power to declare laws unconstitutional. This unbroken practice places the power of judicial review on as solid a precedential foundation as is legally possible.

The best legal interpretation of the precise judicial power asserted in *Marbury* has always been controversial. Many prominent commentators insist that the judicial power detailed by Marshall is very different from the judicial power claimed by contemporary courts. They emphasize three differences in particular. First, *Marbury* sanctioned judicial review, not what has become known as judicial supremacy.[12] The Court in *Marbury,* the argument goes, claimed authority to interpret the Constitution only to resolve the lawsuit before the justices and made no pretense at prescribing rules for other governmental officials. Second, *Marbury* asserts only a power to declare laws of a judiciary nature unconstitutional—that is, laws that specifically relate to such judicial functions as the rules for bringing cases before the Supreme Court.[13] The constitutionality of all other matters, such as the federal power to incorporate a national bank, was left to other branches of government. Third, *Marbury* asserts a power to declare unconstitutional only those laws that no reasonable person could think constitutional.[14] Justices defer to the constitutional judgments made by other officials unless the judgment is so unreasonable as to suggest legislative usurpation rather than legislative mistake.

The merits of these claims about the original legal understanding of judicial review cannot be fully ascertained because of the sparse historical record. Late-eighteenth- and early-nineteenth-century American political and legal thinkers did not speak of judicial review in ways that would resolve late-twentieth- and early-twenty-first-century controversies. Most early constitutionalists refused to speak of judicial review at any length. The brief commentary on judicial review from 1789 to 1798 suggests a general consensus that courts had the power to declare laws unconstitutional, but it is not sufficient or sufficiently consistent to warrant any clear inference about a consensus over the precise nature of that power. Constitutional commentary from 1798 to 1803 was tainted with partisan concerns. Jeffersonians, who in 1798 called on courts to declare the Alien and Sedition Acts constitutional, advocated far narrower understandings of judicial power after courts sustained the constitutionality of those measures. Federalists became uniformly committed to judicial supremacy only after 1801, when Jeffersonians took control of the elected branches of the national government.[15]

What limited evidence exists counsels against claims that the concept of judicial review underlying *Marbury* was far narrower than present practice. Legislators who sat in the first six Congresses called on the Supreme Court to declare unconstitutional a wide variety of legislative measures. Late-eighteenth-century representatives declared that the Supreme Court had the power to determine the constitutionality of the national bank, the carriage tax, the stamp tax, and the Sedition Act. No legislator, justice, or attorney before *Marbury* responded by insisting that federal courts could declare only laws of a judiciary nature unconstitutional. Some early American constitutionalists did insist that justices should declare only laws unconstitutional when no reasonable person would think the law was constitutional. Others did not make that claim. No justice of the Supreme Court sustained a law that that justice declared was probably unconstitutional. Many reasonable persons thought and continue to think that the law struck down in *Marbury* was constitutional.[16] The majority of elected officials who spoke on judicial review before 1800 assumed that justices had the final authority to settle constitutional controversies. Several prominent legislators declared that Congress had no business making any constitutional decisions because that was a judicial function.[17]

Whatever the original legal understanding, the contemporary law of judicial review vests justices with the power to declare unconstitutional virtually every law the justices believe is unconstitutional. Constitutional law at present authorizes the justices to adjudicate all but a number of relatively minor constitutional conflicts. Justices exercise the power of judicial review when determining whether universities may use race when making admissions decisions, when prayers may be said in public schools, the extent to which Congress may punish violence against women, whether Congress may dispose of presidential papers, and many other matters that are clearly not of a distinctively judiciary nature. The political question doctrine is now limited to a few constitutional issues.

Contemporary constitutional law requires justices to call them as they see them. Justices sometimes defer to legislative fact-finding, but they do not defer to legislative constructions of the Constitution. No justice presently claims that courts may strike down only those laws no reasonable person would think constitutional. Michael Klarman observes that

> the rhetoric of judicial restraint has become a commonplace in Burger and Rehnquist era opinions. But the rhetoric is largely a canard. The Burger Court was as activist as any in American history, aggressively constitutionalizing entirely new subject areas. Perhaps most surprisingly of all, in the mid-1990s we have a Supreme Court that engages in unparalleled activism—from the left and the right simultaneously! When Justices [Sandra Day] O'Connor and [Anthony] Kennedy are in their conservative mode, affirmative action, minority voting districts, hate speech regulations, and environmental land use restrictions are all constitutionally suspect, notwithstanding the absence of convincing originalist arguments against them. When these pivotal Justices are in their liberal mode, abortion restrictions, school prayer, restrictions on gay rights, exclusion of women from VMI, and limitations on the right to die fall victim to the Court's constitutional axe.[18]

Justices cannot be seriously said to believe that judicial power may be exercised only when no reasonable person would think the government action constitutional. The more liberal justices interpreted the Fourteenth Amendment in *Roe v. Wade* (1973) as prohibiting state statutes banning abortion. The more conservative justices in *Bush v. Gore* (2000) interpreted the Fourteenth Amendment as being violated by a state court decision ordering a recount of votes during a presidential election.

Judicial review in contemporary constitutional law is judicial supremacy. The Supreme Court for the past fifty years has repeatedly asserted that judicial decisions determine the constitutional rights of parties to lawsuits and provide constitutional standards to which all other governing officials must adhere. The Court first explicitly equated judicial review and judicial supremacy in the aftermath of *Brown v. Board of Education* (1954). Confronted with state officials blocking desegregation and Southern claims that *Brown* was not even a legitimate exercise of constitutional adjudication, every justice signed the opinion in *Cooper v. Aaron* (1958), which maintained that

> [i]n 1803, Chief Justice Marshall, speaking for a unanimous Court, referring to the Constitution as "the fundamental and paramount law of the nation," declared in the notable case of Marbury v. Madison . . . that "It is emphatically the province and duty of the judicial department to say what the law is." This decision declared the basic principle that the federal judiciary is supreme in the exposition of the law of the Constitution, and that principle has ever since been respected by this Court and the Country as a permanent and indispensable feature of our constitutional system. It follows that the interpretation of the Fourteenth Amendment enunciated by this Court in the Brown case is the supreme law of the land, and Art. VI of the Constitution makes it of binding effect on the States "any Thing in the Constitution or Laws of any State to the Contrary notwithstanding." Every state legislator and executive and judicial officer is solemnly committed by oath taken pursuant to Art. VI, cl. 3, "to support this Constitution." . . .
>
> No state legislator or executive or judicial officer can war against the Constitution without violating his undertaking to support it.

Chief Justice Marshall spoke for a unanimous Court in saying that: "If the legislatures of the several states may, at will, annul the judgments of the courts of the United States, and destroy the rights acquired under those judgments, the constitution itself becomes a solemn mockery. . . ." *United States v. Peters,* 5 Cranch 115, 136. A Governor who asserts a power to nullify a federal court order is similarly restrained.[19]

More recently, the Supreme Court, in *City of Boerne v. Flores* (1997), declared unconstitutional a federal law that required states to accommodate religious believers unless a compelling reason existed for a contrary policy. The majority opinion again declared that the Supreme Court determined the content of constitutional rights and that the justices had previously determined that the free exercise clause of the First Amendment and the due process clause of the Fourteenth Amendment merely required that government not discriminate against religious believers. No judge took the position that Congress had any authority to influence what the First or Fourteenth Amendment meant. Congress, the justices agreed, had the power only to implement what the Court thought the First or Fourteenth Amendment meant.

The long-standing requirement that courts declare laws unconstitutional only in the context of a traditional lawsuit is still an important legal limitation on judicial power in the United States. The "case or controversy" provision of Article 3 and much legal precedent forbid justices from making constitutional rulings merely when many people think a government action is unconstitutional. The party seeking to have a law declared unconstitutional must demonstrate that they have been injured by or are in imminent danger of suffering injury from the government policy under constitutional attack. Courts will not make a constitutional ruling when persons merely claim that racial discrimination exists in a housing market or that they might suffer racial discrimination should they decide to buy a house.[20] Courts will determine whether a local housing policy is unconstitutional only if a lawsuit is brought by a person who was prevented by law from buying a house in that market or was forced to pay a higher price because of state discrimination. This "standing" barrier has proven daunting to some plaintiffs. In most areas of the law, persons can usually be found who have suffered the injury necessary to secure a judicial ruling on the constitutional issue.

Many people think the concept of judicial review must have expanded over time because judicial decisions declaring laws unconstitutional dramatically increased over time. The claim that pre–Civil War justices declared federal laws unconstitutional only in *Marbury* and *Scott* is wrong.[21] Still, the Missouri Compromise of 1820 is the only important federal initiative struck down before 1861, and that measure had been repealed at least three years before a Taney Court majority declared it unconstitutional. The contemporary Supreme Court typically declares major political programs unconstitutional on a yearly basis. During June 2002, the justices on the Rehnquist Court declared unconstitutional laws limiting the speech of candidates for judicial offices, *Republican Party v. White* (2002); laws allowing the execution of the mentally retarded, *Atkins v. Virginia* (2002); a regulation requiring persons engaged in door-to-door advocacy to get a permit, *Watchtower Bible and Tract*

Society of New York, Inc. v. Village of Stratton (2002); laws allowing a trial judge to make a finding crucial to the imposition of capital punishment, *Ring v. Arizona* (2002); warrantless searches of homes in the absence of exigent circumstances, *Kirk v. Louisiana* (2002); and the use of a hitching post for punitive purposes, *Hope v. Pelzer* (2002). These decisions declared state practices unconstitutional. By basing the rulings on the Bill of Rights (which limits federal power) as well as the Fourteenth Amendment (which limits state power), the Court made clear that the federal government was equally bound to respect the rules announced in the above cases. Lest states feel they were being singled out, the justices in the previous five weeks had ruled that the federal government could not ban the advertising of compounded drugs, *Thompson v. Western States Medical Center* (2002); ban virtual child pornography, *Ashcroft v. Free Speech Coalition* (2002); or allow federal administrative agencies to hear complaints that a state port authority had violated federal law, *Federal Maritime Commission v. South Carolina State Ports Authority* (2002).

The increase in judicial declarations that laws are unconstitutional is better explained by increased legal opportunities to exercise judicial review than by changes in the legal concept of judicial review.[22] The post–Civil War Constitution significantly expanded the constitutional limits on state governments by declaring that states could not violate the privileges and immunities of citizens, deny to any person the equal protection of the law, or take life, liberty, or property without due process of law. Congress passed several statutes that gave litigants greater opportunities to raise these and other federal constitutional claims in federal courts.[23] The institutionalization of the legal practice and the development of public interest law enabled many persons who could not otherwise afford counsel to bring claims of constitutional right.[24] Finally, legislatures after the Civil War passed many more laws and many more constitutionally controversial laws than had been the case in the antebellum United States. These changes significantly altered the agenda of the Supreme Court. Antebellum justices often had annual terms in which they were never asked by counsel to declare a federal law unconstitutional. Current justices are typically asked on a weekly, if not a daily, basis to declare some measure unconstitutional. Faced with geometrically greater opportunities to exercise judicial review, the justices have, not surprisingly, geometrically increased the occasions upon which they exercise that power.

Many Americans question whether frequent exercises of judicial power are consistent with democratic government. Alexander Bickel famously declared that the act of Supreme Court justices declaring a law unconstitutional "thwarts the will of representatives of the actual people of the here and now."[25] Democracy is commonly thought to entail government by the people or by the people's elected representatives. Federal justices are appointed and enjoy life tenure. Many hold their offices for more than twenty or thirty years, long after their political sponsors have retired from the political scene. From 1995 until November 2002, Americans witnessed five national elections, five changes in the partisan control of one branch of the national government, but no change in the membership of the Supreme Court. Granting any power to such a politically unaccountable institution seems a severe democratic failing.

Judicial review has two possible democratic defects. The obvious defect is that the legal practice authorizes unelected officials to reverse decisions made by elected officials. The less obvious democratic defect is that constitutionalism implemented by any official may violate majoritarian norms. When legal decisions are made by interpreting a constitutional text that cannot be amended by a simple majority, the values and interests of dead majorities are privileged at the expense of the values and interests of present majorities, no matter what the democratic pedigree of the persons doing the interpreting. Why should contemporary majorities be constrained by limits set down in relatively old texts if they believe alternatives would be more just and better policy?

Judicial review and constitutionalism need not be perfectly reconciled to democracy from a purely legal perspective. Judicial review is legally justified if the constitution is fundamental law and best interpreted as authorizing the judicial power to declare laws unconstitutional. The legal question is what the constitution means, not whether the constitution mandates democratic or otherwise desirable practices. Whether Americans should amend the Constitution to modify or abandon judicial review is a political or normative issue, not a legal question about the best interpretation of present law.

Nevertheless, the legal status of judicial review and constitutionalism cannot be neatly separated from more general justifications of judicial review. The Constitution does not explicitly mandate judicial review and says even less about how that power should be exercised. Given the absence of clear textual support, a reasonable legal argument can be made that the Constitution is best interpreted as mandating a particular form of judicial review only if that practice is particularly desirable. Desirable practices must be reasonably consistent with the U.S. commitment to a democratic republic. Judicial review is likely to be constitutional, therefore, only to the extent that vesting justices with the power to declare laws unconstitutional is not inconsistent with democratic principles.

Constitutional commentators have developed numerous theories purporting to demonstrate that constitutionalism and judicial review are democratically desirable practices. The originalist school of constitutional thought emphasizes the democratic commitment to the rule of law.[26] Judicial review promotes rule of law because justices, who are legal experts, are better able to ascertain the original meaning of laws than are elected officials, who have greater expertise in policy matters. The political process school of constitutional thought emphasizes the democratic commitment to fair political procedures.[27] Judicial review promotes political fairness because unelected justices are less tempted than elected officials to manipulate democratic processes in order to stay in power. The fundamental rights school of constitutional thought emphasizes the democratic commitment to certain basic liberties.[28] Judicial review promotes individual freedom because justices are more immune than are elected officials to short-term political pressures for conformity and rights violations. Numerous other theories about judicial review and constitutionalism have been propounded. Several influential commentators insist that judicial review be abandoned as inconsistent with the democratic aspirations of the Constitution.[29]

Legal justifications of judicial review rely heavily on a formalistic understanding of the political system.[30] All assume that government practices under constitutional attack enjoy majoritarian support. When justices declare laws unconstitutional, most constitutional commentators think, they challenge the will of elected officials. Their theories of judicial review explore why and when justices may so oppose majoritarian sentiment. Theories of judicial review also maintain the practice is justified when justices behave in specified ways. Originalists, for example, think judicial review justified when the justices declare unconstitutional only laws inconsistent with the original meaning of a constitutional provision. No theory sets out to justify the actual practice of judicial review, determining whether the historical practice of judicial review has in reality advanced the values that a given commentator claims justify judicial review.

This failure to develop justifications of judicial review that consider actual political practice is puzzling. What needs justification is what courts actually do, not what courts might hypothetically do. Judicial review would be justified if manna fell from the heavens whenever the justices declared laws unconstitutional. In the absence of evidence of such divine favor, judicial review must be known by its actual fruits. This justification requires an examination of the actual political practice of judicial review, not the practice that exists in legal theory.

The Political Foundations of Judicial Review

The practice of judicial review requires political, as well as legal, foundations. These consist of the political support necessary to maintain present practice. That support may be rooted in general beliefs about the legal justification of judicial review. The practice of judicial review has adequate political support whenever enough people believe the constitution authorizes courts to declare laws unconstitutional, even when common justifications for that practice are mistaken. Alternatively, judicial review has adequate political support when crucial political actors believe that vesting courts with the power to declare laws unconstitutional is more likely to advance than retard their political concerns. Political actors may not privately care about the legal foundations of judicial review when they believe courts exercising that power will typically make decisions they favor.

Crucial political actors must support judicial review for that practice to remain viable. The very texts that provide legal foundations for judicial review also provide potential opponents with the tools necessary to undermine those foundations. Justices who declare laws unconstitutional may be impeached. Justices who can be trusted never to declare a law unconstitutional may be added to the court. The judicial power to hear constitutional cases may be curtailed or abolished. A constitutional amendment may be passed barring judicial review. Politicians bent on breaking a wayward judiciary need not limit themselves to constitutional devices. Justices in some countries who defy the wrong people are assassinated. Elected officials in the United States frequently ignore judicial decrees.[31]

The legal foundations for judicial review provide important political foundations for the practice. Most political elites and citizens think courts should have the power to declare laws unconstitutional. This popular belief in judicial review is so entrenched as to go virtually unchallenged in contemporary political life. Modern candidates for the U.S. presidency criticize specific judicial decisions declaring laws unconstitutional, but no national politician when campaigning promises to abolish judicial review. Republican and Democratic presidents nominate to the federal bench only persons who support judicial power. Political debate over controversial nominees focuses on how those nominees will exercise the power to declare laws unconstitutional, not on whether those nominees will exercise that power.

Judicial review benefits from the relatively high regard with which most citizens regard the judicial system. The Supreme Court of the United States typically garners the highest approval ratings of any national institution. Even controversial decisions, such as *Bush v. Gore* (2000), do little to affect judicial approval ratings. What negative effect such decisions have is often only short term.[32] Americans oppose tinkering with the Supreme Court even when that tribunal aggressively strikes down major policy initiatives passed by a majority coalition with strong popular support. During the 1930s Americans first overwhelming voted for Franklin Delano Roosevelt but then opposed Roosevelt's efforts to pack the Supreme Court with supporters of his New Deal.[33] Support for the Supreme Court, however, does not demonstrate either sophisticated awareness of judicial decision making or the arguments for and against judicial review. Studies consistently find that the general public is not particularly aware of what the court does or the arguments for judicial review.[34] Still, given the public's general support for the Supreme Court, politicians

who attack judicial decisions risk losing the support of those citizens who approve the course of judicial policymaking and the even greater number of citizens, many of whom may be unaware of the specific issues, who disapprove of attacks on the courts.

In the United States, the course of judicial decision making over time provides additional political foundations for judicial review. Prominent politicians, political elites, and the general public are far more inclined to support judicial decisions declaring laws unconstitutional than much legal theory suggests. Judicial review is commonly portrayed as "thwarting the will of the people's representatives," but the justices rarely declare a law unconstitutional when such a declaration lacks substantial political support. A famous study of Supreme Court decision making from 1787 to 1957 found only one arena, child labor, where the justices opposed a policy choice made by nationally elected officials for any length of time.[35] Another study concluded that "the modern Court appears neither markedly more nor less consistent with the polls than are other policy makers."[36]

Judicial decisions declaring laws unconstitutional frequently advance prominent political interests. Sometimes the Supreme Court declares unconstitutional those laws passed by deposed political majorities. The white supremacist legislative majorities in the late nineteenth century shed few tears when the Supreme Court declared unconstitutional or inapplicable those laws protecting persons of color passed by more egalitarian legislative majorities during Reconstruction. Other judicial decisions declare unconstitutional those laws passed by local majorities that express values rejected by most national elites. The Supreme

Court in *Griswold v. Connecticut* (1965) declared unconstitutional a ban on birth control on the books in only two of the fifty states. Members of the federal government quite frequently request that the justices strike down local laws inconsistent with national policy goals. The Department of Justice under Presidents Dwight Eisenhower and Harry Truman wrote legal briefs asking the Court to declare unconstitutional state-mandated racial segregation in elementary schools.

Judicial decisions often facilitate the nonpolicy interests of elected officials. The judicial power to declare laws unconstitutional enables legislators to engage in costless position taking. Legislators please their constituents by banning flag burning, knowing that the Supreme Court will probably declare such laws unconstitutional. Legislators eagerly foist on the judiciary the responsibility for making policy on divisive issues, such as slavery and abortion, matters on which taking any clear stand may cost an elected official or a party votes. Judicial review facilitates legislative compromises. Elected officials agree to pass a law with contested provisions, provided that specific procedures are set up to ensure that the Supreme Court quickly gets an opportunity to determine whether those procedures are constitutional. Given the numerous ways judicial review promotes the policy and electoral concerns of elected officials, legislators may suffer some decisions that do not promote their interests rather than weaken the goose that more often than not lays golden eggs.

The fractured structure of U.S. politics provides further political foundations for judicial review. Responsibility for national policymaking is divided between the president, the Senate, and the House of Representatives. Quite frequently, partisan control of these institutions is divided. Judicial decisions castigated by majorities in one institution are celebrated by majorities in another. The Republicans, who controlled both houses of Congress in the late 1990s, exhibited far more enthusiasm than the Clinton administration for the judicial decision in *Clinton v. Jones* (1997) allowing a civil lawsuit to go forth against the president. The greater the divisions between the majorities that control different elected institutions in the federal government, the greater the range of judicial decisions federal justices can make without fear of retaliation. Such countermajoritarian practices as the filibuster and committee system often enable well-placed minorities in the legislative branches of government to provide the support necessary to maintain a line of judicial decisions.

That the legal practice of judicial review has important political foundations hardly reduces constitutional law to an undifferentiated form of politics. All practices involving crucial policy choices require political foundations. Political processes of every sort are maintained only when crucial political actors believe those practices serve their values and interests better than any other attainable practice. The committee system in Congress, the structure of administrative agencies, two-party politics, and judicial review have political foundations even though all are distinctive practices. Judicial review is politics by legal means—one means among many for making political choices.

Conclusion

Much discussion of judicial review in a democracy ignores the diversity of political practices that inevitably characterize contemporary polities. A simple ideal is posited, usually majority rule. Judicial review is scorned to the extent that judicial review does not advance that value. Majoritarianism, however, neither describes the legislative nor any other political process in the United States. The Constitution of 1787 established a moderately complex series of political processes for making public policy. Those processes have become ever more complex over time. Insisting that judicial review conform to pure majoritarianian standards places a demand on the judiciary that no other political institution satisfies or is even asked to satisfy.

Judicial review is justified if that practice, when combined with every other political practice, makes for a more decent society than would otherwise be the case. Judicial review promises to promote various ends. Judicial decisions declaring laws unconstitutional may increase public awareness of political issues, facilitate public participation in constitutional decision making, create a more pluralist political system, increase public control over issues elected officials would rather not resolve, enable lawmaking majorities to pass important legislation, help maintain a politics of rights, be a crucial element of consensus democracy, increase the influence of elites on policymaking, create differences among elites that advantage the less well off, or improve the overall capacity of the political system to reflect popular opinion.[37] Whether judicial review serves any or all of these political functions remains contested. Still, the crucial question is whether these are desirable public purposes, whether judicial review actually serves these desirable purposes, and whether, in the absence or modification of judi-cial review, other political practices will better achieve these or other desired ends.

Notes

1. See Alec Stone Sweet, *Governing with Judges: Constitutional Politics in Europe* (New York: Oxford University Press, 2000), 32–34.
2. James Bradley Thayer, "The Origin and Scope of the American Doctrine of Constitutional Law," *Harvard Law Review* 7 (1893): 129.
3. Abraham Lincoln, "Mr. Lincoln's Speech, Sixth Joint Debate," in *The Lincoln-Douglas Debates,* ed. Robert W. Johannsen (New York: Oxford University Press, 1965), 243.
4. Stephen Douglas, "Mr. Douglas's Rejoinder, Fifth Joint Debate," in Johannsen, *The Lincoln-Douglas Debates,* 243.
5. Robert Lowry Clinton, *Marbury v. Madison and Judicial Review* (Lawrence: University Press of Kansas, 1989), 7.
6. Jeffrey A. Segal and Harold J. Spaeth, *The Supreme Court and the Attitudinal Model* (New York: Cambridge University Press, 1993).
7. See Mark A. Graber and Michael Perhac, eds., *Marbury v. Madison: Documents and Commentary* (Washington, D.C.: CQ Press, 2002).
8. Ibid., 235–269.
9. William W. Van Alstyne, "A Critical Guide to *Marbury v. Madison,*" *Duke Law Journal* (1969): 14–16.
10. Ibid., 30–33.
11. *Marbury v. Madison,* 5 U.S. 137, 176–180 (1803).
12. Larry D. Kramer, "Foreword: We the Court," *Harvard Law Review* 115 (November 2001): 86–87.
13. Clinton, *Marbury v. Madison and Judicial Review.*
14. Sylvia Snowiss, *Judicial Review and the Law of the Constitution* (New Haven: Yale University Press, 1990).
15. Graber and Perhac, *Marbury v. Madison.*
16. Van Alstyne, "A Critical Guide to *Marbury v. Madison,*" 14–16.
17. Graber and Perhac, *Marbury v. Madison.*
18. Michael Klarman, "Majoritarian Judicial Review: The Entrenchment Problem," *Georgetown Law Journal* 85 (1997): 548–549.

19. *Cooper v. Aaron,* 358 U.S. 1, 18–19 (1958).

20. See *Warth v. Seldin,* 422 U.S. 490 (1975).

21. Mark A. Graber, "The Law Professor as Populist," *University of Richmond Law Review* 34 (2000): 373–413.

22. Mark A. Graber, "The Jacksonian Origins of Chase Court Activism," *Journal of Supreme Court History* 25 (2000): 17–39.

23. Howard Gillman, "How Political Parties Can Use the Courts to Advance Their Agendas: Federal Courts in the United States, 1875–1891," *American Political Science Review* 96 (2002).

24. Charles R. Epp, *The Rights Revolution: Lawyers, Activists, and Supreme Courts in Comparative Perspective* (Chicago: University of Chicago Press, 1998).

25. Alexander M. Bickel, *The Least Dangerous Branch: The Supreme Court at the Bar of Politics* (Indianapolis: Bobbs-Merrill, 1962), 16–17.

26. Keith E. Whittington, *Constitutional Interpretation: Textual Meaning, Original Intent, and Judicial Review* (Lawrence: University Press of Kansas, 1999); Antonin Scalia, *A Matter of Interpretation: Federal Courts and the Law* (Princeton, N.J.: Princeton University Press, 1997).

27. John Hart Ely, *Democracy and Distrust: A Theory of Judicial Review* (Cambridge, Mass.: Harvard University Press, 1980).

28. Ronald Dworkin, *Taking Rights Seriously* (Cambridge, Mass.: Harvard University Press, 1978).

29. Mark Tushnet, *Taking the Constitution Away from the Courts* (Princeton, N.J.: Princeton University Press, 1999); Jeremy Waldron, *Law and Disagreement* (New York: Oxford University Press, 1999).

30. See Mark A. Graber, "Constitutional Politics and Constitutional Theory: A Misunderstood and Neglected Relationship," *Law and Social Inquiry* 27 (2002): 317–329.

31. Gerald N. Rosenberg, *The Hollow Hope: Can Courts Bring about Social Change?* (Chicago: University of Chicago Press, 1991).

32. James L. Gibson, Gregory A. Caldeira, and Lester Kenyatta Spence, "The Supreme Court and the U.S. Presidential Election of 2000: Wounds, Self-Inflicted or Otherwise," Working Paper 182, Russell Sage Foundation, New York, 2002.

33. Gregory A. Caldeira, "Public Opinion and the Supreme Court: FDR's Court-Packing Plan," *American Political Science Review* 81 (1987): 1139–1154.

34. Walter F. Murphy and Joseph Tanenhaus, "Publicity, Public Opinion, and the Court," *Northwestern University Law Review* 84 (1990): 991–1004.

35. Robert A. Dahl, "Decision-Making in a Democracy: The Supreme Court as a National Policymaker," *Journal of Public Law* 6 (1957): 279–295.

36. Thomas Marshall, *Public Opinion and the Supreme Court* (New York: Longman, 1989), 80.

37. See Graber, "Law Professor as Populist," 403–410; Terri Jennings Peretti, *In Defense of a Political Court* (Princeton, N.J.: Princeton University Press, 1999).

Chapter Six

The Power to Make War

Nancy Kassop

Resolved, That . . . it is the sense of the Senate that a national commitment by the United States results only from affirmative action taken by the executive and legislative branches of the United States Government by means of a treaty, statute or concurrent resolution of both Houses of Congress specifically providing for such commitment.

National Commitments Resolution
U.S. Senate, 91st Cong., 1st sess., 1969

The National Commitments Resolution represented a Senate effort at the height of the Vietnam War to assert that, henceforth, use of U.S. armed forces would be undertaken only with the expressed agreement of Congress *and* the president through a formal process.[1] Passed in June 1969, this nonbinding "sense of the Senate" resolution was the opening shot across the bow in a legislative battle that would eventually culminate in the War Powers Resolution of 1973.

The remarkable aspect of this simple, one-house resolution was that it was needed at all. In the debates at the Constitutional Convention in 1787, the intent of the framers could scarcely be clearer that Congress and the president should use their collective judgment in making decisions on international affairs and on matters of war and peace. For the first 150

years of the nation's history, this expectation, in large measure, was met. The primary concern for the convention delegates, especially when it came to going to war, was to ensure against absolute, exclusive power—the royal prerogative—enjoyed by British kings. Thus, the framers provided for shared powers between Congress and the president over most aspects of foreign affairs—war making, treaties, and appointment of ambassadors, while allocating sole power to Congress to regulate foreign commerce. The only exclusive authority granted the president in foreign affairs was to receive ambassadors, which was viewed largely as a ceremonial duty at the time but has since taken on the far more substantial function of recognizing foreign states in international law.[2]

If the framers could see the way the government makes foreign policy and commits itself to military hostilities today, they would be stunned by how far these two branches have strayed from their original intent. A dramatic expansion of executive power characterized the latter half of the twentieth century, and with it the usurpation by presidents of Congress's exclusive power to decide when to go to war. According to Arthur Schlesinger Jr., the impetus for the "imperial presidency" rests upon "the capture by the Presidency of . . . the decision to go to war."[3] What the Framers had envisioned as a partnership in foreign policy decision making more than two centuries prior had metamorphosed into the flow of power into one branch, creating an imbalance among the powers they had tried so carefully to calibrate when allocating constitutional authority. David Gray Adler aptly acknowledges this shift as the "wide gulf . . . between constitutional theory and governmental practice" that has occurred in the past fifty years.[4] The causes for this shift in power are many, with each of the three branches bearing partial responsibility for the outcome through executive aggrandizement, legislative deference, and judicial abdication.[5]

Constitutional Powers in Foreign Affairs: The Framers' Intent

As noted, the framers' fear of monarchical power guided their denial of absolute and even primary authority in foreign affairs to the president. With war making, in particular, there was no doubt among them that in the words of delegate James Wilson at the Pennsylvania state ratifying convention, "it will not be in the power of a single man, or a single body of men, to involve us in such distress; for the important power of declaring war is vested in the legislature at large."[6] Thus, Article 1 delegates to Congress the power to "declare war," and Article 2 imparts to the president the designation of "Commander in Chief . . . when called into the actual service of the United States." This division of power has been a source of intense conflict and competition between the legislative and executive branches. Scholars debate whether the "commander-in-chief" clause is merely a title bestowed on the president, with no other substance attached, or whether it is in fact a grant of authority.

Alexander Hamilton, the staunchest proponent of executive power in most other contexts, weighed in on this debate in *Federalist No. 69*, noting that "it would amount to nothing more than the supreme command . . . of the military and naval forces, as First General and Admiral of the Confederacy."[7] Hamilton further sought to allay public fears and make clear the distinctions between the royal prerogative of kings and the powers that the framers had bestowed upon the president. Kings, on their own authority, could make war or peace, conclude treaties with foreign states, and send and receive ambassadors. In contrast, Hamilton notes, the Constitution provides the president with "only the occasional command of such part of the militia of the nation as by legislative provision may be called into the actual service of the Union."[8] Thus, the president would assume the role as commander in chief only, as Article 2 states, "when called into the actual service of the United States." Congress, on the other hand, was given the exclusive authority in Article 1 "to declare war," as well as many other specific powers: to regulate foreign commerce (perhaps the most important power in the eighteenth century, the one considered most likely to provoke war, and, for that very reason, entrusted to Congress alone), to raise and support armies and provide and maintain a navy, to make regulations for land and naval forces, and to call forth the militia and provide for organizing, arming, and disciplining it. The power to conclude treaties and to appoint ambassadors would be, unlike the royal prerogative, shared between the president and the Senate, consonant with the framers' rejection of unilateral executive power in this policy sphere. The president would initiate each process, negotiating agreements with foreign leaders and nominating ambassadors, and the Senate would complete the process, deciding whether to ratify the treaties (by a two-thirds vote) and to confirm appointments (by a simple majority vote).

A sudden attack upon the United States or its troops was the only exception acknowledged by the framers that would permit a president to use military force without congressional approval. As originally drafted, the Constitution delegated to Congress the power to "make war," but James Madison and Elbridge Gerry proposed substituting "declare" for "make," "leaving to the Executive the power to repel sudden attacks."[9] Their rationale was that in an emergency, a president might need to act defensively before Congress could legislate a course of action. The limited nature of this exception reinforces the view that the initiation of offensive hostilities clearly was intended to rest with Congress alone.

The framers' separating the "purse" from the "sword" represents further evidence of their intent to deny the president independent war power. By lodging control over all expenditures in the legislature, they made it necessary for the president to request money from Congress to finance military actions. As Madison explains, "Those who are to *conduct a war* cannot in the nature of things, be proper or safe judges, whether *a war ought* to be *commenced, continued* or *concluded*."[10]

Thus, an unequivocal message can be discerned from the debates at the Constitutional Convention, discussions at state ratifying conventions, and from the *Federalist Papers*: the determination of when and under what circumstances the nation would go from a state of peace to a state of war would be a legislative judgment—the product of a deliberative body—and only after that determination could a president conduct military operations.[11] Early practices by eighteenth- and nineteenth-century presidents adhered generally to this principle, but subsequent Supreme Court decisions and increasingly bolder claims of authority by twentieth-century presidents fueled, in the words of presidential scholar Edward Corwin, a continuing "invitation to struggle for the privilege of directing American foreign policy."[12]

Eighteenth- and Nineteenth-Century Precedents

A trio of early Supreme Court decisions laid to rest any doubt about the allocation of constitutional authority in war making. In *Bas v. Tingy* (1800) and in *Talbot v. Seeman* (1801), the Court ruled that whether military hostilities constituted general ("perfect") war or limited ("imperfect" or "partial") war, some authorization by Congress was necessary, although it could be a formal declaration of war or a statute authorizing an "undeclared" war. Legislation from 1798 to 1800 falling into the latter category includes that authorizing limited responses in the quasi-war with France, which was the subject of these cases. An even more revealing interpretation by the Court was given in *Little v. Barreme* (1804), in which the justices found impermissible the seizure of a foreign vessel by U.S. warships, pursuant to an order by President John Adams that itself exceeded congressional authorization. Congress had legislated the seizure of ships sailing *to* French ports, but Adams's order authorized seizure of ships sailing *to or from* French ports. When a U.S. captain was sued for damages in the seizure of a ship coming *from* a French port, the Court refused to accept his reliance on Adams's order as a defense. In effect, the Court ruled that if a president's order as commander in chief conflicted with congressional authorization, the legislation overruled the presidential order, thus upholding the primacy of Congress in war-making decisions.[13]

In one of the first truly aggressive efforts at presidential war making, President James Polk deceived Congress into passing a declaration of war against Mexico in May 1846, when he ordered General Zachary Taylor to place U.S. troops in disputed territory along the border between Texas and Mexico, thus provoking an attack by Mexico that resulted in the deaths of American soldiers. Mexico declared that a state of war existed, and Congress passed a formal declaration four days later recognizing the state of war. Polk, however, paid a political price for his military provocation and was censured two years later by the House when it rejected its earlier approval of the war and reprimanded Polk for a war "unnecessarily and unconstitutionally begun by the President."[14]

Of particular interest during this affair were the comments written by a first-term House member from Illinois, Abraham Lincoln, to a lawyer in his home state: "Allow the President to invade a neighboring nation . . . *whenever he may choose to say* he deems it necessary . . . and you allow him to make war at pleasure . . . [O]ur Convention . . . resolved to so frame the Constitution that *no one man* should hold the power of bringing this oppression [war] upon us."[15] Lincoln's interpretation of presidential powers during the Civil War would be quite different from those he held as a member of Congress.

The *Prize Cases* (1863) are among the more striking Supreme Court cases involving presidential powers during wartime. The cases were a response to Lincoln's imposition of a naval blockade of Southern ports in April 1861 after the Confederate attack on Fort Sumter. He justified the blockade, along with other unilateral actions—suspending the writ of habeas corpus, calling forth the militia, expanding the army and navy—as wartime necessities under a theory of Lockean emergency power. This theory derives from the seventeenth-century British political philosopher John Locke's *Two Treatises of Government,* in which he wrote of "prerogative" as "this power to act according to discretion, for the public good, without the prescription of the Law, and sometimes even against it."[16] Locke acknowledges the need for discretionary power for the executive during emergencies or when the legislature is not in session, but he also holds that the people would be the ultimate judges of the legitimacy of such use of power.

The constitutionality of the blockade was challenged by owners of seized ships contending before the Supreme Court that Lincoln had exceeded his authority. In a 5-4 decision, the Court upheld the blockade, arguing that the president had a duty "to resist force by force. He does not initiate the war, but is bound to accept the challenge without waiting for any special legislative authority."[17] Justice Samuel Nelson's dissenting opinion was equally as certain that "before it [a civil war] can exist . . .

it must be recognized or declared by the sovereign power of the State, and which sovereign power by our Constitution is lodged in the Congress of the United States. . . . It cannot be delegated or surrendered to the Executive. Congress alone can determine whether war exists or should be declared."[18]

Significantly, Lincoln never claimed that he had independent constitutional power for his actions, and was respectful, instead, of the need for Congress to ratify his decisions.[19] In fact, Lincoln openly conceded that he may have acted beyond his authority, and as soon as Congress reconvened he submitted his actions for retroactive approval, which Congress granted.

The Twentieth Century: Changes in Practice and Purposes

Almost all presidents who committed U.S. military forces prior to the twentieth century used it for limited purposes, such as in defense against pirates or bandits, in "hot pursuit" of criminals across borders, or to protect American lives or property. Although even these limited uses of military power without congressional authorization probably contravened the framers' intent, they became accepted practice during the early days of the Republic. A clear distinction was drawn between defensive uses of force against unorganized bands of intruders and initiation of offensive hostilities against sovereign nations. Presidents acknowledged that the latter action required congressional authorization.[20]

The twentieth century, however, brought about a marked change: presidents no longer hesitated to use force against foreign governments for more expansive purposes without seeking congressional authorization. Thus, the paradox emerged that as the United States became more of a world leader and found itself enmeshed in ever-more complex, broad-scale, and dangerous military ventures, presidents asserted greater independence and autonomy in making military decisions, casting off the constitutional constraints under which their predecessors had operated for most of the nation's history.

Presidents Theodore Roosevelt, William Howard Taft, and Woodrow Wilson introduced this expansion of presidential power in their assorted forays into Mexico, Panama, Cuba, the Dominican Republic, and Nicaragua, sometimes in hot pursuit or to protect American lives and property but also to fight sovereign nations.[21] At times, they justified their interventions as actions in pursuit of broad foreign policy goals. Gradually, the crack in the door widened, as presidents committed U.S. power against foreign governments and Congress became less effective in opposing such actions and in protecting its own war power from usurpation.

Curtiss-Wright: A Mistaken Legacy

Any examination of presidential power in foreign policy inevitably confronts, early on, the Supreme Court decision of *United States v. Curtiss-Wright Export Corp.* (1936), despite the fact that the case had little to do with the foreign policy powers of the president and everything to do with the delegation of power from Congress to the president. Because this ruling was so expansive and generous to presidents, it has since served as the "magic formula" employed by every chief executive when attempting to assert unlimited and independent power in foreign affairs. It is quoted so frequently by government attorneys on behalf of the president that it is called the "*Curtiss-Wright,* so I'm right" cite, suggesting that the invocation of this case should automatically foreclose further argument against the president's powers.[22]

The issue in *Curtiss-Wright* was the constitutionality of Congress's delegation of power to President Franklin Delano Roosevelt to proclaim an arms embargo against companies selling goods to warring countries in South America if he found that it would "contribute to the reestablishment of peace between those countries."[23] The simple answer—that Congress may delegate more broadly in foreign affairs than in domestic affairs—could have been easily reached. Justice George Sutherland used his majority opinion, however, to insert dicta, information irrelevant to the actual ruling, that articulated a theory of inherent, exclusive, and absolute executive power in foreign affairs flowing to the president from extraconstitutional sources. Sutherland describes the president, inaccurately, as "the sole organ of the federal government in the field of international relations,"[24] a description that he took out of context from a speech on the floor of the House in 1800 by Rep. John Marshall, who meant only to refer to the president as the "organ" of communication with foreign governments, not as the sole policymaker.[25] Scholars have criticized Sutherland's opinion for its incorrect interpretation of history and the Constitution, but the decision has never been officially overruled, as it is the dicta—not the decision—that needs to be overturned.[26]

Roosevelt: Pre–World War II

President Franklin Roosevelt's actions in 1940 and 1941, prior to the attack on Pearl Harbor, represented the next phase in the expansion of executive foreign policy powers. By using executive agreements, rather than statutory authorization, Roosevelt committed U.S. military resources to assist England and other Allied nations. In return for leases to British naval bases in the Western Hemisphere, he provided destroyers to England in September 1940. He also made an agreement with Denmark in April 1941 to defend Greenland, ordered U.S. naval vessels to patrol the Atlantic for German submarines in April 1941, agreed in July 1941 to send U.S. troops to Iceland to defend against German occupation, and in fall 1941 instructed U.S. warships to "shoot on sight" German and Italian ships west of the twenty-sixth meridian.[27] He *did* ask Congress for authorization to supply the Allies with defense materiel manufactured in the United States, and Congress obliged with the Lend-Lease Act in March 1941, in effect authorizing retroactively the destroyers-for-bases deal.

Roosevelt's actions pushed the boundaries of presidential power by the nature of the commitments he made to other nations already engaged in war. In effect, coming before formal U.S. entry into hostilities, Roosevelt's actions undermined any U.S. claims of neutrality. Yet, Schlesinger notes, even here, there was a "symbolic concern for Congress" and "a lurking sensitivity to constitutional issues." He adds, "Roosevelt made no general claims to inherent presidential power," "did not claim authority independent of Congress," and rarely relied in his official documents or press conferences on his power as commander in chief as the authority for most of these actions, other than for the destroyers-for-bases deal.[28] Schlesinger finds similarities between Roosevelt and Lincoln, in their understanding of the respective emergencies facing the nation, but explains that both also understood the need, whether political or constitutional, to include Congress, even if retroactively, in most of their decisions.

Truman: A Break with the Past

The same cannot be said for Harry Truman, the president most responsible for charging past the boundaries of the Constitution and beyond the practices of previous presidents. Truman resorted to claims of inherent presidential power, and he bypassed Congress entirely when, on June 26, 1950, he relied instead for authority on a UN Security Council resolution to send U.S. troops to defend South Korea against invasion by North Korea. Action through the United Nations, first convened in October 1945, had not been an option for Truman's predecessors, but his seizure of authority was unprecedented nonetheless. He committed air and sea forces after consultation with executive branch officials, citing the UN resolution as the only authority he needed, and notified congressional leaders of his actions on June 27, the day after making the decision and deploying the troops. When Truman told members of Congress that he planned to increase the U.S. commitment, they suggested that he request the approval of both houses.

Truman had been guided by the opinion of Secretary of State Dean Acheson, who advised on July 3 that he not seek formal congressional approval, but instead rely on his powers as chief executive and as commander in chief.[29] A Department of State memorandum provided to Truman which influenced his decision listed eighty-seven incidents in which presidents had committed U.S. forces to combat without congressional input, often "in the broad interests of American foreign policy."[30] If he had taken a closer look at these precedents, however, Truman would have noticed that they consisted of limited actions against pirates or to protect American citizens and were in no way comparable to a full-scale commitment of U.S. ground and naval forces against a sovereign state. To claim that these incidents served as viable precedents for a major war was not sustainable as a constitutional argument.

Truman's actions in Korea were significant for many reasons: he proceeded on the basis of inapplicable precedents; he did not consult Congress in advance, instead notifying legislative leaders after his decision had been made and implemented; he relied on an unprecedented interpretation of the executive power and commander-in-chief clauses for independent authority to take large-scale military action in circumstances other than "to repel sudden attacks" against the United States or its troops; and he relied on a UN Security Council resolution as a substitute for congressional authorization. It must be noted that the UN Charter and the UN Participation Act of 1945 state that member nations will provide troops to the UN under Security Council resolutions "in accordance with their own constitutional processes." The Senate, in debates on this matter, unequivocally rejected the concept that authorization by the UN Security Council overrode or preempted the Constitution's requirement of congressional authorization for military action.[31]

Bush, Clinton, and the Truman Model

Several presidents have used Truman's actions in Korea as precedents for their own decisions. In August 1990 after the Iraqi invasion of Kuwait, President George Bush committed U.S. troops to the Persian Gulf to defend Saudi Arabia from possible attack. With no indication that Iraq would withdraw from Kuwait, in early November Bush announced that he would substantially increase the U.S. military presence in the Gulf to half a million troops in order to provide "an adequate offensive military option."[32] By late November, the Security Council had passed Resolution 678, authorizing member nations "to use all necessary means" to enforce earlier resolutions calling for Iraqi withdrawal and "to restore international peace and security in the area." Bush asked Congress for a resolution of support in early January 1991. Although Congress eventually authorized the use of force on January 14, 1991, Bush, in his signing statement and in other public announcements, declared that he had the authority as president and as commander in chief to commit troops even without congressional authorization.[33] Like Truman, Bush relied on the president's constitutional authority of Article 2—ignoring Congress's powers in Article 1—and a Security Council resolution. Although he welcomed Congress's "support," he did not believe he needed it.

President Bill Clinton expanded upon Bush's tactic in a number of incidents: the June 1993 air strikes against Iraq in retaliation for an assassination attempt on Bush's life two months earlier; the threatened invasion of Haiti in the summer of 1994; the February 1994 air strikes against the Bosnian Serbs that were carried out by NATO forces under a UN resolution; and the March 1999 air strikes against the Serbs in Kosovo for which Clinton relied wholly on NATO for authority and acted in direct contravention of Congress's refusal to authorize such use of force. (The Senate had agreed to the operation by concurrent resolution on March 23, but the House version failed to pass, on a tie vote, 213-213, on April 28.) It had become routine by this time for presidents to recite that their actions were "pursuant to my constitutional authority with respect to the conduct of foreign relations and as Commander-in-Chief."[34] Any references to Congress's Article 1 power to declare war or to its alternative of authorizing hostilities by statute were conspicuous by their absence. Thus presidents came to possess the full war power in practice and as publicly articulated in theory.

Area Resolutions

An alternative model for commitment of U.S. forces was the use of area resolutions, first employed by President Dwight Eisenhower during the 1950s. These resolutions were congressional enactments authorizing the use of military force in specific nations or regions: their main characteristic was an intention (not always achieved) to pinpoint and, thus, confine hostilities to a particular locale and for a stated objective. Eisenhower displayed a political and constitutional sensitivity to the need for joint action by the legislative and executive branches in making foreign policy commitments, and he wanted to avoid the mistake made by Truman in excluding Congress from the Korean War decision. He employed this approach in the Formosa Resolution of 1955, in which Congress authorized him to "employ the Armed Forces of the United States as he deems necessary for the specific purpose of securing and protecting Formosa and the Pescadores against armed attack,"[35] and in the Middle East Resolution of 1957, "if the President determines the necessity thereof . . . to use armed forces to assist any nation or group of such nations [in the Middle East] requesting assistance against armed aggression from any country controlled by international communism."[36]

Congress later passed resolutions on Cuba in 1962, on the Gulf of Tonkin in 1964, on Lebanon in 1983, and on the Persian Gulf in 1991, although some contained deficiencies or lacked the necessary specificity to make them truly effective and authoritative from a constitutional standpoint. The Gulf of Tonkin Resolution is the most infamous of these in terms of flaws as well as for its unparalleled role in launching an unpopular, decade-long war. In a sense, this resolution represents a combination of the Truman and Eisenhower models: President Lyndon Johnson went to Congress on August 2, 1964, asking for a joint resolution that would give him the "support" of Congress to permit U.S. warships in the waters off South Vietnam to respond to alleged attacks by the North Vietnamese. Two years later, a Department of State legal advisor in a memorandum maintained that Johnson had authority not only from the Gulf of Tonkin Resolution, but also from "the exercise of his presidential powers under Article II," and from mutual defense obligations of the United States under the SEATO Treaty.[37] It could be said that Johnson, thus, combined the concept of Eisenhower's "area resolutions" (though for reasons of political support and not because he believed, as

Eisenhower did, that he needed Congress's express authorization for constitutional legitimacy) with Truman-like assertions of independent executive authority as well as mutual security treaty obligations.

The resolution's most glaring infirmity is its open-ended language: "Congress approves and supports the determination of the President, as Commander in Chief, to take all necessary measures to repel any armed attack against the forces of the United States *and to prevent further aggression.*" It continues, "the United States is prepared, as the President determines, to take all necessary steps, including the use of armed force" to assist any SEATO member or protocol state asking for assistance in defending its freedom.[38] The resolution passed overwhelmingly in both houses—88-2 in the Senate, 416-0 in the House—with the barest of floor debate and conflicting understandings among members as to what they were, in fact, agreeing to pass. Some members, such as Democratic representative Thomas Morgan of Pennsylvania, thought its purpose was limited: "The resolution is definitely not an advance declaration of war. The committee has been assured by the Secretary of State that the constitutional power of Congress in this respect will continue to be scrupulously observed."[39] Other members, such as Democratic senator Wayne Morse of Oregon, one of the two dissenting votes in the Senate, concluded exactly the opposite: "I have called it a predated declaration of war, in clear violation of Article I, Section 8 of the Constitution, which vests the power to declare war in the Congress and not the President. What is proposed is to authorize the President of the United States, without a declaration of war, to commit acts of war."[40]

The deepening of U.S. military involvement in Vietnam was the work of President Johnson, beginning with the Gulf of Tonkin incident. The conflict quickly became known as a "presidential war," an appellation the framers could barely have imagined and an event they surely thought they had foreclosed. Thus, Eisenhower's area resolutions were manipulated by a president to serve his purposes, as Johnson controlled the information on which legislative actions were based.

Vietnam: The Point of No Return

The Vietnam War was a watershed in executive-legislative relations over war powers. Every war powers dispute thereafter has been influenced by the contentious interbranch dynamics of that war's conduct, which involved three presidents and spanned from 1964 to 1975. The war marked a break with earlier times, when Congress generally assumed its constitutional responsibility of monitoring and authorizing military actions, and an abrupt shift toward unilateral presidential war making. This shift set in motion considerable conflict between the branches. Some of the issues involved include the following:

- Who decides when war begins? Who decides to initiate hostilities? Who defines "hostilities" as "war"? Is a congressional declaration of war necessary or can statutory authorization serve the same constitutional purpose as a formal declaration?[41]
- Do congressional appropriations constitute "authorization" if no valid statutory authorization for hostilities exists? Also, if Congress cuts off funding for hostilities, does the prohibition represent conclusive congressional determination that hostilities should cease? In other words, is a funding prohibition the equivalent of insistence on the termination of hostilities?
- What role should the federal courts play in determining the proper constitutional and institutional roles and responsibilities of Congress and the president in war making?

Because so many issues of constitutional significance emerged throughout the Vietnam years, the various parties sought resolution through the federal courts; this route seemed a natural avenue to take. The record of the judiciary during that period, however, is one of almost total disengagement: the courts used a host of doctrines—political question, standing, ripeness, and remedial discretion—to justify their distance from the issues raised. They maintained generally that judges lacked expertise in foreign policy matters and that such questions were more appropriately left to the two "political branches" to resolve. Yet, the Supreme Court had earlier displayed no hesitation in ruling on such matters, as exemplified by its decisions in *Bas v. Tingy, Talbot v. Seeman, Little v. Barreme,* and the *Prize Cases.* Scholars have criticized the Court for its refusal to engage the great issues surrounding the Vietnam War and for its legacy of judicial abdication during that time.[42]

Numerous lawsuits challenged the legality of a "presidential war" and whether the Gulf of Tonkin Resolution and other enactments were sufficient expressions by Congress to authorize the war. The lower federal courts entertained all suits, but none was decided on the merits by the Supreme Court. Three representative cases are *Massachusetts v. Laird* (1971), *Mitchell v. Laird* (1973), and *Holtzman v. Schlesinger* (1973).

In *Massachusetts v. Laird,* the First Circuit Court of Appeals notes that "the war in Vietnam is a product of the jointly supportive actions of the two branches to whom the congeries of the war powers have been committed."[43] The Supreme Court declined to hear the case on appeal on the grounds of lack of standing and nonjusticiability. Thirteen members of Congress brought *Mitchell v. Laird* against the president and other executive branch officials, asking for a declaratory judgment that the war was a violation of Article 1, section 8, clause 11 (the "declare war" clause) and for an injunction to cease prosecution of the war in sixty days unless Congress explicitly authorized it. The D.C. Circuit Court of Appeals refused to address the merits, deeming the matter a "political question." Two federal judges, Charles Wyzanski and David Bazelon, went on record stating that although members of Congress voted for continuing military appropriations, those votes did not automatically constitute consent for the war, but, rather, may have signaled only that members did not want to abandon soldiers already in the field.[44]

The U.S. engaged in bombing communist sanctuaries in Cambodia from 1970 to 1973 on the theory that it was protecting U.S. troops across the border in South Vietnam. By April 1, 1973, all U.S. troops had been withdrawn from Indochina, but the bombing continued. Congress made a series of efforts to deny funding for the bombing, but it was not until an "end-the-war" amendment to a supplemental appropriations bill was adopted by both houses and signed by President Richard Nixon

on July 1, 1973, that Congress was on record as approving an end to all U.S. military involvement in Southeast Asia.

In a suit against Secretary of Defense James Schlesinger, Rep. Elizabeth Holtzman (D-N.Y.) asked a federal district court to determine whether this funding restriction on U.S. combat activities in Southeast Asia after August 15, 1973, applied to the period of July 1 through August 14. The federal district court judge ruled that for that 45-day period "there is no existing Congressional authority to order military forces into combat in Cambodia . . . and that military activities in Cambodia by American armed forces are unauthorized and unlawful."[45] His decision, however, was reversed on appeal to the Second Circuit, which viewed the issue as a political matter, although it went on to interpret the August 15 date as permissive of bombing in Cambodia *until* that date.[46] Thus, two courts offered diametrically opposing interpretations of Congress's intent.

The War Powers Resolution of 1973

The steady stream of efforts by Congress to bring the Vietnam War to an end and the Senate Foreign Relations Committee hearings that resulted in the National Commitments Resolution in 1969 paved the way for the War Powers Resolution of 1973. The first draft of the statute surfaced in 1970 and went through numerous incarnations before emerging as a compromise resolution enacted over President Richard Nixon's veto in November 1973.[47]

The purpose of the original sponsors of the War Powers Resolution was a simple one: to reassert Congress's primacy as the institution designated by the Constitution to make decisions about when to use military force. The statute also incorporated a procedural framework for the sharing of power between Congress and the president, what it called a "collective judgment," and it attempted to create a monitoring role for Congress by directing the president to consult with Congress before taking military action, report to congressional leaders within forty-eight hours after U.S. troops have been introduced into hostilities, and provide reports to Congress every six months on the military situation.[48]

The most controversial part of the legislation is section 5, which provides that "the President shall terminate any use of United States Armed Forces" within sixty days of their introduction unless Congress has declared war or has authorized their use in specific terms, or has officially extended the sixty-day period or is unable to meet. Section 5(c) provides that Congress can direct the president to withdraw forces at any time, even within the first sixty days, if agreed to in a concurrent resolution—that is, one passed by both chambers but not submitted to the president for signing (and is therefore without the force of law).[49]

President Nixon vetoed the measure on October 24, 1973, objecting stridently to "the restrictions which this resolution would impose upon the authority of the President" as "both unconstitutional and dangerous to the best interests of our Nation."[50] Among his concerns were the automatic cutoff after sixty days that required no affirmative congressional action and the concurrent resolution provision, which would permit Congress to withdraw troops at any time. Both houses of Congress overrode Nixon's veto, so the bill became law amid political turbulence and with strong mis-

givings by its sponsors that the compromise bill had drifted far from its original purposes.[51]

It is now fair to conclude, after nearly thirty years of practice, that the War Powers Resolution has not fulfilled the intent of its authors. Its greatest asset has been its symbolic value as a fitful but unsuccessful attempt by Congress to regain its lost power. Every president since 1973 has decried it as an unconstitutional infringement on their constitutional authority as commander in chief, and no president has complied with the prior consultation provision; all "inform" Congress after decisions have been made, rather than including Congress in the making of those decisions. Only President Gerald Ford complied with the reporting requirements under Section 4(a)(1) to start the sixty-day clock, which "folds" the president into all the other provisions that depend upon a report under 4(a)(1). All presidents have consciously reported to Congress "consistent with" the provisions of the War Powers Resolution, but none has reported "pursuant to" it, a significant and determinative difference that would legally obligate them to adhere to all of its provisions.

Presidential defiance of the War Powers Resolution has resulted in a number of lawsuits by frustrated congressional members, who have asked the courts to intervene and to order presidents to comply. The judiciary's position is almost unchanged from that taken during the Vietnam War—refusal to rule on the merits justified by procedural reasons.[52]

A concern raised by courts in these cases was that the claims of a handful of congressional members were not equivalent to the position of Congress as an institution. Thus, if the courts intervened in a dispute in which Congress had not yet "spoken" institutionally, it would short-circuit the legislative process. In essence, a ruling on the merits by a court would encourage one faction—the losing faction or the one with less political influence to carry its chamber's vote—to turn to the courts for relief before (and instead of) utilizing Congress's own processes to resolve a dispute. Only after both houses had acted conclusively and in direct conflict with the president's position would an issue be "ripe," or ready, for judicial resolution. The 1990 district court ruling in *Dellums v. Bush*[53] clearly articulated this view. The case was less concerned with the War Powers Resolution and more with Congress's powers under Article 1, section 8, clause 11 (the "declare war" clause) and represented a breakthrough, of sorts, for the judiciary.

Fifty-four members of Congress had sued President Bush in December 1990, after his November announcement that he intended to increase U.S. troop strength in Saudi Arabia in order to have an "offensive military option" during the Gulf crisis.[54] The congressional plaintiffs asked the court to enjoin Bush from launching an offensive without a declaration of war or statutory authorization. As the suit wended its way through the district court, Congress prepared to act on an authorizing resolution. District court judge Harold Greene adopted the position that "a dispute between Congress and the President is not ready for judicial review unless and until each branch has taken action asserting its constitutional authority." In reviewing the threshold procedural questions, he ruled that the plaintiffs had standing to sue, that the matter was justiciable and not a "political question," that there was no "remedial discretion" available to them— but that the issue was not yet "ripe" for review.

Perhaps the most historic part of the decision was Greene's explanation of Congress's exclusive constitutional authority to determine what constitutes "war": "the Court has no hesitation in concluding that an offensive entry into Iraq by several hundred thousand United States servicemen under the conditions described above could be described as a 'war' within the meaning of Article I, Section 8, Clause 11, of the Constitution. To put it another way: the Court is not prepared to read out of the Constitution the clause granting to the Congress, and to it alone, the authority 'to declare war.' "[55] Finally, a modern-era court had asserted respect for Congress's war-making role as intended by the framers but that had been conspicuously absent for generations. Albeit, a district court decision has limited legal significance, but it was an opening to the possibility that future challenges would no longer be hampered by jurisdictional hurdles and would, if ripe, be considered on the merits. In the matter of the judicial resolution of cases on the constitutional authority to use military force, *Dellums v. Bush* marked the difference between a court saying "not ever" and "not now."[56]

Conclusion

Competition between Congress and the president over the authority to take the nation to war has been a constant part of the constitutional landscape since the framers debated the allocation of power at the Constitutional Convention in Philadelphia in 1787. This ongoing contest is unlikely to abate anytime soon. Under a republican form of government with constitutionally limited powers, each institution interprets its own roles and responsibilities. These interpretations vary over time and with changed circumstances. Although basic, unchanging constitutional values are embedded in the U.S. political system, democratic government encourages flexibility and adaptability, permitting new, and sometimes even unwise, views to be put into practice. An advantage to this system is that it can be tinkered with around the edges, making minor and even major adjustments to institutions and processes as circumstances warrant and to the degree that public consensus will allow.

The history of how the power to commit the nation to hostilities has adapted over time to new conditions is rich in detail and complexity. Certainly, the United States has ventured far from the framers' design of denying exclusive war power to the executive. In 2001 the country embarked on an even more uncertain path, as it began navigating through the war against international terrorism. The president and the rest of the executive branch promptly claimed new and expanded powers, military as well as domestic, as Congress tried to keep a watchful eye to ensure that constitutional limits were respected. The courts were inevitably drawn into what will likely be many controversies about the scope of the executive's reach. There is no better illustration than this to demonstrate the ongoing vitality of the concepts of the separation of powers and checks and balances. They continue to perform the monitoring function in tussles for power that the framers entrusted to them more than two hundred years ago.

Notes

1. S.R. 85, 91st Cong., 1st sess., *Congressional Record*, 115, daily ed. (June 25, 1969): S7153.

2. David Gray Adler, "Court, Constitution and Foreign Affairs," in *The Constitution and the Conduct of American Foreign Policy*, ed. David Gray Adler and Larry N. George (Lawrence: University Press of Kansas, 1996), 21. See also, David Gray Adler, "The President's Recognition Power," in Adler and George, ibid., 133–157.

3. Arthur M. Schlesinger Jr., *The Imperial Presidency* (New York: Popular Library, 1974), 10–11.

4. Adler, "Court, Constitution and Foreign Affairs," 19.

5. Harold Hongju Koh, *The National Security Constitution: Sharing Power after the Iran-Contra Affair* (New Haven: Yale University Press, 1990), chaps. 5 and 6. See also Adler, "Court, Constitution and Foreign Affairs," 19–56.

6. *The Debates in the Several State Conventions on the Adoption of the Federal Constitution*, ed. Jonathan Elliot, 2d ed. (Washington, D.C.: J. Elliot, 1836), 528.

7. Alexander Hamilton, James Madison, and John Jay, *The Federalist Papers*, ed. Clinton Rossiter (New York: New American Library, 1961), 417–418.

8. Ibid., 417.

9. *The Records of the Federal Convention of 1787*, ed. Max Farrand (New Haven: Yale University Press, 1911), 2:318.

10. *The Writings of James Madison*, ed. Gaillard Hunt (New York: Putnam, 1906), 6:148 (emphasis in original).

11. Louis Fisher, *Presidential War Power* (Lawrence: University Press of Kansas, 1995).

12. Edward S. Corwin, *The President: Office and Powers* (New York: New York University Press, 1957), 201.

13. Fisher, *Presidential War Power*, 18–19.

14. *Congressional Globe*, 30th Cong., 1st sess., January 3, 1848, 95.

15. *The Collected Works of Abraham Lincoln*, ed. Roy Basler (New Brunswick, N.J.: Rutgers University Press, 1953), 1:451–452 (emphasis in original).

16. John Locke, *Two Treatises of Government*, ed. Peter Laslett (Cambridge: Cambridge University Press, 1960), Second Treatise, "Of Prerogative," secs. 159–168.

17. *Prize Cases,* 67 U.S. (2 Black) 635, 668 (1863).
18. Ibid., 690.
19. Fisher, *Presidential War Power,* 38–39.
20. U.S. Senate Committee on Foreign Relations, *National Commitments,* 91st Cong., 1st sess., 1969, S. Rept. 129, reprinted in Peter M. Shane and Harold H. Bruff, *Separation of Powers Law: Cases and Materials* (Durham, N.C.: Carolina Academic Press, 1996), 779.
21. Ibid., 780.
22. Koh, *National Security Constitution,* 94.
23. *United States v. Curtiss-Wright Export Corp.,* 299 U.S. 304, 312 (1936).
24. Ibid., 320.
25. David Gray Adler, "The Constitution and Presidential Warmaking," in Adler and George, *The Constitution and the Conduct of American Foreign Policy,* 216.
26. For criticism of the *Curtiss-Wright* decision, see *Youngstown Sheet and Tube Co. v. Sawyer,* 343 U.S. 579, 636 n. 2 (1952), Justice Robert Jackson, concurring; Charles Lofgren, "*United States v. Curtiss-Wright Export Corporation*: An Historical Reassessment," *Yale Law Journal* 83 (1973); David M. Levitan, "The Foreign Relations Power: An Analysis of Mr. Justice Sutherland's Theory," *Yale Law Journal* 55 (1946); David Gray Adler, "The Constitution and Presidential Warmaking: The Enduring Debate," *Political Science Quarterly* 103 (spring 1988): 29–35; *American International Group v. Islamic Republic of Iran,* 657 F. 2d 430, 438 n. 6 (D.C. Cir. 1981).
27. Fisher, *Presidential War Power,* 64–67; Christopher H. Pyle and Richard M. Pious, *The President, Congress and the Constitution: Power and Legitimacy in American Politics* (New York: The Free Press, 1984), 271–272, 329–331; *National Commitments,* in Shane and Bruff, *Separation of Powers Law,* 781.
28. Schlesinger, *Imperial Presidency,* 118–119.
29. Ibid., 135–136.
30. *Department of State Bulletin,* July 31, 1950, 173–179.
31. See Fisher, *Presidential War Power,* 77–84.
32. George Bush, "The President's News Conference on the Persian Gulf Crisis," *Weekly Compilation of Presidential Documents* 26, no. 45 (November 8, 1990): 1790.
33. *Authorization for the Use of Military Force against Iraq Resolution,* P.L. 102-1, 102d Cong., 1st sess. (January 14, 1991); 105 Stat. 3; George Bush, "President's News Conference on Persian Gulf Crisis," *Weekly Compilation of Presidential Documents* 27, no. 2 (January 9, 1991): 25; idem, "Statement on Signing the Resolution Authorizing the Use of Military Force against Iraq," *Weekly Compilation of Presidential Documents* 27, no. 3 (January 14, 1991): 48.
34. Bill Clinton, "Letter to Congressional Leaders on the Strike on Iraqi Intelligence Headquarters," *Weekly Compilation of Presidential Documents* 29, no. 26 (June 28, 1993): 1183.
35. *Joint Resolution on the Defense of Formosa,* P.L. 84-4, 84th Cong., 1st sess. (January 29, 1955); 69 Stat. 7.
36. *Joint Resolution on the Middle East,* P.L. 85-7, 85th Cong., 1st sess. (March 9, 1957); 71 Stat. 5.
37. Leonard Meeker, "The Legality of United States Participation in the Defense of Viet-Nam," *Department of State Bulletin,* March 4, 1966, 474.
38. *The Gulf of Tonkin Resolution,* P.L. 88-408, 88th Cong., 2d sess. (August 10, 1964); 78 Stat. 384 (emphasis added).
39. *Congressional Record,* 88th Cong., 2d sess., 1964, 110:59.
40. Ibid., 110:18426–18427.
41. Even if the Gulf of Tonkin Resolution satisfied the requirement of statutory authorization, evidence brought to light in later years confirms a misinterpretation by the U.S. military of precipitating events, and Johnson chose to use this ambiguous incident as a pretext for congressional support. Eleven years of war rested on a slim reed of misinformation at best, deception at worst. William Goldsmith, *The Growth of Presidential Power* (New York: Chelsea House, 1974), 3:2061–2063; Larry Berman, *Planning a Tragedy: The Americanization of the War in Vietnam* (New York: W. W. Norton, 1982), 33.
42. Koh, *National Security Constitution,* 136–138; Adler, "Court, Constitution and Foreign Affairs," 39–40.
43. *Massachusetts v. Laird,* 451 F. 2d 26 (1st Cir. 1971).
44. *Mitchell v. Laird,* 488 F. 2d 611, 615 (D.C. Cir. 1973).

45. *Holtzman v. Schlesinger,* 361 F. Supp. 553 (E.D.N.Y. 1973).

46. *Holtzman v. Schlesinger,* 484 F. 2d 1307, 1313-1314 (2d Cir. 1973).

47. See Louis Fisher and David Gray Adler, "The War Powers Resolution: Time to Say Goodbye," *Political Science Quarterly* 113 (1998).

48. *War Powers Resolution,* P.L. 93-148, 93d Cong., 1st sess. (November 7, 1973); 87 Stat. 555.

49. This section was undermined by the Supreme Court ruling in *INS v. Chadha,* 462 U.S. 919 (1983), which invalidated the legislative veto. In response to *Chadha,* Congress did not amend the War Powers Resolution but, instead, passed a new law that would require a joint resolution, under an expedited procedure, to order the president to remove troops: 97 Stat. 1062-63, sec. 1013 (1983). See Louis Fisher, *Constitutional Conflicts between Congress and the President,* 4th rev. ed. (Lawrence: University Press of Kansas, 1997), 283.

50. "Veto of the War Powers Resolution," *Public Papers of the Presidents of the United States: Richard M. Nixon, 1973* (Washington, D.C.: Government Printing Office, 1975), 5:893 (October 24, 1973).

51. Nixon's veto occurred four days after the firing of Watergate special prosecutor Archibald Cox and the resultant Saturday Night Massacre. See Fisher, *Presidential War Power,* 130–131.

52. See for example, *Crockett v. Reagan,* 558 F. Supp. 893 (D.D.C.1982), *Sanchez-Espinoza v. Reagan,* 770 F. 2d 202 (D.C. Cir. 1985), and *Lowry v. Reagan,* 676 F. Supp. 333, 340 (D.D.C. 1987), quoting *Baker v. Carr,* 393 U.S. 186, 217, 211 (1962).

53. *Dellums v. Bush,* 752 F. Supp. 1141 (D.D.C. 1990).

54. Bush, "The President's News Conference on the Persian Gulf Crisis," 1790.

55. *Dellums v. Bush,* 1147.

56. Professor Steven Dycus, personal communication, August 8, 2002, paraphrasing from district court decisions by Judge Royce Lambert and Judge Harold Greene.

CHAPTER SEVEN

Emergency Powers

HAROLD C. RELYEA

At various times in U.S. history, emergencies have threatened the well-being of the nation by posing, in varying degrees of severity, the loss of life, property, or public order. In response, presidents have exercised such powers as available by explicit grant or interpretive implication, or otherwise acted of necessity, trusting subsequent acceptance of their actions by Congress, the courts, and the citizenry. As the historical record reflects, however, some responses to these emergencies, whether by the executive, legislature, judiciary, or some combination thereof, endangered citizens' rights and liberties.

Unlike many other democracies or near democracies, the United States does not suspend its Constitution during times of emergency, whether the condition be war, natural disaster, or economic crisis. Other than suspension of the writ of habeas corpus, the Constitution prescribes no arrangement whereby the rights, governmental structure, or procedures specified in its provisions can be temporarily discontinued, in whole or in part, in order to respond to an exigency. The endurance of the United States surely owes much to leaders throughout the federal establishment who relied upon "stretch points" of the Constitution in responding to an emergency.

A national emergency may be said to be one that is gravely threatening to the country and recognizable in its most extreme form as auguring the demise of the nation. The more extreme the threat, the more widespread will be the consensus that a national emergency exists. In political rhetoric, however, the term *emergency* has been artfully used to rally public support and also employed nebulously. According to *Webster's,* an emergency is "an unforeseen combination of circumstances or the resulting state that calls for immediate action."[1] In the midst of the Great Depression, a 1934 majority opinion of the Supreme Court characterized an emergency in terms of urgency and relative infrequency of occurrence, as well as equivalence to a public calamity resulting from fire, flood, or like disaster not reasonably subject to anticipation.[2] Constitutional scholar Edward S. Corwin once explained emergency conditions as being those "which have not attained enough of stability or recurrence to admit of their being dealt with according to rule."[3] During Senate committee hearings on national emergency powers in 1973, political scientist Cornelius P. Cotter described an emergency, stating, "It denotes the existence of conditions of varying nature, intensity and duration, which are perceived to threaten life or well-being beyond tolerable limits."[4] The term, he explained, "connotes the existence of conditions suddenly intensifying the degree of existing danger to life or well-being beyond that which is accepted as normal."[5]

While other understandings of an emergency could be offered, these are sufficient to provide a sense of the concept. An emergency condition appears to have at least four aspects. First is its temporal character: An emergency is sudden, unforeseen, and of unknown duration. Second is its potential gravity: An emergency is dangerous and threatening to life, property, and well-being. Third, in terms of governmental role and authority, is the matter of perception: Who discerns this phenomenon? The Constitution may provide guidance on this question, but it is not always conclusive. Fourth is the matter of response: An emergency requires immediate action but is, as well, unanticipated and, therefore, as Corwin notes, cannot always be "dealt with according to rule." A national emergency is threatening to the nation or some significant portion of its geography, interests, or security.

It should be added that, while some kinds of emergencies may have been unforeseen the first time they occurred, the federal government, over time, as the historical record bears witness, began taking steps to detect and address recurrences. The evolution of civilian and military intelligence capabilities and operations reflects this precautionary development, as do contingency preparations—such as military and other response plans, as well as standby legal authorities—to facilitate quick and effective counteraction to some kinds of emergencies.

Finding the Limits

The exercise of emergency powers was long a concern of classical political theorists, including seventeenth-century English philosopher John Locke, whose ideas had a strong influence on the founding fathers in the United States. A preeminent exponent of a government of laws and not of men, Locke argued that occasions may arise when the executive must exert broad discretion in meeting special exigencies or "emergencies" for which the legislative power provided no relief or existing law granted no necessary remedy. He did not regard this prerogative as limited to wartime, or even to situations of great urgency. It was sufficient if the "public good" might be advanced by its exercise.[6]

The Constitution created a government of limited powers; emergency powers, as such, failed to attract much attention during the 1787 convention at which delegates developed the charter. It may be argued, however, that the grant of emergency powers to Congress is implicit in Article 1, section 8, which allocates to it the authority to "provide for the common Defense and general Welfare"; the commerce clause; its war, armed forces, and militia powers; and the "necessary and proper" clause empowering it to make such laws as are required to fulfill the executions of "the foregoing Powers, and all other Powers vested by this Constitution in the Government of the United States, or in any Department or Officer thereof." The Constitution authorizes the president to call special sessions of Congress, perhaps in order that arrangements for responding to an emergency might be legislated for executive implementation.

One tradition of constitutional interpretation has resulted in so-called implied powers, which may be invoked to respond to an emergency situation. Locke seems to have anticipated this practice. Furthermore, presidents have occasionally taken emergency actions that they assumed to be constitutionally permissible. It has been suggested, as well, that, in the U.S. experience, the exercise of emergency powers "is also contingent upon the personal conception which the incumbent of the presidential office has of the Presidency," so that "the authority of a President is largely determined by the President himself."[7]

A chief executive adopting Theodore Roosevelt's "stewardship" theory—that it was not only the president's "right but his duty to do anything that the needs of the Nation demanded unless such action was forbidden by the Constitution or by the laws"—would seemingly have little reservation about exercising implied executive powers.[8] William Howard Taft, Roosevelt's former secretary of war and personal choice for and actual White House successor, opposed the stewardship theory, and instead held "that the President can exercise no power which cannot be fairly and reasonably traced to some specific grant of power or justly implied and included within such express grant as proper and necessary to its exercise."[9]

Between these two views of the presidency lie various gradations of opinion. Generally, however, those embracing Roosevelt's perspective have been more comfortable with a broad exercise of prerogative powers in times of emergency. If, however, as was proffered earlier, "the authority of a President is largely determined by the President himself," do the constitutional checks of the other two branches have no significance in this regard? To answer this question, the powerful effect of public opinion in times of emergency must be appreciated. If, for example, the nation has been attacked, or a considerable number of Americans have been killed or injured in an overseas assault, such as the sinking of an unarmed ship, public opinion will likely support immediate reprisals ordered by the president as an emergency response. Few in Congress would want to challenge the president's authority to take such actions and incur the enmity of the populace, especially constituents. If, however, the situation evolves to include military reversals and stalemate, increasing casualties, failures at diplomatic resolution, and economic weakening, support for the emergency actions may diminish within the nation and Congress. Constitutional checks may then be exercised, tolerance for dissent as an exercise of First Amendment rights may increase, and courts may become more accepting of cases questioning and seeking to restrain presidential emergency action.

What are the legitimate powers of the legislative, executive, and judicial branches in times of emergency? One answer is the legitimate powers of the three branches supported by the Constitution—that is, those powers explicitly specified, reasonably inferred, or otherwise not prohibited by the fundamental charter. There is a political dimension to be taken into consideration as well. There may be exercises of power by the three branches in times of emergency that are constitutionally suspect: They are neither explicitly specified nor otherwise prohibited, but opinion is divided about whether they may be reasonably inferred. Nonetheless, they are exercised in the absence of effective opposition by the other branches and with the acceptance, if not the support, of a majority of the public. Such exercises of power are often justified as being "of necessity," and usually are of brief duration. In a few instances, the legislature has provided post factum statutory legitimizations of the chief executive's exercise of emergency power. Notable are Abraham Lincoln's emergency actions in response to insurrection in the Southern states prior to the July 1861 convening of Congress and Franklin D. Roosevelt's declaration of a "bank holiday," closing the nation's banking institutions in March 1933.

The Historical Record

Among the initial efforts of Congress to legislate emergency authority were acts of September 29, 1789, and May 8, 1792, authorizing the president to call forth the militia of the states, initially, to protect the inhabitants of the frontiers, and, subsequently, to execute federal laws, suppress insurrections, and repel invasions.[10] In the first presidential response to an emergency, George Washington utilized the 1792 statute to mobilize the militia in August 1794 to suppress the Whiskey Rebellion, the insurrection provoked by a federal excise tax on whiskey that residents of western Pennsylvania, Virginia, and the Carolinas forcefully opposed. Washington personally took command of the forces called up. In the case of the judicial branch, the Supreme Court's ruling in *Marbury v. Madison* (1803) was a critical ruling concerning emergency powers, although it did not deal with the issue specifically. Rather, in declaring for the first time an act of Congress unconstitutional, the Court established

its authority for determining ultimately what is law under the Constitution. Attention here is concentrated on five eras rich in the exercise of emergency powers—the Civil War, World War I, the Great Depression, World War II, and the homeland security period following the September 11, 2001, attacks on the United States.

Civil War

For several decades, controversy and conflict over slavery had steadily grown until it erupted in regional rebellion and insurrection in late 1860. News of the election of a president known to be opposed to slavery—Abraham Lincoln—prompted a public convention in South Carolina that met a few days before Christmas and voted unanimously to dissolve the union between South Carolina and the other states. During the next two months, seven Southern states followed South Carolina in secession. State troops began seizing federal arsenals and forts within the secessionist territories. President James Buchanan, in his fourth and final annual message to Congress on December 3, 1860, conceded that because of the resignation of federal judicial officials throughout South Carolina, "the whole machinery of the Federal Government necessary for the distribution of remedial justice among the people has been demolished." He contended, however, that "the Executive has no authority to decide what shall be the relations between the Federal Government and South Carolina." Any attempt in this regard, he felt, would "be a naked act of usurpation." Consequently, Buchanan indicated that it was his "duty to submit to Congress the whole question in all its bearings," observing that "the emergency may soon arise when you may be called upon to decide the momentous question whether you possess the power by force of arms to compel a State to remain in the Union." Having "arrived at the conclusion that no such power has been delegated to Congress or to any other department of the Federal Government," he proposed that Congress should call a constitutional convention, or ask the states to call one, for purposes of adopting a constitutional amendment recognizing the right of property in slaves in the states where slavery existed or might thereafter occur.[11]

By Lincoln's inauguration, on March 4, 1861, the Confederate provisional government had been established (February 4); Jefferson Davis had been elected (February 9) and installed as the president of the Confederacy (February 18); an army had been assembled by the secessionist states; federal troops, who had been withdrawn to Fort Sumter in Charleston harbor, were becoming desperate for relief and resupply; and the Thirty-sixth Congress had adjourned (March 3). A dissolving nation was poised to witness, as Wilfred Binkley states, "the high-water mark of the exercise of executive power in the United States." Indeed, he continues, "No one can ever know just what Lincoln conceived to be limits of his powers."[12]

A month after Lincoln's inauguration, the new president notified South Carolina authorities that an expedition was en route solely to provision the Fort Sumter troops. In response, Confederate leaders demanded that the garrison's commander immediately surrender. He demurred, and, starting on April 12, the fort and its inhabitants were subjected to continuous, intense fire from shore batteries for thirty-four hours, after which they finally surrendered. The attack galvanized the North for a

defense of the Union. Lincoln, however, did not immediately call Congress into special session. Instead, for reasons not altogether clear, but with broad support in the North, Lincoln engaged in a series of actions that intruded upon the constitutional authority of the legislature. Lincoln's rationale for his conduct may be revealed in a comment he reportedly made in 1864: "I conceive I may in an emergency do things on military grounds which cannot constitutionally be done by the Congress."[13]

In an April 15, 1861, proclamation, Lincoln—recognizing "combinations too powerful to be suppressed by the ordinary course of judicial proceedings" or the U.S. marshals in the seven southernmost states—called 75,000 of "the militia of the several States of the Union" into federal service "to cause the laws to be duly executed." He also called Congress to convene in special session on July 4 "to consider and determine, such measures, as, in their wisdom, the public safety, and interest may seem to demand."[14] Then, in an April 19 proclamation, Lincoln established a blockade of the ports of the secessionist states, "a measure hitherto regarded as contrary to both the Constitution and the law of nations except when the government was embroiled in a declared, foreign war."[15] The next day, the president ordered that nineteen vessels be added to the navy "for purposes of public defense." Shortly thereafter, the blockade was extended to the ports of Virginia and North Carolina.

In a May 3 proclamation, Lincoln ordered that the regular army be enlarged by 22,714 men, that navy personnel be increased by 18,000, and that 42,032 volunteers be accommodated for three-year terms of service. The Constitution, however, specifically empowers only Congress "to raise and support armies." In a July 4 message to the special session of Congress, Lincoln indicated that his actions expanding the armed forces, "whether strictly legal or not, were ventured upon under what appeared to be a popular and a public necessity, trusting then, as now, that Congress would readily ratify them. It is believed," he continued, "that nothing has been done beyond the constitutional competency of Congress." Indeed, in an act of August 6, 1861, Lincoln's "acts, proclamations, and orders" concerning the army, navy, militia, and volunteers from the states were "approved and in all respects legalized and made valid, to the same intent and with the same effect as if they had been issued and done under the previous express authority and direction of the Congress."[16]

The Thirty-seventh Congress, which Lincoln convened in July, initially met for about a month. Members returned in December for a second session, which consumed about two hundred days of the next year, and a third session, beginning in December 1862 and ending in early March 1863. The president had party majorities in both chambers: about two-thirds of the Senate was Republican, and the House counted 106 Republicans, 42 Democrats, and 28 Unionists. The 1862 elections shifted the House balance to 102 Republicans and 75 Democrats. Despite the numerical dominance of the Republicans, presidential leadership was needed for legislative accomplishments because, by one assessment, within the House and the Senate, "no one individual or faction was able to establish firm control of the congressional agendas during the Civil War."[17]

Investigation and oversight activities by congressional committees increased during the war, "when 15 of 35 select committees were primarily concerned with wrongdoing or improper performance of duties," and similar probes were being conducted by at least six standing committees. The war added urgency to proper administrative performance and prompted enlarged federal expenditures. There were, as well, committee examinations of matters more closely connected with the war.[18]

Perhaps the best known of the wartime oversight panels was the Joint Committee on the Conduct of the War. While some of its tactics—secret testimony, leaks to the press, disallowance of an opportunity to confront or cross-examine accusers—and its bias against West Point officers remain unacceptable, its probes of the Fort Pillow massacre, in which black Union troops were murdered and not allowed to surrender, and the poor condition of Union soldiers returned from Confederate prisons "were among its more positive achievements." Indeed, "a number of its investigations exposed corruption, financial mismanagement, and crimes against humanity," with the result that the panel "deserves praise not only for exposing these abuses but also for using such disclosures to invigorate northern public opinion and bolster the resolve to continue the war. Had the committee's work always been modeled on these investigations," it has been rightly concluded, "there would be little debate about its positive, albeit minor, contribution to the Union war effort."[19] Overall, however, congressional overseers appear to have had little restraining effect on the presidential exercise of emergency powers.

In his efforts to suppress the rebellion by the Southern states, Lincoln regarded his war power as including the right to suspend the writ of habeas corpus, to proclaim martial law, and "to place persons under arrest without warrant and without judicially showing the cause of detention." It also encompassed "the right to seize citizens' property if such seizure should become indispensable to the successful prosecution of the war; the right to spend money from the treasury of the United States without congressional appropriation; the right to suppress newspapers; and the right to do unusual things by proclamation, especially to proclaim freedom to the slaves of those in arms against the Government." In these actions, observes historian James G. Randall, Lincoln "was as a rule, though not without exception, sustained by the courts."[20]

At the time of Lincoln's assumption of the presidency, the federal courts in the South had collapsed, and courts in war zones had either temporarily suspended operations or succumbed to declarations of martial law and trials by military tribunals. Many of the federal judges serving in the North, Northwest, and West probably were sympathetic to the new president's antislavery position, but that did not mean that they would necessarily support his exercise of war powers to take extraordinary actions. Similarly, there was uncertainty about how the Supreme Court would evaluate Lincoln's actions. The Court, and particularly Chief Justice Roger B. Taney, had disgraced itself, in the view of many Americans, and engendered the enmity of the Republican Party with its decision in *Dred Scott v. Sandford* (1857).[21] When Lincoln became president, there was one vacancy on the Court because of a death; a month later, death claimed another justice; soon thereafter, a third vacancy occurred when a justice resigned to join the Con-

federate cause. Later, in 1862, Congress created a tenth seat on the Court.[22] Thus, Lincoln had four opportunities to fashion a Supreme Court likely to be supportive of his presidency.[23]

Although Chief Justice Taney declared in May 1861 that the president had improperly suspended the writ of habeas corpus, his ruling was rendered on circuit, and military authorities refused to honor his writ for the release of John Merryman, a Southern sympathizer.[24] Nonetheless, his opinion provided a warning, one clearly understood by Attorney General Edward Bates, who warned Secretary of War Edwin Stanton in January 1863 against seeking Supreme Court review of a Wisconsin case involving the president's suspension power.[25] About a month later, Congress gave final approval to a statute authorizing the president, "during the present rebellion," to suspend habeas corpus.[26] Under the provisions of the act, officers in charge of prisons were required to obey a judge's order for release, and those against whom no violation of federal law was charged could not be held. Also, lists of political prisoners arrested in the past as well as those incarcerated in the future were required to be kept and furnished to the courts. Randall concludes, however, "that the act was not carried out in sufficient degree to make any noticeable difference in the matter of the arrest, confinement, and release of political prisoners."[27]

Arbitrary arrests and the use of the military as the police and the courts continued throughout the war. Because of the controversy the arrests engendered, the administration took pains to explain and justify their utilization and, beginning in February 1862, to temper criticism with grants of amnesty.[28] Court tests of presidential authority in these matters were avoided; Congress reacted by creating the Office of Judge Advocate General in July 1862 to supervise all courts martial and military commission proceedings.[29] In the *Ex parte Vallandigham* decision of 1864, the Supreme Court avoided constitutional issues posed by the exiled traitor, who had been convicted by a military commission, and ruled narrowly that it lacked jurisdiction for an appeal from a military tribunal. Finally, one year after the end of the Civil War, the Supreme Court, noting that "the late wicked Rebellion" had not allowed "that calmness in deliberation and discussion so necessary to a correct conclusion of a purely judicial question," unanimously declared in *Ex parte Milligan* (1866) that military commissions, in an uninvaded and nonrebellious state, in which the federal courts are open and functioning, "had no jurisdiction to try, convict, or sentence for any criminal offense, a citizen who was a resident of a rebellious State, nor a prisoner of war, nor a person in the military or naval service."

In contrast to these developments, almost two years after the beginning of the war, the Supreme Court ruled on the *Prize Cases* (1863), "deemed the most significant decision the Court handed down during the conflict."[30] Technicalities aside, the case addressed the key question of whether the president had the authority to impose a blockade of Southern ports without congressional authorization. If the president's action was determined to be illegal, a vast amount of restitution might be in order. In addition, Lincoln wanted to sustain the blockade as a response to a rebellion rather than a war, the latter condition constituting something of an invitation to foreign powers to recognize and assist the Confederacy. Ulti-

mately, a 5-4 Court majority, which included three Lincoln appointees, supported the president's action and his rebellion theory.[31]

In reviewing the emergency period of the Civil War, scholars generally have concluded "that neither Congress nor the Supreme Court exercised any very effective restraint upon the President."[32] The actions of the chief executive were either unchallenged or sanctioned by Congress, and were either justified, or, because of no opportunity to render judgment, went without evaluation by the Supreme Court. Lincoln sought legislative and judicial support for, or approval of, his actions when he thought he could obtain it, and avoided situations in which disapproval might result. In pursuing this strategy, he remained keenly aware of popular approval of his presidency. For the remainder of the century and throughout the next, no president would exercise emergency powers in quite the same way or under quite the same conditions as did Lincoln.

World War I

The war sweeping across Europe during the latter months of 1914 left the United States unaffected. The presidential contest of 1912 had resulted in the election of Woodrow Wilson, the first Democrat to occupy the White House since 1897. At the start of Wilson's administration, his party held a substantial margin in the House (291-127), an advantage that quickly dwindled during the next two Congresses and disappeared in 1918; an initial seven-seat margin in the Senate grew slightly during the next two Congresses before the opposition gained a two-seat majority in 1918. In March 1913 Wilson had embarked on regularly scheduled conferences with the Washington press corps, an innovation reflective of his intention to gauge, mold, and lead public opinion. The Supreme Court greeting Wilson was largely conservative, and although it had given the commerce clause a little broader reading in the early years of the century, it continued to hold a narrow view of the Constitution's protection of individual rights. Associate Justice Edward D. White was elevated to the position of chief justice in 1910. Wilson would appoint three members to the high court during his two terms.

During the initial months of the war in Europe, the United States adopted a policy of neutrality, but a little later, in September 1915, Wilson reluctantly agreed to allow American bankers to make loans to the belligerent nations. These loans, foreign bond purchases, and foreign trade tended to favor Great Britain and France. Earlier, in February 1915, Germany had proclaimed the waters around the British Isles a war zone that neutral ships entered at their own risk. In May a German submarine sunk the *Lusitania,* a British transatlantic steamer, causing the loss of 1,198 lives, including 128 Americans. Disclosures of German espionage and sabotage in the United States later in the year, unrestricted submarine warfare by Germany as of February 1917, and revelations in March of German attempts to form an alliance with Mexico contributed to Wilson calling a special session of Congress on April 2, when he asked for a declaration of war, which was given final approval four days later.[33]

As Wilson led the nation into war, the "preponderance of his crisis authority," notes Clinton Rossiter, "was delegated to him by statutes of Congress." Indeed, "Wilson chose to demand express legislative authority for almost every unusual step he felt impelled to take." By comparison, the source of Lincoln's power, observes Rossiter, "was the Constitution, and he operated in spite of Congress," while the "basis of Wilson's power was a group of statutes, and he cooperated with Congress.[34]

Wilson also exercised certain discretion over and above that provided by statute, but he did so in a manner that generally did not antagonize the legislature. For example, in February 1917 he armed U.S. merchant ships; in April 1917 he created the Committee on Public Information, a propaganda and censorship entity that had no statutory authority for its limitations on the First Amendment; and he formed various emergency agencies under the broad authority of the Council of National Defense, which had been statutorily mandated in 1916.[35]

"Among the important statutory delegations to the President," recounts Rossiter, "were acts empowering him to take over and operate the railroads and water systems, to regulate and commandeer all ship-building facilities in the United States, to regulate and prohibit exports" and "to raise an army by conscription." Other measures authorized him "to allocate priorities in transportation, to regulate the conduct of resident enemy aliens, to take over and operate the telegraph and telephone systems, to redistribute functions among the executive agencies of the federal government, to control the foreign language press, and to censor all communications to and from foreign countries."[36]

Although Rossiter thinks "limitations on American liberty in World War I were ridiculously few," other observers strongly disagree.[37] His mentor and subsequent faculty colleague, Robert E. Cushman, for example, proffers that "the record of our behavior with respect to civil liberties during World War I is not one in which the thoughtful citizen can take much pride or satisfaction."[38] Although Congress, perhaps with a view to self-protection, refused to give Wilson the authority to censure the American press, it did enact other laws, at the president's request, to truncate freedom of expression. Chief among these was the Espionage Act of 1917, for punishing use of the postal system to advocate or urge treason, insurrection, or forcible resistance to federal law; spying; false reporting or communication with the intent of interfering with armed forces operations, promoting "the success" of the enemy, or causing insubordination, disloyalty, mutiny, or refusal of duty in the armed forces; or willfully obstructing armed forces recruitment or enlistment.[39] Another was the Trading With the Enemy Act of 1917, which expanded the censorship powers of the postmaster general. It also authorized censorship (implemented through a presidential board) of "communications by mail, cable, radio, or other means of transmission passing between the United States and any foreign country."[40] The Sedition Act of 1918, which amended the Espionage Act, was to punish, among other crimes, obstructing the sale of war bonds and willfully uttering, printing, writing, or publishing "any disloyal, profane, scurrilous, or abusive language" about the U.S. form of government, the Constitution, the armed forces or their uniforms, or the flag. Individuals also could be punished for using any language intended to bring any of these entities into contempt, scorn, contumely, or disrepute or "to incite, provoke, or encourage resistance to the United States or to promote the cause of its enemies," or to "urge, incite, or advocate any curtailment" of war production.[41]

By one account, the Department of Justice pursued 2,168 prosecutions under the Espionage Act and the Sedition Act, and obtained 1,055 convictions.[42] In a First Amendment challenge, the Supreme Court unanimously sustained the Espionage Act, with Associate Justice Oliver Wendell Holmes laying out in the opinion of the Court his famous "clear and present danger" test for determining the limits of First Amendment protection of political speech.[43] A unanimous Court also upheld the Sedition Act shortly thereafter, with Holmes again writing the Court's opinion.[44] Several months later, however, the Court divided 7-2 in another Sedition Act case, with Holmes in the minority.[45]

Among the most zealous censors was Postmaster General Albert S. Burleson, who, by one estimate, "exercised his power of censorship with a high hand, excluding from the mails publications which only by far-fetched lines of reasoning could be held to be in violation of the statute."[46] In the view of another analyst, "Burleson used censorship as a bludgeon with which to destroy the left-wing press."[47] For example, "about sixty Socialist papers lost their second-class mailing privileges," and "[m]any lesser papers ceased publication."[48]

A Senate bill providing for trial and punishment of spies and the disloyal by military tribunal engendered Wilson's immediate opposition. The proposal, which Wilson characterized as "unconstitutional . . . unnecessary and uncalled for," had been drafted and supported before a Senate committee by a zealous assistant attorney general, Charles Warren, who had recently left his government position.[49]

In November 1918 Americans elected Republican majorities to both houses of Congress, and an armistice was signed in Europe, bringing a cessation of warfare. As peace negotiations began in Paris in mid-January, with Wilson participating, many temporary wartime authorities began to expire. Most of any remaining war statutes and agencies were terminated by an act of March 3, 1921.[50]

The Great Depression

Calvin Coolidge, in his final state of the union message, transmitted on December 4, 1928, advised the legislators that no previous Congress "has met a more pleasing prospect than that which appears at the present time" and concluded that the "country can regard the present with satisfaction and anticipate the future with optimism."[51] One year later, the dreamworld envisioned by Coolidge vanished and was replaced by a nightmare. On October 24, 1929, an overspeculated stock market suddenly experienced an incredible deluge of selling, which sent prices plummeting. Panic ensued. In the melee of the stock exchange, brokers fought to sell before it was too late. Rapidly, time ran out.

Economic crisis was not new to the United States. The country had experienced financial setbacks of nationwide proportion in 1857, 1875, and 1893. History, however, was an enemy in devising a strategy to deal with the depression that began in 1929. The periods of economic difficulty of the past were but a tum-

ble when compared with the plunge of the Great Depression. This, as it turns out, was the first problem experienced by policymakers attempting to rectify the situation: They did not recognize the ramifications of the crash or the extent of the damage done and continuing to be done. Perhaps, too, the administrative machinery was not available or sufficiently developed to halt the downward economic spiral. It may have been that Herbert Hoover's philosophy of government was inadequate for meeting the exigency. In the face of all efforts to halt the economic slide, it continued, mercilessly devastating American society.

The depression demoralized the nation: It destroyed individual dignity and self-respect, shattered family structure, and begged actions that civilized society had almost forgotten. In brief, it created a most desperate situation, ripe for exploitation by zealots, fanatics, and demagogues. It also created an emergency that, unlike exigencies of the past, dealt a violent blow to the public that neither armed forces nor military weaponry could repel. This new type of crisis led to a broad extension of executive power.

In 1932 a malcontent and despairing electorate voted out Herbert Hoover. Although a dedicated public servant of demonstrated ability, the people replaced him with Franklin Delano Roosevelt, who came to the presidency from the governorship of New York and had previously served as assistant secretary of the navy during the Wilson administration. In his inaugural address, the new president was eloquent, telling the American people "that the only thing we have to fear is fear itself—nameless, unreasoning, unjustified terror which paralyzes needed efforts to convert retreat into advance." More important, he expressed hope that the normal balance of executive and legislative authority would prove to be adequate "to meet the unprecedented tasks before us," but acknowledged that "temporary departure from that normal balance" might be necessary. "I am prepared under my constitutional duty to recommend the measures that a stricken Nation in the midst of a stricken world may require," he said, but, in the event Congress did not cooperate "and in the event that the national emergency is still critical, I shall not evade the clear course of duty that will then confront me"—using "broad Executive power to wage a war against the emergency, as great as the power that would be given to me if we were in fact invaded by a foreign foe."[52]

The day after his inauguration, Roosevelt called a special session of Congress. The proclamation for the gathering did not indicate the purpose for the March 9 assembly. The president's party enjoyed overwhelming majorities in the House (310-117) and Senate (60-35). Roosevelt had arrived in Washington with drafts of two proclamations, one calling for the special session of Congress and the other declaring a so-called bank holiday, which would temporarily close the nation's banks and restrict the export of gold by invoking provisions of the Trading With the Enemy Act.[53] The proclamation of a bank holiday was issued on March 6. Between the evening of the inauguration and the opening of Congress, Roosevelt's lieutenants, aided by Ogden Mills, Hoover's secretary of the Treasury, drafted an emergency banking bill. When Congress convened, the Speaker of the House read to the chamber from a draft text of the legislation. After thirty-eight minutes of debate, the House

passed the bill. That evening, the Senate followed suit. Roosevelt then issued a second proclamation, pursuant to the new banking law, continuing the bank holiday and the terms and provisions of the March 6 proclamation.[54]

Thereafter ensued the famous Hundred Days, when the Seventy-third Congress enacted fifteen major relief and recovery laws, many of which provided specific emergency powers to the president or broad general authority to address the crisis gripping the nation. The Emergency Banking Relief Act, for example, authorized the president to declare a condition of national emergency and, "under such rules and regulations as he may prescribe," regulate banking and related financial matters affecting the economy. This statute also continued the chief executive's authority to suspend the operations of member banks of the Federal Reserve system.[55] Under the authority of the Civilian Conservation Corps Reforestation Relief Act, the president was granted broad power "to provide for employing citizens of the United States who are unemployed, in the construction, maintenance, and carrying on of works of a public nature in connection with the forestation of lands belonging to the United States or to the several States." Authority also was granted to house, care for, and compensate such individuals as might be recruited to carry out programs established pursuant to the act.[56] After declaring the existence of a national emergency with regard to unemployment and the disorganization of industry, the National Industrial Recovery Act authorized the president to establish an industrial code system and a public works program to facilitate the restoration of prosperity. The president could establish administrative agencies to carry out the provisions of the act, and might delegate the functions and powers vested in him by the statute to those entities.[57]

Although Congress was willing to provide Roosevelt emergency authority to bring about the economic recovery of the nation, the Supreme Court soon indicated that some legislative responses to the depression did not pass constitutional muster. The National Industrial Recovery Act was struck down in 1935 for making unconstitutional delegations of legislative power to the executive and, in one case, as well, for improperly relying upon the interstate commerce clause to regulate local commerce. Furthermore, the Court was not swayed by the government's contention that the legislation was justified by the national economic emergency.[58] The following year, in a 6-3 decision, the Court declared a tax provision of the Agricultural Adjustment Act an invasion of the reserved powers of the states, a violation of the Tenth Amendment.[59] These rulings prompted Roosevelt to propose an enlargement of the Court's membership in 1937, a proposition about which many Democratic members of Congress had misgivings. The Court, however, suddenly signaled a change in thinking that produced a new majority more favorably inclined toward statutes supporting the administration's recovery efforts.[60] Moreover, by the end of 1940, Roosevelt had appointed five new justices to the Court.

World War II

The formal entry of the United States into World War II occurred on December 8, 1941, with a declaration of war against Japan in response to the attack on Pearl Harbor the pre-

vious day.[61] Three days later, on December 11, war was declared against Germany and Italy.[62] In the 1940 elections, Americans had returned Roosevelt to office for an unprecedented third term, and his party held large majorities in the House (267-162) and Senate (66-28).

During Roosevelt's first and second terms, 1933–1940, totalitarian regimes had begun threatening the peace of Europe and Asia, and Congress adopted a series of neutrality acts restricting arms shipments and travel by U.S. citizens on the vessels of belligerent nations.[63] Two months after war commenced in Europe in September 1939, Congress, at the president's request, modified the neutrality laws by repealing the arms embargo and authorizing "cash and carry" exports of arms and munitions to belligerent powers.[64] Some advanced weapons—aircraft carriers and long-range bombers—were procured by the U.S. Army and Navy for "defensive" purposes. More bold during the period of professed neutrality was the president's unilateral transfer of fifty retired destroyers to Great Britain in exchange for U.S. bases in British territories in the Caribbean. Roosevelt also negotiated a series of defense agreements whereby U.S. troops were either stationed in foreign territory or were used to replace the troops of nations at war in nonbelligerent tasks so that these countries could commit their military personnel to combat. Such was the case with Canada, when, in August 1940, it was announced that the U.S. Navy, in effect, would police the Canadian and U.S. coasts, providing mutual defense to both borders. Canadian naval personnel would thus be released to aid the British navy. In April 1941 U.S. military and naval personnel, with the agreement of Denmark, were positioned in

Greenland. In November the Netherlands concurred with the introduction of American troops into Dutch Guiana.

With the declarations of war and the impending international crisis, Roosevelt, in Rossiter's estimate, became "a President who went beyond Wilson and even Lincoln in the bold and successful exertion of his constitutional and statutory powers." Congress "gave the President all the power he needed to wage a victorious total war, but stubbornly refused to be shunted to the back of the stage by the leading man."[65] Exemplary among the various congressional committees playing a watchdog role during the war was the Senate Special Committee to Investigate the National Defense Program.[66] The Supreme Court "gave judicial sanction to whatever powers and actions the President and Congress found necessary to the prosecution of the war, and then post bellum had a lot of strong but unavailing things to say about the limits of the Constitution-at-War."[67]

While the First War Powers Act of 1941 authorized the censorship of communications from the United States to foreign countries, the domestic press and radio were controlled by a strictly voluntary and extralegal censorship code.[68] A few allegedly seditious or nearly seditious publications, for example, Father Charles E. Coughlin's *Social Justice,* were suppressed by the postmaster general. The most serious civil liberties violation during the war—although it was not widely criticized at the time—was the internment in camps, at Roosevelt's order, of some 110,000 Japanese Americans, fully 70,000 of whom were legal citizens of the United States. Congress supported the internment directive by legislating a misdemeanor penalty for any action in violation of the restrictions laid down by the president, the secretary of war, or designated military subordinates.[69] The Supreme Court supported the constitutionality of these actions.[70] The Court, meeting in special session, also rejected the habeas corpus applications of seven German saboteurs captured on U.S. soil and prosecuted in secret proceedings by a military tribunal. Six of the prisoners were executed a little more than a week later.[71] When the Roosevelt presidency ended on April 12, 1945, with his sudden death in Warm Springs, Georgia, his experience with the exercise of emergency powers during wartime had been one of little restraint by Congress or the federal courts and, with the exception of the forced internment of American citizens of Japanese ancestry, of respect for constitutionally guaranteed rights.

Homeland Security

President George W. Bush was confronted nine months after his inauguration by the September 11, 2001, attacks on the World Trade Center and the Pentagon. At the time, the 107th Congress sat in session, with the president's party having majority control of the House (221-212), but minority status in the Senate (49-50). Although Bush would request congressional enactment of remedial legislation to address the emergency, he also had available a rich legacy of statutory powers to draw upon. These included, for example, the response and recovery program authorities of the Federal Emergency Management Agency,[72] as well as standby provisions that could be selectively activated pursuant to the National Emergencies Act of 1976 with a national emergency declaration.[73]

A few hours after the attacks, U.S. armed forces around the world were brought to the highest level of readiness; the Capitol grounds and the West Wing of the White House were evacuated. All aircraft over the United States were grounded; most federal employees around the country were sent home; all domestic financial markets were closed; and military defenses for Washington and New York were strengthened. A few days later, Bush formally declared a national emergency and activated provisions of law authorizing the call up of the Ready Reserve and other retired or separated armed services personnel.[74] That same day, September 14, Congress completed action on a $40 billion emergency assistance package for counterterrorism and rescue efforts[75] and enacted a joint resolution authorizing the president to use all necessary force in retaliation for the terrorist attacks.[76] On September 19 Bush ordered the deployment of more than 100 advanced aircraft to the Persian Gulf as part of the initial buildup of U.S. military forces for retaliatory action. Four days later, Bush declared another national emergency, invoked the International Emergency Economic Powers Act of 1977, and ordered its implementation to begin freezing the assets of individuals and organizations believed to be involved in the attacks and in related activities threatening U.S. security interests.[77] On October 7 U.S. and British aircraft and warships began assaults against suspected al-Qaeda and government bases and targets in Afghanistan.

To implement and coordinate new security policies, Bush issued an October 8 order establishing the Office of Homeland Security (OHS) within the Executive Office of the President and creating the Homeland Security

Council.[78] Later that day, he appointed former Pennsylvania governor Tom Ridge to head OHS. On October 26, Bush signed the USA Patriot Act, giving law enforcement officials new and expanded powers to investigate and detain suspected terrorists and to carry out controversial domestic surveillance.[79] A few days later, the Department of Justice authorized the Bureau of Prisons to monitor communications between suspected terrorists and their attorneys, which prompted protests from trial lawyers, the American Bar Association, and civil liberties organizations.[80] Simultaneously, Department of Justice detentions of legal and illegal immigrants of Middle Eastern descent (some of whom were legal residents), its refusals to name publicly those detained, and cessation of the issuance of detention tallies spawned objection. More explosive still was a November 13 military order authorizing the creation of special military tribunals to try suspected terrorists and their collaborators.[81] These matters appeared to be the only ones resulting in any serious conflict between the president and Congress concerning his immediate response to the September attacks. The 107th Congress continued to be generous in providing funds for homeland security; readily enacted new aviation security, border security, and visa entry regulations; and passed bioterrorism preparedness legislation.

Congress also eventually passed legislation for the establishment of a new Department of Homeland Security. The House, where the president's party had majority status, quickly approved legislation establishing the new department. Senate deliberations on the matter were slower due to partisan and parliamentary factors as well as to a few highly contentious issues, such as civil service protections and collective bargaining rights for employees of the new department. Ultimately, Bush largely obtained what he wanted in the legislation mandating the department.

Conclusion

As the historical record recounted here suggests, Congress and the federal courts have not been very effective counterweights to exercises of emergency power by the presidents.[82] Judges, as acknowledged by the Supreme Court in *Milligan,* may defer, delay, or rule narrowly on presidential emergency actions until the period of crisis has passed. Congress also may choose this course as well, as it did when it legislatively terminated unnecessary war statutes and agencies in 1921, well after the end of the fighting in Europe. When enacting legislation vesting emergency authority in the executive, however, Congress may include a sunset provision automatically terminating the statute on the occasion of a particular event or condition marking the end of the emergency, such as the establishment of an armistice or the ratification of a peace treaty.

For many years, Congress has legislated standby delegations of emergency authority that could be activated with a formal national emergency declaration. With the National Emergencies Act in 1976, Congress created procedural arrangements for such declarations, limited their effects to selective activation of standby authorities, and provided itself with a means of canceling unwarranted national emergency declarations or inappropriate activations of standby authorities. Finally, through its power of the purse, Congress can continue to restrain or scale back executive actions responding to a national emergency, as was done abruptly and drastically after the November 1918 armistice in Europe and the immediate years after the end of World War II. The Constitution and the form of government it guarantees have survived many national emergencies in the life of the nation, the three branches not always being in perfect check and balance with one another during these periods of crisis, just as they may not be in less perilous times.

Notes

A version of this chapter was presented by the author in testimony at a February 28, 2002, hearing before the Subcommittee on the Constitution of the House Committee on the Judiciary, Washington, D.C.

1. *Webster's New Collegiate Dictionary,* 8th ed., 372.
2. *Home Building and Loan Association v. Blaisdell,* 290 U.S. 398, 440 (1934).
3. Edward S. Corwin, *The President: Office and Powers, 1787–1957,* 4th rev. ed. (New York: New York University Press, 1957), 3.
4. Senate Special Committee on the Termination of the National Emergency, *National Emergency: Hearings,* 93d Cong., 1st sess., April 11, 1973, 277.
5. Ibid., 279.
6. John Locke, *Two Treatises of Government,* ed. Thomas I. Cook (New York: Hafner, 1947), 203–207; Corwin, *President: Office and Powers,* 147–148.
7. Albert L. Sturm, "Emergencies and the Presidency," *Journal of Politics* 11 (1949): 125–126.
8. Theodore Roosevelt, *Theodore Roosevelt: An Autobiography* (New York: Macmillan, 1913), 388–389.
9. William Howard Taft, *Our Chief Magistrate and His Powers* (New York: Columbia University Press, 1916), 139–140.
10. 1 Stat. 95 (1789), 264 (1792).
11. "Fourth Annual Message," *A Compilation of the Messages and Papers of the Presidents,* ed.

James D. Richardson (New York: Bureau of National Literature, 1897), 7:3165–3167.

12. Wilfred E. Binkley, *President and Congress* (New York: Alfred A. Knopf, 1947), 126.

13. George Fort Milton, *The Use of Presidential Power, 1789–1943* (Boston: Little, Brown, 1944), 111. Contemporary legal support for this point of view can be found in a treatise by a solicitor of the Department of War: William Whiting, *War Powers under the Constitution of the United States* (Boston: Little, Brown, 1862).

14. "By the President of the United States: A Proclamation," *Compilation of the Messages and Papers of the Presidents,* 7:3214–3214.

15. Clinton Rossiter, *Constitutional Dictatorship: Crisis Government in the Modern Democracies* (Princeton, N.J.: Princeton University Press, 1948), 225.

16. 12 Stat. 326 (1861).

17. Allan G. Bogue, *The Congressman's Civil War* (Cambridge: Cambridge University Press, 1989), xiv–xv, xviii, 57.

18. See ibid., 60–88.

19. Bruce Tap, *Over Lincoln's Shoulder: The Committee on the Conduct of the War* (Lawrence: University Press of Kansas, 1998), 253, 255.

20. James G. Randall, *Constitutional Problems under Lincoln,* rev. ed. (Urbana: University of Illinois Press, 1951), 36–37.

21. *Dred Scott v. Sandford,* 60 U.S. 393 (1857) is one of the most important cases in U.S. constitutional history. The 7-2 decision, which played a major role in precipitating the Civil War, was rendered for the majority by Chief Justice Roger Taney, who ruled that Scott remained a slave, that Congress exceeded its authority when it forbade or abolished slavery in the territories because no such power could be inferred from the Constitution, and that slaves were property protected by the Constitution. See Don E. Fehrenbacher, *The Dred Scott Case: Its Significance in American Law and Politics* (New York: Oxford University Press, 1978).

22. 12 Stat. 794 (1822).

23. See David M. Silver, *Lincoln's Supreme Court* (Urbana: University of Illinois Press, 1956), 1–13, 84–85.

24. *Ex parte Merryman,* 17 Fed. Cas. 144 (No. 9487) (C.C.D. Md. 1861); see Silver, *Lincoln's Supreme Court,* 28–36. At the time, Supreme

Court justices also heard cases individually on the federal circuit.

25. See Randall, *Constitutional Problems under Lincoln,* 132; Silver, *Lincoln's Supreme Court,* 123–125.

26. 12 Stat. 755–756 (1863).

27. Randall, *Constitutional Problems under Lincoln,* 166.

28. See Silver, *Lincoln's Supreme Court,* 119–129, 131–137, 147–155, 227–236; Mark E. Neely Jr., *The Fate of Liberty: Abraham Lincoln and Civil Liberties* (New York: Oxford University Press, 1991).

29. 12 Stat. 598 (1862).

30. Silver, *Lincoln's Supreme Court,* 104.

31. *Prize Cases,* 67 U.S. 635 (1863); see Silver, *Lincoln's Supreme Court,* 104–118.

32. Randall, *Constitutional Problems under Lincoln,* 517. For concurrences with this view, see Binkley, *President and Congress,* 124–127; Rossiter, *Constitutional Dictatorship,* 233–234; and Woodrow Wilson, *Constitutional Government in the United States* (New York: Columbia University Press, 1907), 58.

33. 40 Stat. 1 (1917).

34. Rossiter, *Constitutional Dictatorship,* 242.

35. Concerning the Committee on Public Information, see Stephen L. Vaughn, *Holding Fast the Inner Lines: Democracy, Nationalism, and the Committee on Public Information* (Chapel Hill: University of North Carolina Press, 1980). The mandate of the Council of National Defense can be found at 39 Stat. 649–650 (1916), and its operations are discussed in Grosvenor B. Clarkson, *Industrial America in the World War: The Strategy behind the Line, 1917–1918* (Boston: Houghton Mifflin, 1923); also see, generally, William Franklin Willoughby, *Government Organization in War Time and After* (New York: D. Appleton, 1919).

36. Rossiter, *Constitutional Dictatorship,* 243.

37. Ibid., 253.

38. Robert E. Cushman, "Civil Liberty after the War," *American Political Science Review* 38 (February 1944): 6.

39. 40 Stat. 217 (1917).

40. 40 Stat. 411 (1917).

41. 40 Stat. 553 (1918).

42. Harry N. Scheiber, *The Wilson Administration and Civil Liberties, 1917–1921* (Ithaca: Cornell University Press, 1960), 61–63.

43. *Schenck v. United States,* 249 U.S. 47 (1919).
44. *Debs v. United States,* 249 U.S. 211 (1919).
45. *Abrams v. United States,* 250 U.S. 616 (1919).
46. Carl Brent Swisher, *American Constitutional Development* (Boston: Houghton Mifflin, 1943), 610.
47. Scheiber, *Wilson Administration and Civil Liberties,* 32.
48. Dorothy Ganfield Fowler, *Unmailable: Congress and the Post Office* (Athens: University of Georgia Press, 1977), 115.
49. See "Wilson Opposes New Spy Bill," *New York Times,* April 23, 1918, 6; Charles Warren, "Spies, and the Power of Congress to Subject Certain Classes of Civilians to Trial by Military Tribunal," *American Law Review* 53 (March–April 1919): 195–228.
50. 41 Stat. 1359 (1921).
51. "Sixth Annual Message," *The State of the Union Messages of the Presidents, 1790–1966,* ed. Fred L. Israel (New York: Chelsea House–Robert Hector, 1966), 3:2727.
52. "Inaugural Address, March 4, 1933," *The Public Papers and Addresses of Franklin D. Roosevelt,* ed. Samuel I. Rosenman (New York: Random House, 1938), 2:11, 15.
53. Arthur M. Schlesinger Jr., *The Coming of the New Deal* (Boston: Houghton Mifflin, 1959), 4.
54. See 48 Stat. 1 (1933); Samuel I. Rosenman, ed., *The Public Papers and Addresses of Franklin D. Roosevelt,* vol. 2, *The Year of Crisis, 1933* (New York: Random House, 1938), 24–26, 48.
55. 48 Stat. 1 (1933).
56. 48 Stat. 22 (1933).
57. 48 Stat. 195 (1933).
58. See *Panama Refining Co. v. Ryan,* 293 U.S. 388 (1935); *A. L. A. Schechter Poultry Corp. v. United States,* 295 U.S. 495 (1935).
59. See *United States v. Butler,* 297 U.S. 1 (1936).
60. See *West Coast Hotel Co. v. Parrish,* 300 U.S. 379 (1937).
61. 55 Stat. 795 (1941).
62. 55 Stat. 796, 797 (1941).
63. 49 Stat. 1081 (1935), 1152 (1936); 50 Stat. 121 (1937).
64. 54 Stat. 4 (1939).
65. Rossiter, *Constitutional Dictatorship,* 265.
66. See Donald H. Riddle, *The Truman Committee: A Study in Congressional Responsibility* (New Brunswick, N.J.: Rutgers University Press, 1964); Harry A. Toulmin Jr., *Diary of Democracy: The Senate War Investigating Committee* (New York: Richard R. Smith, 1947); Theodore Wilson, "The Truman Committee, 1941," in *Congress Investigates: A Documented History, 1792–1974,* ed. Arthur M. Schlesinger Jr. and Roger Bruns (New York: Chelsea House, 1975), 4:3115–3136.
67. Rossiter, *Constitutional Dictatorship,* 265. For a catalog of emergency powers granted to the president during the war, see U.S. Library of Congress, Legislative Reference Service, *Acts of Congress Applicable in Time of Emergency,* Public Affairs Bulletin 35 (Washington, D.C.: Legislative Reference Service, 1945).
68. 55 Stat. 838 (1941).
69. 56 Stat. 173 (1942).
70. See *Hirabayashi v. United States,* 320 U.S. 81 (1943); *Korematsu v. United States,* 323 U.S. 214 (1944); *Ex parte Endo,* 323 U.S. 283 (1944); Peter Irons, *Justice at War* (New York: Oxford University Press, 1983).
71. *Ex parte Quirin,* 317 U.S. 1 (1942).
72. See 42 U.S.C. 5121 et seq.
73. See 50 U.S.C. 1601 et seq.
74. Proclamation 7463, *Federal Register* 66, no. 181 (September 18, 2001): 48197–48199.
75. 115 Stat. 220 (2001).
76. 115 Stat. 224 (2001).
77. Executive Order 13224, *Federal Register* 66, no. 186 (September 25, 2001): 49079–49082, invoking 50 U.S.C. 1701 et seq.
78. Executive Order 13228, *Federal Register* 66, no. 196 (October 10, 2001): 51812–51817.
79. 115 Stat. 272 (2001).
80. See Department of Justice, Bureau of Prisons, "28 CFR Parts 500 and 501, National Security, Prevention of Acts of Violence and Terrorism. Final Rule," *Federal Register* 66, no. 121 (October 31, 2001): 55061–5506.
81. See President, "Military Order of November 13, 2001—Detention, Treatment, and Trial of Certain Non-Citizens in the War against Terrorism," *Federal Register* 66, no. 222 (November 16, 2001): 57831–57836.
82. A notable exception from outside of the emergency periods considered here is *Youngstown Sheet and Tube Co. v. Sawyer,* 343 U.S. 579 (1952).

CHAPTER EIGHT

Understanding the Impeachment Power: Lessons from the Clinton Case

MICHAEL J. GERHARDT

Impeachment is one of Congress's most formidable, least used, and most misunderstood powers. The popular understanding of Congress's impeachment power has largely been shaped by a few, very well known incidents, the most recent of which is the impeachment of President Bill Clinton by the House of Representatives in 1998 and his acquittal by the Senate in 1999. The other notorious episodes include the nineteenth-century impeachments by the House and acquittals in the Senate of Associate Justice Samuel Chase of the Supreme Court and President Andrew Johnson, the latter of whom avoided conviction in the Senate by only a single vote, and the House Judiciary Committee's approval of three impeachment articles against President Richard Nixon that led to his resignation in 1974. Each of these proceedings featured a conflict in which the fates of national institutions were as much at stake as those of the high-ranking individuals.

The preoccupation with the drama and consequences of high-profile impeachments has produced fundamental misconceptions of the impeachment process, leading many people to miss the critical differences among such proceedings and the relationship between impeachment operations and changes in the constitutional structure. For instance, by diminishing the importance of the electoral college to presidential elections, the Twelfth Amendment and other election reforms arguably helped to transform the presidency into a popularly elected office. Although this development made no difference in the Johnson and Chase impeachments and trials—because neither had been elected—in the case of Presidents Nixon and Clinton, the fact that they each had been popularly elected was an important factor in congressional deliberations on their respective fates. Moreover, the Seventeenth Amendment replaced the system of electing senators in state legislatures with direct election by the people. Consequently, senators became as sensitive to popular opinion as representatives were. Thus, the votes to acquit Clinton largely reflected his high public approval ratings. The fact that these votes were largely cast by Clinton's fellow Democrats—indeed, none of the forty-five Democrats then in the Senate voted to convict him—also reflects the ability of senators from a president's party to block the removal of an impeached president as long as they command enough seats and remain unified.

For the impeachment power to be fully understood, the high-profile exercises of the power must be analyzed in relation to the other impeachment proceedings conducted by the House and the Senate[1] and the circumstances culminating in more than a dozen other officials who have resigned after being threatened with impeachment.[2] Together, these proceedings constitute a set of data that reveals significant patterns and practices of Congress's impeachment power. A single case cannot explain or fully illuminate this power, but the significance of a single case is reflected in what it has in common with and how it differs from other cases. Indeed, the impeachment and trial of President Clinton are a case in point, for they reinforce (rather than expand or revise) the lessons of previous impeachment proceedings: removing a president (or any other impeachable official) without bipartisan support is impossible; impeachment is a relatively ineffective check against a popular president's misconduct; unelected, low-profile officials are relatively more vulnerable than any other officials to impeachment and removal; the burden of proof is squarely on those seeking impeachment and removal of an official; the conduct of impeachment proceedings is nonjusticiable; and the determination of the misconduct that qualifies as impeachable tends to be made on the basis of various factors, including the circumstances in which the misconduct occurred and the relationship between the misconduct and the targeted official's responsibilities.

Historical Background

The discussions of the delegates to the Constitutional Convention and state ratifying conventions provide insights for appreciating the distinctive features of the federal impeachment process. The founders wanted to distinguish the impeachment power set forth in the Constitution from the British practice in a number of important ways:

- First, Article 2, section 4, limits impeachment to "[t]he President, Vice President and all civil Officers of the United Sates"; at the time of the founding of the Republic, in England any officeholder (except for a member of the royal family) could be impeached.
- Second, Article 2, section 4, also narrows the range of impeachable offenses for public officeholders to "Treason, Bribery, or other high Crimes and Misdemeanors"; Parliament always had refused to constrain its jurisdiction over impeachments by restrictively defining impeachable offenses.
- Third, Article 1, section 3, holds that in an impeachment trial held in the Senate, "no Person shall be convicted [and removed from office] without the Concurrence of two thirds of the Members present"; the House of Lords could convict with a bare majority.
- Fourth, Article 1, section 3, clause 7, limits punishment in the federal impeachment process "to removal from Office, and disqualification to hold and enjoy any Office of honor, Trust, or Profit under the United States"; the House of Lords could order any punishment upon conviction.
- Fifth, Article 2 expressly prohibits the president from pardoning an individual for the offenses committed; the king could pardon any person convicted by impeachment.
- Sixth, the Constitution separates criminal procedures and impeachment proceedings;

in England impeachment proceedings were considered to be criminal.[3]

- Seventh, the Constitution provides impeachment as the sole means by which federal judges may be removed for misconduct in office; the British provided for the removal of judges by several means.[4]

Of these features, the one that has been of greatest interest to lawmakers and the public in the twentieth century has been the founders' choice of "Treason, Bribery, or other high Crimes and Misdemeanors" for delineating the scope of impeachable actions. The founders did not extensively debate the meaning of "other high Crimes or Misdemeanors," but the context and content of their discussions about the phrase are important backdrops to contemporary efforts to interpret its meaning.

In the early debates in the Constitutional Convention on the scope of impeachable offenses, every speaker agreed that certain high-ranking officials should not have immunity from prosecution for common law crimes, such as treason and murder. Also, many delegates envisioned a body of offenses for which federal officials could be impeached and believed that, in contrast to the unbounded English system, this body of offenses should be relatively narrow in scope but adequate enough to prevent officials from getting away with conduct not otherwise punishable by law.

In the convention's proceedings, several delegates referred to "mal-" and "corrupt administration," "neglect of duty," and "misconduct in office" as the only impeachable offenses and maintained that such common law crimes as treason and bribery were to be heard in the courts of law.[5] Some delegates, notably William

Paterson, Edmund Randolph, James Wilson, and George Mason, argued that the federal impeachment process should apply to misuse of official power in accordance with their respective state constitutions and experiences. As late as August 20, 1787, the Committee of Detail reported that federal officials "shall be liable to impeachment and removal from office for neglect of duty, malversation, or corruption."[6]

Yet, in its report on September 4, 1787, the Committee of Eleven proposed that the grounds for conviction and removal of the president should be limited to "treason or bribery."[7] On September 8, Mason opened the convention's discussion on this latter proposal by questioning the wisdom of limiting impeachment to those two offenses.[8] He argued that "[t]reason as defined in the Constitution [would] not reach many great and dangerous offences." He used as an example of such subversion the English impeachment of Governor Warren Hastings of the East India Company, whose trial was based in part not upon specific criminal acts, but upon the dangers presented to the government by the governor's wielding of virtually absolute power within the Indian colony.[9] Mason was concerned that "[a]ttempts to subvert the Constitution may not be Treason as . . . defined," and that, since "bills of attainder . . . are forbidden, it is the more necessary to extend[] the power of impeachments."[10] Mason therefore moved to add the term *maladministration* to permit impeachment for less conventionally defined common law offenses.[11] Elbridge Gerry seconded the motion. James Madison, without taking issue with either the appropriateness of including such subversion or the need to expand the standard to include such potentially noncriminal wrongs, responded that "[s]o vague a term will be equivalent to a tenure during pleasure of the Senate."[12] Recalling a debate on June 20 in which he had asked for more "enumerated and defined" impeachable offenses, Gouverneur Morris agreed with Madison.[13] Mason thereupon withdrew his motion and substituted "other high crimes & misdemeanors ag[ain]st the State," which Mason apparently understood as including maladministration.[14] Without further comment, the motion was approved by a vote of eight to three.[15]

Later, the convention delegates, again without discussion, agreed to replace the word *State* with the words *United States.*[16] The Committee of Style and Arrangement, which was responsible for reworking the resolutions without substantive change, eliminated the phrase "against the United States,"[17] presumably because it was thought to be redundant or superfluous. The convention accepted the shortened phrase without further debate on its meaning.

Subsequently, the most substantial discussions of the scope of impeachable offenses, besides those in the *Federalist,* occurred in the ratification conventions in North Carolina and Virginia. For instance, in North Carolina, James Iredell, who later would serve as an associate justice on the Supreme Court, called attention to the complexity, if not impossibility, of defining the scope of impeachable offenses any more precisely than to acknowledge that they would involve serious injustices to the federal government. He understood impeachment as having been "calculated to bring [great offenders] to punishment for crime which it is not easy to describe, but which every one must be convinced is a high crime and misdemeanor against the government. . . . [T]he occasion for

its exercise will arise from acts of great injury to the community."[18] As examples of impeachable offenses, he suggested that the "president must certainly be punishable for giving false information to the Senate" and that "the president would be liable to impeachments [if] he had received a bribe or had acted from some corrupt motive or other."[19] He warned, though, that the purpose of impeachment was not to punish a president for "want of judgment," but rather to hold him responsible for being a "villain" and "willfully abus[ing] his trust."[20] Governor Samuel Johnston, who would later become North Carolina's first U.S. senator, agreed that impeachment "is a mode of trial pointed out for great misdemeanors against the public."[21]

In the Virginia convention, several speakers argued that impeachable offenses were not limited to indictable crimes. For instance, James Madison contended that if the president were to summon only a small number of states in order to try to secure ratification of a treaty that hurt the interests of unrepresented states, "he would be impeached and convicted, as a majority of the states would be affected by his misdemeanor."[22] Madison suggested further that "if the president be connected, in any suspicious manner, with any person, and there be grounds to believe that he will shelter him," the president may be impeached.[23] George Nicholas agreed that a president could be impeached for a nonindictable offense. Edmund Randolph explained that "[i]n England, those subjects which produce impeachments are not opinions. . . . It would be impossible to discover whether the error in opinion resulted from a willful mistake of the heart, or an involuntary fault of the head."[24] He stressed that only the former constituted an impeachable offense.

In the decade following ratification of the Constitution, the federal impeachment process remained the subject of debate and concern. For instance, in the First Congress, Rep. James Madison tried to calm the fears of some of his colleagues about possible presidential abuse of authority to remove executive officials by suggesting that the president "will be impeachable by this House, before the Senate for such an act of mal-administration; for I contend that the wanton removal of meritorious officers would subject him to impeachment and removal from [office]."[25] Although one could construe Madison's comment as meretricious, because it supported a position that he had taken in a partisan debate rather than as a framer—and because it arguably conflicted with his objection in the Constitutional Convention to making "maladministration" a basis for impeachment—Madison's comment is consistent with the stance he took in the Virginia ratifying convention to support presidential impeachment for nonindictable abuses of power.

Justice James Wilson gave a series of lectures as a professor of law at the College of Philadelphia to clarify the foundations of the Constitution. In these talks, presented in 1790–1791 immediately following his appointment to the Supreme Court and published posthumously, Wilson describes the essential character of impeachments as proceedings of a political nature, "confined to political characters, to political crimes and misdemeanors, and to political punishments."[26] He emphasizes that the founders believed that

> [i]mpeachments, and offences and offenders impeachable, [did not] come . . . within the

sphere of ordinary jurisprudence. They are founded on different principles; are governed by different maxims, and are directed to different objects: for this reason, the trial and punishment of an offence on an impeachment, is no bar to a trial and punishment of the same offence at common law.[27]

Hence, Wilson, one of the most thoughtful and influential of the proponents of the new Constitution, strongly endorsed the basic idea that a fundamental feature of the federal impeachment process is its separateness and distinctiveness from judicial proceedings.

"High Crimes and Misdemeanors"

The great majority of commentators who have examined closely the likely meaning of the phrase "other high Crimes and Misdemeanors" have reached the same conclusion: it consists of technical terms of art referring to "political crimes." They also agree that "political crimes" in the eighteenth century were not always necessarily indictable crimes. Instead, they consisted of the kinds of abuses of power or injuries to the Republic that only could be committed by public officials by virtue of the public offices or privileges that they held. Not all indictable offenses committed by political figures were considered political crimes.

To appreciate what would constitute political crimes, one needs to examine the British impeachment practices from which the founders drew the language, "other High crimes or misdemeanors," and thus the concept of political crimes. In the English experience, impeachment was primarily a political proceeding, and impeachable offenses were regarded as "political crimes." Raoul Berger observes in his influential study of impeachment that the

English practice treated "'[h]igh crimes and misdemeanors' [as] a category of *political* crimes against the state."[28] Berger supports this observation with quotations in which speakers use terms equivalent to "political" and "against the state" to identify the distinguishing characteristics of an impeachable event. In England, the critical element of injury regarding an impeachable offense was injury to the state. Eminent legal historian William Blackstone traces this peculiarity to the ancient law of treason, which distinguished "high" treason, which was disloyalty against some superior, from "petit" treason, which was disloyalty to an equal or an inferior.[29] Arthur Bestor further explains that "[t]his element of injury to the commonwealth—that is, to the state itself and to its constitution—was historically the criterion for distinguishing a 'high' crime or misdemeanor from an ordinary one."[30] In summary, the English experience reveals that there was a

> difference of degree, not a difference of kind, separating] 'high' treason from other 'high' crimes and misdemeanors . . . [and that] [t]he common element in [English impeachment proceedings] was . . . injury done to the state and its constitution, whereas among the particular offenses producing such injury some might rank as treasons, some as felonies and some as misdemeanors, among which might be included various offenses that in other contexts would fall short of actual criminality.[31]

In addition, those delegates in the constitutional and state ratifying conventions who supported the Constitution seemed to have a shared understanding of impeachment as a political proceeding and impeachable offenses as essentially "political crimes." The delegates at the Constitutional Convention were intimately familiar with impeachment in colonial America, which, like impeachment in England, had basically been a political proceeding. Although the debates in the convention primarily focused on the offenses for which the president could be impeached and removed, there was general agreement that the president could be impeached only for so-called great offenses.[32] Moreover, the majority of examples presented throughout the convention debates about the scope of impeachable offenses, such as Madison's preference for the phrase "other high Crimes and Misdemeanors" because it encompassed attempts to subvert the Constitution, confirm that impeachable offenses primarily consisted of abuses of power that injured the state (and thus were not necessarily limited to indictable offenses). Neither the debates nor the relevant constitutional language eventually adopted, however, identifies the specific offenses that constitute impeachable abuses against the state.

The ratification campaign further supports the conclusion that "other high Crimes and Misdemeanors" were not limited to indictable offenses, but also included great offenses against the federal government. For example, delegates to state ratification conventions often referred to impeachable offenses as "great" offenses—as opposed to common law crimes—and they frequently spoke of how impeachment should lie if the official "deviates from his duty"[33] or if he "dare[s] to abuse the powers vested in him by the people."[34]

In the *Federalist* No. 65, Alexander Hamilton echoes such sentiments, observing,

> [t]he subjects [of the Senate's] jurisdiction [in an impeachment trial] are those offenses which proceed from the misconduct of public men, or,

in other words, from the abuse or violation of some public trust. They are of a nature which may with peculiar propriety be denominated POLITICAL, as they relate chiefly to injuries done immediately to the society itself.[35]

Believing it unwise to submit the impeachment decision to the Supreme Court because of "the nature of the proceeding,"[36] Hamilton argues that an impeachment court could not be "tied down" by "strict rules, either in the delineation of the offense by the prosecutors [the House of Representatives] or in the construction of it by the judges [the Senate]."[37] Hamilton too believed that impeachable offenses comprised a unique set of transgressions that defied neat delineation.

Justices James Wilson and Joseph Story expressed agreement with Hamilton's understanding of impeachable offenses as political crimes. Wilson's constitutional lectures reflected his understanding of the term *high* in "high Crimes and Misdemeanors" to mean "political," while the term *misdemeanors* refers to conduct against the state.[38] Similarly, Story recognized the unique political nature of impeachable offenses: "The jurisdiction is to be exercised over offences which are committed by public men in violation of their public trust and duties. Those duties are in many cases political. . . . Strictly speaking, then, the power partakes of a political character, as it respects injuries to the society in its political character."[39] Story viewed the penalties of removal and disqualification as "limiting the punishment to such modes of redress as are peculiarly fit for a political tribunal to administer, and as will secure the public against political injuries."[40] Justice Story understood "political injuries" to be "[s]uch kind of misdeeds . . . as

peculiarly injure the commonwealth by the abuse of high offices of trust."[41]

Like Hamilton, Justice Story understood that the framers proceeded as if there would be a federal common law on crimes from which future Congresses could draw the specific or particular offenses for which certain federal officials may be impeached and removed from office. Justice Story explains that "no previous statute is necessary to authorize an impeachment for any official misconduct."[42] In Story's view such a statute could never be drafted, because "political offenses are of so various and complex a character, so utterly incapable of being defined, or classified, that the task of positive legislation would be impracticable, if it were not almost absurd to attempt it."[43] The implicit understanding shared by Hamilton and Story was that subsequent generations would have to define on a case-by-case basis the political crimes serving as contemporary impeachable offenses.

How then to identify the nonindictable offenses for which certain high-level government officials may be impeached? This task is critical for providing notice to impeachable officials as to the conditions of and for narrowing in some meaningful fashion the grounds for their removal. The best place to look for guidance, besides the framers' debates, is historical practice. First, it is noteworthy that of the sixteen men impeached by the House of Representatives, only five were impeached primarily or solely on grounds strictly constituting an indictable offense.[44] One of the five, Alcee Hastings, had been formally acquitted of bribery prior to his impeachment. The House's articles of impeachment against the other eleven include misuses of power that were not indictable federal offenses, at least at the time of impeachment.[45]

Four of the sixteen men convicted and removed from office by the Senate were charged with nonindictable offenses.[46] The remaining three officials who were convicted and removed from office by the Senate were charged with indictable crimes.[47] Prior to the impeachments and removals of these three federal judges from office, two of them, Claiborne and Nixon, had been indicted, convicted in federal court, and exhausted their criminal appeals.

Given that abuses against the state have not always been or necessarily should be confined to indictable offenses, one persistent challenge has been to find contemporary analogues to the abuses that authorities such as Hamilton, Wilson, and Story viewed as suitable grounds for impeachment. On the one hand, these abuses may be reflected in certain statutory crimes.[48] At least one federal criminal statute, for bribery,[49] codifies an impeachable offense because bribery expressly is designated as such in the Constitution. Violations of other federal criminal statutes may also constitute abuses against the state sufficient to subject the perpetrator to impeachment, insofar as the offenses involved demonstrate willful misconduct and serious lack of judgment or respect for the law that is so incompatible with their official duties as to effectively prevent them from continuing to function in office.

On the other hand, not all statutory crimes demonstrate complete unfitness for office. For example, "a President's technical violation of a law making jaywalking [or speeding] a crime obviously would not be an adequate basis for presidential [impeachment and] removal."[50]

Moreover, it is equally obvious that some noncriminal activities may constitute impeachable offenses. As Laurence Tribe observes, "[A] deliberate presidential decision to emasculate our national defenses, or to conduct a private war in circumvention of the Constitution, would probably violate no criminal code,"[51] but probably would constitute a nonindictable, impeachable offense. The full range of such political crimes defies further specification, because it rests on the circumstances under which the offenses occur (including the actor, the forum, the scope of the officer's official duties, and the nature and significance of the offensive act), alternative remedies, and the collective political judgment of Congress.

Lessons from the Clinton Impeachment

As stated above, the founders considered that political crimes constituting impeachable offenses would be clarified over time on a case-by-case basis, while the standard for impeachment would remain constant—that is, whether the official had injured seriously the Republic or the constitutional system. Consequently, congressional practices involving impeachment are important, because they illuminate Congress's deliberate judgments concerning what constitutes an impeachable offense. Given that Congress's judgments on impeachment are immune to presidential veto and judicial review, decisions on impeachment constitute, for all practical purposes, the final word on the scope of the federal impeachment power.[52] Members of Congress thus give special consideration to their impeachment decisions. An analysis of how President Clinton's acquittal fits within congressional impeachment practices illuminates several patterns and lessons to be drawn from impeachment and trial.

The first pattern is the increasing influence of federal prosecutors in triggering impeachment investigations and proceedings.[53] One telling but overlooked fact regarding Clinton's impeachment proceedings is that they marked the sixth occasion in the preceding few decades in which Congress exercised or contemplated seriously using its impeachment power.[54] An important factor linking all six impeachment efforts is that each had been triggered by a referral to Congress from an external investigative authority. The impeachment efforts involving Judges Claiborne, Hastings, Nixon, and Collins were referred to the House by the Judicial Conference of the United States. The other two began with referrals to Congress from special federal prosecutors: Leon Jaworski, who as a special prosecutor appointed by the attorney general referred to the House several boxes of materials relating to possible impeachable misconduct by President Nixon, and former judge and solicitor general Kenneth Starr, who as an independent counsel referred pursuant to a special provision of the Independent Counsel Act[55] evidence that arguably demonstrated Clinton's commission of possible impeachable offenses. Of these six referrals, one resulted in a Senate acquittal (Clinton), three in removals (Claiborne, Nixon, and Hastings), and two in forced resignations (Richard Nixon and Collins).

President Clinton's impeachment stands apart from these other referrals not only as the only one resulting in a Senate acquittal but also as one of only three in which the House undertook no independent fact-finding. The first time the House chose to forgo fact-finding was the impeachment of Andrew Johnson, because it had undertaken limited fact-finding in two prior unsuccessful efforts to impeach him. By firing Secretary of War Edwin Stanton, Johnson had given the proponents of his ouster something that they had not previously had—an act that, in their view, clearly violated a law—the Tenure of Office Act of 1867[56]—and was impeachable. Johnson's impeachment for firing Stanton is widely regarded as perhaps the most intensely partisan impeachment rendered by the House, thereby making it a dubious precedent to follow. Similarly, the House's failure to undertake independent fact-finding prior to impeaching Clinton provided a basis upon which the House's impeachment judgment could be attacked by his defenders as unfair.

The only other instance in which the House failed to undertake independent fact-finding was the Claiborne impeachment. The full House impeached Claiborne within a month of the House Judiciary Committee's formal recommendation of articles of impeachment. Unlike Presidents Johnson and Clinton, Claiborne did not complain about the House proceedings (including its failure to undertake independent fact-finding). Rather, he welcomed a quick impeachment, because he believed the sooner he had a full Senate trial the quicker he would be exonerated. Claiborne's gambit failed.

The fact that the convictions of federal officials as well as the pressure of impending or likely criminal action against high-ranking officials can pressure Congress to initiate impeachment proceedings is an ongoing matter of concern to many members of Congress and many scholars. To them it indicates that under certain circumstances criminal prosecutors can drive the federal impeachment process.

The first lesson from Clinton's impeachment is that in the absence of bipartisan support for removal, acquittal is virtually guaranteed. This is the case because of the constitutional requirement that at least two-thirds of senators concur for removal. A supermajority is difficult to obtain, particularly when the stakes are high. Statistics bear this out, given that most people impeached by the House have been acquitted by the Senate. Of the sixteen officials impeached by the House, two resigned before their Senate trials. The Senate has acquitted eight men. When consensus for removal is achieved, it has been the result of a very compelling and credible case.

Indeed, the uniform opposition of all forty-five Senate Democrats to President Clinton's conviction highlights the enormous difficulty of securing a conviction in a presidential impeachment trial as long as the senators from the president's party unanimously support him.[57] Rarely does a political party control more than two-thirds of the Senate. Hence, a president's removal is likely possible only if the misconduct is sufficiently compelling to draw support from both sides of the aisle for a conviction.

A second lesson of Clinton's trial is that impeachment is a relatively ineffective check against a popular president's misconduct. Clinton's acquittal might have the consequence of leaving subsequent generations uncertain about the resolve of future Congresses to conduct impeachment proceedings against a president with high approval ratings. The congressional investigation into Watergate took more than two years before the "smoking gun"—tapes of conversations in the White House—was discovered that led to President Nixon's resignation.[58] The Clinton impeachment proceedings took roughly six months from start to finish. As such, they are among the shortest in U.S. history; the shortest was Claiborne's, which lasted roughly four months. Yet, the shortness of Clinton's proceedings was too long for most Americans. The majority of people surveyed did not believe that Clinton's case involved offenses for which he should be removed from office and that whatever investigations might be carried out would uncover any such offenses.

Future Congresses thus might think twice before engaging in a relatively prolonged investigation of a president's misconduct for fear that it might alienate the public. In this respect, the Clinton proceedings could be viewed as strengthening rather than weakening the presidency. The Clinton case raises the issue of how serious the misconduct of a popular president must be to convince a majority of Americans to support removal from office. It is possible that impeachment will be effective only for the kinds of misconduct that can galvanize the public to set aside its approval of a president's performance. Indeed, a future Congress might support removal only if it has direct evidence of very serious wrongdoing and unambiguous consensus (in both houses and among the public) on the gravity of such wrongdoing.

The third lesson of Clinton's impeachment proceedings underscores the greater vulnerability to impeachment and removal of those officials who lack a president's resources or popularity. It is conceivable that an unpopular president, such as Andrew Johnson, might meet a different fate in an age in which the media constantly has the president's misconduct and other actions under a microscope and in which daily polls dramatize loss of popularity and increase in support. In such circumstances, removal or resignation might be more likely. To date, the only similar instance was the final days of Nixon's presidency, when the public for the first and only time during the Watergate investigation expressed support for Nixon's ouster based on information revealed in the Watergate tapes. The dynamic of impeachment proceedings is likely to be more problematic for a federal judge, including a Supreme Court justice, whose hearings are unlikely to get anything near the widespread media coverage that Clinton's proceedings received or the outpouring of public opposition to prolonging hearings. A federal judge simply lacks the resources of a (popular) president in opposing political retaliation in the form of an impeachment.

The fourth lesson of the Clinton impeachment proceedings serves as a dramatic reminder that the burden of proof rests with the advocates of impeachment to show that the charges are not based on or motivated by partisanship. No doubt, a proponent of Clinton's removal might claim that the charges were not based on partisanship, but on the need to protect the judicial system's integrity and to ensure the president's compliance with the oath of office (even in regard to a civil lawsuit whose focus is unrelated to official duties). The persons charging Chase and Johnson with impeachable misconduct argued the same thing, claiming that the charges against them were based on the officials' respective abuses of authority, not on partisanship. Ultimately, those seeking Johnson's and Chase's removals failed to carry their burdens. Similarly, those seeking President Clinton's removal failed to convince most Americans, as well as Senate Democrats, that their charges against him were not based or motivated substantially by partisan dislike of Clinton.

This last situation increases the chances that subsequent generations will look unfavorably upon the House's impeachment of Clinton. There have been similar failures in the past—most notably, in the impeachment attempts against Chase and Johnson. The majority votes cast in favor of convicting Chase and Johnson did not preclude either's impeachment from being viewed as lacking political legitimacy by subsequent generations and Congresses. Their acquittals each had the effect of dissuading subsequent Congresses from initiating impeachments based on similar misconduct. The outcomes in the Chase and Johnson trials did not turn on disputes about the underlying facts. Virtually everyone at the time agreed on the facts. They disagreed, however, over the significance of the facts. Unencumbered with having to resolve factual disputes in these cases, future generations have been free to make their own assessments of the legal and constitutional significance of the facts (and thus of Chase's and Johnson's misconduct). They have concluded that the misconduct targeted in each impeachment did not warrant removal from office.

By similar reasoning, the Clinton acquittal could be construed by subsequent Congresses as rejecting the House's judgment on the impeachability of his misconduct. First, the vote to impeach Clinton was (as were the votes in the Chase and Johnson cases) largely cast along party lines. Thus there exists the widespread perception that the proceedings generally were conducted (and resolved) on partisan grounds. Moreover, most people (including most members of Congress) did not disagree much about the underlying facts in the Clinton case; they disagreed, however, over their legal significance. Subsequent Congresses might conclude that if such misconduct did not merit a conviction in Clinton's case, it would be inconsistent or unfair to allow it to support a conviction in another case. In addition, members of Congress could conclude that if a majority vote by the Senate to convict Chase and Johnson could not save either's impeachment from being regarded as illegitimate, the absence of a majority vote in the Senate for either impeachment article against Clinton (coupled with other criticisms of it) could be viewed as a rounder rejection of the legitimacy of the House's case than were the Senate votes in Chase's and Johnson's trials.[59]

The fifth lesson of the Clinton case is that it affirmed the House and the Senate's final, nonreviewable discretion to conduct their respective impeachment proceedings. In the course of Clinton's impeachment proceedings, representatives and senators fully appreciated the significance of (Walter) *Nixon v. United States* (1992), in which the Supreme Court unanimously ruled that challenges to the constitutionality of Senate impeachment trial procedures are nonjusticiable, that is, the Constitution bars judicial review of any challenge to the Senate's authority to devise impeachment trial procedures as it sees fit. Amply familiar with the implications of this ruling, representatives and senators drew on their experiences with or understandings of prior proceedings to fashion their respective impeachment proceedings against President Clinton. For example, in controversial decisions,

the House decided to hold a final vote on the impeachment articles in a lame duck session,[60] to forgo adopting a uniform standard for defining the impeachability of certain misconduct, and not to call witnesses to the chamber or otherwise engage in independent fact-finding. In the Senate, representatives decided for themselves (as had been done in prior proceedings) such questions as the applicability of the Fifth Amendment due process clause, the appropriate burden of proof, and the propriety of allowing three of their colleagues—Jim Bunning, Mike Crapo, and Charles Schumer—to vote on the articles even though each had been elected to the Senate before the final House impeachment vote and scheduled to participate in the president's trial. Before voting, senators decided (as had been done in several prior trials) such procedural questions as the appropriate burden of proof, the applicable rules of evidence, the appropriate standard for determining the impeachability of the president's misconduct, and the propriety of holding closed door hearings on a variety of issues (including final debates on Clinton's guilt or innocence.)

Such conduct affirmed the framers' expectations that Congress would determine on a case-by-case basis what misconduct constituted "other high Crimes or Misdemeanors." Though the constitutional standard was designed to narrow the range of impeachable offenses in England, the standard remains broad. The Constitution contemplates that an impeachable offense is a political crime about whose essential elements the framers agreed only in the abstract (including such general preconditions as serious injury to the Republic). Consequently, every impeachment features a debate over whether the misconduct charged constitutes a political crime. These debates reflect the practical impossibility of getting the House or Senate to adopt a uniform standard for determining the impeachability of misconduct. The resolution of these debates tracks the historic practice in which the members decide how to resolve a series of procedural issues. The debates over the scope of impeachable offenses have featured tugs of war in which those seeking impeachment defend relatively broad, amorphous standards that they can show have been easily met in a given case and those opposing impeachment support very narrow standards that they claim have not been met in the case before them.

While the debates over the scope of impeachable offenses in particular cases have not produced consensus among senators about the offenses, the outcomes of impeachment trials reveal an interesting pattern. The misconduct of the seven federal officials—all judges— whom the Senate convicted and removed from office share two elements: they caused a serious injury to the Republic and involved a nexus between the official's misconduct and the official's duties.[61] In assessing the latter in general, members of Congress have considered the degree to which misconduct has been either so outrageous or so thoroughly disabling or incompatible with an official's duties as to give it no choice but to remove the official. In President Clinton's impeachment trial, several senators explained their acquittal votes on the absence of one or more of these elements.[62]

Yet another possible consequence of President Clinton's impeachment proceedings is that they might have left the public with the impression that impeachment is just another political event. More than 70 percent of Amer-

icans believed that Clinton's trial had been resolved largely on partisan grounds. This is not the outcome desired by the framers. For instance, in *Federalist* No. 65, Hamilton expresses the hope that senators in an impeachment trial would rise above the passions of the moment to do what is in the best interests of the Constitution or the nation.[63] Arguably, President Johnson's acquittal—resulting from seven Republican senators' crossing party lines against their political interests—is an example of this. In contrast, the Clinton impeachment posed a different dynamic from the one that Hamilton explains the founders had tried to guard against. The Senate's failure to convict Clinton followed popular sentiment, but it generally weakened the public's confidence in Congress. The founders were primarily concerned with circumstances in which the public pressured Congress to remove presidents (and senators resisted) and did not address situations in which the public opposed removal while members of Congress intensely supported it.

Last but not least, Clinton's acquittal will hardly qualify as a personal vindication. During the hearings, virtually every senator issued strong public condemnations of his misconduct. Those supporting Clinton's conviction condemned him in the harshest of terms. With one exception, Democrat Tom Harkin of Iowa, the president's defenders strongly condemned his behavior. They contended repeatedly throughout the proceedings that his acquittal should not be construed as foreclosing other fora in which to hold him accountable for his misconduct. This widespread condemnation is likely to have some historical if not constitutional significance (beyond the damage to Clinton's personal reputation and legacy). For example, it might confirm that in the U.S. constitutional system impeachment exists only for a small or rare set of misdeeds, while there are other fora for holding presidents accountable for nonimpeachable misconduct, including civil proceedings, criminal prosecution, public opinion, media scrutiny, and history. Indeed, a similar lesson to be derived from Justice Chase's acquittal is that impeachment is an inappropriate device for retaliating against a federal judge's official rulings. The appropriate forum for dealing with such a matter is the judicial system, particularly the appeals process. A popular lesson drawn from President Johnson's acquittal is that, in spite of the fact that the Senate fell only one vote short of removing him, impeachment is an inappropriate mechanism for redressing a president's bad policy judgments.[64] Appropriate fora for dealing with such erroneous judgments include the court of public opinion, elections, and the judgment of history. A critical lesson for subsequent generations to draw from Clinton's acquittal is that his misconduct did not have a sufficiently public dimension (or harm) to warrant his removal from office. The appropriate fora holding him accountable include public opinion, the judgment of history, possibly censure, civil proceedings (such as Judge Susan Webber Wright's contempt citation of the President),[65] and criminal prosecution (the threat of which led Clinton to enter into a plea bargain that included, among other things, temporarily suspending his license to practice law).

Conclusion

Although many people who endured President Clinton's impeachment ordeal are tempted to think it reveals unique lessons about the federal impeachment power, the opposite is true. Perhaps the most important lesson of the Clinton impeachment proceedings is that they make sense only as part of the pattern and practice of the federal impeachment power. Clinton's impeachment and trial simply reaffirmed what was known about the scope of the federal impeachment power before the proceedings began: First, the requirement of a supermajority makes removal of any impeached official extremely difficult. In fact, the Senate has convicted and removed fewer than half of the officials impeached by the House. Second, Congress has tended to determine the impeachability of misconduct based on various factors, including the responsibilities of the targeted official, the connection between the official's duties and the alleged misconduct, and the exclusivity of impeachment as a remedy for the misconduct in question. Third, impeachment is a relatively ineffective means for sanctioning a popular president for misconduct. Fourth, unelected, low-profile officials are likely to be the most vulnerable targets in impeachment and removal proceedings. Last but not least, as President Clinton's impeachment proceedings demonstrated dramatically, other remedies exist for redressing a president's misconduct for which Congress is unable (or unwilling) to remove him from office. This is particularly true with an official whose popularity is an impediment to removal but not to being held accountable for misconduct in other fora, such as civil and criminal proceedings and the court of history. The Clinton case will long be understood as a testament to this dynamic in the federal impeachment process.

Notes

Information in this text derives from Michael J. Gerhardt, *The Federal Impeachment Process: A Constitutional and Historical Analysis*, 2d ed. (Chicago: University of Chicago Press, 2000); "The Historical and Constitutional Significance of the Impeachment and Trial of President Clinton," *Hofstra Law Review* 28 (1999); and "The Perils of Presidential Impeachment," review of *An Affair of State: The Investigation, Impeachment, and Trial of President Clinton*, by Richard Posner, *University of Chicago Law Review* 67 (2000).

1. The sixteen officials impeached, their positions, and the years of their respective proceedings are as follows: William Blount, senator from Tennessee (1798–1799); John Pickering, U.S. district judge for the District of New Hampshire (1803–1804); Samuel Chase, associate justice on the Supreme Court (1804–1805); James Peck, U.S. district judge for the District of Missouri (1826–1831); West Humphreys, U.S. district judge for the District of Tennessee (1862); Andrew Johnson, president of the United States (1867–1868); William Belknap, secretary of war (1876); Charles Swayne, U.S. district judge for the Northern District of Florida (1903–1905); Robert Archbald, circuit judge, U.S. Court of Appeals for the Third Circuit, then serving as an associate judge of the U.S. Commerce Court (1912–1913); George English, U.S. district judge for the Eastern District of Illinois (1926); Harold Louderback, U.S. district judge for the Northern District of California (1932–1933); Halsted Ritter, U.S. district judge for the Southern District of Florida (1936); Harry Claiborne, U.S. district judge for the District of Nevada (1986); Alcee Hastings, U.S. district judge for the Southern District of Florida (1988–1989); Walter Nixon, U.S. district judge for the Southern District of Mississippi (1988–1989); Bill Clinton, president of the United States (1998–1999). A seventeenth official, Mark Delahay, was a U.S. district judge who resigned from office after the House had voted to impeach him in 1873 but before it had formally approved impeachment articles against him.
2. See, generally, Michael J. Gerhardt, *The Federal Impeachment Process: A Constitutional and*

Historical Analysis, 2d ed. (Chicago: University of Chicago Press, 2000), 60.
3. See generally Michael J. Gerhardt, "The Constitutional Limits To Impeachment and its Alternatives," *Texas Law Review* 68 (1989): 23.
4. See Gerhardt, *Federal Impeachment Process,* 82–102.
5. See Peter Charles Hoffer and N. E. H. Hull, *Impeachment in America, 1635–1805* (New Haven: Yale University Press, 1984), 101; see also *The Records of the Federal Convention of 1787,* ed. Max Farrand, rev. ed. (New Haven: Yale University Press, 1937), 2:64–69.
6. *Records of the Federal Convention of 1787,* 2:101.
7. Ibid., 2:495.
8. Ibid., 2:550.
9. Hastings was ultimately acquitted after proceedings that lasted several years.
10. *Records of the Federal Convention of 1787,* 2:550.
11. Ibid.
12. Ibid.
13. Ibid., 2:65.
14. Ibid., 2:550.
15. Ibid., 2:550.
16. Ibid., 2:551.
17. Ibid., 2:600.
18. *The Debates in the Several State Conventions on the Adoption of the Federal Constitution,* ed. Jonathan Elliot (1836; photo reprint, 1937), 4:113.
19. Ibid., 4:526–527.
20. Ibid., 4:126.
21. Ibid., 4:48.
22. Ibid., 3:500.
23. Ibid., 3:498.
24. Ibid., 3:401.
25. *Annals of Congress,* 1st Cong., 1st sess., 1:498.
26. James Wilson, "Comparison of the Constitution of the United States with That of Great Britain," *The Works of James Wilson,* ed. Robert G. McCloskey (Cambridge, Mass.: Belknap Press of Harvard University Press, 1967), 1: 324.
27. Ibid.
28. Raoul Berger, *Impeachment: The Constitutional Problems* (Cambridge, Mass.: Harvard University Press, 1973), 61.

29. Arthur Bestor, "Impeachment," review of *Impeachment: The Constitutional Problems,* by Raoul Berger, *Washington Law Review* 49 (1973): 255, 264, quoting William Blackstone, *Commentaries on the Laws of England,* 4:75.

30. Ibid., 263–264.

31. Ibid.

32. See Berger, *Impeachment,* 88.

33. *Debates,* 4:32 (James Iredell of North Carolina).

34. Ibid., 2:169 (S. Stillman of Massachusetts).

35. Alexander Hamilton, James Madison, and John Jay, *The Federalist Papers,* ed. Clinton Rossiter (New York: New American Library, 1961), 396.

36. Ibid., 398.

37. Ibid.

38. Wilson, "Comparison."

39. Joseph Story, *Commentaries on the Constitution of the United States,* ed. Melville Bigelow (Boston: Little, Brown, 1891), 1:547, sec. 812.

40. Ibid., 1:591, sec. 812.

41. Ibid., 1:575, sec. 790.

42. Ibid., 1:583, sec. 799.

43. Ibid., 1:581, sec. 797.

44. They are Secretary of War William Belknap, charged with accepting bribes; Judge Harry Claiborne, charged with willfully making false tax statements; Judge Alcee Hastings, charged with conspiring to solicit a bribe and perjury; Judge Walter Nixon, charged with making false statements to a grand jury; and President Bill Clinton, charged with perjury before a grand jury and obstruction of justice.

45. The twelve men impeached by the House for nonindictable offenses are as follows: Senator William Blount, for engaging in a conspiracy to compromise the neutrality of the United States in disregard of the constitutional provision for the conduct of foreign affairs and for an attempt to oust the president's lawful appointee as principal agent for Indian affairs; Judge John Pickering, for mental impairment and public drunkenness; Justice Samuel Chase, for allowing his partisanship to influence his conduct of two trials; Judge James Peck, for vindictive use of his judicial powers against a lawyer who had criticized one of his decisions; Judge West Humphreys, for neglect of duty; President Andrew Johnson, for violating the Tenure of Office Act; Judge Mark Delahay, for intoxication on and off the bench; Judge George English, for using his office for personal monetary gain; Judge Charles Swayne, for maliciously and unlawfully imprisoning two lawyers and a litigant for contempt and for using his office for personal monetary gain; Judge Robert Archbald, for direct and indirect personal monetary gain; Judge Harold Louderback, for indirect and direct personal monetary gain; and Judge Halsted Ritter, for engaging in behavior that brought the judiciary into disrepute.

46. These were Judge John Pickering, for public drunkenness and blasphemy; Judge West Humphreys, for advocating publicly that Tennessee secede from the Union, having organized armed rebellion against the United States, having accepted a judicial commission from the Confederate government, holding court pursuant to that commission, and failing to fulfill his duties as a U.S. district court judge; Judge Robert Archbald, in addition to being convicted and removed was disqualified from future governmental service and benefits for obtaining contracts for himself from persons appearing before his court and others and for adjudicating cases in which he had a financial interest or received payment, offenses for which, as the chairman of the House Impeachment Committee conceded, no criminal charges could be brought; and Judge Halsted Ritter, for bringing "his court into scandal and disrepute, to the prejudice of said court and public confidence in the administration of justice therein, and to the prejudice of public respect for and confidence in the Federal judiciary."

47. These three are Harry Claiborne, income tax invasion; Alcee Hastings, bribery and perjury; and Walter Nixon, making false statements to a grand jury.

48. Moreover, Article 3, section 3, clause 1, of the Constitution defines treason as "consist[ing] only in levying War against [the United States], or, in adhering to their Enemies, giving them Aid and Comfort."

49. 18 U.S.C. sec. 201 (1982).

50. Laurence H. Tribe, *American Constitutional Law,* 3d ed. (New York: Foundation Press, 2000), 294.

51. Ibid.

52. (Walter) *Nixon v. United States*, 113 S.Ct. 732 (1992).

53. Several factors explain this trend, including but not limited to the expansion of the federal judiciary, federal criminal law, and the numbers and resources of federal prosecutors.

54. Besides President Clinton, the following officials were targeted for impeachment by external investigations: President Richard Nixon; Harry Claiborne; Alcee Hastings; Walter Nixon; and Robert Collins, who resigned from a federal district judgeship in 1993 after having been convicted and imprisoned for bribery and threatened with impeachment. See *United States v. Collins*, 972 F. 2d 1385 (5th Cir. 1992). A seventh official, Robert Aguilar, had his conviction for illegally disclosing a wiretap and attempting to obstruct a grand jury investigation overturned by the U.S. Court of Appeals for the Ninth Circuit en banc but resigned from his federal district judgeship as part of a deal to avoid being prosecuted again. In the early 1970s then-Representative Gerald Ford introduced an impeachment resolution in the House against Justice William O. Douglas based in part on his independent lifestyle as well as his association with the Parvin Foundation. The House declined to initiate formal proceedings against the justice.

55. 28 U.S.C. section 595(c) (1994).

56. The Tenure of Office Act, which passed over Johnson's veto, provided in essence that all federal officials whose appointment required Senate confirmation could not be removed by the president without its approval. The Supreme Court declared the act unconstitutional in *Myers v. United States*, 272 U.S. 52 (1926).

57. At the time of Clinton's trial, the Senate had fifty-five Republicans and forty-five Democrats. By a vote of 55-45, strictly along party lines, the Senate found Clinton not guilty of giving "perjurious, false and misleading testimony to a federal grand jury." In a 50-50 vote, with five Republican senators joining the forty-five Democratic senators, the Senate found the president not guilty of at least one of seven acts to obstruct the civil lawsuit brought against him by Paula Jones, who charged that Clinton had sexually harassed her while he had been gov-ernor of Arkansas and she had been a state government employee.

58. On July 25, 1974, the Supreme Court unanimously ruled in *United States v. Nixon,* 418 U.S. 683 (1974), that Nixon must comply with a judicial subpoena to submit tapes of Oval Office conversations to the special prosecutor investigating misconduct, which was the subject of the conversations. During the next several days, the House Judiciary Committee adopted three articles of impeachment against Nixon, charging him with obstruction of justice with respect to the Watergate break-in, abuse of power by misusing executive agencies and violating the rights of the citizenry, and willfully disobeying committee subpoenas to supply copies of the tapes. On August 6, Nixon decided to comply with the Supreme Court decision and made transcripts of the tapes available to the public. On August 9, he resigned.

59. This rejection could be construed consistently with the framers' expectation of the Senate's performing a unique balancing function. See Gordon S. Wood, *The Creation of the American Republic, 1776–1787* (Chapel Hill: University of North Carolina Press, 1969), 513, suggesting that the framers expected that the Senate "would function with more coolness, with more system, and more wisdom, than the popular branch," because its members would be drawn from the elite of society and as a result of its longer term and insulation from direct public pressure.

60. For the arguments for and against the legitimacy of President Clinton's impeachment by a lame duck House, see Michael J. Gerhardt, "The Historical and Constitutional Significance of the Impeachment and Trial of President Clinton," *Hofstra Law Review* 28 (1999): 349, 369 n. 100.

61. It is also fair to say that the vast majority of impeachments brought by the House and the convictions rendered by the Senate are consistent with the paradigmatic case. Most, if not all, of the officials impeached by the House and the seven officials convicted and removed by the Senate were found to have misused their offices or their prerogatives or to have injured seriously the Republic by breaching the special trusts that they held by virtue of their federal offices. For example, in the 1986 case of Judge Claiborne,

at first glance it seems as if his misconduct had no formal relationship to his official duties. Nevertheless, in impeaching and removing Claiborne, Congress reached the judgment that integrity is an indispensable criterion for someone to function as a federal judge. Moreover, as the House report and subsequent Senate debate on Claiborne's impeachment reflected, the members of Congress concluded that the commission of tax evasion robs a federal judge of the moral authority required to oversee the trials and sentencing of others for the same offense. Incontrovertible proof that a federal judge lacks integrity effectively disables a federal judge completely from performing his or her duties.

A variation on this reasoning explains the impeachment and conviction of Judge Walter Nixon in 1989 for making false statements to a grand jury. In a criminal trial, he had been convicted of making false statements to a grand jury about the efforts he had undertaken to influence the criminal prosecution of the son of a business partner. The alleged misconduct did not strictly relate to Nixon's formal actions as a federal judge—for example, he was not formally functioning as a federal judge when talking with the state prosecutor about dropping the case. Nevertheless, whatever influence Nixon had available to exercise on behalf of his business partner's son existed by virtue of the federal judgeship he held. Moreover, making false statements to a grand jury impugns a judge's integrity at least as much, if not more, than does tax evasion (which involves the making of false

statements under oath in a different manner). Again, the House and the Senate each reasonably concluded that the demonstrated lack of integrity robbed Nixon of the most important commodity he must have in order to perform his constitutional function.

62. See, for example, the published closed-door statements of Sens. Max Cleland (D-Ga.), Byron Dorgan (D-N.D.), James Jeffords (R-Vt.), Tim Johnson (D-S.D.), John Kerrey (D-Mass.), Herb Kohl (D-Wis.), Frank Lautenberg (D-N.J.), Joseph Lieberman (D-R.I.), Blanche Lincoln (D-Ark.), Barbara Mikulski (D-Md.), Harry Reid (D-Nev.)., *Congressional Record,* 105th Cong., 2d sess., February 12, 1999.

63. See Alexander Hamilton, James Madison, and John Jay, *Federalist* No. 65, *The Federalist Papers,* ed. I. Kramnick (Harmondsworth: Penguin, 1987), 380–381.

64. The view of Johnson's impeachment as a thoroughly partisan effort by some members of Congress to increase congressional power at the expense of the presidency is not one on which all historians would agree. For instance, Michael Les Benedict suggests that the effort to impeach and remove Johnson from office was not necessarily illegitimate because of Johnson's repeated violations of statutes that had been passed by Congress over his veto and Johnson's efforts to weaken the enforcement of the Fourteenth Amendment. See Michael Les Benedict, *The Impeachment and Trial of Andrew Johnson* (New York: Norton, 1973).

65. See *Jones v. Clinton,* 1999 U.S. Dist. Lexis 4515 (W.D. Ark. April 12, 1999).

CHAPTER NINE

The Delegation of Lawmaking Power to the Executive Branch

THOMAS O. SARGENTICH

The institutional world of U.S. government is more complicated than the classic formula for the separation of powers suggests. The formula holds that Congress makes the law, the executive branch executes the law, and the judiciary interprets the law. This traditional notion implies that the branches perform distinct functions. In fact, it is more accurate to see the institutions of government as sharing powers in a highly interactive system.

Of singular importance in this system is the precept, stated by James Madison in *Federalist* No. 51, that "[a]mbition must be made to counteract ambition."[1] In practical terms, governmental ambitions are checked by the powers of the separate branches. The system of checks and balances is designed to achieve several goals, including the prevention of the undue concentration of power in one institution, the broadening of the base of representation in government by the participation of officials chosen by different electorates, and the promotion of deliberation by government officials having distinct institutional perspectives.

An area that perfectly illustrates the highly interactive nature of the U.S. system of checks and balances involves the broad statutory delegations of lawmaking power to the executive

branch. The practice by Congress of delegating sweeping discretion to construct and enforce legal requirements is pervasive. Indeed, broad delegations to the executive branch are central to all areas of law, including environmental law, health and safety, civil rights law, and other regulatory fields. For example, the Clean Air Act, a major environmental statute, grants the Environmental Protection Agency (EPA), an executive branch body, broad authority to regulate sources of air pollution throughout the country.

This chapter will analyze the delegation of lawmaking power, first, by sketching two major, opposing views about delegation. It will then examine the Supreme Court's major contributions to this area. It will next elaborate on the arguments seeking a more robust delegation principle and consider the implications of the delegation debate for the courts, the president, and agencies.

The Delegation Debate

There are two competing positions on the delegation of lawmaking power to the executive branch. One view asserts that Congress has improperly abandoned its responsibility as the nation's primary lawmaker. From this perspective, Congress has relinquished too much lawmaking authority and needs to be reined in by a rigorous requirement of narrower delegation. Proponents of this critique recommend that federal courts strike down extremely broad delegations in order to breathe new life into the Constitution's principle that "all legislative power herein granted" is vested in Congress.

The opposing view defends the broad delegation of lawmaking authority based on a pragmatic sense of the requisites of modern government; Congress cannot effectively respond to the public's concerns unless it can delegate in generous terms. In part, this argument rests on the limitations in the time and resources that Congress can devote to any subject. Moreover, executive officers are thought to need flexibility, and therefore broad authority, to be able to address unforeseen problems. Furthermore, given the practical difficulties of consensus building, it is generally easier for legislators with differing views to reach agreement on statutory language when the level of generality is relatively high.

Both perspectives have deep roots in theories of U.S. government. Critics of broad delegation rely on a rule-of-law ideal of governmental legitimacy that, they claim, is undermined by existing practices. They charge that defenders of broad delegation are unduly apologetic and complacent about an unaccountable status quo. Delegation defenders, in contrast, invoke a model of pragmatic and effective policymaking that, they insist, requires flexible grants of power to administrators. Delegation defenders charge the critics with being excessively legalistic.

Supreme Court Delegation Decisions

The Supreme Court inevitably has been a focal point in the delegation debate because of its power to determine the constitutionality of statutes and executive actions.[2] The Court has long acknowledged that unlimited delegation to the executive branch violates Article 1, section 1, of the Constitution, which vests "all legislative power herein granted" in Congress. An unlimited delegation is a "nondelegation" in contravention of the constitutional requirement that Congress is the nation's legislator.[3] According to the Court, "[W]e have long insisted that the 'integrity and maintenance of the system of government ordained by the Constitution' mandate that Congress generally cannot delegate its legislative power to another Branch."[4]

In 1928 the Supreme Court enunciated the core requirement that Congress provide in a governing statute an "intelligible principle" that executive officials must follow as they exercise their delegated power.[5] This requirement links the use of administrative discretion to choices made by the representative legislature, reflecting a theory of governmental legitimacy emphasizing the consent of the governed within a framework of constitutional limitations. Also, the requirement that statutory delegations include intelligible principles preserves the concept of judicial checks on agencies. By establishing boundaries on administrative power, an intelligible principle furnishes a legal standard that courts can use in assessing whether a given executive action is within the scope of delegated authority.

At the same time, this rock-bottom constitutional requirement is not terribly demanding. An intelligible principle is not necessarily specific or definite in its references. Indeed, in employing the intelligible principle test, the Supreme Court has upheld notably broad delegations, including ones allowing the Federal Trade Commission (FTC) to prohibit "unfair methods of competition"[6] and authorizing the predecessor of the Federal Communications Commission to regulate the airwaves as the "public convenience, interest or necessity requires."[7]

The high-water mark of the Supreme Court's concern about broad delegations occurred in 1935. In that year the Court struck down two provisions of the National Industrial Recovery Act of 1933 (NIRA), an early New Deal statute designed to restructure the economy in response to the Great Depression. The two decisions, it should be borne in mind, reflected the Court's extreme judicial activism toward Congress in the period preceding 1937.

The first case, *Panama Refining Co. v. Ryan* (1935), involved a challenge to a statutory provision authorizing the president to ban from interstate commerce the shipment of oil that had been produced in violation of a state agency's order. The Court noted that the statute left to the states the determination of what production shall be permitted. The contested provision, the Court concluded, did not specify the circumstances or conditions in which the president would be able to prohibit the transportation of petroleum in excess of a state's allotment. Of the statute, the Court wrote,

> It establishes no criterion to govern the President's course. It does not require any finding by the President as a condition of his action. The Congress . . . thus declares no policy as to the transportation of the excess production. So far as this section is concerned,

it gives to the President an unlimited authority to determine the policy and to lay down the prohibition, or not to lay it down, as he may see fit.[8]

The second case, *A. L. A. Schechter Poultry Corp. v. United States* (1935), involved a challenge to the part of the NIRA provision that authorized the president to adopt "codes of fair competition" for any industry. Industry representatives wrote the codes, which were then submitted to the president for approval.[9] The codes could prescribe prices, wages, hours, working conditions, levels of production, and other practices that would otherwise be determined by the market. The violation of a code constituted a criminal offense. Schechter had been charged with violating, among other provisions, a section of the poultry code banning wholesalers, like Schechter, from allowing retailers to pick the better chickens in a batch. The practice had led to the worst chickens being left behind, with the result that wholesalers had to lower prices to sell the remaining poultry.

The delegation-related issue in *Schechter Poultry* was whether the statute's standards governing codes of fair competition were sufficiently clear and definite to pass constitutional muster. The Court held that the standards were unconstitutional. In doing so, the Court distinguished the standard of "fair competition" in the NIRA from the standards of "unfair competition" in the common law and "unfair methods of competition" in the Federal Trade Commission Act, which had been upheld by the courts. "Unfair competition" was understood to refer to actions beyond the ordinary course of business that are "tainted by fraud, or coercion, or conduct otherwise prohibited by law."[10] "Unfair methods of competition" referred to offenses, defined by the FTC, "in particular instances, upon evidence, in the light of particular competitive conditions and of what is found to be a specific and substantial public interest."[11] In contrast, the NIRA's "fair competition" standard was much broader. The authority conferred did not merely affect behavior offensive under existing law and practice; the statute also called for the formulation of "wise and beneficent measures" for an industry to promote the act's broad purposes.[12] In the Court's view, the NIRA prescribed no clear standards for any industry, but instead unconstitutionally authorized "the making of codes to prescribe them."[13]

In 1937 and thereafter, the Supreme Court adopted a more deferential posture toward legislative action. Some commentators have suggested that the Court's new approach may have been a response to President Franklin Delano Roosevelt's so-called Court-packing plan, which he proposed to Congress in early 1937 out of frustration with the Court's striking down several New Deal statutes. Under Roosevelt's plan, Congress would authorize adding a new member to the Supreme Court for each sitting justice over the age of seventy, a condition that at the time applied to a majority of the justices.[14] The proposal constituted a major assault on the independence of the federal judiciary. As it turned out, the plan's immediate rationale disappeared in spring 1937, when a voting realignment resulted in the majority of the Court repudiating the earlier, narrow view of governmental power, including that of Congress under the commerce clause.[15] There emerged a new jurisprudence of deference to Congress as the older justices left the Court

and Roosevelt made new appointments.

Within a few years of this transition, it became clear that the Supreme Court had abandoned its aggressive use against Congress of the commerce clause as well as the delegation principle. A softening in the Court's approach to delegation was evident in *Yakus v. United States* (1944), in which the Court upheld the Emergency Price Control Act's assignment of power to the price administrator to fix commodity prices. The statute required that regulations establishing commodity prices be "generally fair and equitable" and that they "effectuate the purposes of this act."[16] The Court reasoned that the statute, by setting out the general objectives to be sought, adequately defined the boundaries of the administrator's authority. It also emphasized that Congress need not select the "least possible delegation" to executive officers, but instead can choose "the flexibility attainable by the use of less restrictive standards."[17]

Other decisions in the 1940s upheld delegations of power to the Federal Power Commission to determine just and reasonable rates,[18] to the Securities and Exchange Commission to prevent unfair or inequitable distribution of voting authority among security holders,[19] and to the undersecretary of war to determine excessive profits.[20] Since 1935 the Supreme Court has not followed *Panama Refining* and *Schechter Poultry* in declaring any federal statute to be an impermissible delegation of lawmaking power to the executive branch. The contemporary Court's acceptance of broad delegation is reflected in *Mistretta v. United States* (1989), in which the Court approved a grant of authority to the U.S. Sentencing Commission to promulgate guidelines for determining the punishment of persons convicted of federal crimes.[21] The Court observed that in applying the intelligible principle test in assessing statutory delegations "our jurisprudence has been driven by a practical understanding that in our increasingly complex society, replete with ever changing and more technical problems, Congress simply cannot do its job absent an ability to delegate power under broad general directives."[22]

The Court stressed that since 1935, it had consistently upheld Congress's choices to delegate lawmaking power under broad standards. In view of this pattern, the Court had "no doubt" that the delegation in this case met constitutional requirements. Indeed, the Court observed that the development of "proportionate penalties for hundreds of different crimes by a virtually limitless array of offenders" is "precisely" the type of "intricate, labor-intensive task for which delegation to an expert body is especially appropriate."[23]

More recently, in *Whitman v. American Trucking Associations, Inc.* (2001), the Court unanimously rejected a challenge directed at the Clean Air Act. The U.S. Court of Appeals for the District of Columbia Circuit held that a provision dealing with "ambient air quality standards" as interpreted by the EPA did not provide the required intelligible principle. The Supreme Court disagreed, concluding that the extent of the agency's discretion under the statute was "well within the limits of our nondelegation precedents."[24] The Court pointedly observed that even with respect to "sweeping regulatory schemes," it has never demanded that a statute provide a "determinate criterion" for assessing how much of a regulated harm is "too much."[25]

In light of *Mistretta, American Trucking,* and other modern decisions, a challenge today to a federal statute as an unconstitutional delegation of lawmaking power is unlikely to succeed.[26] At the same time, it would be erroneous to suppose that the Court has evinced no concern about lawmaking delegations to the executive branch. On occasion, justices have adopted the view that Congress, as a matter of statutory intent, meant something narrower than what the words of a statute might suggest, for otherwise, there could be a problem of overly broad delegation.[27] This represents the use of the delegation principle in the context of statutory construction. Such a use assists the Court in interpreting a statute without displacing Congress's power to provide later by law that the Court misunderstood its intent.[28]

The Court and the Legislative Process

In addition, although the modern Supreme Court accepts broad delegations of lawmaking power as a substantive matter, it has actively policed the legislative process by which such delegations are enacted. This development rests on *INS v. Chadha* (1983), which invalidated legislative veto provisions in broadly delegative statutes.[29] Legislative veto provisions were statutes purporting to allow Congress, or a unit of Congress, to adopt a resolution disapproving an executive branch decision implementing a delegation of lawmaking power. The resolution could be adopted in various ways. Some veto provisions authorized one-house resolutions of disapproval, as in *Chadha,* others called for two-house resolutions, and still others provided for committee resolutions. The key characteristic of legislative vetoes was that they were not submitted to the president for approval or veto, unlike standard legislative actions.[30]

The constitutional issue in *Chadha* was whether Congress could establish a more efficient mechanism for acting with the force of law outside the plenary legislative process of bicameral passage and presentment to the president. Congress had sought the power to issue "legislative vetoes" precisely because the process was much easier than complying with bicameralism and presentment, in particular because it avoided the danger of a presidential veto. Legislative vetoes began to appear during the New Deal period of the 1930s, when large-scale delegations of lawmaking power to the executive branch became increasingly common. Scores of such provisions had been enacted by the time *Chadha* was decided.[31] To their defenders, they were important checks on the executive that enhanced its accountability to Congress.

In *Chadha,* an alien, Jagdish Rai Chadha, had sought and received a discretionary determination by the attorney general suspending his deportation. Under the immigration statute in question, suspension decisions could be disapproved by a one-house resolution. Chadha's suspension was "vetoed" by a resolution of the House of Representatives. Chadha's counsel challenged the legislative veto's constitutionality. Although the defendant agreed that the statute was unconstitutional, the INS was bound by law to deport Chadha unless a court struck down the statute. When the Supreme Court took the case, both houses of Congress intervened to defend the statute.[32]

The Court ruled that when Congress exercises its legislative power, it must follow the bi-cameralism and presentment procedures set forth in Article 1, section 7, clauses 2 and 3. Clause 2 speaks of a "Bill," and Clause 3 speaks of an "Order, Resolution, or Vote" by Congress. The key issue in *Chadha* was whether the legislative veto resolution that suspended the alien's deportation order was an exercise of Article 1 legislative power to which bicameralism and presentment apply. The Court read the immigration law as delegating to the attorney general the power to suspend an alien's deportation; it also saw a legislative veto of that decision as a change in the alien's legal rights. Because the purpose and effect of the disapproval resolution were deemed to be "legislative," the resolution must be carried out in compliance with the bicameralism and presentment requirements.[33]

The Court stressed that important values are served by requiring Congress, in general, to comply with the bicameralism and presentment requirements when exercising its Article I power.[34] Bicameralism requires that the two differently constituted chambers of Congress agree on a legislative provision, thus broadening the base of representation underlying the action and assuring wider deliberation about it. Presentment injects the president as a vital actor in the legislative process, especially given the difficulty of achieving a two-thirds vote in both houses of Congress to override a presidential veto. Presentment thus helps to avoid concentration of power in a single branch of government. Also, like bicameralism, presentment broadens the base of representation of legislative action, for the president is elected on different grounds than are senators or representatives, and it promotes deliberation about legislative action. These core values—broadening the base of representation, preventing undue concentrations of power, and promoting deliberation about public policy—are the central principles underlying the system of the separation of powers and checks and balances.

Although *Chadha* represented a legal victory for the executive branch, its effects have been less sweeping than some observers had predicted. First, Congress retains primary legislative power and can limit or eliminate particular delegations to the executive as long as it complies with the plenary legislative process. Second, Congress has the critical "power of the purse," the power to appropriate funds needed for the government to operate. However broad a substantive delegation may be, an agency cannot act if Congress bars its use of funds for a particular purpose. Third, Congress can specifically condition a delegation so that it will expire automatically after a period provided for in a statute.[35] Fourth, Congress can adopt "report-and-wait" provisions that require an executive agency to report its decision to Congress and to wait a certain time before implementing the decision. This procedure allows Congress to review a policy before it becomes a fait accompli.

Beyond these formal lawmaking powers, Congress has broad investigative and oversight authorities, which frequently are used to probe the executive's actions. Oversight hearings can be employed to cajole or embarrass an agency by achieving negative publicity that can lead to a change in the course of events without Congress using its lawmaking power. Also, Congress, speaking through its committees, can take a position that an executive agency as a practical matter will have difficulty ignoring, assuming that it seeks to remain on good terms with its authorizing or appropriating committees. Moreover, as political scientist Louis Fisher has noted, since *Chadha* Congress has continued to enact legislative veto provisions.[36] Although not legally effective, such provisions can have practical weight when Congress invokes them in seeking to "persuade" an agency to pursue certain steps.[37]

To summarize, the modern Supreme Court accepts broad delegations of lawmaking power to the executive branch. It also expects Congress to follow *Chadha* when imposing legally binding duties or conferring legal rights. At the same time, the constitutional system involves ongoing interactions between the legislative and executive branches about the direction of public policy. In the world of broad delegations, Congress retains an impressive array of formal and informal mechanisms for influencing the executive's use of its authority.

Reviving the Principle against Broad Delegations

A number of critics of administrative government have supported the "revival" of a robust delegation principle such as applied by the Supreme Court in *Schechter Poultry*. As noted above, the call to revive *Schechter Poultry* is premised on an activist defense of a rule-of-law ideal, which holds that administrative discretion must be constrained by reasonably determinate rules. In addition, the revivalist position seeks to advance democratic accountability by insisting that public programs be guided by law as crafted by elected legislators, not as devised by bureaucratic actors. Since executive officials with the exception of the president and vice president are unelected, it is arguably undemocratic for such officials to have far-reaching authority to make law.

The revival of a robust delegation principle was endorsed by Justice William Rehnquist in a separate opinion in *Industrial Union Department, AFL-CIO v. American Petroleum Institute* (1980), also know as the *Benzene Case*. The case involved a challenge to the Occupational Safety and Health Administration's (OSHA) standard for employee exposure to benzene, a toxic substance. The standard was promulgated under a statutory provision dealing with toxic materials that authorizes OSHA to create "the standard which most adequately assures, to the extent feasible . . . that no employee will suffer material impairment of health."[38]

Justice Rehnquist urged that the statutory requirement to establish a "feasible" standard was "completely precatory, admonishing the Secretary to adopt the most protective standard if he can, but excusing him from that duty if he cannot."[39] To Rehnquist, it did not matter that a rigorous delegation principle had fallen into disuse. He acknowledged that some had associated the repudiation of a narrow, pre-1937 interpretation of the commerce clause with the demise of a rigorous delegation principle. Yet Rehnquist saw this linkage of doctrines as merely a case of "death by association."[40] He concluded that important values—assuring that significant social policy choices are made by Congress, that Congress specifically guide agencies in their exercise of discretion, and that courts are furnished with a meaningful legal standard in terms of which to evaluate challenged agency conduct—were undermined by the toxic substances provision, which, he concluded, should be held to be unconstitutional.

Criticism of broad delegations has also come from academic quarters. Political scientist Theodore Lowi has prominently decried the tendency in modern statutes to shift policymaking authority from the more politically visible and accountable Congress to administrative agencies.[41] His argument specifically invokes the rule-of-law ideal, according to which the exercise of administrative power needs to be guided by stable, predictable, and reasonably determinate statutory norms.[42] Lowi also has contended that broad delegations exacerbate the problem of factional capture of government. That is, under broad delegations, agencies arguably are more likely to become the captives of well-organized interest groups that lobby agencies for benefits that are obtainable under the discretion they possess. In this view, administrators are seen as the pawns of special interests, rather than as officials acting in the public interest under clear legal standards. To address these concerns, Lowi has urged the federal courts to resuscitate *Schechter Poultry* by strictly reviewing delegations of lawmaking power.

Law professor David Schoenbrod argues against broad delegations by employing a dichotomy between "rules-statutes" and "goals-statutes."[43] A "rules-statute" includes reasonably determinate rules of law to guide an agency. In Schoenbrod's view, such a statute should be upheld under an appropriately rigorous delegation doctrine. In contrast, a "goals-statute" presents a serious problem, for it enunciates the ends that Congress seeks to achieve while leaving to executive officials the hard decisions about how to achieve them.

Schoenbrod's revived delegation doctrine thus would call into question the validity of goals-statutes. In his view, it is simply too tempting for Congress to pass a law that recites general policy objectives, thereby permitting it to claim credit for addressing an issue while shifting decisional responsibility to the executive branch. Furthermore, Schoenbrod argues that a goals-statute undermines the principle of legislative accountability because it allows Congress to avoid blame for unpopular policies by claiming that an agency went beyond what it had contemplated.[44]

In response to the revival position, defenders of broad delegations cite the Supreme Court's delegation decisions since 1935. In reply to critics' rule-of-law contention, defenders invoke the Court's authority for the proposition that intelligible principles in statutes furnish constitutionally adequate legal standards. Also as noted, defenders claim that broad delegations are needed for modern government to work effectively. The breadth of the revival controversy implicates the roles not only of Congress but also of the courts, the president, and the agencies.

The Courts

Critics of broad delegations of lawmaking power contend that the federal courts should revive *Schechter Poultry*, the high-water mark of the Supreme Court's concern about such delegations. In part, such reliance on the courts rests on the fact that they alone are likely to consider pursuing such a path. After all, Congress has incentives to delegate broadly, and presidents, as chief executives, tend to favor sweeping delegations to executive officials. In fact, the judicial branch could expand its power by adopting a highly critical stance to-ward vague delegations, for such an approach would embroil the courts in innumerable disputes about the constitutionality of laws.

The call for courts to revive a rigorous delegation principle implicates the larger debate about judicial review in a democratic society. Since *Marbury v. Madison* (1803), the Supreme Court has assumed the responsibility of reviewing the constitutionality of actions by the legislative and executive branches. This power is premised on the Constitution's supremacy and the practical need for an umpire to decide when the government acts in compliance with constitutional requirements.

From the outset, the practice of judicial review has raised concerns about possible judicial overreaching. A prominent critique starts with the premise that most public choices in a democratic society should be made by majorities of the people, as represented by Congress and the president. When federal judges, who are unelected, review the decisions of the "majoritarian" branches of government, they act in a "countermajoritarian" fashion.[45] This results in pressure against the widespread use of the judicial review power, for it threatens the majoritarian tenets underlying the structure of the U.S. governmental system.

Despite this concern, critics of broad delegations proclaim that the power of judicial review offers an appropriate mechanism for imposing a strict delegation principle on Congress. After all, courts are relatively free from the daily political forces pressing on Congress and the president. They are also the institutions of government most imbued with the ethos of the rule of law. Indeed, judicial decisions about governmental behavior can be envisioned generally as efforts to apply rule-of-law principles to the often unruly products of the political process.

On the other hand, defenders of broad delegation stress the dangers of frequent judicial inquiries into the constitutionality of public laws under a revived delegation principle. The biggest risk is of widespread substitution of judicial judgments for the decisions of the elected branches of government. How could it possibly be legitimate, defenders ask, for courts to arrogate to themselves the general power to second-guess statutes authorizing executive agencies to make law addressing social problems?

Such doubts are exacerbated by the concern that there is no clear test for determining when a statute is or is not constitutional under a demanding delegation principle. That is, there is arguably little clarity in an inquiry designed to ascertain whether a statute is clear enough to be constitutional.[46] Defenders of broad delegations do not find guidance in a distinction between statutes containing rules of law and those calling on agencies to achieve broad goals. To be sure, rules and goals differ in their breadth. Yet, even though goals-statutes are written at a higher level of generality, they can still contain intelligible standards or principles to guide agencies and reviewing courts. Defenders of broad delegations also stress that the law needs standards as well as rules, for it is often socially useful to establish general norms that are not necessarily tied to narrowly conceived factual and legal conditions.[47]

The President

Article 2, section 1, of the Constitution vests "the executive power" in the president. Of particular importance is the president's broad supervisory authority over the heads of executive agencies. Agency heads are officers of the United States chosen after a three-step process consisting of nomination by the president, "advice and consent" of the Senate conveyed by a majority vote in favor of the nominee, and formal appointment by the president. Heads of executive agencies can be removed by the president at will. In contrast, by statute the heads of independent regulatory commissions and other so-called independent agencies are removable by the president only for good cause, such as "inefficiency, neglect of duty, or malfeasance in office."[48] With respect to executive agencies, the president undeniably has broad authority to supervise and guide their execution of the law.[49] This point has two main consequences for the delegation debate.

First, sweeping delegations to executive agencies are in the president's institutional interest. Because such delegations give agency heads broad authority, they also create a wide front across which the president can roam in guiding a law's execution. In particular, the president can urge executive agency heads to use their legal authority in a manner that is most consistent with presidential priorities. If a statute delegates to such an agency broader rather than narrower lawmaking discretion, the president will have a wider range within which to urge action. Hence, efforts to encourage the president to veto legislation because it contains broad delegations will often fall on deaf ears.

Second, the president's power to oversee the law's execution plays a significant part in the defense of broad delegations themselves. Critics of such delegations, again, contend that democratic values are undermined by statutes conferring sweeping lawmaking authority on unelected administrators (read, bureaucrats). This argument implicitly responds to the charge that the pro-*Schechter Poultry* position is unduly legalistic. Supporters of *Schechter Poultry* say it is not because it upholds the values of democratic responsiveness.

A rejoinder to this contention is that although executive agency heads are unelected, they are subject to the supervision and guidance of the president, who is elected. The president's supervision helps to assure the responsiveness of agency action to democratic will. Accordingly, broad delegations to executive agencies arguably do not undermine the principle of democratic responsiveness and may even improve "the responsiveness of the government to the desires of the general electorate."[50]

The emphasis on presidential supervision occurs in other contexts involving the interaction of the branches of government. For instance, when a court is presented with a question of law concerning an executive agency's use of lawmaking authority, the court must determine whether the statute is clear on the precise question at issue, and if it is not whether it should defer to the agency's view of its authorizing statute. In the leading decision of *Chevron U.S.A. Inc. v. Natural Resources Defense Council, Inc.* (1984), the Supreme Court proclaimed that when a statute is not clear, the reviewing court should defer to an agency's view of its authority if the interpretation is reasonable.[51] This direction can result in a high degree of judicial deference to the executive branch. To justify such deference, the Court invoked the practice of presidential supervision of executive agencies, noting that because the agencies are overseen by the president they are more accountable in democratic terms than the courts are.[52]

The argument for agency responsiveness based on presidential supervision is not, of course, without its detractors. First, how active is presidential supervision of most executive decision making? Because of limited resources, centralized reviewers in the White House at most can oversee certain major administrative actions. Moreover, underlying presidential supervision is an assumption that the president represents the public's desires, not those of special or narrow interests. Could the president be swayed by narrow interests? Those who criticize broad delegations argue that Congress is more likely than the president to be faithful to the public's will, in part because Congress is comprised of many representatives from different constituencies.[53] Despite these concerns, however, the notion of presidential supervision plays an important role in justifying broad delegations to the executive branch.

Agencies

Some critics of broad delegation posit a direct relationship between such delegation and an agency's tendency to be "captured" by special interests. The idea is that if a statute specifies what an agency is to do, special interests will have a difficult time convincing it to do something else. After all, agencies will not lightly violate a clear statute if only because they may be challenged and lose in court. On the other hand, the argument goes, if an agency has broad discretion, it can use its discretion to respond to the selfish pleadings of narrow interests. The notion is that with a broad delegation, an agency will have greater flexibility to bargain with special interests. The interests will have incentives to support the agency politically in return for receiving government-derived benefits or avoiding agency-imposed burdens. This analysis reflects a critique of government that emphasizes, among other things, the incentives of narrow, organized groups to advance their selfish aims in the legislative and administrative arenas.[54]

Do broad delegations necessarily promote agency bargaining with narrowly focused interest groups? Defenders of such delegations contend that they do not. Indeed, specific statutory provisions may have a closer connection with interest group bargaining than do vague statutory standards. If a regulatory statute directs an agency not to issue rules in a specific area, for instance, one could justifiably wonder whether that protection had been promoted by special interests.[55] In any event, narrow statutory delegations are valued by interest groups because their consequences are more likely to be predictable and reliable.

Moreover, it is an overstatement to suggest that broad delegations are uncontrolled by law and subject to endless exploitation by special interests. Agencies need to comply with intelligible principles in their statutes, and courts can police their adherence to such principles. Aside from the check of judicial review, there is also the intra-executive check of presidential-level review. An assumption that broad delegations necessarily lead to self-serving deals with special interests disregards the disciplinary effects of such checks.

More generally, the interest group critique of broad delegation reflects a contestable vision of administrative power. Are agencies inevitably prone to making bargains with organ-

ized private groups at the expense of the public interest? Some observers argue that agencies can and do rise above special interest pleading to pursue broader values.[56]

The private interest critique of delegations thus needs to be contrasted with a public interest vision of administration. The latter sees agencies as potential catalysts of social change on behalf of important public aims. During the New Deal, executive power was seen as guided by the exercise of expertise by agency officials.[57] In the modern era, the expertise argument is more qualified. It is widely acknowledged that whereas some regulatory decisions rest on scientific or technical premises, other elements turn on normative choices that reflect policy preferences. Defenders of broad delegations often emphasize that the choices of executive agencies are supervised by the president and, in appropriate cases, reviewed by courts, which can help to assure that the general public's interest is not lost in a shuffle of special interest pleading.

In short, critics of sweeping delegations are skeptical about the worth of broad agency power. They fear its potential to become a pathway for the advancement of narrow societal interests. In contrast, defenders of broad delegations emphasize that checks and balances can restrict the self-interested behavior and factional dominance of agencies. Without denying that bureaucracies can be inefficient and wasteful, delegation defenders stress the potential of agencies to address critical social concerns while advancing public values.

Conclusion

One might suggest that the delegation debate has limited real world importance given the

Supreme Court's acceptance since 1935 of broad delegations. Yet this would be a vast oversimplification. The Court consistently requires that Congress adhere to the intelligible principle test. Although not strenuous, the test does establish a general constraint on legislative action. The Court conceivably could change its view, however unlikely that now appears. It is thus important to understand the main alternative, which calls for narrow delegations. Because the alternative view has powerful grounding in the values of the rule of law and democratic accountability, it forces critics to respond to its challenge to the status quo.

The delegation debate is at the center of contemporary theory and practice of the separation of powers and checks and balances. Studying the delegation debate focuses attention on Congress's institutional limits and strengths as the national legislator. It also cuts to the heart of the controversy surrounding constitutionally based judicial review while directly implicating the conception of the president as an ongoing supervisor of the executive branch. Finally, it compels the asking of basic questions about the role of agencies in the U.S. system of government, for administrative power is as extensive as it is as a direct consequence of broad delegations.

Notes

1. Alexander Hamilton, James Madison, and John Jay, *The Federalist Papers,* ed. Clinton Rossiter (New York: New American Library, 1961), 322.
2. The Supreme Court's decisions on this subject are well summarized in leading legal treatises. See, for example, Erwin Chemerinsky, *Constitutional Law: Principles and Policies,* 2d ed. (New York: Aspen Law and Business, 2002), 319–323; Laurence H. Tribe, *American Constitutional Law,* 3d ed. (New York: Foundation Press, 2000), 1:977–1002.
3. Thus the term *nondelegation doctrine* has been employed to describe this general area of law. In modern cases and commentary, the term *delegation doctrine* has been used synonymously with *nondelegation doctrine.* Both terms deal with whether a broad delegation of lawmaking authority is so unlimited as to violate constitutional norms.
4. *Mistretta v. United States,* 488 U.S. 361, 371–372 (1989), citing *Field v. Clark,* 143 U.S. 649, 692 (1892).
5. See *J. W. Hampton, Jr. & Co. v. United States,* 276 U.S. 394, 409 (1928): "If Congress shall lay down by legislative act an intelligible principle to which the person or body authorized to fix such rates is directed to conform, such legislative action is not a forbidden delegation of legislative power."
6. See *FTC v. Gratz,* 253 U.S. 421 (1920).
7. See *Federal Radio Comm'n v. Nelson Bros. Bond & Mortgage Co.,* 289 U.S. 266, 285 (1933). See also *National Broadcasting Co. v. United States,* 319 U.S. 190, 225–226 (1943).
8. *Panama Refining Co. v. Ryan,* 293 U.S. 388, 415 (1935). Justice Benjamin Cardozo dissented, concluding that "a standard reasonably clear whereby discretion must be governed" was not lacking "when the act with all its reasonable implications is considered as a whole." Ibid., 434.
9. *A. L. A. Schechter Poultry Corp. v. United States,* 295 U.S. 495 (1935), presented the delegation issue and the problem of granting governmental power to private groups.
10. Ibid., 532.
11. Ibid., 533.
12. Ibid., 535.
13. Ibid., 541.
14. See *Encyclopedia of the American Constitution,* 2d ed., s.v. "Court Packing Plans," 696–697. Roosevelt proposed that when a federal judge who had served at least ten years waited more than six months after his or her seventieth birthday to resign or retire, the president might add a new judge to the bench. At the time, this would have allowed for the appointment of as many as six new justices to the Supreme Court

and forty-four new judges to the lower federal courts.

15. The pivotal cases were *West Coast Hotel Co. v. Parrish,* 300 U.S. 379 (1937), interpreting substantive due process to allow greater state regulation of the economy, and *NLRB v. Jones & Laughlin Steel Corp.,* 301 U.S. 1 (1937), interpreting the commerce clause to authorize federal legislation regulating the terms and conditions of employment.

16. *Yakus v. United States,* 321 U.S. 414, 420 (1944).

17. See ibid., 425–426. In dissent, Justice Owen Roberts concluded that the act lacked meaningful standards. Despite the Court's effort to distinguish *Schechter Poultry* on the ground that it involved a broader statutory standard and a delegation of power to private individuals, Roberts stated that *Yakus* "leaves no doubt that the decision is now overruled." Ibid., 452.

18. *FPC v. Hope Natural Gas Co.,* 320 U.S. 591, 600 (1944).

19. *American Power and Light Co. v. SEC,* 329 U.S. 90, 104–105 (1946).

20. *Lichter v. United States,* 334 U.S. 742, 785–786 (1948).

21. The commission is composed of seven presidential appointees, at least three of whom must be federal judges. The commission is designated by statute as part of the judicial branch of the federal government.

22. *Mistretta,* 372.

23. Ibid., 379.

24. *Whitman v. American Trucking Associations, Inc.,* 531 U.S. 457, 474 (2001).

25. Ibid., citing *American Trucking Associations, Inc. v. EPA,* 175 F. 3d 1027, 1034 (D.C. Cir. 1999).

26. See *Loving v. United States,* 517 U.S. 748 (1996), rejecting a delegation doctrine challenge to the president's prescription of aggravating factors for the imposition of the death penalty in the military; *Touby v. United States,* 500 U.S. 160 (1991), rejecting a delegation doctrine challenge to the federal Controlled Substances Act of 1970.

27. In *Industrial Union Department, AFL-CIO v. American Petroleum Institute,* 448 U.S. 607 (1980), four justices voted to overturn an action under the Occupational Safety and Health Act of 1970 by, inter alia, narrowly interpreting the act to avoid an unconstitutionally broad delegation. Ibid., 645–646. The plurality also noted that Congress would not have given the agency such broad power without a clear statement to that effect. Ibid., 645.

28. For discussion of "nondelegation canons" of statutory construction employed by the Court, see Cass R. Sunstein, "Nondelegation Canons," *University of Chicago Law Review* 67 (2000): 315.

29. *INS v. Chadha,* 462 U.S. 919 (1983). The author participated in the *Chadha* litigation on behalf of the Immigration and Naturalization Service as an attorney in the Office of Legal Counsel of the Department of Justice. The views expressed here are, of course, his own.

30. For discussion of legislative vetoes in the pre-*Chadha* world, see Harold H. Bruff and Ernest Gellhorn, "Congressional Control of Administrative Regulation: A Study of Legislative Vetoes," *Harvard Law Review* 90 (1977): 1369.

31. The Court in *Chadha* quoted a study reporting that from 1932 to 1977, 295 legislative veto–type procedures had been inserted in 196 different statutes. See *Chadha,* 944–946.

32. For a survey of *Chadha,* see Barbara Hinkson Craig, *Chadha: The Story of an Epic Constitutional Struggle* (New York: Oxford University Press, 1988).

33. See *Chadha,* 952–954. Congress had urged on the Court the alternative reading of the statute as a conditional grant of power to the attorney general, such that the suspension order was not a final action but merely a recommendation that would become effective only if it were not "vetoed" by one house of Congress. In this reading, the attorney general did not exercise any definite grant of lawmaking power.

From the perspective of the executive branch, this argument was dangerous, as it would allow Congress to transform delegations of power into conditional grants of authority to make mere recommendations to Congress. It also would allow Congress to have the final word on legal matters without complying with bicameralism and presentment, thereby undermining those procedures. For discussion that is critical of the Court's reasoning in *Chadha,* see E. Donald Elliott, "INS v. Chadha: The Administrative Constitution, the Constitution, and the Legislative Veto," *Supreme Court Review* (1983): 125.

34. See *Chadha,* 946–951. The Court also noted that in certain instances, the Constitution provides for one-house actions. These include the Senate's power to give advice and consent on treaties and nominations of officers of the United States, the power of the House of Representatives to impeach an officer of the United States, and the Senate's power to convict following impeachment. See ibid., 955.

35. Such time-limited delegations are commonly referred to as "sunset" provisions.

36. See Louis Fisher, *Constitutional Dialogues: Interpretation as Political Process* (Princeton, N.J.: Princeton University Press, 1988), 225–226.

37. Although, for instance, language in a committee report is not legally binding unless it supports statutory text that has been adopted pursuant to bicameralism and presentment, the committee's views can exert a powerful influence on executive policymaking. See ibid., 228: "Nonstatutory legislative vetoes are not legal in effect. They are, however, in effect legal. Agencies are aware of the penalties that can be invoked by Congress if they decide to violate understandings or working relationships with their review committees." See also, Louis Fisher, *The Politics of Shared Power: Congress and the Executive,* 3d ed. (Washington, D.C.: CQ Press, 1993), 80–84.

38. *Industrial Union Department,* 612.

39. Ibid., 675.

40. Ibid., 686, quoting John Hart Ely, *Democracy and Distrust: A Theory of Judicial Review* (Cambridge, Mass.: Harvard University Press, 1980), 133.

41. See Theodore J. Lowi, *The End of Liberalism: The Second Republic of the United States,* 2d ed. (New York: W. W. Norton and Co., 1979).

42. For discussion of the rule-of-law vision and Lowi's reliance on it, see Thomas O. Sargentich, "The Delegation Debate and Competing Ideals of the Administrative Process," *American University Law Review* 36 (1987): 423–427.

43. See David Schoenbrod, "The Delegation Doctrine: Could the Court Give It Substance?" *Michigan Law Review* 83 (1985): 1252–1260,

1281–1283; idem, "Goals Statutes or Rules Statutes: The Case of the Clean Air Act," *UCLA Law Review* 30 (1983): 740.

44. See David Schoenbrod, "Delegation and Democracy: A Reply to My Critics," *Cardozo Law Review* 20 (1999): 740: "The statutes are framed so that legislators can skirt the hard choices. This permits legislators to claim much of the credit for the benefits of the laws but shift to the unelected agency officials much of the blame for the inevitable costs and disappointments when the agency fails to deliver all the benefits promised." See, generally, idem, *Power without Responsibility: How Congress Abuses the People through Delegation* (New Haven: Yale University Press, 1993).

45. See Alexander M. Bickel, *The Least Dangerous Branch: The Supreme Court at the Bar of Politics,* 2d ed. (New Haven: Yale University Press, 1986).

46. See Sunstein, "Nondelegation Canons," 327: "Without much exaggeration, and with tongue only slightly in cheek, we might even say that judicial enforcement of the conventional [nondelegation] doctrine would violate the constitutional doctrine—since it could not [be] enforced without delegating, without clear standards, a high degree of discretionary lawmaking authority to the judiciary."

47. See Richard J. Pierce Jr., "Accountability and Delegated Power: A Response to Professor Lowi," *American University Law Review* 36 (1987): 401: "Professor Schoenbrod's proposal . . . would also force Congress to choose between declining to intervene in a market at all and intervening through shortsighted and counterproductive statutory instruments."

48. There is a rich literature on presidential supervision of executive and independent agencies. See, for example, Geoffrey P. Miller, "Independent Agencies," *Supreme Court Review* (1986): 41; Peter M. Shane, "Independent Policymaking and Presidential Power: A Constitutional Analysis," *George Washington Law Review* 57 (1989): 596. See, generally, Peter L. Strauss, "The Place of Agencies in Government: Separation of Powers and the Fourth Branch," *Columbia Law Review* 84 (1984): 573.

49. This is not to say that the president can displace an agency head's discretion under a statutory

grant of power to the agency head. Guiding an agency head's use of discretion is not the same as displacing an agency head's discretion.

50. Jerry L. Mashaw, *Greed, Chaos, and Governance: Using Public Choice to Improve Public Law* (New Haven: Yale University Press, 1997), 152. See also idem, "Prodelegation: Why Administrators Should Make Political Decisions," *Journal of Law, Economics, and Organization* 1 (1985): 95–96: "[T]he utilization of vague delegations to administrative agencies takes on significance as a device for facilitating responsiveness to voter preferences expressed in presidential elections."

51. See *Chevron U.S.A., Inc. v. National Resources Defense Council, Inc.* 467 U.S. 837, 842–844 (1984).

52. Ibid., 865: "[W]hile agencies are not directly accountable to the people, the Chief Executive is."

53. See Schoenbrod, "Delegation and Democracy," 751: "The President is not as accountable for agency laws as members of Congress are for enacted laws."

54. See Peter H. Aranson, Ernest Gellhorn, and Glen O. Robinson, "A Theory of Legislative Delegation," *Cornell Law Review* 68 (1982): 1.

55. See Sunstein, "Nondelegation Canons," 324: "Statutory clarity, especially on details, is often a product not of some deliberative judgment by Congress, but of the influence of well organized private groups."

56. See, for example, Mark Seidenfeld, "A Civic Republican Justification for the Bureaucratic State," *Harvard Law Review* 105 (1992): 1511.

57. See James M. Landis, *The Administrative Process* (1938: repr. Westport, Ct.: Greenwood Press, 1974).

CHAPTER TEN

Congressional Power and the States: The Context and Consequences of the U.S. Supreme Court's Federalism Decisions

JOHN DINAN

The conventional account of the Supreme Court's jurisprudence on federalism is that the Court has behaved in a cyclical fashion throughout U.S. history, alternating between periods of strong support for and determined opposition to congressional expansion of power. According to this account, the Marshall Court adhered to a broad construction of congressional power in the early nineteenth century. In the late nineteenth and early twentieth centuries, the Court engaged in a strict construction of congressional power and frustrated a number of efforts by Progressive and New Deal reformers. Then, a series of decisions issued by post–New Deal Courts, notably the Warren Court, brought a return to the expansive interpretation of congressional power that had characterized the decisions of the Marshall Court. In the closing decade of the twentieth century, the Rehnquist Court reversed course and returned to the strict construction of congressional power last seen in the Progressive Era and early New Deal.

If one is concerned primarily with tracking changes in legal doctrine—particularly in regard to the Court's interpretations of the commerce clause, taxing and spending clause, Tenth Amendment, and enforcement clauses of the Civil War amendments—there is little need to move beyond this conventional account. If, however, one is interested in assessing the influence of the Court's decisions, then it is important to take account of the different types of measures on which the Court passed judgment in each of these periods, as well as the particular means by which Congress responded to these rulings. The Marshall and Warren Courts, it is true, both offered broad interpretations of congressional power, but the effects of their decisions were quite different because of the ways in which Congress reacted to their rulings. Similar distinctions need to be made in regard to the influence of the Progressive Era Court, New Deal Court, and Rehnquist Court. Each of them adhered to limited interpretations of congressional power that delayed the enactment of numerous statutes, but the effects of their decisions varied in important ways, depending on the significance of the measures that were struck down and the extent to which Congress was able to overcome these decisions.

The Marshall Court

In 1787 it was clear to nearly all of the assembled delegates at the Constitutional Convention that the central government under the Articles of Confederation had been unable to carry out a number of essential tasks of governance, and, in the words of Alexander Hamilton in *Federalist* No. 15, that "[t]he measures of the union have not been executed; and the delinquencies of the States have step by step matured themselves to an extreme, which has, at length, arrested all the wheels of the national government and brought them to an awful stand."[1] Consequently, in Article 1, section 8, of the Constitution, the delegates authorized the central government to exercise seventeen specific powers, including the power to "regulate commerce . . . among the several States" and to "lay and collect taxes . . . to pay the debts and provide for the common defense and general welfare," as well as to possess all powers "necessary and proper for carrying into execution the foregoing powers." They then stipulated in Article 6 that the "Constitution, and the Laws of the United States which shall be made in pursuance thereof . . . shall be the Supreme Law of the Land." At the same time, few delegates were willing to permit the central government to exercise plenary power, which was a point that James Madison made clear in *Federalist* No. 39, when he wrote that the federal government's jurisdiction "extends to certain enumerated objects only, and leaves to the several States a residuary and inviolable sovereignty over all other objects."[2] The Tenth Amendment reaffirms this position: "The powers not delegated to the United States by the Constitution, nor prohibited by it to the States, are reserved to the States respectively, or to the people."

Although these constitutional provisions settled a number of important issues, they left several questions unresolved and raised still others. It was not entirely clear, for instance, who would be responsible for determining whether a federal law had been "made in pursuance" of the Constitution. Would this task be entrusted solely to the Supreme Court or would state legislatures be permitted to make such a determination? In addition, it was not readily apparent how one ought to interpret the term *commerce* or the phrase *necessary and proper,* each of which admitted of various meanings and could be construed in a broad or narrow fashion.

The first of these issues, which turned out to be the dominant issue in U.S. politics between 1789 and 1865, was resolved primarily through the political, rather than the judicial, process. On a number of occasions during this period, state legislatures issued resolutions claiming the right to determine whether Congress had exceeded its powers. Virginia and Kentucky were the first states to issue such resolutions when they urged the various state legislatures to join forces in opposing the Alien and Sedition Acts of 1798. Several New England states also issued resolutions along these lines out of dissatisfaction with the Embargo Act of 1807 and the War of 1812. South Carolina then took up and extended this line of argument when it responded to the enactment of several federal tariffs in 1828 and 1832 by asserting the right of individual states to nullify acts of Congress.

Although the Supreme Court did not intervene in any of these particular disputes, the legitimacy of independent state legislative interpretation of Congress's constitutional powers was resolved nevertheless.[3] A majority of state legislatures responded to the Virginia and Kentucky resolutions by arguing, as the New Hampshire legislature proclaimed in its 1799 reply, that "the State Legislatures are not the proper tribunals to determine the constitutionality of the laws of the general government; [and] that the duty of such decision is properly and exclusively confided to the judicial department."[4] State legislatures were no more supportive of South Carolina's Ordinance of Nullification in 1832, and with the repeal of this ordinance in 1833 "the use of nullification as a means of resolving constitutional disputes was decisively rejected."[5] By 1865, few states were in a position to maintain that state legislatures had a role to play in determining whether Congress had exceeded its constitutional powers.

The Court played a more significant role in resolving the second outstanding issue—whether constitutional grants of power to Congress should be construed in a broad or narrow fashion. Here as well, though, it is important to be clear about the extent of the influence of the Court's two landmark decisions in *McCulloch v. Maryland* (1819) and *Gibbons v. Ogden* (1824). In *McCulloch*, the principal issue was whether Congress had exceeded its powers by creating a national bank. By the time the case was argued before the Court, the constitutionality and desirability of a bank had been debated at great length by members of the legislative and executive branches. The first national bank had been approved by Congress and signed into law by President George Washington in 1791, at the urging of Secretary of the Treasury Alexander Hamilton and over the objections of Secretary of State Thomas Jefferson and Rep. James Madison. Although the bank's initial twenty-year charter was permit-

ted to expire in 1811, a second national bank was signed into law for another twenty years by President Madison in 1816.

In this context, the Marshall Court's decision in 1819 to uphold the constitutionality of the bank (and to prevent the state of Maryland from taxing the local branch) had little effect on the long-standing controversy surrounding its legitimacy. To be sure, had the Court's decision come down differently, it would have brought an immediate halt to the operation of the bank. In addition, the Court's broad reading of the necessary and proper clause had important long-term effects insofar as future Congresses (and Courts) would come to rely on Marshall's statement that "the sound construction of the constitution must allow to the national legislature that discretion, with respect to the means by which the powers it confers are to be carried into execution, which will enable that body to perform the high duties assigned to it, in the manner most beneficial to the people."[6] As things turned out, however, the bank controversy was eventually resolved through the political process. A bill to recharter the bank for a third time was vetoed by President Andrew Jackson in 1832, thereby bringing about its end, even in the face of the Court's ruling.

In *Gibbons v. Ogden,* the Marshall Court had its first opportunity to interpret the commerce clause. The Court was asked to decide whether a steamboat license obtained pursuant to a 1793 congressional act took precedence over a license obtained through a monopoly granted by the New York legislature. The principal effect of the Court's holding—that congressional power over commerce "cannot stop at the external boundary line of each State, but may be introduced into the interior," and that state laws would be deemed illegitimate if they came "in direct collision with" this grant of congressional authority[7]—was to establish a precedent by which future Courts could invalidate *state* laws that interfered with interstate commerce. In a series of cases over the next several decades, the Marshall Court (1801–1835) and the Taney Court (1836–1864) proceeded to determine whether state laws were best understood as regulations of interstate commerce, in which case they were generally invalidated, or whether they fell within the "completely internal commerce of a state," which, Marshall allowed, could "be considered as reserved for the state itself."[8]

With regard to the extent of *congressional* power, however, the Court's decision in *Gibbons* had a rather limited effect, at least during much of the nineteenth century. To be sure, the language of Marshall's opinion was quite conducive to future exercises of congressional power. He referred to the commerce power as "supreme, unlimited, and plenary," and he disclaimed judicial responsibility for superintending congressional exercise of this power, on the ground that "[t]he wisdom and the discretion of Congress, their identity with the people, and the influence which their constituents possess at election, are . . . the sole restraints on which they have relied, to secure them from its abuse."[9] Felix Frankfurter noted many years later in assessing the consequences of *Gibbons,* however, "Except in the limited fields of the tariff and the hotly contested proposals of internal improvements, government was not yet thought of as a directing agent of social and economic policies."[10] As a result, nineteenth-century Congresses did not take much advantage of the Court's generous interpretation of the commerce clause.

The Court in the Progressive Era

By the close of the nineteenth century, the federal government had come increasingly to be seen as responsible for directing social and economic policies, as a result of the growth in the number and power of interstate corporations and the belief on the part of many citizens that government regulation was the most effective means of restraining these corporations. In many instances, citizens turned to state governments for relief, and state legislatures responded by regulating railroads and trusts, setting limits on working hours, and establishing workmen's compensation systems. In some cases, however, state legislatures were thought to be unable to deal adequately with corporations that did business across state lines, and in these instances Congress was called upon to take action, leading to the passage of a number of statutes: the Interstate Commerce Act of 1887 and the Sherman Anti-Trust Act of 1890, for regulating railroad rates and monopolistic trade practices, respectively; the Safety Appliance Act of 1893, the Erdman Act of 1898, and the Federal Employers' Liability Act of 1906, for regulating the working conditions of employees of interstate carriers; and the Anti-Lottery Act of 1895, the Pure Food and Drug Act of 1906, the White Slave Traffic Act of 1910, and the Child Labor Act of 1916, to prohibit the transportation of various goods or persons across state lines. Finally, Congress provided for an income tax as part of the Wilson Tariff Act of 1894, in part to fund the new regulatory agencies and activities.

Although several of these statutes were sustained—the Anti-Lottery Act, Pure Food and Drug Act, and White Slave Traffic Act—and some that were struck down were quickly revised and upheld—the Federal Employers' Liability Act—conservative majorities on the Fuller Court (1888–1910) and White Court (1910–1921) invalidated or significantly restricted the reach of several important statutes, whether on the ground that they exceeded congressional power under the commerce clause or taxing and spending clause or because they encroached on powers reserved to the states by the Tenth Amendment. Although in each instance the Court's ruling was eventually overcome, some of these reversals were several decades in the making, such that the Progressive Era Court had the effect of delaying the enactment of certain national policies for significant periods of time.[11]

The Court's decision in *Pollock v. Farmers' Loan and Trust Co.* (1895) delayed a federal income tax for nearly two decades. In this case the Court invalidated a recently enacted federal income tax on the ground that Congress had run afoul of the constitutional requirement that direct taxes be collected in proportion to each state's population. In invalidating the statute, which imposed a 2 percent tax on incomes over $4,000, the Court made it clear that any congressional response to the ruling must be in the form of a constitutional amendment. Chief Justice Melville Fuller argued, "The ultimate sovereignty may be thus called into play by a slow and deliberate process, which gives time for mere hypothesis and opinion to exhaust themselves, and for the sober second thought of every part of the country to be asserted."[12] The process of securing such an amendment was indeed a deliberate one. It was not until 1913, a full eighteen years after the Court's decision, that the Sixteenth Amendment was ratified and Congress gained the authority to reenact the tax.

In *United States v. E. C. Knight Co.* (1895), the Court held that the Sherman Act could not be used to prevent the American Sugar Refining Company from gaining a monopoly over the sugar refining business. In issuing its decision, the Court not only prevented the federal government from regulating the sugar trust but also made it more difficult for Congress to regulate various other businesses during this period by virtue of a distinction it introduced between commerce (which could be regulated by Congress) and manufacturing (which was seen as falling outside the reach of congressional power). As Fuller argued, "Commerce succeeds to manufacture, and is not a part of it."[13] It was not until a decade later, in *Swift & Co. v. United States* (1905), a case involving regulation of the Chicago meat-packing industry, that the Court agreed to permit congressional regulation of business practices that could be considered part of a "current of commerce among the States," which was a standard that proved somewhat more favorable to federal trust-busting efforts.[14]

In *Hammer v. Dagenhart* (1918), the Court invalidated the Child Labor Act on the ground that "[i]t not only transcends the authority delegated to Congress over commerce but also exerts a power as to a purely local matter to which the federal authority does not extend."[15] Although Congress responded quickly by enacting the Child Labor Tax Law of 1919, which would have required companies to pay a 10 percent tax on the proceeds of all goods manufactured by underage workers, the Court invalidated this law as well in *Bailey v. Drexel Furniture Co.* (1922). The Court concluded that if such a tax were sustained, "all that Congress would need to do, hereafter, in seeking to take over to its control any one of the great number of subjects of public interest, jurisdiction of which the States have never parted with, and which are reserved to them by the Tenth Amendment, would be to enact a detailed measure of complete regulation of the subject and enforce it by a so-called tax upon departures from it. To give such magic to the word 'tax' would be to break down all constitutional limitation of the powers of Congress and completely wipe out the sovereignty of the States."[16] Congress eventually responded in a different fashion by proposing a constitutional amendment to authorize federal regulation of child labor, but a decade and a half later the amendment had been ratified by only twenty-eight of the requisite thirty-six state legislatures. It was not until 1941—twenty-three years after the Court had originally invalidated the Child Labor Act—that a reconstituted Court finally overruled *Dagenhart*.

The New Deal Court

During the 1920s Congress considered various proposals to go beyond merely regulating businesses and shipments that crossed state lines and to assume primary responsibility for such problems as the alleviation of agricultural surpluses and the provision of electric power for various regions of the country. In several instances, extensions of federal authority into these areas were approved, but other proposals were vetoed because they exceeded the limits of congressional power. By the 1930s, however, after several years of the Great Depression and the election of President Franklin Delano Roosevelt, Congress was prepared to approve, and Roosevelt was quick to sign into law, a number of measures requiring a significant expansion of federal authority. Among the statutes enacted during Roosevelt's first term were the National Industrial Recovery Act of 1933, Agricultural Adjustment Act of 1933, Tennessee Valley Authority Act of 1933, Municipal Bankruptcy Act of 1934, Railroad Retirement Act of 1934, National Labor Relations Act of 1935, Bituminous Coal Conservation Act of 1935, Public Utility Holding Company Act of 1935, and Social Security Act of 1935. These laws were intended for a variety of purposes, including the development of industry codes of conduct and competition, the boosting of farm prices, the protection of the right of unions to engage in collective bargaining, the regulation of assorted business practices, and the provision of pensions and unemployment benefits for workers. The common thread underlying these statutes, however, was a belief that the federal government should assume responsibility for regulating various aspects of the economy that had previously been regulated, if at all, by state governments.

Each of these statutes was eventually challenged in the Supreme Court, just as many of the expansions of congressional power during the Progressive Era had been challenged. Whereas the Fuller and White Courts during the Progressive Era invalidated a relatively small number of the federal statutes adopted over a period of several decades, the Hughes Court (1930–1941) struck down a significant percentage of the federal statutes that it considered in the two terms between 1934 and 1936. As Fred Rodell notes, "Never before Franklin Roosevelt's time had the Court taken almost the entire governmental program of a contemporary President . . . and vetoed it law by law—as the Justices did with the first New Deal."[17] To be sure, several important programs were sustained, such as the Tennessee Valley Authority Act, but far more statutes were overturned, because they were deemed to exceed Congress's enumerated powers, were in violation of the nondelegation doctrine, or encroached on powers reserved to the states. The 1934–1935 term brought *Panama Refining Co. v. Ryan* (1935) and the invalidation of a provision of the National Industrial Recovery Act dealing with the petroleum industry; *Railroad Retirement Board v. Alton* (1935), and the overturning of the Railroad Retirement Act; and *A. L. A. Schechter Poultry Corp. v. United States* (1935), which brought an end to the National Recovery Administration and prompted Roosevelt to complain about the Court's "horse-and-buggy definition of interstate commerce."[18] In the following term, the Court handed down *United States v. Butler* (1936), which invalidated the Agricultural Adjustment Act; *Carter v. Carter Coal Co.* (1936), which overturned the Bituminous Coal Conservation Act; and *Ashton v. Cameron County Water Improvement District* (1936), which struck down the Municipal Bankruptcy Act. The "Four Horsemen"—Justices Pierce Butler, James McReynolds, George Sutherland, and Willis Van Devanter—were determined opponents of all of these measures, and they were joined in each of these decisions by Justice Owen Roberts, in several instances by Chief Justice Charles Evans Hughes, and in one case by every member of the Court.

Roosevelt chose not to publicly criticize the Court after this second round of decisions, but in light of the challenges still pending against the National Labor Relations Act and Social Security Act, he conferred with his advisors about ways in which he might respond to the Court and preserve these programs. Several of the proposals discussed were similar to options that had been considered by Progressive Era critics of the Court, including altering the Court's appellate jurisdiction, requiring a supermajority of the justices to invalidate congressional statutes, and drafting a constitutional amendment to authorize Congress to legislate in a wider range of areas.[19] Eventually, Roosevelt settled on the idea of adding an extra justice for every sitting justice over the age of seventy. In February 1937, several weeks after his second inauguration, he submitted his proposal to Congress.

By July 1937 the Senate had for all practical purposes rejected the Court-packing scheme, but Roosevelt succeeded nonetheless in securing approval for nearly all of his New Deal measures. In the short term, he benefited from Justice Roberts's shift from being a consistent opponent to a reliable supporter of New Deal measures. Although the precise timing and motivation of Roberts's "switch in time that saved nine" are still debated by constitutional historians, there is no denying the consequences, as Roberts cast the decisive votes to uphold the National Labor Relations Act in *NLRB v. Jones & Laughlin Steel Corp.* (1937) and the unemployment compensation and old-age insurance provisions of the Social Security Act in the cases of *Steward Machine Co. v. Davis* (1937) and *Helvering v. Davis* (1937).[20] Beginning in late 1937 and continuing for the next six years, Roosevelt, who had been the only president to serve a full term and not fill a vacancy on the Court, got the opportunity to make more appointments than any president since Washington.

With the contours of the Roosevelt Court beginning to take shape, and with the expectation that the justices would look more favorably on federal regulation of workers' hours and wages, Congress passed the Fair Labor Standards Act of 1938, which was sustained three years later. The Court also proceeded to sustain a number of statutes that had been initially invalidated and subsequently revised by Congress. In the case of the Municipal Bankruptcy Act of 1937, the revised statute was not markedly different from the one that had been struck down several years earlier. In other cases, such as the Bituminous Coal Act of 1937, the Railroad Retirement Act of 1937, and the Agricultural Adjustment Act of 1938, Congress changed the statutes in some fashion to comply with the Court's earlier directive. Ultimately, the National Recovery Administration was the only invalidated program from this period that was not revived after 1937, and this was due to a lack of political support for rewriting the measure.[21]

In the early 1940s the Court signaled in a pair of unanimous rulings that it was unlikely to look favorably on any future challenges to the expansion of congressional power. As Justice Harlan Fiske Stone made clear in *United States v. Darby* (1941), while upholding the Fair Labor Standards Act, "The power of Congress over interstate commerce is not confined to the regulation of commerce among the states. It extends to those activities intrastate

which so affect interstate commerce or the exercise of the power of Congress over it as to make regulation of them appropriate means to the attainment of a legitimate end."[22] In addition, congressional powers were not to be limited in any way by the Tenth Amendment, which, Stone argued, "states but a truism that all is retained which has not been surrendered."[23] Moreover, in *Wickard v. Filburn* (1942), Justice Robert Jackson suggested, in the course of rejecting a challenge to an application of the revised version of the Agricultural Adjustment Act, that it was time for the Court to heed Chief Justice John Marshall's longstanding admonition that restraint on congressional exercise of the commerce power should "proceed from political rather than from judicial processes."[24]

There is no denying that for a two-year period in the mid-1930s, the Supreme Court exerted a significant influence on the balance of power between the federal and state governments, especially insofar as judicial influence is equated with the number and significance of congressional statutes invalidated. To the extent that judicial influence is measured by the length of time that the Court is able to delay the expansion of congressional power, however, the New Deal Court exerted somewhat less influence, especially in comparison with the Progressive Era Court, given that the decisions of the New Deal Court were overcome rather quickly in nearly every case.

The Warren Court

In the decades following the New Deal and World War II, the federal government assumed an even greater degree of responsibility for promoting the economic welfare, as a growing number of citizens came to believe that a national economy required direction from the national government. In the 1950s and 1960s concerns about deprivations of civil rights and liberties in various states, especially in the South, generated additional pressures in favor of centralizing power in the federal government. Scholars, judges, and, occasionally, elected officials began to argue that it was intolerable that some individuals, particularly African Americans, did not enjoy the same rights as other individuals within the same state and that individuals in some states did not enjoy the same rights as individuals in other states. Consequently, they supported the adoption of a national standard that would apply to all individuals, regardless of their race or place of residence. Although some individuals still sought to defend the traditional arrangement under which state officials were primarily responsible for defining and securing individual rights, this position came to be viewed as increasingly untenable. Much more influential during this period was the view expressed by William Riker to the effect that "if in the United States one approves of Southern white racists, then one should approve of American federalism," but "if in the United States one disapproves of racism, one should disapprove of federalism."[25]

To a significant extent during this period, the Warren Court (1953–1969) imposed national standards in regard to civil rights and liberties without much participation from Congress. In several cases, including *Brown v. Board of Education* (1954) and subsequent school desegregation rulings that substantially reduced the degree of state and local control over attendance policies, the Court's decisions were grounded in the equal protection clause of the Fourteenth Amendment. This also formed the basis of the Court's decision in *Reynolds v. Sims* (1964) as well as various other reapportionment rulings requiring state officials to conform to a national policy of one man, one vote in drawing legislative districts. In other cases, the Court continued its project of "incorporating" the Bill of Rights into the due process clause of the Fourteenth Amendment, thereby requiring states to abide by the Court's interpretation of the free speech clause, as in *Roth v. United States* (1957); the religious establishment clause, as in *Engel v. Vitale* (1962); and, especially, the various rights accorded to criminal defendants, as in *Mapp v. Ohio* (1961) and *Miranda v. Arizona* (1966). On each of these occasions, the Court played an independent and significant role in expanding the extent of federal supervision of state courts and legislatures.

In several other instances, Congress took the lead in imposing national standards, and the Warren Court's primary contribution was to remove any uncertainty about the legitimacy of these measures that had been occasioned by previous Court decisions. The first such case derived from the passage of the Civil Rights Act of 1964. A majority of the members of Congress recognized the necessity for a federal law prohibiting racial discrimination in hotels, restaurants, and other establishments. During hearings and debates about the bill, however, several senators raised questions about whether Congress had the power to act in this area given that Congress had at one time sought to regulate similar conduct, by enacting the Civil Rights Act of 1875, and the Court had invalidated it in the *Civil Rights Cases* (1883) for exceeding congressional power under the enforcement clauses of the Thirteenth and Fourteenth Amendments. Despite this history, Congress approved the Civil Rights Act of 1964, arguing that the statute was a legitimate exercise of the commerce power as well as the Fourteenth Amendment. When the Supreme Court heard a pair of challenges to the act later that year, in *Heart of Atlanta Motel v. United States* (1964) and *Katzenbach v. McClung* (1964), the justices unanimously declared that the decision in the *Civil Rights Cases* was "inapposite, and without precedential value in determining the constitutionality of the present Act." Justice Tom Clark explained that "the power of Congress to promote interstate commerce also includes the power to regulate the local incidents thereof, including local activities . . . which might have a substantial and harmful effect upon that commerce." Moreover, he declared that the decision about how best to regulate these activities was "a matter of policy that rests entirely with the Congress not with the courts."[26]

The next year, Congress enacted an equally expansive statute, the Voting Rights Act of 1965, in an effort "to rid the country of racial discrimination in voting."[27] In this area as well, the nineteenth-century Congress had sought to make use of federal power to prevent intimidation and obstruction of African American voters, such as when it passed the Enforcement Act of 1870. Here as well, the nineteenth-century Court had limited the reach of the act, determining in *United States v. Reese* (1875) and *United States v. Cruikshank* (1875) that portions of the act exceeded congressional powers

under the enforcement clauses of the Fourteenth and Fifteenth Amendments. The Voting Rights Act of 1965 was a much more comprehensive statute, and several of its provisions were soon challenged on the ground that they exceeded Congress's powers and intruded on powers reserved to the states. The Court made it clear, however, that it would not stand in the way of Congress's pursuit of the goals embodied in the act. Chief Justice Earl Warren explained in *South Carolina v. Katzenbach* that "[a]s against the reserved powers of the States, Congress may use any rational means to effectuate the constitutional prohibition of racial discrimination in voting," and therefore the Voting Rights Act was "a valid means for carrying out the commands of the Fifteenth Amendment."[28]

The Warren Court's decisions in these cases could be considered a continuation of the approach followed by the Marshall Court a century and a half earlier, insofar as both Courts adhered to broad interpretations of the constitutional powers granted to Congress. In terms of the influence of their decisions, however, the Warren Court's decisions had much more direct and significant consequences. As noted above, Congress did not make much use of the Marshall Court's broad interpretations of the commerce power and the necessary and proper clause until many years later, because there was little expectation that the federal government would assume more responsibilities than it already had. By the mid-twentieth-century, however, the public had begun to look first and foremost to the federal government to address national problems, and Congress was well prepared to take full advantage of the Warren Court's broad interpretations of the commerce power and the enforcement clauses of the Civil War amendments to respond to this desire.

The Rehnquist Court

When William Rehnquist became chief justice in 1986, there was little reason to expect that the Supreme Court would place many barriers in the way of the expansion of congressional power. To be sure, a decade and a half earlier in *Oregon v. Mitchell* (1970), the Court had ruled that Congress had exceeded its powers under the enforcement clause of the Fourteenth Amendment when it reduced the voting age to eighteen in state and local elections. This ruling, however, was overturned six months later with the passage of the Twenty-sixth Amendment. It was also the case that a Rehnquist-authored opinion in *National League of Cities v. Usery* (1976) had invoked the Tenth Amendment to prevent Congress from applying the Fair Labor Standards Act to state and local governments. This ruling, however, was overturned nine years later, when Justice Harry Blackmun, who had voted in the majority in *Usery,* reversed course and wrote the majority opinion in *Garcia v. San Antonio Metropolitan Transit Authority* (1985), which brought an end to this brief effort to prevent Congress from regulating the states in areas of "traditional government functions." In fact, Blackmun's ruling in *Garcia* went farther than any previous majority opinion—including Marshall's opinion in *Gibbons,* Stone's opinion in *Darby,* and Clark's opinion in *Heart of Atlanta*—in declaring that the Court should no longer be in the business of protecting the states against congressional encroachment. As he argued, "State sovereign interests . . . are more properly protected by procedural safeguards inherent in the structure of the federal system than by judicially created limitations on federal power."[29] By the mid-1980s, therefore, there was little reason to expect the Court to be concerned with scrutinizing congressional expansion of power, a view seemingly confirmed when the Rehnquist Court issued its first important federalism decision in *South Dakota v. Dole* (1987), concluding, by a 7-2 vote in a majority opinion written by the chief justice, that Congress was well within its taxing and spending power when it ordered states to raise their drinking age to twenty-one or lose a percentage of their federal transportation funds.

Certainly, few members of Congress expected the Rehnquist Court to be vigorous in enforcing the Constitution's federalism clauses. For most of American history, Congress had conscientiously specified the constitutional clause that legitimated the passage of a particular statute, and congressional committees had been quite diligent in building an evidentiary record to justify the need for federal action in a given area. By the early 1990s, however, Congress had become less and less preoccupied with these matters. When the media began to take note of the presence of guns in and around schools, for instance, members of Congress responded by enacting the Gun-Free School Zones Act of 1990, which made it a federal crime to possess a gun within a thousand feet of a school. Although Congress might have been able to amass evidence to demonstrate that guns in schools affected interstate commerce and that existing state laws were incapable of addressing this problem, there was little reason to go to the trouble given the

Court's deferential approach to the exercise of congressional power in preceding years. As J. Mitchell Pickerill has reported, the Gun-Free School Zones Act was not so much the product of a concern with remedying defects in existing state laws, but rather was the result of a discussion among several Senate staffers, one of whom later explained, "[W]e were just thinking that we wanted to do something in the realm of gun control that we thought could win. And we were sort of kicking around a bunch of ideas, and we thought gee, there was a drug free school zone law, and in Congress we don't generally reinvent the wheel, we just copy good ideas. So why don't we create gun free school zones?"[30] The idea was eventually "introduced on the floor of the Senate, incorporated into the Crime Control Act of 1990 by voice vote, passed both houses of Congress easily, and signed into law by the President" without ever having been "formally debated on the floor of either House." In fact, "[n]owhere in the public record is there evidence that Congress considered the constitutional issue" of whether the law was a legitimate exercise of the commerce power.[31]

In 1992, when the Washington, D.C., area suffered a spate of carjackings, including one high-profile incident in which a woman was dragged to her death by a car thief, Congress responded that year by approving the Anti Car Theft Act and making carjacking a federal crime. In this particular instance, Congress held hearings and solicited testimony about the need for federal legislation, as it would in the cases of the Religious Freedom Restoration Act of 1993 (requiring state and local governments to satisfy a "compelling interest" before burdening an individual's exercise of religion), the

Brady Handgun Violence Prevention Act of 1993 (requiring local law enforcement officials to perform background checks on all prospective handgun buyers), and the Violence Against Women Act of 1994 (providing, in part, for a federal civil remedy for victims of gender-motivated violence). Even so, with the partial exception of the Violence Against Women Act, there was relatively little discussion of whether these measures could be considered legitimate exercises of congressional power under the Constitution.[32]

In the mid-1990s, after several more Reagan and Bush appointees had been named to the Supreme Court, a reliable five-justice majority began to strike down a number of these statutes. This renewed attention to congressional power was in part due to a belief by several justices—Rehnquist, Anthony Kennedy, Sandra Day O'Connor, Antonin Scalia, and Clarence Thomas—that Congress had begun exceeding the already quite generous precedents in this area. In addition, at least one of these justices, Thomas, disagreed with several of these precedents and was eager to reopen the long-dormant debate about their legitimacy. Regardless of the motivation, a bare majority of the Rehnquist Court signaled that it was prepared to be vigilant in enforcing the Constitution's federalism clauses. The commerce clause was deemed insufficient to permit congressional expansions of power in *United States v. Lopez* (1995), which invalidated the Gun-Free School Zones Act, and *United States v. Morrison* (2000), which invalidated the civil remedy provision of the Violence Against Women Act. The enforcement clause of the Fourteenth Amendment was implicated not only in *Morrison*, but also in *City of Boerne v.*

Flores (1997), in which the Court struck down the Religious Freedom Restoration Act insofar as it applied to state and local governments. Meanwhile, the Tenth Amendment served as the basis of the Court's invalidation of a portion of the Low-Level Radioactive Waste Policy Amendments Act in *New York v. United States* (1992) as well as the background check provision of the Brady Act in *Printz v. United States* (1997).

Although the sheer number of congressional statutes invalidated since the mid-1990s might suggest that the Rehnquist Court rivals the Progressive Era Court or the New Deal Court in the extent of its influence on the reach of congressional power, to this point in time the Rehnquist Court's federalism decisions have not been nearly as influential as the decisions rendered by the earlier courts. There is no denying that the Rehnquist Court's federalism decisions have departed in significant respects from rulings issued by previous courts, but a closer examination of the context and consequences of these decisions is helpful for guarding against the temptation (to which both supporters and critics of these rulings have succumbed) to overstate their political significance.

It is important to consider the overall record of the Rehnquist Court in these kinds of cases. As Mark Killenbeck points out, there is "a world of difference between the record fashioned by the pre-1937 Court and that of the Rehnquist Court to date, which has sustained at least as many measures as it has overturned."[33] In fact, whereas in the two-year period between 1934 and 1936 the New Deal Court relied on the commerce clause and the Tenth Amendment to strike down more of Roosevelt's legislative initiatives than it upheld, in the decade between

1992 and 2002 the Rehnquist Court invalidated portions of only two congressional statutes on commerce clause grounds and of two other statutes on Tenth Amendment grounds. Among the many laws that have raised concerns among judges in lower federal courts but have been left undisturbed by the Rehnquist Court are the Child Support Recovery Act, the National Voter Registration Act, and the Driver's Privacy Protection Act.

It is also important to consider the consequences of the Rehnquist Court's federalism rulings for other actors in the political system. When the Fuller Court emasculated the Sherman Act and the White Court ruled against the Child Labor Act, the justices overturned regulations that were central to the political program of the Progressive reformers. Likewise, when the Hughes Court struck down the Agricultural Adjustment Act and the National Industrial Recovery Act, the justices stood in the way of legislation at the heart of the New Deal. It is not so easy to characterize the importance of the Gun-Free School Zones Act, the Religious Freedom Restoration Act, the background check provision of the Brady Act, or the civil remedy provision of the Violence Against Women Act. Certainly, these statutes did not lack for supporters, many of whom were deeply disappointed by the Court's rulings invalidating them. At the same time, as Keith Whittington notes, these measures "do not represent the central legislative goals of any particular political coalition," and the Court's decisions have "had no particular implication for any broad legislative agenda."[34] At the least, one would have to distinguish between the degree to which the measures invalidated by the Rehnquist Court were central to the political debates in the 1990s and the degree to which the measures invalidated by the Progressive Era and New Deal Courts struck at the heart of contemporary political programs.

An assessment of the significance of the Rehnquist Court's federalism decisions must take account, finally, of the extent to which Congress has been able to overcome the effects of these rulings. Although it will be some time before a final verdict can be reached on this matter, it does not appear that these decisions have placed insurmountable barriers in the way of congressional regulatory efforts. In the aftermath of the invalidation of the Gun-Free School Zones Act, Congress turned around a year later and enacted a revised statute that applies to any individual possessing a firearm that has moved through interstate commerce. Three years after the Court struck down the Religious Freedom Restoration Act, Congress responded by enacting a somewhat narrower version, the revised focus of which was expressed in its new title, the Religious Land Use and Institutionalized Persons Act. After the invalidation of the background check provision of the Brady Act, Congress saw no need to respond because it had always intended that the local background checks would be a temporary measure; within a year of the Court's decision, a national computerized background check system was up and running, as scheduled. Finally, although Congress has not yet responded to the invalidation of the civil remedy provision of the Violence Against Women Act in 2000, members of the House of Representatives drafted a Violence Against Women Civil Rights Restoration Act later that year that was intended to comply with the Court's decision and that would achieve many of the goals of

the original statute.[35]

To conclude that the effects of the Rehnquist Court's federalism decisions have been modest is not to say that these rulings have been inconsequential.[36] The Rehnquist Court has made a difference insofar as the justices have signaled to members of Congress that it is no longer enough for them to justify the passage of a congressional statute by merely pointing to the existence of a national problem that has attracted media attention. Members of Congress have, in effect, been put on notice that they will have to demonstrate that the statute is a legitimate exercise of an enumerated power and that it does not encroach on any powers reserved to the states, and moreover, that congressional judgments will not necessarily be treated as final. These decisions have also had the effect of encouraging the efforts of various members of Congress, as well as other groups and individuals, who seek to limit federal power and expand the role of state governments. It is in this sense that the Rehnquist Court's federalism decisions have been influential, not so much in placing a temporary veto on a presidential program, as in the New Deal, or in delaying for several decades the passage of important legislation, as in the Progressive Era, but rather in signaling that statutes whose constitutionality had previously been taken for granted would be reviewed carefully and in emboldening political actors committed to limiting congressional power in various areas.

Conclusion

Taking account of the context and consequences of Supreme Court federalism decisions makes it possible to distinguish among the various ways in which Court decisions have been influential in the course of U.S history. It is not enough to say that the Court has alternated between sustaining and limiting congressional power in regard to the states. One must also consider the significance of the statutes that were upheld or struck down as well as the extent to which Congress has been able to overcome the effects of these decisions.

The Marshall Court and the Warren Court both issued decisions that sustained important congressional statutes. The Marshall Court approved several statutes whose constitutionality was uncertain because they raised novel questions of law. Many years later, the Warren Court legitimized various statutes whose constitutionality was in question due to previous judicial decisions. Because the Warren Court handed down its decisions at a time when Congress was much more prepared than in previous times to take advantage of generous interpretations of congressional power, however, its decisions were much more influential than those handed down by the Marshall Court.

The Progressive Era Court, early New Deal Court, and Rehnquist Court each invalidated a number of congressional statutes, but to quite different effects. The Progressive Era Court was the most influential, in that it delayed the enactment of several important statutes for as long as several decades. The New Deal Court also proved to be quite influential because of its brief but wide-ranging assault on the major components of a presidential program. The Rehnquist Court has not struck down any statutes that rise to the significance of the measures invalidated in either the Progressive Era or the New Deal or occasioned the sorts of lengthy delays in the reenactment of statutes as were seen in the Progressive Era, but it has been influential nevertheless, insofar as it has forced Congress to be more conscious of the Constitution's federalism clauses and the Court's interpretations of those clauses.

Notes

1. Alexander Hamilton, James Madison, and John Jay, *The Federalist Papers* ed. Clinton Rossiter (New York: Mentor, 1999), 80.
2. Ibid., 213.
3. The Court's involvement during this period was limited to issuing several decisions that established the supremacy of the federal courts over state legislatures and courts. On several occasions between 1809 and 1821, the legislatures and courts of Pennsylvania and Virginia, among other states, claimed the power to interpret federal law independently of the federal judiciary. In a series of cases, the Marshall Court issued a clear rejection of these claims: *United States v. Peters,* 9 U.S. 115 (1809), *Martin v. Hunter's Lessee,* 14 U.S. 304 (1816), and *Cohens v. Virginia,* 19 U.S. 264 (1821).
4. Herman V. Ames, *State Documents on Federal Relations: The States and the United States* (Philadelphia: University of Pennsylvania, 1906), 25.
5. Keith E. Whittington, *Constitutional Construction: Divided Powers and Constitutional Meaning* (Cambridge, Mass.: Harvard University Press, 1999), 112.
6. *McCulloch v. Maryland,* 17 U.S. 316, 421 (1819).
7. *Gibbons v. Ogden,* 22 U.S. 1, 194, 221 (1824).
8. Ibid., 195.
9. Ibid., 59, 185.
10. Felix Frankfurter, *The Commerce Clause under Marshall, Taney and Waite* (1937; repr. Chicago: Quadrangle Books, 1964), 39. This point about the limited effects of these Marshall Court rulings is made more recently in Stephen M. Griffin, "Constitutional Theory Transformed," *Yale Law Journal* 108 (1999): 2115, 2121–2129.

11. In addition to the cases discussed below, one could also point to *Cincinnati, New Orleans and Texas Pacific Railway Co. v. ICC,* 162 U.S. 184 (1896), in which the Court prevented the Interstate Commerce Commission from setting railroad rates for nearly a decade. One could also take note of *Adair v. United States,* 208 U.S. 161 (1908), in which the Court struck down a provision of the Erdman Act of 1898 that prohibited interstate carriers from issuing yellow-dog contracts, whereby workers were hired only if they agreed not to join a union. This decision effectively prevented for several decades the enactment of federal legislation protecting the right to unionize.

12. *Pollock v. Farmers' Loan and Trust Co.,* 158 U.S. 601, 635 (1895).

13. *United States v. E. C. Knight Co.,* 156 U.S. 1, 112 (1895).

14. *Swift & Co. v. United States,* 196 U.S. 375, 398 (1905).

15. *Hammer v. Dagenhart,* 247 U.S. 251, 276 (1918).

16. *Bailey v. Drexel Furniture Co.,* 259 U.S. 20, 38 (1922).

17. Fred Rodell, *Nine Men: A Political History of the Supreme Court of the United States from 1790 to 1955* (New York: Random House, 1955), 214.

18. *The Public Papers and Addresses of Franklin D. Roosevelt,* ed. Samuel I. Rosenman (New York: Random House, 1938), 4:221.

19. A comprehensive discussion of the Court-curbing proposals that were considered during the Progressive Era and the New Deal can be found in William G. Ross, *A Muted Fury: Populists, Progressives, and Labor Unions Confront the Courts: 1890–1937* (Princeton, N.J.: Princeton University Press, 1994).

20. Roberts's change first became apparent in March 1937, when he cast the deciding vote to uphold a state minimum wage law in *West Coast Hotel v. Parrish,* 300 U.S. 379 (1937). The decision in the National Labor Relations Board case was issued in April, and the Social Security Act cases were handed down in May.

21. The congressional responses are discussed in Carl Brent Swisher, *American Constitutional Development,* 2d ed. (New York: Houghton Mifflin, 1954), 920–954; William E. Leuchtenburg, *The Supreme Court Reborn: The Constitutional Revolution in the Age of Roosevelt* (New York: Oxford University Press), 220–228.

22. *United States v. Darby,* 312 U.S. 100, 118 (1941).

23. Ibid., 124.

24. *Wickard v. Filburn,* 317 U.S. 111, 120 (1942).

25. William E. Riker, *Federalism: Origin, Operation, Significance* (Boston: Little, Brown, 1964), 155.

26. *Heart of Atlanta Motel v. United States,* 379 U.S. 241, 250, 258, 261 (1964).

27. *South Carolina v. Katzenbach,* 383 U.S. 301, 315 (1965).

28. Ibid., 324, 337. In *Katzenbach v. Morgan,* 384 U.S. 641 (1966), in the course of resolving another challenge to the Voting Rights Act, the Court offered a similarly expansive interpretation of the enforcement clause of the Fourteenth Amendment.

29. *Garcia v. San Antonio Metropolitan Transit Authority,* 469 U.S. 528, 552 (1985).

30. Quoted in J. Mitchell Pickerill, "Congress and Constitutional Deliberation: The Role of Judicial Review in a Separated System" (Ph.D diss., University of Wisconsin, 2000), 161.

31. Ibid., 2.

32. On the origin of the Anti Car Theft Act, see Liz Spayd, "Tragedy Spurs Call for Tougher Car Theft Laws," *Washington Post,* September 11, 1992, D1. On the debates over the Religious Freedom Restoration Act, see Neal Devins, "Congress as Culprit: How Lawmakers Spurred on the Court's Anti-Congress Crusade," *Duke Law Journal* 51 (2001): 435, 449–450. On the deliberations over the Brady Act and Violence Against Women Act, see Pickerill, "Congress and Constitutional Deliberation," 175–181, 184–188.

33. Mark R. Killenbeck, "Revolution or Retreat?" in *The Tenth Amendment and State Sovereignty: Constitutional History and Contemporary Issues,* ed. Mark R. Killenbeck (Lanham, Md.: Rowman and Littlefield, 2002), 184.

34. Keith E. Whittington, "Taking What They Give Us: Explaining the Court's Federalism Offensive," *Duke Law Journal* 51 (2001): 477, 514, 515.

35. These congressional responses are discussed in more detail in John Dinan, "Congressional

Responses to the Rehnquist Court's Federalism Decisions," *Publius: The Journal of Federalism* (forthcoming).

36. A discussion of the Supreme Court's Eleventh Amendment jurisprudence is beyond the scope of this chapter, but several of the Rehnquist Court's Eleventh Amendment decisions are deserving of mention. In a series of cases handed down since the mid-1990s, the Court invoked the Eleventh Amendment (coupled in some cases with interpretations of the commerce clause and enforcement clause of the Fourteenth Amendment, among other constitutional provisions) to restrict the ability of Congress to permit federal suits to be filed against unconsenting state governments: *Seminole Tribe of Florida v. Florida,* 517 U.S. 44 (1996), *Alden v. Maine,* 527 U.S. 706 (1999), *Florida Prepaid Postsecondary Education Expense Board v. College Savings Bank,* 527 U.S. 627 (1999), *College Savings Bank v. Florida Prepaid Postsecondary Education Expense Board,* 527 U.S. 666 (1999), *Kimel v. Florida,* 528 U.S. 62 (2000), and *Board of Trustees of University of Alabama v. Garrett,* 531 U.S. 356 (2001). Although Congress has a variety of means by which it can overcome the effects of these decisions, at this point in time it has failed to approve any of the proposed statutes that are intended to accomplish this goal.

CHAPTER ELEVEN

Executive Privilege and Congressional and Independent Investigations

NEAL DEVINS

Battles over the executive's obligation to turn over information to lawmakers and prosecutors are legion. Starting with George Washington's 1796 refusal to provide the House of Representatives with correspondence relating to the negotiation of Jay's Treaty, presidents and their legal advisors have argued that neither Congress nor the courts have an unqualified right of access to executive branch materials. Instead, the White House argues that the separation of powers protects the confidentiality of deliberations between the president and top advisors, especially on national security matters.

Congress and independent prosecutors, not surprisingly, advance a much narrower view of presidential prerogatives than does the White House. What is surprising is that the subpoena power—Congress's ultimate weapon for bringing the executive into compliance with its information requests—is very much dependent on executive branch officials. Specifically, were Congress to conclude that such an official was in contempt for failing to comply with a congressional subpoena, the matter would be turned over to the Department of Justice, an executive branch department. In sharp contrast, the raison d'être for the independent prosecutor statute, enacted in 1978 but since expired, was to allow someone outside of the executive branch to seek judicial enforcement of information access requests.

The fact that Congress cannot go into court, however, does not mean that Congress cannot get the information it wants from the executive. Congress and the executive have had a long-standing reliance on negotiation and compromise that has resulted in satisfactory nonjudicial settlements of disputes. Countervailing institutional interests have guided this process, balancing congressional oversight and the executive's control of its own officials and agencies. While the terms of these solutions are often defined by how long and how hard each branch is willing to push its agenda, neither the executive nor Congress is willing to trade concrete political solutions for something as abstract as the defense of executive or legislative prerogatives under the separation of powers. More to the point, Congress and the executive need not worry about the binding effect of the ad hoc deals that they make with each other, which would not be the case if the outcome were litigated. Independent prosecutor investigations, in contrast, were far more likely to produce binding judicial precedents. For this and other reasons, the dance between independent prosecutors and the executive was often bitter and drawn out.

This chapter will describe how it is that Congress and the executive bargain with each other over information access disputes. Moreover, by examining independent prosecutor battles with the president, attention will be called to the virtues of the current arrangement between Congress and the executive. In particular, reform proposals that would create a judicial resolution of conflicts that are now solved without judicial involvement would encourage obstinacy, bitterness, and legal precedents that could stand in the way of future constructive bargaining.

Executive Privilege

The Constitution makes no mention of the president's power to withhold information. This power, instead, is considered ancillary to other presidential powers. For example, the constitutional command to the president to "take Care that the Laws be faithfully executed" has been interpreted by the Department of Justice as an "exclusive [grant of] constitutional authority to enforce federal laws."[1] Thus, according to this argument, the president need not share with Congress conversations held with advisors or memoranda to or from advisors.

When arguing that certain categories of information possessed by the executive branch are privileged and not subject to release, the executive invariably turns to *United States v. Nixon* (1974), the Supreme Court's only ruling on executive privilege. *Nixon* involved President Richard Nixon's efforts to resist a court-ordered subpoena requiring him to turn over tapes and other materials relevant to a grand jury investigation of White House involvement in the failed 1972 burglary at Democratic National Committee headquarters at the Watergate Hotel. In "declin[ing] to obey the command of that subpoena," Nixon argued that the president "is not subject to compulsory process from the courts."[2] Federal district court judge John Sirica rejected this argument, prompting the White House to try to end run the decision by having Attorney General Elliot Richardson dismiss Archibald Cox, the special prosecutor appointed by Richardson to handle the case. Richardson refused and resigned over the issue, but Acting Attorney General Robert Bork ultimately fired Cox on Nixon's order, prompting a public uproar and the call by eighty-four members of Congress for Nixon's impeachment. Responding to these events, Nixon released some of the tapes and had Bork appoint a new prosecutor to the case, Leon Jaworski.

The legal dispute over the release of materials made its way to the Supreme Court after Jaworski went to court seeking sixty-four conversations, most of them involving Nixon, that took place after the Watergate burglary. In *Nixon,* the Court formally recognized that some presidential communications are privileged. At the same time, however, the president's generalized assertion of executive privilege had to yield to the demonstrated, specific need for evidence in a pending criminal trial.

Nixon left open as many questions as it answered. Rather than establishing how courts should balance the competing interests of the president, Congress, and the judiciary, the *Nixon* Court left it for subsequent litigation to detail the precise contours of executive privilege.

Following *Nixon,* executive privilege has generally been defined as the privilege, available only to the president and those acting under the president's orders, to refuse to release information that falls under one of two categories. The first category covers all communications between the president and the president's closest advisors that occur during the process of deliberation and debate on matters coming before the chief executive. The second category comprises information relating to matters that are "within the exclusive province of" the executive branch.

Among the areas protected by the privilege, several are easily identifiable. These include powers that are constitutionally committed to the executive branch, such as details of foreign policy and treaty negotiation, nominations before they are made, possible pardons, and matters of current military significance. Such information is made available at executive discretion and cannot be compelled. Congress may not inquire into deliberative communications between the president and White House advisors so that openness, honesty, trust, and confidentiality will prevail in high-level policy discussions. This rationale was well stated in a 1984 memorandum prepared by the Office of Legal Counsel: "Human experience teaches that those who expect public dissemination of their remarks may well temper candor with a concern for appearances and for their own interests to the detriment of the decisionmaking process."[3]

The Competing Interests of Congress and the Executive

Information access disputes between Congress and the executive are animated by two themes: tension, which makes disputes likely to occur, and cooperation, which moderates potentially explosive conflicts between the branches. Tension is rooted in the ongoing tug-of-war between the executive and Congress over what information access is necessary for Congress to perform its legislative duties or, alternatively, whether information access requests improperly intrude upon the executive's duty to administer governmental programs. Cooperation speaks to the incentives for Congress and the executive to reach an accommodation over information access, namely, Congress's desire to maintain control over executive operations and the executive's concomitant desire for Congress to delegate authority to it through broadly worded legislative mandates.

Tension

Although the Constitution speaks of legislative power being vested in Congress and executive power belonging to the president, it does not demarcate the boundaries that divide executive and legislative powers. Without clear borders, each branch sometimes claims authority for itself that the other sees as its own. The executive often characterizes Congress's desire to expand its lawmaking function as micromanagement, which intrudes upon its power of implementation. From Congress's perspective, the executive seeks to expand its authority to implement into the gray area of lawmaking. Both branches see the Constitution—and their inherent powers under it—as supporting their competing interpretations. This attitude bolsters their willingness to engage in conflict over them.

As noted above, claims of executive privilege are grounded in the belief that legislative inquiries unduly tread into essential executive branch operations. For its part, Congress bases its broad investigatory powers in history and the Constitution's text. Article 1 declares that "[a]ll legislative powers . . . shall be vested in a Congress of the United States." A key element of Congress's ability to carry out this mandate depends on how much information is made available to it as it deliberates and then legislates. At the Constitutional Convention, Virginia delegate George Mason emphasized that members of Congress "are not only Legislators but they possess inquisitorial powers. They must meet frequently to inspect the Conduct of the public offices."[4]

Absent access to accurate, relevant information, it would probably be impossible to legislate effectively or wisely. Woodrow Wilson wrote that Congress's free exercise of its investigative power, especially when applied to gain information from the executive branch, is one of the most important protectors of liberty, as well as being an indispensable element for wise legislation.[5] The Supreme Court, too, has given great weight to the congressional power of inquiry. In *Barenblatt v. United States* (1959), the Court held that the power to inquire and compel response is "as penetrating and far-reaching as the potential power to enact and appropriate under the Constitution."[6] In the words of Chief Justice Earl Warren,

> The power of the Congress to conduct investigations is inherent in the legislative process. That power is broad. It encompasses inquiries concerning the administration of existing laws as well as proposed or possibly needed statutes. It includes surveys of defects in our social, economic or political system for the purpose of enabling the Congress to remedy them. It comprehends probes into departments of the Federal Government to expose corruption, inefficiency or waste.[7]

The subpoena is Congress's sole formal tool for compelling the production of information it desires. The subpoena power has been held to be an "indispensable ingredient" of Congress's legislative powers,[8] for mere requests for information "often are unavailing, and also that information which is volunteered is not always accurate or complete, so some means of compulsion are essential to obtain what is needed."[9] At the same time, "[s]ince Congress may only investigate into those areas in which it may potentially legislate or appropriate, it cannot inquire into matters which are within the exclusive province of one of the other branches of the Government."[10]

With no clear line separating permissible congressional inquiries of the executive from impermissible meddling, the president and Congress both have strong incentive to broadly interpret their powers under the Constitution. Moreover, after Watergate, with the cementing of changes to executive and legislative branch operations and increasing polarization of the political parties, the invocation of executive privilege in response to congressional information requests is more likely now than ever before: "On the executive side, the bureaucracy directly reporting to the president . . . has tried repeatedly to increase centralized control over [executive branch programs]. . . . Correspondingly, the increasing number and complexity of administrative tasks at the national level has prompted a burgeoning of congressional staff and oversight."[11]

Cooperation

The prospect of repeated acrimonious conflicts between the legislative and executive branches is acute. Nevertheless, Congress rarely makes use of its subpoena power, and the president rarely invokes executive privilege. The infrequency of such battles is the result of the availability of alternative mechanisms to resolve disputes between the branches and the benefits that each branch receives by cooperating with the other.

Congress, for example, can make use of its appropriations and confirmation powers to pressure the executive to turn over information. For its part, presidents sometimes sidestep executive privilege claims by engaging in delaying strategies, including deliberations over whether it should invoke executive privilege, by claiming attorney-client privilege, or by claiming that one or another statute forbids the release of requested information. By making use of these alternative mechanisms, presidents and Congress need not risk court decisions that may limit their prerogatives in subsequent information access disputes.

More significant, Congress and the executive have strong incentives to work with each other. For Congress, broadly worded statutes that set forth generalized objectives but are silent on the details of administration are far easier to enact than highly detailed legislation that specifies the distribution of benefits and burdens. At the same time, Congress has strong incentive to couch its delegation to the executive with mechanisms that enable it to "veto" administrative decisions of which it disapproves without enacting legislation. Likewise, Congress has strong incentives to insist that the executive share with it information necessary to monitor the administration of federal programs.

The executive also benefits from these power-sharing arrangements. Witness the White House's participation in the establishment and growth of the legislative veto, a procedure by which departments or agencies would make administrative proposals that would become law unless Congress rejected them by a majority vote of either one or both houses of Congress. The legislative veto, originally proposed by President Herbert Hoover in 1929, enabled Hoover to "make law" and reorganize executive branch operations without subjecting his plan to the cumbersome and uncertain lawmaking process. Indeed, notwithstanding the 1983 Supreme Court decision in *INS v. Chadha* striking down the legislative veto, more than four hundred legislative vetoes have been approved in the past two decades. Preferring to informally resolve disputes with each other, "[n]either Congress nor the executive branch wanted the static model of government offered by the Court."[12]

Information access disputes tell nearly identical stories. The two sides, despite sometimes laying claim to each other's power, are mutually dependent on one another. Congress needs to delegate in order to forge the coalitions necessary to enact legislation. The executive needs to accept conditions on delegated authority in order to facilitate Congress's willingness to transfer power through delegations.

The Politics of Information Access Disputes

Cooperation dominates most congressional requests for information, with the executive turning over the information as a matter of routine. On rare occasions, however, the executive resists information requests. When this occurs, a (generally unworkable) statutory enforcement scheme gives way to a negotiation process that brings together the themes of tension and cooperation.

Congress has available to it several formal mechanisms to secure enforcement of its subpoenas. The most basic option is its inherent power to punish contempt of Congress. First used to compel the release of information in 1812, contempt of Congress is invoked by sending the sergeant-at-arms to arrest and imprison the offending individual. This power, last used in 1945, is of little practical relevance. As a result, refusals to comply with congressional subpoenas are enforced through one of two statutory alternatives, one criminal and the other civil.

Criminal contempt originated in 1857, when Congress supplemented its inherent contempt power with a statute providing for criminal contempt. The law holds that a witness who fails to appear before a congressional committee or who appears but fails to testify or produce requested evidence is guilty of a misdemeanor. Criminal contempt prosecutions are filed by the U.S. attorney for the District of Columbia and punish a witness for defiance. Consequently, the defendant cannot purge himself or herself of contempt by turning over the withheld documents or testimony.

Congress may also enforce its subpoenas under 1978 legislation authorizing the Senate (but not the House) to bring a civil suit on its own behalf to enforce its subpoenas.[13] The civil enforcement option is limited, however, because it authorizes a suit against any subpoena except that which is issued to an officer or employee of the federal government. Therefore, the statute cannot be used to subpoena agency employees as a part of the oversight process.

The feasibility of the above statutory scheme was severely challenged in the fall of 1982, when a bitter dispute erupted between the Environmental Protection Agency (EPA) and two House subcommittees. EPA was asked to turn over files relating to its enforcement activities. The EPA initially indicated that it would cooperate with the investigation. The Department of Justice's Office of Legal Counsel, however, instructed the EPA to hold onto the files after it concluded that they contained confidential information regarding evidence and litigation strategy. Responding to this claim of privilege, the House found EPA administrator Anne Burford in contempt.

Before the Speaker of the House could certify the contempt, however, a suit was filed by the Department of Justice, seeking a declaratory judgment that Burford had acted lawfully in refusing to release the subpoenaed documents. The D.C. district court refused to hear the suit, concluding that the proper forum to raise a constitutional argument would be as a defense to a criminal contempt prosecution.[14] The court's ruling seemed to prompt a resolution: After two months of negotiations, the information was released to the subcommittees.

Although Congress succeeded in getting the information it requested, the Burford controversy demonstrates that Congress's subpoena enforcement powers are inadequate if the subpoenaed party refuses to cooperate. In order for Congress to satisfy its information needs, it must rely on the cooperation of the U.S. attorney. When a request is made of an executive branch official, the Department of Justice may have considerable incentives to refuse to cooperate. Claims of executive privilege, the oath of office, and basic considerations of separation of powers all may persuade the executive that cooperation is inconsistent with its institutional duty to preserve and defend the Constitution. Indeed, in an Office of Legal Counsel opinion issued in the aftermath of the Burford dispute, the Department of Justice concluded that "[a]s a matter of statutory construction and separation of powers analysis, a United States Attorney is not required . . . to prosecute an Executive Branch official who carries out the President's instructions to invoke the President's claim of executive privilege before a committee of Congress."[15]

Congress, however, did not seek to beef up its subpoena enforcement authority in the wake of this controversy. One explanation is that, throughout the dispute, it was the Department of Justice, not the EPA, that sought to withhold the documents. In other words, the Burford dispute was a bit of an anomaly. Agency heads have the ability to (and incentive to) skirt Department of Justice participation in nearly every instance. Furthermore, Congress has available to it effective alternatives to subpoena enforcement actions.

Negotiating Information

As noted, the EPA controversy stands outside of the pattern of information access disputes between the executive and legislative branches. Indeed, in the midst of this controversy, President Ronald Reagan issued a memorandum to the heads of executive departments and agencies making it administration policy to "comply with Congressional requests for information."[16] While the memorandum exempts "*substantial* question[s] of executive privilege from this policy," the determination of whether an information access request raises a substantial question of executive privilege is left to the agency or department head.[17] Given the costs to an agency or department of a protracted executive privilege fight with its congressional overseers, department and agency referrals are quite rare. For this reason, ethereal concerns of separation of powers typically give way to more immediate pressures of maximizing political capital.

Executive privilege concerns, when raised, are typically resolved through a process of compromise and negotiation. The mechanisms for some compromises have been formalized. For example, the House and Senate committees on intelligence have adopted a standing order that defines the procedures by which information between the branches is shared.[18] Outside of foreign relations, where the possibility is substantial that information access requests will raise executive privilege concerns, formalized procedures are unnecessary. In some instances, the executive will waive executive privilege claims in order to accomplish its political objective. In other instances, an intermediate solution is reached. Types of intermediate options include the executive providing the requested information in stages, releasing expurgated or redacted versions of the information, or preparing summaries of the information. Also, Congress may promise to maintain the confidentiality of the information, or it may inspect the material while it remains in executive custody.[19]

Waivers of Executive Privilege

It is hardly unusual for the president to forego an executive privilege claim by releasing information to advance a political agenda. For example, fearing that Congress would refuse to appropriate funds for a treaty with Morocco and Algiers, President George Washington forwarded confidential letters to the House and Senate leadership. Washington's secretary of state, Thomas Jefferson, explained that even though the House plays no formal role in the ratification of treaties, "[w]e must go to Algiers with cash in our hands" and if the House needs to fund a treaty "why should they not expect to be consulted."[20]

Even when presidents and their advisors hold back information from Congress, the executive rarely invokes executive privilege in doing so. In a 2001–2002 dispute between Vice President Dick Cheney and the General Accounting Office (GAO) over an energy task force headed by Cheney, the Bush administration sought to sidestep the executive privilege question. Cheney and his lawyers focused their efforts on federal statutes limiting the scope of GAO investigations, while also arguing that the GAO, an investigative arm of Congress, was seeking to inquire "into the exercise of the authorities committed to the Executive by the Constitution" and that the law protects "the candor in Executive deliberations necessary to effective government."[21]

Sometimes, of course, presidents do formally invoke executive privilege. Even in such instances, however, presidents often waive executive privilege claims after Congress or one of its committees holds a high-ranking executive official in contempt. Consider, for example, the Clinton White House's handling of a 1995 House Committee on Government Reform Oversight investigation into the firing of seven White House Travel Office employees.

After invoking executive privilege—rather than turn over thousands of disputed documents—the Committee found White House Counsel Jack Quinn in contempt. In response, the White House, notwithstanding its earlier invocation of executive privilege, turned over the disputed documents.[22]

Another example of White House backpedaling occurred in 1986. At that time, Congress requested copies of internal memoranda written by William Rehnquist when he served in the Department of Justice under President Nixon between 1969 and 1971. Congress demanded access after President Reagan nominated Rehnquist as chief justice of the United States.[23] Reagan initially refused to release the memoranda on the ground that they were protected by the deliberative process privilege and, indeed, a strong argument could be made that these memoranda constituted the sort of deliberative remarks among presidents and advisors eligible for protection under executive privilege. Despite Reagan's right to assert the privilege, he decided to release the documents.[24] By doing so, the executive was able to ease the effect of confirmation politicking and to move Rehnquist's nomination through the Senate.

Intermediate Solutions

Information access disputes are typically worked out through one of several intermediate options. Sometimes these accommodations seem little more than a device enabling one or the other branch (usually the executive) to save face. For example, when Gerald Ford's secretary of commerce, Rogers Morton, released copies of all boycott requests filed by U.S. companies under the Export Administration Act, the House Committee on Interstate and Foreign Commerce agreed to protect the confidentiality of the documents.[25] This agreement was a symbolic concession to Morton, who feared an imminent contempt of Congress resolution. Jimmy Carter's secretary of energy, James B. Edwards, likewise sought to escape a contempt citation by agreeing to present to the House Committee on Governmental Operations all requested documents concerning a petroleum import fee program.[26] Unlike Morton's case, the committee refused to promise confidentiality, agreeing only to review the materials in executive session.

Many intermediate approaches represent true compromises between the branches. The standing order of the intelligence committees, mentioned above, represents one such intermediate approach. Most intermediate options, however, are ad hoc solutions to legislative-executive conflicts. In a dispute between Reagan secretary of the interior James Watt and the House Energy and Commerce Subcommittee on Oversight, materials related to the implementation of the Mineral Lands Leasing Act were "made available for one day at Congress under the custody of a representative from the Office of Counsel to the President. Minimal note-taking, but no photocopying, was permitted; the documents were available for examination by Members Only."[27] Another intermediate solution was reached in a 1989 dispute between a subcommittee of the House Committee on Governmental Operations and the Internal Revenue Service (IRS) over congressional examination of alleged corruption in IRS auditing. The subcommittee and the IRS agreed to an elaborate procedure in which "(1) [subcommittee] staff would have access at IRS

to all the information requested, (2) staff could take notes on the documents, (3) the documents would remain within IRS custody, and (4) the subcommittee would not publicly rely on any data garnered from the documents unless it was confirmed from another source."[28]

Intermediate approaches, while avoiding much of the acrimony of Burford-like controversies, are hardly a panacea. Dispute resolutions can cut into valuable staff resources (on both sides) and can take several months. Furthermore, negotiations, since they are principally conducted on an ad hoc basis, are as dependent on the skills of the negotiators and the political climate as much as they are on the strengths of the executive's claim of privilege and the Congress's claim of relevancy.

Congress, as noted above, almost always gets the information it wants without having to resort to the subpoenaing of executive officials or contempt of Congress findings. Executive compliance, however, does not mean that the executive is convinced of the appropriateness of the information request. Rather, Congress's success is often a byproduct of the numerous weapons in its arsenal that can be used to punish recalcitrant executive branch officials.

These congressional powers can be potent. For example, executive branch officials have no interest in seeing "Congress Subpoenas Documents" as a newspaper headline nor do they want to be publicly humiliated at a legislative hearing. When an agency official is called to testify, committee members occupy a position of some strength. If a dispute over information access is in process, the hearing is the committee's chance to apply political and personal pressure. Along the same lines, agencies seem particularly willing to work with

Congress when the nomination of a high-rank-ing agency official is held up pending executive branch compliance with oversight requests.

Are executive branch interests served through such regular compliance? The answer is a qualified yes. Presidents can make use of delaying techniques to negotiate with Congress and to control when information is made pub-lic.[29] Perhaps more significant, at the agency and departmental level, it is critically impor-tant to maintain good relations with legislative overseers. Consequently, it is rarely sensible to place abstract principles of separation of pow-ers ahead of this day-to-day working relation-ship. Furthermore, there is often as much or more of an identity of interests between agency officials and legislative overseers as there is be-tween these officials and the Office of Legal Counsel attorneys, who are interested in pro-tecting the prerogatives of the presidency writ large.

The divide between Department of Justice and EPA approaches to information access re-quests reveals the complexity of executive branch interests. While an academic debate rages over whether the executive is a unitary entity, executive branch operations often re-semble a hydra. In other words, for Depart-ment of Justice and White House attorneys in-terested in the preservation and expansion of presidential power, the current system may ap-pear in a state of disrepair, whereas for agency officials and department heads, the current sys-tem may reflect an appropriate quid pro quo for legislative appropriations and delegations of authority.

Were the executive interested in protecting presidential prerogatives from possible legisla-tive overreaching, the current set of presiden-tial memoranda and Department of Justice procedures would need significant alteration. Under the current regime, the threshold deter-mination of whether an information request raises a "substantial claim of executive pri-vilege" rests with those with the least inter-est in asserting an executive privilege claim against congressional overseers—department and agency heads. While presidential and De-partment of Justice materials provide guidance as to what types of legislative requests are problematic, there is little reason to think that agency heads will place these values ahead of maintaining good day-to-day relations with their congressional overseers.

Judicial Intervention in Information Access Disputes

Information access disputes between Congress and the executive rarely make their way into court. In contrast, independent prosecutor in-vestigations of the executive branch, especially during the Clinton years, resulted in acrimo-nious court fights over the scope of executive privilege. While the expiration of the inde-pendent counsel statute signals the end of such litigation, it is nevertheless useful to compare the courts' active role in these independent prosecutions with the courts' limited role in Congress-executive disputes. This comparison suggests that executive privilege disputes are better resolved politically than judicially.

Federal courts generally steer clear of infor-mation access disputes between Congress and the White House. In *United States v. AT&T* (1977), for example, a federal appeals court made clear that it did not want to police such disagreements. Speaking of the framers' intention that such disputes be resolved politically and that "a spirit of dynamic compromise would promote resolution of the dispute in the manner most likely to result in efficient and effective functioning of our governmental system,"[30] the court pressured both sides to reach a political compromise. "[E]ach branch," wrote the court "should take cognizance of an implicit constitutional mandate to seek optimal accommodation through a realistic evaluation of the needs of the conflicting branches in the particular fact situation."[31] This they did, and the case was dismissed after the Department of Justice and the Subcommittee on Oversight and Investigations of the House Committee on Interstate and Foreign Commerce reached a political settlement of their differences. D.C. district court judge John Lewis Smith Jr. advanced similar arguments in the Reagan-EPA dispute. Claiming that judicial intervention in executive-legislative disputes "should be delayed until all avenues for [political] settlement have been exhausted,"[32] the Department of Justice's challenge to the subpoena was thrown out on ripeness grounds. In the end, recourse to the judiciary accomplished little else than delaying political settlement between the executive and Congress.

Such judicial reluctance is to be expected. For better or worse, the courts are extremely hesitant to play a lead role in defining executive-legislative relations. On such issues as war powers, the veto power, the incompatibility clause, and recess appointments, the courts have used justiciability and other devices to sidestep resolution of executive-legislative disputes. In this way, "the Court maximizes utility among the branches and, thus, minimizes the chance of retaliation against its own inter-

ests."[33] Specifically, by ducking the substantive issues raised in these disputes, the courts have found a "graceful way" of avoiding substantive decisions against one or the other elected branch. Although legislative proposals calling on the courts to participate in information access disputes might change the present calculus, this judicial hesitancy nonetheless calls into question the ultimate usefulness of elected government delegating to the courts the resolution of information access disputes.

Although the courts have taken a standoffish approach to disputes between Congress and the executive, they have played a defining role in settling information access disputes between independent prosecutors and the executive. The Clinton White House, for example, fought several pitched battles with Kenneth Starr and other independent prosecutors over the release of information. One byproduct of these battles is a series of federal court rulings on the scope of executive privilege that have generally limited the breadth of privilege claims.

None of this comes as a surprise. The independent prosecutor statute, by allowing a court-appointed prosecutor to pursue individual cases of wrongdoing by executive branch officials, placed the investigative and prosecutorial interests of the United States ahead of the attorney general's need to balance a multitude of governmental interests.[34] Independent prosecutors, in other words, had no incentive to think about subsequent cases; their incentives, instead, were to vigorously pursue the case before them. For its part, the White House too had no incentive to see the independent prosecutor as a repeat player. Because investigations by independent prosecutors often sought politically embarrassing (if not criminal) information from the executive, presidents were often willing to risk a court defeat, even one that might make it harder to successfully invoke executive privilege in another dispute.

The costs to the executive of litigating executive privilege disputes were on full display during the Clinton years. In a case involving Secretary of Agriculture Mike Espy, the White House refused to turn over documents to a grand jury convened by independent prosecutor Donald Smaltz. The claim of executive privilege in this case resulted in a federal appeals court decision limiting privilege claims to "official government matters" involving "direct decisionmaking by the President."[35] The Clinton White House also raised privilege claims in several lawsuits with independent prosecutor Starr. In cases involving First Lady Hillary Clinton, attorneys from the White House counsel's office, and White House aides Bruce Lindsey and Sidney Blumenthal, Clinton was unsuccessful in invoking executive privilege.[36]

Clinton White House battles with independent prosecutors underscore several truths about executive privilege litigation. First, in cases involving allegations of criminal wrongdoing, courts are likely to place a very high value on the judiciary's need to know all relevant facts. In litigation between Starr and Clinton aides, for example, the court did not question the legitimacy of the executive privilege claim; instead, the court concluded that the judiciary's need to have access to relevant testimony outweighed the president's interests. Second, the stench of Watergate remains sufficiently strong that presidents will rarely succeed when raising privilege claims that smell of a White House cover-up of wrongdoing. Third (and most important), the presidency is

harmed when expansive claims of privilege are pursued in court: "[T]he rise (and success) of the modern Presidency is the story of the gradual expansion of executive power, seized or ceded to it often in times of crisis."[37] Presidents therefore should avoid litigation that freezes or restricts the scope of presidential authority.

No doubt, with the demise of the independent prosecutor statute, there will be far fewer occasions for the White House to litigate executive privilege disputes. When those occasions do arise, however, presidents should view privilege assertions as a claim of last resort. The executive, as independent prosecutor litigation makes clear, is better served through a dynamic political process than through the court system.

Conclusion

Adversarial winner-take-all litigation is a poor substitute for the dance that now takes place between legislative and executive interests over information access. Congress and the White House are constantly reacting to and making accommodations with each other. This repeat player element to separation of powers is best served by the political process. In particular, since Congress and the White House are almost always able to accommodate each other, it is hard to see how either branch would benefit from a judicial resolution, especially one that could produce precedents that might constrain future bargaining between the branches.

The saga of independent prosecutor investigations supports this conclusion. Fights between independent prosecutors and the White House were especially bitter because both sides looked to the courts, not bargaining, for answers. Moreover, these fights ill suited a repeat player dynamic. Instead, it often seemed as if the White House and independent prosecutors saw each other as irresolute enemies engaged in a fight to the death. That the White House would invoke executive privilege claims in these disputes is hardly surprising. There was simply no reason to hold back or think about the future. Congress–White House information access disputes, in contrast, take place in a context of constant bargaining and accommodation. In such a system, it is best to leave the precise contours of the separation of powers to the political process.

Notes

Portions of this chapter are drawn from Neal Devins, "Congressional-Executive Information Access Disputes: A Modest Proposal—Do Nothing," *Administrative Law Review* 48 (1996).

1. "Prosecution for Contempt of Congress of an Executive Branch Official Who Has Asserted a Claim of Executive Privilege," *Opinions of the Office of Legal Counsel* 8 (1984): 113.
2. *Public Papers of the Presidents of the United States: Richard Nixon, 1973* (Washington, D.C.: Government Printing Office, 1975), 669–670.
3. "Prosecution for Contempt of Congress," 116. In 1982 Attorney General William French Smith also asserted that "the interest of Congress in obtaining information for oversight purposes is . . . considerably weaker than its interest when specific legislative proposals are in question." *Executive Privilege: Legal Opinions Regarding Claim of President Ronald Reagan in Response to a Subpoena Issued to James G. Watt, Secretary of the Interior,* report prepared for the U.S. House Committee on Energy and Commerce, 97th Cong., 1st sess., 1981, Committee Print, 3.
4. *The Records of the Federal Convention of 1787,* ed. Max Farrand (New Haven: Yale University Press, 1937), 2:206.
5. Woodrow Wilson, *Congressional Government: A Study in American Politics,* 15th ed. (Boston: Houghton Mufflin, 1913), 303.
6. *Barenblatt v. United States,* 360 U.S. 109, 111 (1959).
7. *Watkins v. United States,* 354 U.S. 178, 187 (1957).
8. *Eastland v. United States Servicemen's Fund,* 421 U.S. 491, 505 (1975).
9. *McGrain v. Daugherty,* 273 U.S. 135, 175 (1927).
10. *Barenblatt,* 112.
11. Peter M. Shane, "Legal Disagreement and Negotiation in a Government of Laws: The Case of Executive Privilege Claims against Congress," *Minnesota Law Review* 71 (1987): 461, 463–464.
12. Louis Fisher, "The Legislative Veto: Invalidated, It Survives," *Law and Contemporary Problems* 56 (autumn 1993): 273, 292; *INS v. Chadha,* 462 U.S. 919 (1983), holding that the legislative veto violates the Constitution's command that legislative action be approved by both houses of Congress and presented to the president for his signature or veto.
13. *Ethics in Government Act of 1978,* P.L. 95-521, 95th Cong., 2d sess. (October 26, 1978); 92 Stat. 1824 (1978). See also 2 U.S.C. sec. 288(d) (1993); 28 U.S.C. sec. 1365 (1988).
14. *United States v. House of Representatives,* 556 F. Supp. 150, 152–153 (D.D.C. 1983).
15. "Prosecution for Contempt of Congress," 101.
16. "Memorandum from President Ronald Reagan to the Heads of Executive Departments and Agencies, Procedures Governing Responses to Congressional Requests for Information," November 4, 1982. Reprinted in *Investigation of the Role of the Department of Justice in the Withholding of Environmental Protection Agency Documents from Congress in 1982–83,* 99th Cong., 1st sess., 1986, H. Rept. 99-435, 2:1106.
17. Ibid.
18. See Peter M. Shane, "Negotiating for Knowledge: Administrative Responses to Congressional Demands for Information," *Administrative Law Review* 44 (1992): 197, 215.
19. See ibid., 218–219.
20. "The Anas," in *Writings of Thomas Jefferson,* ed. Albert Ellery Bergh (Washington, D.C.:

Thomas Jefferson Memorial Association of the United States, 1903), 1:294. For a fuller discussion, see Louis Fisher, "Congressional Access to Information: Using Legislative Will and Leverage," *Duke Law Journal* (forthcoming).

21. Letter of May 16, 2001, from David S. Addington, counsel to the vice president, to Anthony Gamboa, GAO general counsel. On December 9, 2002, the D.C. District Court dismissed the GAO-Cheney lawsuit on jurisdictional grounds. See Adam Clymer, "Judge Says Cheney Needn't Give Energy Policy Records to Agency," *New York Times,* December 10, 2002, A1.

22. See David Johnston, "Panel Moves to Gain Travel Office Files," *New York Times,* May 26, 1996, A26; Eric Schmitt, "White House Gives Committee More Papers in Dismissal Case," *New York Times,* May 31, 1996, A2.

23. Al Kamen and Ruth Marcus, "Reagan Uses Executive Privilege to Keep Rehnquist Memos Secret: Senate Denied Access of Nixon-Era Papers," *Washington Post,* August 1, 1986, A1.

24. Howard Kurtz and Al Kamen, "Rehnquist Bid Not in Danger over Papers: Sen. Mathias Finds 'Nothing Dramatic,' " *Washington Post,* August 7, 1986, A1.

25. See Shane, "Negotiating for Knowledge," 202–203.

26. See House Committee on Governmental Operations, *The Petroleum Import Fee: Department of Energy Oversight,* 96th Cong., 2d sess., 1980, H. Rept. 1099, 28.

27. "History of Refusals by Executive Branch Officials to Provide Information Demanded by Congress," *Opinions of the Office of Legal Counsel* 6 (1982): 751.

28. Shane, "Negotiating for Knowledge," 214.

29. See Mark J. Rozell, "Executive Privilege and the Modern Presidents: In Nixon's Shadow," *Minnesota Law Review* 83 (1999): 1069.

30. *United States v. AT&T,* 567 F. 2d 121, 127 (D.C. Cir. 1977).

31. Ibid.

32. *House of Representatives,* 152.

33. John O. McGinnis, "Constitutional Review by the Executive in Foreign Affairs and War Powers: A Consequence of Rational Choice in the Separation of Powers," *Law and Contemporary Problems* 56 (autumn 1993): 293, 307.

34. See William K. Kelly, "The Constitutional Dilemma of Litigation under the Independent Counsel System," *Minnesota Law Review* 83 (1999): 1197.

35. *In re Sealed Case,* 121 F. 3d 729, 752 (D.C. Cir. 1997).

36. This litigation is detailed in Rozell, "Executive Privilege and the Modern Presidents," 1117–1125.

37. John C. Yoo, "The First Claim: The Burr Trial, *United States v Nixon,* and Presidential Power," *Minnesota Law Review* 83 (1999): 1435, 1469.

CHAPTER TWELVE

The Supreme Court and Constitutional Dialogue

LOUIS FISHER

Too often, especially in recent years, it is assumed that the judiciary has a monopoly on constitutional interpretation. Under this model, the president, Congress, and the states dutifully fall in line behind whatever rulings (regardless of merit) are announced by federal courts. U.S. government has never functioned this way. At the national level during the early decades of the Republic, Congress and the president decided almost exclusively most of the important constitutional issues. Federal courts issued few decisions to guide elected officials. The states reached independent and differing results based on their individual constitutions.

It was not until the twentieth century that scholars, judges, and public officials began to claim that the Supreme Court has the "last word" on the meaning of the Constitution. What if elected branches disagree with a Court ruling? Is their only alternative to pass a constitutional amendment to overturn the Court? No. Judicial rulings are often overturned and modified through the political process. The misguided belief in judicial supremacy overlooks much of the flexibility and adaptability that characterize the relationship between the judiciary and other participants that help shape the Constitution: Congress, the president, the states, and the general public.

What About *Marbury*?

For the past half century, the Supreme Court has claimed final authority on constitutional matters by citing language from Chief Justice John Marshall, in *Marbury v. Madison* (1803), that it is "emphatically the province and duty of the judicial department to say what the law is." In the unanimous ruling in the desegregation case of *Cooper v. Aaron* (1958), the Court said that *Marbury* "declared the basic principle that the federal judiciary is supreme in the exposition of the law of the Constitution." The Court reasserted that same principle in the reapportionment case of *Baker v. Carr* (1962): "Deciding whether a matter has in any measure been committed by the Constitution to another branch of government, or whether action of that branch exceeds whatever authority has been committed, is itself a delicate exercise in constitutional interpretation, and a responsibility of this Court as ultimate interpreter of the Constitution." Seven years later, in *Powell v. McCormack* (1969), concerning the exclusion of Representative Adam Clayton Powell from

Congress, the Court again referred to itself as the "ultimate interpreter" of the Constitution.

These statements, no matter how frequently repeated, wildly distort what Chief Justice Marshall ruled in *Marbury*. While it is "emphatically the province and duty of the judicial department to say what the law is," the same can be said of Congress, the president, and the states. The legislative, executive, and judicial branches at the national and state levels interpret the law, the Supreme Court rules on the constitutionality of the law, and then the law may be changed by the elected branches.

In 1803 Marshall did not think he was powerful enough to give orders to Congress and the president. After the elections of 1800, with the Jeffersonians in control of Congress and the presidency, the Federalist Court was hardly in a position to dictate to the other branches. Far from claiming supremacy, Marshall did everything he could to simply survive. A likely collision occurred when the Federalist Congress, with a few weeks remaining in 1801, passed two statutes creating positions for a number of federal judges and justices of the peace in the District of Columbia. President John Adams nominated Federalists to the posts, the Senate confirmed the names, but some of the commissions (including William Marbury's) were never delivered by the Adams administration. When Thomas Jefferson became president, he ordered that the commissions be withheld. Marbury took his grievance directly to the Supreme Court.

Marbury's case required the Court to interpret the meaning of section 13 of the Judiciary Act of 1789. Did that statute empower the Court to direct Secretary of State James Madison to deliver the commissions to the disap-

pointed would-be judges, including Marbury? Marshall knew that President Jefferson and Madison would have ignored a judicial order. The Court had no compulsory powers over the other branches.

The political context of *Marbury* is important. It was decided on February 24, 1803, at which time Congress was considering the impeachments of district judge Thomas Pickering and Justice Samuel Chase. The House impeached Pickering on March 2, 1803, and the Senate convicted him on March 12, 1804. Next the House directed its guns at Chase. Had its campaign succeeded, Marshall had reason to believe he was next in line. With these threats pressing upon the Court, Marshall wrote to Chase on January 23, 1805, pointing out that if members of Congress objected to judicial opinions it was not necessary to resort to impeachment. Lawmakers could simply review and reverse objectionable decisions through the regular legislative process. Here is Marshall's language to Chase: "I think the modern doctrine of impeachment should yield to an appellate jurisdiction in the legislature. A reversal of those legal opinions deemed unsound by the legislature would certainly better comport with the mildness of our character than [would] a removal of the Judge who has rendered them unknowing of his fault."[1]

Marshall's language is somewhat ambiguous. He could have been referring to legislative reversals of statutory interpretation, not constitutional interpretation, but given the temper of the times and the specific dispute at issue, the broader view is far more likely. Marshall's options were circumscribed by one overpowering fact: Whatever technical ground he might use to rule against the Jefferson administration, he had no power to compel the other branches. If the Court's order could be dismissed with impunity, the judiciary's power and prestige would suffer greatly. Chief Justice Warren Burger later noted, "The Court could stand hard blows, but not ridicule, and the ale house would rock with hilarious laughter" if Marshall issued a mandamus ignored by Jefferson and Madison.[2]

The meaning and breadth of *Marbury* are placed in proper perspective when it is recalled that Marshall never again struck down a congressional statute during his tenure, which lasted from 1801 to 1835. Instead, he played a consistently supportive role in defending congressional interpretations of the Constitution. In the years following *Marbury,* Marshall upheld the power of Congress to exercise the commerce power, to create a national bank (although the Constitution does not expressly grant such power), and to discharge other constitutional responsibilities. The judiciary functioned and thrived as an affirmative, not a negative, branch.

Several Supreme Court decisions in the 1850s reflect the Court's respect for congressional judgments. In 1852 the Court held that the height of a bridge in Pennsylvania made it "a nuisance." Congress promptly passed legislation to declare the bridges to be "lawful structures." Did the Court then lecture Congress that it had already decided that issue and that its ruling was final and binding on other branches? Hardly. In 1856 the Court faced reality and ruled that the bridges were no longer unlawful obstructions.[3] In the second decision, Justices John McLean, Robert C. Grier, and James M. Wayne expressed astonishment that the Court's work could be set aside so easily by

Congress. Objecting that Congress could not annul or vacate a court decree, they attacked the congressional statute as an exercise of judicial—not legislative—power. That position has never prevailed. As the Court noted in 1946, "whenever Congress' judgment has been uttered affirmatively to contradict the Court's previously expressed view that specific action taken by the states in Congress' silence was forbidden by the commerce clause, this body has accommodated its previous judgment to Congress' expressed approval."[4] That is, when lawmakers and the judiciary collide on their interpretations in this area, the branch that accommodates is the Court, not Congress.

Interpreting the Law

The legislative, executive, and judicial branches interpret the law at the state and national levels at various times: before the Court decides, after the Court upholds the constitutionality of a measure, and after the Court decides that a measure is unconstitutional. In none of these three areas is the meaning of the Constitution irrevocably fixed by a single branch. Rather, constitutional meaning is the product of all three branches acting in concert with the states and the public.

Before the Court Decides

The elected branches frequently act on constitutional questions before there are useful precedents from the courts. Many difficult issues, such as those related to the veto power, the pocket veto, recess appointments, war powers, covert operations, executive privilege, and congressional investigations, are generally resolved by the legislative and executive branches with little input from the courts.[5] The judiciary expects other branches to interpret the Constitution in their initial deliberations. As the Court noted in *United States v. Nixon* (1974), "In the performance of assigned constitutional duties each branch of the Government must initially interpret the Constitution, and the interpretation of its powers by any branch is due great respect from the others."

Occasionally a constitutional issue moves toward the Supreme Court, but just as quickly it is turned back by various self-imposed judicial limits. In the 1970s covert funding of the Central Intelligence Agency (CIA) was challenged as a violation of the constitutional language that "a regular Statement and Account of the Receipts and Expenditures of all public Money shall be published from time to time."[6] Since 1949 the CIA and the rest of the intelligence community had been funded without a public appropriation. In 1974 the Court held in *United States v. Richardson* that the litigant lacked standing to bring the suit. The "injury" he identified was too small to merit a judicial decision on the merits. In short, the constitutional issue was left to Congress and the president to decide.

Similarly, in 1987 it appeared that the Court in *Burke v. Barnes* would decide the constitutionality of a pocket veto issued by President Ronald Reagan. The Constitution provides that any bill not returned by the president within ten days (Sundays excepted) shall become law unless adjournment by Congress prevents its return. In such cases, the bill does not become law and therefore is "pocket vetoed." Several decisions effectively eliminate the use of the pocket veto *during* a session of Congress. The legal issue concerned the president's power to pocket veto a bill *between* the first and second sessions. That was the issue before the Court in 1987. The Court dismissed the case, however, on the ground of mootness, returning this constitutional issue to elected officials to resolve. A variety of other judicial doctrines—political questions, ripeness, prudential considerations, nonjusticiability, and equitable discretion—have been and continue to be used by the courts to sidestep constitutional questions.

When the Court Upholds Constitutionality

Even when the Court decides that a congressional statute or a presidential action is constitutional, the controversy may remain open for different treatments by the elected branches. For example, President Andrew Jackson received a bill in 1832 to recharter the national bank. Several presidents before him and previous Congresses had decided that the bank was constitutional. In *McCulloch v. Maryland* (1819), the Court ruled that the bank was, indeed, constitutional. Nevertheless, Jackson vetoed the bill on the ground that it was unconstitutional. His veto message explained that he had taken an oath of office to support the Constitution "as he understands it, and not as it is understood by others."[7] Unless Congress has the votes to override, the president's veto is the "final word" on a particular constitutional dispute. Subsequent presidents adopted Jackson's position on the scope of the veto power. Regardless of constitutional decisions reached by Congress and the courts, presidents may independently analyze and assess the constitutionality of bills presented to them. Congress has the same capacity to reach independent decisions on constitutional questions.

In *Goldman v. Weinberger* (1986), the Court upheld the constitutionality of an air force regulation that prohibited Capt. Simcha Goldman from wearing his yarmulke indoors while on duty. By defending the regulation as necessary for military discipline, unity, and order, the Court permitted air force needs to outweigh Goldman's free exercise of religion. The "last word" on this issue? Not at all. Under the Constitution, it is Congress, not the Court, that is empowered to "make rules for the Government and Regulations of the land and naval Forces." Within a year, Congress attached language to a military authorization bill permitting military personnel to wear conservative, unobtrusive religious apparel indoors, provided that it does not interfere with their military duties.[8] The debate in the House and the Senate demonstrated that lawmakers were capable of analyzing constitutional rights and giving greater protection to individuals than could be obtained from the Court. The justices decided the conflict between air force needs and religious freedom one way, but Congress decided it the opposite way.

Congress and President Jimmy Carter agreed on legislation to create the Office of Independent Counsel to prosecute high-level executive officials. In *Morrison v. Olson* (1988), the Court upheld the constitutionality of the statute. Presidents Ronald Reagan and Bill Clinton later signed bills reauthorizing the independent counsel statute. Nevertheless, either president had the option of vetoing a reauthorization bill on the ground that the office encroached upon the executive power granted to

the president by the Constitution. Presidents are not bound by the Court's reasoning. They have an independent duty to protect their own branch. Similarly, lawmakers are free to decide that reauthorization would violate the Constitution. In that sense, *Morrison* simply means that Congress and the president may create the office if they want to. The elected branches may rethink and revisit the statute at any time and reach independent judgments on the constitutionality of the office. Congress allowed the statute to expire in 1999.

Recess appointments are another example of independent legislative and executive analysis. The president's constitutional authority to make recess appointments to the federal courts was upheld by the Second Circuit in 1962 and the Ninth Circuit in 1985.[9] Although this practice was sanctioned by the courts, Congress has consistently expressed opposition to these appointments. In 1960 the Senate had adopted a resolution objecting to recess appointments, and the House Judiciary Committee conducted a study of them. Both houses pointed to serious constitutional issues: circumvention of the Senate's role in confirming regular appointments, judges serving in a recess capacity without the independence of a lifetime appointment, and litigants forced to argue their case before a part-time federal judge.[10]

Because of opposition to this practice, no president since Dwight Eisenhower has used the recess appointment power to place someone on the Supreme Court. President Carter used the power for a federal district judge, and President Clinton relied on a recess appointment to place Roger Gregory on an appellate court. Similar to the independent counsel issue, the courts have told the political branches that they may place recess appointments on the federal courts if they want to, but the branches are free to reach their own constitutional judgment that it is harmful to the Senate, the judiciary, and to litigants to rely on part-time judges. If a president decided that recess appointments to the courts offered political benefits, the Senate could protect its constitutional interests by rejecting the nominee when the president offers the name for a lifetime position. Faced with that prospect, most nominees for the federal courts would refuse to accept a recess appointment.

When the Court Finds Unconstitutionality

If the Court decides that a governmental action is unconstitutional, it is somewhat more difficult for the elected branches to challenge and override the judiciary. Difficult, but not impossible. Some legislative and executive actions have effectively reversed court rulings.

In 1857 President James Buchanan announced in his inaugural address that the dispute over slavery in the territories "is a judicial question, which legitimately belongs to the Supreme Court of the United States, before whom it is now pending, and will, it is understood, be speedily and finally settled."[11] Two days later Chief Justice Roger Taney issued the Court's decision in *Dred Scott v. Sandford,* holding that Congress could not prohibit slavery in the territories and that blacks were not citizens. Far from settling the matter and providing the final word on the slavery issue, the Court's decision split the country and contributed to the momentum leading to civil war.

Scott was eventually overturned by the Thirteenth, Fourteenth, and Fifteenth Amend-

ments, ratified from 1865 to 1870. By that time, however, Congress and the president had already taken other steps to reverse the decision. President Abraham Lincoln regarded the Court as a coequal, not a superior, branch of government. In his 1861 inaugural address, he denied that constitutional questions could be settled solely by the Court. If government policy on "vital questions affecting the whole people is to be irrevocably fixed" by the Court, "the people will have ceased to be their own rulers, having to that extent practically resigned their Government into the hands of that eminent tribunal."[12]

In 1862 Congress passed legislation to prohibit slavery in the territories. If Supreme Court decisions on constitutional matters can be overturned only by constitutional amendments, it would seem that someone during the congressional debate would have objected to nullifying *Scott* by statute. That decision was not even mentioned. Members of Congress never doubted their constitutional authority to prohibit slavery in the territories and proceeded to announce their independent interpretation, with or without the Court.

Also in 1862, Attorney General Edward Bates released a long opinion, holding that neither color nor race could deny American blacks the right of citizenship. He pointed out that "freemen of all colors" had voted in some of the states. The idea of denying citizenship on the ground of color was received by other nations "with incredulity, if not disgust." The Constitution was "silent about *race* as it is about *color.*" With regard to *Scott,* Bates said that the case, "as it stands of record, does not determine, nor purport to determine," the question of blacks to be citizens. What Chief

Justice Taney said about citizenship was pure dicta and "of no authority as a judicial decision." Bates concluded, "the *free man of color*, . . . if born in the United States, is a citizen of the United States."[13]

In 1916 Congress relied on the commerce power to enact a child labor law. After the Court in *Hammer v. Dagenhart* (1918) declared the statute unconstitutional, a year later Congress passed new child labor legislation, this time relying on the taxing power. With the constitutionality of this legislation challenged, Solicitor General James Beck advised the Court that congressional statutes should be struck down only when "an *invincible, irreconcilable, and indubitable repugnancy* develops between a statute and the Constitution." He further cautioned: "The impression is general—and I believe that it is a mischievous one—that the judiciary has an unlimited power to nullify a law if its incidental effect is in excess of the governmental sphere of the enacting body." He said it was an "erroneous idea" that the Court is the "sole guardian and protector of our constitutional form of government," for that belief would lead to an impairment within Congress and the people of "what may be called the constitutional conscience."[14]

In *Bailey v. Drexel Furniture* Co. (1922), the Court struck down this second effort to enact child labor legislation. Congress responded by drafting a constitutional amendment in 1924 to give it the power to regulate child labor. By 1937 only twenty-eight of the necessary thirty-six states had ratified the amendment, and there was little hope of securing additional states. After major collisions between the Court and the political branches throughout the 1930s that culminated in Franklin Roo-

sevelt's 1937 Court-packing plan, Congress returned to the commerce power and included a child labor provision in the Fair Labor Standards Act of 1938. The issue was taken to the Supreme Court, which in *United States v. Darby* (1941) unanimously upheld the child labor section.

This record on child labor—from 1916 to 1941—marked an exceptionally lengthy dialogue between Congress and the Court, with the legislative branch eventually prevailing. The Court later admitted in *Prudential Ins. Co. v. Benjamin* (1946) that "the history of judicial limitation of congressional power over commerce, when exercised affirmatively, has been more largely one of retreat than of ultimate victory."

In 1956 the Supreme Court invalidated a state sedition law because the Smith Act of 1940, amended in 1948, passed by Congress, regulated the same subject. The Court concluded in *Pennsylvania v. Nelson* (1956) that it had been the intent of Congress to occupy the whole field of sedition. Lawmakers lost no time in telling the Court that it misunderstood legislative intent. The author of the Smith Act, Democratic representative Howard W. Smith of Virginia, denied that he had intended the result reached by the Court. Even before the Court decided on the issue, Smith introduced a bill to prohibit the courts from construing a congressional statute "as indicating an intent on the part of Congress to occupy a field in which such act operates, to the exclusion of all State laws on the same subject matter, unless such act contains an express provision to that effect."[15]

In Smith's second attempt, congressional committees reported legislation to permit concurrent jurisdiction by the federal government and the states in the areas of sedition and subversion. The legislation would also have prohibited courts from using intent or implication to decide questions of federal exemption over state activities. Those bills were never enacted. Smith's bill, however, was debated at length on the House floor in 1958. He explained that the purpose of his bill was to tell the Supreme Court, "Do not undertake to read the minds of the Congress; we, in the Congress, think ourselves more capable of knowing our minds than the Supreme Court has proved itself capable of in the past; and we will do our own mind reading; and we are telling you that when we get ready to repeal a State law or preempt a field, we will say so and we will not leave it to the Supreme Court to guess whether we are or not."[16] His bill, after passing the House 241-155, was never taken up by the Senate for a floor vote.

In 1959 these bills were again under consideration. Shortly before the House debated the legislation, the Court "distinguished" its 1956 decision by holding that a state could investigate subversive activities against itself. This decision in *Uphaus v. Wyman* (1959) allowed that, at least in this area, state and federal sedition laws could coexist. The Court's modification satisfied congressional critics, who thought the 1956 preemption doctrine intruded upon state sovereignty.

Congress and the courts clashed again in 1970, when the House Committee on Internal Security prepared a report on the honoraria given to guest speakers at colleges and universities. The study included the names of leftist and antiwar speakers and the amounts they received. The American Civil Liberties Union ob-

tained a copy of the galleys and asked a federal district court to enjoin their publication. In *Hentoff v. Ichord* (1970), district judge Gerhard Gesell ruled that the report served no legislative purpose and was issued solely for the sake of exposure or intimidation. He ordered the public printer and the superintendent of documents not to print the report "or any portion, restatement or facsimile thereof," with the possible exception of placing the report in the *Congressional Record*.[17]

The House of Representatives rebelled, passing a resolution that told the courts, in essence, to back off. During the course of the debate, lawmakers explained that it was not the practice of the House to print committee reports in the *Congressional Record*. Moreover, the representatives contended that Judge Gesell's order "runs afoul not only of the speech and debate clause—article I, section 6—of the Constitution, but obstructs the execution of other constitutional commitments of the House as well, including article I, section 5, which authorizes each House to determine the rules of its proceedings, and requires each House to publish its proceedings." With an eye toward Judge Gesell and others who might stand in the way, the resolution provided that all persons "are further advised, ordered, and enjoined to refrain from molesting, intimidating, damaging, arresting, imprisoning, or punishing any person because of his participation in" publishing the report.[18] After the resolution passed by a large bipartisan majority, 302-54, the report was printed without further judicial interference.

This collision between Congress and the judiciary was unusually sharp and combative. The legislative-judicial dialogue is generally more nuanced and subtle. In *INS v. Chadha* (1983), the Supreme Court struck down the "legislative veto" as an unconstitutional technique used by Congress to oversee the executive branch. Since 1932 Congress had used two-house, one-house, and even committee or subcommittee vetoes to control executive actions. Presidents and agencies would submit to Congress certain proposals for congressional review within a specific period of days, at which time the House, the Senate, committees, or subcommittees could disapprove. The *Chadha* Court held that legislative efforts to control the executive branch would have to satisfy two tests: bicameralism and presentment. That is, congressional action would have to pass both Houses of Congress and be presented to the president for signing or veto.

Congress complied only in part with *Chadha*. It no longer attempts to use one-house or two-house legislative vetoes to control the executive branch. On the other hand, it continues to use committee and subcommittee vetoes to approve or disapprove agency actions.[19] By misreading history, congressional procedures, and executive-legislative relations, the Court in *Chadha* commanded the political branches to follow a lawmaking process that was impracticable and unworkable. Neither executive agencies nor Congress wanted the static model advanced by the Court. Legislative vetoes remain an important technique for reconciling legislative and executive interests.

Judicial Invitations

On several occasions the courts have decided a constitutional question while at the same time inviting Congress to reenter the debate. In *Leisy v. Hardin* (1890), the Supreme Court ruled that a state's prohibition of intoxicating liquors could not be applied to "original packages" or kegs. Only after the original package had been broken into smaller packages could the state exercise control. The Court qualified its opinion by saying that the states could not exclude incoming articles "without congressional permission." Within a matter of months, Congress debated legislation to overturn the decision. During debate, Sen. George Edmunds of Vermont stated that the opinions of the Court regarding Congress "are of no more value to us than ours are to it. We are just as independent of the Supreme Court of the United States as it is of us, and every judge will admit it." If lawmakers concluded that the Court had made an error "are we to stop and say that is the end of the law and the mission of civilization in the United States for that reason? I take it not." As he noted, further consideration by the Court might produce a different result "as they have often done, it may be their mission next year to change their opinion and say that the rule ought to be the other way."[20]

Congress quickly overturned the Court's decision by passing legislation that made intoxicating liquors, upon their arrival in a state or territory, subject to the police power of a state "to the same extent and in the same manner as though such liquids or liquors had been produced in such State or Territory, and shall not be exempt therefrom by reason of being introduced therein in original packages or otherwise."[21] A year later, in *In re Rahrer* (1891), the Court upheld the constitutionality of this statute.

During the 1930s and 1940s the Supreme Court told Congress it should feel free to pass legislation that challenged judicial rulings. In

Helvering v. Griffiths (1943), the Court put it this way: "There is no reason to doubt that this Court may fall into error as may other branches of the Government. Nothing in the history or attitude of this Court should give rise to legislative embarrassment if in the performance of its duty a legislative body feels impelled to enact laws which may require the Court to reexamine its previous judgment or doctrine." The Court explained that it is less able than other branches "to extricate itself from error," because it can reconsider a matter "only when it is again properly brought before it as a case or controversy." By overruling itself, the Court admits its ability on an earlier occasion to commit error. Justice Harlan Fiske Stone reminded his colleagues in *United States v. Butler* (1936), "Congress and the courts both unhappily may falter or be mistaken in the performance of their constitutional duty."

A 1957 decision by the Supreme Court involved access by defendants to government files bearing on their trial. On the basis of statements by two informers for the Federal Bureau of Investigation, the government prosecuted Clinton Jencks for failing to state that he was a member of the Communist Party. He asked that the FBI reports be turned over to the trial judge for examination to determine whether they had value in impeaching the statements of the two informers. In *Jencks v. United States* (1957), the Court exceeded Jencks's request by ordering the government to produce for his inspection all FBI reports "touching the events and activities" at issue in the trial. The Court specifically rejected the option of producing government documents to the trial judge for determining relevance and materiality.

In a concurrence, Justices Harold Burton and John Harlan argued that Jencks was only entitled to have the records submitted to the trial judge. A dissent by Justice Tom Clark, agreeing that the documents should be delivered only to the judge, encouraged Congress to act: "Unless the Congress changes the rule announced by the Court today, those intelligence agencies of our Government engaged in law enforcement may as well close up shop, for the Court has opened their files to the criminal and thus afforded him a Roman holiday for rummaging through confidential information as well as vital national secrets."

The Court had announced its decision on June 3, 1957. Both houses of Congress quickly held hearings and reported remedial legislation. The "Jencks Bill" passed the Senate by voice vote on August 26 and shot through the House on August 27 by a vote of 351-17. The conference report was adopted with huge majorities: 74-2 in the Senate and 315-0 in the House. The bill became law on September 2, 1957.[22] The statute provides that in any federal criminal prosecution, no statement or report in the possession of the government "which was made by a Government witness or prospective Government witness (other than the defendant) to an agent of the Government shall be the subject of subpoena, discovery, or inspection unless said witness has testified on direct examination in the trial of the case." If a witness testifies, statements may be delivered to the defendant for examination and use unless the United States claims that the statement contains irrelevant matter, in which case the statement shall be inspected by the court *in camera*. The judge may excise irrelevant portions of the statement before submitting it to the defendant.

Collisions between Congress and the judiciary can result in the passage of statutes that give greater protection to privacy rights. In *Zurcher v. Stanford Daily* (1978), the Court reviewed the constitutionality of a police search of a student newspaper that had taken photographs of a clash between demonstrators and police. A search warrant was issued to obtain the photos and learn the identities of those who had assaulted police officers. The Court held that police are not prevented from issuing a search warrant simply because the owner of a place is not reasonably suspected of criminal involvement. Law enforcement officials could obtain a warrant and enter the premises of a newspaper to conduct a search for evidence against another party.

The Court's approval of third-party searches and the threat to a free press triggered nationwide protests and congressional hearings. Newspapers denounced the decision as "a first step toward a police state," an assault that "stands on its head the history of both the first and the fourth amendments," and a threat to the "privacy rights of the law-abiding."[23] In an amicus brief, Solicitor General Wade McCree argued that the use of a warrant to search third parties was constitutional and that there was no need to adopt a "subpoena-first" policy to obtain materials, even if the parties were newspapers with First Amendment interests.

Congress had other ideas. In fact, the Court had invited Congress to legislate if it considered the Court's decision too restrictive on free press rights. The Court stated that nothing in the Fourth Amendment prevented legislative or executive efforts to establish "nonconstitutional protections against possible abuses of the search procedure." Although the elected branches could not pass legislation to weaken the Fourth Amendment, they could act to strengthen its protections. The word *nonconstitutional* was the Court's way of pretending that it had a monopoly on constitutional questions. Yet Congress had to do precisely what the Court had done: balance the interests of law enforcement against a free press.

The Privacy Protection Act of 1980 limited newsroom searches by requiring, with certain exceptions, a subpoena instead of the more intrusive warrant.[24] If a newspaper or anyone with a First Amendment interest is required by subpoena to respond, they surrender only the requested documents. Law enforcement officials do not enter their space to begin a general search through files, wastepaper baskets, or other areas. Thus, First Amendment protections unavailable in the courts were secured by Congress.

Independent State Actions

States can reach constitutional decisions that are markedly different from Supreme Court rulings by interpreting their own constitutions and statutes. The U.S. Constitution provides only a minimum, or floor, for the protection of individual rights and liberties. As the Court noted in *PruneYard Shopping Center v. Robins* (1980), each state has the "sovereign right to adopt in its own Constitution individual liberties more expansive than those conferred by the Federal Constitution." When states want to express these independent views, they must make clear that their rulings depend exclusively on the constitution and laws of the states. If state courts base their decisions on "bona fide separate, adequate and independent grounds," the Court stated in *Michigan v. Long* (1983), it will not undertake a review. Under these circumstances, the final word on constitutional law rests with the states, not with the federal government.

Many so-called innovations by the U.S. Supreme Court were established first at the state level. The Warren Court has been praised for issuing *Gideon v. Wainright* (1963), which granted indigent defendants the right to counsel provided by the government. Many states, a century earlier, had already recognized that right. The Supreme Court of Indiana stated in 1854 that "a civilized community" could not prosecute a poor person and withhold counsel. In 1859 the Wisconsin Supreme Court called it a "mockery" to promise a pauper a fair trial but tell him that he must employ his own counsel. Congress passed legislation in 1892 to provide counsel to represent poor persons.[25]

In 1914 the Court ruled that papers illegally seized by federal officers had to be excluded in federal court as evidence—the exclusionary rule. For years, many states had been following that policy. When the Court applied the exclusionary rule to all of the states in 1961, it acknowledged that states were moving increasingly in that direction anyway. Even now, the exclusionary rule leaves plenty of room for independent state action. Evidence admissible in federal court is not necessarily admissible in state court.

State independence is strengthened by more explicit language in state constitutions. Although the Supreme Court has accepted the use of public funds for sectarian schools to pay for such expenses as transportation and textbooks, many state courts invalidated that type of assistance because of highly restrictive language in their constitutions prohibiting the appropriation of public funds for any religious worship or instruction.[26]

Similarly, state constitutions are often far more explicit in protecting the rights of speech, assembly, and privacy. Through interpretation, state courts can issue rulings that depart dramatically from U.S. Supreme Court doctrines. In *Bowers v. Hardwick* (1986), the Court held that the Constitution does not confer a fundamental right upon homosexuals to engage in sodomy. In so deciding, it emphasized that its decision "raises no question about the right or propriety of state legislative decisions to repeal their laws that criminalize homosexual sodomy, or of state-court decisions invalidating those laws on state constitutional grounds." A number of state courts, including those in Georgia, Kentucky, Montana, New York, Pennsylvania, Texas, and Tennessee have invalidated state statutes that criminalize consensual sodomy. More than two dozen states have repealed their sodomy laws. Independent constitutional interpretations by the states can satisfy the values some people place on diversity, pluralism, representative government, and a distrust of centralized authority.

In 1980 the Supreme Court of Washington held that a university police officer had exceeded his authority in seizing incriminating evidence in a student's room. The officer stopped the student, who was carrying a bottle of gin and appeared to be under age. When the student asked permission to return to his dormitory room to retrieve his identification card, the officer followed. From an open doorway the officer noticed what appeared to be marijuana seeds and a pipe. He entered the room, confirmed that the seeds were marijuana, and concluded that the pipe smelled of marijuana. The Supreme Court of Washington held that the evidence had been obtained illegally and could not be admitted at the trial.

The U.S. Supreme Court reversed the state court decision, holding that its "plain view" doctrine permits a law enforcement officer to seize incriminating evidence or contraband "when it is discovered in a place where the officer has a right to be." The Court returned the case to the state court for "further proceedings not inconsistent with this opinion." In fact, in this next round, the Supreme Court of Washington refused to accept the plain view analysis of the U.S. Supreme Court. Whereas the Washington court's 1980 decision had cited several federal decisions, this time it based its reasoning "solely and exclusively on the constitution and laws of the state of Washington." It concluded that it was right the first time and excluded the evidence.[27] Who had the final word? The state.

Settling Constitutional Disputes

In the *Harvard Law Review* in 1997, Larry Alexander and Frederick Schauer argue that the Supreme Court should be the exclusive and authoritative interpreter of the Constitution. Although they caution that their study was not based on historical precedents, they conclude that the Court is best situated to decide and settle constitutional issues. Concentrating constitutional analysis in the judiciary, they insist, will achieve "a degree of settlement and stability" and remove "a series of transcendent questions from short-term majoritarian control."[28]

Alexander and Schauer could reach that conclusion only by ignoring history. It is difficult to find an example when the Court ever "settled" a constitutional issue, transcendent or otherwise. Certainly the decision in *Scott*

did not settle the slavery issue. Toward the end of the nineteenth century, the judiciary tried to resist legislative efforts to regulate the economy. The elected branches eventually prevailed, after a struggle that lasted almost forty years. Writing in 1951, Justice Owen Roberts explained why the judiciary capitulated: "Looking back, it is difficult to see how the Court could have resisted the popular urge for uniform standards throughout the country—for what in effect was a unified economy."[29] Eventually the courts accepted the constitutional judgments reached by the legislative and executive branches. Who can argue that the nation would have been better off to allow the judiciary final say on such issues as child labor?

Roe v. Wade (1973) did not settle the abortion issue. After almost two decades of fierce national debate, the Court in *Planned Parenthood v. Casey* (1992) jettisoned its trimester standard, which had been bitterly criticized as the work of a legislative body. The Court's decision in *Furman v. Georgia* (1972) to strike down death penalty statutes in Georgia and Texas as cruel and unusual did not settle that constitutional dispute. Reacting to a national revolt, the Court later acknowledged in *Gregg v. Georgia* (1976) that the death penalty—if accompanied by appropriate procedures—was constitutional.

Even in regard to more popular decisions, such as the desegregation case of *Brown v. Board of Education* (1954), little has been settled by judicial rulings. More than a decade after that important decision, a federal appellate court noted, "A national effort, bringing together Congress, the executive, and the judiciary may be able to make meaningful the right of Negro children to equal educational opportunities. *The courts acting alone have failed.*"[30]

To deal effectively with racism and segregation, it was necessary for Congress and the president, backed by strong bipartisan majorities, to pass such landmark statutes as the Civil Rights Act of 1964 and the Voting Rights Act of 1965.

Conclusion

At certain points in U.S. constitutional history, there has been a compelling need for an authoritative and binding decision by the Supreme Court. The unanimous ruling in *Cooper v. Aaron,* signed by each justice, was essential in dealing with the Little Rock desegregation crisis. The unanimous decision in *United States v. Nixon* (1974) disposed of the confrontation between President Nixon and the judiciary over the Watergate tapes. For the most part, however, judicial decisions are tentative and reversible like other political events.

In *Brown v. Allen* (1953), Justice Robert H. Jackson said, "We are not final because we are infallible, but we are infallible only because we are final." A cute turn of phrase, but even the most casual observer of U.S. history knows that the Court has been neither final nor infallible. Justice Byron White was closer to the truth when he said in a dissenting opinion in *Welsh v. United States* (1970) that "this Court is not alone in being obliged to construe the Constitution in the course of its work; nor does it even approach having a monopoly on the wisdom and insight appropriate to the task."

There is no reason for elected officials to defer automatically to the judiciary because of its supposed technical skills and political independence. Much of constitutional law depends on fact-finding and the balancing of competing values, areas in which the legislative branch can claim substantial expertise. Each decision by a court is subject to scrutiny by private citizens and public officials. What is "final" at one stage of political development may be reopened at some later date, leading to revisions, fresh interpretations, and reversals of Supreme Court doctrines. Elected officials have the authority and the capability of participating constructively in constitutional interpretation.[31]

Through this process of interaction among the three branches of government, each institution is able to expose weaknesses, hold excesses in check, and gradually forge a consensus on constitutional values. Also through this process, the public has an opportunity to add legitimacy and meaning to what might otherwise be an alien and short-lived document. Judicial decisions are entitled to respect, not adoration. Just because a court issues its judgment does not mean that the people should suspend theirs. In the search for a harmony between constitutional law and self-government, all citizens have a right and a need to participate.

Notes

The themes of this article are drawn from Louis Fisher, *American Constitutional Law,* 4th ed. (Durham, N.C.: Carolina Academic Press, 2001).

1. Albert J. Beveridge, *The Life of John Marshall* (Boston: Houghton Mifflin, 1919), 3:177. Marshall actually dated the letter January 23, 1804, but modern scholarship fixes the date a year later. See *The Papers of John Marshall,* ed. Charles F. Hobson (Chapel Hill: University of North Carolina Press, 1990), 6:348 n. 1. Like others of us, Marshall forgot the switch to the new year.
2. Warren E. Burger, "The Doctrine of Judicial Review: Mr. Marshall, Mr. Jefferson, and Mr. Marbury," in *Views from the Bench,* ed. Mark W. Cannon and David M. O'Brien (Chatham, N.J.: Chatham House Publishers, 1985), 14.

3. *Pennsylvania v. Wheeling &c. Bridge Co.,* 13 How. (54 U.S.) 518 (1852); 10 Stat. 112, sec. 6 (1852); *Pennsylvania v. Wheeling and Belmont Bridge Co.,* 18 How. (59 U.S) 421 (1856).

4. *Prudential Ins. Co. v. Benjamin,* 326 U.S. 408, 425 (1946). In 1985 the Court said that when Congress "so chooses, state actions which it plainly authorizes are invulnerable to constitutional attack under the Commerce Clause." *Northeast Bancorp v. Board of Governors, FRS,* 472 U.S. 159, 174 (1985). In a concurrence in 1995, Justices Anthony Kennedy and Sandra Day O'Connor noted, "if we invalidate a state law, Congress can in effect overturn our judgment." *United States v. Lopez,* 514 U.S. 549, 580 (1995).

5. Louis Fisher, *American Constitutional Law,* 4th ed. (Durham, N.C.: Carolina Academic Press, 2001); idem, "Separation of Powers: Interpretation outside the Courts," *Pepperdine Law Review* 18 (1990): 57–93; idem, *Constitutional Dialogues: Interpretation as Political Process* (Princeton, N.J.: Princeton University Press, 1987).

6. U.S. Constitution, art. 1, sec. 9, cl. 7.

7. *A Compilation of the Messages and Papers of the Presidents,* ed. James D. Richardson (New York: Bureau of National Literature, 1897), 3:1145.

8. 101 Stat. 1086-87, sec. 508 (1987).

9. *United States v. Allocco,* 305 F. 2d 704 (2d Cir. 1962), cert. denied, 371 U.S. 964 (1963); *United States v. Woodley,* 751 F. 2d 1008 (9th Cir. 1985), cert. denied, 475 U.S. 1048 (1986).

10. Louis Fisher, *Constitutional Conflicts between Congress and the President,* 4th ed. (Lawrence: University Press of Kansas, 1997), 43–45.

11. *Compilation of the Messages and Papers of the Presidents,* 7:2962.

12. Ibid., 7:3210.

13. 12 Stat. 432 (1862); 10 Ops. Att'y Gen. 382 (1862).

14. *Landmark Briefs and Arguments of the Supreme Court of the United States: Constitutional Law,* ed. P. Kurland and G. Casper ([Washington, D.C.]: University Publications of America, 1975), 21:46, 47, 59.

15. *Congressional Record,* 84th Cong., 1st sess., 1955, 101:142.

16. *Congressional Record,* 85th Cong., 2d sess., 1958, 104:14139–14140.

17. 318 F. Supp. 1175, 1183 (D.D.C. 1970).

18. *Congressional Record,* 91st Cong., 2d sess., 1970, 116:41357. See also pp. 41358–41374.

19. These provisions typically require agencies to obtain the prior approval of the appropriations committees. See, for example, 110 Stat. 3009-321 (1996). Louis Fisher, "The Legislative Veto: Invalidated, It Survives," *Law and Contemporary Problems* 56 (1993): 272–292.

20. *Congressional Record,* 51st Cong., 1st sess., 1890, 21:4964.

21. 26 Stat. 313, ch. 728 (1890).

22. 71 Stat. 595 (1957).

23. Fisher, *American Constitutional Law,* 771.

24. 94 Stat. 1879 (1980).

25. *Gideon v. Wainright,* 372 U.S. 335 (1963); *Webb v. Baird,* 6 Ind. 13 (1854); *Carpenter v. Dane,* 9 Wis. 249 (1859); 27 Stat. 252 (1892).

26. Fisher, *American Constitutional Law,* 661.

27. *State v. Chrisman,* 619 P.2d 971 (Wash. 1980); *Washington v. Chrisman,* 455 U.S. 1 (1982); *State v. Chrisman,* 676 P.2d 419 (Wash. 1984).

28. Larry Alexander and Frederick Schauer, "On Extrajudicial Constitutional Interpretation," *Harvard Law Review* 110 (1997): 1359–1387. For a rebuttal to this article, see Neal Devins and Louis Fisher, "Judicial Exclusivity and Political Instability," *Virginia Law Review* 84 (1998): 83–106.

29. Owen J. Roberts, *The Court and the Constitution* (Cambridge, Mass.: Harvard University Press, 1951), 61.

30. *United States v. Jefferson County Bd. of Educ.,* 372 F. 2d 836, 847 (5th Cir. 1966), cert. denied sub nom., East Baton Rouge Parish Sch. Bd. of Davis, 389 U.S. 840 (1967) (emphasis in original).

31. Neal Devins, "Congressional Factfinding and the Scope of Judicial Review: A Preliminary Analysis," *Duke Law Journal* 50 (2001): 1169–1214; Charles Tiefer, "Comparing Alternative Approaches about Congress's Role in Constitutional Law," *University of Richmond Law Review* 34 (2000): 489–508; Louis Fisher, "Congress and the Fourth Amendment," *Georgia Law Review* 21 (1986): 107–170; idem, "Constitutional Interpretation by Members of Congress," *North Carolina Law Review* 63 (1985): 707–747.

Introduction to the Documents

K ATY J. H ARRIGER

In the *Federalist Papers* James Madison argued that a separation of powers could not be maintained by mere "parchment barriers." Historical experience teaches us, he contended, that for the separation to be maintained, each branch must be armed with the necessary constitutional means to defend its prerogatives against attack by the other branches. The documents here reveal important insights about the separation of powers doctrine reflected in Madison's concerns.

The philosophical and historical documents reveal that the doctrine has been conceived of in a number of ways over the centuries and that the U.S. model is derived from yet is different from the preceding models of the Roman Empire, the British constitutional system, and early experiments in the American colonies and their fledgling successor. The congressional, presidential, and judicial documents illustrate the various ways in which the branches of government have viewed their places in the federal system and their attempts to defend the powers provided them under the Constitution. These documents represent the raw material of U.S. constitutional development.

Documents 1–13

Philosophical and Historical Roots of the Separation of Powers Doctrine

Political philosophers have always recognized that a central question of governance is how to allocate and manage power in a way that allows decision makers to accomplish the ends of government. Of course, there has been considerable disagreement over what those ends are, and thus, how power should be dispersed. The separation of powers doctrine grew out of a tradition that viewed concentrated power as dangerous. The doctrine was particularly of interest to those who would challenge monarchy. It appealed to the framers of the U.S. Constitution because of the high value they placed on liberty and the belief that only separated powers could insure government that was limited and accountable. The documents in this section reveal the ancient and varied roots of the doctrine of separated powers and demonstrate the influence of this earlier thinking on the founding generation.

Documents 14–26

Congressional Responses to Boundary Struggles

The framers of the Constitution intended that Congress be the most powerful branch of government, so they sought to structure the federal system to allow internal and external checks on congressional power. The legislature's power to write laws, raise and allocate money, and declare war ensures that despite these checks, Congress will remain the branch with the most potential power. The executive and judicial branches have not, however, hesitated to use their powers to challenge and check Congress. Indeed, the branches have fought epic battles over issues as profound as the war power, federal spending, judicial review, the nature of federalism, and impeachment. Congress has initiated impeachment proceedings against presidents three times. On numerous occasions, Congress has challenged the Supreme Court's interpretation of statutes and of the Constitution as well. Although in the twentieth century Congress's power waned in contrast to presidential power, these documents demonstrate that the federal legislature remains a powerful institution, with substantial means to challenge the actions of the executive and judicial branches.

Documents 27–36

Presidential Responses to Boundary Struggles

The framers carefully delineated some presidential powers in Article 2 of the Constitution—for example, the power to appoint and to negotiate treaties—but they left other powers less clear. The president is undisputedly the commander in chief of the armed forces, but what exactly that means has been the focus of an ongoing struggle between the executive branch and Congress. The president negotiates treaties, but is it acceptable for the executive to withhold from Congress information relevant to the making of treaties? The president has the duty to "take care that the laws be faithfully executed," but how much discretion is allowable in interpreting the law and challenging in-

terpretations of the Supreme Court? The documents in this section demonstrate that presidents throughout U.S. history have been forthright in defending what they perceive as executive prerogative. In doing so, they have helped shape the meaning of Article 2 and the separation of powers doctrine.

Documents 37–56

Supreme Court Responses to Boundary Struggles

The Supreme Court has had substantial opportunity over the years to weigh in on the separation of powers doctrine. It has refereed numerous conflicts between Congress and the executive branch and between Congress and the states. Further, it has shaped significantly its own powers through its justification and exercise of judicial review and through its interpretations enhancing federal power and upholding the supremacy of the Constitution. Its decisions concerning the separation of powers should not, however, be viewed independent of executive and legislative branch actions, as it is clear that Congress and presidents have also had much to say about the doctrine and have helped shape it through the exercise of their powers and through resolution of the struggles between them. The Court is *one* authoritative interpreter of the Constitution, not the *only* interpreter in the U.S. system of divided and shared powers. The case law excerpted here illustrates the role the Court plays as an interpreter of the Constitution and referee for the separation of powers system.

Document 1

Plato, *Laws*
360 B.C.E.

Plato's political philosophy reflects the Greek interest in balance, as does the thought of other prominent Greek philosophers. The notion of balancing power is central in Plato's imaginings of the ideal political society. Many of the framers of the Constitution were educated in the classics, exposing them to the ancients' experience with and philosophy about government. The concept of balancing power forms the root of the separation of powers doctrine, highlighting the enduring concern that power concentrated is power made dangerous.

. . . [I]f any one gives too great a power to anything, too large a sail to a vessel, too much food to the body, too much authority to the mind, and does not observe the mean, everything is overthrown, and, in the wantonness of excess runs in the one case to disorders, and in the other to injustice, which is the child of excess. I mean to say, my dear friends, that there is no soul of man, young and ir- responsible, who will be able to sustain the temp- tation of arbitrary power—no one who will not, under such circumstances, become filled with folly, that worst of diseases, and be hated by his nearest and dearest friends: when this happens, his king- dom is undermined, and all his power vanishes from him. And great legislators who know the mean should take heed of the danger.

Source: Plato, *Laws,* bk. 3, trans. Benjamin Jowett. Accessible at http://classics.mit.edu/Plato/laws.3.iii.html.

Document 2

Polybius, Analysis of Roman Government
2d Century B.C.E.

The Greek historian Polybius spent years as a hostage in Rome after the conquest of Macedonia in 168 B.C.E. He later wrote an extensive history attempting to explain how the Romans created their empire. In his history, Polybius describes power within the Roman government as being divided on the basis of social status among the monarchy, the aristocracy, and the people—an early version of the separation of powers. The Romans also devised a system of checks and balances to constrain the power of each of these groups.

THE THREE kinds of government, monarchy, aristocracy and democracy, were all found united in the commonwealth of Rome. And so even was the balance between them all, and so regular the administration that resulted from their union, that it was no easy thing to determine with as- surance, whether the entire state was to be esti- mated an aristocracy, a democracy, or a monar- chy. For if they turned their view upon the power of the consuls, the government appeared to be purely monarchical and regal. If, again, the au- thority of the senate was considered, it then seemed to wear the form of aristocracy. And, lastly, if regard was to be had to the share which the people possessed in the administration of affairs, it could then scarcely fail to be denominated a popular state. The several powers that were appropriated to each of these distinct branches of the constitution at the time of which we are speaking, and which, with very little variation, are even still preserved, are these which follow.

The consuls, when they remain in Rome, before they lead out the armies into the field, are the masters of all public affairs. For all other magistrates, the tribunes alone excepted, are subject to them, and bound to obey their commands. They introduce ambassadors into the senate. They propose also to the senate the subjects of debates; and direct all forms that are observed in making the decrees. Nor is it less a part of their office likewise, to attend to those affairs that are transacted by the people; to call together general assemblies; to report to them the resolutions of the senate; and to ratify whatever is determined by the greater number. In all the preparations that are made for war, as well as in the whole administration in the field, they possess an almost absolute authority. For to them it belongs to impose upon the allies whatever services they judge expedient; to appoint the military tribunes; to enroll the legions, and make the necessary levies, and to inflict punishments in the field, upon all that are subject to their command. Add to this, that they have the power likewise to expend whatever sums of money they may think convenient from the public treasury; being attended for that purpose by a quaestor; who is always ready to receive and execute their orders. When any one therefore, directs his view to this part of the constitution, it is very reasonable for him to conclude that this government is no other than a simple royalty. . . .

To the senate belongs, in the first place, the sole care and management of the public money. For all returns that are brought into the treasury, as well as all the payments that are issued from it, are directed by their orders. Nor is it allowed to the quaestors to apply any part of the revenue to particular occasions as they arise, without a decree of the senate; those sums alone excepted which are expended in the service of the consuls.

And even those more general, as well as greatest disbursements, which are employed at the return every five years, in building and repairing the public edifices, are assigned to the censors for that purpose, by the express permission of the Senate. To the Senate also is referred the cognizance of all the crimes, committed in any part of Italy, that demand a public examination and inquiry: such as treasons, conspiracies, poisonings, and assassinations. Add to this, that when any controversies arise, either between private men, or any of the cities of Italy, it is the part of the senate to adjust all disputes; to censure those that are deserving of blame: and to yield assistance to those who stand in need of protection and defense. When any embassies are sent out of Italy; either to reconcile contending states; to offer exhortations and advice; or even, as it sometimes happens, to impose commands; to propose conditions of a treaty; or to make a denunciation of war; the care and conduct of all these transactions is entrusted wholly to the senate. When any ambassadors also arrive in Rome, it is the senate likewise that determines how they shall be received and treated, and what answer shall be given to their demands.

In all these things that have now been mentioned, the people has no share. To those, therefore, who come to reside in Rome during the absence of the consuls, the government appears to be purely aristocratic. . . .

There is, however, a part still allotted to the people; and, indeed, the most important part. For, first, the people are the sole dispensers of rewards and punishments; which are the only bands by which states and kingdoms, and, in a word, all human societies, are held together. For when the difference between these is overlooked, or when they are distributed without due distinction, nothing but disorder can ensue. Nor is it possible, indeed, that the government should be maintained if the wicked stand in equal estimation with the good. The people, then, when any such offences demand such punishment, frequently condemn citizens to the payment of a fine: those especially who have been invested with the dignities of the state. To the people alone belongs the right to sentence any one to die. Upon this occasion they have a custom which deserves to be mentioned with applause. The person accused is allowed to withdraw himself in open view, and embrace a voluntary banishment, if only a single tribe remains that has not yet given judgment; and is suffered to retire in safety to Praeneste, Tibur, Naples, or any other of the confederate cities. The public magistrates are allotted also by the people to those who are esteemed worthy of them: and these are the noblest rewards that any government can bestow on virtue. To the people belongs the power of approving or rejecting laws and, which is still of greater importance, peace and war are likewise fixed by their deliberations. When any alliance is concluded, any war ended, or treaty made; to them the conditions are referred, and by them either annulled or ratified. And thus again, from a view of all these circumstances, it might with reason be imagined, that the people had engrossed the largest portion of the government, and that the state was plainly a democracy.

Such are the parts of the administration, which are distinctly assigned to each of the three forms of government, that are united in the commonwealth of Rome. It now remains to be considered, in what manner each several form is enabled to counteract the others, or to cooperate with them. . . .

Thus, while each of these separate parts is enabled either to assist or obstruct the rest, the government, by the apt contexture of them all in the general frame, is so well secured against every accident, that it seems scarcely possible to invent a more perfect system. For when the dread of any common danger, that threatens from abroad, constrains all the orders of the state to unite together, and cooperate with joint assistance; such

is the strength of the republic that as, on the one hand, no measures that are necessary are neglected, while all men fix their thoughts upon the present exigency; so neither is it possible, on the other hand, that their designs should at any time be frustrated through the want of due celerity, because all in general, as well as every citizen in particular, employ their utmost efforts to carry what has been determined into execution. Thus the government, by the very form and peculiar nature of its constitution, is equally enabled to resist all attacks, and to accomplish every purpose. And when again all apprehensions of foreign enemies are past, and the Romans being now settled in tranquility, and enjoying at their leisure all the fruits of victory, begin to yield to the seduction of ease and plenty, and, as it happens usually in such conjunctures, become haughty and ungovernable; then chiefly may we observe in what manner the same constitution likewise finds in itself a remedy against the impending danger. For whenever either of the separate parts of the republic attempts to exceed its proper limits, excites contention and dispute, and struggles to obtain a greater share of power, than that which is assigned to it by the laws, it is manifest, that since no one single part, as we have shown in this discourse, is in itself supreme or absolute, but that on the contrary, the powers which are assigned to each are still subject to reciprocal control, the part, which thus aspires, must soon be reduced again within its own just bounds, and not be suffered to insult or depress the rest. And thus the several orders, of which the state is framed, are forced always to maintain their due position: being partly counter-worked in their designs; and partly also restrained from making any attempt, by the dread of falling under that authority to which they are exposed. . . .

Source: The Library of Original Sources, vol. 3, *The Roman World*, ed. Oliver J. Thatcher (Milwaukee: University Research Extension, 1907). Accessible at http://www.fordham.edu/halsall/ancient/polybius6.html.

Document 3   John Locke, *The Second Treatise of Civil Government*
1690

British philosopher John Locke profoundly influenced political thought during the American Revolution and the founding of the United States. In his writings, Locke challenged the notion of the divine right of kings to govern, instead insisting that the only legitimate government was one based on popular sovereignty in which the legislative power, derived as it was from the people, represented supreme governmental power. Locke's work also reflected the fundamental concern at the root of the separation of powers doctrine: Power—even that of a legislature—must be constrained by law and checked by the people and by other parts of government. John Jay, Alexander Hamilton, and James Madison iterated many of Locke's ideas in the Federalist Papers *(Doc. 11), which they wrote in defense of the proposed U.S. Constitution of 1787.*

Of the Forms of a Common-wealth

Sec. 132. THE majority having, as has been shewed, upon men's first uniting into society, the whole power of the community naturally in them, may employ all that power in making laws for the community from time to time, and executing those laws by officers of their own appointing; and then the form of the government is a perfect democracy: or else may put the power of making laws into the hands of a few select men, and their heirs or successors; and then it is an oligarchy: or else into the hands of one man, and then it is a monarchy: if to him and his heirs, it is an hereditary monarchy: if to him only for life, but upon his death the power only of nominating a successor to return to them;

an elective monarchy. And so accordingly of these the community may make compounded and mixed forms of government, as they think good. And if the legislative power be at first given by the majority to one or more persons only for their lives, or any limited time, and then the supreme power to revert to them again; when it is so reverted, the community may dispose of it again anew into what hands they please, and so constitute a new form of government: for the form of government depending upon the placing the supreme power, which is the legislative, it being impossible to conceive that an inferior power should prescribe to a superior, or any but the supreme make laws, according as the power of making laws is placed, such is the form of the common-wealth.

Source: John Locke, *The Second Treatise of Civil Government* (1690). Accessible at http://www.constitution.org/jl/2ndtr10.htm.

Of the Extent of the Legislative Power

Sec. 134. THE great end of men's entering into society, being the enjoyment of their properties in peace and safety, and the great instrument and means of that being the laws established in that society; the first and fundamental positive law of all common-wealths is the establishing of the legislative power; as the first and fundamental natural law, which is to govern even the legislative

itself, is the preservation of the society, and (as far as will consist with the public good) of every person in it. This legislative is not only the supreme power of the common-wealth, but sacred and unalterable in the hands where the community have once placed it; nor can any edict of any body else, in what form soever conceived, or by what power soever backed, have the force and obligation of a law, which has not its sanction from that legislative which the public has chosen and appointed: for without this the law could not have that, which is absolutely necessary to its being a law, the consent of the society, over whom no body can have a power to make laws, but by their own consent, and by authority received from them; and therefore all the obedience, which by the most solemn ties any one can be obliged to pay, ultimately terminates in this supreme power, and is directed by those laws which it enacts: nor can any oaths to any foreign power whatsoever, or any domestic subordinate power, discharge any member of the society from his obedience to the legislative, acting pursuant to their trust; nor oblige him to any obedience contrary to the laws so enacted, or farther than they do allow; it being ridiculous to imagine one can be tied ultimately to obey any power in the society, which is not the supreme.

Sec. 135. Though the legislative, whether placed in one or more, whether it be always in being, or only by intervals, though it be the supreme power in every common-wealth; yet,

First, It is not, nor can possibly be absolutely arbitrary over the lives and fortunes of the people: for it being but the joint power of every member of the society given up to that person, or assembly, which is legislator; it can be no more than those persons had in a state of nature before they entered into society, and gave up to the community: for no body can transfer to another more power than he has in himself; and no body has an absolute arbitrary power over himself, or over any other, to destroy his own life, or take away the life or property of another. . . . Their power, in the utmost bounds of it, is limited to the public good of the society. It is a power, that hath no other end but preservation, and therefore can never have a right to destroy, enslave, or designedly to impoverish the subjects. . . .

Sec. 136. Secondly, The legislative, or supreme authority, cannot assume to its self a power to rule by extemporary arbitrary decrees, but is bound to dispense justice, and decide the rights of the subject by promulgated standing laws, and known authorized judges: for the law of nature being unwritten, and so no where to be found but in the minds of men, they who through passion or interest shall miscite, or misapply it, cannot so easily be convinced of their mistake where there is no established judge: and so it serves not, as it ought, to determine the rights, and fence the properties of those that live under it, especially where every one is judge, interpreter, and executioner of it too, and that in his own case: and he that has right on his side, having ordinarily but his own single strength, hath not force enough to defend himself from injuries, or to punish delinquents. To avoid these inconveniences, which disorder men's properties in the state of nature, men unite into societies, that they may have the united strength of the whole society to secure and defend their properties, and may have standing rules to bound it, by which every one may know what is his. To this end it is that men give up all their natural power to the society which they enter into, and the community put the legislative power into such hands as they think fit, with this trust, that they shall be governed by declared laws, or else their peace, quiet, and property will still be at the same uncertainty, as it was in the state of nature.

Sec. 137. Absolute arbitrary power, or governing without settled standing laws, can neither of them consist with the ends of society and government, which men would not quit the freedom of the state of nature for, and tie themselves up under, were it not to preserve their lives, liberties and fortunes, and by stated rules of right and property to secure their peace and quiet. It cannot be supposed that they should intend, had they a power so to do, to give to any one, or more, an absolute arbitrary power over their persons and estates, and put a force into the magistrate's hand to execute his unlimited will arbitrarily upon them. This were to put themselves into a worse condition than the state of nature, wherein they had a liberty to defend their right against the injuries of others, and were upon equal terms of force to maintain it, whether invaded by a single man, or many in combination. Whereas by supposing they have given up themselves to the absolute arbitrary power and will of a legislator, they have disarmed themselves, and armed him, to make a prey of them when he pleases; he being in a much worse condition, who is exposed to the arbitrary power of one man, who has the command of 100,000, than he that is exposed to the arbitrary power of 100,000 single men; no body being secure, that his will, who has such a command, is better than that of other men, though his force be 100,000 times stronger. And therefore, whatever form the common-wealth is under, the ruling power ought to govern by declared and received laws, and not by extemporary dictates and undetermined resolutions: for then mankind will be in a far worse condition than in the state of nature, if they shall have armed one, or a few men with the joint power of a multitude, to force them to obey at pleasure the exorbitant and unlimited decrees of their sudden thoughts, or unrestrained, and till that moment unknown wills, without having any measures set down which may guide and justify their actions: for all the power the government has, being only for the good of the society, as it ought not to be arbitrary and at pleasure, so it ought to be exercised by established and promulgated laws; that both the people may know their duty, and be safe and secure within the limits of the law; and the rulers too kept within their bounds, and not be tempted, by the power they have in their hands, to employ it to such purposes, and by such measures, as they would not have known, and own not willingly. . . .

Sec. 140. It is true, governments cannot be supported without great charge, and it is fit every one who enjoys his share of the protection, should pay out of his estate his proportion for the maintenance of it. But still it must be with his own consent, i.e. the consent of the majority, giving it either by themselves, or their representatives chosen by them: for if any one shall claim a power to lay and levy taxes on the people, by his own authority, and without such consent of the people, he thereby invades the fundamental law of property, and subverts the end of government: for what property have I in that, which another may by right take, when he pleases, to himself?

Sec. 141. Fourthly, The legislative cannot transfer the power of making laws to any other

hands: for it being but a delegated power from the people, they who have it cannot pass it over to others. The people alone can appoint the form of the common-wealth, which is by constituting the legislative, and appointing in whose hands that shall be. And when the people have said, We will submit to rules, and be governed by laws made by such men, and in such forms, no body else can say other men shall make laws for them; nor can the people be bound by any laws, but such as are enacted by those whom they have chosen, and authorized to make laws for them. The power of the legislative, being derived from the people by a positive voluntary grant and institution, can be no other than what that positive grant conveyed, which being only to make laws, and not to make legislators, the legislative can have no power to transfer their authority of making laws, and place it in other hands.

Sec. 142. These are the bounds which the trust, that is put in them by the society, and the law of God and nature, have set to the legislative power of every common-wealth, in all forms of government.

First, They are to govern by promulgated established laws, not to be varied in particular cases, but to have one rule for rich and poor, for the favourite at court, and the country man at plough.

Secondly, These laws also ought to be designed for no other end ultimately, but the good of the people.

Thirdly, They must not raise taxes on the property of the people, without the consent of the people, given by themselves, or their deputies. And this properly concerns only such governments where the legislative is always in being, or at least where the people have not reserved any part of the legislative to deputies, to be from time to time chosen by themselves.

Fourthly, The legislative neither must nor can transfer the power of making laws to any body else, or place it any where, but where the people have.

Source: John Locke, *The Second Treatise of Civil Government* (1690). Accessible at http://www.constitution.org/jl/2ndtr11.htm.

Of the Legislative, Executive, and Federative Power of the Common-wealth

Sec. 143. THE legislative power is that, which has a right to direct how the force of the common-wealth shall be employed for preserving the community and the members of it. But because those laws which are constantly to be executed, and whose force is always to continue, may be made in a little time; therefore there is no need, that the legislative should be always in being, not having always business to do. And because it may be too great a temptation to human frailty, apt to grasp at power, for the same persons, who have the power of making laws, to have also in their hands the power to execute them, whereby they may exempt themselves from obedience to the laws they make, and suit the law, both in its making, and execution, to their own private advantage, and thereby come to have a distinct interest from the rest of the community, contrary to the end of society and government: therefore in well ordered commonwealths, where the good of the whole is so considered, as it ought, the legislative power is put into the hands of divers persons, who duly assembled, have by themselves, or jointly with others, a power to make laws, which when they have done, being separated again, they are themselves subject to the laws they have made; which is a new and near tie upon them, to take care, that they make them for the public good.

Sec. 144. But because the laws, that are at once, and in a short time made, have a constant and lasting force, and need a perpetual execution, or an attendance thereunto; therefore it is necessary there should be a power always in being, which should see to the execution of the laws that are made, and remain in force. And thus the legislative and executive power come often to be separated.

Sec. 145. There is another power in every common-wealth, which one may call natural, because it is that which answers to the power every man naturally had before he entered into society: for though in a common-wealth the members of

it are distinct persons still in reference to one another, and as such as governed by the laws of the society; yet in reference to the rest of mankind, they make one body, which is, as every member of it before was, still in the state of nature with the rest of mankind. Hence it is, that the controversies that happen between any man of the society with those that are out of it, are managed by the public; and an injury done to a member of their body, engages the whole in the reparation of it. So that under this consideration, the whole community is one body in the state of nature, in respect of all other states or persons out of its community.

Sec. 146. This therefore contains the power of war and peace, leagues and alliances, and all the transactions, with all persons and communities without the common-wealth, and may be called federative, if any one pleases. So the thing be understood, I am indifferent as to the name.

Sec. 147. These two powers, executive and federative, though they be really distinct in themselves, yet one comprehending the execution of the municipal laws of the society within its self, upon all that are parts of it; the other the management of the security and interest of the public without, with all those that it may receive benefit or damage from, yet they are always almost united. And though this federative power in the well or ill management of it be of great moment to the common-wealth, yet it is much less capable to be directed by antecedent, standing, positive laws, than the executive; and so must necessarily be left to the prudence and wisdom of those, whose hands it is in, to be managed for the public good: for the laws that concern subjects one amongst another, being to direct their actions, may well enough precede them. But what is to be done in reference to foreigners, depending much upon their actions, and the variation of designs and interests, must be left in great part to the prudence of those, who have this power committed to them, to be managed by the best of their skill, for the advantage of the common-wealth.

Sec. 148. Though, as I said, the executive and federative power of every community be really distinct in themselves, yet they are hardly to be separated, and placed at the same time, in the hands of distinct persons: for both of them requiring the force of the society for their exercise, it is almost impracticable to place the force of the common-wealth in distinct, and not subordinate hands; or that the executive and federative power should be placed in persons, that might act separately, whereby the force of the public would be under different commands: which would be apt some time or other to cause disorder and ruin.

Source: John Locke, *The Second Treatise of Civil Government* (1690). Accessible at http://www.constitution.org/jl/2ndtr12.htm.

Of the Subordination of the Powers of the Common-wealth

Sec. 149. THOUGH in a constituted common-wealth, standing upon its own basis, and acting according to its own nature, that is, acting for the preservation of the community, there can be but one supreme power, which is the legislative, to which all the rest are and must be subordinate, yet the legislative being only a fiduciary power to act for certain ends, there remains still in the people a supreme power to remove or alter the legislative, when they find the legislative act contrary to the trust reposed in them: for all power given with trust for the attaining an end, being limited by that end, whenever that end is manifestly neglected, or opposed, the trust must necessarily be forfeited, and the power devolve into the hands of those that gave it, who may place it anew where they shall think best for their safety and security. And thus the community perpetually retains a supreme power of saving themselves from the attempts and designs of any body, even of their legislators, whenever they shall be so foolish, or so wicked, as to lay and carry on designs against the liberties and properties of the subject: for no man or society of men, having a power to deliver up their preservation, or consequently the means of it, to the absolute will and arbitrary dominion of another; when ever any one shall go about to bring them into such a slavish condition, they will always have a right to preserve, what they have not a power to part with; and to rid themselves of those, who invade this fundamental, sacred, and unalterable law of self-preservation, for which they entered into society. And thus the community may be said in this respect to be always the supreme power, but not as considered under any form of government, because this power of the people can never take place till the government be dissolved. . . .

Sec. 153. It is not necessary, no, nor so much as convenient, that the legislative should be always in being; but absolutely necessary that the executive power should, because there is not always need of new laws to be made, but always need of execution of the laws that are made. When the legislative hath put the execution of the laws, they make, into other hands, they have a power still to resume it out of those hands, when they find cause, and to punish for any maladministration against the laws. The same holds also in regard of the federative power, that and the executive being both ministerial and subordinate to the legislative, which, as has been shewed, in a constituted common-wealth is the supreme. The legislative also in this case being supposed to consist of several persons (for if it be a single person, it cannot but be always in being, and so will, as supreme, naturally have the supreme executive power, together with the legislative) may assemble, and exercise their legislature, at the times that either their original constitution, or their own adjournment, appoints, or when they please; if neither of these hath appointed any time, or there be no other way prescribed to convoke them: for the supreme power being placed in them by the people, it is always in them, and they may exercise it when they please, unless by their original constitution they are limited to certain seasons, or by an act of their supreme power they have adjourned to a certain time; and when that time comes, they have a right to assemble and act again. . . .

Sec. 155. It may be demanded here, What if the executive power, being possessed of the force of the common-wealth, shall make use of that force to hinder the meeting and acting of the legislative, when the original constitution, or the public exigencies require it? I say, using force upon the people without authority, and contrary to the trust put in him that does so, is a state of war with the people, who have a right to reinstate their legislative in the exercise of their power: for having erected a legislative, with an intent they should exercise the power of making laws, either at certain set times, or when there is need of it, when they are hindered by any force from what is so necessary to the society, and wherein the safety and preservation of the people consists, the people have a right to remove it by force. In all states and conditions, the true remedy of force without authority, is to oppose force to it. The use of force without authority, always puts him that uses it into a state of war, as the aggressor, and renders him liable to be treated accordingly. . . .

Source: John Locke, *The Second Treatise of Civil Government* (1690). Accessible at http://www.constitution.org/jl/2ndtr13.htm.

Document 4   Montesquieu, *Spirit of the Laws*
1748

On the matter of a separation of powers, no European theorist was more influential in the founders' thinking than Charles de Secondat, Baron de Montesquieu, the French writer and theorist who rose to prominence with his satirical critiques of French politics and institutions and whose work influenced the French Revolution. Montesquieu was an admirer of the British constitutional arrangement, which he believed had a proper balance between the legislative, executive, and judicial powers. In the United States, Federalists and Anti-Federalists used Montesquieu's arguments in attacking and defending ratification of the Constitution and the governmental structure therein.

Of the Constitution of England. In every government there are three sorts of power: the legislative; the executive in respect to things dependent on the law of nations; and the executive in regard to matters that depend on the civil law.

By virtue of the first, the prince or magistrate enacts temporary or perpetual laws, and amends or abrogates those that have been already enacted. By the second, he makes peace or war, sends or receives embassies, establishes the public security, and provides against invasions. By the third, he punishes criminals, or determines the disputes that arise between individuals. The latter we shall call the judiciary power, and the other simply the executive power of the state.

The political liberty of the subject is a tranquillity of mind arising from the opinion each person has of his safety. In order to have this liberty, it is requisite the government be so constituted as one man need not be afraid of another.

When the legislative and executive powers are united in the same person, or in the same body of magistrates, there can be no liberty; because apprehensions may arise, lest the same monarch or senate should enact tyrannical laws, to execute them in a tyrannical manner.

Again, there is no liberty, if the judiciary power be not separated from the legislative and executive. Were it joined with the legislative, the life and liberty of the subject would be exposed to arbitrary control; for the judge would be then the legislator. Were it joined to the executive power, the judge might behave with violence and oppression.

There would be an end of everything, were the same man or the same body, whether of the nobles or of the people, to exercise those three powers, that of enacting laws, that of executing the public resolutions, and of trying the causes of individuals. . . .

As in a country of liberty, every man who is supposed a free agent ought to be his own governor; the legislative power should reside in the whole body of the people. But since this is impossible in large states, and in small ones is subject to many inconveniences, it is fit the people should transact by their representatives what they cannot transact by themselves.

The inhabitants of a particular town are much better acquainted with its wants and interests than with those of other places; and are better judges of the capacity of their neighbours than of that of the rest of their countrymen. The members, therefore, of the legislature should not be chosen from the general body of the nation; but it is proper that in every considerable place a representative should be elected by the inhabitants.

The great advantage of representatives is, their capacity of discussing public affairs. For this the people collectively are extremely unfit, which is one of the chief inconveniences of a democracy. . . .

All the inhabitants of the several districts ought to have a right of voting at the election of a representative, except such as are in so mean a situation as to be deemed to have no will of their own.

One great fault there was in most of the ancient republics, that the people had a right to active resolutions, such as require some execution, a thing of which they are absolutely incapable. They ought to have no share in the government

but for the choosing of representatives, which is within their reach. For though few can tell the exact degree of men's capacities, yet there are none but are capable of knowing in general whether the person they choose is better qualified than most of his neighbours.

Neither ought the representative body to be chosen for the executive part of government, for which it is not so fit; but for the enacting of laws, or to see whether the laws in being are duly executed, a thing suited to their abilities, and which none indeed but themselves can properly perform.

In such a state there are always persons distinguished by their birth, riches, or honours: but were they to be confounded with the common people, and to have only the weight of a single vote like the rest, the common liberty would be their slavery, and they would have no interest in supporting it, as most of the popular resolutions would be against them. The share they have, therefore, in the legislature ought to be proportioned to their other advantages in the state; which happens only when they form a body that has a right to check the licentiousness of the people, as the people have a right to oppose any encroachment of theirs.

The legislative power is therefore committed to the body of the nobles, and to that which represents the people, each having their assemblies and deliberations apart, each their separate views and interests.

Of the three powers above mentioned, the judiciary is in some measure next to nothing: there remain, therefore, only two; and as these have need of a regulating power to moderate them, the part of the legislative body composed of the nobility is extremely proper for this purpose.

The body of the nobility ought to be hereditary. In the first place it is so in its own nature; and in the next there must be a considerable interest to preserve its privileges—privileges that in themselves are obnoxious to popular envy, and of course in a free state are always in danger.

But as a hereditary power might be tempted to pursue its own particular interests, and forget those of the people, it is proper that where a singular advantage may be gained by corrupting the nobility, as in the laws relating to the supplies, they should have no other share in the legislation than the power of rejecting, and not that of resolving.

By the *power of resolving* I mean the right of ordaining by their own authority, or of amending what has been ordained by others. By the *power of rejecting* I would be understood to mean the right of annulling a resolution taken by another; which was the power of the tribunes at Rome. And though the person possessed of the privilege of rejecting may likewise have the right of approving, yet this approbation passes for no more than a declaration that he intends to make no use of his privilege of rejecting, and is derived from that very privilege.

The executive power ought to be in the hands of a monarch, because this branch of government, having need of despatch, is better administered by one than by many: on the other hand, whatever depends on the legislative power is oftentimes better regulated by many than by a single person.

But if there were no monarch, and the executive power should be committed to a certain number of persons selected from the legislative body, there would be an end then of liberty; by reason the two powers would be united, as the same persons would sometimes possess, and would be always able to possess, a share in both.

Were the legislative body to be a considerable time without meeting, this would likewise put an end to liberty. For of two things one would naturally follow: either that there would be no longer any legislative resolutions, and then the state would fall into anarchy; or that these resolutions would be taken by the executive power, which would render it absolute. . . .

Were the executive power not to have a right of restraining the encroachments of the legislative body, the latter would become despotic; for as it might arrogate to itself what authority it pleased, it would soon destroy all the other powers.

But it is not proper, on the other hand, that the legislative power should have a right to stay the executive. For as the execution has its natural limits, it is useless to confine it; besides, the executive power is generally employed in momentary operations. . . .

Though, in general, the judiciary power ought not to be united with any part of the legislative, yet this is liable to three exceptions, founded on the particular interest of the party accused.

The great are always obnoxious to popular envy; and were they to be judged by the people, they might be in danger from their judges, and would, moreover, be deprived of the privilege which the meanest subject is possessed of in a free state, of being tried by his peers. The nobility, for this reason, ought not to be cited before the ordinary courts of judicature, but before that part of the legislature which is composed of their own body.

It is possible that the law, which is clear-sighted in one sense, and blind in another, might, in some cases, be too severe. But as we have already observed, the national judges are no more than the mouth that pronounces the words of the law, mere passive beings, incapable of moderating either its force or rigour. That part, therefore, of the legislative body, which we have just now observed to be a necessary tribunal on another occasion, is also a necessary tribunal in this; it belongs to its supreme authority to moderate the law in favour of the law itself, by mitigating the sentence.

It might also happen that a subject entrusted with the administration of public affairs may infringe the rights of the people, and be guilty of crimes which the ordinary magistrates either could not or would not punish. But, in general, the legislative power cannot try causes: and much less can it try this particular case, where it represents the party aggrieved, which is the people. It can only, therefore, impeach. But before what court shall it bring its impeachment? Must it go and demean itself before the ordinary tribunals, which are its inferiors, and, being composed, moreover, of men who are chosen from the people as well as itself, will naturally be swayed by the authority of so powerful an accuser? No: in order to preserve the dignity of the people, and the security of the subject, the legislative part which represents the people must bring in its charge before the legislative part which represents the nobility, who have neither the same interests nor the same passions.

Here is an advantage which this government has over most of the ancient republics, where this abuse prevailed, that the people were at the same time both judge and accuser.

The executive power, pursuant of what has been already said, ought to have a share in the legislature by the power of rejecting, otherwise it would soon be stripped of its prerogative. But should the legislative power usurp a share of the executive, the latter would be equally undone.

If the prince were to have a part in the legislature by the power of resolving, liberty would be lost. But as it is necessary he should have a share in the legislature for the support of his own prerogative, this share must consist in the power of rejecting. . . .

Here then is the fundamental constitution of the government we are treating of. The legislative body being composed of two parts, they check one another by the mutual privilege of rejecting. They are both restrained by the executive power, as the executive is by the legislative.

These three powers should naturally form a state of repose or inaction. But as there is a ne-cessity for movement in the course of human affairs, they are forced to move, but still in concert.

As the executive power has no other part in the legislative than the privilege of rejecting, it can have no share in the public debates. It is not even necessary that it should propose, because as it may always disapprove of the resolutions that shall be taken, it may likewise reject the decisions on those proposals which were made against its will. . . .

To prevent the executive power from being able to oppress, it is requisite that the armies with which it is entrusted should consist of the people, and have the same spirit as the people, as was the case at Rome till the time of Marius. To obtain this end, there are only two ways, either that the persons employed in the army should have sufficient property to answer for their conduct to their fellow-subjects, and be enlisted only for a year, as was customary at Rome: or if there should be a standing army, composed chiefly of the most despicable part of the nation, the legislative power should have a right to disband them as soon as it pleased; the soldiers should live in common with the rest of the people; and no separate camp, barracks, or fortress should be suffered.

When once an army is established, it ought not to depend immediately on the legislative, but on the executive, power; and this from the very nature of the thing, its business consisting more in action than in deliberation. . . .

Source: Charles de Secondat, Baron de Montesquieu, *Spirit of the Laws* (1748), bk. 11, chap. 6. Accessible at http://www.constitution.org/cm/sol_11.htm#006.

Document 5 **Albany Plan of Union**
1754

In 1754 representatives from New England, New York, Pennsylvania, Maryland, and the Iroquois Confederacy held the Albany Congress to improve relations between the colonies and the confederacy in anticipation of war with France. Delegates to the Congress endorsed the Albany Plan of Union, which had been drafted by Benjamin Franklin. The plan, which was never adopted, became the model for the federal union established first under the Articles of Confederation and later under the Constitution of 1787. The plan divided power at the national level between a representative legislative council elected by the colonies and a king-appointed president-general with executive power. The plan demonstrates recognition of the need for checks and balances between executive and legislative powers.

It is proposed that humble application be made for an act of Parliament of Great Britain, by virtue of which one general government may be formed in America, including all the said colonies, within and under which government each colony may retain its present constitution, except in the particulars wherein a change may be directed by the said act, as hereafter follows.

1. That the said general government be administered by a President-General, to be appointed and supported by the crown; and a Grand Council, to be chosen by the representatives of the people of the several Colonies met in their respective assemblies.

2. That within ___ months after the passing such act, the House of Representatives that happen to be sitting within that time, or that shall be especially for that purpose convened, may and shall choose members for the Grand Council. . . .

3. —who shall meet for the first time at the city of Philadelphia, being called by the President-General as soon as conveniently may be after his appointment.

4. That there shall be a new election of the members of the Grand Council every three years; and, on the death or resignation of any member, his place should be supplied by a new choice at the next sitting of the Assembly of the Colony he represented. . . .

6. That the Grand Council shall meet once in every year, and oftener if occasion require, at such time and place as they shall adjourn to at the last preceding meeting, or as they shall be called to meet at by the President-General on any emergency; he having first obtained in writing the consent of seven of the members to such call, and sent duly and timely notice to the whole.

7. That the Grand Council have power to choose their speaker; and shall neither be dissolved, prorogued, nor continued sitting longer than six weeks at one time, without their own consent or the special command of the crown. . . .

9. That the assent of the President-General be requisite to all acts of the Grand Council, and that it be his office and duty to cause them to be carried into execution.

10. That the President-General, with the advice of the Grand Council, hold or direct all Indian treaties, in which the general interest of the Colonies may be concerned; and make peace or declare war with Indian nations.

11. That they make such laws as they judge necessary for regulating all Indian trade.

12. That they make all purchases from Indians, for the crown, of lands not now within the bounds of particular Colonies, or that shall not be within their bounds when some of them are reduced to more convenient dimensions.

13. That they make new settlements on such purchases, by granting lands in the King's name, reserving a quitrent to the crown for the use of the general treasury.

14. That they make laws for regulating and governing such new settlements, till the crown shall think fit to form them into particular governments.

15. That they raise and pay soldiers and build forts for the defence of any of the Colonies, and equip vessels of force to guard the coasts and protect the trade on the ocean, lakes, or great rivers; but they shall not impress men in any Colony, without the consent of the Legislature.

16. That for these purposes they have power to make laws, and lay and levy such general duties, imposts, or taxes, as to them shall appear most equal and just (considering the ability and other circumstances of the inhabitants in the several Colonies), and such as may be collected with the least inconvenience to the people; rather discouraging luxury, than loading industry with unnecessary burdens.

17. That they may appoint a General Treasurer and Particular Treasurer in each government when necessary; and, from time to time, may order the

sums in the treasuries of each government into the general treasury; or draw on them for special payments, as they find most convenient.

18. Yet no money to issue but by joint orders of the President-General and Grand Council; except where sums have been appropriated to particular purposes, and the President-General is previously empowered by an act to draw such sums. . . .

21. That the laws made by them for the purposes aforesaid shall not be repugnant, but, as near as may be, agreeable to the laws of England, and shall be transmitted to the King in Council for approbation, as soon as may be after their passing; and if not disapproved within three years after presentation, to remain in force.

22. That, in case of the death of the President-General, the Speaker of the Grand Council for the time being shall succeed, and be vested with the same powers and authorities, to continue till the King's pleasure be known.

23. That all military commission officers, whether for land or sea service, to act under this general constitution, shall be nominated by the President-General; but the approbation of the Grand Council is to be obtained, before they receive their commissions. And all civil officers are to be nominated by the Grand Council, and to receive the President-General's approbation before they officiate.

24. But, in case of vacancy by death or removal of any officer, civil or military, under this constitution, the Governor of the Province in which such vacancy happens may appoint, till the pleasure of the President-General and Grand Council can be known.

25. That the particular military as well as civil establishments in each Colony remain in their present state, the general constitution notwithstanding; and that on sudden emergencies any Colony may defend itself, and lay the accounts of expense thence arising before the President-General and General Council, who may allow and order payment of the same, as far as they judge such accounts just and reasonable.

Source: Papers of Benjamin Franklin, ed. Leonard Larrabee (New Haven: Yale University Press, 1959), 5:387–392. Accessible at http://www.constitution.org/bcp/albany.htm.

Document 6   **James Otis, "The Rights of the British Colonies Asserted and Proved"**
1764

James Otis was a Massachusetts lawyer who defended colonial merchants in their challenges to royal customs law and became an important spokesperson for the argument that the colonists' rights as British subjects were being violated through the acts of Parliament and the king. This pamphlet excerpt demonstrates the influence of John Locke's thought on the colonists' claims of injustice and reveals their distaste for concentrated power. The colonial experience would be a driving force behind the rejection of monarchy and nobility and the insistence on a separation of powers scheme in the U.S. Constitution.

Government having been proved to be necessary by the law of nature, it makes no difference in the thing to call it from a certain period, *civil*. This term can only relate to form, to additions to, or deviations from, the substance of government: This being founded in nature, the super-structures and the whole administration should be conformed to the law of universal reason. A supreme legislative and supreme executive power, must be placed *somewhere* in every common-wealth: Where there is no other positive provision or compact to the contract, those powers remain in the *whole body of the people.* It is also evident there can be but *one* best way of depositing those powers; but what that way is, mankind have been disputing in peace and in war more than five thousand years. If we could suppose the individuals of a community met to deliberate, whether it were best to keep those powers in *their own* hands, or dispose of them in *trust,* the following questions would occur—Whether those two great powers of *Legislation* and *Execution* should remain united? If so, whether in the hands of the many, or jointly or severally in the hands of a few, or jointly in some one individual? If both those powers are retained in the hands of the many, where nature seems to have placed them originally, the government is a simple *democracy,* or a government of all over all. This can be administered, only by establishing it as a first principle, that the votes of the majority shall be taken as the voice of the whole. If those powers are lodged in the hands of a few, the government is an *Aristocracy* or *Oligarchy.* Here too the first principles of a practicable administration is that the majority rules the whole. If those great powers are both lodged in the hands of one man, the government is a *simple Monarchy,* commonly, though falsly called *absolute,* if by that term is meant a right to do as one pleases.—*Sic volo, sic jubeo, stet pro ratione voluntas,* belongs not of right to any mortal man.

The same law of nature and of reason is equally obligatory on a *democracy,* an *aristocracy,* and a *monarchy:* Whenever the administrators, in any of those forms, deviate from truth, justice and equity, they verge towards tyranny, and are to be opposed; and if they prove incorrigible, they will be *deposed* by the people, if the people are not rendered too abject. . . .

The first principle and great end of government being to provide for the best good of all the people, this can be done only by a supreme legislative and executive ultimately in the people, or whole community, where God has placed it; but the inconveniencies, not to say impossibility, attending the consultations and operations of a large body of people have made it necessary to transfer the power of the whole to a *few:* This necessity gave rise to deputation, proxy or a right of representation.

Source: Accessible at http://teachingamericanhistory.org/library/index.asp?document=267.

Document 7   **Sir William Blackstone, *Commentaries***
                               1765–1769

British jurist Sir William Blackstone influenced not only British jurisprudence with his opus Commentaries on the Laws of England, *but he also established the foundations of the U.S. legal system. Although the parliamentary system of Britain clearly differed in substantial ways from the separation of powers system adopted by the founders, Blackstone's assessment of the balance of power in Britain demonstrates that there is more than one way to "separate" power and therefore check its arbitrary use. In the British system, the instruments for doing so included bicameralism in Parliament, with one house representing the people and the other the nobility, and the veto power held by the Crown.*

Preserving the Ballance of the Constitution

The constituent parts of a parliament are the next objects of our inquiry. And these are, the king's majesty, sitting there in his royal political capacity, and the three estates of the realm: the lords spiritual, the lords temporal, (who sit, together with the king, in one house) and the commons, who sit by themselves in another. And the king and these three estates, together, form the great corporation or body politic of the kingdom of which the king is said to be *caput, principium, et finis*. . . .

It is highly necessary for preserving the ballance of the constitution, that the executive power should be a branch, though not the whole, of the legislative. The total union of them, we have seen, would be productive of tyranny; the total disjunction of them, for the present, would in the end produce the same effects, by causing that union against which it seems to provide. The legislature would soon become tyrannical, by making continual encroachments, and gradually assuming to itself the rights of the executive power. Thus the long parliament of Charles the first, while it acted in a constitutional manner, with the royal concurrence, redressed many heavy grievances and established many salutary laws. But, when the two houses assumed the power of legislation, in exclusion of the royal authority, they soon after assumed likewise the reins of administration; and, in consequence of these united powers, overturned both church and state, and established a worse oppression than any they pretended to remedy. To hinder therefore any such encroachments, the king is himself a part of the parliament: and, as this is the reason of his being so, very properly therefore the share of legislation, which the constitution has placed in the crown, consists in the power of *rejecting* rather than *resolving;* this being sufficient to answer the end proposed. For we may apply to the royal negative, in this instance, what Cicero observes of the negative of the Roman tribunes, that the crown has not any power of *doing* wrong, but merely of *preventing* wrong from being done. The crown cannot begin of itself any alterations in the present established law; but it may approve or disapprove of the alterations suggested and consented to by the two houses. The legislative, therefore, cannot abridge the executive power of any rights which it now has by law, without its own consent; since the law must perpetually stand as it now does, unless all the powers will agree to alter it. And herein indeed consists the true excellence of the English government, that all the parts of it form a mutual check upon each other. In the legislature, the people are a check upon the nobility, and the nobility a check upon the people; by the mutual privilege of rejecting what the other has resolved: while the king is a check upon both, which preserves the executive power from encroachments. And this very executive power is again checked, and kept within due bounds, by the two houses, through the privilege they have of inquiring into, impeaching, and punishing the conduct (not indeed of the king, which would destroy his constitutional independence; but, which is more beneficial to the public) of his evil and pernicious counsellors. Thus, every branch of our civil polity supports and is supported, regulates and is regulated, by the rest: for the two houses naturally drawing in two directions of opposite interest, and the prerogative in another still different from them both, they mutually keep each other from exceeding their proper limits; while the whole is prevented from separation, and artificially connected together by the mixed nature of the crown, which is a part of the legislative, and the sole executive magistrate. Like three distinct powers in mechanics, they jointly impel the machine of government in a direction different from what either, acting by itself, would have done; but, at the same time, in a direction partaking of each, and formed out of all: a direction which constitutes the true line of the liberty and happiness of the community.

Source: St. George Tucker, *Blackstone's Commentaries: With Notes of Reference, to the Constitution and Laws, of the Federal Government of the United States, and of the Commonwealth of Virginia,* ed. Paul Finkelman and David Cobin, vol. 2 (Union, N.J.: The Lawbook Exchange, 1996). Accessible at http://www.constitution.org/tb/tb2.htm.

Document 8   **Virginia Declaration of Rights**
1776

The year that the American colonies signed the Declaration of Independence, Virginia adopted its own constitution and declaration of rights. Planter, legislator, and states-men George Mason drafted it. Schooled in the classics and a delegate to the 1787 Con-stitutional Convention, Mason refused to sign the document because of his objection to the centralization of power at the national level and the lack of a bill of rights. The Bill of Rights added to the Constitution in 1789, authored by Virginian James Madi-son, was modeled after the Virginia declaration. For Mason and other framers, govern-ment based on the separation of powers was the crucial element for preserving indi-vidual liberty.

Section 1. That all men are by nature equally free and independent, and have certain inherent rights, of which, when they enter into a state of society, they cannot, by any compact, deprive or divest their posterity; namely, the enjoyment of life and liberty, with the means of acquiring and possessing property, and pursuing and obtaining happiness and safety.

Sec. 2. That all power is vested in, and conse-quently derived from, the people; that magistrates are their trustees and servants, and at all times amenable to them.

Sec. 3. That government is, or ought to be, in-stituted for the common benefit, protection, and security of the people, nation or community; of all the various modes and forms of government that is best, which is capable of producing the great-est degree of happiness and safety and is most ef-fectually secured against the danger of malad-ministration; and that, whenever any government shall be found inadequate or contrary to these purposes, a majority of the community hath an indubitable, unalienable, and indefeasible right to reform, alter or abolish it, in such manner as shall be judged most conducive to the public weal.

Sec. 4. That no man, or set of men, are entitled to exclusive or separate emoluments or privileges from the community, but in consideration of pub-lic services; which, not being descendible, neither ought the offices of magistrate, legislator, or judge be hereditary.

Sec. 5. That the legislative and executive pow-ers of the state should be separate and distinct from the judicative; and, that the members of the two first may be restrained from oppression by feeling and participating the burthens of the people, they should, at fixed periods, be reduced to a private station, return into that body from which they were originally taken, and the vacan-cies be supplied by frequent, certain, and regular elections in which all, or any part of the former members, to be again eligible, or ineligible, as the laws shall direct. . . .

Sec. 7. That all power of suspending laws, or the execution of laws, by any authority without con-sent of the representatives of the people is injurious to their rights and ought not to be exercised. . . .

Sec. 13. That a well regulated militia, com-posed of the body of the people, trained to arms, is the proper, natural, and safe defense of a free state; that standing armies, in time of peace, should be avoided as dangerous to liberty; and that, in all cases, the military should be under strict subordination to, and be governed by, the civil power.

Sec. 14. That the people have a right to uni-form government; and therefore, that no govern-ment separate from, or independent of, the gov-ernment of Virginia, ought to be erected or established within the limits thereof.

Sec. 15. That no free government, or the blessings of liberty, can be preserved to any people but by a firm adherence to justice, moderation, temperance, frugality, and virtue and by frequent recurrence to fundamental principles. . . .

Source: The Federal and State Constitutions, Colonial Charters, and Other Organic Laws of the States[s], Territories, and Colonies Now and Heretofore Forming the United States of America, ed. Francis Newton Thorpe (Washington, D.C.: Government Printing Office, 1909), 7:3812–3814. Accessible at http://www.constitution.org/bcp/virg_dor.htm.

Document 9   ### Articles of Confederation
1777, Ratified in 1781

In 1776 the Continental Congress decided that it needed a binding agreement among the states. John Dickinson of Pennsylvania set about drafting the Articles of Confederation, which were adopted with little change by Congress in 1777 and, with the exception of Maryland, agreed to by all the states by 1781, when they became effective. The Articles established a highly decentralized government with power resting in the states and unanimous agreement required for Congress to take action. Missing was a provision for judicial or executive power, the effect of which was to weaken substantially the ability of the federal government to act. The problems resulting from the Articles' shortcomings led to calls for the 1787 Constitutional Convention in Philadelphia, where the current Constitution was crafted.

ARTICLE I. The Stile of this Confederacy shall be "The United States of America".

ARTICLE II. Each state retains its sovereignty, freedom, and independence, and every power, jurisdiction and right, which is not by this Confederation expressly delegated to the United States, in Congress assembled. . . .

ARTICLE V. For the most convenient management of the general interests of the United States, delegates shall be annually appointed in such manner as the legislatures of each State shall direct, to meet in Congress on the first Monday in November, in every year, with a power reserved to each State to recall its delegates, or any of them, at any time within the year, and to send others in their stead for the remainder of the year.

No State shall be represented in Congress by less than two, nor by more than seven members; and no person shall be capable of being a delegate for more than three years in any term of six years; nor shall any person, being a delegate, be capable of holding any office under the United States, for which he, or another for his benefit, receives any salary, fees or emolument of any kind.

Each State shall maintain its own delegates in a meeting of the States, and while they act as members of the committee of the States.

In determining questions in the United States in Congress assembled, each State shall have one vote.

Freedom of speech and debate in Congress shall not be impeached or questioned in any court or place out of Congress, and the members of congress shall be protected in their persons from arrests and imprisonments, during the time of their going to and from, and attendence on Congress, except for treason, felony, or breach of the peace.

ARTICLE VI. No State, without the consent of the United States in Congress assembled, shall send any embassy to, or receive any embassy from, or enter into any conference, agreement, alliance or treaty with any King, Prince or State; nor shall any person holding any office of profit or trust under the United States, or any of them, accept any present, emolument, office or title of any kind whatever from any King, Prince or foreign State; nor shall the United States in Congress assembled, or any of them, grant any title of nobility.

No two or more States shall enter into any treaty, confederation or alliance whatever between them, without the consent of the United States in Congress assembled, specifying accurately the purposes for which the same is to be entered into, and how long it shall continue.

No State shall lay any imposts or duties, which may interfere with any stipulations in treaties, entered into by the United States in Congress assembled, with any King, Prince or State, in pursuance of any treaties already proposed by Congress, to the courts of France and Spain.

No vessel of war shall be kept up in time of peace by any state, except such number only, as shall be deemed necessary by the United States in congress assembled, for the defense of such State, or its trade; nor shall any body of forces be kept up by any State in time of peace, except such number only, as in the judgment of the United States in Congress assembled, shall be deemed requisite to garrison the forts necessary for the defense of such State; but every State shall always keep up a well-regulated and disciplined militia, sufficiently armed and accoutered, and shall provide and constantly have ready for use, in public stores, a due number of field pieces and tents, and a proper quantity of arms, ammunition and camp equipage.

No State shall engage in any war without the consent of the United States in Congress assembled, unless such State be actually invaded by enemies, or shall have received certain advice of a resolution being formed by some nation of Indians to invade such State, and the danger is so imminent as not to admit of a delay till the United States in Congress assembled can be consulted; nor shall any State grant commissions to any ships or vessels of war, nor letters of marque or reprisal, except it be after a declaration of war by the United States in Congress assembled, and

then only against the Kingdom or State and the subjects thereof, against which war has been so declared, and under such regulations as shall be established by the United States in Congress assembled, unless such State be infested by pirates, in which case vessels of war may be fitted out for that occasion, and kept so long as the danger shall continue, or until the United States in Congress assembled shall determine otherwise.

ARTICLE VII. When land forces are raised by any State for the common defense, all officers of or under the rank of colonel, shall be appointed by the legislature of each State respectively, by whom such forces shall be raised, or in such manner as such State shall direct, and all vacancies shall be filled up by the State which first made the appointment.

ARTICLE VIII. All charges of war, and all other expenses that shall be incurred for the common defense or general welfare, and allowed by the United States in Congress assembled, shall be defrayed out of a common treasury, which shall be supplied by the several States in proportion to the value of all land within each State, granted or surveyed for any person, as such land and the buildings and improvements thereon shall be estimated according to such mode as the United States in Congress assembled, shall from time to time direct and appoint.

The taxes for paying that proportion shall be laid and levied by the authority and direction of the legislatures of the several States within the time agreed upon by the United States in Congress assembled.

ARTICLE IX. The United States in Congress assembled, shall have the sole and exclusive right and power of determining on peace and war, except in the cases mentioned in the sixth article— of sending and receiving ambassadors—entering into treaties and alliances, provided that no treaty of commerce shall be made whereby the legislative power of the respective States shall be restrained from imposing such imposts and duties on foreigners, as their own people are subjected to, or from prohibiting the exportation or importation of any species of goods or commodities, whatsoever—of establishing rules for deciding in all cases, what captures on land or water shall be legal, and in what manner prizes taken by land or naval forces in the service of the United States shall be divided or appropriated—of granting letters of marque and reprisal in times of peace—appointing courts for the trial of piracies and felonies committed on the high seas and establishing courts for receiving and determining finally appeals in all cases of captures, provided that no member of Congress shall be appointed a judge of any of the said courts.

The United States in Congress assembled shall also be the last resort on appeal in all disputes and differences now subsisting or that hereafter may arise between two or more States concerning boundary, jurisdiction or any other cause whatever; which authority shall always be exercised in the manner following. Whenever the legislative or executive authority or lawful agent of any State in controversy with another shall present a petition to Congress stating the matter in question and praying for a hearing, notice thereof shall be given by order of Congress to the legislative or executive authority of the other State in controversy, and a day assigned for the appearance of the parties by their lawful agents, who shall then be directed to appoint by joint consent, commissioners or judges to constitute a court for hearing and determining the matter in question: but if they cannot agree, Congress shall name three persons out of each of the United States, and from the list of such persons each party shall alternately strike out one, the petitioners beginning, until the number shall be reduced to thirteen; and from that number not less than seven, nor more than nine names as Congress shall direct, shall in the presence of Congress be drawn out by lot, and the persons whose names shall be so drawn or any five of them, shall be commissioners or judges, to hear and finally determine the controversy, so always as a major part of the judges who shall hear the cause shall agree in the determination: and if either party shall neglect to attend at the day appointed, without showing reasons, which Con-

gress shall judge sufficient, or being present shall refuse to strike, the Congress shall proceed to nominate three persons out of each State, and the secretary of Congress shall strike in behalf of such party absent or refusing; and the judgment and sentence of the court to be appointed, in the manner before prescribed, shall be final and conclusive; and if any of the parties shall refuse to submit to the authority of such court, or to appear or defend their claim or cause, the court shall nevertheless proceed to pronounce sentence, or judgment, which shall in like manner be final and decisive, the judgment or sentence and other proceedings being in either case transmitted to Congress, and lodged among the acts of Congress for the security of the parties concerned: provided that every commissioner, before he sits in judgment, shall take an oath to be administered by one of the judges of the supreme or superior court of the State, where the cause shall be tried, 'well and truly to hear and determine the matter in question, according to the best of his judgment, without favor, affection or hope of reward': provided also, that no State shall be deprived of territory for the benefit of the United States.

All controversies concerning the private right of soil claimed under different grants of two or more States, whose jurisdictions as they may respect such lands, and the States which passed such grants are adjusted, the said grants or either of them being at the same time claimed to have originated antecedent to such settlement of jurisdiction, shall on the petition of either party to the Congress of the United States, be finally determined as near as may be in the same manner as is before prescribed for deciding disputes respecting territorial jurisdiction between different States.

The United States in Congress assembled shall also have the sole and exclusive right and power of regulating the alloy and value of coin struck by their own authority, or by that of the respective States—fixing the standards of weights and measures throughout the United States—regulating the trade and managing all affairs with the Indians, not members of any of the States, provided that the legislative right of any State within its own limits be not infringed or violated—establishing or regulating post offices from one State to another, throughout all the United States, and exacting such postage on the papers passing through the same as may be requisite to defray the expences of the said office—appointing all officers of the land forces, in the service of the United States, excepting regimental officers—appointing all the officers of the naval forces, and commissioning all officers whatever in the service of the United States—making rules for the government and regulation of the said land and naval forces, and directing their operations.

The United States in Congress assembled shall have authority to appoint a committee, to sit in the recess of Congress, to be denominated 'A Committee of the States', and to consist of one delegate from each state; and to appoint such other committees and civil officers as may be necessary for managing the general affairs of the United States under their direction—to appoint one of their members to preside, provided that no person be allowed to serve in the office of president more than one year in any term of three years; to ascertain the necessary sums of money to be raised for the service of the United States, and to appropriate and apply the same for defraying the public expences—to borrow money, or emit bills on the credit of the United States, transmitting every half-year to the respective States an account of the sums of money so borrowed or emitted—to build and equip a navy—to agree upon the number of land forces, and to make requisitions from each State for its quota, in proportion to the number of white inhabitants in such State; which requisition shall be binding, and thereupon the legislature of each State shall appoint the regimental officers, raise the men and cloath, arm and equip them in a solid-like manner, at the expense of the United States; and the officers and men so cloathed, armed and equipped shall march to the place appointed, and within the time agreed on by the United States in Congress assembled. But if the United States in Congress assembled shall, on consideration of circumstances judge

proper that any State should not raise men, or should raise a smaller number than its quota, and that any other State should raise a greater number of men than the quota thereof, such extra number shall be raised, officered, cloathed, armed and equipped in the same manner as the quota of each State, unless the legislature of State shall judge that such extra number cannot be safely spread out in the same, in which case they shall raise, officer, cloath, arm and equip as many of such extra number as they judge can be safely spared. And the officers and men so cloathed, armed, and equipped, shall march to the place appointed, and within the time agreed on by the United States in Congress assembled.

The United States in Congress assembled shall never engage in a war, nor grant letters of marque and reprisal in time of peace, nor enter into any treaties or alliances, nor coin money, nor regulate the value thereof, nor ascertain the sums and expences necessary for the defence and welfare of the United States, or any of them, nor emit bills, nor borrow money on the credit of the United States, nor appropriate money, nor agree upon the number of vessels of war, to be built or purchased, or the number of land or sea forces to be raised, nor appoint a commander in chief of the army or navy, unless nine States assent to the same: nor shall a question on any other point, except for adjourning from day to day be determined, unless by the votes of a majority of the United States in Congress assembled. . . .

ARTICLE XII. All bills of credit emitted, monies borrowed, and debts contracted by, or under the authority of Congress, before the assembling of the United States, in pursuance of the present confederation, shall be deemed and considered as a charge against the United States, for payment and satisfaction whereof the said United States, and the public faith are hereby solemnly pledged.

ARTICLE XIII. Every State shall abide by the determinations of the United States in Congress assembled, on all questions which by this confederation are submitted to them. And the Articles of this Confederation shall be inviolably observed by every State, and the Union shall be perpetual; nor shall any alteration at any time hereafter be made in any of them; unless such alteration be agreed to in a Congress of the United States, and be afterwards confirmed by the legislatures of every State. . . .

Source: The Avalon Project at Yale Law School, http://www.yale.edu/lawweb/avalon/artconf.htm.

Document 10   **Constitution of the United States of America (Abridged) 1787, Ratified in 1789**

Amended twenty-seven times since its inception, the U.S. Constitution delineates a governing system with distinct separations of power. The first three articles define and limit the powers of the legislature, executive, and judiciary. The Constitution is notable in its brevity and, some would say, its ambiguity. The boundaries between the branches have been a matter of struggle throughout the history of the Republic.

[Preamble:] We the People of the United States, in Order to form a more perfect Union, establish Justice, insure domestic Tranquility, provide for the common defence, promote the general Welfare, and secure the Blessings of Liberty to ourselves and our Posterity, do ordain and establish this Constitution for the United States of America.

ARTICLE I

Section 1. All legislative Powers herein granted shall be vested in a Congress of the United States, which shall consist of a Senate and House of Representatives.

Section 2. The House of Representatives shall be composed of Members chosen every second Year by the People of the several States, and the Electors in each State shall have the Qualifications requisite for Electors of the most numerous Branch of the State Legislature.

No Person shall be a Representative who shall not have attained to the age of twenty five Years, and been seven Years a Citizen of the United States, and who shall not, when elected, be an Inhabitant of that State in which he shall be chosen.

[Representatives and direct Taxes shall be apportioned among the several States which may be included within this Union, according to their respective Numbers, which shall be determined by adding to the whole Number of free Persons, including those bound to Service for a Term of Years, and excluding Indians not taxed, three fifths of all other Persons.] The actual Enumeration shall be made within three Years after the first Meeting of the Congress of the United States, and within every subsequent Term of ten Years, in such Manner as they shall by Law direct. The Number of Representatives shall not exceed one for every thirty Thousand, but each State shall have at Least one Representative; and until such enumeration shall be made, the State of New Hampshire shall be entitled to chuse three, Massachusetts eight, Rhode-Island and Providence Plantations one, Connecticut five, New-York six, New Jersey four, Pennsylvania eight, Delaware one, Maryland six, Virginia ten, North Carolina five, South Carolina five, and Georgia three.

When vacancies happen in the Representation from any State, the Executive Authority thereof shall issue Writs of Election to fill such Vacancies.

The House of Representatives shall chuse their Speaker and other Officers; and shall have the sole Power of Impeachment.

Section 3. The Senate of the United States shall be composed of two Senators from each State, [chosen by the Legislature thereof,] for six Years; and each Senator shall have one Vote.

Immediately after they shall be assembled in Consequence of the first Election, they shall be divided as equally as may be into three Classes. The Seats of the Senators of the first Class shall be vacated at the Expiration of the second Year, of the second Class at the Expiration of the fourth Year, and of the third Class at the Expiration of the sixth Year, so that one third may be chosen every second Year; [and if Vacancies happen by Resignation, or otherwise, during the Recess of the Legislature of any State, the Executive thereof may make temporary Appointments until the next Meeting of the Legislature, which shall then fill such Vacancies.]

No Person shall be a Senator who shall not have attained to the Age of thirty Years, and been nine Years a Citizen of the United States, and who shall not, when elected, be an Inhabitant of that State for which he shall be chosen.

The Vice President of the United States shall be President of the Senate, but shall have no Vote, unless they be equally divided.

The Senate shall chuse their other Officers, and also a President pro tempore, in the Absence of the Vice President, or when he shall exercise the Office of President of the United States.

The Senate shall have the sole Power to try all Impeachments. When sitting for that Purpose, they shall be on Oath or Affirmation. When the President of the United States is tried, the Chief Justice shall preside: And no Person shall be convicted without the Concurrence of two thirds of the Members present.

Judgment in Cases of Impeachment shall not extend further than to removal from Office, and disqualification to hold and enjoy any Office of honor, Trust or Profit under the United States: but the Party convicted shall nevertheless be liable and subject to Indictment, Trial, Judgment and Punishment, according to Law.

Section 4. The Times, Places and Manner of holding Elections for Senators and Representatives, shall be prescribed in each State by the Legislature thereof; but the Congress may at any time by Law make or alter such Regulations, except as to the Places of chusing Senators.

The Congress shall assemble at least once in every Year, and such Meeting shall [be on the first Monday in December], unless they shall by Law appoint a different Day.

Section 5. Each House shall be the Judge of the Elections, Returns and Qualifications of its own Members, and a Majority of each shall constitute a Quorum to do Business; but a smaller Number may adjourn from day to day, and may be authorized to compel the Attendance of absent Members, in such Manner, and under such Penalties as each House may provide.

Each House may determine the Rules of its Proceedings, punish its Members for disorderly Behaviour, and, with the Concurrence of two thirds, expel a Member.

Each House shall keep a Journal of its Proceedings, and from time to time publish the same, excepting such Parts as may in their Judgment require Secrecy; and the Yeas and Nays of the Members of either House on any question shall, at the Desire of one fifth of those Present, be entered on the Journal.

Neither House, during the Session of Congress, shall, without the Consent of the other, adjourn for more than three days, nor to any other Place than that in which the two Houses shall be sitting.

Section 6. The Senators and Representatives shall receive a Compensation for their Services, to be ascertained by Law, and paid out of the Treasury of the United States. They shall in all Cases, except Treason, Felony and Breach of the Peace, be privileged from Arrest during their Attendance at the Session of their respective Houses, and in going to and returning from the same; and for any Speech or Debate in either House, they shall not be questioned in any other Place.

No Senator or Representative shall, during the Time for which he was elected, be appointed to any civil Office under the Authority of the United States, which shall have been created, or the Emoluments whereof shall have been increased during such time; and no Person holding any Office under the United States, shall be a Member of either House during his Continuance in Office.

Section 7. All Bills for raising Revenue shall originate in the House of Representatives; but the Senate may propose or concur with Amendments as on other Bills.

Every Bill which shall have passed the House of Representatives and the Senate, shall, before it become a Law, be presented to the President of the United States; If he approve he shall sign it, but if not he shall return it, with his Objections to that House in which it shall have originated, who shall enter the Objections at large on their Journal, and proceed to reconsider it. If after such Reconsideration two thirds of that House shall agree to pass the Bill, it shall be sent, together with the Objections, to the other House, by which it shall likewise be reconsidered, and if approved by two thirds of that House, it shall become a Law. But in all such Cases the Votes of both Houses shall be determined by Yeas and Nays, and the Names of the Persons voting for and against the Bill shall be entered on the Journal of each House respectively. If any Bill shall not be returned by the President within ten Days (Sundays excepted) after it shall have been presented to him, the Same shall be a Law, in like Manner as if he had signed it, unless the Congress by their Adjournment prevent its Return, in which Case it shall not be a Law.

Every Order, Resolution, or Vote to which the Concurrence of the Senate and House of Representatives may be necessary (except on a question of Adjournment) shall be presented to the President of the United States; and before the Same shall take Effect, shall be approved by him, or being disapproved by him, shall be repassed by two thirds of the Senate and House of Representatives, according to the Rules and Limitations prescribed in the Case of a Bill.

Section 8. The Congress shall have Power To lay and collect Taxes, Duties, Imposts and Excises, to pay the Debts and provide for the common Defence and general Welfare of the United States; but all Duties, Imposts and Excises shall be uniform throughout the United States;

To borrow Money on the credit of the United States;

To regulate Commerce with foreign Nations, and among the several States, and with the Indian Tribes;

To establish an uniform Rule of Naturalization, and uniform Laws on the subject of Bankruptcies throughout the United States;

To coin Money, regulate the Value thereof, and of foreign Coin, and fix the Standard of Weights and Measures;

To provide for the Punishment of counterfeiting the Securities and current Coin of the United States;

To establish Post Offices and post Roads;

To promote the Progress of Science and useful Arts, by securing for limited Times to Authors and Inventors the exclusive Right to their respective Writings and Discoveries;

To constitute Tribunals inferior to the supreme Court;

To define and punish Piracies and Felonies committed on the high Seas, and Offences against the Law of Nations;

To declare War, grant Letters of Marque and Reprisal, and make Rules concerning Captures on Land and Water;

To raise and support Armies, but no Appropriation of Money to that Use shall be for a longer Term than two Years;

To provide and maintain a Navy;

To make Rules for the Government and Regulation of the land and naval Forces;

To provide for calling forth the Militia to execute the Laws of the Union, suppress Insurrections and repel Invasions;

To provide for organizing, arming, and disciplining, the Militia, and for governing such Part of them as may be employed in the Service of the United States, reserving to the States respectively, the Appointment of the Officers, and the Authority of training the Militia according to the discipline prescribed by Congress;

To exercise exclusive Legislation in all Cases whatsoever, over such District (not exceeding ten Miles square) as may, by Cession of particular States, and the Acceptance of Congress, become the Seat of the Government of the United States, and to exercise like Authority over all Places purchased by the Consent of the Legislature of the State in which the Same shall be, for the Erection of Forts, Magazines, Arsenals, dock-Yards, and other needful Buildings;—And

To make all Laws which shall be necessary and proper for carrying into Execution the foregoing Powers, and all other Powers vested by this Constitution in the Government of the United States, or in any Department or Officer thereof.

Section 9. The Migration or Importation of such Persons as any of the States now existing shall think proper to admit, shall not be prohibited by the Congress prior to the Year one thousand eight hundred and eight, but a Tax or duty may be imposed on such Importation, not exceeding ten dollars for each Person.

The Privilege of the Writ of Habeas Corpus shall not be suspended, unless when in Cases of Rebellion or Invasion the public Safety may require it.

No Bill of Attainder or ex post facto Law shall be passed.

No Capitation, or other direct, Tax shall be laid, unless in Proportion to the Census or Enumeration herein before directed to be taken.

No Tax or Duty shall be laid on Articles exported from any State.

No Preference shall be given by any Regulation of Commerce or Revenue to the Ports of one State over those of another; nor shall Vessels bound to, or from, one State, be obliged to enter, clear, or pay Duties in another.

No Money shall be drawn from the Treasury, but in Consequence of Appropriations made by Law; and a regular Statement and Account of the Receipts and Expenditures of all public Money shall be published from time to time.

No Title of Nobility shall be granted by the United States: And no Person holding any Office of Profit or Trust under them, shall, without the Consent of the Congress, accept of any present, Emolument, Office, or Title, of any kind whatever, from any King, Prince, or foreign State.

Section 10. No State shall enter into any Treaty, Alliance, or Confederation; grant Letters of Marque and Reprisal; coin Money; emit Bills of Credit; make any Thing but gold and silver Coin a Tender in Payment of Debts; pass any Bill of Attainder, ex post facto Law, or Law impairing the Obligation of Contracts, or grant any Title of Nobility.

No State shall, without the Consent of the Congress, lay any Imposts or Duties on Imports or Exports, except what may be absolutely necessary for executing it's inspection Laws: and the net Produce of all Duties and Imposts, laid by any State on Imports or Exports, shall be for the Use of the Treasury of the United States; and all such Laws shall be subject to the Revision and Controul of the Congress.

No State shall, without the Consent of Congress, lay any Duty of Tonnage, keep Troops, or Ships of War in time of Peace, enter into any Agreement or Compact with another State, or with a foreign Power, or engage in War, unless actually invaded, or in such imminent Danger as will not admit of delay.

ARTICLE II

Section 1. The executive Power shall be vested in a President of the United States of America. He shall hold his Office during the Term of four Years, and, together with the Vice President, chosen for the same Term, be elected, as follows:

Each State shall appoint, in such Manner as the Legislature thereof may direct, a Number of Electors, equal to the whole Number of Senators and Representatives to which the State may be entitled in the Congress: but no Senator or Representative, or Person holding an Office of Trust or Profit under the United States, shall be appointed an Elector.

[The Electors shall meet in their respective States, and vote by Ballot for two Persons, of whom one at least shall not be an Inhabitant of the same State with themselves. And they shall make a List of all the Persons voted for, and of the Number of Votes for each; which List they shall sign and certify, and transmit sealed to the Seat of the Government of the United States, directed to the President of the Senate. The President of the Senate shall, in the Presence of the Senate and House of Representatives, open all the Certificates, and the Votes shall then be counted. The Person having the greatest Number of Votes shall be the President, if such Number be a Majority of the whole Number of Electors appointed; and if there be more than one who have such Majority, and have an equal Number of Votes, then the House of Representatives shall immediately chuse by Ballot one of them for President; and if no Person have a Majority, then from the five highest on the list the said House shall in like Manner chuse the President. But in chusing the President, the Votes shall be taken by States, the Representation from each State having one Vote; a quorum for this Purpose shall consist of a Member or Members from two thirds of the States, and a Majority of all the States shall be necessary to a Choice. In every Case, after the Choice of the President, the Person having the greatest Number of Votes of the Electors shall be the Vice President. But if there should remain two or more who have equal Votes, the Senate shall chuse from them by Ballot the Vice President.]

The Congress may determine the Time of chusing the Electors, and the Day on which they shall give their Votes; which Day shall be the same throughout the United States.

No Person except a natural born Citizen, or a Citizen of the United States, at the time of the Adoption of this Constitution, shall be eligible to the Office of President; neither shall any Person be eligible to that Office who shall not have attained to the Age of thirty five Years, and been fourteen Years a Resident within the United States.

In Case of the Removal of the President from Office, or of his Death, Resignation, or Inability to discharge the Powers and Duties of the said Office, the Same shall devolve on the Vice President, and the Congress may by Law provide for the Case of Removal, Death, Resignation or Inability, both of the President and Vice President, declaring what Officer shall then act as President, and such Officer shall act accordingly, until

the Disability be removed, or a President shall be elected.

The President shall, at stated Times, receive for his Services, a Compensation, which shall neither be encreased nor diminished during the Period for which he shall have been elected, and he shall not receive within that Period any other Emolument from the United States, or any of them.

Before he enter on the Execution of his Office, he shall take the following Oath or Affirmation:—"I do solemnly swear (or affirm) that I will faithfully execute the Office of President of the United States, and will to the best of my Ability, preserve, protect and defend the Constitution of the United States."

Section 2. The President shall be Commander in Chief of the Army and Navy of the United States, and of the Militia of the several States, when called into the actual Service of the United States; he may require the Opinion, in writing, of the principal Officer in each of the executive Departments, upon any Subject relating to the Duties of their respective Offices, and he shall have Power to grant Reprieves and Pardons for Offences against the United States, except in Cases of Impeachment.

He shall have Power, by and with the Advice and Consent of the Senate, to make Treaties, provided two thirds of the Senators present concur; and he shall nominate, and by and with the Advice and Consent of the Senate, shall appoint Ambassadors, other public Ministers and Consuls, Judges of the supreme Court, and all other Officers of the United States, whose Appointments are not herein otherwise provided for, and which shall be established by Law: but the Congress may by Law vest the Appointment of such inferior Officers, as they think proper, in the President alone, in the Courts of Law, or in the Heads of Departments.

The President shall have Power to fill up all Vacancies that may happen during the Recess of the Senate, by granting Commissions which shall expire at the End of their next Session.

Section 3. He shall from time to time give to the Congress Information of the State of the

Union, and recommend to their Consideration such Measures as he shall judge necessary and expedient; he may, on extraordinary Occasions, convene both Houses, or either of them, and in Case of Disagreement between them, with Respect to the Time of Adjournment, he may adjourn them to such Time as he shall think proper; he shall receive Ambassadors and other public Ministers; he shall take Care that the Laws be faithfully executed, and shall Commission all the Officers of the United States.

Section 4. The President, Vice President and all civil Officers of the United States, shall be removed from Office on Impeachment for, and Conviction of, Treason, Bribery, or other high Crimes and Misdemeanors.

ARTICLE III

Section 1. The judicial Power of the United States, shall be vested in one supreme Court, and in such inferior Courts as the Congress may from time to time ordain and establish. The Judges, both of the supreme and inferior Courts, shall hold their Offices during good Behaviour, and shall, at stated Times, receive for their Services, a Compensation, which shall not be diminished during their Continuance in Office.

Section 2. The judicial Power shall extend to all Cases, in Law and Equity, arising under this Constitution, the Laws of the United States, and Treaties made, or which shall be made, under their Authority;—to all Cases affecting Ambassadors, other public Ministers and Consuls;—to all Cases of admiralty and maritime Jurisdiction;—to Controversies to which the United States shall be a Party;—to Controversies between two or more States; —between a State and Citizens of another State; —between Citizens of different States;—between Citizens of the same State claiming Lands under Grants of different States, and between a State, or the Citizens thereof, and foreign States, Citizens or Subjects.

In all Cases affecting Ambassadors, other public Ministers and Consuls, and those in which a State shall be Party, the supreme Court shall have original Jurisdiction. In all the other Cases before mentioned, the supreme Court shall have appellate Jurisdiction, both as to Law and Fact, with such Exceptions, and under such Regulations as the Congress shall make.

The Trial of all Crimes, except in Cases of Impeachment, shall be by Jury; and such Trial shall be held in the State where the said Crimes shall have been committed; but when not committed within any State, the Trial shall be at such Place or Places as the Congress may by Law have directed.

Section 3. Treason against the United States, shall consist only in levying War against them, or in adhering to their Enemies, giving them Aid and Comfort. No Person shall be convicted of Treason unless on the Testimony of two Witnesses to the same overt Act, or on Confession in open Court.

The Congress shall have Power to declare the Punishment of Treason, but no Attainder of Treason shall work Corruption of Blood, or Forfeiture except during the Life of the Person attainted. . . .

ARTICLE VI

All Debts contracted and Engagements entered into, before the Adoption of this Constitution, shall be as valid against the United States under this Constitution, as under the Confederation.

This Constitution, and the Laws of the United States which shall be made in Pursuance thereof; and all Treaties made, or which shall be made, under the Authority of the United States, shall be the supreme Law of the Land; and the Judges in every State shall be bound thereby, any Thing in the Constitution or Laws of any State to the Contrary notwithstanding.

The Senators and Representatives before mentioned, and the Members of the several State Legislatures, and all executive and judicial Officers, both of the United States and of the several States, shall be bound by Oath or Affirmation, to support this Constitution; but no religious Test shall ever be required as a Qualification to any Office or public Trust under the United States. . . .

AMENDMENTS (First ten amendments ratified December 15, 1791)

Amendment I

Congress shall make no law respecting an establishment of religion, or prohibiting the free exercise thereof; or abridging the freedom of speech, or of the press; or the right of the people peaceably to assemble, and to petition the Government for a redress of grievances.

Amendment II

A well regulated Militia, being necessary to the security of a free State, the right of the people to keep and bear Arms, shall not be infringed.

Amendment III

No Soldier shall, in time of peace be quartered in any house, without the consent of the Owner, nor in time of war, but in a manner to be prescribed by law.

Amendment IV

The right of the people to be secure in their persons, houses, papers, and effects, against unreasonable searches and seizures, shall not be violated, and no Warrants shall issue, but upon probable cause, supported by Oath or affirmation, and particularly describing the place to be searched, and the persons or things to be seized.

Amendment V

No person shall be held to answer for a capital, or otherwise infamous crime, unless on a presentment or indictment of a Grand Jury, except in cases arising in the land or naval forces, or in the Militia, when in actual service in time of War or public danger; nor shall any person be

subject for the same offence to be twice put in jeopardy of life or limb; nor shall be compelled in any criminal case to be a witness against himself, nor be deprived of life, liberty, or property, without due process of law; nor shall private property be taken for public use, without just compensation.

Amendment VI

In all criminal prosecutions, the accused shall enjoy the right to a speedy and public trial, by an impartial jury of the State and district wherein the crime shall have been committed, which district shall have been previously ascertained by law, and to be informed of the nature and cause of the accusation; to be confronted with the witnesses against him; to have compulsory process for obtaining witnesses in his favor, and to have the Assistance of Counsel for his defence.

Amendment VII

In Suits at common law, where the value in controversy shall exceed twenty dollars, the right of trial by jury shall be preserved, and no fact tried by a jury, shall be otherwise re-examined in any Court of the United States, than according to the rules of the common law.

Amendment VIII

Excessive bail shall not be required, nor excessive fines imposed, nor cruel and unusual punishments inflicted.

Amendment IX

The enumeration in the Constitution, of certain rights, shall not be construed to deny or disparage others retained by the people.

Amendment X

The powers not delegated to the United States by the Constitution, nor prohibited by it to the

States, are reserved to the States respectively, or to the people.

Amendment XI (Ratified February 7, 1795)

The Judicial power of the United States shall not be construed to extend to any suit in law or equity, commenced or prosecuted against one of the United States by Citizens of another State, or by Citizens or Subjects of any Foreign State.

Amendment XII (Ratified June 15, 1804)

The Electors shall meet in their respective states and vote by ballot for President and Vice-President, one of whom, at least, shall not be an inhabitant of the same state with themselves; they shall name in their ballots the person voted for as President, and in distinct ballots the person voted for as Vice-President, and they shall make distinct lists of all persons voted for as President, and of all persons voted for as Vice-President, and of the number of votes for each, which lists they shall sign and certify, and transmit sealed to the seat of the government of the United States, directed to the President of the Senate;—The President of the Senate shall, in the presence of the Senate and House of Representatives, open all the certificates and the votes shall then be counted;—The person having the greatest number of votes for President, shall be the President, if such number be a majority of the whole number of Electors appointed; and if no person have such majority, then from the persons having the highest numbers not exceeding three on the list of those voted for as President, the House of Representatives shall choose immediately, by ballot, the President. But in choosing the President, the votes shall be taken by states, the representation from each state having one vote; a quorum for this purpose shall consist of a member or members from two-thirds of the states, and a majority of all the states shall be necessary to a choice. [And if the House of Representatives shall not choose a President whenever the right of choice shall devolve upon them, before the

fourth day of March next following, then the Vice-President shall act as President, as in the case of the death or other constitutional disability of the President.] The person having the greatest number of votes as Vice-President, shall be the Vice-President, if such number be a majority of the whole number of Electors appointed, and if no person have a majority, then from the two highest numbers on the list, the Senate shall choose the Vice-President; a quorum for the purpose shall consist of two-thirds of the whole number of Senators, and a majority of the whole number shall be necessary to a choice. But no person constitutionally ineligible to the office of President shall be eligible to that of Vice-President of the United States.

Amendment XIII (Ratified December 6, 1865)

Section 1. Neither slavery nor involuntary servitude, except as a punishment for crime whereof the party shall have been duly convicted, shall exist within the United States, or any place subject to their jurisdiction.

Section 2. Congress shall have power to enforce this article by appropriate legislation.

Amendment XIV (Ratified July 9, 1868)

Section 1. All persons born or naturalized in the United States, and subject to the jurisdiction thereof, are citizens of the United States and of the State wherein they reside. No State shall make or enforce any law which shall abridge the privileges or immunities of citizens of the United States; nor shall any State deprive any person of life, liberty, or property, without due process of law; nor deny to any person within its jurisdiction the equal protection of the laws.

Section 2. Representatives shall be apportioned among the several States according to their respective numbers, counting the whole number of persons in each State, excluding Indians not taxed. But when the right to vote at any election for the choice of electors for President and Vice President of the United States, Representatives in Congress, the Executive and Judicial officers of a State, or the members of the Legislature thereof, is denied to any of the male inhabitants of such State, being twenty-one years of age, and citizens of the United States, or in any way abridged, except for participation in rebellion, or other crime, the basis of representation therein shall be reduced in the proportion which the number of such male citizens shall bear to the whole number of male citizens twenty-one years of age in such State.

Section 3. No person shall be a Senator or Representative in Congress, or elector of President and Vice President, or hold any office, civil or military, under the United States, or under any State, who, having previously taken an oath, as a member of Congress, or as an officer of the United States, or as a member of any State legislature, or as an executive or judicial officer of any State, to support the Constitution of the United States, shall have engaged in insurrection or rebellion against the same, or given aid or comfort to the enemies thereof. But Congress may by a vote of two-thirds of each House, remove such disability.

Section 4. The validity of the public debt of the United States, authorized by law, including debts incurred for payment of pensions and bounties for services in suppressing insurrection or rebellion, shall not be questioned. But neither the United States nor any State shall assume or pay any debt or obligation incurred in aid of insurrection or rebellion against the United States, or any claim for the loss or emancipation of any slave; but all such debts, obligations and claims shall be held illegal and void.

Section 5. The Congress shall have power to enforce, by appropriate legislation, the provisions of this article.

Amendment XV (Ratified February 3, 1870)

Section 1. The right of citizens of the United States to vote shall not be denied or abridged by the United States or by any State on account of race, color, or previous condition of servitude.

Section 2. The Congress shall have power to enforce this article by appropriate legislation.

Amendment XVI (Ratified February 3, 1913)

The Congress shall have power to lay and collect taxes on incomes, from whatever source derived, without apportionment among the several States, and without regard to any census or enumeration.

Amendment XVII (Ratified April 8, 1913)

The Senate of the United States shall be composed of two Senators from each State, elected by the people thereof, for six years; and each Senator shall have one vote. The electors in each State shall have the qualifications requisite for electors of the most numerous branch of the State legislatures.

When vacancies happen in the representation of any State in the Senate, the executive authority of such State shall issue writs of election to fill such vacancies: Provided, That the legislature of any State may empower the executive thereof to make temporary appointments until the people fill the vacancies by election as the legislature may direct.

This amendment shall not be so construed as to affect the election or term of any Senator chosen before it becomes valid as part of the Constitution.

[Amendment XVIII (Ratified January 16, 1919)

Section 1. After one year from the ratification of this article the manufacture, sale, or transportation of intoxicating liquors within, the importation thereof into, or the exportation thereof from the United States and all territory subject to the jurisdiction thereof for beverage purposes is hereby prohibited.

Section 2. The Congress and the several States shall have concurrent power to enforce this article by appropriate legislation.

Section 3. This article shall be inoperative unless it shall have been ratified as an amendment to the Constitution by the legislatures of the several States, as provided in the Constitution, within seven years from the date of the submission hereof to the States by the Congress.]

Amendment XIX (Ratified August 18, 1920)

The right of citizens of the United States to vote shall not be denied or abridged by the United States or by any State on account of sex.

Congress shall have power to enforce this article by appropriate legislation.

Amendment XX (Ratified January 23, 1933)

Section 1. The terms of the President and Vice President shall end at noon on the 20th day of January, and the terms of Senators and Representatives at noon on the 3d day of January, of the years in which such terms would have ended if this article had not been ratified; and the terms of their successors shall then begin.

Section 2. The Congress shall assemble at least once in every year, and such meeting shall begin at noon on the 3d day of January, unless they shall by law appoint a different day.

Section 3. If, at the time fixed for the beginning of the term of the President, the President elect shall have died, the Vice President elect shall become President. If a President shall not have been chosen before the time fixed for the beginning of his term, or if the President elect shall have failed to qualify, then the Vice President elect shall act as President until a President shall have qualified; and the Congress may by law provide for the case wherein neither a President elect nor a Vice President elect shall have qualified, declaring who shall then act as President, or the manner in which one who is to act shall be selected, and such person shall act accordingly until a President or Vice President shall have qualified.

Section 4. The Congress may by law provide for the case of the death of any of the persons from whom the House of Representatives may choose a President whenever the right of choice shall have devolved upon them, and for the case of the death of any of the persons from whom the Senate may choose a Vice President whenever the right of choice shall have devolved upon them.

Section 5. Sections 1 and 2 shall take effect on the 15th day of October following the ratification of this article.

Section 6. This article shall be inoperative unless it shall have been ratified as an amendment to the Constitution by the legislatures of three-fourths of the several States within seven years from the date of its submission.

Amendment XXI (Ratified December 5, 1933)

Section 1. The eighteenth article of amendment to the Constitution of the United States is hereby repealed.

Section 2. The transportation or importation into any State, Territory, or possession of the United States for delivery or use therein of intoxicating liquors, in violation of the laws thereof, is hereby prohibited.

Section 3. This article shall be inoperative unless it shall have been ratified as an amendment to the Constitution by conventions in the several States, as provided in the Constitution, within seven years from the date of the submission hereof to the States by the Congress.

Amendment XXII (Ratified February 27, 1951)

Section 1. No person shall be elected to the office of the President more than twice, and no person who has held the office of President, or acted as President, for more than two years of a term to which some other person was elected President shall be elected to the office of the President more than once. But this Article shall not apply to any person holding the office of President when this Article was proposed by the Congress, and shall not prevent any person who may be holding the office of President, or acting as President, during the term within which this Article become operative from holding the office of President or acting as President during the remainder of such term.

Section 2. This article shall be inoperative unless it shall have been ratified as an amendment to the Constitution by the legislatures of three-fourths of the several States within seven years from the date of its submission to the States by the Congress.

Amendment XXIII (Ratified March 29, 1961)

Section 1. The District constituting the seat of Government of the United States shall appoint in such manner as the Congress may direct:

A number of electors of President and Vice President equal to the whole number of Senators and Representatives in Congress to which the District would be entitled if it were a State, but in no event more than the least populous State; they shall be in addition to those appointed by the States, but they shall be considered, for the purposes of the election of President and Vice President, to be electors appointed by a State; and they shall meet in the District and perform such duties as provided by the twelfth article of amendment.

Section 2. The Congress shall have power to enforce this article by appropriate legislation.

Amendment XXIV (Ratified January 23, 1964)

Section 1. The right of citizens of the United States to vote in any primary or other election for President or Vice President, for electors for President or Vice President, or for Senator or Representative in Congress, shall not be denied or abridged by the United States or any State by reason of failure to pay any poll tax or other tax.

Section 2. The Congress shall have power to enforce this article by appropriate legislation.

Amendment XXV (Ratified February 10, 1967)

Section 1. In case of the removal of the President from office or of his death or resignation, the Vice President shall become President.

Section 2. Whenever there is a vacancy in the office of the Vice President, the President shall nominate a Vice President who shall take office upon confirmation by a majority vote of both Houses of Congress.

Section 3. Whenever the President transmits to the President pro tempore of the Senate and the Speaker of the House of Representatives his written declaration that he is unable to discharge the powers and duties of his office, and until he transmits to them a written declaration to the contrary, such powers and duties shall be discharged by the Vice President as Acting President.

Section 4. Whenever the Vice President and a majority of either the principal officers of the executive departments or of such other body as Congress may by law provide, transmit to the President pro tempore of the Senate and the Speaker of the House of Representatives their written declaration that the President is unable to discharge the powers and duties of his office, the Vice President shall immediately assume the powers and duties of the office as Acting President.

Thereafter, when the President transmits to the President pro tempore of the Senate and the Speaker of the House of Representatives his written declaration that no inability exists, he shall resume the powers and duties of his office unless the Vice President and a majority of either the principal officers of the executive department or of such other body as Congress may by law provide, transmit within four days to the President pro tempore of the Senate and the Speaker of the House of Representatives their written declaration that the President is unable to discharge the powers and duties of his office. Thereupon Congress shall decide the issue, assembling within forty-eight hours for that purpose if not in session. If the Congress, within twenty-one days after receipt of the latter written declaration, or, if Congress is not in session, within twenty-one days after Congress is required to assemble, determines by two-thirds vote of both Houses that the President is unable to discharge the powers and duties of his office, the Vice President shall continue to discharge the same as Acting President; otherwise, the President shall resume the powers and duties of his office.

Amendment XXVI (Ratified July 1, 1971)

Section 1. The right of citizens of the United States, who are eighteen years of age or older, to vote shall not be denied or abridged by the United States or by any State on account of age.

Section 2. The Congress shall have power to enforce this article by appropriate legislation.

Amendment XXVII (Ratified May 7, 1992)

No law varying the compensation for the services of the Senators and Representatives shall take effect, until an election of Representatives shall have intervened.

Source: Accessible at http://caselaw.lp.findlaw.com/data/constitution/articles.html and http://caselaw.lp.findlaw.com/data/constitution/amendments.html.

Document 11   *The Federalist Papers*
                    1787–1788

Alexander Hamilton, John Jay, and James Madison wrote the Federalist Papers *under the pseudonym Publius during the debate over the ratification of the U.S. Constitution in New York state. Today, the essays are considered some of the most important works of American political thought, explaining and defending as they do the new constitutional structure. Hamilton, Jay, and Madison wrote them in response to critics of the Constitution and to ease the concerns of those who feared, among other things, the concentration of power in a central government, the blending of the powers of the three branches of government through checks and balances, and the particular powers given each of the branches.*

James Madison, the "Father of the Constitution," provided the primary intellectual leadership in the writing of the document. His long career in public service included positions as a state assemblyman and congressman for Virginia, secretary of state, and U.S. president. Alexander Hamilton, a prominent New York lawyer who had served as George Washington's aide-de-camp and personal secretary during the Revolutionary War, took a leading role in calling for a constitutional convention to revise the Articles of Confederation. His influence at the 1787 Philadelphia convention was limited because fellow delegates did not share his desire for a strong central government. He did, however, exert considerable influence in the ratification battle in New York, enlisting Madison and prominent jurist John Jay to assist in writing the Federalist Papers *essays. Hamilton later served as secretary of the Treasury under George Washington.*

Federalist *No. 22*

Many critics of the Constitution argued that it strayed too far from the principles established in the first U.S. constitution—the Articles of Confederation (Doc. 9)—which put a premium on state power and autonomy. Hamilton outlined the problems that had resulted from the Articles' weaknesses, making the case for a radically revised constitutional structure.

In addition to the defects already enumerated in the existing Foederal system, there are others of not less importance, which concur in rendering it altogether unfit for the administration of the affairs of the Union.

The want of a power to regulate commerce is by all parties allowed to be of the number. . . . It is indeed evident, on the most superficial view, that there is no object, either as it respects the interests of trade or finance that more strongly demands a Federal superintendence. The want of it has already operated as a bar to the formation of beneficial treaties with foreign powers; and has given occasions of dissatisfaction between the States. No nation acquainted with the nature of our political association would be unwise enough to enter into stipulations with the United States, by which they conceded privileges of any importance to them, while they were apprised that the engagements on the part of the Union, might at any moment be violated by its members; and while they found from experience that they might enjoy every advantage they desired in our markets, without granting us any return, but such as their momentary convenience might suggest. . . .

A circumstance, which crowns the defects of the confederation, remains yet to be mentioned—the want of a judiciary power. Laws are a dead letter without courts to expound and define their true meaning and operation. The treaties of the United States to have any force at all, must be considered as part of the law of the land. Their true import as far as respects individuals, must, like all other laws, be ascertained by judicial determinations. To produce uniformity in these determinations, they ought to be submitted in the last resort, to one SUPREME TRIBUNAL. And this tribunal ought to be instituted under the same authority which forms the treaties themselves. These ingredients are both indispensable. If there is in each State, a court of final jurisdiction, there may be as many different final determinations on the same point, as there are courts. There are endless diversities in the opinions of men. We often see not only different

courts, but the Judges of the same court differing from each other. To avoid the confusion which would unavoidably result from the contradictory decisions of a number of independent judicatories, all nations have found it necessary to establish one court paramount to the rest—possessing a general superintendance, and authorised to settle and declare in the last resort, an uniform rule of civil justice.

This is the more necessary where the frame of the government is so compounded, that the laws of the whole are in danger of being contravened by the laws of the parts. In this case if the particular tribunals are invested with a right of ultimate jurisdiction, besides the contradictions to be expected from difference of opinion, there will be much to fear from the bias of local views and prejudices, and from the interference of local regulations. As often as such an interference was to happen, there would be reason to apprehend, that the provisions of the particular laws might be preferred to those of the general laws; for nothing is more natural to men in office, than to look with peculiar deference towards that authority to which they owe their official existence. . . .

The organization of Congress [under the Articles of Confederation], is itself utterly improper for the exercise of those powers which are necessary to be deposited in the Union. A single Assembly may be a proper receptacle of those slender, or rather fettered authorities, which have been heretofore delegated to the federal head; but it would be inconsistent with all the principles of good government, to intrust it with those additional powers which even the moderate and more rational adversaries of the proposed constitution admit ought to reside in the United States. If that plan should not be adopted; and if the necessity of union should be able to withstand the ambitious aims of those men, who may indulge magnificent schemes of personal aggrandizement from its dissolution; the probability would be, that we should run into the project of conferring supplementary powers upon Congress as they are now constituted; and either the machine, from the intrinsic feebleness of its structure, will moulder into pieces in spite of our ill-judged efforts to prop it; or by successive augmentations of its force and energy, as necessity might prompt, we shall finally accumulate in a single body, all the most important prerogatives of sovereignty; and thus entail upon our posterity, one of the most execrable forms of government that human infatuation ever contrived. Thus we should create in reality that very tyranny, which the adversaries of the new constitution either are, or affect to be solicitous to avert. . . .

Source: Alexander Hamilton, James Madison, and John Jay, *The Federalist,* ed. Jacob E. Cooke (Middletown, Conn.: Wesleyan University Press, 1961), 135–146. Accessible at http://press-pubs.uchicago.edu/founders/documents/v1ch5s23.html.

Federalist No. 44

The necessary and proper clause of Article 1 drew particular criticism, as Anti-Federalists viewed it as a blank check to congressional power. James Madison sought to justify Congress's power based on the needs of government and the governing experience under the Articles of Confederation (Doc. 9).

Few parts of the Constitution have been assailed with more intemperance than this; yet on a fair investigation of it, no part can appear more completely invulnerable. Without the *substance* of this power, the whole Constitution would be a dead letter. Those who object to the article therefore as a part of the Constitution, can only mean that the *form* of the provision is improper. But have they considered whether a better form could have been substituted?

There are four other possible methods which the Convention might have taken on this subject. They might have copied the second article of the existing confederation which would have prohibited the exercise of any power not *expressly* delegated; they might have attempted a positive enumeration of the powers comprehended under the general terms "necessary and proper"; they might have attempted a negative enumeration of them, by specifying the powers excepted from the general definition: They might have been altogether silent on the subject; leaving these necessary and proper powers, to construction and inference.

Had the Convention taken the first method of adopting the second article of confederation; it is evident that the new Congress would be continually exposed as their predecessors have been, to the alternative of construing the term *"expressly"* with so much rigor as to disarm the government of all real authority whatever, or with so much latitude as to destroy altogether the force of the restriction. It would be easy to show if it were necessary, that no important power, delegated by the articles of confederation, has been or can be executed by Congress, without recurring more or less to the doctrine of *construction* or *implication.* As the powers delegated under the new system are more extensive, the government which is to administer it would find itself still more distressed with the alternative of betraying the public interest by doing nothing; or of violating the Constitution by exercising powers, indispensably necessary and proper; but at the same time, not *expressly* granted.

Had the convention attempted a positive enumeration of the powers necessary and proper for carrying their other powers into effect; the attempt would have involved a complete digest of laws on every subject to which the Constitution relates; accommodated too not only to the existing state of things, but to all the possible changes which futurity may produce: For in every new application of a general power, the *particular powers,* which are the means of attaining the *object* of the general power, must always necessarily vary with that object; and be often properly varied whilst the object remains the same.

Had they attempted to enumerate the particular powers or means, not necessary or proper for carrying the general powers into execution, the task would have been no less chimerical; and would have been liable to this further objection; that every defect in the enumeration, would have been equivalent to a positive grant of authority. If to avoid this consequence they had attempted a partial enumeration of the exceptions, and described the residue by the general terms, *not necessary or proper*: It must have happened that the enumeration would comprehend a few of the excepted powers only; that these would be such as would be least likely to be assumed or tolerated, because the enumeration would of course select such as would be least necessary or proper, and that the unnecessary and improper powers included in the residuum, would be less *forceably* excepted, than if no partial enumeration had been made.

Had the Constitution been silent on this head, there can be no doubt that all the particular powers, requisite as means of executing the general powers, would have resulted to the government, by unavoidable implication. No axiom is more clearly established in law, or in reason, than that wherever the end is required, the means are authorized; wherever a general power to do a thing is given, every particular power necessary for doing it, is included. Had this last method therefore been pursued by the Convention, every objection now urged against their plan, would remain in all its plausibility; and the real inconveniency would be incurred, of not removing a pretext which may be seized on critical occasions for drawing into question the essential powers of the Union.

If it be asked, what is to be the consequence, in case the Congress shall misconstrue this part of the Constitution, and exercise powers not warranted by its true meaning? I answer the same as if they should misconstrue or enlarge any other power vested in them, as if the general power had been reduced to particulars, and any one of these were to be violated; the same in short, as if the State Legislatures should violate their respective constitutional authorities. In the first instance, the success of the usurpation will depend on the executive and judiciary departments, which are to expound and give effect to the legislative acts; and in the last resort, a remedy must be obtained from the people, who can by the election of more faithful representatives, annul the acts of the usurpers. The truth is, that this ultimate redress may be more confided in against unconstitutional acts of the federal than of the State Legislatures, for this plain reason, that as every such act of the former, will be an invasion of the rights of the latter, these will be ever ready to mark the innovation, to sound the alarm to the people, and to exert their local influence in effecting a change of foederal representatives. There being no such intermediate body between the State Legislatures and the people, interested in watching the conduct of the former, violations of the State Constitutions are more likely to remain unnoticed and unredressed.

Source: Alexander Hamilton, James Madison, and John Jay, *The Federalist,* ed. Jacob E. Cooke (Middletown, Conn.: Wesleyan University Press, 1961), 303–305. Accessible at http://press-pubs.uchicago.edu/founders/documents/a1_8_18s7.html.

Federalist No. 51

Many of the Constitution's critics objected to what they saw as too much overlapping of power among the legislative, executive, and judicial branches. James Madison justified the system of checks and balances as a means of ensuring that the basic separation of the branches would be maintained in practice. In addition, he contended that two levels of government, national and state, would provide additional checks on abuse of power.

To what expedient then shall we finally resort for maintaining in practice the necessary partition of power among the several departments, as laid down in the constitution? The only answer that can be given is, that as all these exterior provisions are found to be inadequate, the defect must be supplied, by so contriving the interior structure of the government, as that its several constituent parts may, by their mutual relations, be the means of keeping each other in their proper places. Without presuming to under-take a full development of this important idea, I will hazard a few general observations, which may perhaps place it in a clearer light, and enable us to form a more correct judgment of the principles and structure of the government planned by the convention.

In order to lay a due foundation for that separate and distinct exercise of the different powers of government, which to a certain extent, is admitted on all hands to be essential to the preservation of liberty, it is evident that each department should have a will of its own; and consequently should be so constituted, that the members of each should have as little agency as possible in the appointment of the members of the others. Were this principle rigorously adhered to, it would require that all the appointments for the supreme executive, legislative, and judiciary magistracies, should be drawn from the same fountain of authority, the people, through channels, having no communication whatever with one another. Perhaps such a plan of constructing the several departments would be less difficult in practice than it may in contemplation appear. Some difficulties however, and some additional expence, would attend the execution of it. Some deviations therefore from the principle must be admitted. In the constitution of the judiciary department in particular, it might be inexpedient to insist rigorously on the principle; first, because peculiar qualifications being essen-

tial in the members, the primary consideration ought to be to select that mode of choice, which best secures these qualifications; secondly, because the permanent tenure by which the appointments are held in that department, must soon destroy all sense of dependence on the authority conferring them.

It is equally evident that the members of each department should be as little dependent as possible on those of the others, for the emoluments annexed to their offices. Were the executive magistrate, or the judges, not independent of the legislature in this particular, their independence in every other would be merely nominal.

But the great security against a gradual concentration of the several powers in the same department, consists in giving to those who administer each department, the necessary constitutional means, and personal motives, to resist encroachments of the others. The provision for defence must in this, as in all other cases, be made commensurate to the danger of attack. Ambition must be made to counteract ambition. The interest of the man must be connected with the constitutional rights of the place. It may be a reflection on human nature, that such devices should be necessary to controul the abuses of government. But what is government itself but the greatest of all reflections on human nature? If men were angels, no government would be necessary. If angels were to govern men, neither external nor internal controuls on government would be necessary. In framing a government which is to be administered by men over men, the great difficulty lies in this: You must first enable the government to controul the governed; and in the next place, oblige it to controul itself. A dependence on the people is no doubt the primary controul on the government; but experience has taught mankind the necessity of auxiliary precautions.

This policy of supplying by opposite and rival interests, the defect of better motives, might be traced through the whole system of human affairs, private as well as public. We see it particularly displayed in all the subordinate distributions of power; where the constant aim is to divide and arrange the several offices in such a manner as that each may be a check on the other; that the private interest of every individual, may be a centinel over the public rights. These inventions of prudence cannot be less requisite in the distribution of the supreme powers of the state.

But it is not possible to give to each department an equal power of self defence. In republican government the legislative authority, necessarily, predominates. The remedy for this inconveniency is, to divide the legislature into different branches; and to render them by different modes of election, and different principles of action, as little connected with each other, as the nature of their common functions, and their common dependence on the society, will admit. It may even be necessary to guard against dangerous encroachments by still further precautions. As the weight of the legislative authority requires that it should be thus divided, the weakness of the executive may require, on the other hand, that it should be fortified. An absolute negative, on the legislature, appears at first view to be the natural defence with which the executive magistrate should be armed. But perhaps it would be neither altogether safe, nor alone sufficient. On ordinary occasions, it might not be exerted with the requisite firmness; and on extraordinary occasions, it might be perfidiously abused. May not this defect of an absolute negative be supplied, by some qualified connection between this weaker department, and the weaker branch of the stronger department, by which the latter may be led to support the constitutional rights of the former, without being too much detached from the rights of its own department? . . .

There are moreover two considerations particularly applicable to the federal system of America, which place that system in a very interesting point of view.

First. In a single republic, all the power surrendered by the people, is submitted to the administration of a single government; and usurpations are guarded against by a division of the government into distinct and separate departments. In the compound republic of America, the power surrendered by the people, is first divided between two distinct governments, and then the portion allotted to each, subdivided among distinct and separate departments. Hence a double security arises to the rights of the people. The different governments will controul each other; at the same time that each will be controuled by itself.

Second. It is of great importance in a republic, not only to guard the society against the oppression of its rulers; but to guard one part of the society against the injustice of the other part. Different interests necessarily exist in different classes of citizens. If a majority be united by a common interest, the rights of the minority will be insecure. There are but two methods of providing against this evil: The one by creating a will in the community independent of the majority, that is, of the society itself; the other by comprehending in the society so many separate descriptions of citizens, as will render an unjust combination of a majority of the whole, very improbable, if not impracticable. The first method prevails in all governments possessing an hereditary or self appointed authority. This at best is but a precarious security; because a power independent of the society may as well espouse the unjust views of the major, as the rightful interests, of the minor party, and may possibly be turned against both parties. The second method will be exemplified in the federal republic of the United States. Whilst all authority in it will be derived from and dependent on the society, the society itself will be broken into so many parts, interests and classes of citizens, that the rights of individuals or of the minority, will be in little danger from interested combinations of the majority. In a free government, the security for civil rights must be the same as for religious rights. It consists in the one case in the multiplicity of interests, and in the other, in the multiplicity of sects. The degree of security in both cases will depend on the number of interests and sects; and this may be presumed to depend on the extent of country and number of people comprehended under the same government. This view of the subject must particularly recommend a proper federal system to all the sincere and considerate friends of republican government: Since it shews that in exact proportion as the territory of the union may be formed into more circumscribed confederacies or states, oppressive combinations of a majority will be facilitated, the best security under the republican form, for the rights of every class of citizens, will be diminished; and consequently, the stability and independence of some member of the government, the only other security, must be proportionally increased. Justice is the end of government. It is the end of civil so-

ciety. It ever has been, and ever will be pursued, until it be obtained, or until liberty be lost in the pursuit. In a society under the forms of which the stronger faction can readily unite and oppress the weaker, anarchy may as truly be said to reign, as in a state of nature where the weaker individual is not secured against the violence of the stronger: And as in the latter state even the stronger individuals are prompted by the uncertainty of their condition, to submit to a government which may protect the weak as well as themselves: So in the former state, will the more powerful factions or parties be gradually induced by a like motive, to wish for a government which will protect all parties, the weaker as well as the more powerful. . . .

Source: Alexander Hamilton, James Madison, and John Jay, *The Federalist,* ed. Jacob E. Cooke (Middletown, Conn.: Wesleyan University Press, 1961), 347–353. Accessible at http://press-pubs.uchicago.edu/founders/documents/v1ch10s16. html.

Federalist No. 65

The Constitution allows the legislative branch to sit in judgment of executive and judicial officers through the impeachment process, which the Anti-Federalists objected to on the grounds that powers were blended. Alexander Hamilton explained how the impeachment process was to work and why the Senate was the best institution for trials following impeachment.

A well constituted court for the trial of impeachments, is an object not more to be desired than difficult to be obtained in a government wholly elective. The subjects of its jurisdiction are those offenses which proceed from the misconduct of public men, or in other words from the abuse or violation of some public trust. They are of a nature which may with peculiar propriety be denominated POLITICAL, as they relate chiefly to injuries done immediately to the society itself. The prosecution of them, for this reason, will seldom fail to agitate the passions of the whole community, and to divide it into parties, more or less friendly or inimical, to the accused. In many cases, it will connect itself with the pre-existing factions, and will inlist all their ani-

mosities, partialities, influence and interest on one side, or on the other; and in such cases there will always be the greatest danger, that the decision will be regulated more by the comparative strength of parties than by the real demonstrations of innocence or guilt. . . .

What it may be asked is the true spirit of the institution itself? Is it not designed as a method of NATIONAL INQUEST into the conduct of public men? If this be the design of it, who can so properly be the inquisitors for the nation, as the representatives of the nation themselves? It is not disputed that the power of originating the inquiry, or in other words of preferring the impeachment ought to be lodged in the hands of one branch of the legislative body; will not the reasons which indicate the propriety of this arrangement, strongly plead for an admission of the other branch of that body to a share in the inquiry? . . .

Where else, than in the Senate could have been found a tribunal sufficiently dignified, or sufficiently independent? What other body would be likely to feel *confidence enough in its own situation,* to preserve unawed and uninfluenced the necessary impartiality between an *individual* accused, and the *representatives of the people, his accusers*?

Could the Supreme Court have been relied upon as answering this description? It is much to be doubted whether the members of that tribunal would, at all times, be endowed with so eminent a portion of fortitude, as would be called for in the execution of so difficult a task; & it is still more to be doubted, whether they would possess the degree of credit and authority, which might, on certain occasions, be indispensable, towards reconciling the people to a decision, that should happen to clash with an accusation brought by their immediate representatives. A deficiency in the first would be fatal to the accused; in the last, dangerous to the public tranquillity. The hazard in both these respects could only be avoided, if at all, by rendering that tribunal more numerous than would consist with a reasonable attention to oeconomy. The necessity of a numerous court for the trial of impeachments is equally dictated by the nature of the proceeding. This can never be tied down by such strict rules, either in the delineation of the offence by the prosecutors, or in the construction of it by the Judges, as in common cases serve to limit the discretion of courts in favor of personal security. There will be no jury to stand between the Judges, who are to pronounce the sentence of the law and the party who is to receive or suffer it. The awful discretion, which a court of impeachments must necessarily have, to doom to honor or to infamy the most confidential and the most distinguished characters of the community, forbids the commitment of the trust to a small number of persons.

These considerations seem alone sufficient to authorize a conclusion, that the Supreme Court would have been an improper substitute for the Senate, as a court of impeachments. There remains a further consideration which will not a little strengthen this conclusion. It is this. The punishment, which may be the consequence of conviction upon impeachment, is not to terminate the chastisement of the offender. After having been sentenced to a perpetual ostracism from the esteem and confidence, and honors and emoluments of his country; he will still be liable to prosecution and punishment in the ordinary course of law. Would it be proper that the persons, who had disposed of his fame and his most valuable rights as a citizen in one trial, should in another trial, for the same offence, be also the disposers of his life and his fortune? Would there not be the greatest reason to apprehend, that error in the first sentence would be the parent of error in the second sentence? That the strong bias of one decision would be apt to overrule the influence of any new lights, which might be brought to vary the complexion of another decision? Those, who know any thing of human nature, will not hesitate to answer these questions in the affirmative; and will be at no loss to perceive, that by making the same persons Judges in both cases, those who might happen to be the objects of prosecution would in a great measure be deprived of the double security, intended them by a double trial. . . .

Would it have been an improvement of the plan, to have united the Supreme Court with the Senate, in the formation of the court of impeachments? This Union would certainly have been attended with several advantages; but would they not have been overballanced by the signal disadvantage, already stated, arising from the agency of the same Judges in the double prosecution to which the offender would be liable? To a certain extent, the benefits of that Union will be obtained from making the Chief Justice of the Supreme Court the President of the court of impeachments, as is proposed to be done in the plan of the Convention; while the inconveniences of an intire incorporation of the former into the latter will be substantially avoided. This was perhaps the prudent mean. I forbear to remark upon the additional pretext for clamour, against the Judi-ciary, which so considerable an augmentation of its authority would have afforded. . . .

Source: Alexander Hamilton, James Madison, and John Jay, *The Federalist,* ed. Jacob E. Cooke (Middletown, Conn.: Wesleyan University Press, 1961), 439–445. Accessible at http://press-pubs.uchicago.edu/founders/documents/a1_2_5s9. html.

Federalist No. 66

In further defense of the impeachment arrangement (see Federalist No. 65), *Hamilton responded to critics' concerns about the separation of powers and the power of the Senate in particular.*

A review of the principal objections that have appeared against the proposed court for the trial of impeachments, will not improbably eradicate the remains of any unfavourable impressions, which may still exist, in regard to this matter.

The *first* of these objections is, that the provision in question confounds legislative and judiciary authorities in the same body; in violation of that important and well established maxim, which requires a separation between the different departments of power. The true meaning of this maxim has been discussed and ascertained in another place, and has been shewn to be entirely compatible with a partial intermixture of those departments for special purposes, preserving them in the main distinct and unconnected. This partial intermixture is even in some cases not only proper, but necessary to the mutual defence of the several members of the government, against each other. An absolute or qualified negative in the executive, upon the acts of the legislative body, is admitted by the ablest adepts in political science, to be an indefensible barrier against the encroachments of the latter upon the former. And it may perhaps with not less reason be contended that the powers relating to impeachments are as before intimated, an essential check in the hands of that body upon the encroachments of the executive. The division of them between the two branches of the legislature; assigning to one the right of accusing, to the other the right of judging; avoids the inconve-nience of making the same persons both accusers and judges; and guards against the danger of persecution from the prevalency of a factious spirit in either of those branches. As the concurrence of two-thirds of the senate will be requisite to a condemnation, the security to innocence, from this additional circumstance, will be as complete as itself can desire. . . .

A *second* objection to the senate, as a court of impeachments, is, that it contributes to an undue accumulation of power in that body, tending to give to the government a countenance too aristocratic. The senate, it is observed, is to have concurrent authority with the executive in the formation of treaties, and in the appointment to offices: If, say the objectors, to these prerogatives is added that of deciding in all cases of impeachment, it will give a decided predominancy to senatorial influence. To an objection so little precise in itself, it is not easy to find a very precise answer. Where is the measure or criterion to which we can appeal, for determining what will give the senate too much, too little, or barely the proper degree of influence? Will it not be more safe, as well as more simple, to dismiss such vague and uncertain calculations, to examine each power by itself, and to decide on general principles where it may be deposited with most advantage and least inconvenience? . . .

But this hypothesis, such as it is has already been refuted in the remarks applied to the duration in office prescribed for the senators. It was by them shewn, as well on the credit of historical examples, as from the reason of the thing, that the most popular branch of every government, partaking of the republican genius, by being generally the favorite of the people, will be as generally a full match, if not an overmatch, for every other member of the government.

But independent of this most active and operative principle; to secure the equilibrium of the national house of representatives, the plan of the convention has provided in its favor, several important counterpoises to the additional authorities, to be conferred upon the senate. The exclusive privilege of originating money bills will belong to the house of representatives. The same house will possess the sole right of instituting impeachments: Is not this a complete counterbalance to that of determining them? The same house will be the umpire in all elections of the president, which do not unite the suffrages of a majority of the whole number of electors; a case which it cannot be doubted will sometimes, if not frequently, happen. The constant possibility of the thing must be a fruitful source of influence to that body. The more it is contemplated, the more important will appear this ultimate, though contingent power of deciding the competitions of the most illustrious citizens of the union, for the first office in it. It would not perhaps be rash to pre-

dict, that as a mean of influence it will be found to outweigh all the peculiar attributes of the senate.

A third objection to the senate as a court of impeachments is drawn from the agency they are to have in the appointments to office. It is imagined that they would be too indulgent judges of the conduct of men, in whose official creation they had participated. . . .

It will be the office of the president to *nominate*, and with the advice and consent of the senate to *appoint*. There will of course be no exertion of *choice* on the part of the senate. They may defeat one choice of the executive, and oblige him to make another; but they cannot themselves *choose*—they can only ratify or reject the choice, of the president. They might even entertain a preference to some other person, at the very moment they were assenting to the one proposed; because there might be no positive ground of opposition to him; and they could not be sure, if they withheld their assent, that the subsequent nomination would fall upon their own favorite, or upon any other person in their estimation more meritorious than the one rejected. Thus it could hardly happen that the majority of the senate would feel any other complacency towards the object of an appointment, than such, as the appearances of merit, might inspire, and the proofs of the want of it, destroy. . . .

Source: Alexander Hamilton, James Madison, and John Jay, *The Federalist,* ed. Jacob E. Cooke (Middletown, Conn.: Wesleyan University Press, 1961), 445–451. Accessible at http://press-pubs.uchicago.edu/founders/documents/a1_2_5s10.html.

Federalist No. 70

The Articles of Confederation (Doc. 9) had established a legislature but not an executive power to carry out or enforce legislative decisions. The creation of a presidency and executive branch thus frightened many Anti-Federalists, who argued instead for multiple executives or a council of advisors to constrain presidential power. Hamilton's response to their concerns is a classic defense of a unitary executive.

There is an idea, which is not without its advocates, that a vigorous executive is inconsistent with the genius of republican government. The enlightened well wishers to this species of government must at least hope that the supposition is destitute of foundation; since they can never admit its truth, without at the same time admitting the condemnation of their own principles.

Energy in the executive is a leading character in the definition of good government. It is essential to the protection of the community against foreign attacks: It is not less essential to the steady administration of the laws, to the protection of property against those irregular and high handed combinations, which sometimes interrupt the ordinary course of justice, to the security of liberty against the enterprises and assaults of ambition, of faction and of anarchy. . . .

A feeble executive implies a feeble execution of the government. A feeble execution is but another phrase for a bad execution: And a government ill executed, whatever it may be in theory, must be in practice a bad government.

Taking it for granted, therefore that all men of sense will agree in the necessity of an energetic executive; it will only remain to inquire, what are the ingredients which constitute this energy—how far can they be combined with those other ingredients which constitute safety in the republican sense? And how far does this combination characterize the plan, which has been reported by the convention?

The ingredients, which constitute energy in the executive, are first unity, secondly duration, thirdly an adequate provision for its support, fourthly competent powers.

The circumstances which constitute safety in the republican sense are, 1st. a due dependence on the people, secondly a due responsibility.

Those politicians and statesmen, who have been the most celebrated for the soundness of their principles, and for the justness of their views, have declared in favor of a single executive and a numerous legislature. They have with great propriety considered energy as the most necessary qualification of the former, and have regarded this as most applicable to power in a single hand; while they have with equal propriety considered the latter as best adapted to deliberation and wisdom, and best calculated to conciliate the confidence of the people and to secure their privileges and interests.

That unity is conducive to energy will not be disputed. Decision, activity, secrecy, and dispatch will generally characterize the proceedings of one man, in a much more eminent degree, than the proceedings of any greater number; and in proportion as the number is increased, these qualities will be diminished.

This unity may be destroyed in two ways; either by vesting the power in two or more magistrates of equal dignity and authority; or by vesting it ostensibly in one man, subject in whole or in part to the control and co-operation of others, in the capacity of counselors to him. . . .

Wherever two or more persons are engaged in any common enterprize or pursuit, there is always danger of difference of opinion. If it be a public trust or office in which they are cloathed with equal dignity and authority, there is peculiar danger of personal emulation and even animosity. From either and especially from all these causes, the most bitter dissentions are apt to spring. Whenever these happen, they lessen the respectability, weaken the authority, and distract the plans and operations of those whom they divide. If they should unfortunately assail the supreme executive magistracy of a country, consisting of a plurality of persons, they might impede or frustrate the most important measures of the government, in the most critical emergencies of the state. And what is still worse, they might split the community into the most violent and irreconcilable factions, adhering differently to the different individuals who composed the magistracy. . . .

Upon the principles of a free government, inconveniencies from the source just mentioned must necessarily be submitted to in the formation of the legislature; but it is unnecessary and therefore unwise to introduce them into the constitution of the executive. It is here too that they may be most pernicious. In the legislature, promptitude of decision is oftener an evil than a benefit. The differences of opinion, and the jarrings of parties in that department of the government, though they may sometimes obstruct salutary plans, yet often promote deliberation and circumspection; and serve to check excesses in the majority. When a resolution too is once taken, the opposition must be at an end. That resolution is a law, and resistance to it punishable. But no favourable circumstances palliate or atone for the disadvantages of dissention in the executive department. Here they are pure and unmixed. There is no point at which they cease to operate. They serve to embarrass and weaken the execution of the plan or measure, to which they relate, from the first step to the final conclusion of it. They constantly counteract those qualities in the executive, which are the most necessary ingredients in its composition, vigor and expedition, and this without any counterballancing good. In the conduct of war, in which the energy of the executive is the bulwark of the national security, every thing would be to be apprehended from its plurality.

It must be confessed that these observations apply with principal weight to the first case supposed, that is to a plurality of magistrates of equal dignity and authority; a scheme the advocates for which are not likely to form a numerous sect: But they apply, through not with equal, yet with considerable weight, to the project of a council, whose concurrence is made constitutionally necessary to the operations of the ostensible executive. An artful cabal in the council would be able to distract and to enervate the whole system of administration. If no such cabal should exist, the mere diversity of views and opinions would alone be sufficient to tincture the exercise of the executive authority with a spirit of habitual feebleness and dilatoriness.

But one of the weightiest objections to a plurality in the executive, and which lies as much against the last as the first plan, is that it tends to conceal faults, and destroy responsibility. Responsibility is of two kinds, to censure and to punishment. The first is the most important of the two; especially in an elective office. Man, in public trust, will much oftener act in such a manner as to render him unworthy of being any longer trusted, than in such a manner as to make him obnoxious to legal punishment. But the multiplication of the executive adds to the difficulty of detection in ei-

ther case. It often becomes impossible, amidst mutual accusations, to determine on whom the blame or the punishment of a pernicious measure, or series of pernicious measures ought really to fall. It is shifted from one to another with so much dexterity, and under such plausible appearances, that the public opinion is left in suspense about the real author. The circumstances which may have led to any national miscarriage or misfortune are sometimes so complicated, that where there are a number of actors who may have had different degrees and kinds of agency, though we may clearly see upon the whole that there has been mismanagement, yet it may be impracticable to pronounce to whose account the evil which may have been incurred is truly chargeable.

"I was overruled by my council. The council were so divided in their opinions, that it was impossible to obtain any better resolution on the point." These and similar pretexts are constantly at hand, whether true or false. And who is there that will either take the trouble or incur the odium of a strict scrutiny into the secret springs of the transaction? Should there be found a citizen zealous enough to undertake the unpromising task, if there happen to be a collusion between the parties concerned, how easy is it to cloath the circumstances with so much ambiguity, as to render it uncertain what was the precise conduct of any of those parties? . . .

It is evident from these considerations, that the plurality of the executive tends to deprive the people of the two greatest securities they can have for the faithful exercise of any delegated power; first, the restraints of public opinion, which lose their efficacy as well on account of the division of the censure attendant on bad measures among a number, as on account of the uncertainty on whom it ought to fall; and secondly, the opportunity of discovering with facility and clearness the misconduct of the persons they trust, in order either to their removal from office, or to their actual punishment, in cases which admit of it. . . .

Source: Alexander Hamilton, James Madison, and John Jay, *The Federalist,* ed. Jacob E. Cooke (Middletown, Conn.: Wesleyan University Press, 1961), 471–480. Accessible at http://press-pubs.uchicago.edu/founders/documents/a2_1_1s13.html.

Federalist No. 76

The role of the Senate in the appointment process troubled some critics of the Constitution. Hamilton explained why a sharing of this power was a desirable arrangement.

It will be agreed on all hands, that the power of appointment in ordinary cases ought to be modified in one of three ways. It ought either to be vested in a single man—or in a *select* assembly of a moderate number—or in a single man with the concurrence of such an assembly. The exercise of it by the people at large, will be readily admitted to be impracticable; as, waving every other consideration it would leave them little time to do any thing else. When therefore mention is made in the subsequent reasonings of an assembly or body of men, what is said must be understood to relate to a select body or assembly of the description already given. The people collectively from their number and from their dispersed situation cannot be regulated in their movements by that systematic spirit of cabal and intrigue, which will be urged as the chief objections to reposing the power in question in a body of men.

Those who have themselves reflected upon the subject, or who have attended to the observations made in other parts of these papers, in relation to the appointment of the President, will I presume agree to the position that there would always be great probability of having the place supplied by a man of abilities, at least respectable. Premising this, I proceed to lay it down as a rule, that one man of discernment is better fitted to analyze and estimate the peculiar qualities adapted to particular offices, than a body of men of equal, or perhaps even of superior discernment.

The sole and undivided responsibility of one man will naturally beget a livelier sense of duty and a more exact regard to reputation. He will on this account feel himself under stronger obligations, and more interested to investigate with care the qualities requisite to the stations to be filled, and to prefer with impartiality the persons who may have the fairest pretensions to them. He will have fewer personal attachments to grat-

ify than a body of men, who may each be supposed to have an equal number, and will be so much the less liable to be misled by the sentiments of friendship and of affection. A single well directed man by a single understanding, cannot be distracted and warped by that diversity of views, feelings and interests, which frequently distract and warp the resolutions of a collective body. There is nothing so apt to agitate the passions of mankind as personal considerations, whether they relate to ourselves or to others, who are to be the objects of our choice or preference. Hence, in every exercise of the power of appointing to offices by an assembly of men, we must expect to see a full display of all the private and party likings and dislikes, partialities and antipathies, attachments and animosities, which are felt by those who compose the assembly. The choice which may at any time happen to be made under such circumstances will of course be the result either of a victory gained by one party over the other, or of a compromise between the parties. In either case, the intrinsic merit of the candidate will be too often out of sight. In the first, the qualifications best adapted to uniting the suffrages of the party will be more considered than those which fit the person for the station. In the last the coalition will commonly turn upon some interested equivalent—"Give us the man we wish for this office, and you shall have the one you wish for that." This will be the usual condition of the bargain. And it will rarely happen that the advancement of the public service will be the primary object either of party victories or of party negociations.

The truth of the principles here advanced seems to have been felt by the most intelligent of those who have found fault with the provision made in this respect by the Convention. They contend that the President ought solely to have been authorized to make the appointments under the Federal Government. But it is easy to shew that every advantage to be expected from such an arrangement would in substance be derived from the power of *nomination*, which is proposed to be conferred upon him; while several disadvantages which might attend the absolute power of appointment in the hands of that officer, would be avoided. In the act of nomination his judgment alone would be exercised; and as it would be his sole duty to point out the man, who with the approbation of the Senate should fill an office, his responsibility would be as complete as if he were to make the final appointment. There can in this view be no difference between nominating and appointing. The same motives which would influence a proper discharge of his duty in one case would exist in the other. And as no man could be appointed, but upon his previous nomination, every man who might be appointed would be in fact his choice.

But might not his nomination be overruled? I grant it might, yet this could only be to make place for another nomination by himself. The person ultimately appointed must be the object of his preference, though perhaps not in the first degree. It is also not very probable that his nomination would often be overruled. The Senate could not be tempted by the preference they might feel to another to reject the one proposed; because they could not assure themselves that the person they might wish would be brought forward by a second or by any subsequent nomination. They could not even be certain that a future nomination would present a candidate in any degree more acceptable to them: And as their dissent might cast a kind of stigma upon the individual rejected; and might have the appearance of a reflection upon the judgment of the chief magistrate; it is not likely that their sanction would often be refused, where there were not special and strong reasons for the refusal.

To what purpose then require the co-operation of the Senate? I answer that the necessity of their concurrence would have a powerful, though in general a silent operation. It would be an excellent check upon a spirit of favoritism in the President, and would tend greatly to preventing the appointment of unfit characters from State prejudice, from family connection, from personal attachment, or from a view to popularity. And, in addition to this, it would be an efficacious source of stability in the administration.

It will readily be comprehended, that a man, who had himself the sole disposition of offices, would be governed much more by his private inclinations and interests, than when he was bound to submit the propriety of his choice to the discussion and determination of a different and independent body; and that body an entire branch of the Legislature. The possibility of rejection would be a strong motive to care in proposing. The danger to his own reputation, and, in the case of an elective magistrate, to his political existence, from betraying a spirit of favoritism, or an unbecoming pursuit of popularity, to the observation of a body, whose opinion would have great weight in forming that of the public, could not fail to operate as a barrier to the one and to the other. He would be both ashamed and afraid to bring forward for the most distinguished or lucrative stations, candidates who had no other merit, than that of coming from the same State to which he particularly belonged, or of being in some way or other personally allied to him, or of possessing the necessary insignificance and pliancy to render them the obsequious instruments of his pleasure. . . .

Source: Alexander Hamilton, James Madison, and John Jay, *The Federalist,* ed. Jacob E. Cooke (Middletown, Conn.: Wesleyan University Press, 1961), 509–515. Accessible at http://press-pubs.uchicago.edu/founders/documents/a2_2_2-3s39.html.

Federalist No. 78

The Constitution granted federal judges life tenure and made them removable only through the impeachment process. In justifying this apparently undemocratic arrangement, Hamilton argued that the judicial branch was the weakest of the three branches, having neither the power of the purse nor the power of the sword, "only judgment." He contended that life tenure would provide judges with the necessary independence to exercise constitutional review over the acts of the legislature. Chief Justice John Marshall would later take up his argument in justifying judicial review in Marbury v. Madison *(1803) (Doc. 37).*

Some perplexity respecting the right of the courts to pronounce legislative acts void, because contrary to the constitution, has arisen from an imagination that the doctrine would imply a superiority of the judiciary to the legislative power. It is urged that the authority which can declare the acts of another void, must necessarily be superior to the one whose acts may be declared void. As this doctrine is of great importance in all the American constitutions, a brief discussion of the grounds on which it rests cannot be unacceptable.

There is no position which depends on clearer principles, than that every act of a delegated authority, contrary to the tenor of the commission under which it is exercised, is void. No legislative act therefore contrary to the constitution can be valid. To deny this would be to affirm that the deputy is greater than his principal; that the servant is above his master; that the representatives of the people are superior to the people themselves; that men acting by virtue of powers may do not only what their powers do not authorize, but what they forbid.

If it be said that the legislative body are themselves the constitutional judges of their own powers, and that the construction they put upon them is conclusive upon the other departments, it may be answered, that this cannot be the natural presumption, where it is not to be collected from any particular provisions in the constitution. It is not otherwise to be supposed that the constitution could intend to enable the representatives of the people to substitute their *will* to that of their constituents. It is far more rational to suppose that the courts were designed to be an intermediate body between the people and the legislature, in order, among other things, to keep the latter within the limits assigned to their authority. The interpretation of the laws is the proper and peculiar province of the courts. A constitution is in fact, and must be, regarded by the judges as a fundamental law. It therefore belongs to them to ascertain its meaning as well as the meaning of any particular act proceeding from the legislative body. If there should happen to be an irreconcilable variance between the two, that which has the superior obligation and validity ought of course to be preferred; or in other words, the constitution ought to be preferred to the statute, the intention of the people to the intention of their agents.

Nor does this conclusion by any means suppose a superiority of the judicial to the legislative power. It only supposes that the power of the people is superior to both; and that where the will of the legislature declared in its statutes, stands in opposition to that of the people declared in the constitution, the judges ought to be governed by the latter, rather than the former. They ought to regulate their decisions by the fundamental laws, rather than by those which are not fundamental.

Source: Alexander Hamilton, James Madison, and John Jay, *The Federalist,* ed. Jacob E. Cooke (Middletown, Conn.: Wesleyan University Press, 1961), 524–525. Accessible at http://press-pubs.uchicago.edu/founders/documents/v1ch17s24.html.

Document 12   *The Anti-Federalist Papers*
                1787–1788

Because the defenders of the Constitution had already laid claim to the mantle "Feder-alists," those who objected to the new document were labeled "Anti-Federalists," even though many of them would have considered themselves the true proponents of federal-ism. Opposition to the Constitution varied, but the primary reasons centered on the centralization of power and whether a distant central government could adequately represent the people. There was also concern about the states surviving as sovereign governments under the new arrangement. Finally, many objected to the absence of a Bill of Rights in the original document. A number of prominent Anti-Federalists used letters to the newspapers to make their case against the Constitution. They used various pseudonyms, such as The Federal Farmer, Cato, Brutus, and Cincinnatus. These letters and several speeches became known as the "Anti-Federalist Papers."

Brutus No. 1

Historians are uncertain of Brutus's identity, although many believe him to be Robert Yates, a prominent political figure and judge from New York. He warned of a number of arrangements in the Constitution that threatened state sovereignty, including the nec-essary and proper clause of Article 1, the supremacy clause in Article 6, and the cre-ation of federal judicial authority in Article 3.

The first question that presents itself on the sub-ject is, whether a confederated government be the best for the United States or not? Or in other words, whether the thirteen United States should be reduced to one great republic, governed by one legislature, and under the direction of one executive and judicial; or whether they should continue thirteen confederated republics, under the direction and controul of a supreme federal head for certain defined national purposes only?

This inquiry is important, because, although the government reported by the convention does not go to a perfect and entire consolidation, yet it approaches so near to it, that it must, if exe-cuted, certainly and infallibly terminate in it.

This government is to possess absolute and uncontroulable power, legislative, executive and judicial, with respect to every object to which it extends, for by the last clause of section 8th, ar-ticle 1st, it is declared "that the Congress shall have power to make all laws which shall be nec-essary and proper for carrying into execution the foregoing powers, and all other powers vested by this constitution, in the government of the United States; or in any department or office thereof." And by the 6th article, it is declared "that this constitution, and the laws of the United States, which shall be made in pursuance thereof, and the treaties made, or which shall be made, under the authority of the United States, shall be the supreme law of the land; and the judges in every state shall be bound thereby, any thing in the constitution, or law of any state to the contrary notwithstanding." It appears from these articles that there is no need of any inter-vention of the state governments, between the Congress and the people, to execute any one power vested in the general government, and that the constitution and laws of every state are nullified and declared void, so far as they are or shall be inconsistent with this constitution, or the laws made in pursuance of it, or with treaties

made under the authority of the United States—
The government then, so far as it extends, is a
complete one, and not a confederation. It is as
much one complete government as that of New-
York or Massachusetts, has as absolute and perfect powers to make and execute all laws, to appoint officers, institute courts, declare offences,
and annex penalties, with respect to every object
to which it extends, as any other in the world. So
far therefore as its powers reach, all ideas of confederation are given up and lost. It is true this
government is limited to certain objects, or to
speak more properly, some small degree of
power is still left to the states, but a little attention to the powers vested in the general government, will convince every candid man, that if it
is capable of being executed, all that is reserved
for the individual states must very soon be anni-
hilated, except so far as they are barely necessary
to the organization of the general government.
The powers of the general legislature extend to
every case that is of the least importance—there
is nothing valuable to human nature, nothing
dear to freemen, but what is within its power. It
has authority to make laws which will affect the
lives, the liberty, and property of every man in
the United States; nor can the constitution or
laws of any state, in any way prevent or impede
the full and complete execution of every power
given. The legislative power is competent to lay
taxes, duties, imposts, and excises;—there is no
limitation to this power, unless it be said that the
clause which directs the use to which those taxes,
and duties shall be applied, may be said to be a
limitation: but this is no restriction of the power
at all, for by this clause they are to be applied to
pay the debts and provide for the common defence and general welfare of the United States;
but the legislature have authority to contract
debts at their discretion; they are the sole judges
of what is necessary to provide for the common
defence, and they only are to determine what is
for the general welfare; this power therefore is
neither more nor less, than a power to lay and
collect taxes, imposts, and excises, at their pleasure; not only [is] the power to lay taxes unlim-

ited, as to the amount they may require, but it is
perfect and absolute to raise them in any mode
they please. No state legislature, or any power in
the state governments, have any more to do in
carrying this into effect, than the authority of
one state has to do with that of another. In the
business therefore of laying and collecting taxes,
the idea of confederation is totally lost, and that
of one entire republic is embraced. It is proper
here to remark, that the authority to lay and collect taxes is the most important of any power
that can be granted; it connects with it almost all
other powers, or at least will in process of time
draw all other after it; it is the great mean of protection, security, and defence, in a good government, and the great engine of oppression and
tyranny in a bad one. . . .

It might be here shewn, that the power in the
federal legislative, to raise and support armies at
pleasure, as well in peace as in war, and their
controul over the militia, tend, not only to a consolidation of the government, but the destruction
of liberty.—I shall not, however, dwell upon
these, as a few observations upon the judicial
power of this government, in addition to the preceding, will fully evince the truth of the position.

The judicial power of the United States is to
be vested in a supreme court, and in such inferior
courts as Congress may from time to time ordain
and establish. The powers of these courts are
very extensive; their jurisdiction comprehends all
civil causes, except such as arise between citizens
of the same state; and it extends to all cases in
law and equity arising under the constitution.
One inferior court must be established, I presume, in each state, at least, with the necessary
executive officers appendant thereto. It is easy to
see, that in the common course of things, these
courts will eclipse the dignity, and take away
from the respectability, of the state courts. These
courts will be, in themselves, totally independent
of the states, deriving their authority from the
United States, and receiving from them fixed
salaries; and in the course of human events it is
to be expected, that they will swallow up all the
powers of the courts in the respective states.

How far the clause in the 8th section of the 1st article may operate to do away all idea of confederated states, and to effect an entire consolidation of the whole into one general government, it is impossible to say. The powers given by this article are very general and comprehensive, and it may receive a construction to justify the passing almost any law. A power to make all laws, which shall be *necessary and proper*, for carrying into execution, all powers vested by the constitution in the government of the United States, or any department or officer thereof, is a power very comprehensive and definite [indefinite?], and may, for ought I know, be exercised in a such manner as entirely to abolish the state legislatures. Suppose the legislature of a state should pass a law to raise money to support their government and pay the state debt, may the Congress repeal this law, because it may prevent the collection of a tax which they may think proper and necessary to lay, to provide for the general welfare of the United States? For all laws made, in pursuance of this constitution, are the supreme law of the land, and the judges in every state shall be bound thereby, any thing in the constitution or laws of the different states to the contrary notwithstanding.—By such a law, the government of a particular state might be overturned at one stroke, and thereby be deprived of every means of its support.

It is not meant, by stating this case, to insinuate that the constitution would warrant a law of this kind; or unnecessarily to alarm the fears of the people, by suggesting, that the federal legislature would be more likely to pass the limits assigned them by the constitution, than that of an individual state, further than they are less responsible to the people. But what is meant is, that the legislature of the United States are vested with the great and uncontrollable powers, of laying and collecting taxes, duties, imposts, and excises: of regulating trade, raising and supporting armies, organizing, arming, and disciplining the militia, instituting courts, and other general powers. And are by this clause invested with the power of making all laws, *proper and necessary*, for carrying all these into execution; and they may so exercise this power as entirely to annihilate all the state governments, and reduce this country to one single government. And if they may do it, it is pretty certain they will; for it will be found that the power retained by individual states, small as it is, will be a clog upon the wheels of the government of the United States; the latter therefore will be naturally inclined to remove it out of the way. Besides, it is a truth confirmed by the unerring experience of ages, that every man, and every body of men, invested with power, are ever disposed to increase it, and to acquire a superiority over every thing that stands in their way. This disposition, which is implanted in human nature, will operate in the federal legislature to lessen and ultimately to subvert the state authority, and having such advantages, will most certainly succeed, if the federal government succeeds at all. It must be very evident then, that what this constitution wants of being a complete consolidation of the several parts of the union into one complete government, possessed of perfect legislative, judicial, and executive powers, to all intents and purposes, it will necessarily acquire in its exercise and operation.

Source: The Complete Anti-Federalist, ed. Herbert J. Storing (Chicago: University of Chicago Press, 1981). Accessible at http://press-pubs.uchicago.edu/founders/documents/v1ch8s13.html.

Brutus No. 5

Brutus warned against the taxing power granted Congress and suggested that with such power the states could be destroyed.

1st. To detail the particulars comprehended in the general terms, taxes, duties, imposts and excises, would require a volume, instead of a single piece in a news-paper. . . . Under this clause may be imposed a poll-tax, a land-tax, a tax on houses and buildings, on windows and fire places, on cattle and on all kinds of personal property:—It extends to duties on all kinds of goods to any amount, to tonnage and poundage on vessels, to duties on written instruments, newspapers, almanacks, and books:—It comprehends an excise on all kinds of liquors, spirits, wines, cyder, beer, etc. and indeed takes in duty or excise on every necessary or conveniency of life; whether of foreign or home growth or manufactory. In short, we can have no conception of any way in which a government can raise money from the people, but what is included in one or other of [these] general terms. We may say then that this clause commits to the hands of the general legislature every conceivable source of revenue within the United States. Not only are these terms very comprehensive, and extend to a vast number of objects, but the power to lay and collect has great latitude; it will lead to the passing a vast number of laws, which may affect the personal rights of the citizens of the states, expose their property to fines and confiscation, and put their lives in jeopardy: it opens a door to the appointment of a swarm of revenue and excise officers to prey upon the honest and industrious part of the community, eat up their substance, and riot on the spoils of the country.

2d. We will next enquire into what is implied in the authority to pass all laws which shall be necessary and proper to carry this power into execution.

It is, perhaps, utterly impossible fully to define this power. The authority granted in the first clause can only be understood in its full extent, by descending to all the particular cases in which a revenue can be raised; the number and variety of these cases are so endless, and as it were infinite, that no man living has, as yet, been able to reckon them up. . . . A case cannot be conceived of, which is not included in this power. . . . The command of the revenues of a state gives the command of every thing in it.—He that has the purse will have the sword, and they that have both, have every thing; so that the legislature having every source from which money can be drawn under their direction, with a right to make all laws necessary and proper for drawing forth all the resource of the country, would have, in fact, all power. . . .

I shall only remark, that this power, given to the federal legislature, directly annihilates all the powers of the state legislatures. There cannot be a greater solecism in politics than to talk of power in a government, without the command of any revenue. . . . Now the general government having in their controul every possible source of revenue, and authority to pass any law they may deem necessary to draw them forth, or to facilitate their collection; no source of revenue is therefore left in the hands of any state. Should any state attempt to raise money by law, the general government may repeal or arrest it in the execution, for all their laws will be the supreme law of the land: If then any one can be weak enough to believe that a government can exist without having the authority to raise money to pay a door-keeper to their assembly, he may believe that the state government can exist, should this new constitution take place.

. . . The legislature of the United States will have a right to exhaust every source of revenue in every state, and to annul all laws of the states which may stand in the way of effecting it; unless therefore we can suppose the state governments can exist without money to support the officers who execute them, we must conclude they will exist no longer than the general legislature choose they should. Indeed the idea of any government existing, in any respect, as an independent one, without any means of support in their own hands, is an absurdity. If therefore, this constitution has in view, what many of its framers and advocates say it has, to secure and guarantee to the separate states the exercise of certain powers of government[,] it certainly ought to have left in their hands some sources of revenue. It should have marked the line in which the general government should have raised money, and set bounds over which they should not pass, leaving to the separate states other means to raise supplies for the support of their governments, and to discharge their respective debts. To this it is objected, that the general government ought to have power competent to the purposes of the union; they are to provide for the common defence, to pay the debts of the United States, support foreign ministers, and the civil establishment of the union, and to do these they ought to have authority to raise money adequate to the purpose. . . . The great and only security the people can have against oppression from this kind of taxes, must rest in their representatives. If they are sufficiently numerous to be well informed of the circumstances, and ability of those who send them, and have a proper regard for the people, they will be secure. The general legislature . . . will not be thus qualified, and therefore, on this account, ought not to exercise the power of direct taxation. . . .

Source: The Complete Anti-Federalist, ed. Herbert J. Storing (Chicago: University of Chicago Press, 1981). Accessible at http://press-pubs.uchicago.edu/founders/documents/a1_8_1s7.html.

Brutus No. 12

Many Anti-Federalists feared the new federal judicial branch for its potential to interfere with state courts and law. Brutus argued that the exercise of judicial review would be an essential power of the court, and that coupled with the broad grants of power to Congress and the national government—including those involving the necessary and proper clause and the supremacy clause—this practice would have a grave impact on the states.

First. Let us enquire how the judicial power will effect an extension of the legislative authority.

Perhaps the judicial power will not be able, by direct and positive decrees, ever to direct the legislature, because it is not easy to conceive how a question can be brought before them in a course of legal discussion, in which they can give a decision, declaring, that the legislature have certain powers which they have not exercised, and which, in consequence of the determination of the judges, they will be bound to exercise. But it is easy to see, that in their adjudications they may establish certain principles, which being received by the legislature, will enlarge the sphere of their power beyond all bounds.

It is to be observed, that the supreme court has the power, in the last resort, to determine all questions that may arise in the course of legal discussion, on the meaning and construction of the constitution. This power they will hold under the constitution, and independent of the legislature. The latter can no more deprive the former of this right, than either of them, or both of them together, can take from the president, with the advice of the senate, the power of making treaties, or appointing ambassadors.

In determining these questions, the court must and will assume certain principles, from which they will reason, in forming their decisions. These principles, whatever they may be, when they become fixed, by a course of decisions, will be adopted by the legislature, and will be the rule by which they will explain their own powers. This appears evident from this consideration, that if the legislature pass laws, which, in the judgment of the court, they are not authorized to do by the constitution, the court will not take notice of them; for it will not be denied, that the constitution is the highest or supreme law. And the courts are vested with the supreme and uncontroulable power, to determine, in all cases that come before them, what the constitution means;

they cannot, therefore, execute a law, which, in their judgment, opposes the constitution, unless we can suppose they can make a superior law give way to an inferior. The legislature, therefore, will not go over the limits by which the courts may adjudge they are confined. And there is little room to doubt but that they will come up to those bounds, as often as occasion and opportunity may offer, and they may judge it proper to do it. For as on the one hand, they will not readily pass laws which they know the courts will not execute, so on the other, we may be sure they will not scruple to pass such as they know they will give effect, as often as they may judge it proper.

From these observations it appears, that the judgment of the judicial, on the constitution, will become the rule to guide the legislature in their construction of their powers.

What the principles are, which the courts will adopt, it is impossible for us to say; but taking up the powers as I have explained them in my last number, which they will possess under this clause, it is not difficult to see, that they may, and probably will, be very liberal ones.

We have seen, that they will be authorized to give the constitution a construction according to its spirit and reason, and not to confine themselves to its letter.

To discover the spirit of the constitution, it is of the first importance to attend to the principal ends and designs it has in view. These are expressed in the preamble, in the following words, viz. "We, the people of the United States, in order to form a more perfect union, establish justice, insure domestic tranquility, provide for the common defence, promote the general welfare, and secure the blessings of liberty to ourselves and our posterity, do ordain and establish this constitution," &c. If the end of the government is to be learned from these words, which are clearly designed to declare it, it is obvious it has in view every object which is embraced by any government. The preservation of internal peace—the due administration of justice—and to provide for the defence of the community, seems to include all the objects of government; but if

they do not, they are certainly comprehended in the words, "to provide for the general welfare." If it be further considered, that this constitution, if it is ratified, will not be a compact entered into by states, in their corporate capacities, but an agreement of the people of the United States, as one great body politic, no doubt can remain, but that the great end of the constitution, if it is to be collected from the preamble, in which its end is declared, is to constitute a government which is to extend to every case for which any government is instituted, whether external or internal. The courts, therefore, will establish this as a principle in expounding the constitution, and will give every part of it such an explanation, as will give latitude to every department under it, to take cognizance of every matter, not only that affects the general and national concerns of the union, but also of such as relate to the administration of private justice, and to regulating the internal and local affairs of the different parts.

Such a rule of exposition is not only consistent with the general spirit of the preamble, but it will stand confirmed by considering more minutely the different clauses of it.

The first object declared to be in view is, "To form a perfect union." It is to be observed, it is not an union of states or bodies corporate; had this been the case the existence of the state governments, might have been secured. But it is a union of the people of the United States considered as one body, who are to ratify this constitution, if it is adopted. Now to make a union of this kind perfect, it is necessary to abolish all inferior governments, and to give the general one compleat legislative, executive and judicial powers to every purpose. The courts therefore will establish it as a rule in explaining the constitution to give it such a construction as will best tend to perfect the union or take from the state governments every power of either making or executing laws. The second object is "to establish justice." This must include not only the idea of instituting the rule of justice, or of making laws which shall be the measure or rule of right, but also of providing for the application of this rule or of administering justice under it. And under this the courts will in their decisions extend the power of the government to all cases they possibly can, or otherwise they will be restricted in doing what appears to be the intent of the constitution they should do, to wit, pass laws and provide for the execution of them, for the general distribution of justice between man and man. Another end declared is "to insure domestic tranquility." This comprehends a provision against all private breaches of the peace, as well as against all public commotions or general insurrections; and to attain the object of this clause fully, the government must exercise the power of passing laws on these subjects, as well as of appointing magistrates with authority to execute them. And the courts will adopt these ideas in their expositions. I might proceed to the other clause, in the preamble, and it would appear by a consideration of all of them separately, as it does by taking them together, that if the spirit of this system is to be known from its declared end and design in the preamble, its spirit is to subvert and abolish all the powers of the state government, and to embrace every object to which any government extends.

As it sets out in the preamble with this declared intention, so it proceeds in the different parts with the same idea. Any person, who will peruse the 8th section with attention, in which most of the powers are enumerated, will perceive that they either expressly or by implication extend to almost every thing about which any legislative power can be employed. But if this equitable mode of construction is applied to this part of the constitution; nothing can stand before it.

This will certainly give the first clause in that article a construction which I confess I think the most natural and grammatical one, to authorise the Congress to do any thing which in their judgment will tend to provide for the general welfare, and this amounts to the same thing as general and unlimited powers of legislation in all cases.

This same manner of explaining the constitution, will fix a meaning, and a very important one too, to . . . the clause . . . which authorises the Congress to make all laws which shall be proper and necessary for carrying into effect the foregoing powers, &c. A voluminous writer in favor of this system, has taken great pains to convince the public, that this clause means nothing: for that the same powers expressed in this, are implied in other parts of the constitution. Perhaps it is so, but still this will undoubtedly be an excellent auxilliary to assist the courts to discover the spirit and reason of the constitution, and when applied to any and every of the other clauses granting power, will operate powerfully in extracting the spirit from them.

I might instance a number of clauses in the constitution, which, if explained in an *equitable* manner, would extend the powers of the government to every case, and reduce the state legislatures to nothing; but, I should draw out my remarks to an undue length, and I presume enough has been said to shew, that the courts have sufficient ground in the exercise of this power, to determine, that the legislature have no bounds set to them by this constitution, by any supposed right the legislatures of the respective states may have, to regulate any of their local concerns.

Source: The Complete Anti-Federalist, ed. Herbert J. Storing (Chicago: University of Chicago Press, 1981). Accessible at http://press-pubs.uchicago.edu/founders/documents/a3_2_1s20.html.

Cato No. 4

Cato, believed to be New York governor George Clinton, takes up the concerns of the Anti-Federalists about the presidency created in the Constitution. Many Americans, only recently removed from the domination of a king, feared that the new executive arrangement simply replaced the old king with a new one.

It is remarked by Montesquieu, in treating of republics, that *in all magistracies, the greatness of the power must be compensated by the brevity of the duration; and that a longer time than a year, would be dangerous.* It is therefore obvious to the least intelligent mind, to account why, great power in the hands of a magistrate, and that power connected, with a considerable duration, may be dangerous to the liberties of a republic—the deposit of vast trusts in the hands of a single magistrate, enables him in their exercise, to create a numerous train of dependants—this tempts his *ambition*, which in a republican magistrate is also remarked, *to be pernicious* and the duration of his office for any considerable time favors his views, gives him the means and time to perfect and execute his designs—*he therefore fancies that he may be great and glorious by oppressing his fellow citizens, and raising himself to permanent grandeur on the ruins of his country.*—And here it may be necessary to compare the vast and important powers of the president, together with his continuance in office with the foregoing doctrine—his eminent magisterial situation will attach many adherents to him, and he will be surrounded by expectants and courtiers—his power of nomination and influence on all appointments—the strong posts in each state comprised within his superintendance, and garrisoned by troops under his direction—his controul over the army, militia, and navy—the unrestrained power of granting pardons for treason, which may be used to screen from punishment, those whom he had secretly instigated to commit the crime, and thereby prevent a discovery of his own guilt—his duration in office for four years: these, and various other principles evidently prove the truth of the position—that if the president is possessed of ambition, he has power and time sufficient to ruin his country.

Though the president, during the sitting of the legislature, is assisted by the senate, yet he is without a constitutional council in their recess—he will therefore be unsupported by proper information and advice, and will generally be directed by minions and favorites, or a council of state will grow out of the principal officers of the great departments, the most dangerous council in a free country.

The ten miles square, which is to become the seat of government, will of course be the place of residence for the president and the great officers of state—the same observations of a great man will apply to the court of a president possessing the powers of a monarch, that is observed of that of a monarch—*ambition with idleness—baseness with pride—the thirst of riches without labour—aversion to truth—flattery—treason—perfidy—violation of engagements—contempt of civil duties—hope from the magistrate's weakness; but above all, the perpetual ridicule of virtue*—these, he remarks, are the characteristics by which the courts in all ages have been distinguished. . . .

The establishment of a vice-president is as unnecessary as it is dangerous. This officer, for want of other employment, is made president of the senate, thereby blending the executive and legislative powers, besides always giving to some one state, from which he is to come, an unjust preeminence. . . .

Will not the exercise of these powers therefore tend either to the establishment of a vile and arbitrary aristocracy, or monarchy? The safety of the people in a republic depends on the share or proportion they have in the government; but experience ought to teach you, that when a man is at the head of an elective government invested with great powers, and interested in his re-election, in what circle appointments will be made; by which means *an imperfect aristocracy* bordering on monarchy may be established. . . .

Source: The Complete Anti-Federalist, ed. Herbert J. Storing (Chicago: University of Chicago Press, 1981). Accessible at http://press-pubs.uchicago.edu/founders/documents/a2_1_1s6.html.

Document 13   **Additional Founding Era Documents**
                1787–1804

While the Federalist and Anti-Federalist writings (Docs. 11–12) are the primary documents for studying the debates over the Constitution and the new U.S. government, other documents have value in presenting the philosophical concerns that shaped U.S. governance. James Madison's notes of the debate at the Constitutional Convention provide insight into how particular delegations voted and the major concerns of delegates about the wording of the Constitution and how the document might be interpreted. Debates in the first Congresses and documents from the executive branch are also valuable in understanding this period because many of the Constitution's writers came to hold positions of power in the new government. This firsthand experience has given their early interpretations of the document particular authority.

Records of the Federal Convention
August 17, 1787

James Madison took notes on the debate at the Constitutional Convention that were published after his death. Here delegates discuss how to allocate the power to declare and make war.

"To make war"

Mr Pinkney opposed the vesting this power in the Legislature. Its proceedings were too slow. It wd. meet but once a year. The Hs. of Reps. would be too numerous for such deliberations. The Senate would be the best depositary, being more acquainted with foreign affairs, and most capable of proper resolutions. If the States are equally represented in Senate, so as to give no advantage to large States, the power will notwithstanding be safe, as the small have their all at stake in such cases as well as the large States. It would be singular for one authority to make war, and another peace.

Mr Butler. The Objections agst the Legislature lie in a great degree agst the Senate. He was for vesting the power in the President, who will have all the requisite qualities, and will not make war but when the Nation will support it.

Mr. Madison and Mr Gerry moved to insert "declare," striking out "make" war; leaving to the Executive the power to repel sudden attacks.

Mr Sharman thought it stood very well. The Executive shd. be able to repel and not to com-

mence war. "Make" better than "declare" the latter narrowing the power too much.

Mr Gerry never expected to hear in a republic a motion to empower the Executive alone to declare war.

Mr. Elseworth. There is a material difference between the cases of making war, and making peace. It shd. be more easy to get out of war, than into it. War also is a simple and overt declaration. Peace attended with intricate & secret negociations.

Mr. Mason was agst giving the power of war to the Executive, because not safely to be trusted with it; or to the Senate, because not so constructed as to be entitled to it. He was for clogging rather than facilitating war; but for facilitating peace. He preferred "declare" to "make".

On the Motion to insert declare—in place of Make, it was agreed to.

N.H. no. Mas. abst. Cont. no.1 Pa ay. Del. ay. Md. ay. Va. ay. N.C. ay. S.C. ay. Geo- ay. [Ayes—7; noes—2; absent—1.]

Mr. Pinkney's motion to strike out whole clause, disagd. to without call of States.

Mr Butler moved to give the Legislature power of peace, as they were to have that of war.

Mr Gerry 2ds. him. 8 Senators may possibly exercise the power if vested in that body, and 14 if all should be present; and may consequently give up part of the U. States. The Senate are more liable to be corrupted by an Enemy than the whole Legislature.

On the motion for adding "and peace" after "war"

N.H. no. Mas. no. Ct. no. Pa. no. Del. no. Md. no. Va. no. N.C. no S.C. no. Geo. no. [Ayes—0; noes—10.]

1. On the remark by Mr. King that "make" war might be understood to "conduct" it which was an Executive function, Mr. Elseworth gave up his objection and the vote of Cont was changed to—ay.

Source: The Records of the Federal Convention of 1787, ed. Max Farrand, rev. ed. (New Haven: Yale University Press, 1937), 2:318.

Alexander Hamilton, *Report on Manufactures* 1791

As the secretary of the Treasury, Alexander Hamilton worked aggressively to convince the national government that it had an active role to play in promoting the development of commerce in the new nation. His attempts drew considerable resistance from Anti-Federalists. In Report on Manufactures, *Hamilton used the Constitution to defend the national role in promoting economic expansion.*

A Question has been made concerning the Constitutional right of the Government of the United States to apply this species of encouragement, but there is certainly no good foundation for such a question. The National Legislature has express authority "To lay and Collect taxes, duties, imposts and excises, to pay the debts and provide for the *Common defence* and *general welfare*" with no other qualifications than that "all duties, imposts and excises, shall be *uniform* throughout the United states, that no capitation or other direct tax shall be laid unless in proportion to numbers ascertained by a census or enumeration taken on the principles prescribed in the Constitution, and that "no tax or duty shall be laid on articles exported from any state." These three qualifications excepted, the power to *raise money* is *plenary*, and *indefinite*; and the objects to which it may be *appropriated* are no less comprehensive, than the payment of the public debts and the providing for the common defence and "*general Welfare.*" The terms

"*general Welfare*" were doubtless intended to signify more than was expressed or imported in those which Preceded; otherwise numerous exigencies incident to the affairs of a Nation would have been left without a provision. The phrase is as comprehensive as any that could have been used; because it was not fit that the constitutional authority of the Union, to appropriate its revenues *shou'd* have been restricted within narrower limits than the "General Welfare" and because this necessarily embraces a vast variety of particulars, which are susceptible neither of specification nor of definition.

It is therefore of necessity left to the discretion of the National Legislature, to pronounce, upon the objects, which concern the general Welfare, and for which under that description, an appropriation of money is requisite and proper. And there seems to be no room for a doubt that whatever concerns the general Interests of *learning* of *Agriculture* of *Manufactures* and of *Commerce* are within the sphere of the national Councils *as far as regards an application of Money.*

The only qualification of the generality of the Phrase in question, which seems to be admissible, is this—That the object to which an appropriation of money is to be made be *General* and not *local*; its operation extending in fact, or by possibility, throughout the Union, and not being confined to a particular spot.

No objection ought to arise to this construction from a supposition that it would imply a power to do whatever else should appear to Congress conducive to the General Welfare. A power to appropriate money with this latitude which is granted too in *express terms* would not carry a power to do any other thing, not authorised in the constitution, either expressly or by fair implication.

Source: The Papers of Alexander Hamilton, ed. Harold C. Syrett et al. (New York: Columbia University Press, 1961–1979), 10:302–304. Accessible at http://press-pubs.uchicago.edu/founders/documents/a1_8_1s21.html.

Luther Martin, Speech at the Impeachment Trial of Justice Samuel Chase 1804

The Anti-Federalists, many of whom found a home with the Jeffersonian Democratic-Republicans under the new government, continued to distrust the judiciary after ratification of the Constitution. Most historians view the effort to impeach Justice Samuel Chase as politically motivated by this partisan dislike for the nationalist rulings of the Marshall Court. At Chase's impeachment hearing, Luther Martin, a Federalist from Maryland, pondered why the framers of the Constitution placed impeachment trials in the Senate, reminding his listeners that impeachment involved only removal from office. Impeached officials could still be indicted and tried in a court of law for crimes that they were alleged to have committed.

We have been told by an honorable Manager, (Mr. Campbell,) that the power of trying impeachments was lodged in the Senate with the most perfect propriety; for two reasons—the one, that the person impeached would be tried before those who had given their approbation to his appointment to office. This certainly was not the reason by which the framers of the Constitution were influenced, when they gave this power to the Senate. Who are the officers liable to impeachment? The President, the Vice President, and all civil officers of Government. In the election of the two first, the Senate have no control, either as to nomination or approbation. As to other civil officers, who hold their appointments during good behavior, it is extremely probable that, though they were approved by one Senate, yet from lapse of time, and the fluc-tuations of that body, an officer may be impeached before a Senate, not one of whom had sanctioned his appointment, not one of whom, perhaps, had he been nominated after their election, would have given him their sanction.

This, then, could not have been one of the reasons for thus placing the power over these officers. But as a second reason, he assigned, that, if any other inferior tribunal had been entrusted with the trial of impeachments, the members might have an interest in the conviction of an officer, thereby to have him removed in order to obtain his place; but, that no Senator could have such inducement.

I see two honorable members of this Court, (Messrs. Dayton and Baldwin,) who were with me in Convention, in 1787, who as well as myself, perfectly knew why this power was invested in the Senate. It was because, among all our speculative systems, it was thought this power could no where be more properly placed, or where it would be less likely to be abused. A sentiment, sir, in which I perfectly concurred, and I have no doubt but the event of this trial will show that we could not have better disposed of that power. . . .

The President, Vice President, and other civil officers, can only be impeached. They only in that case are deprived of a trial by jury; they, when they accept their offices, accept them on those terms, and, as far as relates to the tenure of their offices, relinquish that privilege; they, therefore, cannot complain. Here, it appears to me, the framers of the Constitution have so expressed themselves as to leave not a single doubt on this subject.

In the first article, section the third, of the Constitution, it is declared that, judgment in all cases of impeachment, shall not extend further than removal from office, and disqualification to hold any office of honor, trust, or profit, under the United States. This clearly evinces, that no persons but those *who hold offices* are liable to impeachment. They are to lose their offices; and, having misbehaved themselves in such manner as to lose their offices, are, with propriety, to be rendered ineligible thereafter.

The truth is, the framers of the Constitution, for many reasons, which influenced them, did not think proper to place the officers of Government in the power of the two branches of the Legislature, further than the tenure of their office. Nor did they choose to permit the tenure of their offices to depend upon the passions or prejudices of jurors. The very clause in the Constitution, of itself, shows that it was intended the persons impeached and removed from office might still be indicted and punished for the same offence, else the provision would have been not only nugatory, but a reflection on the enlightened body who framed the Constitution; since no person ever could have dreamed that a conviction on impeachment and a removal from office, in consequence, for one offense, could prevent the same person from being indicted and punished for another and different offence. . . .

Source: Annals of Congress, 14:429–432, 436. Accessible at http://press-pubs.uchicago.edu/founders/documents/a1_2_5s16. html.

Thomas Jefferson on the Separation of Powers
1816–1819

Although Thomas Jefferson was not present at the Constitutional Convention, he is without a doubt among the founders. He supported ratification of the Constitution despite misgivings about the lack of a Bill of Rights and the national government retaining too much power. As the third president of the United States and the leader of the Democratic-Republican Party in its battle with the Federalists over how the new constitutional order would unfold, Jefferson played a leading role in shaping the early Republic. Upon his retirement from the presidency, his views continued to be sought by those who would carry his party's banner and who believed that with ratification of the Constitution their worst fears had come to pass. In the following correspondence, Jefferson responds to letters from fellow Democratic-Republicans regarding the extent to which the Virginian and federal systems meet the requirements of republicanism and whether their constitutions ought to be amended to better reflect these principles. Critics of the separation of powers have often noted the limitations it appears to place on popular sovereignty. Jefferson appears to agree with them.

Jefferson to John Taylor, May 28, 1816

DEAR SIR

On my return from a long journey and considerable absence from home, I found here the copy of your "Enquiry into the principles of our government," which you had been so kind as to send me; and for which I pray you to accept my thanks. . . .

I see in it much matter for profound reflection; much which should confirm our adhesion, in practice, to the good principles of our constitution, and fix our attention on what is yet to be made good. . . . The further the departure from direct and constant control by the citizens, the less has the government of the ingredient of republicanism. . . .

In the General Government, the House of Representatives is mainly republican; the Senate scarcely so at all, as not elected by the people directly, and so long secured even against those who do elect them; the Executive more republican than the Senate, from its shorter term, its election by the people, in *practice,* (for they vote for A only on an assurance that he will vote for B,) and because, *in practice also,* a principle of rotation seems to be in a course of establishment; the judiciary independent of the nation, their coercion by impeachment being found nugatory.

If, then, the control of the people over the organs of their government be the measure of its republicanism, and confess I know no other measure, it must be agreed that our governments have much less of republicanism than ought to have been expected; in other words, that the people have less regular control over their agents, than their rights and their interests require. And this I ascribe, not to any want of republican dispositions in those who formed these constitutions, but to a submission of true principle to European authorities, to speculators on government, whose fears of the people have been inspired by the populace of their own great cities, and were unjustly entertained against the independent, the happy, and therefore orderly citizens of the United States. Much

apprehend that the golden moment is past for reforming these heresies. The functionaries of public power rarely strengthen in their dispositions to abridge it, and an unorganized call for timely amendment is not likely to prevail against an organized opposition to it. We are always told that things are going on well; why change them? *"Chi sta bene, non si muove,"* said the Italian, "let him who stands well, stand still." This is true; and I verily believe they would go on well with us under an absolute monarch, while our present character remains, of order, industry and love of peace, and restrained, as he would be, by the proper spirit of the people. But it is while it remains such, we should provide against the consequences of its deterioration. And let us rest in the hope that it will yet be done, and spare ourselves the pain of evils which may never happen.

On this view of the import of the term *republic,* instead of saying, as has been said, "that it may mean anything or nothing," we may say with truth and meaning, that governments are more or less republican as they have more or less of the element of popular election and control in their composition; and believing, as I do, that the mass of the citizens is the safest depository of their own rights, and especially, that the evils flowing from the duperies of the people, are less injurious than those from the egoism of their agents, I am a friend to that composition of government which has in it the most of this ingredient. And I sincerely believe, with you, that banking establishments are more dangerous than standing armies; and that the principle of spending money to be paid by posterity, under the name of funding, is but swindling futurity on a large scale.

I salute you with constant friendship and respect.

Jefferson to Samuel Kercheval, July 12, 1816

SIR,—I duly received your favor of June the 13th, with the copy of the letters on the calling a convention, on which you are pleased to ask my opinion. . . .

But it will be said, it is easier to find faults than to amend them. I do not think their amendment so difficult as is pretended. Only lay down true principles, and adhere to them inflexibly. Do not be frightened into their surrender by the alarms of the timid, or the croakings of wealth against the ascendency of the people. If experience be called for, appeal to that of our fifteen or twenty governments for forty years, and show me where the people have done half the mischief in these forty years, that a single despot would have done in a single year; or show half the riots and rebellions, the crimes and the punishments, which have taken place in any single nation, under kingly government, during the same period. The true foundation of republican government is the equal right of every citizen, in his person and property, and in their management. Try by this, as a tally, every provision of our constitution, and see if it hangs directly on the will of the people. Reduce your legislature to a convenient number for full, but orderly discussion. Let every man who fights or pays, exercise his just and equal right in their election. Submit them to approbation or rejection at short intervals. Let the executive be chosen in the same way, and for the same term, by those whose agent he is to be; and leave no screen of a council behind which to skulk from responsibility. It has been thought that the people are not competent electors of judges *learned in the law.* But I do not know that this is true, and, if doubtful, we should follow principle. In this, as in many other elections, they would be guided by reputation, which would not err oftener, perhaps, than the present mode of appointment. In one State of the Union, at least, it has long been tried, and with the most satisfactory success. The judges of Connecticut have been chosen by the people every six months, for nearly two centuries, and believe there has hardly ever been an instance of change; so powerful is the curb of incessant responsibility. If prejudice, however, derived from a monarchical institution, is still to prevail against the vital elective principle of our own, and if the existing example among ourselves of periodical election of judges by the people be still mistrusted, let us at least not adopt the evil, and reject the good, of the English precedent; let us retain amovability on the concurrence of the executive and legislative branches, and nomination by the executive alone. Nomination to office is an executive function. To give it to the legislature, as we do, is a violation of the principle of the separation of powers. It swerves the members from correctness, by temptations to intrigue for office themselves, and to a corrupt barter of votes; and destroys responsibility by dividing it among a multitude. By leaving nomination in its proper place, among executive functions, the principle of the distribution of power is preserved, and responsibility weighs with its heaviest force on a single head. . . .

We should thus marshal our government into, 1, the general federal republic, for all concerns foreign and federal; 2, that of the State, for what relates to our own citizens exclusively; 3, the county republics, for the duties and concerns of the county; and 4, the ward republics, for the small, and yet numerous and interesting concerns of the neighborhood; and in government, as well as in every other business of life, it is by division and subdivision of duties alone, that all matters, great and small, can be managed to perfection. And the whole is cemented by giving to every citizen, personally, a part in the administration of the public affairs.

The sum of these amendments is, 1. General Suffrage. 2. Equal representation in the legislature. 3. An executive chosen by the people. 4. Judges elective or amovable. 5. Justices, jurors, and sheriffs elective. 6. Ward divisions. And 7. Periodical amendments of the constitution.

I have thrown out these as loose heads of amendment, for consideration and correction; and their object is to secure self-government by the republicanism of our constitution, as well as by the spirit of the people; and to nourish and perpetuate that spirit. I am not among those who fear the people. They, and not the rich, are our dependence for continued freedom. . . .

Some men look at constitutions with sanctimonious reverence, and deem them like the arc of the covenant, too sacred to be touched. They ascribe to the men of the preceding age a wisdom more than human, and suppose what they did to be beyond amendment. I knew that age well; I belonged to it, and labored with it. It deserved well of its country. It was very like the present, but without the experience of the present; and forty years of experience in government is worth a century of book-reading; and this they would say themselves, were they to rise from the dead. I am certainly not an advocate for frequent and untried changes in laws and constitutions. I think moderate imperfections had better be borne with; because, when once known, we accommodate ourselves to them, and find practical means of correcting their ill effects. But I know also, that laws and institutions must go hand in hand with the progress of the human mind. As that becomes more developed, more enlightened, as new discoveries are made, new truths disclosed, and manners and opinions change with the change of circumstances, institutions must advance also, and keep pace with the times. We might as well require a man to wear still the coat which fitted him when a boy, as civilized society to remain ever under the regimen of their barbarous ancestors. It is this preposterous idea which has lately deluged Europe in blood. Their monarchs, instead of wisely yielding to the gradual change of circumstances, of favoring progressive accommodation to progressive improvement, have clung to old abuses, entrenched themselves behind steady habits, and obliged their subjects to seek through blood and violence rash and ruinous innovations, which, had they been referred to the peaceful deliberations and collected wisdom of the nation, would have been put into acceptable and salutary forms. Let us follow no such examples, nor weakly believe that one generation is not as capable as another of taking care of itself, and of ordering its own affairs.

Let us, as our sister States have done, avail ourselves of our reason and experience, to correct the crude essays of our first and unexperienced, although wise, virtuous, and well-meaning councils. And lastly, let us provide in our constitution for its revision at stated periods. What these periods should be, nature herself indicates. By the European tables of mortality, of the adults living at any one moment of time, a majority will be dead in about nineteen years. At the end of that period, then, a new majority is come into place; or, in other words, a new generation. Each generation is as independent as the one preceding, as that was of all which had gone before. It has then, like them, a right to choose for itself the form of government it believes most promotive of its own happiness; consequently, to accommodate to the circumstances in which it finds itself, that received from its predecessors; and it is for the peace and good of mankind, that a solemn opportunity of doing this every nineteen or twenty years, should be provided by the constitution; so that it may be handed on, with periodical repairs, from generation to generation, to the end of time, if anything human can so long endure. It is now forty years since the constitution of Virginia was formed. The same tables inform us, that, within that period, two-thirds of the adults then living are now dead. Have then the remaining third, even if they had the wish, the right to hold in obedience to their will, and to laws heretofore made by them, the other two-thirds, who, with themselves, compose the present mass of adults? If they have not, who has? The dead? But the dead have no rights. They are nothing; and nothing cannot own something. Where there is no substance, there can be no accident. This corporeal globe, and everything upon it, belong to its present corporeal inhabitants, during their generation. They alone have a right to direct what is the concern of themselves alone, and to declare the law of that direction; and this declaration can only be made by their majority. That majority, then, has a right to depute representatives to a convention, and to make the constitution what they think will be the best for themselves. . . .

Jefferson to Judge Spencer Roane, September 6, 1819

DEAR SIR,—I had read in the Enquirer, and with great approbation, the pieces signed Hampden,

and have read them again with redoubled approbation, in the copies you have been so kind as to
send me. I subscribe to every tittle of them. They
contain the true principles of the revolution of
1800, for that was as real a revolution in the principles of our government as that of 1776 was in
its form; not effected indeed by the sword, as
that, but by the rational and peaceable instrument of reform, the suffrage of the people. The
nation declared its will by dismissing functionaries of one principle, and electing those of another,
in the two branches, executive and legislative,
submitted to their election. Over the judiciary department, the constitution had deprived them of
their control. That, therefore, has continued the
reprobated system, and although new matter has
been occasionally incorporated into the old, yet
the leaven of the old mass seems to assimilate to
itself the new, and after twenty years' confirmation of the federal system by the voice of the nation, declared through the medium of elections,
we find the judiciary on every occasion, still driving us into consolidation.

In denying the right they usurp of exclusively
explaining the constitution, I go further than
you do, if [I] understand rightly your quotation
from the Federalist, of an opinion that "the judiciary is the last resort in relation *to the other
departments* of the government, but not in relation to the rights of the parties to the compact
under which the judiciary is derived." If this
opinion be sound, then indeed is our constitution a complete *felo de se.* For intending to establish three departments, co-ordinate and independent, that they might check and balance
one another, it has given, according to this opinion, to one of them alone, the right to prescribe
rules for the government of the others, and to
that one too, which is unelected by, and independent of the nation. For experience has already shown that the impeachment it has provided is not even a scare-crow; that such
opinions as the one you combat, sent cautiously
out, as you observe also, by detachment, not belonging to the case often, but sought for out of
it, as if to rally the public opinion beforehand to

their views, and to indicate the line they are to
walk in, have been so quietly passed over as
never to have excited animadversion, even in a
speech of any one of the body entrusted with impeachment. The constitution, on this hypothesis, is a mere thing of wax in the hands of the judiciary, which they may twist and shape into any
form they please. It should be remembered, as
an axiom of eternal truth in politics, that whatever power in any government is independent, is
absolute also; in theory only, at first, while the
spirit of the people is up, but in practice, as fast
as that relaxes. Independence can be trusted
nowhere but with the people in mass. They are
inherently independent of all but moral law. My
construction of the constitution is very different
from that you quote. It is that each department
is truly independent of the others, and has an
equal right to decide for itself what is the meaning of the constitution in the cases submitted to
its action; and especially, where it is to act ultimately and without appeal. I will explain myself
by examples, which, having occurred while I
was in office, are better known to me, and the
principles which governed them.

A legislature had passed the sedition law. The
federal courts had subjected certain individuals to
its penalties of fine and imprisonment. On coming
into office, I released these individuals by the
power of pardon committed to executive discretion, which could never be more properly exercised than where citizens were suffering without
the authority of law, or, which was equivalent,
under a law unauthorized by the constitution, and
therefore null. In the case of Marbury and Madison, the federal judges declared that commissions,
signed and sealed by the President, were valid, although not delivered. [I] deemed delivery essential
to complete a deed, which, as long as it remains in
the hands of the party, is as yet no deed, it is in
posse only, but not in *esse,* and I withheld delivery of the commissions. They cannot issue a mandamus to the President or legislature, or to any of
their officers. . . . When the British treaty . . .
arrived, without any provision against the im-
pressment of our seamen, I determined not to

ratify it. The Senate thought I should ask their advice. I thought that would be a mockery of them, when I was predetermined against following it, should they advise its ratification. The constitution had made their advice necessary to confirm a treaty, but not to reject it. This has been blamed by some; but I have never doubted its soundness. In the cases of two persons, *antenati,* under exactly similar circumstances, the federal court had determined that one of them (Duane) was not a citizen; the House of Representatives nevertheless determined that the other (Smith, of South Carolina) was a citizen, and admitted him to his seat in their body. Duane was a republican, and Smith a federalist, and these decisions were made during the federal ascendancy.

These are examples of my position, that each of the three departments has equally the right to decide for itself what is its duty under the constitution, without any regard to what the others may have decided for themselves under a similar question. . . .

Source: Electronic Text Center, University of Virginia Library, *Jefferson Digital Archive,* http://etext.virginia.edu/toc/modeng/public/JefLett.html.

Document 14   Judiciary Act of 1789

Article 3 of the Constitution established the Supreme Court and "such inferior courts as Congress shall from time to time consider." It says little about the actual operating procedures for the federal judiciary, which meant that one of the first orders of business for the First Congress was to establish through statute a federal judicial structure. The Judiciary Act of 1789 was one of the more significant pieces of legislation from the First Congress. Some of its provisions became sources of constitutional disputes that would go before the Supreme Court for resolution. Section 13, which gives the Court the power to issue a writ of mandamus ordering government officials to do their duty, was struck down in Marbury v. Madison *(1803) as an unconstitutional expansion of the Court's jurisdiction. Section 25, which gives the Supreme Court appellate jurisdiction over the decisions of state supreme courts, was challenged in* Martin v. Hunter's Lessee *(1816). Here, the Court upheld the provision, finding it compatible with the supremacy clause of Article 6 and the nature of a federal system.*

CHAP. XX.—An Act to establish the Judicial Courts of the United States.

SECTION 1. *Be it enacted by the Senate and House of Representatives of the United States of America in Congress assembled,* That the supreme court of the United States shall consist of a chief justice and five associate justices, any four of whom shall be a quorum, and shall hold annually at the seat of government two sessions, the one commencing the first Monday of February, and the other the first Monday of August. . . .

SEC. 2. *And be it further enacted,* That the United States shall be, and they hereby are divided into thirteen districts, . . .

SEC. 3. *And be it further enacted,* That there be a court called a District Court, in each of the afore mentioned districts, to consist of one judge, who shall reside in the district for which he is appointed, and shall be called a District Judge, and shall hold annually four sessions, . . .

SEC. 4. *And be it further enacted,* That the before mentioned districts, except those of Maine and Kentucky, shall be divided into three circuits, and be called the eastern, the middle, and the southern circuit . . . and that there shall be held annually in each district of said circuits, two courts, which shall be called Circuit Courts, and shall consist of any two justices of the Supreme Court, and the district judge of such districts, any two of whom shall constitute a quorum: *Provided,* That no district judge shall give a vote in any case of appeal or error from his own decision; but may assign the reasons of such his decision. . . .

SEC. 8. *And be it further enacted,* That the justices of the Supreme Court, and the district judges, before they proceed to execute the duties of their respective offices, shall take the following oath or affirmation, to wit: "I, A. B., do solemnly swear or affirm, that I will administer justice without respect to persons, and do equal right to the poor and to the rich, and that I will faithfully and impartially discharge and perform all the duties incumbent on me as [title], according to the best of my abilities and understanding, agreeably to the constitution, and laws of the United States. So help me God."

SEC. 9. *And be it further enacted,* That the district courts shall have, exclusively of the courts of the several States, cognizance of all crimes and offences that shall be cognizable under the authority of the United States, committed within their respective districts, or upon the high seas; where no other punishment than whipping, not exceeding thirty stripes, a fine not exceeding one hundred dollars, or a term of imprisonment not exceeding six months, is to be inflicted; and shall also have exclusive original cognizance of all civil causes of admiralty and maritime jurisdiction, including all seizures under laws of impost, navigation or trade of the United States, where the seizures are made, on waters which are navigable from the sea by vessels of ten or more tons burthen, within their respective districts as well as upon the high seas; saving to suitors, in all cases, the right of a common law remedy, where the common law is competent to give it; and shall also have exclusive original cognizance of all seizures on land,

or other waters than as aforesaid, made, and of all suits for penalties and forfeitures incurred, under the laws of the United States. And shall also have cognizance, concurrent with the courts of the several States, or the circuit courts, as the case may be, of all causes where an alien sues for a tort only in violation of the law of nations or a treaty of the United States. And shall also have cognizance, concurrent as last mentioned, of all suits at common law where the United States sue, and the matter in dispute amounts, exclusive of costs, to the sum or value of one hundred dollars. And shall also have jurisdiction exclusively of the courts of the several States, of all suits against consuls or vice-consuls, except for offences above the description aforesaid. And the trial of issues in fact, in the district courts, in all causes except civil causes of admiralty and maritime jurisdiction, shall be by jury. . . .

SEC. 11. *And be it further enacted,* That the circuit courts shall have original cognizance, concurrent with the courts of the several States, of all suits of a civil nature at common law or in equity, where the matter in dispute exceeds, exclusive of costs, the sum or value of five hundred dollars, and the United States are plaintiffs, or petitioners; or an alien is a party, or the suit is between a citizen of the State where the suit is brought, and a citizen of another State. And shall have exclusive cognizance of all crimes and offences cognizable under the authority of the United States, except where this act otherwise provides, or the laws of the United States shall otherwise direct, and concurrent jurisdiction with the district courts of the crimes and offences cognizable therein. But no person shall be arrested in one district for trial in another, in any civil action before a circuit or district court. And no civil suit shall be brought before either of said courts against an inhabitant of the United States, by any original process in any other district than that whereof he is an inhabitant, or in which he shall be found at the time of serving the writ, nor shall any district or circuit court have cognizance of any suit to recover the contents of any promissory note or other chose in action in favour of an assignee, unless a suit might have been prosecuted in such court to recover the said contents if no assignment had been made, except in cases of foreign bills of exchange. And the circuit courts shall also have appellate jurisdiction from the district courts under the regulations and restrictions herein after provided. . . .

SEC. 13. *And be it further enacted,* That the Supreme Court shall have exclusive jurisdiction of all controversies of a civil nature, where a state is a party, except between a state and its citizens; and except also between a state and citizens of other states, or aliens, in which latter case it shall have original but not exclusive jurisdiction. And shall have exclusively all such jurisdiction of suits or proceedings against ambassadors, or other public ministers, or their domestics, or domestic servants, as a court of law can have or exercise consistently with the law of nations; and original, but not exclusive jurisdiction of all suits brought by ambassadors, or other public ministers, or in which a consul, or vice consul, shall be a party. And the trial of issues in fact in the Supreme Court, in all actions at law against citizens of the United States, shall be by jury. The Supreme Court shall also have appellate jurisdiction from the circuit courts and courts of the several states, in the cases herein after specially provided for; and shall have power to issue writs of prohibition to the district courts, when proceeding as courts of admiralty and maritime jurisdiction, and writs of *mandamus,* in cases warranted by the principles and usages of law, to any courts appointed, or persons holding office, under the authority of the United States.

SEC. 14. *And be it further enacted,* That all the before-mentioned courts of the United States, shall have power to issue writs of *scire facias, habeas corpus,* and all other writs not specially provided for by statute, which may be necessary for the exercise of their respective jurisdictions, and agreeable to the principles and usages of law. And that either of the justices of the Supreme Court, as well as judges of the district courts, shall have power to grant writs of *habeas corpus* for the purpose of an inquiry into the cause of commitment.—*Provided,* That writs of *habeas corpus* shall in no case extend to prisoners in gaol, unless where they are in custody, under or by colour of the authority of the United States, or are committed for trial before some court of the same, or are necessary to be brought into court to testify. . . .

SEC. 25. *And be it further enacted,* That a final judgment or decree in any suit, in the highest court of law or equity of a State in which a decision in the suit could be had, where is drawn in question the validity of a treaty or statute of, or an authority exercised under the United States, and the decision is against their validity; or where is drawn in question the validity of a statute of, or an authority exercised under any State, on the ground of their being repugnant to the constitution, treaties or laws of the United States, and the decision is in favour of such their validity, or where is drawn in question the construction of any clause of the Constitution, or of a treaty, or statute of, or commission held under the United States, and the decision is against the title, right, privilege or exemption specially set up or claimed by either party, under such clause of the said Constitution, treaty, statute or commission, may be re-examined and reversed or affirmed in the Supreme Court of the United States upon a writ of error, the citation being signed by the chief justice, or judge or chancellor of the court rendering or passing the judgment or decree complained of, or by a justice of the Supreme Court of the United States, in the same manner and under the same regulations, and the writ shall have the same effect, as if the judgment or decree complained of had been rendered or passed in a circuit court, and the proceeding upon the reversal shall also be the same, except that the Supreme Court, instead of remanding the cause for a final decision as before provided, may at their discretion, if the cause shall have been once remanded before, proceed to a final decision of the same, and award execution. But no other error shall be assigned or regarded as a ground of reversal in any such case as aforesaid, than such as appears on the face of the record, and immediately respects the before mentioned questions of validity or construction of the said Constitution, treaties, statutes, commissions, or authorities in dispute. . . .

APPROVED, September 24, 1789.

Source: 1 Stat. 73 (1789).

Document 15   Senate Debate concerning the Louisiana Purchase and the Governance Act of 1804

The 1803 Louisiana Purchase has been called one of the greatest real estate deals in history. It doubled the size of the United States, adding to it more than 900,000 square miles at a cost of $15 million dollars. When President Thomas Jefferson learned that Napoleon had reclaimed the Louisiana Territory from the Spanish, he instructed his ambassador to France to negotiate its purchase. Napoleon, persuaded that France could not defend the vast area, agreed to the sale through a treaty. The Senate ratified the treaty in October 1803. Implementation of the treaty required that Congress allocate funds for the purchase, which prompted congressional debate about whether Jefferson had gone beyond his constitutional authority. Even those members of Congress who endorsed the purchase had serious qualms about its constitutionality. Like Jefferson, they welcomed the agreement but worried about the effect it might have on the federal system.

LOUISIANA TREATY.

The Senate resumed the second reading of the bill, entitled "An act authorizing the creation of a tock to the amount of eleven millions two hundred and fifty thousand dollars, for the purpose of carrying into effect the convention of the 30th of April, 1803, between the United States of America and the French Republic, and making provision for the payment of the same;" and having amended the bill. . . .

Mr. WHITE rose and made the following remarks:

. . . Gentlemen may say this money is to be paid upon the responsibility of the President of the United States, and not until after the delivery of possession to us of the territory; but why case from ourselves all the responsibility upon this subject and impose the whole weight upon the President, which may hereafter prove dangerous and embarrassing to him? Why make the Presi-

dent the sole and absolute judge of what shall be a faithful delivery of possession under the treaty? What he may think a delivery of possession sufficient to justify the payment of this money, we might not; and I have no hesitation in saying that if, in acquiring this territory under the treaty, we have to fire a single musket, to charge a bayonet, or to lose a drop of blood, it will not be such a cession on the part of France as should justify to the people of this country the payment of any, and much less so enormous a sum of money. What would the case be, sir? It would be buying of France authority to make war upon Spain; it would be giving the First Consul fifteen millions of dollars to stand aloof until we can settle our differences with His Catholic Majesty. Would honorable gentlemen submit to the degradation of purchasing even his neutrality at so inconvenient a price? . . .

Mr. WELLS said: Mr. President, having always held to the opinion that, when a treaty was duly made under the constituted authorities of the United States, Congress was bound to pass the laws necessary to carry it into effect; and as the vote which I am about to give may not at first seem to conform itself to this opinion, I feel an obligation imposed upon me to state, in as concise a manner as I can, the reasons why I withhold my assent from the passage of this bill.

There are two acts necessary to be performed to carry the present treaty into effect—one by the French Government, the other by our own. They are to deliver us a fair and effectual possession of the ceded territory; and then, and not till then, are we to pay the purchase money. We have already authorized the President to receive possession. This co-operation on our part was requisite to enable the French to comply with the stipulation they had made; they could not deliver unless somebody was appointed to receive. In this view of the subject, the question which presents itself to my mind is, who shall judge whether the French Government does, or does not, faithfully comply with the previous condition? The bill . . . gives to the President this power. I am for our retaining and exercising it ourselves. I may be asked, why not delegate this power to the President? Sir, I answer by inquiring why we should delegate it? To us it properly belongs; and, unless some advantage will be derived to the United States, it should not be transferred with my consent. . . .

Mr. JACKSON . . .

Mr. President, the honorable gentleman appears to be extremely apprehensive of vesting the powers delegated by the bill, now on its passage, in the President, and wishes to retain it in the Legislature. Is this a Legislative or Executive business? Assuredly, in my mind, of the latter nature. The President gave instruction for, and, with our consent, ratified the treaty. We have given him the power to take possession, which his officers are, perhaps, at this moment doing; and surely, as the ostensible party, the representative of the sovereignty to whom France will alone look, he ought to possess the power of fulfilling our part of the contract. Gentlemen, indeed, had doubted, on a former occasion, the propriety of giving the President the power of taking possession and organizing a temporary government. . . . For my part, sir, I have none of those fears. I believe the President will be as cautious as ourselves, and the bill is as carefully worded as possible; for the money is not to be paid until after Louisiana shall be placed in our possession. . . .

Mr. TAYLOR . . .

Recollect, sir, that it has been proved that the United States may acquire territory. Territory, so acquired, becomes from the acquisition itself a portion of the territories of the United States, or may be united with their territories without being erected into a State. An union of territory is one thing; of States another. Both are exemplified by an actual existence. The United States possess territory, comprised in the union of territory, and not in the union of States. Congress is empowered to regulate or dispose of territorial sections of the Union, and have exercised the power; but it is not empowered to regulate or dispose of State sections of the Union. The citizens of these territorial sections are citizens of the United S[t]ates, and they have all the rights of citizens of the United States; but such rights do not include those political rights arising from State compacts or governments, which are dissimilar in different States. Supposing the General Government or treaty-making power have no right to add or unite States and State citizens to the Union, yet they have a power of adding or uniting to it territory and territorial citizens of the United States.

. . . The Constitution recognises and the practice warrants an incorporation of a Territory and its inhabitants into the Union, without admitting either as a State. . . .

The same gentleman . . . observes, that although Congress may admit new States, the President and Senate who are but a component part, cannot. Apply this doctrine to the case before us. How could Congress by any mode of legislation admit this country into the Union until it was acquired? And how can this acquisition be made except through the treaty-making power? Could the gentleman rise in his place and move for leave to bring in a bill for the purchase of Louisiana and its admission into the Union? I take it that no transaction of this or any other kind with a foreign Power can take place except through the Executive Department, and that in the form of a treaty, agreement, or convention. When the acquisition is made, Congress can then make such disposition of it as may be expedient.

. . . If you reject this treaty, with what face can you open another negotiation? What President would venture another mission, or what Minister could be prevailed on to be made the instrument of another negotiation? You adopt the treaty, direct possession to be taken of the country, and then refuse to pay for it!

What palliation can we offer to our Western citizens for a conduct like this? . . . Will it be satisfactory to them to be told that the title is good, the price low, the finances competent, and the authority, at least to purchase, Constitutional; but that the country is too extensive, and that the admission of these people to all the privileges we ourselves enjoy, is not permitted by the Constitution? It will not, sir.

. . . There is a point of endurance beyond which even the advocates for passive obedience and non-resistance cannot expect men to pass. That point is at once reached the moment you solemnly declare, by your vote, that a part of your citizens shall not enjoy those natural rights and advantages of which they are unjustly deprived, and which you have not the complete power to restore to them. Then it is that gentlemen may talk of danger to the Union; then it is I shall begin to tremble for my country; and then it is, and not till then, I shall agree with gentlemen that the Confederacy is in danger. . . .

Source: *Annals of Congress: Debates and Proceedings of the Congress of the United States,* 8th Cong., 2d sess., 1804, 31–44, 49–51, 63–65.

Document 16   Articles of Impeachment, Andrew Johnson 1868

The post–Civil War impeachment of President Andrew Johnson demonstrates how political struggles between branches of government can become constitutional issues. Johnson's firing of Secretary of War Edwin M. Stanton violated the Tenure of Office Act of 1867, a law passed over the president's veto requiring the advice and consent of the Senate for removal of executive officers. Johnson claimed that the statute imposed an unconstitutional limitation on the executive power of appointment. The last two articles of impeachment demonstrate that this battle went beyond the dispute over the Tenure of Office Act, extending to the struggle over Reconstruction. The Senate fell one vote short of convicting Johnson. His view ultimately prevailed when the Supreme Court decided Myers v. United States *(1926) (Doc. 43).*

ARTICLE 1. That said Andrew Johnson, President of the United States, on the 21st day of February, in the year of our Lord 1868, at Washington, in the District of Columbia, unmindful of the high duties of his oath of office and of the requirements of the Constitution, that he should take care that the laws be faithfully executed, did unlawfully, in violation of the Constitution and laws of the United States, issue an order in writing for the removal of Edwin M. Stanton from the office of Secretary of the Department of War, said Edwin M. Stanton having been, therefore, duly appointed and commissioned by and with the advice and consent of the Senate of the United States as such Secretary; and said Andrew Johnson, President of the United States, on the 12th day of August, in the year of our Lord 1867, and during the recess of said Senate, having suspended by his order Edwin M. Stanton from said office, and within twenty days after the first day of the next meeting of said Senate, on the 12th day of December, in the year last aforesaid, having reported to said Senate such suspension, with the evidence and reasons for his action in the case, and the name of the person designated to perform the duties of such office temporarily, until the next meeting of the Senate, and said Senate thereafterwards, on the 13th day of January, in the year of our Lord 1868, having duly considered the evidence and reasons reported by said Andrew Johnson for said suspension, did refuse to concur in said suspension; whereby and by force of the provisions of an act entitled "an act regulating the tenure of civil officers," passed March 2, 1867, said Edwin M. Stanton did forthwith resume the functions of his office, whereof the said Andrew Johnson had then and there notice, and the said Edwin M. Stanton, by reason of the premises, on said 21st day of February, was lawfully entitled to hold said office of Secretary for the Department of War, which said order for the removal of said Edwin M. Stanton is, in substance, as follows, that is to say:

Executive Mansion, Washington, D.C., Feb. 21, 1868.

Sir: By virtue of the power and authority vested in me, as President, by the Constitution and laws of the United States, you are hereby removed from the office of Secretary for the Department of War, and your functions as such will terminate upon receipt of their communication. You will transfer to Brevet Major-General L. Thomas, Adjutant-General of the Army, who has this day been authorized and empowered to act as Secretary of War ad interim, all books, paper and

other public property now in your custody and charge.

Respectfully, yours, Andrew Johnson.

To the Hon. E. M. Stanton, Secretary of War

Which order was unlawfully issued, and with intent then are there to violate the act entitled "An act regulating the tenure of certain civil offices," passed March 2, 1867, and contrary to the provisions of said act, and in violation thereof, and contrary to the provisions of the Constitution of the United States, and without the advice and consent of the Senate of the United States, the said Senate then and there being in session, to remove said E. M. Stanton from the office of Secretary for the Department of War, whereby said Andrew Johnson, President of the United States, did then and there commit, and was guilty of a high misdemeanor in office.

ARTICLE 2. That on the 21st day of February, in the year of our Lord 1868, at Washington, in the District of Columbia, said Andrew Johnson, President of the United States, unmindful of the high duties of his oath of office, and in violation of the Constitution of the United States, and contrary to the provisions of an act entitled "An act regulating the tenure of certain civil offices," passed March 2, 1867, without the advice and consent of the Senate, then and there being in session, and without authority of law, did appoint one L. Thomas to be Secretary of War ad interim. . . .

Whereby said Andrew Johnson, President of the United States, did then and there commit, and was guilty of a high misdemeanor in office.

ARTICLE 3. That said Andrew Johnson, President of the United States, on the 21st day of February, in the year of our Lord one thousand eight hundred and sixty-eight, at Washington, in the District of Columbia, did commit, and was guilty of a high misdemeanor in office, in this: That without authority of law, while the Senate of the United States was then and there in session, he did appoint one Lorenzo Thomas to be

Secretary for the Department of War, ad interim, without the advice and consent of the Senate, and in violation of the Constitution of the United States, no vacancy having happened in said office of Secretary for the Department of War during the recess of the Senate, and no vacancy existing in said office at the time. . . .

ARTICLE 4. That said Andrew Johnson, President of the United States, unmindful of the high duties of his office, and of his oath of office, in violation of the Constitution and laws of the United States, on the 21st day of February, in the year of our Lord 1868, at Washington, in the District of Columbia, did unlawfully conspire with one Lorenzo Thomas, and with other persons to the House of Representatives unknown, with intent, by intimidation and threats, to hinder and prevent Edwin M. Stanton, then and there, the Secretary for the Department of War, duly appointed under the laws of the United States, from holding said office of Secretary for the Department of War, contrary to and in violation of the Constitution of the United States, and of the provisions of an act entitled "An act to define and punish certain conspiracies," approved July 31, 1861, whereby said Andrew Johnson, President of the United States, did then and there commit and was guilty of high crime in office.

ARTICLE 5. That said Andrew Johnson, President of the United States, unmindful of the high duties of his office and of his oath of office, on the 21st of February, in the year of our Lord one thousand eight hundred and sixty-eight, and on divers others days and time in said year before the 28th day of said February, at Washington, in the District of Columbia, did unlawfully conspire with one Lorenzo Thomas, and with other persons in the House of Representatives unknown, by force to prevent and hinder the execution of an act entitled "An act regulating the tenure of certain civil office," passed March 2, 1867, and in pursuance of said conspiracy, did attempt to prevent E. M. Stanton, then and there being Secretary for the Department of War, duly appointed and commissioned under the laws of

the United States, from holding said office, whereby the said Andrew Johnson, President of the United States, did then and there commit and was guilty of high misdemeanor in office.

ARTICLE 6. That Andrew Johnson, President of the United States, unmindful of the duties of his high office and of his oath of office, on the 21st day of February, in the year of our Lord 1868, at Washington, in the District of Columbia, did unlawfully conspire with one Lorenzo Thomas, by force to seize, take and possess the property of the United Sates at the War Department, contrary to the provisions of an act entitled "An act to define and punish certain conspiracies," approved July 31, 1861, and with intent to violate and disregard an act entitled "An act regulating the tenure of certain civil offices," passed March 2, 1867, whereby said Andrew Johnson, President of the United States, did then and there commit a high crime in office.

ARTICLE 7. That said Andrew Johnson, President of the United States, unmindful of the high duties of his office, and of his oath of office, on the 21st day of February, in the year of our Lord 1868, and on diverse other days in said year, before the 28th day of said February, at Washington, in the District of Columbia, did unlawfully conspire with one Lorenzo Thomas to prevent and hinder the execution of an act of the United States, entitled "An act regulating the tenure of certain civil offices," passed March 2, 1867, and in pursuance of said conspiracy, did unlawfully attempt to prevent Edwin M. Stanton, then and there being Secretary for the Department of War, under the laws of the United States, from holding said office to which he had been duly appointed and commissioned, whereby said Andrew Johnson, President of the United States, did there and then commit and was guilty of a high misdemeanor in office.

ARTICLE 8. That said Andrew Johnson, President of the United States, unmindful of the high duties of his office, and of his oath of office, on the 21st day of February, in the year of our Lord 1868, at Washington, in the District of Columbia, did unlawfully conspire with one

Lorenzo Thomas, to seize, take and possess the property of the United States in the War Department, with intent to violate and disregard the act entitled "An act regulating the tenure of certain civil offices," passed March 2, 1867, whereby said Andrew Johnson, President of the United States, did then and there commit a high misdemeanor in office.

ARTICLE 9. That said Andrew Johnson, President of the United States, on the 22nd day of February, in the year of our Lord 1868, at Washington, in the District of Columbia, in disregard of the Constitution and the law of Congress duly enacted, as Commander-in-Chief, did bring before himself, then and there, William H. Emory, a Major-General by brevet in the Army of the United States, actually in command of the Department of Washington and the military forces therefore, and did and there, as Commander-in-Chief, declare to, and instruct said Emory, that part of the law of the United States, passed March 2, 1867, entitled "an act for making appropriations for the support of the army for the year ending June 30, 1868, and for other purposes," especially the second section thereof, which provides, among other things, that all orders and instructions relating to military operations issued by the President and Secretary of War, shall be issued through the General of the Army, and in case of his inability, through the next in rank was unconstitutional, and in contravention of the commission of Emory, and therefore not binding on him, as an officer in the Army of the United States, which said provisions of law had been therefore duly and legally promulgated by General Order for the government and direction of the Army of the United States, as the said Andrew Johnson then and there well knew, with intent thereby to induce said Emory, in his official capacity as Commander of the Department of Washington, to violate the provisions of said act, and to take and receive, act upon and obey such orders as he, the said Andrew Johnson, might make and give, and which should not be issued through the General of the Army of the United States, according to the pro-

visions of said act, whereby said Andrew Johnson, President of the United States, did then and there commit, and was guilty of a high misdemeanor in office; and the House of Representatives, by protestation, saving to themselves the liberty of exhibition, at any time hereafter, any further articles of their accusation or impeachment against the said Andrew Johnson, President of the United States, and also or replying to his answers, which will make up the articles herein preferred against him, and of offering proof to the same and every part thereof, and to all and every other article, accusation or impeachment which shall be exhibited by them as the case shall require, do demand that the said Andrew Johnson may be put to answer the high crimes and misdemeanors in office herein charged against him, and that such proceedings, examinations, trials and judgments may be thereupon had and given had and given as may be agreeable to law and justice.

[Subsequently, two additional articles were added.]

ARTICLE 10. That said Andrew Johnson, President of the United States, unmindful of the high duties of his high office and the dignity and proprieties thereof, and of the harmony and courtesies which ought to exist and be maintained between the executive and legislative branches of the Government of the United States, designing and intending to set aside the rightful authorities and powers of Congress, did attempt to bring into disgrace, ridicule, hatred, contempt and reproach, the Congress of the United States, and the several branches thereof, to impair and destroy the regard and respect of all the good people of the United States for the Congress and the legislative power thereof, which all officers of the government ought inviolably to preserve and maintain, and to excite the odium and resentment of all good people of the United States against Congress and the laws by it duly and constitutionally enacted; and in pursuance of his said design and intent, openly and publicly and before diverse assemblages of citizens of the United States, convened in diverse parts thereof, to meet and receive said Andrew Johnson as the Chief Magistrate of the United States, did, on the eighteenth day of August, in the year of our Lord one thousand eight hundred and sixty-six, and on diverse other days and times, as well before as afterwards, make and declare, with a loud voice, certain intemperate, inflammatory and scandalous harangues, and therein utter loud threats and bitter menaces, as well against Congress as the laws of the United States duly enacted thereby, amid the cries, jeers and laughter of the multitudes then assembled in hearing. . . .

Which said utterances, declarations, threats and harangues, highly censurable in any, are peculiarly indecent and unbecoming in the Chief Magistrate of the United States, by means whereof the said Andrew Johnson has brought the high office of the President of the United States into contempt, ridicule and disgrace, to the great scandal of all good citizens, whereby said Andrew Johnson, President of the United States, did commit, and was then and there guilty of a high misdemeanor in office.

ARTICLE 11. That the said Andrew Johnson, President of the United States, unmindful of the high duties of his office and his oath of office, and in disregard of the Constitution and laws of the United States, did, heretofore, to wit: On the 18th day of August, 1866, at the city of Washington, and in the District of Columbia, by public speech, declare and affirm in substance, that the Thirty-ninth Congress of the United States was not a Congress of the United States authorized by the Constitution to exercise legislative power under the same, but on the contrary, was a Congress of only part of the States, thereby denying and intending to deny, that the legisla-

tion of said Congress was valid or obligatory upon him, the said Andrew Johnson, except in so far as he saw fit to approve the same, and also thereby denying the power of the said Thirty-ninth Congress to propose amendments to the Constitution of the United States. And in pursuance of said declaration, the said Andrew Johnson, President of the United States, afterwards, to wit: On the 21st day of February, 1868, at the city of Washington, D.C., did, unlawfully and in disregard of the requirements of the Constitution that he should take care that the laws be faithfully executed, attempt to prevent the execution of an act entitled "An act regulating the tenure of certain civil office," passed March 2, 1867, by unlawfully devising and contriving and attempting to devise and contrive means by which he should prevent Edwin M. Stanton from forthwith resuming the functions of the office of Secretary for the Department of War, notwithstanding the refusal of the Senate to concur in the suspension theretofore made by the said Andrew Johnson of said Edwin M. Stanton from said office of Secretary for the Department of War; and also by further unlawfully devising and contriving, and attempting to devise and contrive means then and there to prevent the execution of an act entitled "An act making appropriations for the support of the army for the fiscal year ending June 30, 1868, and for other purposes," approved March 20, 1867. And also to prevent the execution of an act entitled "An act to provide for the more efficient government of the Rebel States," passed March 2, 1867. Whereby the said Andrew Johnson, President of the United States, did then, to wit, on the 21st day of February, 1868, at the city of Washington, commit and was guilty of a high misdemeanor in office.

Source: Congressional Globe, House of Representatives, 40th Cong., 2d sess., 1868, 1613–18; 1638–1642. Also accessible at "Finding Precedent: The Impeachment of Andrew Johnson," *HarpWeek,* http://www.impeach-andrewjohnson.com.

Document 17 Senate Debate on the Court-Packing Plan of Franklin Delano Roosevelt
July 9, 1937

President Franklin Delano Roosevelt and the Democratic majority in Congress suc-
ceeded in implementing an unprecedented legislative agenda to address the Great De-
pression. Significant pieces of that agenda were, however, struck down by the Supreme
Court as unconstitutional, prompting Roosevelt to propose a "Court-packing" plan.
Roosevelt argued that the Court was out of step with the times and was holding up the
work of the more democratic branches of government. "New blood" on the Court
would alleviate this crisis, Roosevelt contended. He, therefore, proposed a plan permit-
ting him to appoint a new justice for each sitting justice over the age of seventy who re-
fused to resign. The plan was met with considerable resistance even in the Democrat-
controlled Congress. The debate in the Senate, with Burton K. Wheeler (D-Mont.)
leading the opposition, demonstrates that institutional interest in checking exercises of
power can prevail over party allegiance.

Mr. WHEELER. . . . Never before in the history of the Senate of the United States . . . have I seen such appeals to the prejudices of the people, to the uninformed, as have been made with reference to this proposed legislation. Never before have I seen on both sides such deep feeling aroused. The reason for it, of course, is that this is a fundamental issue which everyone who has any feeling at all and who knows anything about the proposal realizes goes to the very foundation of our Government.

When the bill was first introduced the Attorney General of the United States in a radio speech used this language:

Ladies and gentlemen, only 9 short days have passed since the President sent to the Congress recommendations for the reorganization of the Federal judiciary. Yet in that brief time unfriendly voices have filled the air with lamentations and have vexed our ears with insensate clamor calculated to divert attention from the merits of his proposal.

Why was it that immediately there was aroused such feeling that protests came from the masses of the people of the country against the proposal? It was because they felt that the bill was an attempt on the part of the administration to do by indirection what it did not want to do by direction.

Again, Mr. President, after the appeal was made to the drought-stricken farmers in the Dust Bowl that we must immediately pack the Supreme Court in order to afford relief to those farmers, and after an appeal was made to the flood victims along the Ohio River in order to get them up in favor of the proposal and to cause them to send protests to their Senators who were opposed to it, we found another kind of appeal being made. We found an appeal being made by the Postmaster General of the United States on the ground of party loyalty. He contended that every Democrat ought to support the bill because of party loyalty regardless of its effect upon the Constitution of the United States and regardless of its violation of the spirit of the Constitution.

We heard Mr. Farley saying, "It is in the bag." In another place and at another time he said, "We will let the Senate talk and then we will let the House talk. Then we will call the roll. We have the votes." The press of the country after the last election pronounced Mr. Farley one of the great prognosticators the country had ever seen. Think of it, Mr. President, here in the United States the Postmaster General has said, "We will let the Senate talk." Certainly our constituents ought to feel very grateful to the Postmaster General for permitting the Members of the Senate of the United States, whom they have elected to office, to speak their minds in the Senate. The constituents of the Members of the House of Representatives ought to feel very grateful to the Postmaster General for condescending to let their Representatives speak with reference to the bill.

Then men were sent into nearly every State in the Union to arouse the labor leaders for the purpose of having them send protests and denunciations of Members of the Senate of the United States who were opposed to the bill. Men were sent into my State. One man was sent there who went to every labor organization in the State. I am told that he was on the Government pay roll. He was seeking to persuade the labor organizations to adopt resolutions not only in favor of the President's bill, but denouncing me. They went even further than that; one of the farm leaders told me that for the first time in his life he was invited to the White House, and it was suggested to him that he should go out and line up the farm organizations in the Northwest against every Member of the House and every Member of the Senate who dared to voice his opposition to the President's bill.

Something has been said about propaganda. We found the Secretary of Agriculture, by the medium of the radio, trying to line up the farmers of the country. Why? Not because he knew anything about the Court proposal, not because he was particularly interested in this piece of proposed legislation, but because the Congress of the United States had appropriated money and placed it in his hands to take care of the drought-stricken farmers or those in need of relief; he alone could disburse this money to them, and the implication, of course, was that unless a bill should be passed then the farmers would not be able perhaps to get further appropriations from the Congress.

Then we find the Postmaster General lining up the postmasters throughout the country. We find Mr. Harry Hopkins, of the W.P.A., on the radio, talking about the Democratic Party and about the Court proposal. Why? Why should the head of Works Progress Administration of the United States be propagandizing and trying to influence the people on relief against Members of the Senate? Hopkins' great influence over relief clients comes from the fact that he disburses money to them. But who appropriated that money? Whose money was it? It was the money of the people of the United States, appropriated by the Congress and turned over to Mr. Hopkins, and yet he is stirring up W.P.A. workers and their dependents against Members of the Senate and Members of the House, and that is the only reason why Hopkins spoke.

That spirit of intolerance with reference to the pending bill has prevailed and pervaded the discussion right down to the present moment. Everyone who does not agree with the administration on this proposal or who disagrees with the Attorney General is denounced as an "economic royalist" and as one who has sold out to Wall Street.

Then we found the same spirit of intolerance prevailing in this chamber yesterday, disclosed by the amazing situation which developed here. When the debate had been proceeding for only a couple of days and the opponents of the bill had not spoken at all, but had merely asked questions of the proponents of the bill who were talking, a practice which has been indulged in by the Senate from time immemorial, when no question of a filibuster was involved at all, but only bona-fide debate on the issues involved in the bill, we were confronted with a sudden appeal for strict application of the rules. Was it because the proponents of the bill are afraid of real debate? . . .

Thank God, I did not ride in on the coattails of the President of the United States! Thank God, I do not have to go to him and ask him whether or not I have to follow the Democratic leader in this new proposal! Those of you who rode in on the coattails of the President of the United States will ride out on the coattails of the President of the United States if that is the only reason you are here.

I did not ride in on the coattails of any President of the United States. I did not come here because I had promised to be 100 percent for the administration and to vote for everything the President wanted.

There are those who were elected to the United States Senate on a platform of "100 percent Roosevelt," but after assuming their seats in this body, when it was politically expedient, they unhesitatingly cast their votes against the administration. Now, however, some such Senators assert that they must vote for this bill because of their campaign promise of supporting the President 100 percent—that pledge is one that they keep or follow, utilize or discard as they deem it politically expedient.

No, Mr. President, I did not come to the Senate on the coattails of anyone; I came to the Senate on my own, and I am responsible for what I do in the Senate. I expect the people of my State to hold me responsible for my actions; and if I go out, I will go out riding on my own coattails and not upon the coattails of anyone else. . . .

I do not propose to be intimidated, and the rest of us do not propose to be intimidated, by name callers, or by anyone else, and our opponents might just as well make up their minds to that fact first as last. We are going to have a legitimate debate upon this question before the Senate, regardless of whether Mr. Farley wants us to or whether anybody else wants us to. The country is entitled to it.

Mr. HUGHES. Then the objection of the Senator from Montana is not, as I understand, to the purpose of the bill but to the method by which it is sought to effectuate the purpose?

Mr. WHEELER. My contention is that the bill proposes to do something in an unconstitutional way. I want to see the people themselves vote upon the constitutional amendment or upon the proposed; and I say that the people of this country have a right to vote upon such a measure. No President, no Congress, has a right to change the Constitution. When I say that, I say upon the best authority, because I repeat what Presidents of the United States have said, and what the present Attorney General of the United States has said in a speech before the American Bar Association, to which I shall call the Senate's attention.

Mr. HUGHES. Then, as I understand, the contention of the Senator from Montana is that changing the number of members of the Supreme Court by an act of Congress is changing the Constitution in an unconstitutional way?

Mr. WHEELER. No. Of course, the Congress of the United States has the power to increase the membership of the Supreme Court of the United States.

Mr. HUGHES. Or to decrease it.

Mr. WHEELER. Or to decrease the number of members of the Supreme Court. The Congress of the United States has the power to withhold appropriations for the salaries of the members of the Supreme Court of the United States.

Mr. TYDINGS. Or the salary of the President of the United States.

Mr. WHEELER. Or the salary of the President of the United States; but such would be against the spirit the Constitution. If Senators want to get rid of Mr. Justice Roberts, if Senators want to get rid of Mr. Justice Butler, why do they not do what they can do under the Constitution; that is, refuse to appropriate money to pay the salaries of those Justices? Why do they not do that? Because they know that the people of the United States would not stand for it, and that it would be against the spirit of the Constitution.

Mr. HUGHES. I think I can assure the Senator from Montana that, so far as I am concerned, I would not think of doing any such action with respect to any Justice of the Supreme Court. I would not tear down any Federal institution by denying the necessary support for it. That is as far from my mind as anything possibly can be.

Mr. BARKLEY. Mr. President, may I ask the Senator a question in order to clarify the matter?

Mr. WHEELER. Yes.

Mr. BARKLEY. Is it the Senator's contention that under the Constitution the pending bill is unconstitutional?

Mr. WHEELER. Of course, it is constitutional, just as it would be constitutional for the Congress to refuse to appropriate money to pay the salaries of Federal judges. That would be constitutional but it would be against the spirit of the Constitution.

Mr. BARKLEY. Whatever the reasoning and the comparison, the Senator admits that Congress can do this in the way proposed?

Mr. WHEELER. Congress, of course, can refuse to appropriate money for the President of the United States and make it impossible for him to act in the capacity of President. The Congress of the United States can refuse, I repeat, to appropriate the money for Justice Butler, for Justice McReynolds, or for any other Justice of the Supreme Court of the United States by saying that no part of the money appropriated shall be used to pay the salary of a particular Justice.

Mr. BURKE. Mr. President, will the Senator yield there?

Mr. WHEELER. I yield.

Mr. BURKE. On the point raised by the Senator from Kentucky [Mr. Barkley], while it must be admitted that the Constitution leaves it to the Congress entirely to fix the number of the members of the Court, does that necessarily mean that Congress is vested with the authority to turn over to somebody else the right to determine whether the Supreme Court shall consist of 9, 10, 11, or some other number of Justices?

Mr. WHEELER. I wish to consider that point a little later on.

Mr. BURKE. Very well.

Mr. CONNALLY. Mr. President, will the Senator yield for a question?

Mr. BURKE. I yield.

Mr. CONNALLY. In connection with the question of the Senator from Kentucky, let me ask the Senator from Montana a question. The Senator from Kentucky asked if Congress had not the constitutional power to increase the number of judges. Is it not true that Congress has the power to regulate the number of Justices on the Supreme Court for the purpose of making the Court of sufficient size to transact its business and efficiently to dispose of that business, but that Congress has no constitutional power to subtract from or to add to the Court for the purpose of destroying the Court?

Mr. WHEELER. Of course, such an act would be against the spirit of the Constitution. I am sorry

the junior Senator from Kentucky [Mr. Logan] is not present, for he said yesterday that the spirit of the Constitution and the letter of the Constitution were the same thing. Let me quote what James Truslow Adams says about that. He says:

To use the letter of the Constitution for a purpose not intended, and subversive to the whole constitutional structure, cannot be considered a constitutional act, although it may be a legal one. . . .

After all, speaking of 5-to-4 decisions, do we want a Supreme Court that simply will agree entirely with our viewpoint? Is that what we want? Let me call attention to the fact that it is out of the clash of opinions that the truth comes. The worse thing that could happen to Congress, the worst thing that could happen to the country, would be to have but one strong political party. We get better legislation in this body because we have a clash of opinions as to proposed legislation. We get better bills out of committees when we have a clash of opinions. The American form of government depends upon the clash of opinions of its people, and not upon a subservient people who are voting as they are told to vote because they are getting hand-outs from the Treasury of the United States.

If the contention of those who favor the bill is correct, why have a written Constitution at all? A great many persons in this country think there is not any need for a written Constitution; but why do we have one? We have one, my friends. because my forefathers like the forefathers of most of the Senators, had left foreign shores, where they had seen the tyranny of one-man government in Europe. Some of them had been driven out of England by James I, who said to them, "Unless you conform, I will harass you out of the country"; and he did harass them until they left that country. He drove them to Holland, and then they came to America and settled upon the shores of this great country of ours. They fought the American Revolution; they spilled their blood and many of them died, all up and down the Atlantic seaboard, in order that you and I, their posterity, might have a democratic form of government assured by a written Constitution.

When the framers of the Constitution met in the assembly in Philadelphia, they did not write the Constitution simply to protect themselves, but they remembered some of the things that had occurred before. . . .

Mr. President, I say that there is nothing liberal about the proposal before us; there is nothing progressive about it. It has been dressed up in gaudy clothes for the purpose of attracting the fancy of some of the younger generation, who have not given it any serious thought and do not know that the liberties which have become commonplace to us were earned by the lifeblood of our forefathers. Our liberties are so commonplace that few people give any serious consideration to them.

Why should we be zealous about this cause? When we look at world affairs we realize that in Germany there is a dictator, under whose iron heel are 70,000,000 people. How did he come into power? On what plea did he come into office? He came in under the constitution of Germany. Every step that was taken by him at first was taken in a constitutional way. Mr. Hitler acted "to meet the needs of the times."

Mussolini came into office upon the plea that he would improve economic conditions and he assumed the power of a dictator and abolished the legislative body of Italy and set up his own court, in order that he might "meet the needs of the times" in that country. In every place where a dictatorship has been set up it has been done "in order to meet the needs of the times." . . .

There are courts in Germany, there are courts in Italy, there are courts in Russia, and men are placed on them to meet the needs of the times as the dictators see the needs, and those judges do what the dictators want them to do. Can the Democratic Party afford to be placed in the position of saying to the people of this country, "We are going to put men on the Supreme Bench to meet the needs of the times as we see them"?

So, my friends, the needs of the times, I repeat, are like shifting sands upon the beach. The needs of the times are one thing today and some-

thing else tomorrow. When men are appointed upon the Supreme Court Bench to interpret the Constitution to meet the needs of the times, I say that a step is being taken which is reactionary. A step is being taken which, while it is within the letter of the Constitution, is against the spirit of the Constitution, and I defy anyone who knows the difference between the spirit of the law and the letter of the law to deny that statement. . . .

It is distressing to have to stand up here and disagree with the President of the United States, with any President of the United States, upon a vital, fundamental issue before the country. Particularly is it distressing for a Senator of the United States to have to stand up and disagree with the President of the United States when he is of his own party. It is even more distressing to me to have to stand up here and disagree with the President of the United States when he has been a personal friend of mine over many years. There is no judgeship dangling before my face, though. [Laughter.] I am not seeking a place upon the circuit court of appeals or upon any other court. The President has been most generous in his treatment of me; he has probably been as friendly to me as he has to any other Member of this body; but there comes a time in the life of every man, whether he was elected on the coattails of the President or not, when his own conscience must tell him whether or not he is going blindly to support the President. . . .

But when we want to amend the Constitution, let us not amend it by subterfuge. Let us do it in the way that every great President of the United States including Washington, Jefferson, Jackson, and Wilson has said it should be done. Let us do it under the Constitution. Let us have the amendment submitted to the people of the country. Let us have a vote upon it by the people. Let us not be afraid of it.

As I have previously said, I give the President all credit for the great things he has accomplished during the last 4 years for the people of this Nation. We have given him more power than any President of the United States has ever had in peacetime or in war. He has powers that no other President ever had. . . . I am not complaining. Conditions in the country were such that we had to give him that power and I am not complaining about the way he has used it.

But with a subservient Congress, with such tremendous power in the Executive, has not the time come in this Nation when we should say there is a line beyond which no man should pass? Has not the time come when we should say,

"No matter how beloved you may be, no matter how profound and wonderful you may be, no matter how much your sympathies are with the masses of the people of the United States, no matter what you want to do, the time has come when we should say there is a line beyond which, under this American Government of ours and under our Constitution, no man shall pass."

Source: Congressional Record, 75th Cong., 1st sess., July 9, 1937, 6966–6981.

Document 18   **Gulf of Tonkin Resolution 1964**

When North Vietnamese naval vessels attacked several U.S. ships in the Gulf of Tonkin, Congress authorized President Lyndon Johnson to respond with force. Johnson and his successor, Richard Nixon, used the Gulf of Tonkin Resolution—formally the Southeast Asia Resolution—to justify escalation of the conflict in Vietnam, claiming that the resolution was tantamount to a declaration of war. As the conflict became increasingly unpopular at home, Congress repealed the resolution. This experience over the right to declare war led Congress to pass the War Powers Resolution in 1973 (Doc. 19).

To promote the maintenance of international peace and security in Southeast Asia.

WHEREAS naval units of the Communist regime in Vietnam, in violation of the principles of the Charter of the United Nations and of international law, have deliberately and repeatedly attacked United States naval vessels lawfully present in international waters, and have thereby created a serious threat to international peace; and

WHEREAS these attacks are part of a deliberate and systematic campaign of aggression that the Communist regime in North Vietnam has been waging against its neighbors and the nations joined with them in the collective defense of their freedom; and

WHEREAS the United States is assisting the peoples of Southeast Asia to protect their freedom and has no territorial, military or political ambitions in that area, but desires only that these peoples should be left in peace to work out their own destinies in their own way; Now, therefore be it

Resolved by the Senate and House of Representatives of the United States of America in Congress assembled, That the Congress approves and supports the determination of the President, as Commander in Chief, to take all necessary measures to repel any armed attack against the forces of the United States and to prevent further aggression.

SECTION 2. The United States regards as vital to its national interest and to world peace the maintenance of international peace and security in Southeast Asia. Consonant with the Constitution of the US and Charter of the UN and in accordance with its obligations under the Southeast Asia Collective Defense Treaty [SACDT], the US is, therefore, prepared, as the President determines, to take all necessary steps, including the use of armed force, to assist any member or protocol state of the SACDT requesting assistance in defense of its freedom.

SECTION 3. This resolution shall expire when the President shall determine that the peace and security of the area is reasonably assured by international conditions created by action of the United Nations or otherwise, except that it may be terminated earlier by concurrent resolution of the Congress.

Source: House Joint Resolution 1145, August 7, 1964. P.L. 88-408; 78 Stat. 384

Document 19   **War Powers Resolution**
1973

Members of Congress believed that Presidents Lyndon Johnson and Richard Nixon, in their conduct of the Vietnam War, had gone beyond what they had authorized under the Gulf of Tonkin Resolution. Concerned about the executive's ability and willingness to take preemptive action in the commitment of troops, Congress passed the War Powers Resolution in an attempt to rein in presidential prerogative in this area. Passed over Nixon's veto, this resolution continues to be a source of controversy between presidents and Congress.

Resolved by the Senate and House of Representatives of the United States of America in Congress assembled, That:

Section 1. This joint resolution may be cited as the "War Powers Resolution."

Section 2. (a) It is the purpose of this joint resolution to fulfill the intent of the framers of the Constitution of the United States and insure that the collective judgment of both the Congress and the President will apply to the introduction of United States Armed Forces into hostilities, or into situations where imminent involvement in hostilities is clearly indicated by the circumstances, and to the continued use of such forces in hostilities or in such situations.

(b) Under Article 1, section 8, of the Constitution, it is specifically provided that the Congress shall have the power to make all laws necessary and proper for carrying into execution, not only its own powers but also all other powers vested by the Constitution in the Government of the United States, or in any department or officer thereof.

(c) The constitutional powers of the President as Commander-in-Chief to introduce United States Armed Forces into hostilities, or into situations where imminent involvement in hostilities is clearly indicated by the circumstances, are exercised only pursuant to (1) a declaration of war, (2) specific statutory authorization, or (3) a national emergency created by attack upon the United States, its territories or possessions, or its armed forces.

Section 3. The President in every possible instance shall consult with Congress before introducing United States Armed Forces into hostilities or into situations where imminent involvement in hostilities is clearly indicated by the circumstances, and after every such introduction shall consult regularly with Congress until United States Armed Forces are no longer engaged in hostilities or have been removed from such situations.

Section 4. (a) In the absence of a declaration of war, in any case in which United States Armed Forces are introduced—

(1) into hostilities or into situations where imminent involvement in hostilities is clearly indicated by the circumstances;

(2) into the territory, airspace or waters of a foreign nation, while equipped for combat, except for deployments which relate solely to supply, replacement, repair or training of such forces; or

(3) in numbers which substantially enlarge United States Armed Forces equipped for combat already located in a foreign nation; the President shall submit within 48 hours to the Speaker of the House of Representatives and to the President pro tempore of the Senate a report, in writing, setting forth—

   (A) the circumstances necessitating the introduction of United States Armed Forces;

   (B) the constitutional and legislative authority under which such introduction took place; and

   (C) the estimated scope and duration of the hostilities or involvement.

(b) The President shall provide such other information as Congress may request in the fulfillment of its constitutional responsibilities with respect to committing the Nation to war and the use of United States Armed Forces abroad.

(c) Whenever United States Armed Forces are introduced into hostilities or into any situation described in subsection (a) of this section, the President shall, so long as such armed forces continue to be engaged in such hostilities or situation, report to the Congress periodically on the status of such hostilities or situation, as well as on the scope and duration of such hostilities or situation, but in no event shall he report to Congress less often than once every six months.

Section 5. (a) Each report submitted pursuant to section 4(a)(1) shall be transmitted to the Speaker of the House of Representatives and to the President pro tempore of the Senate on the same calendar day. Each report so transmitted shall be referred to the Committee on Foreign Affairs of the House of Representatives and to the Committee on Foreign Relations of the Senate for appropriate action. If, when the report is transmitted, the Congress is adjourned sine die or has adjourned for any period in excess of

three calendar days, the Speaker of the House of Representatives and the President pro tempore of the Senate, if they deem it advisable (or if petitioned by at least 30 percent of the membership of their respective Houses) shall jointly request the President to convene Congress in order that it may consider the report and take appropriate action pursuant to this section.

(b) Within sixty calendar days after a report is submitted or is required to be submitted pursuant to section 4(a)(1), whichever is earlier, the President shall terminate any use of United States Armed Forces with respect to which such report was submitted (or required to be submitted), unless the Congress (1) has declared war or has enacted a specific authorization for such use of United States Armed Forces, (2) has extended by law such sixty-day period, or (3) is physically unable to meet as a result of an armed attack upon the United States. Such sixty-day period shall be extended for not more than an additional thirty days if the President determines and certifies to the Congress in writing that unavoidable military necessity respecting the safety of United States Armed Forces requires the continued use of such armed forces in the course of bringing about a prompt removal of such forces.

(c) Notwithstanding subsection (b), at any time that United States Armed Forces are engaged in hostilities outside the territory of the United States, its possessions and territories without a declaration of war or specific statutory authorization, such forces shall be removed by the President if Congress so directs by concurrent resolution.

[Sections 6 and 7 lay out the procedure Congress is to follow in passing such concurrent resolutions.]

Section 8. (a) Authority to introduce United States Armed Forces into hostilities or into situations wherein involvement in hostilities is clearly indicated by the circumstances shall not be inferred—

(1) from any provision of law (whether or not in effect before the date of enactment of this

joint resolution), including any provisions contained in any appropriation Act, unless such provision specifically authorizes the introduction of United States Armed Forces into hostilities or into such situations and states that it is intended to constitute specific statutory authorization within the meaning of this joint resolution; or

(2) from any treaty heretofore or hereafter ratified unless such treaty is implemented by legislation specifically authorizing the introduction of United States Armed Forces into hostilities or into such situations and states that it is intended to constitute specific statutory authorization within the meaning of this joint resolution.

(b) Nothing in this joint resolution shall be construed to require any further specific statutory authorization to permit members of United States Armed Forces to participate jointly with members of the armed forces of one or more foreign countries in the headquarters operations of high-level military commands which were established prior to the date of enactment of this joint resolution and pursuant to the United Nations Charter or any treaty ratified by the United States prior to such date.

(c) For purposes of this joint resolution, the term "introduction of United States Armed Forces" includes the assignment of members of such armed forces to command, coordinate, participate in the movement of, or accompany the regular or irregular military forces of any foreign country or government when such military forces are engaged or there exists an imminent threat that such forces will become engaged, in hostilities.

(d) Nothing in this joint resolution—

(1) is intended to alter the constitutional authority of the Congress or the President, or the provisions of existing treaties, or

(2) shall be construed as granting any authority to the President with respect to the introduction of United States Armed Forces into hostilities or into situations wherein involvement in hostilities is clearly indicated by the circumstances which authority he would not have had in the absence of the joint resolution.

Section 9. If any provision of this joint resolution or the application thereof to any person or circumstance is held invalid, the remainder of the joint resolution and the application of such provision to any other person or circumstance shall not be affected thereby.

Source: 87 Stat. 555 (1973).

Document 20 Articles of Impeachment, Richard M. Nixon
1974

In 1974 the House Judiciary Committee passed three articles of impeachment against President Richard Nixon, charging him with preventing, obstructing, and impeding the administration of justice in the Watergate scandal, which began as a burglary at Democratic National Committee headquarters in 1972. The committee passed the first of the three articles three days after Nixon complied with the Supreme Court ruling in United States v. Nixon *(1974) (Doc. 50) to relinquish to special prosecutor Leon Jaworski tapes of conversations with White House aides. A week later Nixon announced his resignation and left the presidency before the impeachment process could proceed further.*

Resolved, That Richard M. Nixon, President of the United States, is impeached for high crimes and misdemeanors, and that the following articles of impeachment be exhibited to the Senate:

Articles of impeachment exhibited by the House of Representatives of the United States of America in the name of itself and of all of the people of the United States of America, against Richard M. Nixon, President of the United States of America, in maintenance and support of its impeachment against him for high crimes and misdemeanors.

Article I

In his conduct of the office of the President of the United States, Richard M. Nixon, in violation of his constitutional oath faithfully to execute the office of the President of the United States and, to the best of his ability, preserve, protect, and defend the Constitution of the United States, and in violation of his constitutional duty to take care that the laws be faithfully executed, has prevented, obstructed, and impeded the administration of justice, in that:

On June 17, 1972, and prior thereto, agents of the Committee for the Re-election of the President committed unlawful entry of the headquarters of the Democratic National Committee in Washington, District of Columbia, for the purpose of securing political intelligence. Subsequent thereto, Richard M. Nixon, using the powers of his high office, engaged, personally and through his subordinates and agents, in a course of conduct or plan designed to delay, impede, and obstruct the investigation of such unlawful entry; to cover-up, conceal and protect those responsible; and to conceal the existence and scope of other unlawful covert activities.

The means used to implement this course of conduct or plan included one or more of the following:

1. Making or causing to be made false and misleading statements to lawfully authorized investigative officers and employees of the United States;

2. Withholding relevant and material evidence or information from lawfully authorized investigative officers and employees of the United States;

3. Approving, condoning, and acquiescing in, and counseling witnesses with respect to the giving of false or misleading statements to lawfully authorized investigative officers and employees of the United States and false or misleading testimony in duly instituted judicial and congressional proceedings;

4. Interfering and endeavoring to interfere with the conduct of investigations by the Department of Justice of the United States, the Federal Bureau of Investigation, the Office of Watergate Special Prosecution Force, and Congressional committees;

5. Approving, condoning, and acquiescing in, the surreptitious payment of substantial sums of money for the purpose of obtaining the silence or influencing the testimony of witnesses, potential witnesses or individuals who participated in such illegal entry or other illegal activities;

6. Endeavoring to misuse the Central Intelligence Agency, an agency of the United States;

7. Disseminating information received from officers of the Department of Justice of the United States to subjects of investigations conducted by lawfully authorized investigative officers and employees of the United States, for the purpose of aiding and assisting such subjects in their attempts to avoid criminal liability;

8. Making false or misleading public statements for the purpose of deceiving the people of the United States into believing that a thorough and complete investigation had been conducted with respect to allegations of misconduct on the part of the personnel of the executive branch of the United States and personnel of the Committee for the Re-election of the President, and that there was no involvement of such personnel in such misconduct; or

9. Endeavoring to cause prospective defendants, and individuals duly tried and convicted, to expect favored treatment and consideration in return for their silence or false testimony, or rewarding individuals for their silence or false testimony.

In all of this, Richard M. Nixon has acted in a manner contrary to his trust as President and subversive of constitutional government, to the great prejudice of the cause of law and justice and to the manifest injury of the people of the United States.

Wherefore Richard Nixon, by such conduct, warrants impeachment and trial, and removal from office.

Article II

Using the powers of the office of president of the United States, Richard M. Nixon, in violation of his constitutional oath faithfully to execute the office of president of the United States and, to the best of his ability, preserve, protect and defend the Constitution of the United States, and in disregard of his constitutional duty to take care that the laws be faithfully executed, has repeatedly engaged in conduct violating the constitutional rights of citizens, impairing the due and proper administration of justice and the conduct of lawful inquiries, or contravening the laws governing agencies of the executive branch and the purposes of these agencies.

This conduct has included one or more of the following:

1. He has, acting personally and through his subordinates and agents, endeavored to obtain from the Internal Revenue Service, in violation of the constitutional rights of citizens, confidential information contained in income tax returns for purposes not authorized by law, and to cause, in violation of the constitutional rights of citizens, income tax audits or other income tax investigations to be initiated or conducted in a discriminatory manner.

2. He misused the Federal Bureau of Investigation, the Secret Service and other executive personnel in violation or disregard of the constitutional rights of citizens by directing or authorizing such agencies or personnel to conduct or continue electronic surveillance or other investigations for purposes unrelated to national security, the enforcement of laws or any other lawful function of this office; and he did direct the concealment of certain records made by the Federal Bureau of Investigation of electronic surveillance.

3. He has, acting personally and through his subordinates and agents, in violation or disregard of the constitutional rights of citizens, authorized and permitted to be maintained a secret investigative unit within the office of president, financed in part with money derived from campaign contributions to him, which unlawfully utilized the resources of the Central Intelligence Agency, engaged in covert and unlawful activities and attempted to prejudice the constitutional right of an accused to a fair trial.

4. He has failed to take care that the laws are faithfully executed by failing to act when he knew or had reason to know that his close subordinates endeavored to impede and frustrate lawful inquiries by duly constituted executive, judicial, and legislative entities concerning the unlawful entry into the headquarters of the Democratic National Committee and the cover-up thereof, and concerning other unlawful activities including those relating to the confirmation of Richard Kleindienst as attorney general of the United States, the electronic surveillance of private citizens, the break-in into the office of Dr. Lewis Fielding and the campaign practices of the Committee to Re-elect the President.

5. In disregard of the rule of law, he knowingly misused the executive power by interfering with agencies of the executive branch, including the Federal Bureau of Investigation, the Criminal Division and the Office of Watergate Special Prosecution Force, of the Department of Justice and the Central Intelligence Agency, in violation of his duty to take care that the laws be faithfully executed.

In all of this, Richard M. Nixon has acted in a manner contrary to his trust as president and subversive of constitutional government, to the great prejudice of the cause of law and justice and to manifest injury of the people of the United States.

Wherefore Richard M. Nixon, by such conduct, warrants impeachment and trial and removal from office.

Article III

In his conduct of the office of president of the United States, Richard M. Nixon, contrary to his oath faithfully to execute the office of president of the United States and, to the best of his ability, preserve, protect and defend the Constitution of the United States, and in violation of his constitutional duty to take care that the laws be faithfully executed, has failed without lawful cause or excuse to produce papers and things directed by duly authorized subpoenas issued by the Committee on the Judiciary of the House of Representatives on April 11, 1974; May 15, 1974; May 30, 1974, and June 24, 1974, and willfully disobeyed such subpoenas.

The subpoenaed papers and things were deemed necessary by the committee in order to resolve by direct evidence fundamental, factual questions relating to presidential direction, knowledge or approval of actions demonstrated by other evidence to be substantial grounds for impeachment of the president.

In refusing to produce these papers and things Richard M. Nixon substituting his judgment as to what materials were necessary for the inquiry, interposed the powers of the presidency against the lawful subpoenas of the House of Representatives, thereby assuming to himself functions and judgments necessary to the exercise of the sole power of impeachment vested by the Constitution in the House of Representatives.

In all of this, Richard M. Nixon has acted in a manner contrary to his trust as president and subversive of constitutional government, to the great prejudice of the cause of law and justice and to the manifest injury of the people of the United States.

Wherefore, Richard M. Nixon by such conduct, warrants impeachment and trial and removal from office.

Source: House Committee on the Judiciary, *Debate on Articles of Impeachment: Hearings of the Committee on the Judiciary,* 93d Cong., 2d sess., pursuant to H.R. 803 (Washington, D.C.: Government Printing Office, 1974).

Document 21   **Senate Debate on the Gulf War**
January 1991

In August 1990 Iraq invaded neighboring Kuwait. The United States decried the invasion and through the United Nations worked to form a multinational military coalition against the invasion and to impose sanctions on Iraq in an effort to force its withdrawal. In fall 1990 Congress gave its support for sanctions and their enforcement. The Bush administration argued later, however, that sanctions were insufficient and that military force was necessary. President George Bush sought congressional support for the use of force after obtaining UN Security Council agreement on a resolution giving Iraq a deadline for withdrawal, after which time it would face military attack if its forces remained in Kuwait. In early January 1991 Congress debated and ultimately passed a resolution supporting military action. In the following excerpt of the debate in the Senate, the members' discussion reveals the extent to which the president's role had evolved in foreign and military affairs, and the difficulty faced by Congress in resisting that new reality.

Mr. MOYNIHAN. . . . Here are two countries, neither of them very attractive: Kuwait openly contemptuous of and hostile to the United States; Iraq the beneficiary of the United States.

Suddenly, on behalf of Kuwait and in opposition to Iraq we have seen the largest array of armed forces since the Second World War. We see the President declaring that he has the right to send those forces into battle, independently of any judgment of the Senate.

How could this happen in the first post–cold-war crisis?

I would like to suggest, Mr. President, and I hope this might help us think about the subject, that the way in which the President initially proceeded obtained the universal support of the country and the Senate. Suddenly, however, there was an institutional lurch back into the manner and mode of the cold war. . . .

From 1914 to 1989, there was a 75-year "war" which inevitably changed attitudes and institutions. In our hearings we were looking at the attitudes and institutions that had changed, and the ways in which they did. I chaired the hearings, so I took the opportunity to organize our inquiry around an extraordinary speech which Woodrow Wilson gave in St. Louis, MO, on September 5, 1919. It was on that trip around the country, pleading for public support to influence the Senate to consent to the ratification of the Treaty of Versailles which contained the League of Nations covenant. Wilson was asking for that support. He was 20 days from Pueblo, CO, where he would collapse. It would be, in effect, the end of his Presidency.

I see the Senator representing St. Louis is on the floor, and I think the senior Senator from Missouri would recognize that Wilson's remarks had about them the quality of prophecy: It was the end of his life. He was trying to tell America what he would leave behind him, what would happen if we did not establish a world order where there was law, where there were procedures, where peace was enforced. And if we did not, what would come instead.

He said, "Very well, then. If we must stand apart and be the hostile rivals of the rest of the world, we must do something else: We must be physically ready for anything to come. We must have a great standing army. We must see to it that every man in America is trained in arms, and we must see to it that there are munitions and guns enough for an army. And that means a mobilized nation; that they are not only laid up in store, but that they are kept up to date; that they are ready to use tomorrow; that we are a nation in arms."

Then he said, "What would a nation in arms be? Well, you know, you have to think of the President of the United States not as the chief counselor of the Nation, elected for a little while, but as the man meant constantly and every day to be Commander in Chief of the Army and Navy of the United States, ready to order it to any part of the world with a threat of war, as a menace to his own people."

Then he said, "And you can't do that under free debate; you can't do that under public counsel. Plans must be kept secret. Knowledge must be accumulated by a system which we have condemned, because we called it a spying system. The more polite call it a system of intelligence."

Then he went on a little further to say, in effect, how this world would shape itself up into one of continuing crises. And so, Mr. President, in that speech in St. Louis, which, as I say, had a prophetic quality which haunts one to this day, Woodrow Wilson said that we would see the emergence of a system of Government in which the President had become Commander in Chief, head of the Armed Forces. That did happen. And nothing is more extraordinary evidence of it having happened than the assertions we have heard in the past month after the lurching from a defensive, deterrent position, which we responded to very well, into an offensive position on November 8. This was a decision reached in secret. It suddenly turned what had been a collective security operation with the complete support of the country and the world into an offensive, military crisis situation.

Wilson's prediction in action: The President as Commander in Chief, secretly moving in an atmosphere of ongoing, permanent, Orwellian crisis, asserting that this is entirely in his own hands. The President told a press conference on

November 30, when asked, "What do you think your responsibilities are to Congress and the people that elect them," he said, "Full consultation." Nothing more. When asked on December 28 by David Frost, "Don't you need an authorization from Congress, in effect, for war?" He said, "We have used military force 200 times in history. I think there have been five declarations of war."

In effect, he claimed that he did not need congressional support to do what, clearly, the Constitution requires of him.

This is an idea—that Congress decides whether to go to war—that simply eroded in the cold war with the prospect of nuclear confrontation, permitting no time for reflection and consultation. The *New York Times* wrote this morning, very ably, I think, that Congress' constitutional warmaking authority fell into disuse during the cold war, so much that we can scarcely even remember the number of times that we have declared war. There is a notion that we declared war once during World War II. We declared war three times against six different countries in one form or another.

Mr. Specter. As I was saying, Mr. President, there is a conclusion by the administration that sanctions are not working. There may be a disagreement on that, but I think it ought to be recognized that this is the position of the President and this is the position of the administration.

I offer one comment on information which has been brought to me just recently by one of the ex-hostages who was held in Kuwait, a man named Christopher Folsom from Doylestown, PA, who was in Kuwait on August 2 and who was later taken to Iraq on September 23. Mr. Folsom, having been in Iraq and having seen some of the stores there and having some firsthand knowledge, makes a very forceful representation that the sanctions are not working.

I further call the attention of the Senate to a representation made by a group of former American hostages from Kuwait, some 30 in number. They make a number of points, but I shall limit my current presentation to simply one,

and that is that sanctions are having little impact on Iraq.

Mr. President, the third issue that I would address with respect to the Mitchell resolution is that I believe it is late in the day, frankly, too late in the day, for the Congress meaningfully to disagree with the President's request and the content of U.N. Resolution 678.

Had I my preference, I would not have opted for a January 15 date, and I would have given sanctions more of an opportunity to work. However, I believe as a matter of U.S. policy that we are well beyond that alternative.

The U.N. resolution was enacted on November 29, 1990. The Members of the Senate and the House had ample notice of what was being accomplished with the establishment of January 15 as a deadline for Iraqi withdrawal. The Congress of the United States has taken no action. It is only today, 5 days before January 15, that the Congress is finally beginning.

Mr. President, even a week ago today, when the new Senate was sworn in, there was no assurance that the Senate or the House would address this issue in advance of January 15.

I wrote to the majority leader last month and made the point I thought the Senate and the House should be assembled to vote, up or down, on authorization for use of force. . . . We know that when the distinguished Senator from Iowa [Mr. Harkin] and the distinguished Senator from Washington [Mr. Adams] pressed to have a date for Senate action a week ago today, that none was forthcoming. Now, at the very last moment in a very complex process, there is a resolution which is being offered which guts, eliminates the thrust of U.N. Resolution 678.

It is my judgment, Mr. President, that if the Congress of the United States does not back the President and the Congress of the United States does not back Resolution 678, then our leadership in the coalition will fail completely, the sanctions will disintegrate, and the coalition will disintegrate. We are much past the point of changing U.S. or U.N. policy in this important respect.

I say that, Mr. President, because even as we speak there is no assurance that the Senate will vote on any resolution before January 15. There has not even been the scheduling of this matter in a timely way so that, if the Senate is faced with a filibuster, cloture could be filed, if that was the will of the Senate, and a vote would occur in advance of January 15. It seems to this Senator that we are very, very late in the day to be stepping forward and articulating the fundamental disagreement with the U.N. resolution and with what the President has requested.

It is my view, again repeating, that my preferences would have been contrary to current policy in a number of important respects. However, if we do not follow through at this stage, if Iraq does not withdraw voluntarily from Kuwait, and if the U.N. resolution does not proceed, we will be building a more powerful Iraq, and we will be fighting this war at another day and in a more destructive way with greater loss of life, American lives.

That, Mr. President, brings me to what I consider to be a core of disagreement as to what is the best way to avoid war at this time. I personally remain hopeful that war will be avoided. But it seems to me that the best way to avoid a war is to put Iraq squarely on notice, with very strong support by the Congress for the U.N. resolution and the President, that we mean business and we are prepared to fight.

We have an opportunity to come to a conclusion by Saturday, as the majority leader has articulated a wish or proposed a schedule. If we can conclude our debate, we can put Iraq and President Saddam Hussein squarely on notice that there is unity.

Source: Congressional Record, 102d Cong., 1st sess., January 3, 1991, 137, S107.

Document 22 **Senator Robert Byrd on the Line-Item Veto**
October 18, 1993

The federal budget deficit grew substantially in the 1980s as a result of a combination of economic factors, including tax reductions, increased defense spending, and burgeoning costs for such entitlement programs as Social Security and Medicare. One of the proposals for reining in the budget deficit called for providing the president with a line-item veto, a device available to many state governors that permits the executive to reject particular items within a bill without having to veto the entire bill. In debates on the line-item veto, Senator Robert Byrd (D-W. Va.) invoked the history of the Roman Empire and its influence on the framer's notion of the proper distribution of powers in arguing that the line-item veto would undermine the separation of powers. Congress passed a line-item veto after Republicans took control of the House in 1994, but the Supreme Court struck it down in Clinton v. City of New York *(1998) (Doc. 56).*

Mr. BYRD. Mr. President, this is the 14th in my series of speeches on the line-item veto, with particular reference to the Roman Republic and the Roman Senate. When I began this series of 1-hour speeches on May 5, I spoke of Montesquieu, the eminent French philosopher and author who had greatly influenced the Founding Fathers with his political theory of checks and balances and separation of powers.

What influenced Montesquieu in his espousal of this political system? Montesquieu was greatly influenced by the history of the development of the English constitution and by the history of the people of Rome. So impressed was Montesquieu with the Romans that he, in fact, developed and published a work of his own on the subject. Almost midway between the "Persian Letters" in 1721 and the "Spirit of the Laws" in 1748, Montesquieu published, in 1734, his "Considerations on the Causes of the Greatness of the Romans and their Decline," which is the least well-known of the three.

I have also stated a number of times that if we are to have a better appreciation and understanding of the Constitution—its separation of powers, and checks and balances, and the power over the purse—then we should follow in Montesquieu's tracks and study Roman history as he did, and that is what we have been doing together during these past several months.

What have we acquired to pay us for our pains? What have we learned that can be applicable to our own time, our own country, and to the political questions of today concerning checks and balances and the control over the purse? Let us see. . . .

During the centuries of the early and middle Republic, public office in Rome could be obtained only through virtue, and brought with it no pay, no salary, no benefit other than honor, and the opportunity to prove one's self worthy of being preferred for further toils on behalf of the State.

In the last century of the Republic, the old citizen soldiery and the old moral structure of integrity and dedication to the cause of country gave way to greed, graft, corruption, venality, and political demagoguery, much of which we see in our own time and in our own country. The self-serving ambitions of Roman generals and politicians led to violence, civil wars, and military domination by standing armies made up of professional soldiers. In our own Republic today, the military-industrial complex, against which President Eisenhower warned, can pose a threat to the system.

So, Mr. President, there are sundry similarities between our own history and the history of the Romans.

Now, let us turn to the consideration of the Roman political system. In the Roman Republic, the political organization was complex, and it was also experimental, unlike that of Lycurgus, the Spartan lawgiver of the ninth century B.C.

Lycurgus united in his constitution all of the good and distinctive features of the best governments, so that none of the principal parts should unduly grow and predominate. But inasmuch as the force of each part would be neutralized by that of the others, neither of them should prevail and outbalance another. Therefore, the constitution should remain in a state of equilibrium.

Lycurgus then, foreseeing by a process of reasoning whence and how events would naturally happen, constructed his constitution untaught by adversity. But, while the Romans would achieve the same final result, according to Polybius, they did not reach it by any process of reasoning but by the discipline of many trials and struggles. And, by always choosing the best, in the light of the experience gained, they reached the same result as Lycurgus.

Let us consider the Roman system as it was seen by Polybius, the Greek historian, who lived in Rome from 168 B.C. after the Battle of Pydna, until after 150 B.C., at a time when the Roman Republic was at a pinnacle of majesty that excited his admiration and comment.

Polybius viewed the Roman constitution as having three elements: the Executive, the Senate, and the people, with their respective share of power in the state regulated by a scrupulous regard to equality and equilibrium.

Let us examine the separation of powers in the Roman Republic as explained by Polybius. The consuls—representing the Executive—were the supreme masters of the administration of the government when remaining in Rome. All of the other magistrates, except the tribunes, were under the consuls and took their orders from the consuls. The consuls brought matters before the Senate that required its deliberation and they saw to the execution of the Senate's decrees. In matters requiring the authorization of the people, the consuls summoned the popular meetings, presented the proposals for their decision, and carried out the decrees of the majority.

In matters of war, the consuls imposed such levies upon the allies as the consuls deemed appropriate, and made up the roll for soldiers and selected those who were suitable. Consuls had absolute power to inflict punishment upon all who were under their command, and had all but absolute power in the conduct of military campaigns.

As to the Senate—we are talking about the separation of powers—as to the Senate, it had complete control over the treasury and regulated receipts and disbursements alike. The quaestors could not issue any public money to the various departments of the state without a decree of the Senate. The Senate controlled the money for the repair and construction of public works and public buildings throughout Italy, but this money could not be obtained by the censors, who oversaw the contracts for public works and public buildings, except by the grant of the Senate. . . .

What part of the constitution was left to the people? The people participated in the ratification of treaties and alliances, and decided questions of war and peace. The people passed and repealed laws, and bestowed public offices on the deserving, which, according to Polybius, "are the most honorable rewards for virtue."

Polybius, having described the separation of powers under the Roman constitution, how did the three parts of state check and balance each other?

Mr. President, during the past several months, I have often referred to the various checks that the consuls, the tribunes, the Senate and the assemblies exercised against each other. And I have paid particular attention to the veto power of the Roman Senate and the tribunes.

Incidentally, Henry Clay, who believed that the veto power of American Presidents was "despotic" and ought to be circumscribed, stated in a Senate floor speech that the veto "originated in the institution of the tribunician power in ancient Rome," and had "been introduced from the practice under the empire into the monarchies of Europe."

Polybius explains the checks and balances of the Roman constitution, as he had observed them firsthand. Remember, he was living in Rome at the time.

What were the checks upon the consuls, the executive? The consul—whose power over the administration of the government when in the city, and over the military when in the field, appeared absolute—still had need of the support of the Senate and the people. The consul needed supplies for his legions, but without a decree of the Senate, his soldiers could be supplied with neither corn nor clothes nor pay. Moreover, all of his plans would be futile if the Senate shrank from danger, or if the Senate opposed his plans or sought to hamper them. Therefore, whether the consul could bring any undertaking to a successful conclusion depended upon the Senate, which had the absolute power, at the end of his one-year term, to replace him with another consul or to extend his command.

Even to the successes of the consuls on the field of battle, the Senate had the power to add distinction and glory, or to obscure their merits, for unless the Senate concurred in recognizing the achievements of the consuls and in voting the money, there could be no celebration or public triumph.

The consuls were also obliged to court the favor of the people, so here is the check of the people against the consul, for it was the people who would ratify, or refuse to ratify, the terms of peace. But most of all, the consuls, when laying down their office at the conclusion of their 1-year term, would have to give an accounting of their administration, both to the Senate and to the people. So, it was necessary that the consuls maintain the good will of both the Senate and the people.

What were the checks against the Senate? The Senate was obliged to take the multitude into account and respect the wishes of the people, for in matters directly affecting the Senators—for instance, in the case of a law diminishing the Senate's traditional authority, or depriving Senators of certain dignities, or even actually reducing the property of Senators—in such cases, the people had the power to pass or reject the law in their assembly.

In addition, according to Polybius, if the tribunes imposed their veto, the Senate would not only be unable to pass a decree, but could not even hold a meeting. And because the tribunes must always have a regard for the people's wishes, the Senate stood in awe of the multitude and could not neglect the feelings of the people.

But as a counterbalance, what check was there against the people? We have seen the checks against the consuls; we have described the checks against the Senate. What about the people? According to Polybius, the people were far from being independent of the Senate, and were bound to take its wishes into account, both collectively and individually.

For example, contracts were given out in all parts of Italy by the censors for the repair and construction of public works and public buildings. Then there was the matter of the collection of revenues from rivers and harbors and mines and lands—everything, in a word, that came under the control of the Roman government. In all of these things, the people were engaged, either as contractors or as pledging their property as security for the contractors, or in selling supplies, or making loans to the contractors, or as engaging in the work and in the employ of the contractors.

"Over all these transactions," says Polybius, "the Senate has complete control." For example, it could extend the time on a contract and thus assist the contractors; or in the case of unforeseen accident, it could relieve the contractors of a portion of their obligation; or it could even release them altogether if they were absolutely unable to fulfill the contract.

So, there were many ways in which the Senate could inflict great hardships upon the contractors; or, on the other hand, grant great indulgences to the contractors. But in every case, the appeal was to the Senate.

The Senate's ace card lay in its control over the purse strings. Also, the judges were selected from the Senate, at the time of Polybius, for the majority of trials in which the charges were heavy. Consequently, the people were cautious about resisting or actively opposing the will of the Senate, because they were uncertain as to when they might need the Senate's aid. For a similar reason, the people did not rashly resist the will of the consuls, because one and all might, in one way or another, become subject to the absolute power of the consuls at some point in time.

Polybius sums it up in this way: "When any one of the three classes becomes puffed up, and manifests an inclination to be contentious and unduly encroaching, the mutual interdependency of all the three, and the possibility of the pretensions of any one being checked and thwarted by the others, must plainly check this tendency. And so the proper equilibrium is maintained by the impulsiveness of the one part being checked by its fear of the other."

The theory of a mixed constitution—that is what ours is, a mixed constitution, checks and balances, and separation of powers—the theory of a mixed constitution had had its great measure of success in the Roman Republic. It is not surprising, therefore, that the Founding Fathers of the United States should have been familiar with the works of Polybius, or that Montesquieu should have been influenced by the checks and balances and separation of powers in the Roman constitutional system, a clear element of which was the control over the purse, vested solely in the Senate in the heyday of the Republic.

Mr. President, in my presentations today and heretofore on this subject, I have drawn many parallels between our own Republic and the historical meanderings of that ancient Republic. . . . It is my own sincere prayer, however, that the United States will not follow a course parallel to the Roman Republic into an inexorable decline and decadence. . . .

The political causes of decay were rooted in one fact—increasing despotism destroyed the citizens' civic sense and dried up statesmanship at its source. . . . The Senate, losing ever more of its power and prestige, . . . relapsed into indolence, subservience, or venality; and the last barrier fell that might have saved the state from militarism and anarchy.

In short, Rome's fate was sealed by the one-by-one donations of power and prerogative that the Roman Senate plucked from its own quiver and voluntarily delivered into the hands, first, of Julius Caesar and Octavian, and then into the trust of the succession of Caligulas, Neros, Commoduses, and Elagabaluses who followed, until at last, the ancient and noble ideals of the Roman Republic had been dissolved into the stinking brew of imperial debauchery, tyranny, megalomania, and rubble into which the Roman Empire eventually sank.

At the height of the Republic, the Roman Senate had been the one agency with the authority, the perspective, and the popular aura to debate, investigate, commission, and correct the problems that confronted the Roman state and its citizens. But the Senate's loss of will and its eagerness to hand its responsibilities over to a one-man government—a man on a "white horse"—a dictator, and later an emperor, doomed Rome and predestined Rome's decline and ultimate fall.

Mr. President, those "political midwives" attendant on the birth of our own Republic—George Washington, Alexander Hamilton, Benjamin Franklin, James Madison, James Wilson, Elbridge Gerry, Oliver Elsworth, and others—were some of the wisest men alive at that time, in this or any other country. Many had served in the Continental and Confederation Congresses and in State legislatures. All of them were experienced and reflective men.

Many of those constitutional framers were well acquainted with Cicero, Polybius, Livius, Tacitus, and Plutarch, and the glories of the classical Roman Republic. Those brilliant men borrowed freely from the best of ancient Rome, and purposefully and deliberately christened the upper Chamber of the Congress "the Senate."

Just as carefully, they set in place a system of checks and balances and separation of powers, and lodged the control of the purse in the "people's branch" to prevent the rise of a new coinage of imperial executives in the federation that they created.

Mr. President, in our own times we see the same problems, the same kinds of dilemmas that the hand of history wrote large upon Rome's slate, being written upon America's slate. In difficult times or in crises, many people grow impatient, as they grew impatient during the French revolution and elevated Napoleon to the emperorship; as they grew impatient during the Russian revolution and elevated Lenin to head of state; as they grew impatient in depression-era Germany and elevated Adolf Hitler to the presidency and the chancellorship; as they grew impatient in Cuba and elevated Fidel Castro to the dictatorship.

We, too, have reached a stage where we seem to remain in a state of crisis, semicrisis, or pseudocrisis. The American people have grown impatient and are demanding solutions to serious problems—problems that do not lend themselves to easy and quick solutions. The solutions to these problems will be painful and will take time, perhaps years, to succeed.

This is not a truth that some people want to hear. Many would rather believe that quack remedies such as line-item vetoes and enhanced rescissions powers in the hands of Presidents will somehow miraculously solve our current fiscal situation and eliminate our monstrous budget deficits.

Of course, some people would, perhaps, prefer to abolish the Congress altogether and institute one-man government from now on. Some people have no patience with constitutions, for that matter.

Mr. President, let us study Rome. The basic lesson that we should remember for our purposes here is, that when the Roman Senate gave away its control of the purse strings, it gave away its power to check the Executive. From that point on, the Senate declined and, as we have seen, it was only a matter of time. Once the mainstay was weakened, the structure collapsed and the Roman Republic fell.

This lesson is as true today as it was 2,000 years ago. Does anyone really imagine that the splendors of this capital city stand or fall with mansions, monuments, buildings, and piles of masonry? These are but bricks and mortar, lifeless things, and their collapse or restoration means little or nothing when measured on the great clock-tower of time.

But the survival of the American constitutional system, the foundation upon which the superstructure of the Republic rests, finds its firmest support in the continued preservation of the delicate mechanism of checks and balances, separation of powers, and the control of the purse, solemnly instituted by the Founding Fathers. For over 200 years, from the beginning of the Republic to this very hour, it has survived in unbroken continuity. We received it from our fathers. Let us as surely hand it on to our sons and daughters.

Mr. President, I close my series of reflections on the ancient Roman Republic with the words of Daniel Webster from his speech in 1832 on the centennial anniversary of George Washington's birthday:

Other misfortunes may be borne or their effects overcome. If disastrous war should sweep our commerce from the ocean, another genera-

tion may renew it. If it exhaust our Treasury, future industry may replenish it. If it desolate and lay waste our fields, still, under a new cultivation, they will grow green again and ripen to future harvests. It were but a trifle even if the walls of yonder Capitol were to crumble, if its lofty pillars should fall, and its gorgeous decorations be all covered by the dust of the valley. All these might be rebuilt. But who shall reconstruct the fabric of demolished government? Who shall rear again the well-proportioned columns of constitutional liberty? Who shall frame together the skillful architecture which unites national sovereignty with State rights, individual security, and public prosperity? No. If these columns fall, they will be raised not again. Like the Colosseum and the Parthenon, they will be destined to a mournful, a melancholy immortality. Bitterer tears, however, will flow over them than were ever shed over the monuments of Roman or Grecian art. For they will be the remnants of a more glorious edifice than Greece or Rome ever saw: the edifice of constitutional American liberty.

Source: Congressional Record, 103d Cong., 1st sess., October 18, 1993, S13561–13565.

Document 23   Senate Debate on the Religious Freedom Restoration Act of 1993

In Employment Division, Department of Human Resources of Oregon v. Smith *(1990) the Supreme Court decided that the constitutional test for whether a generally applicable law violates religious freedom should be lowered from strict judicial scrutiny, which had been the Court's test since* Sherbert v. Verner *(1963), to one more deferential to governments. A "generally applicable law" is one that has as its purpose some legitimate government interest other than the restriction of religious freedom. For example, in the Oregon case, it involved the application of generally applicable drug laws to Native Americans using peyote for religious purposes. Religious and libertarian groups joined in urging Congress to reestablish* Sherbert's *compelling state interest test for cases involving religious freedom. In response, Congress passed the Religious Freedom Restoration Act of 1993. The Supreme Court struck down the act in* City of Boerne v. Flores *(1997) on the grounds that it was an unconstitutional use of Congress's enforcement powers (delegated in the Fourteenth Amendment) and a violation of the separation of power in that it invaded the Court's authority to interpret the Constitution. In the following excerpts from the debate prior to enactment of the statute, senators consider their constitutional authority to challenge the Court's interpretation and the possible impact of the Religious Freedom Restoration Act on prisoner lawsuits and other governmental functions.*

Wednesday, October 27, 1993.

Mr. SIMPSON. There is a not a single thing that has come up in this debate that should lead anyone to believe anything other than that we all believe in religious freedom for everybody. It is absurd, to describe any person who would deign to vote against this bill as being bigoted, or having some great prejudice, or some horrid antireligious feeling. Although, I have had some of that characterization from some of the local media clowns in Wyoming, at least in Casper. So I know what that is. And it is unfortunate.

I have heard many of my colleagues say that "All we should do is go back to the law as it was before the Supreme Court decision." I would be the first one to do that. The Supreme Court decision was 6 to 3. It had to do with a couple of guys doing peyote in Oregon. It was not a case involving the great fabric of our society, or any such thing. They were not supposed to use controlled substances or drugs. They did. They got canned. They went through the unemployment system to get benefits and the case that they brought to assert their rights ultimately went to the Supreme Court.

The Supreme Court made a decision, 6 to 3. It was not the liberals versus the conservatives, or the "in's" versus the "out's." It was a sensible decision. And now most of us agree to go back to where the law was—but this bill does not go back to that point. As is typical in these situations, we have gone too far. If we remove this evidentiary standard of "reasonableness," we will have tons of problems in some of the worst places. These are not social places for social engineering—These are prisons. You put people in the "clink" and you keep them there. This is to avoid terrible evidentiary burdens placed upon prison administrators and attorneys general. That is what the amendment is all about.

How ironic that today is "National Unfunded Mandate Day." Legislation addressing "unfunded mandates" now has 47 cosponsors. Yet today we are considering a bill—the Religious Freedom Restoration Act—which is an unfunded Federal mandate requiring the State and local governments to pay for more frequent, expensive, and protracted prisoner suits in the name of religious freedom. The taxpayer will lose again. . . .

COLLOQUY OF SENATORS HATCH AND GRASSLEY, SENATE JUDICIARY COMMITTEE, MAY 6, 1993

Mr. GRASSLEY. What is the basis for congressional power to enact this bill? Do we have authority to prescribe a specific standard for the Supreme Court?

Mr. HATCH. In my view there is congressional authority to defend the first amendment's protection of our religious freedom. Congress has the power to regulate state action under section 5 of the 14th amendment to the Constitution. The due process clause of the 14th amendment provides that authority and it has consistently been held to incorporate and apply the First Amendment to the States. Constitutional scholars, including professor Douglas Laycock of the University of Texas, have testified before our Committee to this effect.

Mr. GRASSLEY. How does the bill apply to the military and prisons—where I believe—and the court has stated—the government has a very strong interest in order and discipline?

Mr. HATCH. I believe the United States military will certainly be able to maintain good order, discipline, and security under this bill. The courts have always recognized the compelling nature of our military's interest in order, discipline, and security in the regulation of our armed forces and have always extended to them significant deference. I would expect this deference to continue under the bill.

With respect to prisons, the bottom line is that prison administrators' interest in order, safety, security, and discipline [is] going to be deemed compelling, and that is certainly my intention.

As a practical matter, I should emphasize, prison administrators will have to articulate their security concerns and demonstrate the connection between their legitimate concern and the regulations. I do not think that is too much to ask on behalf of the free exercise of religion, even for prisoners. Indeed, prisoners are especially needful of the influence of religion. I would rather have prisoners trying to practice their faith than learning how to become better criminals once released. Obviously, when the practice of religion collides with the need to maintain order and security, the prison administrators will win their case under this bill.

Mr. GRASSLEY. How will this bill apply in cases the courts have decided on the basis of the need to conduct the internal affairs of the government? In one case—*Bowen v. Roy*—the Court denied a free exercise challenge to the government's use of Social Security numbers for internal management. In another case, *Lyng v. Northwest Indian Cemetery Protective Association,* the Court rejected a free exercise challenge to the government's use of government's lands. Instead of using the compelling interest test, the Court in these cases found that the religious claims of particular citizens were outweighed by the government's need to conduct internal affairs. Are these cases essentially overruled by this bill?

Mr. HATCH. RFRA would have no effect on cases like *Bowen v. Roy,* 476 U.S. 673 (1986), involving the use of social security numbers, because the incidental impact on a religious practice does not constitute a cognizable "burden" on anyone's free exercise of religion. Unless such a burden is demonstrated, there can be no free exercise violation. Thus, a claimant never gets to the compelling interest test where there is no burden demonstrated. RFRA language intentionally includes terminology requiring a "burden" on

one's exercise of religion. RFRA also does not effect *Lyng v. Northwest Indian Cemetery Protective Assn.,* 485 U.S. 439 (1987), a case concerning the use and management of government resources, because, like *Bowen v. Roy,* the incidental impact on a religious practice does not "burden" anyone's free exercise of religion. In *Lyng,* the court ruled that the way in which government manages its affairs and uses its own property does not impose a burden on religious exercise. Unless a burden is demonstrated, there can be no free exercise violation.

Mr. GRASSLEY. Does this bill change the way courts assess a "compelling state interest"? Will it still be up to the judge—who will look at all the factors in the case—to say whether there is a compelling interest? In other words, this bill does not purport to legislate a definition of compelling interest, does it?

Mr. HATCH. RFRA reestablishes a very familiar and traditional standard of review that the courts have been applying since the 1963 decision *Sherbert v. Verner.* That is why we do not attempt to define the standard in the bill. This bill does not dictate the proper result in a particular free exercise case nor does it identify specific governmental interests that are compelling. The courts will continue to determine whether burdens on religious exercise are justified based upon a consideration and weighing of all relevant facts and circumstances. Historically, the courts have had little difficulty identifying important governmental interests. For example, the courts have found eradication of racial discrimination to be compelling governmental interest.

Source: Congressional Record, 103d Cong., 1st sess., 1993, 139, S14461.

Document 24   Articles of Impeachment, William J. Clinton
1998

In December 1998 the House Judiciary Committee approved four articles of impeachment against President Bill Clinton relating to his relationship with White House intern Monica Lewinsky. Two of the four articles passed by a majority vote in the full House, and in January 1999 they were presented to the Senate for a vote on a trial. In the Senate, neither article gained even a majority of votes, let alone the extraordinary majorities required by the Constitution. That outcome was widely attributed to the lack of public support for the impeachment. In fact, Clinton's popularity ratings rose during the scandal and impeachment, revealing the political nature of the process and suggesting that the president's popularity can be a factor in the willingness of Congress to remove him from office.

Resolution Impeaching William Jefferson Clinton, President of the United States, for high crimes and misdemeanors.

Resolved, that William Jefferson Clinton, President of the United States, is impeached for high crimes and misdemeanors, and that the following articles of impeachment be exhibited to the United States Senate:

Articles of impeachment exhibited by the House of Representatives of the United States of America in the name of itself and of the people of the United States of America, against William Jefferson Clinton, President of the United States of America, in maintenance and support of its impeachment against him for high crimes and misdemeanors.

Article I

In his conduct while President of the United States, William Jefferson Clinton, in violation of his constitutional oath faithfully to execute the office of President of the United States and, to the best of his ability, preserve, protect, and defend the Constitution of the United States, and in violation of his constitutional duty to take care that the laws be faithfully executed, has willfully corrupted and manipulated the judicial process of the United

States for his personal gain and exoneration, impeding the administration of justice, in that:

On August 17, 1998, William Jefferson Clinton swore to tell the truth, the whole truth, and nothing but the truth before a Federal grand jury of the United States. Contrary to that oath, William Jefferson Clinton willfully provided perjurious, false and misleading testimony to the grand jury concerning one or more of the following: (1) the nature and details of his relationship with a subordinate Government employee; (2) prior perjurious, false and misleading testimony he gave in a Federal civil rights action brought against him; (3) prior false and misleading statements he allowed his attorney to make to a Federal judge in that civil rights action; and (4) his corrupt efforts to influence the testimony of witnesses and to impede the discovery of evidence in that civil rights action.

In doing this, William Jefferson Clinton has undermined the integrity of his office, has brought disrepute on the Presidency, has betrayed his trust as President, and has acted in a manner subversive of the rule of law and justice, to the manifest injury of the people of the United States.

Wherefore, William Jefferson Clinton, by such conduct, warrants impeachment and trial, and removal from office and disqualification to hold and enjoy any office of honor, trust or profit under the United States.

[Article I passed on a 21–16 vote in the House Judiciary Committee. In the full House it passed 228–206. In the Senate it failed 45–55.]

Article II

In his conduct while President of the United States, William Jefferson Clinton, in violation of his constitutional oath faithfully to execute the office of President of the United States and, to the best of his ability, preserve, protect, and defend the Constitution of the United States, and in violation of his constitutional duty to take care that the laws be faithfully executed, has willfully corrupted and manipulated the judicial process of the United States for his personal gain and exoneration, impeding the administration of justice, in that:

(1) On December 23, 1997, William Jefferson Clinton, in sworn answers to written questions asked as part of a Federal civil rights action brought against him, willfully provided perjurious, false and misleading testimony in response to questions deemed relevant by a Federal judge concerning conduct and proposed conduct with subordinate employees.

(2) On January 17, 1998, William Jefferson Clinton swore under oath to tell the truth, the whole truth, and nothing but the truth in a deposition given as part of a Federal civil rights action brought against him. Contrary to that oath, William Jefferson Clinton willfully provided perjurious, false and misleading testimony in response to questions deemed relevant by a Federal judge concerning the nature and details of his relationship with a subordinate Government employee, his knowledge of that employee's involvement and participation in the civil rights action brought against him, and his corrupt efforts to influence the testimony of that employee.

In all of this, William Jefferson Clinton has undermined the integrity of his office, has brought disrepute on the Presidency, has betrayed his trust as President, and has acted in a manner subversive of the rule of law and justice, to the manifest injury of the people of the United States.

Wherefore, William Jefferson Clinton, by such conduct, warrants impeachment and trial, and removal from office and disqualification to hold and enjoy any office of honor, trust or profit under the United States.

[Article II passed on a 20–17 vote in the House Judiciary Committee. It failed by a vote of 205–229 in the full House.]

Article III

In his conduct while President of the United States, William Jefferson Clinton, in violation of his constitutional oath faithfully to execute the office of President of the United States and, to the best of his ability, preserve, protect, and defend the Constitution of the United States, and in violation of his constitutional duty to take care that the laws be faithfully executed, has prevented, obstructed, and impeded the administration of justice, and has to that end engaged personally, and through his subordinates and agents, in a course of conduct or scheme designed to delay, impede, cover up, and conceal the existence of evidence and testimony related to a Federal civil rights action brought against him in a duly instituted judicial proceeding.

The means used to implement this course of conduct or scheme included one or more of the following acts:

(1) On or about December 17, 1997, William Jefferson Clinton corruptly encouraged a witness in a Federal civil rights action brought against him to execute a sworn affidavit in that proceeding that he knew to be perjurious, false and misleading.

(2) On or about December 17, 1997, William Jefferson Clinton corruptly encouraged a witness in a Federal civil rights action brought against him to give perjurious, false and misleading testimony if and when called to testify personally in that proceeding.

(3) On or about December 28, 1997, William Jefferson Clinton corruptly engaged in, encouraged, or supported a scheme to conceal evidence that had been subpoenaed in a Federal civil rights action brought against him.

(4) Beginning on or about December 7, 1997, and continuing through and including January 14, 1998, William Jefferson Clinton intensified and succeeded in an effort to secure job assistance to a witness in a Federal civil rights action brought against him in order to corruptly prevent the truthful testimony of that witness in that proceeding at a time when the truthful testimony of that witness would have been harmful to him.

(5) On January 17, 1998, at his deposition in a Federal civil rights action brought against him, William Jefferson Clinton corruptly allowed his attorney to make false and misleading statements to a Federal judge characterizing an affidavit, in order to prevent questioning deemed relevant by the judge. Such false and misleading statements were subsequently acknowledged by his attorney in a communication to that judge.

(6) On or about January 18 and January 20–21, 1998, William Jefferson Clinton related a false and misleading account of events relevant to a Federal civil rights action brought against him to a potential witness in that proceeding, in order to corruptly influence the testimony of that witness.

(7) On or about January 21, 23 and 26, 1998, William Jefferson Clinton made false and misleading statements to potential witnesses in a Federal grand jury proceeding in order to corruptly influence the testimony of those witnesses. The false and misleading statements made by William Jefferson Clinton were repeated by the witnesses to the grand jury, causing the grand jury to receive false and misleading information.

In all of this, William Jefferson Clinton has undermined the integrity of his office, has brought disrepute on the Presidency, has betrayed his trust as President, and has acted in a manner subversive of the rule of law and justice, to the manifest injury of the people of the United States.

Wherefore, William Jefferson Clinton, by such conduct, warrants impeachment and trial, and removal from office and disqualification to hold and enjoy any office of honor, trust or profit under the United States.

[Article III passed on a 21–16 vote in the House Judiciary Committee. It passed by a vote of 221–212 in the full House. It failed by a vote of 50–50 in the Senate.]

Article IV

Using the powers and influence of the office of President of the United States, William Jefferson Clinton, in violation of his constitutional oath faithfully to execute the office of President of the United States and, to the best of his ability, preserve, protect, and defend the Constitution of the United States, and in disregard of his constitutional duty to take care that the laws be faithfully executed, has engaged in conduct that resulted in misuse and abuse of his high office, impaired the due and proper administration of justice and the conduct of lawful inquiries, and contravened the authority of the legislative branch and the truth-seeking purpose of a coordinate investigative proceeding in that, as President, William Jefferson Clinton, refused and failed to respond to certain written requests for admission and willfully made perjurious, false and misleading sworn statements in response to certain written requests for admission propounded to him as part of the impeachment inquiry authorized by the House of Representatives of the Congress of the United States.

William Jefferson Clinton, in refusing and failing to respond, and in making perjurious, false and misleading statements, assumed to himself functions and judgments necessary to the exercise of the sole power of impeachment vested by the Constitution in the House of Representatives and exhibited contempt for the inquiry.

In doing this, William Jefferson Clinton has undermined the integrity of his office, has brought disrepute on the Presidency, has betrayed his trust as President, and has acted in a manner subversive of the rule of law and justice, to the manifest injury of the people of the United States.

Wherefore, William Jefferson Clinton, by such conduct, warrants impeachment and trial, and removal from office and disqualification to hold and enjoy any office of honor, trust or profit under the United States.

[Article IV passed on a 21–16 vote in the House Judiciary Committee. It failed in the full House by a vote of 148–285.]

Source: H.R. 611, 105th Cong., 2d sess., *Congressional Record*, 144, December 19, 1998, H12040–12042. Also accessible at PBS, "The Impeachment Trial," http://www.pbs.org/newshour/impeachment/hearings/committee_vote1.html.

Document 25   Senate Debate on the Independent Counsel Reform Act of 1999

Richard Nixon's resignation from the presidency in 1974, as a result of his role in the Watergate consipiracy, significantly affected the modern presidency. One result was the decision by Congress to pass the Ethics in Government Act of 1978, which, among other things, provided for the appointment of an independent counsel by a panel of judges in cases implicating the president, vice president, and other executive branch officials. The act included a "sunset clause" that required Congress to reauthorize the statute every five years, which it did in 1982 and 1987 despite the Reagan administration's assertions that it was an unconstitutional intrusion on executive power.

The Supreme Court resolved the question of the statute's constitutionality, upholding it in Morrison v. Olson *(1988). Other questions persisted concerning the fairness of the arrangement and the length and cost of investigations. In 1992 the statute was allowed to expire but was reauthorized in 1994, when Congress decided it was needed for an independent investigation of President Bill Clinton's involvement in the Whitewater development scandal. The controversy surrounding Whitewater, including Clinton's impeachment, ultimately led to the statute's demise when it expired on June 30, 1999.The following excerpt—from debates on reauthorization of the independent counsel statute in 1999—details the history of the controversy surrounding the measure. As the comments make clear, the supporters of reauthorization knew the bill would not be passed.*

Senator SPECTER: Mr. President, I seek recognition today to join my colleagues Senators Levin, Lieberman, and Collins in introducing the Independent Counsel Reform Act of 1999. Our bill would accomplish two important goals. First, it would reauthorize the institution of the independent counsel for another 5 years. Second, our bill would make significant changes to the existing independent counsel statute to correct a number of problems which have become clear to all of us during the course of the past few years.

Tomorrow, the independent counsel statute will sunset. The law is dying because there appears to be a consensus that it created more problems than it solved. Many of us have forgotten the very serious problems and conflicts that led us to pass the statute in the first place. Any problems with the law can be fixed, and our bill addresses the issues that have caused the most serious complaints. But it would be a serious error to eliminate the institution of the independent counsel.

Many years have passed since President Nixon's infamous Saturday Night Massacre. Yet it is important that we remember this episode because it is such a powerful reminder of why we passed the independent counsel statute and why the statute is still needed today.

Before there was an independent counsel, the Attorney General appointed special prosecutors under his control to conduct investigations of Presidents and other high ranking officials. After the Watergate break-in, Attorney General Elliot Richardson appointed Archibald Cox to serve as the Watergate Special Prosecutor. When President Nixon decided that Cox's investigation was getting too close to the truth, he sought to have Cox fired. The President was legally entitled to fire Cox, of course, since Cox was a Justice Department employee like any other. When Attorney General Elliot Richardson refused to fire Cox, Richardson was fired. When Deputy Attorney General William Ruckelshaus refused to fire Cox, Ruckelshaus was also fired. Finally, Solicitor General Robert Bork agreed to fire Cox.

After Archibald Cox was fired, the White House announced that the office of the Watergate special prosecutor was to be closed and the President's chief of staff sent the FBI to surround Cox's offices and seize the records he had compiled. Henry Ruth, an old friend of mine who was working at the time as Archibald Cox's top deputy, described the following scene in his testimony before the Governmental Affairs Committee on March 3 of this year:

> In anticipation of adverse action, we had secured copies of key documents in secret locations around Washington, D.C. and even removed some key items from the office that Saturday night hidden in underwear and other unlikely locations. We did not know whether the military would raid our homes looking for documents. Unanimously, the staff of the Watergate prosecutor's office just refused to leave or to change any-

thing we were doing unless someone physically removed us. And if an unprecedented 450,000 telegrams of spontaneous protest had not descended upon Washington, D.C. in the few days after that Saturday night, no one really knows if President Nixon would have succeeded in aborting the investigation. In other words, we do not feel that the Department of Justice was an adequate instrument for investigating the President and other high officials of government.

Eventually, as a result of these telegrams and enormous public pressure, Leon Jaworski was appointed as a special prosecutor and the Watergate investigation was continued. But this positive outcome was far from guaranteed. As Mr. Ruth reminded the committee, "it is impossible to describe how thin a thread existed at that time, and for three weeks, for the continuation of what was going on."

It was this dark episode, perhaps more than any other, which convinced the nation that the individual investigating the President must be truly independent of the President. This is a lesson we should have to learn only once. While recent independent counsels have made some mistakes, none of these mistakes are on the scale of a Saturday Night Massacre. With this history as our guide, let us move to fix the statute, not eliminate it.

First of all, we all agreed that too many independent counsels have been appointed for matters which simply do not warrant this high level of review. . . . To address this issue, we have raised the evidentiary standard which must be met before the Attorney General is required to appoint an independent counsel. The statute currently requires that an independent counsel be appointed when there are "reasonable grounds to believe that further investigation is warranted." Our bill provides that an independent counsel must be appointed only when there are "substantial grounds to believe that further investigation is warranted." This change will give an Attorney General the discretion to decide that evidence she receives is not sufficiently strong to justify an independent counsel investigation.

As a further step to control the number of independent counsel investigations, our legislation limits the number of "covered persons" under the statute to the President, Vice President, members of the President's Cabinet, and the President's chief of staff. Accordingly, it would no longer be possible to appoint an independent counsel to investigate lower officials and staff whom an Attorney General could properly investigate on his or her own.

The four of us also agreed that it is a mistake to give an independent counsel jurisdiction over more than one investigation. For instance, Kenneth Starr started as the independent counsel for Whitewater. Attorney General Reno later expanded his jurisdiction to cover Travelgate, Filegate, the death of Vince Foster, and, of course, Monica Lewinsky. Unfortunately, the Attorney General's repeated expansion of Mr. Starr's jurisdiction created the mistaken impression that Mr. Starr was on a personal crusade against President Clinton, opening new lines of inquiry when prior ones failed to bear fruit.

The four of us also agreed that some independent counsel investigations drag on too long. Lawrence Walsh's Iran/Contra investigation lasted 6 years. Kenneth Starr's investigation of President Clinton has been going on for almost 5 years. Investigations of this length are really an anomaly in our criminal justice system. Federal grand juries are empaneled for a period of 18 months. As district attorney of Philadelphia, I had a series of grand juries on complex topics such as municipal corruption, police corruption and drugs all of which lasted 18 months. If you can't find certain facts in 18 months, I think the odds are pretty good that you will never find them.

Our bill sets a 2-year time limit for independent counsel investigations. Since there are some who would try to take advantage of this time limit and "run out the clock" on an investigation, our bill also empowers the special division of the court to extend this original 2-year period for as long as necessary to make up for dilatory tactics.

Another complaint about the Starr investigation was that his report to Congress was a partisan document making an argument for impeachment rather than providing an impartial recitation of evidence. While I believe that Mr. Starr was merely doing his job when he submitted this report, I do agree that requiring such a report inserts an independent counsel into a process—impeachment—which should be left entirely to Congress. Accordingly, our bill deletes the requirement that the independent counsel submit a report to Congress of any substantial and credible information that may constitute grounds for an impeachment.

While Kenneth Starr was blamed for many things that were not his fault, I do believe he made a mistake when he decided to continue his private law practice while he was serving as an independent counsel. The job of being an independent counsel is a privilege and an enormous responsibility—it deserves someone's full time attention. Accordingly, our bill requires that an independent counsel serve on a full-time basis for the duration of his or her investigation.

It appears that a majority of our colleagues believe that it is better to let the independent counsel statute die and return to the old days when special prosecutors appointed and controlled by the Attorney General will investigate the President and his Cabinet. I am confident, however, that after the dust settles and tempers abate, our colleagues will realize that the independent counsel statute provides a better way to handle investigations of the President and his cabinet than any of the alternatives.

We must all remember that the independent counsel statute was passed to address a serious problem inherent in our system of government—the potential for abuse and conflicts of interest when the Attorney General investigates the President and other high-level executive branch officials. After all, it is the President who appoints the Attorney General and is the Attorney General's boss. Often the Attorney General and the President are close friends. Accordingly, there is an inherent conflict of interest in having the Attorney General control an investigation of the President or the President's closest associates.

Even if an Attorney General were capable of conducting an impartial investigation, the appearance of a conflict of interest is serious enough to discredit the Attorney General's findings, especially a finding of innocence.

The independent counsel statute is the only way to address this inherent conflict of interest. As memories of the Saturday Night Massacre have been supplanted by memories of Kenneth Starr, the pendulum of public opinion has swung too far against the statute. I am confident that as soon as the Attorney General begins to investigate his or her colleagues in the White House,

the pendulum will swing back in the opposite direction. When this occurs, I believe that our colleagues will see that our approach is the best approach—to fix the problems in the statute, not abandon it.

Sooner or later a crisis will arise in Washington. It happens all the time. The crisis will be about the need to investigate the President or the Vice President or some ranking official. The question will present itself about the inherent conflict of interest of the Attorney General, and this statute will be available to deal with the problem.

Source: Congressional Record, 106th Cong., 1st sess., Tuesday, June 29, 1999, 145, S7766.

Document 26
House Debate on the USA PATRIOT Act
2001

In the immediate aftermath of the September 11, 2001, attacks on the United States, President George W. Bush asked Congress to pass legislation giving law enforcement officers greater authority to investigate and apprehend potential terrorists and disrupt their organizations. Six weeks later, Congress passed the Uniting and Strengthening America by Providing Appropriate Tools Required to Intercept and Obstruct Terrorism Act of 2001, also known as the USA PATRIOT Act.

Although there was widespread public and congressional support for the act, some members of Congress, particularly those on the House Judiciary Committee, raised concerns about civil liberties and sought to alter the statute to better protect them. The majority of the House, however, appeared not to have such reservations and passed a bill that excluded the committee's provisions for the protection of civil liberties. In this excerpt, House members debate whether their concerns have been adequately met in the conference bill reconciling the House and Senate versions. The debate demonstrates the trade-offs indicative in a bicameral legislature and the difficulty of slowing down initiatives in a climate of fear and demand for action.

Mr. WATT: I voted for the Committee on the Judiciary's version of the anti-terrorism bill. I voted against the bill that came to the floor because it was a far cry from the Committee on the Judiciary's bill. I voted in the Committee on Financial Services for the money laundering provisions of the bill. And I feel like I am in a really, really difficult position with these bills, now having

been put together, because the money laundering provisions which were reported out of the Committee on Banking and Financial Services, I think, are worthwhile and needed provisions and strike a good balance in terms of protecting the rights of individuals in our country.

I would have thought that if any committee would have been overstepping due process bounds, it might have been the Committee on Financial Services, not the Committee on the Judiciary. So I find myself in the same position that the gentleman from Michigan (Mr. Conyers) has expressed. Were the money laundering provisions a freestanding bill, I would certainly support them. But I think the Committee on the Judiciary part of this bill goes too far.

And let me be blunt. Some of us, who have a different history in America, with delegation of authority to the Government and the abuse of that authority, proceed a lot differently than others when we talk about giving authority to the Government that can be abused. And I think that is why we are having so much trouble in this debate. We cannot just come in the middle of a terrorism episode and forget all of the history that has occurred in our country.

Some groups in our country have had their rights violated, trampled on by the law enforcement authorities in this country; and so we do not have the luxury of being able to just sit back and give more authority than is warranted, the authority possibly to abuse due process through law enforcement, even in the context of what we are going through now. This is a very difficult time. I acknowledge that it is. But I think we are giving the Government and law enforcement too much authority in this bill.

We drew a very, very delicate, fine balance in the Committee on the Judiciary. Unfortunately, we took several giant steps backwards when we passed the House version of the bill; and now we have taken a couple of steps forward, more toward the Judiciary bill. But I cannot justify voting for this bill only because it is better than what the House previously passed. It still does not measure up, and I encourage my colleagues to vote against it.

Mr. OXLEY. Mr. Speaker, this has been a legislative process at its best, the Congress coming together, recognizing a very, very serious problem: the fact that our law enforcement people, the Secretary of the Treasury, currently do not have the powers and the tools necessary to deal with this horrible threat known as terrorism, this

new kind of war. The Congress came together, both Republicans and Democrats from both sides of the Capitol, to craft this legislation.

This is going to pass by an overwhelming margin. I think we all understand that. Because the Members recognize . . . that the committees have done their work, have made the compromises, have made the necessary changes to get a piece of legislation that can pass, be sent to the President, and can indeed solve this very, very difficult problem. Nothing could be more important in our careers here in the Congress, no matter how long we stay, than to protect the American people and to make certain that the people who seek to terrorize us and to kill our citizens are brought to justice, and, indeed, even more importantly stop these individuals before they commit these heinous acts.

So from my perspective, this is one of the proudest moments of my 20 years here in the Congress, to participate in this wonderful exercise of democracy and positive legislation. For that, I think all of us deserve a great deal of credit.

Mr. DELAHUNT. Mr. Speaker, I thank the chairman for yielding me this time, and let me respond for a moment to the gentleman from North Carolina. There is no one for whom I have such profound respect as I do the gentleman from North Carolina (Mr. Watt), and I listen carefully to what he says, because what he says always rings true.

In this particular case, however, I do have a disagreement, because we hear much about roving wiretaps, we hear much about expanded powers; but I think it is absolutely essential to note that the expansion of powers do not go to the criminal side of the bill that is before us. In other words, the safeguards that are inculcated in our jurisprudence through the fourth amendment of the Constitution are still there. All those checks and balances are still there.

Clearly, there is an unease; and I share some of these concerns. I do not think that there was any doubt in the aftermath of September 11 that it was clear that the administration was going to come to the Congress to seek additional authorities to deal with the terrorist attacks on our Nation. And while all of us were ready to and willing to grant them, what was appropriate, many, including myself, also braced for a frontal assault on civil liberties. In that regard, even the administration proposal was most notable, in my opinion, for what it did not contain: no new death penalty provisions, no new mandatory sentences.

On the other hand, the proposal did contain a number of profoundly disturbing features, including provisions that would have authorized the indefinite detention of nonresident aliens, the use in evidence in a criminal prosecution of information illegally obtained by foreign intelligence services operating abroad in criminal prosecutions in the United States, and the use of wiretap authority under the so-called FISA Act, even when the real purpose of the wiretap had little or nothing to do with intelligence gathering. Now, we all know what happened here on the floor of the House when the committee bill came before the body.

Much was accomplished in that committee. It has been mentioned time and time again that it was a unanimous vote, and both the chairman and the staffs on both sides and the gentleman from Michigan (Mr. Conyers) really do deserve our gratitude.

However, in the aftermath of what happened here, many of us could not support the bill. I was one of those who voted against it. But the good news is that there were subsequent negotiations with the Senate, and it has resulted in a better bill. Among other things, and it has been mentioned again and again, that there is a sunset provision.

The sunset provision obviously will give us a second look and correct the problems that we hope will not arise, but many of us fear. At this point in time I want to commend the gentleman from Massachusetts (Mr. Frank) because he participated in those negotiations and really did improve the bill that left the floor of this House.

Having said that, I still harbor reservations about some aspects of the bill. For example, it allows disclosure of secret grand jury information to intelligence and national security officials without a court order. This is a serious departure from our criminal jurisprudence, and I cannot understand why it is included because securing a court order is a simple procedure. It would not hinder an investigation. However, notwithstanding such reservations, I have to acknowledge we have come a long way and I will support the bill.

Mr. UDALL of New Mexico. Mr. Speaker, I supported the bipartisan bill that came out of the Committee on the Judiciary; and sadly, that is not before us today and it is not the bill that we would have been able to support and that I could have supported with enthusiasm.

The bill that passed the House was improved upon by the conference. Court supervision was added to the grand jury provisions. Money laundering provisions are now in the bill; and as we know, the first shot that was fired by this administration was one using the freezing of assets and monetary measures.

Probably the saving grace here is that the sunset provision forces us to come back and to look at these issues again when heads are cooler and when we are not in the heat of battle.

Mr. FRANK. What I want to talk about now is my deep disappointment in the procedure. The gentleman from Wisconsin (Mr. Sensenbrenner), the chairman of the committee, has fought hard for a fair chance for the Members to look at things; but on the whole, his efforts have not been honored.

We now, for the second time, are debating on the floor a bill of very profound significance for the constitutional structure and security of our country. In neither case has any Member been allowed to offer a single amendment. At no point in the debate in this very profound set of issues have we had a procedure whereby the most democratic institution in our government, the House of Representatives, engages in democracy.

Who decided that to defend democracy we had to degrade it? Who decided that the very openness and participation and debate and weighing of issues, who decided that was a defect at a time of crisis? This is a chance for us to show the world that democracy is a source of strength; that with our military strength and our determination and our unity of purpose goes a continued respect for the profound way in which a democracy functions.

This bill, ironically, which has been given all of these high-flying acronyms, it is the PATRIOT bill, it is the U.S.A. bill, it is the stand up and sing the Star Spangled Banner bill, has been debated in the most undemocratic way possible, and it is not worthy of this institution.

There is no reason why we could not have had this open to amendment tonight. This bill should not be debated now. Was it really necessary to debate one of the most profound pieces of legislation and its impact on our society that we have had, was it really necessary to debate it at night after all of the Members who have been working all day were told to go home? Why could this not have been a full-fledged debate with some amendments? I think because leadership of the House thought Members might have voted for a 3-year sunset. They might have voted not to have the burden of proof be on someone to prove his innocence in a criminal trial.

Mr. Speaker, the House has not been well served by a procedure which degrades democracy in the name of defending it.

Mr. CONYERS. Mr. Speaker, no one has appreciated the attempts at fairness more than the ranking member of the Committee on the Judiciary. The members of the Committee on the Judiciary had a free and open debate; and we came to a bill that even though imperfect, was unanimously agreed on. That was removed from us, and we are now debating at this hour of night, with only two copies of the bill that we are being asked to vote on available to Members on this side of the aisle. I am hoping on the other side of the aisle they at least have two copies.

Mr. Speaker, there is something wrong with that process. The gentleman from Wisconsin (Mr. Obey) first put his finger on it in the debate in which 79 Members were not able to go along with the bill, is that a legislative body that does not debate is being railroaded whether they know it or not, whether they want to accede to it or not.

Although I like the money laundering provisions in the bill, I detest the work product that bears the name of my committee on it that has now been joined with this bill. For those reasons as we close this debate, my inclination is not to support the bill. I hate to say that to Members because a number have asked me what I was going to do, and I have said up to now I was not sure.

Mr. Speaker, why should I put my name down in history for all time that I went for this ridiculous procedure which has been outlined? I do not feel inclined to support it tonight or tomorrow morning either.

Mr. SENSENBRENNER. Mr. Speaker, this is the latest step in a long process to attempt to pass a bill and send to the President a bill that is vitally needed. It is vitally needed by our law enforcement officials who are fighting the battle at home. We do not know how this battle will be fought. We do not know what tactics the enemy will take. We do not know what agents the enemy will use.

What we need is we need to get the intelligence necessary to protect the people of the United States of America from whatever the enemy has up its sleeve. . . .

There is no surprise in any of these issues. This is a bill that is vitally needed. The President has called for it. The Attorney General has called for it, and we should not delay in passing it.

I think the urgency of getting this job done is very, very great. . . . We have done a good job in balancing the need for stronger law enforcement powers and civil liberties. I would urge support of this bill.

Source: *Congressional Record*, 107th Cong., 1st sess., October 23, 2001, 147, H7205–7207.

Document 27   George Washington, Message to the House regarding
                  Documents Relative to Jay's Treaty
                  March 30, 1796

Federalist and Anti-Federalist sentiments carried over into the new government formed in 1789, affected domestic and foreign policy. The new Jeffersonian Republicans disliked the Federalists' alignment with Great Britain and sought closer relations with France, their ally in the Revolutionary War. When France and Great Britain went to war in 1793, the Federalist and Anti-Federalist debate in the United States became even more heated. President George Washington issued a proclamation declaring U.S. neutrality, a move criticized by Jefferson and his supporters as an abuse of executive power. In 1794 Jay's Treaty, which settled conflicts over navigation and commerce between the two countries, was negotiated in London and ratified by the Senate. Republicans opposed the treaty, arguing that it maintained peace with Great Britain by submitting to its superior naval forces and risking war with France. Some provisions of the treaty required congressional appropriations. The House of Representatives, which had a Republican majority, demanded that Washington present to them documents related to John Jay's negotiation of the treaty. Washington refused their request, arguing that the House of Representatives had no constitutional authority regarding the treaty-making process. This exchange marks the beginning of the practice of executive privilege and the ongoing battle between the legislative and executive branches over such claims.

To the House of Representatives of the United States:

With the utmost attention I have considered your resolution . . . requesting me to lay before your House a copy of the instructions to the minister of the United States who negotiated the treaty with the King of Great Britain, together with the correspondence and other documents relative to that treaty, excepting such of the said papers as any existing negotiation may render improper to be disclosed.

In deliberating upon this subject it was impossible for me to lose sight of the principle which some have avowed in its discussion, or to avoid extending my views to the consequences which must flow from the admission of that principle.

I trust that no part of my conduct has ever indicated a disposition to withhold any information which the Constitution has enjoined upon the President as a duty to give, or which could be required of him by either House of Congress as a right; and with truth I affirm that it has been, as it will continue to be while I have the honor to preside in the Government, my constant endeavor to harmonize with the other branches thereof so far as the trust delegated to me by the people of the United States and my sense of the obligation it imposes to "preserve, protect, and defend the Constitution" will permit.

The nature of foreign negotiations requires caution, and their success must often depend on secrecy; and even when brought to a conclusion a full disclosure of all the measures, demands, or eventual concessions which may have been proposed or contemplated would be extremely impolitic; for this might have a pernicious influence on future negotiations, or produce immediate inconveniences, perhaps danger and mischief, in relation to other powers. The necessity of such caution and secrecy was one cogent reason for vesting the power of making treaties in the President, with the advice and consent of the Senate, the principle on which that body was formed confining it to a small number of members. To admit, then, a right in the House of Representatives to demand and to have as a matter of course all the papers respecting a negotiation with a foreign power would be to establish a dangerous precedent.

It does not occur that the inspection of the papers asked for can be relative to any purpose under the cognizance of the House of Representatives, except that of an impeachment, which the resolution has not expressed. I repeat that I have no disposition to withhold any information which the duty of my station will permit or the public good shall require to be disclosed; and, in fact, all the papers affecting the negotiation with Great Britain were laid before the Senate when the treaty itself was communicated for their consideration and advice. . . .

Having been a member of the General Convention, and knowing the principles on which the Constitution was formed, I have ever entertained but one opinion on this subject; and from the first establishment of the Government to this moment my conduct has exemplified that opinion that the power of making treaties is exclusively vested in the President, by and with the advice and consent of the Senate, provided two-thirds of the Senators present concur; and that every treaty so made and promulgated thenceforward became the law of the land. It is thus that the treaty-making power has been understood by foreign nations, and in all the treaties made with them we have declared and they have believed that, when ratified by the President, with the advice and consent of the Senate, they became obligatory. In this construction of the Constitution every House of Representatives has heretofore acquiesced, and until the present time not a doubt or suspicion has appeared, to my knowledge, that this construction was not the true one. Nay, they have more than acquiesced; for till now, without controverting the obligation of such treaties, they have made all the requisite provisions for carrying them into effect.

There is also reason to believe that this construction agrees with the opinions entertained by the State conventions when they were deliberating on the Constitution, especially by those who objected to it because there was not required in com-

mercial treaties the consent of two-thirds of the whole number of the members of the Senate instead of two-thirds of the Senators present, and because in treaties respecting territorial and certain other rights and claims the concurrence of three-fourths of the whole number of the members of both Houses, respectively, was not made necessary.

It is a fact declared by the General Convention and universally understood that the Constitution of the United States was the result of a spirit of amity and mutual concession; and it is well known that under this influence the smaller States were admitted to an equal representation in the Senate with the larger States, and that this branch of the Government was invested with great powers, for on the equal participation of those powers the sovereignty and political safety of the smaller States were deemed essentially to depend.

If other proofs than these and the plain letter of the Constitution itself be necessary to ascertain the point under consideration, they may be found in the journals of the General Convention, which I have deposited in the office of the Department of State. In those journals it will appear that a proposition was made "that no treaty should be binding on the United States which was not ratified by a law," and that the proposition was explicitly rejected.

As, therefore, it is perfectly clear to my understanding that the assent of the House of Representatives is not necessary to the validity of a treaty; as the treaty with Great Britain exhibits in itself all the objects requiring legislative provision, and on these the papers called for can throw no light, and as it is essential to the due administration of the Government that the boundaries fixed by the Constitution between the different departments should be preserved, a just regard to the Constitution and to the duty of my office, under all the circumstances of this case, forbids a compliance with your request.

Go WASHINGTON.

Source: A Compilation of the Messages and Papers of the Presidents (New York: Bureau of National Literature, 1897). Also accessible at www.yale.edu/lawweb/avalon/presiden/messages/gw003.htm.

Document 28   Andrew Jackson, Veto Message on the National Bank Bill
1832

A continuous source of conflict between early political parties involved whether the federal government could establish a national bank. In McCulloch v. Maryland *(1819) (Doc. 38), Chief Justice John Marshall found the establishment of a bank to be within the legislative powers of Congress. This ruling, however, did not resolve the controversy. In 1832, when Congress passed a bill extending the bank's charter, President Andrew Jackson, a long-time opponent of the bank, vetoed it. In his veto message, Jackson challenged the notion that the Court's opinion was the final word on the constitutionality of the bank.*

. . . It is maintained by the advocates of the bank that its constitutionality in all its features ought to be considered as settled by precedent and by the decision of the Supreme Court. To this conclusion I can not assent. Mere precedent is a dangerous source of authority, and should not be regarded as deciding questions of constitutional power except where the acquiescence of the people and the States can be considered as well settled. So far from this being the case on this subject, an argument against the bank might be based on precedent. One Congress, in 1791, decided in favor of a bank; another, in 1811, decided against it. One Congress, in 1815, decided against a bank; another, in 1816, decided in its favor. Prior to the present Congress, therefore, the precedents drawn from that source were equal. If we resort to the States, the expressions of legislative, judicial, and executive opinions against the bank have been probably to those in its favor as 4 to 1. There is nothing in precedent, therefore, which, if its authority were admitted, ought to weigh in favor of the act before me.

If the opinion of the Supreme Court covered the whole ground of this act, it ought not to control the coordinate authorities of this Government. The Congress, the Executive, and the Court must each for itself be guided by its own opinion of the Constitution. Each public officer who takes an oath to support the Constitution swears that he will support it as he understands it, and not as it is understood by others. It is as much the duty of the House of Representatives, of the Senate, and of the President to decide upon the constitutionality of any bill or resolution which may be presented to them for passage or approval as it is of the supreme judges when it may be brought before them for judicial decision. The opinion of the judges has no more authority over Congress than the opinion of Congress has over the judges, and on that point the President is independent of both. The authority of the Supreme Court must not, therefore, be permitted to control the Congress or the Executive when acting in their legislative capacities, but to have only such influence as the force of their reasoning may deserve.

But in the case relied upon the Supreme Court have not decided that all the features of this corporation are compatible with the Constitution. It is true that the court have said that the law incorporating the bank is a constitutional exercise of power by Congress; but taking into view the whole opinion of the court and the reasoning by which they have come to that conclusion, I understand them to have decided that inasmuch as a bank is an appropriate means for carrying into effect the enumerated powers of the General Government, therefore the law incorporating it is in accordance with that provision of the Constitution which declares that Congress shall have power "to make all laws which shall be necessary and proper for carrying those powers into execution." Having satisfied themselves that the word *"necessary"* in the Constitution means *"needful," "requisite," "essential," "conducive* to," and that "a bank" is a convenient, a useful, and essential instrument in the prosecution of the Government's "fiscal operations," they conclude that to "use one must be within the discretion of Congress" and that "the act to incorporate the Bank of the United States is a law made in pursuance of the Constitution;" "but," say they, *"where the law is not prohibited and is really calculated to effect any of the objects entrusted to the Government, to undertake here to inquire into the degree of its necessity would be to pass the line which circumscribes the judicial department and to tread on legislative ground."*

The principle here affirmed is that the "degree of its necessity," involving all the details of a banking institution, is a question exclusively for legislative consideration. A bank is constitutional, but it is the province of the Legislature to determine whether this or that particular power, privilege, or exemption is "necessary and proper" to enable the bank to discharge its duties to the Government, and from their decision there is no appeal to the courts of justice. Under the decision of the Supreme Court, therefore, it is the exclusive province of Congress and the President to decide whether the particular features of this act are *necessary* and *proper* in order to enable the bank to perform conveniently and efficiently the public duties assigned to it as a fiscal agent, and therefore constitutional, or *unnecessary* and *improper*, and therefore unconstitutional. . . .

The Government is the only *"proper"* judge where its agents should reside and keep their offices, because it best knows where their presence will be *"necessary."* It can not, therefore, be *"necessary"* or *"proper"* to authorize the bank to locate branches where it pleases to perform the public service, without consulting the Government, and contrary to its will. The principle laid down by the Supreme Court concedes that Congress can not establish a bank for purposes of private speculation and gain, but only as a means of executing the delegated powers of the General Government. By the same principle a branch bank can not constitutionally be established for other than public purposes. The power which this act gives to establish two branches in any State, without the injunction or request of the Government and for other than public purposes, is not *"necessary"* to the due *execution* of the powers delegated to Congress. . . .

It is maintained by some that the bank is a means of executing the constitutional power "to coin money and regulate the value thereof." Congress have established a mint to coin money and passed laws to regulate the value thereof. The money so coined, with its value so regulated, and such foreign coins as Congress may adopt are the only currency known to the Constitution. But if they have other power to regulate the currency, it was conferred to be exercised by themselves, and not to be transferred to a corporation. If the bank be established for that purpose, with a charter unalterable without its consent, Congress have parted with their power for a term of years, during which the Constitution is a dead letter. It is neither necessary nor proper to transfer its legislative power to such a bank, and therefore unconstitutional. . . .

The bank is professedly established as an agent of the executive branch of the Government, and its constitutionality is maintained on that ground. Neither upon the propriety of present action nor upon the provisions of this act was the Executive consulted. It has had no opportunity to say that it neither needs nor wants an agent clothed with such powers and favored by such exemptions. There is nothing in its legitimate functions which makes it necessary or proper. Whatever interest or influence, whether public or private, has given birth to this act, it can not be found either in the wishes or necessities of the executive department, by which present action is deemed premature, and the powers conferred upon its agent not only unnecessary, but dangerous to the Government and country. . . .

Source: A Compilation of the Messages and Papers of the Presidents (New York: Bureau of National Literature, 1897), 2:576–591.

Document 29

Abraham Lincoln on the *Scott* Decision
1857

In 1858 Abraham Lincoln was a little-known Republican candidate for the U.S. Senate, running against Democrat Stephen Douglas, a nationally renowned politician who had served as a judge and was the incumbent senator from Illinois. In the famous statewide Lincoln-Douglas debates, the issue of slavery and the Supreme Court's decision in Dred Scott v. Sandford *(1857) were central issues. Lincoln's party had formed in part to resist the expansion of slavery into the territories, and Lincoln was an outspoken critic of the Court's ruling that Congress had no power to prohibit slavery in new states.*

In one of his early speeches, Lincoln argued that the Court's decision applied to the parties in the suit but that others were not bound to respect it, because the issue was clearly unsettled and because the Court was wrong in its interpretation of history and the meaning of the Declaration of Independence. Lincoln lost the 1858 race, but the prominence he gained during the campaign helped earn him the party's nomination for the presidency in 1860.

And now as to the Dred Scott decision. That decision declares two propositions—first, that a negro cannot sue in the U.S. Courts; and secondly, that Congress cannot prohibit slavery in the Territories. It was made by a divided court—dividing differently on the different points. . . .

[Douglas] denounces all who question the correctness of that decision, as offering violent resistance to it. But who resists it? Who has, in spite of the decision, declared Dred Scott free, and resisted the authority of his master over him?

Judicial decisions have two uses—first, to absolutely determine the case decided, and secondly, to indicate to the public how other similar cases will be decided when they arise. For the latter use, they are called "precedents" and "authorities."

We believe, as much as Judge Douglas, (perhaps more) in obedience to, and respect for the judicial department of government. We think its decisions on Constitutional questions, when fully settled, should control, not only the particular cases decided, but the general policy of the country, subject to be disturbed only by amendments of the Constitution as provided in that instrument itself. More than this would be revolution. But we think the Dred Scott decision is erroneous. We know the court that made it, has often over-ruled its own decisions, and we shall do what we can to have it to over-rule this. We offer no resistance to it.

Judicial decisions are of greater or less authority as precedents, according to circumstances. That this should be so, accords both with common sense, and the customary understanding of the legal profession.

If this important decision had been made by the unanimous concurrence of the judges, and without any apparent partisan bias, and in accordance with legal public expectation, and with the steady practice of the departments throughout our history, and had been in no part, based on assumed historical facts which are not really true; or, if wanting in some of these, it had been before the court more than once, and had there been affirmed and re-affirmed through a course of years, it then might be, perhaps would be, factious, nay, even revolutionary, to not acquiesce in it as a precedent.

But when, as it is true we find it wanting in all these claims to the public confidence, it is not resistance, it is not factious, it is not even disrespectful, to treat it as not having yet quite established a settled doctrine for the country—But Judge Douglas considers this view awful. . . .

Why this same Supreme Court once decided a national bank to be constitutional; but Gen. Jackson, as President of the United States, disregarded the decision, and vetoed a bill for a recharter, partly on constitutional ground, declaring that each public functionary must support the Constitution, "as he understands it." . . .

In these the Chief Justice does not directly assert, but plainly assumes, as a fact, that the public estimate of the black man is more favorable now than it was in the days of the Revolution. This assumption is a mistake. In some trifling particulars, the condition of that race has been ameliorated; but, as a whole, in this country, the change between then and now is decidedly the other way; and their ultimate destiny has never appeared so hopeless as in the last three or four years. In two of the five States—New Jersey and North Carolina—that then gave the free negro the right of voting, the right has since been taken away; and in a third—New York—it has been greatly abridged; while it has not been extended, so far as I know, to a single additional State, though the number of the States has more than doubled. In those days, as I understand, masters could, at their own pleasure, emancipate their slaves; but since then, such legal restraints have been made upon emancipation, as to amount almost to prohibition. In those days, Legislatures held the unquestioned power to abolish slavery in their respective States; but now it is becoming quite fashionable for State Constitutions to withhold that power from the Legislatures. In those days, by common consent, the spread of the black man's bondage to new countries was prohibited; but now, Congress decides that it *will* not continue the prohibition, and the Supreme Court decides that it *could* not if it would. In those days, our Declaration of Independence was held sacred by all, and thought to include all; but now, to aid in making the bondage of the negro universal and eternal, it is assailed, and sneered at, and construed, and hawked at, and torn, till, if its framers could rise from their graves, they could not at all recognize it. All the powers of earth seem rapidly combining against him. . . .

Chief Justice Taney, in his opinion in the Dred Scott case, admits that the language of the Declaration is broad enough to include the whole human family, but he and Judge Douglas argue that the authors of that instrument did not intend to include negroes, by the fact that they did not at once, actually place them on an equality with the whites. Now this grave argument comes to just nothing at all, by the other fact, that they did not at once, *or ever afterwards,* actually place all white people on an equality with one or another. And this is the staple argument of both the Chief Justice and the Senator, for doing this obvious violence to the plain unmistakable language of the Declaration. I think the authors of that notable instrument intended to include *all* men, but they did not intend to declare all men equal *in all respects.* They did not mean to say all were equal in color, size, intellect, moral developments, or social capacity. They defined with tolerable distinctness, in what respects they did consider all men created equal—equal in "certain inalienable rights, among which are life, liberty, and the pursuit of happiness." This they said, and this they meant. They did not mean to assert the obvious untruth, that all were then actually enjoying that equality, nor yet, that they were about to confer it immediately upon them. In fact they had no power to confer such a boon. They meant simply to declare the *right*, so that the *enforcement* of it might follow as fast as circumstances should permit. They meant to set up a standard maxim for free society, which should be familiar to all, and revered by all; constantly looked to, constantly labored for, and even though never perfectly attained, constantly approximated, and thereby constantly spreading and deepening its influence, and augmenting the happiness and value of life to all people of all colors everywhere. The assertion that "all men are created equal" was of no practical use in effecting our separation from Great Britain; and it was placed in the Declaration, nor for that, but for future use. Its authors meant it to be, thank God, it is now proving itself, a stumbling block to those who in after times might seek to turn a free people back into the hateful paths of despotism. They knew the proneness of prosperity to breed tyrants, and they meant when such should re-appear in this fair land and commence their vocation they should find left for them at least one hard nut to crack. . . .

Source: The Collected Works of Abraham Lincoln, ed. Roy P. Basler (New Brunswick, N.J.: Rutgers University Press, 1953), 2:398–410. Accessible at http://www.hti.umich.edu/l/lincoln.

Document 30

Abraham Lincoln, Emancipation Proclamation
January 1, 1863

The Emancipation Proclamation, issued by Abraham Lincoln at a critical point in the conduct of the Civil War, freed the slaves in the rebellious states. The proclamation represented a significant exercise of the presidential authority as commander in chief, committing the "Executive Government of the United States, including the military and naval authority thereof" to recognize and maintain "the freedom of such persons." While the proclamation did not rest on congressional authorization, Congress had already approved through legislation compensation for slave owners who freed their slaves, the emancipation of all slaves in the District of Columbia through this method, and the prohibition of slavery in the territories (thus directly challenging the Supreme Court decision in Dred Scott v. Sandford *[1857]).*

Whereas, on the twenty-second day of September, in the year of our Lord one thousand eight hundred and sixty-two, a proclamation was issued by the President of the United States, containing, among other things, the following, to wit:

"That on the first day of January, in the year of our Lord one thousand eight hundred and sixty-three, all persons held as slaves within any State or designated part of a State, the people whereof shall then be in rebellion against the United States, shall be then, thenceforward, and forever free; and the Executive Government of the United States, including the military and naval authority thereof, will recognize and maintain the freedom of such persons, and will do no act or acts to repress such persons, or any of them, in any efforts they may make for their actual freedom.

"That the Executive will, on the first day of January aforesaid, by proclamation, designate the States and parts of States, if any, in which the people thereof, respectively, shall then be in rebellion against the United States; and the fact that any State, or the people thereof, shall on that day be, in good faith, represented in the Congress of the United States by members chosen thereto at elections wherein a majority of the qualified voters of such State shall have participated, shall, in the absence of strong countervailing testimony, be deemed conclusive evidence that such State, and the people thereof, are not then in rebellion against the United States."

Now, therefore I, Abraham Lincoln, President of the United States, by virtue of the power in me vested as Commander-in-Chief, of the Army and Navy of the United States in time of actual armed rebellion against the authority and government of the United States, and as a fit and necessary war measure for suppressing said rebellion, do, on this first day of January, in the year of our Lord one thousand eight hundred and sixty-three, and in accordance with my purpose so to do publicly proclaimed for the full period of one hundred days, from the day first above mentioned, order and designate as the States and parts of States wherein the people thereof respectively, are this day in rebellion against the United States, the following, to wit:

Arkansas, Texas, Louisiana, (except the Parishes of St. Bernard, Plaquemines, Jefferson, St. John, St. Charles, St. James Ascension, Assumption, Terrebonne, Lafourche, St. Mary, St. Martin, and Orleans, including the City of New Orleans) Mississippi, Alabama, Florida, Georgia, South Carolina, North Carolina, and Virginia, (except the forty-eight counties designated as West Virginia, and also the counties of Berkley, Accomac, Northampton, Elizabeth City, York, Princess Ann, and Norfolk, including the cities of Norfolk and Portsmouth[)], and which excepted parts, are for the present, left precisely as if this proclamation were not issued.

And by virtue of the power, and for the purpose aforesaid, I do order and declare that all persons held as slaves within said designated States, and parts of States, are, and henceforward shall be free; and that the Executive government of the United States, including the military and naval authorities thereof, will recognize and maintain the freedom of said persons.

And I hereby enjoin upon the people so declared to be free to abstain from all violence, unless in necessary self-defence; and I recommend to them that, in all cases when allowed, they labor faithfully for reasonable wages.

And I further declare and make known, that such persons of suitable condition, will be received into the armed service of the United States to garrison forts, positions, stations, and other places, and to man vessels of all sorts in said service.

And upon this act, sincerely believed to be an act of justice, warranted by the Constitution, upon military necessity, I invoke the considerate judgment of mankind, and the gracious favor of Almighty God.

In witness whereof, I have hereunto set my hand and caused the seal of the United States to be affixed.

Done at the City of Washington, this first day of January, in the year of our Lord one thousand eight hundred and sixty three, and of the Independence of the United States of America the eighty-seventh.

By the President: ABRAHAM LINCOLN
WILLIAM H. SEWARD, Secretary of State.

Source: The Collected Works of Abraham Lincoln, ed. Roy P. Basler (New Brunswick, N.J.: Rutgers University Press, 1953), 6:28–31.

Document 31   Franklin Delano Roosevelt, "A Fireside Chat" Discussing the
Plan for Reorganization of the Judiciary
March 9, 1937

Roosevelt's first term in office was characterized by great success with Congress, which passed his New Deal legislative agenda, and great frustration as a closely divided Supreme Court struck down the central pieces of that agenda. After the public returned him to office in 1936 by a huge margin, Roosevelt proposed changing the Court by adding one new justice for each sitting justice over the age of seventy. He would have enlarged the Court by six justices and created a majority supportive of his policies. In this radio address, Roosevelt explains why the enlargement of the Court is necessary. The Congress ultimately defeated the plan, but within a few short years Roosevelt was able to replace all of his opponents on the Court and, as a consequence, fundamentally transform its jurisprudence.

. . . The American people have learned from the depression. For in the last three national elections an overwhelming majority of them voted a mandate that the Congress and the President begin the task of providing that protection—not after long years of debate, but now.

The Courts, however, have cast doubts on the ability of the elected Congress to protect us against catastrophe by meeting squarely our modern social and economic conditions.

We are at a crisis in our ability to proceed with that protection. It is a quiet crisis. There are no lines of depositors outside closed banks. But to the far-sighted it is far-reaching in its possibilities of injury to America.

I want to talk with you very simply tonight about the need for present action in this crisis—the need to meet the unanswered challenge of one-third of a Nation ill-nourished, ill-clad, ill-housed.

Last Thursday I described the American form of Government as a three-horse team provided by the Constitution to the American people so that their field might be plowed. The three horses are, of course, the three branches of government—the Congress, the Executive and the Courts. Two of the horses, the Congress and the executive, are pulling in unison today; the third is not. Those who have intimated that the President of the United States is trying to drive the team, overlook the simple fact that the President, as Chief Executive, is himself one of the three horses.

It is the American people themselves who are in the driver's seat.

It is the American people themselves who want the furrow plowed.

It is the American people themselves who expect the third horse to pull in unison with the other two. . . .

But since the rise of the modern movement for social and economic progress through legislation, the Court has more and more often and more and more boldly asserted a power to veto laws passed by Congress and State Legislatures in complete disregard for this original limitation which I have just read.

In the last four years the sound rule of giving statutes the benefit of all reasonable doubt has been cast aside. The Court has been acting not as a judicial body, but as a policy-making body.

When the Congress has sought to stabilize national agriculture, to improve the conditions of labor, to safeguard business against unfair competition, to protect our national resources, and in many other ways, to serve our clearly national needs, the majority of the Court has been assuming the power to pass on the wisdom of these Acts of the Congress—to approve or disapprove the public policy written into these laws. . . .

The Court in addition to the proper use of its judicial functions has improperly set itself up as a third House of the Congress—a superlegislature, as one of the Justices called it—reading into the Constitution words and implications which are not there, and which were never intended to be there.

We have therefore reached the point as a Nation where we must take action to save the Constitution from the Court and the Court from itself. We must find a way to take an appeal from the Supreme Court to the Constitution itself. We want a Supreme Court which will do justice under the Constitution and not over it. In our Courts we want a government of laws and not of men.

When I commenced to review the situation with the problem squarely before me, I came by a process of elimination to the conclusion that short of amendments the only method which was clearly constitutional, and would at the same time carry out other much needed reforms, was to infuse new blood into all our Courts. We must have men worthy and equipped to carry out impartial justice. But, at the same time, we must have Judges who will bring to the Courts a present-day sense of the Constitution—Judges who will retain in the Courts the judicial functions of a court, and reject the legislative powers which the courts have today assumed. . . .

What is my proposal? It is simply this: whenever a Judge or Justice of any Federal Court has reached the age of seventy and does not avail himself of the opportunity to retire on a pension, a new member shall be appointed by the President then in office, with the approval, as required by the Constitution, of the Senate of the United States.

That plan has two chief purposes. By bringing into the Judicial system a steady and continuing stream of new and younger blood, I hope, first, to make the administration of all Federal justice, from the buttom to the top, speedier and, therefore, less costly; secondly, to bring to the decision of social and economic problems younger men who have had the personal experience and contact with modern facts and circumstances under which average men have to work and live. This plan will save our national Constitution from hardening of the judicial arteries. . . .

Like all lawyers, like all Americans, I regret the necessity of this controversy. But the welfare of the United States, and indeed of the Constitution itself, is what we all must think about first. Our difficulty with the Court today rises not from the Court as an institution but from the human beings within it. But we cannot yield our constitutional destiny to the personal judgment of a few men who, being fearful of the future, would deny the necessary means of dealing with the present.

This plan of mine is no attack on the Court; it seeks to restore the Court to its rightful and historic place in our system of Constitutional Government and to have it resume its high task of building anew on the Constitution "a system of living law." . . .

Source: Public Papers and Addresses of Franklin D. Roosevelt, 1937 (New York: McMillan, 1941), 122–133.

Document 32   **Richard Nixon, Veto Message on the War Powers Resolution 1973**

As the Vietnam War became increasingly unpopular, Congress's original support dwindled. Many members felt that Presidents Lyndon Johnson and Richard Nixon's use of the Gulf of Tonkin Resolution as the equivalent of a declaration of war went well beyond the legislative intent of the authorization. The War Powers Resolution was an effort to rein in the presidential commitment of troops without congressional authorization. Nixon vetoed the measure and explained in his veto message why he believed it to be unconstitutional. Within weeks Congress overrode Nixon's veto, and the resolution became law without the president's signature. The resolution remains controversial, however, as presidents resist invoking its provisions.

To the House of Representatives:

I hereby return without my approval House Joint Resolution 542—the War Powers Resolution. While I am in accord with the desire of the Congress to assert its proper role in the conduct of our foreign affairs, the restrictions which this resolution would impose upon the authority of the President are both unconstitutional and dangerous to the best interests of our Nation.

The proper roles of the Congress and the Executive in the conduct of foreign affairs have been debated since the founding of our country. Only recently, however, has there been a serious challenge to the wisdom of the Founding Fathers in choosing not to draw a precise and detailed line of demarcation between the foreign policy powers of the two branches.

The Founding Fathers understood the impossibility of foreseeing every contingency that might arise in this complex area. They acknowledged the need for flexibility in responding to changing circumstances. They recognized that foreign policy decisions must be made through close cooperation between the two branches and not through rigidly codified procedures.

These principles remain as valid today as they were when our Constitution was written. Yet House Joint Resolution 542 would violate those principles by defining the President's powers in ways which would strictly limit his constitutional authority.

House Joint Resolution 542 would attempt to take away, by a mere legislative act, authorities which the President has properly exercised under the Constitution for almost 200 years. One of its provisions would automatically cut off certain authorities after sixty days unless the Congress extended them. Another would allow the Congress to eliminate certain authorities merely by the passage of a concurrent resolution—an action which does not normally have the force of law, since it denies the President his constitutional role in approving legislation.

I believe that both of these provisions are unconstitutional. The only way in which the constitutional powers of a branch of Government can be altered is by amending the Constitution—and any attempt to make such alterations by legislation alone is clearly without force.

While I firmly believe that a veto . . . is warranted solely on constitutional grounds, I am also deeply disturbed by the practical consequences of this resolution. For it would seriously undermine this Nation's ability to act decisively and convincingly in times of international crisis. As a result, the confidence of our allies in our ability to assist them could be diminished and the respect of our adversaries for our deterrent posture could decline. A permanent and substantial element of unpredictability would be injected into the world's assessment of American behavior, further increasing the likelihood of miscalculation and war.

If this resolution had been in operation, America's effective response to a variety of challenges in recent years would have been vastly complicated or even made impossible. We may well have been unable to respond in the way we did during the Berlin crisis of 1961, the Cuban missile crisis of 1962, the Congo rescue operation in 1964, and the Jordanian crisis of 1970—to mention just a few examples. In addition, our recent actions to bring about a peaceful settlement of the hostilities in the Middle East would have been seriously impaired if this resolution had been in force.

I am particularly disturbed by the fact that certain of the President's constitutional powers as Commander in Chief of the Armed Forces would terminate automatically under this resolution 60 days after they were involved. No overt Congressional action would be required to cut off these powers—they would disappear automatically unless the Congress extended them. In effect, the Congress is here attempting to increase its policymaking role through a provision which requires it to take absolutely no action at all.

In my view, the proper way for the Congress to make known its will on such foreign policy questions is through a positive action, with full debate on the merits of the issue and with each member taking the responsibility of casting a yes or no vote after considering those merits. The authorization and appropriations process represents one of the ways in which such influence can be exercised. I do not, however, believe that the Congress can responsibly contribute its considered, collective judgment on such grave questions without full debate and without a yes or no vote. Yet this is precisely what the joint resolution would allow. It would give every future Congress the ability to handcuff every future President merely by doing nothing and sitting still. In my view, one cannot become a responsible partner unless one is prepared to take responsible action.

Source: Public Papers of the Presidents of the United States: Richard Nixon, 1973 (Washington, D.C.: Government Printing Office, 1975), 893–895.

Document 33   Bill Clinton on the Line-Item Veto
April 9, 1996

The federal budget deficit that began in the 1970s and ballooned in the 1980s led to a call for a line-item veto, which would allow the president to reject lines in the budget that might be considered unnecessary, such as certain pork barrel projects, which contribute to government spending. Several governors had this power, and presidents and opponents of deficit spending began to argue that the president needed a similar device to help balance budgets. The Republican Party's 1994 Contract With America included the promise to pass a line-item veto. The Republicans won control of the House that year and, in keeping with their contract promises, passed a line-item veto. The provisions were slated to go into effect after the 1996 presidential election, which Bill Clinton won. In his signing statement, Clinton addressed the policy and the constitutional issues surrounding the veto. Ultimately, the Supreme Court struck down the line-item veto in Clinton v. City of New York *(1998), declaring it an unconstitutional alteration of the balance of power between Congress and the president. To exercise a change of such magnitude, the Court said, supporters of the veto would need to amend the Constitution.*

THE PRESIDENT. Good morning. . . .

It gives me great pleasure today to sign into law the line item veto. This is a bipartisan achievement that has been long sought by Presidents, long supported by Members of Congress and by Governors. It will help us to cut waste and to balance the budget. For years, Presidents of both parties have pounded this very desk in frustration at having to sign necessary legislation that contained special interest boondoggles, tax loopholes, and pure pork. The line item veto will give us a chance to change that, to permit Presidents to better represent the public interest by cutting waste, protecting taxpayers, and balancing the budget.

We all know that this is needed because too often, as vital bills move through Congress, they can become clogged with items that would never pass on their own. Presidents often have no choice but to sign these bills because of their main purpose. This new law will give the President the power to cancel specific spending items and specific tax loopholes that benefit special interests. These proposals can then be debated and subject to an open vote on the floor of Congress.

A fresh air of public accountability will blow through the Federal budget.

This law gives the President tools to cut wasteful spending, and even more important, it empowers our citizens, for the exercise of this veto or even the possibility of its exercise will throw a spotlight of public scrutiny onto the darkest corners of the Federal budget.

I have advocated the line item veto for a long time. When I was Governor, I used it, and it helped us to balance 12 budgets in a row. Forty-three of our 50 Governors have the line item veto. Governor Romer is with us because so many of the Nation's Governors have supported this measure for so long. The line item veto will help us to bring common sense to our Nation's Capital, just as it has to State capitals all across America.

Let me say, I am particularly pleased that this measure received support from both parties, working together for the public good. That's the way we should meet all of our challenges in America, and it's the only way we can balance the budget in the right way. . . .

Thank you.

Q. Doesn't this transcend the Founding Fathers' separation of powers and give the President too much power?

THE PRESIDENT. I don't think so. We've worked hard to—we anticipate that it will be challenged. We've worked hard to provide for a means for it to be resolved quickly. But this leaves ultimate hands in the authority of the Congress. They can take all these separate issues back and vote on them separately. And I think all of us believe that as long as that is done, that we don't violate the constitutional separation of powers doctrine.

And the constitutions of our various States are modeled pretty closely on the Federal Constitution. They all have separation of powers doctrines, and the Governors have had this authority in almost all the States and have used it well and without any upsetting of the constitutional framework.

As long as the practical impact of this is to force these matters to be considered separately, I don't think there's any question that it's not a violation of the separation of powers. Now of course, others in authority and the judicial branch will have their opportunity to say differently, but I believe it will be upheld. . . .

Q. Mr. President your critics of the line item veto have said that it will allow a President to wheel and deal with a Senator or a Congressman or a group of Senators or Congressmen, and to threaten them with this power. What could you say—not to question your integrity or whatever—what would you say to the American people that you would not, and your successors would not, abuse this power?

THE PRESIDENT. Well, first of all, every power given to the Congress or to the President or to the courts is, I suppose, susceptible to some abuse, and we have a system of checks and balances there. My argument is, number one, there's obviously some negotiations that go on over legislation all the time now and almost always, by the way, fully reported by you and the press, whether we like it or not. [Laughter]

Number two, keep in mind, the protection the Members have is that if the President goes overboard and says, if you don't vote for me on some other bill, or this bill, I'm not going to allow your project in here—if the President started doing that, and it was unrelated to the real merits of the underlying spending provision, then I believe the Congress would respond by passing these bills separately.

Keep in mind the ultimate protection the Congress has: If the President abuses his authority, the ultimate protection the Congress has is the clear ability to have these bills voted on separately and publicly. And then the President's veto gets singled out. The President could veto it, that spending bill again, too. Then the President would be ultimately held accountable by the people, through the reporting of the process in the press.

And let me also say that I found—you know, I was a Governor for quite a long time before I came here, and what I found was—and I'm sure Governor Romer could corroborate this—is that once this mechanism is in place and people understand that the Executive is prepared to use it, it becomes necessary to use it less, that its main benefit after a few years is that it exists in reserve, because it changes the whole shape of the budget negotiations and makes these bills less subject to this sort of catch-all spending.

Now, it will take some years, perhaps, for that to happen here, but we are doing this for the long run. None of us who have supported this—and I'm sure the representatives from the business groups, the taxpayers unions, and others would say the same thing—none of us have ever pretended that this was some sort of miraculous cureall. But we believe it will put discipline into this budget, and it will really help over the long run to give the American people a kind of budgeting process they need, as well as reducing waste and helping to move the budget into balance.

Thank you. . . .

Source: Weekly Compilation of Presidential Documents (Washington, D.C.: Government Printing Office, 1996), 32: 635–637.

Document 34   Department of Justice, Executive Branch Immunity from
Compelled Congressional Testimony
September 3, 1996

Since the early days of the Republic, the legislative and executive branches have battled over congressional access to testimony and documentary evidence from the executive (see Doc. 27). The Supreme Court endorsed the constitutional legitimacy of executive privilege in United States v. Nixon *(1974) (Doc. 50), in which it found some such claims to be essential to the ability of the president to fulfill executive functions. During the Clinton administration, Congress launched a number of investigations into alleged wrongdoings by the president, the first lady, and members of their staff. Because of the likelihood that the White House counsel, who acts as legal adviser to the president on official matters, would be called to testify in one of these investigations, the White House sought from the Department of Justice an explanation of the legal status of the counsel in claims of executive privilege. A Justice official responded that executive privilege was assertable because the counsel serves as an immediate adviser to the president and would therefore be immune from compelled congressional testimony.*

LETTER OPINION FOR THE COUNSEL TO THE PRESIDENT

You have asked whether it would be consistent with precedent and governing legal principles to assert executive privilege should a subpoena be issued by a congressional committee to you, in your capacity as Counsel to the President, to compel your testimony at a committee hearing concerning the performance of your official duties. We believe that executive privilege would be assertable on the basis that you serve as an immediate adviser to the President and are therefore immune from compelled congressional testimony.

It is the longstanding position of the executive branch that "the President and his immediate advisors are absolutely immune from testimonial compulsion by a Congressional committee."[1] This position is constitutionally based:

The President is a separate branch of government. He may not compel congressmen to appear before him. As a matter of separation of powers, Congress may not compel him to appear before it. The President's close advisors are an extension of the President.[2]

Accordingly, "[n]ot only can the President invoke executive privilege to protect [his personal staff] from the necessity of answering questions posed by a congressional committee, but he can

————

1. Memorandum for all Heads of Offices, Divisions, Bureaus and Boards of the Department of Justice, from John M. Harmon, Acting Assistant Attorney General, Office of Legal Counsel, *Re: Executive Privilege* at 5 (May 23, 1977).

————

2. Memorandum for Edward C. Schmults, Deputy Attorney General, from Theodore B. Olson, Assistant Attorney General, Office of Legal Counsel at 2 (Jul. 29, 1982) (discussing subpoena for testimony of the Counsel to the President). *See also* Memorandum for the Honorable John W. Dean, III, Counsel to the President, from Roger C. Cramton, Assistant Attorney General, Office of Legal Counsel, *Re: Availability of Executive Privilege Where Congressional Committee Seeks Testimony of Former White House Official on Advice Given President on Official Matters* at 6 (Dec. 21, 1972) (since "[a]n immediate assistant to the President may be said to serve as his alter ego . . . the same considerations that were persuasive to former President Truman [when he declined to comply with a congressional subpoena for his testimony] would apply to justify a refusal to appear by . . . a former staff member"); Letter for Senator Orrin G. Hatch, Chairman, United States Senate, Committee on Labor and Human Resources, and Senator Edward M.

also direct them not even to appear before the committee."[3]

An often-quoted statement of this position is contained in an opinion by Assistant Attorney General William Rehnquist:

> The President and his immediate advisers— that is, those who customarily meet with the President on a regular or frequent basis— should be deemed absolutely immune from testimonial compulsion by a congressional committee. They not only may not be examined with respect to their official duties, but they

may not even be compelled to appear before a congressional committee.[4]

There is no question that the Counsel to the President falls within Assistant Attorney General Rehnquist's description of the type of Presidential advisers who are immune from testimonial compulsion.

CHRISTOPHER H. SCHROEDER
Acting Assistant Attorney General
Office of Legal Counsel

Kennedy, Ranking Minority Member, United States Senate, Committee on Labor and Human Resources, from Edward C. Schmults, Deputy Attorney General at 2 (Apr. 19, 1983) ("[O]ur concern regarding your desire for the sworn testimony of [the Counsel to the President] is based upon important principles relative to the powers, duties and prerogatives of the Presidency. We share with previous Presidents and their advisers serious reservations regarding the implications for established constitutional doctrines arising from the separation of powers of a Congressional demand for the sworn testimony of close presidential advisers on the White House staff.").

3. Memorandum for Margaret McKenna, Deputy Counsel to the President, from John M. Harmon, Assistant Attorney General, Office of Legal Counsel, *Re: Dual-purpose Presidential Advisers,* Appendix at 7 (Aug. 11, 1977).

4. Memorandum for the Honorable John D. Ehrlichman, Assistant to the President for Domestic Affairs, from William H. Rehnquist, Assistant Attorney General, Office of Legal Counsel, *Re: Power of Congressional Committee to Compel Appearance or Testimony of "White House Staff"* at 7 (Feb. 5, 1971).

Source: Accessible at http://www.usdoj.gov/olc/execpric.htm.

Document 35 **George W. Bush, Executive Order Authorizing Military Tribunals**
November 13, 2001

> *How to handle legal cases against alleged terrorists was among the many questions raised by the September 11, 2001, attacks on the United States. In one response, President George W. Bush issued an executive order authorizing the use of military tribunals, in which the due process rights that would be afforded defendants in a criminal trial are substantially reduced. The order created considerable controversy. Civil libertarians argued that it was an abuse of power that threatened the rights of defendants and that a president could not establish such tribunals without congressional authorization (Ex parte Milligan [1866]). Bush's supporters pointed to the Supreme Court precedent permitting such tribunals in World War II (Ex parte Quirin [1942]) and argued that such an order was within the president's powers as commander in chief. In addition, they contended, such provision had been implicitly sanctioned by Congress's post–September 11 authorization for the president to use military force to respond to the attacks. The order was ultimately revised in ways that satisfied some, but not all, of the concerns of its critics.*

By the authority vested in me as President and as Commander in Chief of the Armed Forces of the

United States by the Constitution and the laws of the United States of America, including the Authorization for Use of Military Force Joint Resolution (Public Law 107-40, 115 Stat. 224) and sections 821 and 836 of title 10, United States Code, it is hereby ordered as follows:

Section 1. Findings.

(a) International terrorists, including members of al Qaida, have carried out attacks on United States diplomatic and military personnel and facilities abroad and on citizens and property within the United States on a scale that has created a state of armed conflict that requires the use of the United States Armed Forces.

(b) In light of grave acts of terrorism and threats of terrorism, including the terrorist attacks on September 11, 2001, on the headquarters of the United States Department of Defense in the national capital region, on the World Trade Center in New York, and on civilian aircraft such as in Pennsylvania, I proclaimed a national emergency on September 14, 2001 (Proc. 7463, Declaration of National Emergency by Reason of Certain Terrorist Attacks).

(c) Individuals acting alone and in concert involved in international terrorism possess both the capability and the intention to undertake further terrorist attacks against the United States that, if not detected and prevented, will cause mass deaths, mass injuries, and massive destruction of property, and may place at risk the continuity of the operations of the United States Government.

(d) The ability of the United States to protect the United States and its citizens, and to help its allies and other cooperating nations protect their nations and their citizens, from such further terrorist attacks depends in significant part upon using the United States Armed Forces to identify terrorists and those who support them, to disrupt their activities, and to eliminate their ability to conduct or support such attacks.

(e) To protect the United States and its citizens, and for the effective conduct of military operations and prevention of terrorist attacks, it is necessary for individuals subject to this order pursuant to section 2 hereof to be detained, and, when tried, to be tried for violations of the laws of war and other applicable laws by military tribunals.

(f) Given the danger to the safety of the United States and the nature of international terrorism, and to the extent provided by and under this order, I find consistent with section 836 of title 10, United States Code, that it is not practicable to apply in military commissions under this order the principles of law and the rules of evidence generally recognized in the trial of criminal cases in the United States district courts.

(g) Having fully considered the magnitude of the potential deaths, injuries, and property destruction that would result from potential acts of terrorism against the United States, and the probability that such acts will occur, I have determined that an extraordinary emergency exists for national defense purposes, that this emergency constitutes an urgent and compelling government interest, and that issuance of this order is necessary to meet the emergency. . . .

Sec. 3. Detention Authority of the Secretary of Defense. Any individual subject to this order shall be—

(a) detained at an appropriate location designated by the Secretary of Defense outside or within the United States;

(b) treated humanely, without any adverse distinction based on race, color, religion, gender, birth, wealth, or any similar criteria;

(c) afforded adequate food, drinking water, shelter, clothing, and medical treatment;

(d) allowed the free exercise of religion consistent with the requirements of such detention; and

(e) detained in accordance with such other conditions as the Secretary of Defense may prescribe.

Sec. 4. Authority of the Secretary of Defense Regarding Trials of Individuals Subject to this Order.

(a) Any individual subject to this order shall, when tried, be tried by military commission for any and all offenses triable by military commission that such individual is alleged to have committed, and may be punished in accordance with the penalties provided under applicable law, including life imprisonment or death.

(b) As a military function and in light of the findings in section 1, including subsection (f) thereof, the Secretary of Defense shall issue such orders and regulations, including orders for the appointment of one or more military commissions, as may be necessary to carry out subsection (a) of this section.

(c) Orders and regulations issued under subsection (b) of this section shall include, but not be limited to, rules for the conduct of the proceedings of military commissions, including pretrial, trial, and post-trial procedures, modes of proof, issuance of process, and qualifications of attorneys, which shall at a minimum provide for—

(1) military commissions to sit at any time and any place, consistent with such guidance regarding time and place as the Secretary of Defense may provide;

(2) a full and fair trial, with the military commission sitting as the triers of both fact and law;

(3) admission of such evidence as would, in the opinion of the presiding officer of the military commission (or instead, if any other member of the commission so requests at the time the presiding officer renders that opinion, the opinion of the commission rendered at that time by a majority of the commission), have probative value to a reasonable person;

(4) in a manner consistent with the protection of information classified or classifiable under Executive Order 12958 of April 17, 1995, as amended, or any successor Executive Order, protected by statute or rule from unauthorized disclosure, or otherwise protected by law, (A) the handling of, admission into evidence of, and access to materials and information, and (B) the conduct, closure of, and access to proceedings;

(5) conduct of the prosecution by one or more attorneys designated by the Secretary of Defense and conduct of the defense by attorneys for the individual subject to this order;

(6) conviction only upon the concurrence of two-thirds of the members of the commission present at the time of the vote, a majority being present;

(7) sentencing only upon the concurrence of two-thirds of the members of the commission present at the time of the vote, a majority being present; and

(8) submission of the record of the trial, including any conviction or sentence, for review and final decision by me or by the Secretary of Defense if so designated by me for that purpose. . . .

Sec. 7. Relationship to Other Law and Forums.

(a) Nothing in this order shall be construed to—

(1) authorize the disclosure of state secrets to any person not otherwise authorized to have access to them;

(2) limit the authority of the President as Commander in Chief of the Armed Forces or the power of the President to grant reprieves and pardons; or

(3) limit the lawful authority of the Secretary of Defense, any military commander, or any other officer or agent of the United States or of any State to detain or try any person who is not an individual subject to this order.

(b) With respect to any individual subject to this order—

(1) military tribunals shall have exclusive jurisdiction with respect to offenses by the individual; and

(2) the individual shall not be privileged to seek any remedy or maintain any proceeding, directly or indirectly, or to have any such remedy or proceeding sought on the individual's behalf, in (i) any court of the United States, or any State thereof, (ii) any court of any foreign nation, or (iii) any international tribunal.

(c) This order is not intended to and does not create any right, benefit, or privilege, substantive or procedural, enforceable at law or equity by any party, against the United States, its departments, agencies, or other entities, its officers or employees, or any other person.

(d) For purposes of this order, the term "State" includes any State, district, territory, or possession of the United States.

(e) I reserve the authority to direct the Secretary of Defense, at any time hereafter, to transfer to a governmental authority control of any individual subject to this order. Nothing in this order shall be construed to limit the authority of any such governmental authority to prosecute any individual for whom control is transferred. . . .

GEORGE W. BUSH
THE WHITE HOUSE

Source: White House Press Release, November 13, 2001. Accessible at http://www.whitehouse.gov/news/releases/2001/11/20011113-27.html.

Document 36   **George W. Bush, Memo on Executive Privilege**
December 12, 2001

One of the battles between Congress and the Clinton administration involved allegations that the president and the Democratic Party had violated campaign finance laws during the 1996 election. The conflict became particularly heated when Attorney General Janet Reno refused congressional committees' pressure to seek an appointment of an independent counsel to investigate the charges and resisted turning over internal Department of Justice memos regarding her decision. After the election of George W. Bush, congressional Republicans hoped that they might finally gain access to the Justice documents and made such a request. Bush's response demonstrates that defending executive privilege as a prerogative of the presidency can override partisan interests in exposing wrongdoing by opponents.

Memo for Attorney General on Executive Branch Documents

December 12, 2001

MEMORANDUM FOR THE ATTORNEY GENERAL
SUBJECT: Congressional Subpoena for Executive Branch Documents

I have been advised that the Committee on Government Reform of the House of Representatives has subpoenaed confidential Department of Justice documents. The documents consist of memoranda from the Chief of the Campaign Financing Task

Force to former Attorney General Janet Reno recommending that a Special Counsel be appointed to investigate a matter under review by the Task Force, memoranda written in response to those memoranda, and deliberative memoranda from other investigations containing advice and recommendations concerning whether particular criminal prosecutions should be brought. I understand that, among other accommodations the Department has provided the Committee concerning the matters that are the subject of these documents, the Department has provided briefings with explanations of the reasons for the prosecutorial decisions, and is willing to provide further briefings. I also understand that you believe it would be inconsistent with the constitutional doctrine of separation of powers and the Department's law enforcement responsibilities to release these documents to the Committee or to make them available for review by Committee representatives.

It is my decision that you should not release these documents or otherwise make them available to the Committee. Disclosure to Congress of confidential advice to the Attorney General regarding the appointment of a Special Counsel and confidential recommendations to Department of Justice officials regarding whether to bring criminal charges would inhibit the candor necessary to the effectiveness of the deliberative processes by which the Department makes prosecutorial decisions. Moreover, I am concerned that congressional access to prosecutorial decisionmaking documents of this kind threatens to politicize the criminal justice process. The Founders' fundamental purpose in establishing the separation of powers in the Constitution was to protect individual liberty. Congressional pressure on executive branch prosecutorial decision-making is inconsistent with separation of powers and threatens individual liberty. Because I believe that congressional access to these documents would be contrary to the national interest, I have decided to assert executive privilege with respect to the documents and to instruct you not to release them or otherwise make them available to the Committee.

I request that you advise the Committee of my decision. I also request that the Department remain willing to work informally with the Committee to provide such information as it can, consistent with these instructions and without violating the constitutional doctrine of separation of powers.

GEORGE W. BUSH

Source: White House Press Release, December 13, 2001. Accessible at http://www.whitehouse.gov/news/releases/2001/12/20011213-1.html.

Document 37   *Marbury v. Madison* (1803)

In Federalist No. 78 (Doc. 11), *Alexander Hamilton argued that one of the reasons that the federal judiciary needed life tenure was to free its members from political pressure that might interfere with their ability to uphold the Constitution in the face of legislation that conflicted with that document. The Constitution was the fundamental law of the land, and legislation was subordinate to it. If a written constitution was to mean anything, its limits had to be enforced against legislative usurpations of power.*

Hamilton's argument is evidence that the power of judicial review was not a concept newly created by Chief Justice John Marshall when the Court claimed the power of judicial review in Marbury v. Madison. *The case arose out of a political conflict between the newly elected Democratic Republicans, who took control of the government in the election of 1800, and the Federalists, who had controlled the government since the founding. Between the election and the inaugural and the seating of Congress, the Federalists created a number of new judicial offices and filled them with their partisans. The commissions of a few appointees, including that of William Marbury, were not delivered before the change in government. Angered by the Federalists' attempt to stack the judiciary, President Thomas Jefferson refused to turn over the commissions, and Marbury sued in the Supreme Court for a writ of mandamus forcing the new secretary of state, James Madison, to deliver the commissions.*

Mr. Chief Justice MARSHALL delivered the opinion of the Court. . . .

It is then the opinion of the court,

1. That by signing the commission of Mr. Marbury, the president of the United States appointed him a justice of peace for the county of Washington in the district of Columbia; and that the seal of the United States, affixed thereto by the secretary of state, is conclusive testimony of the verity of the signature, and of the completion of the appointment; and that the appointment conferred on him a legal right to the office for the space of five years.

2. That, having this legal title to the office, he has a consequent right to the commission; a refusal to deliver which is a plain violation of that right, for which the laws of his country afford him a remedy.

It remains to be inquired whether,

3. He is entitled to the remedy for which he applies. This depends on,

1. The nature of the writ applied for. And,
2. The power of this court.

1. The nature of the writ. . . .

This writ, if awarded, would be directed to an officer of government, and its mandate to him would be, to use the words of Blackstone, "to do a particular thing therein specified, which appertains to his office and duty, and which the court has previously determined or at least supposes to be consonant to right and justice." Or, in the words of Lord Mansfield, the applicant, in this case, has a right to execute an office of public concern, and is kept out of possession of that right.

These circumstances certainly concur in this case.

Still, to render the mandamus a proper remedy, the officer to whom it is to be directed, must be one to whom, on legal principles, such writ may be directed; and the person applying for it must be without any other specific and legal remedy. . . .

It is not by the office of the person to whom the writ is directed, but the nature of the thing to be done, that the propriety or impropriety of issuing a mandamus is to be determined. Where the head of a department acts in a case in which executive discretion is to be exercised; in which he is the mere organ of executive will; it is again repeated, that any application to a court to control, in any respect, his conduct, would be rejected without hesitation.

But where he is directed by law to do a certain act affecting the absolute rights of individuals, in the performance of which he is not placed under the particular direction of the president, and the performance of which the president cannot lawfully forbid, and therefore is never presumed to have forbidden; as for example, to record a commission, or a patent for land, which has received all the legal solemnities; or to give a copy of such record; in such cases, it is not perceived on what ground the courts of the country are further excused from the duty of giving judgment, that right to be done to an injured individual, than if the same services were to be performed by a person not the head of a department. . . .

The doctrine . . . now advanced is by no means a novel one.

It is true that the mandamus, now moved for, is not for the performance of an act expressly enjoined by statute.

It is to deliver a commission; on which subjects the acts of congress are silent. This difference is not considered as affecting the case. It has already been stated that the applicant has, to that commission, a vested legal right, of which the executive cannot deprive him. He has been appointed to an office, from which he is not removable at the will of the executive; and being so appointed, he has a right to the commission which the secretary has received from the president for his use. The act of congress does not indeed order the secretary of state to send it to him, but it is placed in his hands for the person entitled to it; and cannot be more lawfully withheld by him, than by another person. . . .

This, then, is a plain case of a mandamus, either to deliver the commission, or a copy of it from the record; and it only remains to be inquired,

Whether it can issue from this court.

The act to establish the judicial courts of the United States authorizes the supreme court "to issue writs of mandamus, in cases warranted by the principles and usages of law, to any courts appointed, or persons holding office, under the authority of the United States."

The secretary of state, being a person, holding an office under the authority of the United States, is precisely within the letter of the description; and if this court is not authorized to issue a writ of mandamus to such an officer, it must be because the law is unconstitutional, and therefore absolutely incapable of conferring the authority, and assigning the duties which its words purport to confer and assign.

The constitution vests the whole judicial power of the United States in one supreme court, and such inferior courts as congress shall, from time to time, ordain and establish. This power is expressly extended to all cases arising under the laws of the United States; and consequently, in some form, may be exercised over the present case; because the right claimed is given by a law of the United States.

In the distribution of this power it is declared that "the supreme court shall have original jurisdiction in all cases affecting ambassadors, other public ministers and consuls, and those in which a state shall be a party. In all other cases, the supreme court shall have appellate jurisdiction."

It has been insisted at the bar, that as the original grant of jurisdiction to the supreme and inferior courts is general, and the clause, assigning original jurisdiction to the supreme court, contains no negative or restrictive words; the power remains to the legislature to assign original jurisdiction to that court in other cases than those specified in the article which has been recited; provided those cases belong to the judicial power of the United States.

If it had been intended to leave it in the discretion of the legislature to apportion the judicial power between the supreme and inferior courts according to the will of that body, it would certainly have been useless to have proceeded further than to have defined the judicial power, and the tribunals in which it should be vested. The subsequent part of the section is mere surplusage, is entirely without meaning, if such is to be the construction. If congress remains at liberty to give this court appellate jurisdiction, where the constitution has declared their jurisdiction shall be original; and original jurisdiction where the constitution has declared it shall be appellate; the distribution of jurisdiction made in the constitution, is form without substance.

Affirmative words are often, in their operation, negative of other objects than those affirmed; and in this case, a negative or exclusive sense must be given to them or they have no operation at all.

It cannot be presumed that any clause in the constitution is intended to be without effect; and therefore such construction is inadmissible, unless the words require it. If the solicitude of the convention, respecting our peace with foreign powers, induced a provision that the supreme court should take original jurisdiction in cases which might be supposed to affect them; yet the clause would have proceeded no further than to provide for such cases, if no further restriction on the powers of congress had been intended. That they should have appellate jurisdiction in all other cases, with such exceptions as congress might make, is no restriction; unless the words be deemed exclusive of original jurisdiction.

When an instrument organizing fundamentally a judicial system, divides it into one supreme, and so many inferior courts as the legislature may ordain and establish; then enumerates its powers, and proceeds so far to distribute them, as to define the jurisdiction of the supreme court by declaring the cases in which it shall take original jurisdiction, and that in others it shall take appellate jurisdiction, the plain import of the words seems to be, that in one class of cases its jurisdiction is original, and not appellate; in the other it is appellate, and not original. If any other construction would render the clause inoperative, that is an additional reason for rejecting such other construction, and for adhering to the obvious meaning.

To enable this court then to issue a mandamus, it must be shown to be an exercise of appellate jurisdiction, or to be necessary to enable them to exercise appellate jurisdiction.

It has been stated at the bar that the appellate jurisdiction may be exercised in a variety of forms, and that if it be the will of the legislature that a mandamus should be used for that purpose, that will must be obeyed. This is true; yet the jurisdiction must be appellate, not original.

It is the essential criterion of appellate jurisdiction, that it revises and corrects the proceedings in a cause already instituted, and does not create that case. Although, therefore, a mandamus may be directed to courts, yet to issue such a writ to an officer for the delivery of a paper, is in effect the same as to sustain an original action for that paper, and therefore seems not to belong to appellate, but to original jurisdiction. Neither is it necessary in such a case as this, to enable the court to exercise its appellate jurisdiction.

The authority, therefore, given to the supreme court, by the act establishing the judicial courts of the United States, to issue writs of mandamus to public officers, appears not to be warranted by the constitution; and it becomes necessary to inquire whether a jurisdiction, so conferred, can be exercised.

The question, whether an act, repugnant to the constitution, can become the law of the land, is a question deeply interesting to the United States; but, happily, not of an intricacy proportioned to its interest. It seems only necessary to recognise certain principles, supposed to have been long and well established, to decide it.

That the people have an original right to establish, for their future government, such principles as, in their opinion, shall most conduce to their own happiness, is the basis on which the whole American fabric has been erected. The exercise of this original right is a very great exertion; nor can it nor ought it to be frequently repeated. The principles, therefore, so established are deemed fundamental. And as the authority, from which they proceed, is supreme, and can seldom act, they are designed to be permanent.

This original and supreme will organizes the government, and assigns to different departments their respective powers. It may either stop here; or establish certain limits not to be transcended by those departments.

The government of the United States is of the latter description. The powers of the legislature are defined and limited; and that those limits may not be mistaken or forgotten, the constitution is written. To what purpose are powers limited, and to what purpose is that limitation committed to writing; if these limits may, at any time, be passed by those intended to be restrained? The distinction between a government with limited and unlimited powers is abolished, if those limits do not confine the persons on whom they are imposed, and if acts prohibited and acts allowed are of equal obligation. It is a proposition too plain to be contested, that the constitution controls any legislative act repugnant to it; or, that the legislature may alter the constitution by an ordinary act.

Between these alternatives there is no middle ground. The constitution is either a superior, paramount law, unchangeable by ordinary means, or it is on a level with ordinary legislative acts, and like other acts, is alterable when the legislature shall please to alter it.

If the former part of the alternative be true, then a legislative act contrary to the constitution is not law: if the latter part be true, then written constitutions are absurd attempts, on the part of the people, to limit a power in its own nature illimitable.

Certainly all those who have framed written constitutions contemplate them as forming the fundamental and paramount law of the nation, and consequently the theory of every such government must be, that an act of the legislature repugnant to the constitution is void.

This theory is essentially attached to a written constitution, and is consequently to be considered by this court as one of the fundamental principles of our society. It is not therefore to be lost sight of in the further consideration of this subject.

If an act of the legislature, repugnant to the constitution, is void, does it, notwithstanding its invalidity, bind the courts and oblige them to give it effect? Or, in other words, though it be not law, does it constitute a rule as operative as if it was a law? This would be to overthrow in fact what was established in theory; and would seem, at first view, an absurdity too gross to be insisted on. It shall, however, receive a more attentive consideration.

It is emphatically the province and duty of the judicial department to say what the law is. Those who apply the rule to particular cases, must of necessity expound and interpret that rule. If two laws conflict with each other, the courts must decide on the operation of each. So if a law be in opposition to the constitution: if both the law and the constitution apply to a particular case, so that the court must either decide that case conformably to the law, disregarding the constitution; or conformably to the constitution, disregarding the law: the court must determine which of these conflicting rules governs the case. This is of the very essence of judicial duty.

If then the courts are to regard the constitution; and the constitution is superior to any ordinary act of the legislature; the constitution, and not such ordinary act, must govern the case to which they both apply.

Those then who controvert the principle that the constitution is to be considered, in court, as a paramount law, are reduced to the necessity of maintaining that courts must close their eyes on the constitution, and see only the law.

This doctrine would subvert the very foundation of all written constitutions. It would declare that an act, which, according to the principles and theory of our government, is entirely void, is yet, in practice, completely obligatory. It would declare, that if the legislature shall do what is expressly forbidden, such act, notwithstanding the express prohibition, is in reality effectual. It would be giving to the legislature a practical and real omnipotence with the same breath which professes to restrict their powers within narrow limits. It is prescribing limits, and declaring that those limits may be passed at pleasure.

That it thus reduces to nothing what we have deemed the greatest improvement on political institutions—a written constitution, would of itself be sufficient, in America where written constitutions have been viewed with so much reverence, for rejecting the construction. But the peculiar expressions of the constitution of the United States furnish additional arguments in favour of its rejection.

The judicial power of the United States is extended to all cases arising under the constitution. Could it be the intention of those who gave this power, to say that, in using it, the constitution should not be looked into? That a case arising under the constitution should be decided without examining the instrument under which it arises?

. . . [I]t is apparent, that the framers of the constitution contemplated that instrument as a rule for the government of courts, as well as of the legislature.

Why otherwise does it direct the judges to take an oath to support it? This oath certainly applies, in an especial manner, to their conduct in their official character. How immoral to impose it on them, if they were to be used as the instruments, and the knowing instruments, for violating what they swear to support! . . .

It is also not entirely unworthy of observation, that in declaring what shall be the supreme law of the land, the constitution itself is first mentioned; and not the laws of the United States generally, but those only which shall be made in pursuance of the constitution, have that rank.

Thus, the particular phraseology of the constitution of the United States confirms and strengthens the principle, supposed to be essential to all written constitutions, that a law repugnant to the constitution is void, and that courts, as well as other departments, are bound by that instrument. . . .

Source: 1 Cranch (5 U.S.) 137 (1803). Also available in Mark A. Graber and Michael Perhac, eds., *Marbury v. Madison: Documents and Commentary* (Washington, D.C.: CQ Press, 2002).

Document 38   McCulloch v. Maryland (1819)

For the first several decades of the United States, the parties in Congress fought over whether the legislature had the authority to establish a national bank. Congress first established a bank in 1791. In 1811, however, Congress decided against reauthorizing it. Reestablishment of the bank was rejected again in 1815 but approved in 1816. Proponents of the bank argued that it was needed to fulfill the federal government's financial responsibilities, including collecting taxes and securing loans. Opponents of the bank argued that its establishment went beyond the delegated powers of Congress and was, rather, a power reserved to the states. Despite the bank's reauthorization in 1816 there remained strong opposition in the states. The controversy in McCulloch v. Maryland resulted from Maryland's effort to tax a branch of the national bank. Clearly designed to challenge the bank's legitimacy, Maryland's law imposed an annual tax of $15,000 on all banks not chartered by the state government. James W. McCulloch, who worked for the national bank, refused to pay the tax. Maryland sued McCulloch, who in turn appealed to the Supreme Court. Chief Justice John Marshall's opinion is considered a classic statement on how the Constitution is to be interpreted, as well as a very significant federalist reading of the legislative powers of Congress.

Mr. Chief Justice MARSHALL delivered the opinion of the Court. . . .

The first question made in the cause is—has congress power to incorporate a bank? It has been truly said, that this can scarcely be considered as an open question, entirely unprejudiced by the former proceedings of the nation respecting it. The principle now contested was introduced at a very early period of our history, has been recognised by many successive legislatures, and has been acted upon by the judicial department, in cases of peculiar delicacy, as a law of undoubted obligation. . . .

The power now contested was exercised by the first congress elected under the present constitution. The bill for incorporating the Bank of the United States did not steal upon an unsuspecting legislature, and pass unobserved. Its principle was completely understood, and was opposed with equal zeal and ability. After being resisted, first, in the fair and open field of debate, and afterwards, in the executive cabinet, with as much persevering talent as any measure has ever

experienced, and being supported by arguments which convinced minds as pure and as intelligent as this country can boast, it became a law. The original act was permitted to expire; but a short experience of the embarrassments to which the refusal to revive it exposed the government, convinced those who were most prejudiced against the measure of its necessity, and induced the passage of the present law. It would require no ordinary share of intrepidity, to assert that a measure adopted under these circumstances, was a bold and plain usurpation, to which the constitution gave no countenance. . . .

This government is acknowledged by all, to be one of enumerated powers. The principle, that it can exercise only the powers granted to it, would seem too apparent, to have required to be enforced by all those arguments, which its enlightened friends, while it was depending before the people, found it necessary to urge; that principle is now universally admitted. But the question respecting the extent of the powers actually granted, is perpetually arising, and will probably continue to arise, so long as our system shall exist. In discussing these questions, the conflicting powers of the general and state governments must be brought into view, and the supremacy of their respective laws, when they are in opposition, must be settled.

If any one proposition could command the universal assent of mankind, we might expect it would be this—that the government of the Union, though limited in its powers, is supreme within its sphere of action. This would seem to result, necessarily, from its nature. It is the government of all; its powers are delegated by all; it represents all, and acts for all. Though any one state may be willing to control its operations, no state is willing to allow others to control them. The nation, on those subjects on which it can act, must necessarily bind its component parts. But this question is not left to mere reason: the people have, in express terms, decided it, by saying, "this constitution, and the laws of the United States, which shall be made in pursuance thereof," "shall be the supreme law of the land," and by requiring that the members of the state legislatures, and the officers of the executive and judicial departments of the states, shall take the oath of fidelity to it. The government of the United States, then, though limited in its powers, is supreme; and its laws, when made in pursuance of the constitution, form the supreme law of the land, "anything in the constitution or laws of any state to the contrary notwithstanding."

Among the enumerated powers, we do not find that of establishing a bank or creating a corporation. But there is no phrase in the instrument which, like the articles of confederation, excludes incidental or implied powers; and which requires that everything granted shall be expressly and minutely described. Even the 10th amendment, which was framed for the purpose of quieting the excessive jealousies which had been excited, omits the word "expressly," and declares only, that the powers "not delegated to the United States, nor prohibited to the states, are reserved to the states or to the people;" thus leaving the question, whether the particular power which may become the subject of contest, has been del-

egated to the one government, or prohibited to the other, to depend on a fair construction of the whole instrument. . . . A constitution, to contain an accurate detail of all the subdivisions of which its great powers will admit, and of all the means by which they may be carried into execution, would partake of the prolixity of a legal code, and could scarcely be embraced by the human mind. It would, probably, never be understood by the public. Its nature, therefore, requires, that only its great outlines should be marked, its important objects designated, and the minor ingredients which compose those objects, be deduced from the nature of the objects themselves. That this idea was entertained by the framers of the American constitution, is not only to be inferred from the nature of the instrument, but from the language. . . . In considering this question, then, we must never forget that it is a constitution we are expounding.

Although, among the enumerated powers of government, we do not find the word "bank" or "incorporation," we find the great powers, to lay and collect taxes; to borrow money; to regulate commerce; to declare and conduct a war; and to raise and support armies and navies. The sword and the purse, all the external relations, and no inconsiderable portion of the industry of the nation, are intrusted to its government. It can never be pretended, that these vast powers draw after them others of inferior importance, merely because they are inferior. Such an idea can never be advanced. But it may with great reason be contended, that a government, intrusted with such ample powers, on the due execution of which the happiness and prosperity of the nation so vitally depends, must also be intrusted with ample means for their execution. The power being given, it is the interest of the nation to facilitate its execution. It can never be their interest, and cannot be presumed to have been their intention, to clog and embarrass its execution, by withholding the most appropriate means. . . .

But the constitution of the United States has not left the right of congress to employ the necessary means, for the execution of the powers conferred on the government, to general reasoning. To its enumeration of powers is added, that of making "all laws which shall be necessary and proper, for carrying into execution the foregoing powers, and all other powers vested by this constitution, in the government of the United States, or in any department thereof." . . .

. . . Congress is not empowered by [this clause] to make all laws, which may have relation to the powers conferred on the government, but such only as may be "necessary and proper" for carrying them into execution. The word "necessary" is considered as controlling the whole sentence, and as limiting the right to pass laws for the execution of the granted powers, to such as are indispensable, and without which the power would be nugatory. That it excludes the choice of means, and leaves to congress, in each case, that only which is most direct and simple.

Is it true, that this is the sense in which the word "necessary" is always used? Does it always import an absolute physical necessity, so strong, that one thing to which another may be termed necessary, cannot exist without that other? We think it does not. If reference be had to its use, in the common affairs of the world, or in approved authors, we find that it frequently imports no more than that one thing is convenient, or useful, or essential to another. To employ the means necessary to an end, is generally understood as employing any means calculated to produce the end, and not as being confined to those single means, without which the end would be entirely unattainable. Such is the character of human language, that no word conveys to the mind, in all situations, one single definite idea; and nothing is more common than to use words in a figurative sense.

. . . The word "necessary" is of this description. It has not a fixed character, peculiar to itself. It admits of all degrees of comparison; and is often connected with other words, which increase or diminish the impression the mind receives of the urgency it imports. A thing may be necessary, very necessary, absolutely or indispensably necessary. . . . This word, then, like others, is used in various senses; and, in its construction, the subject, the context, the intention of the person using them, are all to be taken into view.

Let this be done in the case under consideration. The subject is the execution of those great powers on which the welfare of a nation essentially depends. It must have been the intention of those who gave these powers, to insure, so far as human prudence could insure, their beneficial execution. This could not be done, by confiding the choice of means to such narrow limits as not to leave it in the power of congress to adopt any which might be appropriate, and which were conducive to the end. This provision is made in a constitution, intended to endure for ages to come, and consequently, to be adapted to the various crises of human affairs. To have prescribed the means by which government should, in all future time, execute its powers, would have been to change, entirely, the character of the instrument, and give it the properties of a legal code. It would have been an unwise attempt to provide, by immutable rules, for exigencies which, if foreseen at all, must have been seen dimly, and which can be best provided for as they occur. To have declared, that the best means shall not be used, but those alone, without which the power given would be nugatory, would have been to deprive the legislature of the capacity to avail itself of experience, to exercise its reason, and to accommodate its legislation to circumstances. If we apply this principle of construction to any of the powers of the government, we shall find it so pernicious in its operation that we shall be compelled to discard it. . . .

The result of the most careful and attentive consideration bestowed upon this clause is, that if it does not enlarge, it cannot be construed to restrain the powers of congress, or to impair the right of the legislature to exercise its best judgment in the selection of measures to carry into execution the constitutional powers of the government. If no other motive for its insertion can be suggested, a sufficient one is found in the desire to remove all doubts respecting the right to legislate on that vast mass of incidental powers which must be involved in the constitution, if that instrument be not a splendid bauble.

We admit, as all must admit, that the powers of the government are limited, and that its limits are not to be transcended. But we think the sound construction of the constitution must allow to the national legislature that discretion, with respect to the means by which the powers it confers are to be carried into execution, which will enable that body to perform the high duties assigned to it, in the manner most beneficial to the people. Let the end be legitimate, let it be within the scope of the constitution, and all means which are appropriate, which are plainly adapted to that end, which are not prohibited, but consist with the letter and spirit of the constitution, are constitutional. . . .

After the most deliberate consideration, it is the unanimous and decided opinion of this court, that the act to incorporate the Bank of the United States is a law made in pursuance of the constitution, and is a part of the supreme law of the land. . . .

Source: 4 Wheaton (17 U.S.) 316 (1819). Also available in Gerald Gunther, ed., *John Marshall's Defense of McCulloch vs. Maryland* (Stanford: Stanford University Press, 1969).

Document 39   *Gibbons v. Ogden* (1824)

> *The Supreme Court decision in* Gibbons v. Ogden *lays the groundwork for an expansive reading of Congress's powers under the interstate commerce clause. Aaron Ogden had been granted an exclusive license by New York to operate his steamboat between New York City and New Jersey. Thomas Gibbons also operated a ferry in the same waters. Ogden sued in a New York court to stop Gibbons, claiming that his license gave him exclusive rights to the route. Gibbons claimed that he was operating under a congressional statute regulating coastal vessels. The New York courts upheld Ogden's claim, so Gibbons appealed to the U.S. Supreme Court. The Court's decision, in favor of Gibbons, became the classic statement on the definition of commerce.*

Mr. Chief Justice MARSHALL delivered the opinion of the Court. . . .

. . . "Congress shall have power to regulate commerce with foreign nations, and among the several States, and with the Indian tribes." . . .

We are now arrived at the inquiry-What is this power?

It is the power to regulate; that is, to prescribe the rule by which commerce is to be governed. This power, like all others vested in Congress, is complete in itself, may be exercised to its utmost extent, and acknowledges no limitations, other than are prescribed in the constitution. These are expressed in plain terms, and do not affect the questions which arise in this case, or which have been discussed at the bar. If, as has always been understood, the sovereignty of Congress, though limited to specified objects, is plenary as to those objects, the power over commerce with foreign nations, and among the several States, is vested in Congress as absolutely as it would be in a single government, having in its constitution the same restrictions on the exercise of the power as are found in the constitution of the United States. The wisdom and the discretion of Congress, their identity with the people, and the influence which their constituents possess at elections, are, in this, as in many other instances, as that, for example, of declaring war, the sole restraints on which they have relied, to secure them from its abuse. They are the restraints on which the people must often rely solely, in all representative governments.

The power of Congress, then, comprehends navigation, within the limits of every State in the Union; so far as that navigation may be, in any manner, connected with "commerce with foreign nations, or among the several States, or with the Indian tribes." It may, of consequence, pass the jurisdictional line of New-York, and act upon the very waters to which the prohibition now under consideration applies.

. . . The sole question is, can a State regulate commerce with foreign nations and among the States, while Congress is regulating it?

. . . It is obvious, that the government of the Union, in the exercise of its express powers, that, for example, of regulating commerce with foreign nations and among the States, may use means that may also be employed by a State, in the exercise of its acknowledged powers; that, for example, of regulating commerce within the State. If Congress license vessels to sail from one port to another, in the same State, the act is supposed to be, necessarily, incidental to the power expressly granted to Congress, and implies no claim of a direct power to regulate the purely internal commerce of a State, or to act directly on its system of police. So, if a State, in passing laws on subjects acknowledged to be within its control, and with a view to those subjects, shall adopt a measure of the same character with one which Congress may adopt, it does not derive its authority from the particular power which has been granted, but from some other, which remains with the State, and may be executed by the same means. All experience shows, that the same measures, or measures scarcely distinguishable from each other, may flow from distinct powers; but this does not prove that the powers themselves are identical. Although the means used in their execution may sometimes approach each other so nearly as to be confounded, there are other situations in which they are sufficiently distinct to establish their individuality.

In our complex system, presenting the rare and difficult scheme of one general government, whose action extends over the whole, but which possesses only certain enumerated powers; and of numerous State governments, which retain and exercise all powers not delegated to the Union, contests respecting power must arise. Were it even otherwise, the measures taken by the respective governments to execute their acknowledged powers, would often be of the same description, and might, sometimes, interfere. This, however, does not prove that the one is exercising, or has a right to exercise, the powers of the other. . . .

Since . . . in exercising the power of regulating their own purely internal affairs, whether of trading or police, the States may sometimes enact laws, the validity of which depends on their interfering with, and being contrary to, an act of Congress passed in pursuance of the constitution, the Court will enter upon the inquiry, whether the laws of New-York, as expounded by the highest tribunal of that State, have, in their application to this case, come into collision with an act of Congress, and deprived a citizen of a right to which that act entitles him. Should this collision exist, it will be immaterial whether those laws were passed in virtue of a concurrent power "to regulate commerce with foreign nations and among the several States," or, in virtue of a power to regulate their domestic trade and police. In one case and the other, the acts of New-York must yield to the law of Congress; and the decision sustaining the privilege they confer, against a right given by a law of the Union, must be erroneous. . . .

But the framers of our constitution foresaw this state of things, and provided for it, by declaring the supremacy not only of itself, but of the laws made in pursuance of it. . . . The appropriate application of that part of the clause which confers the same supremacy on laws and treaties, is to such acts of the State Legislatures as do not transcend their powers, but, though enacted in the execution of acknowledged State powers, interfere with, or are contrary to the laws of Congress, made in pursuance of the constitution, or some treaty made under the authority of the United States. In every such case, the act of Congress, or the treaty, is supreme; and the law of the State, though enacted in the exercise of powers not controverted, must yield to it. . . .

Powerful and ingenious minds, taking, as postulates, that the powers expressly granted to the government of the Union, are to be contracted by construction, into the narrowest possible compass, and that the original powers of the States are retained, if any possible construction will retain them, may, by a course of well digested, but refined and metaphysical reasoning, founded on these premises, explain away the constitution of our country, and leave it, a magnificent structure, indeed, to look at, but totally unfit for use. They may so entangle and perplex the understanding, as to obscure principles, which were before thought quite plain, and induce doubts where, if the mind were to pursue its own course, none would be perceived. In such a case, it is peculiarly necessary to recur to safe and fundamental principles to sustain those principles, and when sustained, to make them the tests of the arguments to be examined. . . .

Source: 9 Wheaton (22 U.S.) 1 (1824).

Document 40   *The Prize Cases* (1863)

When the Civil War began in April 1861, President Abraham Lincoln imposed on Southern ports a blockade without congressional approval, which would ultimately be granted in a special session of Congress. The owners of several captured ships brought suit in federal court claiming that the blockade was illegal and that their property had been unlawfully confiscated. Their suits failed in the lower courts, so they appealed to the Supreme Court. The cases have legitimized the notion that the president must be able to act in an emergency without prior congressional authorization. In fact, Lincoln's actions during the early days of the war are often cited as evidence of such a need and the potential dangers if immediate action is denied.

Mr. Justice GRIER delivered the opinion of the Court. . . .

. . . 1st. Had the President a right to institute a blockade of ports in possession of persons in armed rebellion against the Government, on the principles of international law, as known and acknowledged among civilized States? . . .

The parties belligerent in a public war are independent nations. But it is not necessary to constitute war, that both parties should be acknowledged as independent nations or sovereign States. A war may exist where one of the belligerents, claims sovereign rights as against the other.

Insurrection against a government may or may not culminate in an organized rebellion, but a civil war always begins by insurrection against the lawful authority of the Government. A civil war is never solemnly declared; it becomes such by its accidents—the number, power, and organization of the persons who originate and carry it on. When the party in rebellion occupy and hold in a hostile manner a certain portion of territory; have declared their independence; have cast off their allegiance; have organized armies; have commenced hostilities against their former sovereign, the world acknowledges them as belligerents, and the contest a war. They claim to be in arms to establish their liberty and independence, in order to become a sovereign State, while the sovereign party treats them as insurgents and rebels who owe allegiance, and who should be punished with death for their treason. . . .

As a civil war is never publicly proclaimed, eo nomine, against insurgents, its actual existence is a fact in our domestic history which the Court is bound to notice and to know. . . .

By the Constitution, Congress alone has the power to declare a national or foreign war. It cannot declare war against a State, or any number of States, by virtue of any clause in the Constitution. The Constitution confers on the President the whole Executive power. He is bound to take care that the laws be faithfully executed. He is Commander-in-chief of the Army and Navy of the United States, and of the militia of the several States when called into the actual service of the United States. He has no power to initiate or declare a war either against a foreign nation or a domestic State. But by the Acts of Congress of February 28th, 1795, and 3d of March, 1807, he is authorized to call out the militia and use the military and naval forces of the United States in case of invasion by foreign nations, and to suppress insurrection against the government of a State or of the United States.

If a war be made by invasion of a foreign nation, the President is not only authorized but bound to resist force by force. He does not initiate the war, but is bound to accept the challenge without waiting for any special legislative authority. And whether the hostile party be a foreign invader, or States organized in rebellion, it is none the less a war, although the declaration of it be "unilateral." . . . After . . . official recognition [of war] by the sovereign, a citizen of a foreign State is estopped to deny the existence of a war with all its consequences as regards neutrals. They cannot ask a Court to affect a technical ignorance of the existence of a war, which

all the world acknowledges to be the greatest civil war known in the history of the human race, and thus cripple the arm of the Government and paralyze its power by subtle definitions and ingenious sophisms.

The law of nations is also called the law of nature; it is founded on the common consent as well as the common sense of the world. It contains no such anomalous doctrine as that which this Court are now for the first time desired to pronounce, to wit: That insurgents who have risen in rebellion against their sovereign, expelled her Courts, established a revolutionary government, organized armies, and commenced hostilities, are not enemies because they are traitors; and a war levied on the Government by traitors, in order to dismember and destroy it, is not a war because it is an "insurrection."

Whether the President in fulfilling his duties, as Commander-in-chief, in suppressing an insurrection, has met with such armed hostile resistance, and a civil war of such alarming proportions as will compel him to accord to them the character of belligerents, is a question to be decided by him, and this Court must be governed by the decisions and acts of the political department of the Government to which this power was entrusted. "He must determine what degree of force the crisis demands." The proclamation of blockade is itself official and conclusive evidence to the Court that a state of war existed which demanded and authorized a recourse to such a measure, under the circumstances peculiar to the case. . . .

If it were necessary to the technical existence of a war, that it should have a legislative sanction, we find it in almost every act passed at the extraordinary session of the Legislature of 1861, which was wholly employed in enacting laws to enable the Government to prosecute the war with vigor and efficiency. And finally, in 1861, we find Congress "ex majore cautela" and in anticipation of such astute objections, passing an act "approving, legalizing, and making valid all the acts, proclamations, and orders of the President, &c., as if they had been issued and done under the previous express authority and direction of the Congress of the United States." . . .

On this first question therefore we are of the opinion that the President had a right, *jure belli*, to institute a blockade of ports in possession of the States in rebellion, which neutrals are bound to regard. . . .

Source: 2 Black (67 U.S.) 635 (1863).

Document 41   *Ex parte Milligan* (1866)

Article 1 of the Constitution authorizes Congress to suspend the writ of habeas corpus if necessary in an emergency. In 1862 President Abraham Lincoln suspended the writ and ordered that those disloyal to the Union be tried in military courts. The next year Congress passed legislation endorsing the suspension. Lambdin P. Milligan was an active Confederate sympathizer in Indiana, a state not in rebellion but where there was considerable sympathy for the Confederacy. He was arrested and sentenced to death by a military commission. He appealed to a federal circuit court for a writ of habeas corpus and a declaration that the military commissions were unconstitutional. The circuit court certified the questions to the Supreme Court. The Court's decision stands as an important statement about the rule of law in times of emergency.

Mr. Justice DAVIS delivered the opinion of the Court. . . .

Milligan insists that said military commission had no jurisdiction to try him upon the charges preferred, or upon any charges whatever; because he was a citizen of the United States and the State of Indiana, and had not been, since the commencement of the late Rebellion, a resident of any of the States whose citizens were arrayed against the government, and that the right of trial by jury was guaranteed to him by the Constitution of the United States. . . .

1st. "On the facts stated in said petition and exhibits, ought a writ of habeas corpus to be issued?"

2d. "On the facts stated in said petition and exhibits, ought the said Lambdin P. Milligan to be discharged from custody as in said petition prayed?"

3d. "Whether, upon the facts stated in said petition and exhibits, the military commission mentioned therein had jurisdiction legally to try and sentence said Milligan in manner and form as in said petition and exhibits is stated?" . . .

But Milligan claimed his discharge from custody by virtue of the act of Congress "relating to habeas corpus, and regulating judicial proceedings in certain cases," approved March 3d, 1863. Did that act confer jurisdiction on the Circuit Court of Indiana to hear this case?

In interpreting a law, the motives which must have operated with the legislature in passing it are proper to be considered. This law was passed in a time of great national peril, when our heritage of free government was in danger. An armed rebellion against the national authority, of greater proportions than history affords an example of, was raging; and the public safety required that the privilege of the writ of habeas corpus should be suspended. The President had practically suspended it, and detained suspected persons in custody without trial; but his authority to do this was questioned. It was claimed that Congress alone could exercise this power; and that the legislature, and not the President, should judge of the political considerations on which the right to suspend it rested. The privilege of this great writ had never before been withheld from the citizen; and as the exigence of the times demanded immediate action, it was of the highest importance that the lawfulness of the suspension should be fully established. It was under these circumstances, which were such as to arrest the attention of the country, that this law was passed. The President was authorized by it to suspend the privilege of the writ of habeas corpus, whenever, in his judgment, the public safety required; and he did, by proclamation, bearing date the 15th of September, 1863, reciting, among other things, the authority of this statute, suspend it. The suspension of the writ does not authorize the arrest of any one, but simply denies to one arrested the privilege of this writ in order to obtain his liberty. . . . The controlling question in the case is this: Upon the facts stated in Milligan's petition, and the exhibits filed, had the military commission mentioned in it jurisdiction, legally, to try and sentence him? Milligan, not a resident of one of the rebellious states, or a prisoner of war, but a citizen of Indiana for twenty years past, and never in the military or naval service, is, while at his home, arrested by the military power of the United States, imprisoned, and, on certain criminal charges preferred against him, tried, convicted, and sentenced to be hanged by a military commission, organized under the direction of the military commander of the military district of Indiana. Had this tribunal the legal power and authority to try and punish this man?

No graver question was ever considered by this court, nor one which more nearly concerns the rights of the whole people; for it is the birthright of every American citizen when charged with crime, to be tried and punished according to law. The power of punishment is, alone through the means which the laws have provided for that purpose, and if they are ineffectual, there is an immunity from punishment, no matter how great an offender the individual may be, or how much his crimes may have shocked the sense of justice of the country, or endangered its safety. By the protection of the law human rights are secured; withdraw that protection, and they are at the mercy of wicked rulers or the clamor of an excited people. If there was law to justify this military trial, it is not our province to interfere; if there was not, it is our duty to declare the nullity of the whole proceedings. The decision of this question does not depend on argument or judicial precedents, numerous and highly illustrative as they are. These precedents inform us of the extent of the struggle to preserve liberty and to relieve those in civil life from military trials. The founders of our government were familiar with the history of that struggle; and secured in a written constitution every right which the people had wrested from power during a contest of ages. By that Constitution and the laws authorized by it this question must be determined. The provisions of that instrument on the administration of criminal justice are too plain and direct, to leave room for misconstruction or doubt of their true meaning. Those applicable to this case are found in that clause of the original Constitution which says, "That the trial of all crimes, except in case of impeachment, shall be by jury;" and in the fourth, fifth, and sixth articles of the amendments. The fourth proclaims the right to be secure in person and effects against unreasonable search and seizure; and directs that a judicial warrant shall not issue "without proof of probable cause supported by oath or affirmation." The fifth declares "that no person shall be held to answer for a capital or otherwise infamous crime unless on presentment by a grand jury, except in cases arising in the land or naval forces, or in the militia, when in actual service in time of war or public danger, nor be deprived of life, liberty, or property, without due process of law." And the sixth guarantees the right of trial by jury, in such manner and with such regulations that with upright judges, impartial juries, and an able bar, the innocent will be saved and the guilty punished. It is in these words: "In all criminal prosecutions the accused shall enjoy the right to a speedy and public trial by an impartial jury of the state and district wherein the crime shall have been committed, which district shall have been previously ascertained by law, and to be informed of the nature and cause of the accusation, to be confronted with the witnesses against him, to have compulsory process for obtaining witnesses in his favor, and to have the assistance of counsel for his defence."

These securities for personal liberty thus embodied, were such as wisdom and experience had demonstrated to be necessary for the protection of those accused of crime. And so strong was the sense of the country of their importance, and so jealous were the people that these rights, highly prized, might be denied them by implication, that when the original Constitution was proposed for adoption it encountered severe opposition; and, but for the belief that it would be so amended as to embrace them, it would never have been ratified.

. . . The Constitution of the United States is a law for rulers and people, equally in war and in peace, and covers with the shield of its protection all classes of men, at all times, and under all circumstances. No doctrine, involving more pernicious consequences, was ever invented by the wit of man than that any of its provisions can be suspended during any of the great exigencies of government. Such a doctrine leads directly to anarchy or despotism, but the theory of necessity on which it is based is false; for the government, within the Constitution, has all the powers granted to it, which are necessary to preserve its existence; as has been happily proved by the result of the great effort to throw off its just authority.

Have any of the rights guaranteed by the Constitution been violated in the case of Milligan? and if so, what are they?

Every trial involves the exercise of judicial power; and from what source did not military commission that tried him derive their authority? Certainly no part of judicial power of the country was conferred on them; because the Constitution expressly vests it "in one supreme court

and such inferior courts as the Congress may from time to time ordain and establish," and it is not pretended that the commission was a court ordained and established by Congress. They cannot justify on the mandate of the President; because he is controlled by law, and has his appropriate sphere of duty, which is to execute, not to make, the laws; and there is "no unwritten criminal code to which resort can be had as a source of jurisdiction."

But it is said that the jurisdiction is complete under the "laws and usages of war."

It can serve no useful purpose to inquire what those laws and usages are, whence they originated, where found, and on whom they operate; they can never be applied to citizens in states which have upheld the authority of the government, and where the courts are open and their process unobstructed. This court has judicial knowledge that in Indiana the Federal authority was always unopposed, and its courts always open to hear criminal accusations and redress grievances; and no usage of war could sanction a military trial there for any offence whatever of a citizen in civil life, in nowise connected with the military service. Congress could grant no such power; and to the honor of our national legislature be it said, it has never been provoked by the state of the country even to attempt its exercise. One of the plainest constitutional provisions was, therefore, infringed when Milligan was tried by a court not ordained and established by Congress, and not composed of judges appointed during good behavior.

Why was he not delivered to the Circuit Court of Indiana to be proceeded against according to law? No reason of necessity could be urged against it; because Congress had declared penalties against the offences charged, provided for their punishment, and directed that court to hear and determine them. And soon after this military tribunal was ended, the Circuit Court met, peacefully transacted its business, and adjourned. It needed no bayonets to protect it, and required no military aid to execute its judgments. It was held in a state, eminently distinguished for patriotism, by judges commissioned during the Rebellion, who were provided with juries, upright, intelligent, and selected by a marshal appointed by the President. The government had no right to conclude that Milligan, if guilty, would not receive in that court merited punishment; for its records disclose that it was constantly engaged in the trial of similar offences, and was never interrupted in its administration of criminal justice. If it was dangerous, in the distracted condition of affairs, to leave Milligan unrestrained of his liberty, because he "conspired against the government, afforded aid and comfort to rebels, and incited the people to insurrection," the law said arrest him, confine him closely, render him powerless to do further mischief; and then present his case to the grand jury of the district, with proofs of his guilt, and, if indicted, try him according to the course of the common law. If this had been done, the Constitution would have been vindicated, the law of 1863 enforced, and the securities for personal liberty preserved and defended. . . .

The discipline necessary to the efficiency of the army and navy, required other and swifter modes of trial than are furnished by the common law courts; and, in pursuance of the power conferred by the Constitution, Congress has declared the kinds of trial, and the manner in which they shall be conducted, for offences committed while the party is in the military or naval service. Every one connected with these branches of the public service is amenable to the jurisdiction which Congress has created for their government, and, while thus serving, surrenders his right to be tried by the civil courts. All other persons, citizens of states where the courts are open, if charged with crime, are guaranteed the inestimable privilege of trial by jury. This privilege is a vital principle, underlying the whole administration of criminal justice; it is not held by sufferance, and cannot be frittered away on any plea of state or political necessity. When peace prevails, and the authority of the government is undisputed, there is no difficulty of preserving the safeguards of liberty; for the ordinary modes of trial are never neglected, and no one wishes it otherwise; but if society is disturbed by civil commotion—if the passions of men are aroused and the restraints of law weakened, if not disregarded—these safeguards need, and should receive, the watchful care of those intrusted with the guardianship of the Constitution and laws. In no other way can we transmit to posterity unimpaired the blessings of liberty, consecrated by the sacrifices of the Revolution.

It is claimed that martial law covers with its broad mantle the proceedings of this military commission. The proposition is this: that in a time of war the commander of an armed force (if in his opinion the exigencies of the country demand it, and of which he is to judge), has the power, within the lines of his military district, to suspend all civil rights and their remedies, and subject citizens as well as soldiers to the rule of his will; and in the exercise of his lawful authority cannot be restrained, except by his superior officer or the President of the United States.

If this position is sound to the extent claimed, then when war exists, foreign or domestic, and the country is subdivided into military departments for mere convenience, the commander of one of them can, if he chooses, within his limits, on the plea of necessity, with the approval of the Executive, substitute military force for and to the exclusion of the laws, and punish all persons, as he thinks right and proper, without fixed or certain rules.

. . . Martial law, established on such a basis, destroys every guarantee of the Constitution, and effectually renders the "military independent of and superior to the civil power". . . .

This nation, as experience has proved, cannot always remain at peace, and has no right to expect that it will always have wise and humane rulers, sincerely attached to the principles of the Constitution. Wicked men, ambitious of power, with hatred of liberty and contempt of law, may fill the place once occupied by Washington and Lincoln; and if this right is conceded, and the calamities of war again befall us, the dangers to human liberty are frightful to contemplate. If our fathers had failed to provide for just such a contingency, they would have been false to the trust reposed in them. They . . . secured the inheritance they had fought to maintain, by incorporating in a written constitution the safeguards which time had proved were essential to its preservation. Not one of these safeguards can the President, or Congress, or the Judiciary disturb, except the one concerning the writ of habeas corpus.

It is essential to the safety of every government that, in a great crisis, like the one we have just passed through, there should be a power somewhere of suspending the writ of habeas corpus. In every war, there are men of previously good character, wicked enough to counsel their fellow-citizens to resist the measures deemed necessary by a good government to sustain its just authority and overthrow its enemies; and their influence may lead to dangerous combinations. In the emergency of the times, an immediate public investigation according to law may not be possible; and yet, the period to the country may be too imminent to suffer such persons to go at large. Unquestionably, there is then an exigency which demands that the government, if it should see fit in the exercise of a proper discretion to make arrests, should not be required to produce the persons arrested in answer to a

writ of habeas corpus. The Constitution goes no further. . . .

It is difficult to see how the safety for the country required martial law in Indiana. If any of her citizens were plotting treason, the power of arrest could secure them, until the government was prepared for their trial, when the courts were open and ready to try them. It was as easy to protect witnesses before a civil as a military tribunal; and as there could be no wish to convict, except on sufficient legal evidence, surely an ordained and established court was better able to judge of this than a military tribunal composed of gentlemen not trained to the profession of the law.

It follows, from what has been said on this subject, that there are occasions when martial rule can be properly applied. . . . Martial rule can never exist where the courts are open, and in the proper and unobstructed exercise of their jurisdiction. It is also confined to the locality of actual war. Because, during the late Rebellion it could have been enforced in Virginia, where the national authority was overturned and the courts driven out, it does not follow that it should obtain in Indiana, where that authority was never disputed, and justice was always administered. And so in the case of a foreign invasion, martial rule may become a necessity in one state, when, in another, it would be "mere lawless violence." . . .

Source: 4 Wallace (71 U.S.) 2 (1866).

Document 42   *Hammer v. Dagenhart* (1918)

The decision in Gibbons v. Ogden *(1824) (Doc. 39), while clearly federal in its outlook, did make a distinction between interstate and intrastate commerce. Chief Justice John Marshall suggested that had the framers intended for Congress's power to extend to all commerce, they would not have used the qualifying language of "among the several states." This distinction gained importance in the late nineteenth and early twentieth centuries as Congress began to more aggressively regulate commerce, and the Supreme Court, now more sympathetic to states' rights and less sympathetic to the regulation of business, limited Congress's ability to exert control in the areas of manufacturing, production, farming, and mining. In* Hammer v. Dagenhart, *the Court thwarted temporarily efforts to regulate child labor through legislation under the commerce clause.*

Mr. Justice DAY delivered the opinion of the Court. . . .

Commerce "consists of intercourse and traffic . . . and includes the transportation of persons and property, as well as the purchase, sale and exchange of commodities." The making of goods and the mining of coal are not commerce, nor does the fact that these things are to be afterwards shipped, or used in interstate commerce, make their production a part thereof.

Over interstate transportation, or its incidents, the regulatory power of Congress is ample, but the production of articles, intended for interstate commerce, is a matter of local regulation. . . . If it were otherwise, all manufacture intended for interstate shipment would be brought under federal control to the practical exclusion of the authority of the states, a result certainly not contemplated by the framers of the Constitution when they vested in Congress the authority to regulate commerce among the States.

It is further contended that the authority of Congress may be exerted to control interstate commerce in the shipment of child made goods because of the effect of the circulation of such goods in other states where the evil of this class of labor has been recognized by local legislation, and the right to thus employ child labor has been more rigorously restrained than in the state of production. In other words, that the unfair competition, thus engendered, may be controlled by closing the channels of interstate commerce to manufacturers in those states where the local laws do not meet what Congress deems to be the more just standard of other states.

There is no power vested in Congress to require the states to exercise their police power so as to prevent possible unfair competition. Many causes may co-operate to give one state, by reason of local laws or conditions, an economic advantage over others. The commerce clause was not intended to give to Congress a general authority to equalize such conditions. In some of the states laws have been passed fixing minimum wages for women, in others the local law regulates the hours of labor of women in various employments. Business done in such states may be at an economic disadvantage when compared with states which have no such regulations; surely, this fact does not give Congress the power to deny transportation in interstate commerce to those who carry on business where the hours of labor and the rate of compensation for women have not been fixed by a standard in use in other states and approved by Congress. . . .

The grant of authority over a purely federal matter was not intended to destroy the local power always existing and carefully reserved to the states in the Tenth Amendment to the Constitution. . . .

In interpreting the Constitution it must never be forgotten that the nation is made up of states to which are entrusted the powers of local government. And to them and to the people the powers not expressly delegated to the national government are reserved. The power of the states to regulate their purely internal affairs by such laws as seem wise to the local authority is inherent and has never been surrendered to the general government. To sustain this statute would not be in our judgment a recognition of the lawful exertion of congressional authority over interstate commerce, but would sanction an invasion by the federal power of the control of a matter purely local in its character, and over which no authority has been delegated to Congress in conferring the power to regulate commerce among the states. . . .

Mr. Justice HOLMES, dissenting. . . .

. . . Regulation means the prohibition of something, and when interstate commerce is the matter to be regulated I cannot doubt that the regulation may prohibit any part of such commerce that Congress sees fit to forbid. . . .

The notion that prohibition is any less prohibition when applied to things now thought evil I do not understand. But if there is any matter upon which civilized countries have agreed—far more unanimously than they have with regard to intoxicants and some other matters over which

this country is now emotionally aroused—it is the evil of premature and excessive child labor. I should have thought that if we were to introduce our own moral conceptions where is my opinion they do not belong, this was preeminently a case for upholding the exercise of all its powers by the United States.

But I had thought that the propriety of the exercise of a power admitted to exist in some cases was for the consideration of Congress alone and that this Court always had disavowed the right to intrude its judgment upon questions of policy or morals. It is not for this Court to pronounce when prohibition is necessary to regulation if it ever may be necessary—to say that it is permissible as against strong drink but not as against the product of ruined lives. The Act does not meddle with anything belonging to the States. They may regulate their internal affairs and their domestic commerce as they like. But when they seek to send their products across the State line they are no longer within their rights. If there were no Constitution and no Congress their power to cross the line would depend upon their neighbors. Under the Constitution such commerce belongs not to the States but to Congress to regulate. It may carry out its views of public policy whatever indirect effect they may have upon the activities of the States. . . . The national welfare as understood by Congress may require a different attitude within its sphere from that of some self-seeking State. It seems to me entirely constitutional for Congress to enforce its understanding by all the means at its command. . . .

Source: 247 U.S. 251 (1918).

Document 43   *Myers v. United States* (1926)

While the appointments clause in Article 2 of the Constitution states in fairly specific detail the procedure for appointing primary "Officers of the United States" and "inferior" positions that Congress may create, the Constitution says nothing about the removal of such officers other than outlining the impeachment process. The First Congress debated extensively this issue as it relates to primary officers, such as cabinet secretaries, and concluded that the removal power was vested in the executive. This decision, however, did not resolve the conflict between Congress and the president over removal of a whole host of officers sanctioned by Congress over the years. President Andrew Jackson's use of the removal power to appoint his supporters to government positions helped motivate Congress to institute civil service reform that would make "spoils system" appointments less likely. Congressional efforts to limit the president's removal powers heightened conflict between the branches.

One of the primary issues in President Andrew Johnson's impeachment was his removal of the secretary of war in violation of the Tenure of Office Act of 1867. This statute was eventually repealed, but other statutes creating various positions and agencies continued to limit the president's removal power, including the statute creating postmasters, the position at the center of the controversy in Myers v. United States. *The Supreme Court's decision connects the president's power to remove executive officers to the constitutional duty to take care that the laws are faithfully executed. It stands as a classic statement about the unitary executive and the presidential need to control all those who exercise executive power. The opinions in the case offer extensive treatment of the historical debate over removal powers.*

Mr. Chief Justice TAFT delivered the opinion of the Court.

This case presents the question whether under the Constitution the President has the exclusive power of removing executive officers of the United States whom he has appointed by and with the advice and consent of the Senate.

Myers . . . was on July 21, 1917, appointed by the President, by and with the advice and consent of the Senate, to be a postmaster of the first class at Portland, Or., for a term of four years. On January 20, 1920, Myers' resignation was demanded. He refused the demand. On February 2, 1920, he was removed from office by order of the Postmaster General, acting by direction of the President. . . . He protested to the department against his removal, and continued to do so until the end of his term. He pursued no other occu-

pation and drew compensation for no other service during the interval. On April 21, 1921, he brought this suit in the Court of Claims for his salary from the date of his removal. . . . The Court of Claims gave judgment against Myers and this is an appeal from that judgment. . . .

By the sixth section of the Act of Congress of July 12, 1876, under which Myers was appointed with the advice and consent of the Senate as a first-class postmaster, it is provided that:

Postmasters of the first, second, and third classes shall be appointed and may be removed by the President by and with the advice and consent of the Senate, and shall hold their offices for four years unless sooner removed or suspended according to law.

The Senate did not consent to the President's removal of Myers during his term. If this statute in its requirement that his term should be four years unless sooner removed by the President by and with the consent of the Senate is valid, the appellant, Myers' administratrix, is entitled to recover his unpaid salary for his full term and the judgment of the Court of Claims must be reversed. The government maintains that the requirement is invalid, for the reason that under article 2 of the Constitution the President's power of removal of executive officers appointed by him with the advice and consent of the Senate is full and complete without consent of the Senate. . . .

The question where the power of removal of executive officers appointed by the President by and with the advice and consent of the Senate was vested, was presented early in the first session of the First Congress. There is no express provision respecting removals in the Constitution, except as section 4 of article 2, above quoted, provides for removal from office by impeachment. The subject was not discussed in the Constitutional Convention. . . .

The vesting of the executive power in the President was essentially a grant of the power to execute the laws. But the President alone and unaided could not execute the laws. He must execute them by the assistance of subordinates. This view has since been repeatedly affirmed by this court. As he is charged specifically to take care that they be faithfully executed, the reasonable implication, even in the absence of express words, was that as part of his executive power he should select those who were to act for him under his direction in the execution of the laws. The further implication must be, in the absence of any express limitation respecting removals, that as his selection of administrative officers is essential to the execution of the laws by him, so must be his power of removing those for whom he cannot continue to be responsible. . . .

The requirement of the second section of article 2 that the Senate should advise and consent to the presidential appointments, was to be strictly construed. The words of section 2, following the general grant of executive power under section 1, were either an enumeration and emphasis of specific functions of the executive,

not all inclusive, or were limitations upon the general grant of the executive power, and as such, being limitations, should not be enlarged beyond the words used. The executive power was given in general terms strengthened by specific terms where emphasis was regarded as appropriate, and was limited by direct expressions where limitation was needed, and the fact that no express limit was placed on the power of removal by the executive was convincing indication that none was intended. . . .

Under section 2 of article 2 . . . the power of appointment by the executive is restricted in its exercise by the provision that the Senate, a part of the legislative branch of the government, may check the action of the executive by rejecting the officers he selects. Does this make the Senate part of the removing power? And this, after the whole discussion in the House is read attentively, is the real point which was considered and decided in the negative by the vote already given.

The history of the clause by which the Senate was given a check upon the President's power of appointment makes it clear that it was not prompted by any desire to limit removals. . . . The power to prevent the removal of an officer who has served under the President is different from the authority to consent to or reject his appointment. When a nomination is made, it may be presumed that the Senate is, or may become, as well advised as to the fitness of the nominee as the President, but in the nature of things the defects in ability or intelligence or loyalty in the administration of the laws of one who has served as an officer under the President are facts as to which the President, or his trusted subordinates, must be better informed than the Senate, and the power to remove him may therefor be regarded as confined for very sound and practical reasons, to the governmental authority which has administrative control. The power of removal is incident to the power of appointment, not to the power of advising and consenting to appointment, and when the grant of the executive power is enforced by the express mandate to take care that the laws be faithfully executed, it emphasizes the necessity for including within the executive power as conferred the exclusive power of removal. . . .

The constitutional construction that excludes Congress from legislative power to provide for the removal of superior officers finds support in the second section of article 2. By it the appointment of all officers, whether superior or inferior, by the President is declared to be subject to the advice and consent of the Senate. In the absence of any specific provision to the contrary, the power of appointment to executive office carries with it, as a necessary incident, the power of removal. Whether the Senate must concur in the removal is aside from the point we now are considering. That point is that by the specific constitutional provision for appointment of executive officers with its necessary incident of removal, the power of appointment and removal is clearly provided for by the Constitution, and the legislative power of Congress in respect to both is excluded save by the specific exception as to inferior offices in the clause that follows. This is "but the Congress may by law vest the appointment of such inferior officers, as they think proper, in the President alone, in the Courts of Law, or in the Heads of Departments." These words, it has been held by this court, give to Congress the power to limit and regulate removal of such inferior officers by heads of departments when it exercises its constitutional power to lodge the power of appointment with them. Here then is an express provision introduced in words of exception for the exercise by Congress of legislative power in the matter of appointments and removals in the case of inferior executive officers. The phrase, "But Congress may by law vest," is equivalent to "excepting that Congress may by law vest." By the plainest implication it excludes congressional dealing with appointments or removals of executive officers not falling within the exception and leaves unaffected the executive power of the President to appoint and remove them.

A reference of the whole power of removal to general legislation by Congress is quite out of keeping with the plan of government devised by the framers of the Constitution. It could never have been intended to leave to Congress unlimited discretion to vary fundamentally the operation of the great independent executive branch of government and thus most seriously to weaken it. It would be a delegation by the convention to Congress of the function of defining the primary boundaries of another of the three great divisions of government. The inclusion of removals of executive officers in the executive power vested in the President by article 2 according to its usual definition, and the implication of his power of removal of such officers from the provision of section 2 expressly recognizing in him the power of their appointment, are a much more natural and appropriate source of the removing power.

It is reasonable to suppose also that had it been intended to give to Congress power to regulate or control removals in the manner suggested, it would have been included among the specifically enumerated legislative powers in article 1, or in the specified limitations on the executive power in article 2. The difference between the grant of legislative power under article 1 to Congress which is limited to powers therein enumerated, and the more general grant of the executive power to the President under article 2 is significant. The fact that the executive power is given in general terms strengthened by specific terms where emphasis is appropriate, and limited by direct expressions where limitation is needed, and that no express limit is placed on the power of removal by the executive is a convincing indication that none was intended. . . .

In all such cases, the discretion to be exercised is that of the President in determining the national public interest and in directing the action to be taken by his executive subordinates to protect it. In this field his cabinet officers must do his will. He must place in each member of his official family, and his chief executive subordinates, implicit faith. The moment that he loses confidence in the intelligence, ability, judgment, or loyalty of any one of them, he must have the power to remove him without delay. To require him to file charges and submit them to the consideration of the Senate might make impossible that unity and co-ordination in executive administration essential to effective action. . . .

The power to remove inferior executive officers, like that to remove superior executive officers, is an incident of the power to appoint them, and is in its nature an executive power. The authority of Congress given by the excepting clause to vest the appointment of such inferior officers in the heads of departments carries with it authority incidentally to invest the heads of departments with power to remove. It has been the practice of Congress to do so and this court has recognized that power. The court also has recognized in the Perkins Case that Congress, in committing the appointment of such inferior officers to the heads of departments, may prescribe incidental regulations controlling and restricting the latter in the exercise of the power of removal. But the court never has held, nor reasonably could hold, although it is argued to the contrary on behalf of the appellant, that the excepting clause enables Congress to draw to itself, or to either branch of it, the power to remove or the right to participate in the exercise of that power. To do this would be to go beyond the words and implications of that clause, and to infringe the constitutional principle of the separation of governmental powers.

Assuming, then, the power of Congress to regulate removals as incidental to the exercise of its constitutional power to vest appointments of inferior officers in the heads of departments, certainly so long as Congress does not exercise that power, the power of removal must remain where the Constitution places it, with the President, as part of the executive power. . . .

We come now to a period in the history of the government when both houses of Congress attempted to reverse this constitutional construction, and to subject the power of removing executive officers appointed by the President and confirmed by the Senate to the control of the Senate, indeed finally to the assumed power in

Congress to place the removal of such officers anywhere in the government.

This reversal grew out of the serious political difference between the two houses of Congress and President Johnson. There was a two-thirds majority of the Republican party, in control of each house of Congress, which resented what it feared would be Mr. Johnson's obstructive course in the enforcement of the reconstruction measures in respect to the states whose people had lately been at war against the national government. This led the two houses to enact legislation to curtail the then acknowledged powers of the President. It is true that during the latter part of Mr. Lincoln's term two important voluminous acts were passed, each containing a section which seemed inconsistent with the legislative decision of 1789; but they were adopted without discussion of the inconsistency and were not tested by executive or judicial inquiry. The real challenge to the decision of 1789 was begun by the Act of July 13, 1866, forbidding dismissals of Army and Navy officers in time of peace without a sentence by court-martial, which this court in *Blake v. United States* attributed to the growing difference between President Johnson and Congress. . . .

But the chief legislation in support of the reconstruction policy of Congress was the Tenure of Office Act of March 2, 1867, providing that all officers appointed by and with the consent of the Senate should hold their offices until their successors should have in like manner been appointed and qualified; that certain heads of departments, including the Secretary of War, should hold their offices during the term of the President by whom appointed and one month thereafter, subject to removal by consent of the Senate. The Tenure of Office Act was vetoed, but it was passed over the veto. The House of Representatives preferred articles of impeachment against President Johnson for refusal to comply with, and for conspiracy to defeat, the legislation above referred to, but he was acquitted for lack of a two- thirds vote for conviction in the Senate. . . .

[I]t is contended that, since the passage of the Tenure of Office Act, there has been general acquiescence by the executive in the power of Congress to forbid the President alone to remove executive officers, an acquiescence which has changed any formerly accepted constitutional construction to the contrary. . . .

In the use of congressional legislation to support or change a particular construction of the Constitution by acquiescence, its weight for the purpose must depend not only upon the nature of the question, but also upon the attitude of the executive and judicial branches of the government, as well as upon the number of instances in the execution of the law in which opportunity for objection in the courts or elsewhere is afforded. When instances which actually involve the question are rare or have not in fact occurred, the weight of the mere presence of acts on the statute book for a considerable time as showing general acquiescence in the legislative assertion of a questioned power is minimized. . . .

What, then, are the elements that enter into our decision of this case? We have, first, a construction of the Constitution made by a Congress which was to provide by legislation for the organization of the government in accord with the Constitution which had just then been adopted, and in which there were, as Representatives and Senators, a considerable number of those who had been members of the convention that framed the Constitution and presented it for ratification. It was the Congress that launched the government. It was the Congress that rounded out the Constitution itself by the proposing of the first 10 amendments, which had in effect been promised to the people as a consideration for the ratification. It was the Congress in which Mr. Madison, one of the first in the framing of the Constitution, led also in the organization of the government under it. It was a Congress whose constitutional decisions have always been regarded, as they should be regarded, as of the greatest weight in the interpretation of that fundamental instrument. This construction was fol-

lowed by the legislative department and the executive department continuously for 73 years. . . . This court has repeatedly laid down the principle that a contemporaneous legislative exposition of the Constitution, when the founders of our government and framers of our Constitution were actively participating in public affairs, acquiesced in for a long term of years, fixes the construction to be given its provisions.

We are now asked to set aside this construction thus buttressed and adopt an adverse view, because the Congress of the United States did so during a heated political difference of opinion between the then President and the majority leaders of Congress over the reconstruction measures adopted as a means of restoring to their proper status the states which attempted to withdraw from the Union at the time of the Civil War. . . .

For the reasons given, we must therefore hold that the provision of the law of 1876 by which the unrestricted power of removal of first-class postmasters is denied to the President is in violation of the Constitution and invalid. This leads to an affirmance of the judgment of the Court of Claims.

Judgment affirmed.

The separate opinion of Mr. Justice McREYNOLDS.

A certain repugnance must attend the suggestion that the President may ignore any provision of an act of Congress under which he has proceeded. He should promote and not subvert orderly government. The serious evils which followed the practice of dismissing civil officers as caprice or interest dictated, long permitted under congressional enactments, are known to all. It brought the public service to a low estate and caused insistent demand for reform. "Indeed, it is utterly impossible not to feel, that, if this unlimited power of removal does exist, it may be made, in the hands of a bold and designing man, of high ambition and feeble principles, an instrument of the worst oppression and most vindictive vengeance." . . .

. . . Nothing short of language clear beyond serious disputation should be held to clothe the President with authority wholly beyond congressional control arbitrarily to dismiss every officer whom he appoints except a few judges. There are no such words in the Constitution, and the asserted inference conflicts with the heretofore accepted theory that this government is one of carefully enumerated powers under an intelligible charter. . . .

If the phrase "executive power" infolds the one now claimed, many others heretofore totally unsuspected may lie there awaiting future supposed necessity, and no human intelligence can define the field of the President's permissible activities. "A masked battery of constructive powers would complete the destruction of liberty."

. . . Constitutional provisions should be interpreted with the expectation that Congress will discharge its duties no less faithfully than the executive will attend to his. The Legislature is charged with the duty of making laws for orderly administration obligatory upon all. It possesses supreme power over national affairs and may wreck as well as speed them. It holds the purse; every branch of the government functions under statutes which embody its will; it may impeach and expel all civil officers. The duty is upon it "to make all laws which shall be necessary and proper for carrying into execution" all powers of the federal government. We have no such thing as three totally distinct and independent departments; the others must look to the legislative for direction and support. "In republican government the legislative authority necessarily predominates." Perhaps the chief duty of the President is to carry into effect the will of Congress through such instrumentalities as it has chosen to provide. Arguments, therefore, upon the assumption that Congress may willfully impede executive action are not important. . . .

The Legislature may create post offices and prescribe qualifications, duties, compensation, and term. And it may protect the incumbent in the enjoyment of his term unless in some way restrained therefrom. The real question, therefore, comes to this: Does any constitutional provision definitely limit the otherwise plenary power of Congress over postmasters, when they are appointed by the President with the consent of the Senate? The question is not the much-mooted one whether the Senate is part of the appointing power under the Constitution and therefore must participate in removals.

Here the restriction is imposed by statute alone and thereby made a condition of the tenure. I suppose that beyond doubt Congress could authorize the Postmaster General to appoint all postmasters and restrain him in respect of removals.

Concerning the insistence that power to remove is a necessary incident of the President's duty to enforce the laws, it is enough now to say: The general duty to enforce all laws cannot justify infraction of some of them. Moreover, Congress, in the exercise of its unquestioned power, may deprive the President of the right either to appoint or to remove any inferior officer, by vesting the authority to appoint in another. Yet in that event his duty touching enforcement of the laws would remain. He must utilize the force which Congress gives. He cannot, without permission, appoint the humblest clerk or expend a dollar of the public funds.

It is well to emphasize that our present concern is with the removal of an "inferior officer," within article 2, 2, of the Constitution, which the statute positively prohibits without consent of the Senate. This is no case of mere suspension. The demand is for salary, and not for restoration to the service. We are not dealing with an ambassador, public minister, consul, judge, or "superior officer." Nor is the situation the one which arises when the statute creates an office without a specified term, authorizes appointment and says nothing of removal. In the latter event, under long-continued practice and supposed early legislative construction, it is now accepted doctrine that the President may remove at pleasure. This is entirely consistent with implied legislative assent; power to remove is commonly incident to the right to appoint when not forbidden by law. But there has never been any such usage where the statute prescribed restrictions. From its first session down to the last one Congress has consistently asserted its power to prescribe conditions concerning the removal of inferior officers. The executive has habitually observed them, and this court has affirmed the power of Congress therein. . . .

The Constitution empowers the President to appoint ambassadors, other public ministers, consuls, judges of the Supreme Court and superior officers, and no statute can interfere therein. But Congress may authorize both appointment and removal of all inferior officers without regard to the President's wishes—even in direct opposition to them. This important distinction must not be overlooked. And consideration of the complete control which Congress may exercise over inferior officers is enough to show the hollowness of the suggestion that a right to remove them may be inferred from the President's duty to "take care that the laws be faithfully executed." He cannot appoint any inferior officer, however humble, without legislative authorization; but such officers are essential to execution of the laws. Congress may provide as many or as few of them as it likes. It may place all of them beyond the President's control; but this would not suspend his duty concerning faithful execution of the laws. Removals, however important, are not so necessary as appointments.

. . . If the framers of the Constitution had intended "the executive power," in article 2, 1, to include all power of an executive nature, they would not have added the carefully defined grants of section 2. They were scholarly men, and it exceeds belief" that the known advocates in the convention for a jealous grant and cautious definition of federal powers should have silently permitted the introduction of words and phrases in a sense rendering fruitless the restrictions and definitions elaborated by them." Why say, the President shall be commander-in-chief; may require opinions in writing of the principal officers in each of the executive departments; shall have power to grant reprieves and pardons; shall give information to Congress concerning the state of the union; shall receive ambassadors; shall take care that the laws be faithfully executed—if all of these things and more had already been vested in him by the general words? The Constitution is exact in statement. That the general words of a grant are limited, when followed by those of special import, is an established canon; and an accurate writer would hardly think of emphasizing a general grant by adding special and narrower ones without explanation. . . .

Mr. Justice BRANDEIS, dissenting.

The simple answer to the argument is this: The ability to remove a subordinate executive officer, being an essential of effective government, will, in the absence of express constitutional provision to the contrary, be deemed to have been vested in some person or body. But it is not a power inherent in a chief executive. The President's power of removal from statutory civil inferior offices, like the power of appointment to them, comes immediately from Congress. It is true that the exercise of the power of removal is said to be an executive act, and that when the Senate grants or withholds consent to a removal by the President, it participates in an executive act. But the Constitution has confessedly granted to Congress the legislative power to create offices, and to prescribe the tenure thereof; and it has not in terms denied to Congress the power to control removals. To prescribe the tenure involves prescribing the conditions under which incumbency shall cease. For the possibility of removal is a condition or qualification of the tenure. When Congress provides that the incumbent shall hold the office for four years unless sooner removed with the consent of the Senate, it prescribes the term of the tenure. . . .

The separation of the powers of government did not make each branch completely autonomous. It left each in some measure, dependent upon the others, as it left to each power to exercise, in some respects, functions in their nature executive, legislative and judicial. Obviously the President cannot secure full execution of the laws, if Congress denies to him adequate means of doing so. Full execution may be defeated because Congress declines to create offices indispensable for that purpose; or because Congress, having created the office, declines to make the indispensable appropriation; or because Congress, having both created the office and made the appropriation, prevents, by restrictions which it imposes, the appointment of officials who in quality and character are indispensable to the efficient execution of the law. If, in any such way, adequate means are denied to the President, the fault will lie with Congress. The President performs his full constitutional duty, if, with the means and instruments provided by Congress and within the limitations prescribed by it, he uses his best endeavors to secure the faithful execution of the laws enacted. . . .

Checks and balances were established in order that this should be "a government of laws and not of men." . . . The doctrine of the separation of powers was adopted by the convention of 1787 not to promote efficiency but to preclude the exercise of arbitrary power. The purpose was not to avoid friction, but, by means of the inevitable friction incident to the distribution of the governmental powers among three departments, to save the people from autocracy. In order to prevent arbitrary executive action, the Constitution provided in terms that presidential appointments be made with the consent of the Senate, unless Congress should otherwise provide; and this clause was construed by Alexander Hamilton in The Federalist, No. 77, as requiring like consent to removals. Limiting further executive prerogatives customary in monarchies, the Constitution empowered Congress to vest the appointment of inferior officers, "as we think proper, in the President alone, in the Courts of Law, or in the Heads of Departments." Nothing in support of the claim of uncontrollable power can be inferred from the silence of the convention of 1787 on the subject of removal. . . .

Mr. Justice HOLMES, dissenting. . . .

We have to deal with an office that owes its existence to Congress and that Congress may abolish tomorrow. Its duration and the pay attached to it while it lasts depend on Congress alone. Congress alone confers on the President the power to appoint to it and at any time may transfer the power to other hands. With such power over its own creation, I have no more trouble in believing that Congress has power to prescribe a term of life for it free from any interference than I have in accepting the undoubted power of Congress to decree its end. I have equally little trouble in accepting its power to prolong the tenure of an incumbent until Congress or the Senate shall have assented to his removal. The duty of the President to see that the laws be executed is a duty that does not go beyond the laws or require him to achieve more than Congress sees fit to leave within his power.

Source: 272 U.S. 52 (1926).

Document 44   *A. L. A. Schechter Poultry Corp. v. United States* (1935)

One of the central constitutional questions in the rise of the modern administrative state was Congress's ability to delegate legislative power to other agencies and actors to empower them to write rules and regulations governing their area of jurisdiction. In early cases testing the validity of independent regulatory agencies, the Supreme Court upheld the ability to delegate, as long as Congress provided clear guidance and "intelligible principles" by which the discretion of those exercising the power would be channeled.

A. L. A. Schechter Poultry Corp. v. United States challenged the National Industrial Recovery Act of 1933, which was designed to address the problems of the Great Depression by establishing codes for fair business practice and regulating working conditions. The provision in question delegated power to the president and the National Recovery Administration to establish the codes for the various industries that operated in interstate commerce. The A. L. A. Schechter Poultry Corporation ran afoul of the Live Poultry Code established under this process. While Schechter stands for the notion that Congress may not delegate unlimited power to executive actors, it in fact appears to have had little impact beyond the conflict between President Franklin Delano Roosevelt and the Supreme Court over the New Deal. Once Roosevelt prevailed, the Court took a decidedly "hands-off" approach to the question of the breadth of delegation, contributing to the rise of the modern administrative state.*

Mr. Chief Justice HUGHES delivered the opinion of the Court. . . .

. . . The Question of the Delegation of Legislative Power—We recently had occasion to review the pertinent decisions and the general principles which govern the determination of this question. The Constitution provides that "All legislative powers herein granted shall be vested in a Congress of the United States, which shall consist of a Senate and House of Representatives." And the Congress is authorized "To make all Laws which shall be necessary and proper for carrying into Execution" its general powers. The Congress is not permitted to abdicate or to transfer to others the essential legislative functions with which it is thus vested. We have repeatedly recognized the necessity of adapting legislation to complex conditions involving a host of details with which the national Legislature cannot deal directly. We pointed out in the Panama Refining Company

Case that the Constitution has never been regarded as denying to Congress the necessary resources of flexibility and practicality, which will enable it to perform its function in laying down policies and establishing standards, while leaving to selected instrumentalities the making of subordinate rules within prescribed limits and the determination of facts to which the policy as declared by the Legislature is to apply. But we said that the constant recognition of the necessity and validity of such provisions, and the wide range of administrative authority which has been developed by means of them, cannot be allowed to obscure the limitations of the authority to delegate, if our constitutional system is to be maintained.

Accordingly, we look to the statute to see whether Congress has overstepped these limitations—whether Congress in authorizing "codes of fair competition" has itself established the standards of legal obligation, thus performing its essential legislative function, or, by the failure to enact such standards, has attempted to transfer that function to others. . . .

The question, then, turns upon the authority which section 3 of the Recovery Act vests in the President to approve or prescribe. If the codes have standing as penal statutes, this must be due to the effect of the executive action. But Congress cannot delegate legislative power to the President to exercise an unfettered discretion to make whatever laws he thinks may be needed or advisable for the rehabilitation and expansion of trade or industry.

Accordingly we turn to the Recovery Act to ascertain what limits have been set to the exercise of the President's discretion: First, the President, as a condition of approval, is required to find that the trade or industrial associations or groups which propose a code "impose no inequitable restrictions on admission to membership" and are "truly representative." That condition, however, relates only to the status of the initiators of the new laws and not to the permissible scope of such laws. Second, the President is required to find that the code is not "designed to promote monopolies or to eliminate or oppress small enterprises and will not operate to discriminate against them." And to this is added a proviso that the code "shall not permit monopolies or monopolistic practices." But these restrictions leave virtually untouched the field of policy envisaged by section 1, and, in that wide field of legislative possibilities, the proponents of a code, refraining from monopolistic designs, may roam at will, and the President may approve or disapprove their proposals as he may see fit. That is the precise effect of the further finding that the President is to make—that the code "will tend to effectuate the policy of this title." While this is called a finding, it is really but a statement of an opinion as to the general effect upon the promotion of trade or industry of a scheme of laws. These are the only findings which Congress has made essential in order to put into operation a legislative code having the aims described in the "Declaration of Policy." . . .

Such a sweeping delegation of legislative power finds no support in the decisions upon which the government especially relies. . . .

To summarize and conclude upon this point: Section 3 of the Recovery Act is without precedent. It supplies no standards for any trade, industry, or activity. It does not undertake to prescribe rules of conduct to be applied to particular states of fact determined by appropriate administrative procedure. Instead of prescribing rules of conduct, it authorizes the making of codes to prescribe them. For that legislative undertaking, section 3 sets up no standards, aside from the statement of the general aims of rehabilitation, correction, and expansion described in section 1. In view of the scope of that broad declaration and of the nature of the few restrictions that are imposed, the discretion of the President in approving or prescribing codes, and thus enacting laws for the government of trade and industry throughout the country, is virtually unfettered. We think that the code-making authority thus conferred is an unconstitutional delegation of legislative power. . . .

Mr. Justice CARDOZO (concurring).

The delegated power of legislation which has found expression in this code is not canalized within banks that keep it from overflowing. It is unconfined and vagrant, if I may borrow my own words in an earlier opinion.

. . . Here, in the case before us, is an attempted delegation not confined to any single act nor to any class or group of acts identified or described by reference to a standard. Here in effect is a roving commission to inquire into evils and upon discovery correct them. I have said that there is no standard, definite or even approximate, to which legislation must conform. Let me make my meaning more precise. If codes of fair competition are codes eliminating "unfair" methods of competition ascertained upon inquiry to prevail in one industry or another, there is no unlawful delegation of legislative functions when the President is directed to inquire into such practices and denounce them when discovered. For many years a like power has been committed to the Federal Trade Commission with the approval of this court in a long series of decisions. Delegation in such circumstances is born of the necessities of the occasion. The industries of the country are too many and diverse to make it possible for Congress, in respect of matters such as these, to legislate directly with adequate appreciation of varying conditions. Nor is the substance of the power changed because the President may act at the instance of trade or industrial associations having special knowledge of the facts. Their function is strictly advisory; it is the imprimatur of the President that begets the quality of law. . . .

Source: 295 U.S. 495 (1935)

Document 45   *Humphrey's Executor v. United States* (1935)

The decision in Myers v. United States *(1926) (Doc. 43) implied that the president's power of removal might also apply to officers of independent regulatory agencies if the president disagreed with their decisions. That particular issue arose in* Humphrey's Executor v. United States. *President Franklin Delano Roosevelt removed a member of the Federal Trade Commission for policy reasons, rather than those outlined in the authorizing statute. By 1935 the Supreme Court had demonstrated considerable concern about (some might say, hostility toward) the expansion of presidential power under Roosevelt's leadership. In the same year, for example, it struck down several New Deal statutes. In* Humphrey's *the Court drew a distinction between the removal power over "purely executive officers" (established in* Myers) *and those whom Congress intended to make independent of the executive and who were exercising "quasi-legislative" and "quasi-judicial" powers. The importance of this decision to the development of the modern administrative state was substantial.*

Mr. Justice SUTHERLAND delivered the opinion of the Court. . . .

William E. Humphrey, the decedent, on December 10, 1931, was nominated by President Hoover to succeed himself as a member of the Federal Trade Commission, and was confirmed by the United States Senate. He was duly commissioned for a term of seven years, expiring September 25, 1938; and, after taking the required oath of office, entered upon his duties. On July 25, 1933, President Roosevelt addressed a letter to the commissioner asking for his resignation, on the ground "that the aims and purposes of the Administration with respect to the work of the Commission can be carried out most effectively with personnel of my own selection," but disclaiming any reflection upon the commissioner personally or upon his services. The commissioner replied, asking time to consult his friends. After some further correspondence upon the subject, the President on August 31, 1933, wrote the commissioner expressing the hope that the resignation would be forthcoming, and saying: "You will, I know, realize that I do not feel that your mind and my mind go along together on either the policies or the administering of the Federal Trade Commission, and, frankly, I think it is best for the people of this country that I should have a full confidence."

The commissioner declined to resign; and on October 7, 1933, the President wrote him: "Effective as of this date you are hereby removed from the office of Commissioner of the Federal Trade Commission."

Humphrey never acquiesced in this action, but continued thereafter to insist that he was still a member of the commission, entitled to perform its duties and receive the compensation provided by law at the rate of $10, 000 per annum. Upon these and other facts set forth in the certificate, . . . the following questions are certified:

"1. Do the provisions of section 1 of the Federal Trade Commission Act, stating that 'any commissioner may be removed by the President for inefficiency, neglect of duty, or malfeasance in office', restrict or limit the power of the President to remove a commissioner except upon one or more of the causes named?

"If the foregoing question is answered in the affirmative, then—

"2. If the power of the President to remove a commissioner is restricted or limited . . . is such a restriction or limitation valid under the Constitution of the United States?" . . .

The commission is to be nonpartisan; and it must, from the very nature of its duties, act with entire impartiality. It is charged with the enforcement of no policy except the policy of the law. Its duties are neither political nor executive, but predominantly quasi judicial and quasi legislative. Like the Interstate Commerce Commission, its members are called upon to exercise the trained judgment of a body of experts "appointed by law and informed by experience."

The legislative reports in both houses of Congress clearly reflect the view that a fixed term was necessary to the effective and fair administration of the law. In the report to the Senate the Senate Committee on Interstate Commerce, in support of the bill which afterwards became the act in question, after referring to the provision fixing the term of office at seven years, so arranged that the membership would not be subject to complete change at any one time, said: "The work of this commission will be of a most exacting and difficult character, demanding persons who have experience in the problems to be met—that is, a proper knowledge of both the public requirements and the practical affairs of industry. It is manifestly desirable that the terms of the commissioners shall be long enough to give them an opportunity to acquire the expertness in dealing with these special questions concerning industry that comes from experience." The report declares that one advantage which the commission possessed over the Bureau of Corporations (an executive subdivision in the Department of Commerce which was abolished by the act) lay in the fact of its independence, and that it was essential that the commission should not be open to the suspicion of partisan direction. . . .

Thus, the language of the act, the legislative reports, and the general purposes of the legislation as reflected by the debates, all combine to demonstrate the congressional intent to create a body of experts who shall gain experience by length of service; a body which shall be independent of executive authority, except in its selection, and free to exercise its judgment without the leave or hindrance of any other official or any department of the government. To the accomplishment of these purposes, it is clear that Congress was of the opinion that length and certainty of tenure would vitally contribute. And to hold that, nevertheless, the members of the commission continue in office at the mere will of the President, might be to thwart, in large measure, the very ends which Congress sought to realize by definitely fixing the term of office.

We conclude that the intent of the act is to limit the executive power of removal to the causes enumerated, the existence of none of which is claimed here; and we pass to the second question.

Second. To support its contention that the removal provision of section 1, as we have just construed it, is an unconstitutional interference with the executive power of the President, the government's chief reliance is *Myers v. United States.* That case has been so recently decided, and the prevailing and dissenting opinions so fully review the general subject of the power of executive removal, that further discussion would add little of value to the wealth of material there collected. . . . Nevertheless, the narrow point actually decided was only that the President had power to remove a postmaster of the first class, without the advice and consent of the Senate as required by act of Congress. In the course of the opinion of the court, expressions occur which tend to sustain the government's contention, but these are beyond the point involved and, therefore, do not come within the rule of stare decisis. In so far as they are out of harmony with the views here set forth, these expressions are disapproved. . . .

The office of a postmaster is so essentially unlike the office now involved that the decision in the Myers Case cannot be accepted as controlling our decision here. A postmaster is an executive officer restricted to the performance of executive functions. He is charged with no duty at all related to either the legislative or judicial power. . . . Putting aside dicta, which may be followed if sufficiently persuasive but which are not controlling, the necessary reach of the decision goes far enough to include all purely executive officers. It goes no farther; much less does it include an officer who occupies no place in the executive department and who exercises no part of the executive power vested by the Constitution in the President.

The Federal Trade Commission is an administrative body created by Congress to carry into effect legislative policies embodied in the statute in accordance with the legislative standard therein prescribed, and to perform other specified duties as a legislative or as a judicial aid. Such a body cannot in any proper sense be characterized as an arm or an eye of the executive. Its duties are performed without executive leave and, in the contemplation of the statute, must be free from executive control. In administering the provisions of the statute in respect of "unfair methods of competition," that is to say, in filling in and administering the details embodied by that general standard, the commission acts in part quasi legislatively and in part quasi judicially. In making investigations and reports thereon for the information of Congress under section 6, in aid of the legislative power, it acts as a legislative agency. Under section 7, which authorizes the commission to act as a master in chancery under rules prescribed by the court, it acts as an agency of the judiciary. To the extent that it exercises any executive function, as distinguished from executive power in the constitutional sense, it does so in the discharge and effectuation of its quasi legislative or quasi judicial powers, or as an agency of the legislative or judicial departments of the government. If Congress is without authority to prescribe causes for removal of members of the trade commission and limit executive power of removal accordingly, that power at once becomes practically all-inclusive in respect of civil officers with the exception of the judiciary provided for by the Constitution. . . .

We are thus confronted with the serious question whether not only the members of these quasi legislative and quasi judicial bodies, but the judges of the legislative Court of Claims, exercising judicial power, continue in office only at the pleasure of the President.

We think it plain under the Constitution that illimitable power of removal is not possessed by the President in respect of officers of the character of those just named. The authority of Congress, in creating quasi legislative or quasi judicial agencies, to require them to act in discharge of their duties independently of executive control cannot well be doubted; and that authority includes, as an appropriate incident, power to fix the period during which they shall continue, and to forbid their removal except for cause in the meantime. For it is quite evident that one who holds his office only during the pleasure of another cannot be depended upon to maintain an attitude of independence against the latter's will.

The fundamental necessity of maintaining each of the three general departments of government entirely free from the control or coercive influence, direct or indirect, of either of the others, has often been stressed and is hardly open to serious question. So much is implied in the very fact of the separation of the powers of these departments by the Constitution; and in the rule which recognizes their essential coequality. The sound application of a principle that makes one master in his own house precludes him from imposing his control in the house of another who is master there. . . .

The power of removal here claimed for the President falls within this principle, since its coercive influence threatens the independence of a commission, which is not only wholly disconnected from the executive department, but which, as already fully appears, was created by Congress as a means of carrying into operation legislative and judicial powers, and as an agency of the legislative and judicial departments. . . .

Source: 295 U.S. 602 (1935).

Document 46   ***United States v. Curtiss-Wright Export Corp.*** **(1936)**

In 1934 Congress passed a resolution against the sale of arms to combatants in the Chaco War, a small regional conflict between Bolivia and Paraguay. The resolution authorized the president to prohibit sales based on whether he thought the cause of peace would be advanced by such an embargo. President Franklin Delano Roosevelt imposed the prohibition, and the Curtiss-Wright Export Corporation was found to have violated the order by selling arms to Bolivia. At trial, Curtiss-Wright contended that the resolution unconstitutionally delegated power to the executive without adequate standards for guiding the president's discretion. In A. L. A. Schechter Poultry Corp. v. United States (1935) (Doc. 44), the Supreme Court had struck down a piece of New Deal legislation regulating fair trade as an unconstitutional delegation of legislative power to the president. Justice George Sutherland's opinion in United States v. Curtiss-Wright Export Corp. draws the important distinction between the president's authority in domestic and foreign affairs that presidents have since used to justify foreign policy initiatives.

Mr. Justice SUTHERLAND delivered the opinion of the Court.

On January 27, 1936, an indictment was returned in the court below, the first count of which charges that appellees, beginning with the 29th day of May, 1934, conspired to sell in the United States certain arms of war, namely, fifteen machine guns, to Bolivia, a country then engaged in armed conflict in the Chaco, in violation of the Joint Resolution of Congress approved May 28, 1934, and the provisions of a proclamation issued on the same day by the President of the United States pursuant to authority conferred by section 1 of the resolution. . . . The Joint Resolution follows: "Resolved by the Senate and House of Representatives of the United States of America in Congress assembled, That if the President finds that the prohibition of the sale of arms and munitions of war in the United States to those countries now engaged in armed conflict in the Chaco may contribute to the reestablishment of peace between those countries, and if after consultation with the governments of other American Republics and with their cooperation, as well as that of such other governments as he may deem necessary, he makes proclamation to that effect, it shall be unlawful to sell, except under such limitations and exceptions as the President prescribes, any arms or munitions of war in any place in the United States to the countries now engaged in that armed conflict, or to any person, company, or association acting in the interest of either country, until otherwise ordered by the President or by Congress." . . .

First. It is contended that by the Joint Resolution the going into effect and continued operation of the resolution was conditioned (a) upon the President's judgment as to its beneficial effect upon the re-establishment of peace between the countries engaged in armed conflict in the Chaco; (b) upon the making of a proclamation, which was left to his unfettered discretion, thus constituting an attempted substitution of the President's will for that of Congress; (c) upon the making of a proclamation putting an end to the operation of the resolution, which again was left to the President's unfettered discretion; and (d) further, that the extent of its operation in particular cases was subject to limitation and exception by the President, controlled by no standard. In each of these particulars, appellees urge that Congress abdicated its essential functions and delegated them to the Executive.

. . . The determination which we are called to make . . . is whether the Joint Resolution, as applied to that situation, is vulnerable to attack under the rule that forbids a delegation of the lawmaking power. . . .

It is important to bear in mind that we are here dealing not alone with an authority vested in the President by an exertion of legislative power, but with such an authority plus the very delicate, plenary and exclusive power of the President as the sole organ of the federal government in the field of international relations— a power which does not require as a basis for its exercise an act of Congress, but which, of course, like every other governmental power, must be exercised in subordination to the applicable provisions of the Constitution. It is quite apparent that if, in the maintenance of our international relations, embarrassment—perhaps serious embarrassment—is to be avoided and success for our aims achieved, congressional legislation which is to be made effective through negotiation and inquiry within the international field must often accord to the President a degree of discretion and freedom from statutory restriction which would not be admissible were domestic affairs alone involved. Moreover, he, not Congress, has the better opportunity of knowing the conditions which prevail in foreign countries, and especially is this true in time of war. He has his confidential sources of information. He has his agents in the form of diplomatic, consular and other officials. Secrecy in respect of information gathered by them may be highly necessary, and the premature disclosure of it productive of harmful results. . . . The marked difference between foreign affairs and domestic affairs in this respect is recognized by both houses of Congress in the very form of their requisitions for information from the executive departments. In the case of every department except the Department of State, the resolution directs the official to furnish the information. In the case of the State Department, dealing with foreign affairs, the President is requested to furnish the information "if not incompatible with the public interest." A statement that to furnish the information is not compatible with the public interest rarely, if ever, is questioned.

When the President is to be authorized by legislation to act in respect of a matter intended to affect a situation in foreign territory, the legislator properly bears in mind the important consideration that the form of the President's action—or, indeed, whether he shall act at all—may well depend, among other things, upon the nature of the confidential information which he has or may thereafter receive, or upon the effect which his action may have upon our foreign relations. This consideration, in connection with what we have already said on the subject discloses the unwisdom of requiring Congress in this field of governmental power to lay down narrowly definite standards by which the President is to be governed. . . .

In the light of the foregoing observations, it is evident that this court should not be in haste to apply a general rule which will have the effect of condemning legislation like that under review as constituting an unlawful delegation of legislative power. The principles which justify such legislation find overwhelming support in the unbroken legislative practice which has prevailed almost from the inception of the national government to the present day. . . .

The result of holding that the joint resolution here under attack is void and unenforceable as constituting an unlawful delegation of legislative power would be to stamp this multitude of comparable acts and resolutions as likewise invalid. And while this court may not, and should not, hesitate to declare acts of Congress, however many times repeated, to be unconstitutional if beyond all rational doubt it finds them to be so, an impressive array of legislation such as we have just set forth, enacted by nearly every Congress from the beginning of our national existence to the present day, must be given unusual weight in the process of reaching a correct determination of the problem. A legislative practice such as we have here, evidenced not by only occasional instances, but marked by the movement of a steady stream for a century and a half of time, goes a long way in the direction of proving the presence of unassailable ground for the constitutionality of the practice, to be found in the origin and history of the power involved, or in its nature, or in both combined. . . .

Source: 299 U.S. 304 (1936).

Document 47   **United States v. Darby (1941)**

The Supreme Court's continued resistance to national efforts at regulation of the economy eventually led to the "constitutional crisis" of 1937. Key pieces of New Deal legislation had been struck down in 1935 and 1936. After President Franklin Delano Roosevelt's landslide reelection in 1936, he proposed a plan to get "new blood" on the Supreme Court. His "Court-packing" plan would have added one new justice for each justice over the age of seventy who chose not to retire (see Docs. 17 and 31). The plan failed in the Democrat-controlled Congress, but in the end Roosevelt got what he wanted: Justice Owen Roberts, who had been voting in the five-member majority striking down New Deal legislation, voted with the dissenters to uphold the National Labor Relations Board's oversight of the steel industry in NLRB v. Jones & Laughlin Steel Corp. (1937). The next year Congress, relying on its interstate commerce powers, passed the Fair Labor Standards Act (FSLA) to regulate the minimum wage and the maximum hours of workers. Within a few years, justices who had resisted the New Deal had left the Court and been replaced by Roosevelt nominees. In 1941 the Court unanimously upheld the FSLA in United States v. Darby, and in doing so overruled the production exception used in Hammer v. Dagenhart (1918) (Doc. 42).

Mr. Justice STONE delivered the opinion of the Court.

The two principal questions raised by the record in this case are, first, whether Congress has constitutional power to prohibit the shipment in interstate commerce of lumber manufactured by employees whose wages are less than a prescribed minimum or whose weekly hours of labor at that wage are greater than a prescribed maximum, and, second, whether it has power to prohibit the employment of workmen in the production of goods "for interstate commerce" at other than prescribed wages and hours. A subsidiary question is whether in connection with such prohibitions Congress can require the employer subject to them to keep records showing the hours worked each day and week by each of his employees including those engaged "in the production and manufacture of goods to wit, lumber, for "interstate commerce." . . .

While manufacture is not of itself interstate commerce the shipment of manufactured goods interstate is such commerce and the prohibition of such shipment by Congress is indubitably a regulation of the commerce. The power to regulate commerce is the power "to prescribe the rule by which commerce is to be governed." It extends not only to those regulations which aid, foster and protect the commerce, but embraces those which prohibit it. It is conceded that the power of Congress to prohibit transportation in interstate commerce includes noxious articles, stolen articles, Kidnapped persons, and articles such as intoxicating liquor or convict made goods, traffic in which is forbidden or restricted by the laws of the state of destination.

But it is said that the present prohibition falls within the scope of none of these categories; that while the prohibition is nominally a regulation of the commerce its motive or purpose is regulation of wages and hours of persons engaged in manufacture, the control of which has been reserved to the states and upon which Georgia and some of the states of destination have placed no restriction; that the effect of the present statute

is not to exclude the prescribed articles from interstate commerce in aid of state regulation . . . but instead, under the guise of a regulation of interstate commerce, it undertakes to regulate wages and hours within the state contrary to the policy of the state which has elected to leave them unregulated.

The power of Congress over interstate commerce "is complete in itself, may be exercised to its utmost extent, and acknowledges no limitations, other than are prescribed by the constitution." That power can neither be enlarged nor diminished by the exercise or non-exercise of state power. Congress, following its own conception of public policy concerning the restrictions which may appropriately be imposed on interstate commerce, is free to exclude from the commerce articles whose use in the states for which they are destined it may conceive to be injurious to the public health, morals or welfare, even though the state has not sought to regulate their use. . . .

The motive and purpose of the present regulation are plainly to make effective the Congressional conception of public policy that interstate commerce should not be made the instrument of competition in the distribution of goods produced under substandard labor conditions, which competition is injurious to the commerce and to the states from and to which the commerce flows. The motive and purpose of a regulation of interstate commerce are matters for the legislative judgment upon the exercise of which the Constitution places no restriction and over which the courts are given no control. . . .

Whatever their motive and purpose, regulations of commerce which do not infringe some constitutional prohibition are within the plenary power conferred on Congress by the Commerce Clause. Subject only to that limitation, presently to be considered, we conclude that the prohibition of the shipment interstate of goods produced under the forbidden substandard labor conditions is within the constitutional authority of Congress. . . .

Without attempting to define the precise limits of the phrase, we think the acts alleged in the indictment are within the sweep of the statute. The obvious purpose of the Act was not only to prevent the interstate transportation of the proscribed product, but to stop the initial step toward transportation, production with the purpose of so transporting it. Congress was not unaware that most manufacturing businesses shipping their product in interstate commerce make it in their shops without reference to its ultimate destination and then after manufacture select some of it for shipment interstate and some intrastate according to the daily demands of their business, and that it would be practically impossible, without disrupting manufacturing businesses, to restrict the prohibited kind of production to the particular pieces of lumber, cloth, furniture or the like which later move in interstate rather than intrastate commerce. . . .

There remains the question whether such restriction on the production of goods for commerce is a permissible exercise of the commerce power. The power of Congress over interstate commerce is not confined to the regulation of commerce among the states. It extends to those activities intrastate which so affect interstate commerce or the exercise of the power of Congress over it as to make regulation of them appropriate means to the attainment of a legitimate end, the exercise of the granted power of Congress to regulate interstate commerce. . . .

Congress, having by the present Act adopted the policy of excluding from interstate commerce all goods produced for the commerce which do not conform to the specified labor standards, it may choose the means reasonably adapted to the attainment of the permitted end, even though they involve control of intrastate activities. Such legislation has often been sustained with respect to powers, other than the commerce power granted to the national government, when the means chosen, although not themselves within the granted power, were nevertheless deemed appropriate aids to the accomplishment of some purpose within an admitted power of the national government.

A familiar like exercise of power is the regulation of intrastate transactions which are so commingled with or related to interstate commerce that all must be regulated if the interstate commerce is to be effectively controlled. Similarly Congress may require inspection and preventive treatment of all cattle in a disease infected area in order to prevent shipment in interstate commerce of some of the cattle without the treatment. It may prohibit the removal, at destination, of labels required by the Pure Food & Drugs Act, to be affixed to articles transported in interstate commerce. And we have recently held that Congress in the exercise of its power to require inspection and grading of tobacco shipped in interstate commerce may compel such inspection and grading of all tobacco sold at local auction rooms from which a substantial part but not all of the tobacco sold is shipped in interstate commerce. . . .

REVERSED.

Source: 312 U.S. 100 (1941).

Document 48   *Korematsu v. United States* (1944)

After the attack by the Japanese on Pearl Harbor on December 7, 1941, President Franklin Delano Roosevelt, through executive order, established military zones in which military commanders were authorized to use curfews and exclusion to maintain security and order. Congress followed with legislative authorization. Under such authority the military commander on the West Coast rounded up aliens and citizens of Japanese origin or descent and removed them to internment camps inland. Toyosaburo Korematsu refused to comply with the exclusion order and was arrested and convicted. After losing his appeal to a federal circuit court, he sought review by the Supreme Court of the constitutionality of the orders. Citing the authority of Congress, the president, and military commanders in times of war, the majority of the Court upheld the conviction. In the long term, however, the dissenters' views prevailed. In 1988 Congress passed legislation for the payment of reparations to those who had been interned.

Mr. Justice BLACK delivered the opinion of the Court. . . .

In the light of the principles we announced in the Hirabayashi [v. United States (1943)] case, we are unable to conclude that it was beyond the war power of Congress and the Executive to exclude those of Japanese ancestry from the West Coast war area at the time they did. True, exclusion from the area in which one's home is located is a far greater deprivation than constant confinement to the home from 8 p.m. to 6 a.m. Nothing short of apprehension by the proper military authorities of the gravest imminent danger to the public safety can constitutionally justify either. But exclusion from a threatened area, no less than curfew, has a definite and close relationship to the prevention of espionage and sabotage. The military authorities, charged with the primary responsibility of defending our shores, concluded that curfew provided inadequate protection and ordered exclusion. They did so, as pointed out in our Hirabayashi opinion, in accordance with Congressional authority to the military to say who should, and who should not, remain in the threatened areas. . . .

Here, as in the Hirabayashi case, " . . . we cannot reject as unfounded the judgment of the military authorities and of Congress that there were disloyal members of that population, whose number and strength could not be precisely and quickly ascertained. We cannot say that the war-making branches of the Government did not have ground for believing that in a critical hour such persons could not readily be isolated and separately dealt with, and constituted a menace to the national defense and safety, which demanded that prompt and adequate measures be taken to guard against it." . . .

AFFIRMED.

Mr. Justice FRANKFURTER, concurring. . . .

The provisions of the Constitution which confer on the Congress and the President powers to enable this country to wage war are as much part of the Constitution as provisions looking to a nation at peace. . . . Therefore, the validity of action under the war power must be judged wholly in the context of war. That action is not to be stigmatized as lawless because like action in times of peace would be lawless. To talk about a military order that expresses an allowable judgment of war needs by those entrusted with the duty of conducting war as "an unconstitutional order" is to suffuse a part of the Constitution with an atmosphere of unconstitutionality. The respective spheres of action of military authorities and of judges are of course very different. But within their sphere, military authorities are no more outside the bounds of obedience to the Constitution than are judges within theirs. "The war power of the United States, like its other powers . . . is subject to applicable constitutional limitations." To recognize that military orders are "reasonably expedient military precautions" in time of war and yet to deny them constitutional legitimacy makes of the Constitution an instrument for dialetic subtleties not reasonably to be attributed to the hard-headed Framers, of whom a majority had had actual participation in war. If a military order such as that under review does not transcend the means appropriate for conducting war, such action by the military is as constitutional as would be any authorized action by the Interstate Commerce Commission within the limits of the constitutional power to regulate commerce. And being an exercise of the war power explicitly granted by the Constitution for safeguarding the national life by prosecuting war effectively, I find nothing in the Constitution which denies to Congress the power to enforce such a valid military order by making its violation an offense triable in the civil courts. To find that the Constitution does not forbid the military measures now complained of does not carry with it approval of that which Congress and the Executive did. That is their business, not ours. . . .

Mr. Justice MURPHY, dissenting. . . .

In dealing with matters relating to the prosecution and progress of a war, we must accord great respect and consideration to the judgments of the military authorities who are on the scene and who have full knowledge of the military facts. The scope of their discretion must, as a matter of necessity and common sense, be wide. And their judgments ought not to be overruled lightly by those whose training and duties ill-equip them to

deal intelligently with matters so vital to the physical security of the nation.

At the same time, however, it is essential that there be definite limits to military discretion, especially where martial law has not been declared. Individuals must not be left impoverished of their constitutional rights on a plea of military necessity that has neither substance nor support. Thus, like other claims conflicting with the asserted constitutional rights of the individual, the military claim must subject itself to the judicial process of having its reasonableness determined and its conflicts with other interests reconciled. . . .

The judicial test of whether the Government, on a plea of military necessity, can validly deprive an individual of any of his constitutional rights is whether the deprivation is reasonably related to a public danger that is so "immediate, imminent, and impending" as not to admit of delay and not to permit the intervention of ordinary constitutional processes to alleviate the danger. Civilian Exclusion Order No. 34, banishing from a prescribed area of the Pacific Coast "all persons of Japanese ancestry, both alien and non-alien," clearly does not meet that test. Being an obvious racial discrimination, the order deprives all those within its scope of the equal protection of the laws as guaranteed by the Fifth Amendment. It further deprives these individuals of their constitutional rights to live and work where they will, to establish a home where they choose and to move about freely. In excommunicating them without benefit of hearings, this order also deprives them of all their constitutional rights to procedural due process. Yet no reasonable relation to an "immediate, imminent, and impending" public danger is evident to support this racial restriction which is one of the most sweeping and complete deprivations of constitutional rights in the history of this nation in the absence of martial law.

It must be conceded that the military and naval situation in the spring of 1942 was such as to generate a very real fear of invasion of the Pacific Coast, accompanied by fears of sabotage and espionage in that area. The military command was therefore justified in adopting all reasonable means necessary to combat these dangers. In adjudging the military action taken in light of the then apparent dangers, we must not erect too high or too meticulous standards; it is necessary only that the action have some reasonable relation to the removal of the dangers of invasion, sabotage and espionage. But the exclusion, either temporarily or permanently, of all persons with Japanese blood in their veins has no such reasonable relation. And that relation is lacking because the exclusion order necessarily must rely for its reasonableness upon the assumption that all persons of Japanese ancestry may have a dangerous tendency to commit sabotage and espionage and to aid our Japanese enemy in other ways. It is difficult to believe that reason, logic or experience could be marshalled in support of such an assumption. . . .

. . . A military judgment based upon such racial and sociological considerations is not entitled to the great weight ordinarily given the judgments based upon strictly military considerations. Especially is this so when every charge relative to race, religion, culture, geographical location, and legal and economic status has been substantially discredited by independent studies made by experts in these matters. . . .

Mr. Justice JACKSON, dissenting. . . .

. . . [T]he "law" which this prisoner is convicted of disregarding is not found in an act of Congress, but in a military order. Neither the Act of Congress nor the Executive Order of the President, nor both together, would afford a basis for this conviction. It rests on the orders of General DeWitt. And it is said that if the military commander had reasonable military grounds for promulgating the orders, they are constitutional and become law, and the Court is required to enforce them. There are several reasons why I cannot subscribe to this doctrine.

It would be impracticable and dangerous idealism to expect or insist that each specific military command in an area of probable operations will conform to conventional tests of constitutionality. When an area is so beset that it must be put under military control at all, the paramount consideration is that its measures be successful, rather than legal. The armed services must protect a society, not merely its Constitution. The very essence of the military job is to marshal physical force, to remove every obstacle to its effectiveness, to give it every strategic advantage. Defense measures will not, and often should not, be held within the limits that bind civil authority in peace. No court can require such a commander in such circumstances to act as a reasonable man; he may be unreasonably cautious and exacting. Perhaps he should be. But a commander in temporarily focusing the life of a community on defense is carrying out a military program; he is not making law in the sense the courts know the term. He issues orders, and they may have a certain authority as military commands, although they may be very bad as constitutional law.

But if we cannot confine military expedients by the Constitution, neither would I distort the Constitution to approve all that the military may deem expedient. This is what the Court appears to be doing, whether consciously or not. I cannot say, from any evidence before me, that the orders of General DeWitt were not reasonably expedient military precautions, nor could I say that they were. But even if they were permissible military procedures, I deny that it follows that they are constitutional. If, as the Court holds, it does follow, then we may as well say that any military order will be constitutional and have done with it. . . .

In the very nature of things military decisions are not susceptible of intelligent judicial appraisal. They do not pretend to rest on evidence, but are made on information that often would not be admissible and on assumptions that could not be proved. Information in support of an order could not be disclosed to courts without danger that it would reach the enemy. Neither can courts act on communications made in confidence. Hence courts can never have any real alternative to accepting the mere declaration of the authority that issued the order that it was reasonably necessary from a military viewpoint.

Much is said of the danger to liberty from the Army program for deporting and detaining these citizens of Japanese extraction. But a judicial construction of the due process clause that will sustain this order is a far more subtle blow to liberty than the promulgation of the order itself. A military order, however unconstitutional, is not apt to last longer than the military emergency. Even during that period a succeeding commander may revoke it all. But once a judicial opinion rationalizes such an order to show that it conforms to the Constitution, or rather rationalizes the Constitution to show that the Constitution sanctions such an order, the Court for all time has validated the principle of racial discrimination in criminal procedure and of transplanting American citizens. The principle then lies about like a loaded weapon ready for the hand of any authority that can bring forward a plausible claim of an urgent need. Every repetition imbeds that principle more deeply in our law and thinking and expands it to new purposes. All who observe the work of courts are familiar with what Judge Cardozo described as "the tendency of a principle to expand itself to the limit of its logic." A military commander may overstep the bounds of constitutionality, and it is an incident. But if we review and approve, that passing incident becomes the doctrine of the Constitution. There it has a generative power of its own, and all that it creates will be in its own image. Nothing better illustrates this danger than does the Court's opinion in this case. . . .

Source: 323 U.S. 214 (1944).

Document 49   *Youngstown Sheet and Tube Co. v. Sawyer* (1952)

In 1952, in order to avert a strike in the steel industry, President Harry Truman ordered Secretary of Commerce Charles Sawyer to seize the steel mills and keep them operating. He justified his actions as necessary to sustain the war effort in Korea and under his inherent presidential powers to respond to an emergency and conduct war. The Supreme Court found the president to have acted beyond his authority, but the number of opinions by individual justices made it difficult to conclude the actual precedential value of the opinion as to the parameters of presidential power. Justice Robert H. Jackson's concurring opinion has endured as a succinct summary of the three levels of presidential power, varying by the degree to which the president acts with congressional authorization or alone.

MR. JUSTICE BLACK delivered the opinion of the Court.

We are asked to decide whether the President was acting within his constitutional power when he issued an order directing the Secretary of Commerce to take possession of and operate most of the Nation's steel mills. The mill owners argue that the President's order amounts to lawmaking, a legislative function which the Constitution has expressly confided to the Congress and not to the President. The Government's position is that the order was made on findings of the President that his action was necessary to avert a national catastrophe which would inevitably result from a stoppage of steel production, and that in meeting this grave emergency the President was acting within the aggregate of his constitutional powers as the Nation's Chief Executive and the Commander in Chief of the Armed Forces of the United States. . . .

Two crucial issues have developed: First. Should final determination of the constitutional validity of the President's order be made in this case which has proceeded no further than the preliminary injunction stage? Second. If so, is the seizure order within the constitutional power of the President?

[The Court concluded that it should resolve the dispute given the importance to the nation of the issue.]

The President's power, if any, to issue the order must stem either from an act of Congress or from the Constitution itself. There is no statute that expressly authorizes the President to take possession of property as he did here. Nor is there any act of Congress to which our attention has been directed from which such a power can fairly be implied. Indeed, we do not understand the Government to rely on statutory authorization for this seizure. There are two statutes which do authorize the President to take both personal and real property under certain conditions. However, the Government admits that these conditions were not met and that the President's order was not rooted in either of the statutes. The Government refers to the seizure provisions of one of these statutes (201(b) of the Defense Production Act) as "much too cumbersome, involved, and time-consuming for the crisis which was at hand." . . .

It is clear that if the President had authority to issue the order he did, it must be found in some provision of the Constitution. And it is not claimed that express constitutional language grants this power to the President. The contention is that presidential power should be implied from the aggregate of his powers under the Constitution. Particular reliance is placed on provisions in Article II which say that "The ex-

ecutive Power shall be vested in a President . . ."; that "he shall take Care that the Laws be faithfully executed"; and that he "shall be Commander in Chief of the Army and Navy of the United States."

The order cannot properly be sustained as an exercise of the President's military power as Commander in Chief of the Armed Forces. The Government attempts to do so by citing a number of cases upholding broad powers in military commanders engaged in day-to-day fighting in a theater of war. Such cases need not concern us here. Even though "theater of war" be an expanding concept, we cannot with faithfulness to our constitutional system hold that the Commander in Chief of the Armed Forces has the ultimate power as such to take possession of private property in order to keep labor disputes from stopping production. This is a job for the Nation's lawmakers, not for its military authorities.

Nor can the seizure order be sustained because of the several constitutional provisions that grant executive power to the President. In the framework of our Constitution, the President's power to see that the laws are faithfully executed refutes the idea that he is to be a lawmaker. The Constitution limits his functions in the lawmaking process to the recommending of laws he thinks wise and the vetoing of laws he thinks bad. And the Constitution is neither silent nor equivocal about who shall make laws which the President is to execute. The first section of the first article says that "All legislative Powers herein granted shall be vested in a Congress of the United States. . . ." After granting many powers to the Congress, Article I goes on to provide that Congress may "make all Laws which shall be necessary and proper for carrying into Execution the foregoing Powers, and all other Powers vested by this Constitution in the Government of the United States, or in any Department or Officer thereof."

The President's order does not direct that a congressional policy be executed in a manner prescribed by Congress—it directs that a presidential policy be executed in a manner prescribed by the President. The preamble of the order itself, like that of many statutes, sets out reasons why the President believes certain policies should be adopted, proclaims these policies as rules of conduct to be followed, and again, like a statute, authorizes a government official to promulgate additional rules and regulations consistent with the policy proclaimed and needed to carry that policy into execution. . . .

The Founders of this Nation entrusted the lawmaking power to the Congress alone in both good and bad times. It would do no good to recall the historical events, the fears of power and the hopes for freedom that lay behind their choice. Such a review would but confirm our holding that this seizure order cannot stand.

The judgment of the District Court is Affirmed. . . .

MR. JUSTICE FRANKFURTER, concurring. . . .

The issue before us can be met, and therefore should be, without attempting to define the President's powers comprehensively. I shall not attempt to delineate what belongs to him by virtue of his office beyond the power even of Congress to contract; what authority belongs to him until Congress acts; what kind of problems may be dealt with either by the Congress or by the President or by both; what power must be exercised by the Congress and cannot be delegated to the President. It is as unprofitable to lump together in an undiscriminating hotch-potch past presidential actions claimed to be derived from occupancy of the office, as it is to conjure up hypothetical future cases. The judiciary may, as this case proves, have to intervene in determining where authority lies as between the democratic forces in our scheme of government. But in doing so we should be wary and humble. Such is the teaching of this Court's role in the history of the country.

. . . In formulating legislation for dealing with industrial conflicts, Congress could not more clearly and emphatically have withheld author-

ity than it did in 1947. Perhaps as much so as is true of any piece of modern legislation, Congress acted with full consciousness of what it was doing and in the light of much recent history. Previous seizure legislation had subjected the powers granted to the President to restrictions of varying degrees of stringency. Instead of giving him even limited powers, Congress in 1947 deemed it wise to require the President, upon failure of attempts to reach a voluntary settlement, to report to Congress if he deemed the power of seizure a needed shot for his locker. The President could not ignore the specific limitations of prior seizure statutes. No more could he act in disregard of the limitation put upon seizure by the 1947 Act. . . .

It is one thing to draw an intention of Congress from general language and to say that Congress would have explicitly written what is inferred, where Congress has not addressed itself to a specific situation. It is quite impossible, however, when Congress did specifically address itself to a problem, as Congress did to that of seizure, to find secreted in the interstices of legislation the very grant of power which Congress consciously withheld. To find authority so explicitly withheld is not merely to disregard in a particular instance the clear will of Congress. It is to disrespect the whole legislative process and the constitutional division of authority between President and Congress. . . .

MR. JUSTICE DOUGLAS, concurring.

There can be no doubt that the emergency which caused the President to seize these steel plants was one that bore heavily on the country. But the emergency did not create power; it merely marked an occasion when power should be exercised. And the fact that it was necessary that measures be taken to keep steel in production does not mean that the President, rather than the Congress, had the constitutional authority to act. The Congress, as well as the President, is trustee of the national welfare. The President can act more quickly than the Congress. The President with the armed services at his disposal can move with force as well as with speed. All executive power—from the reign of ancient kings to the rule of modern dictators—has the outward appearance of efficiency.

Legislative power, by contrast, is slower to exercise. There must be delay while the ponderous machinery of committees, hearings, and debates is put into motion. That takes time; and while the Congress slowly moves into action, the emergency may take its toll in wages, consumer goods, war production, the standard of living of the people, and perhaps even lives. Legislative action may indeed often be cumbersome, time-consuming, and apparently inefficient. . . .

We therefore cannot decide this case by determining which branch of government can deal most expeditiously with the present crisis. The answer must depend on the allocation of powers under the Constitution. . . .

If we sanctioned the present exercise of power by the President, we would be expanding Article II of the Constitution and rewriting it to suit the political conveniences of the present emergency. Article II which vests the "executive Power" in the President defines that power with particularity. Article II, Section 2 makes the Chief Executive the Commander in Chief of the Army and Navy. But our history and tradition rebel at the thought that the grant of military power carries with it authority over civilian affairs. Article II, Section 3 provides that the President shall "from time to time give to the Congress Information of the State of the Union, and recommend to their Consideration such Measures as he shall judge necessary and expedient." The power to recommend legislation, granted to the President, serves only to emphasize that it is his function to recommend and that it is the function of the Congress to legislate. Article II, Section 3 also provides that the President "shall take Care that the Laws be faithfully executed." But, as MR. JUSTICE BLACK and MR. JUSTICE FRANK-FURTER point out, the power to execute the laws starts and ends with the laws Congress has enacted. . . .

We could not sanction the seizures and condemnations of the steel plants in this case without reading Article II as giving the President not only the power to execute the laws but to make some. Such a step would most assuredly alter the pattern of the Constitution.

We pay a price for our system of checks and balances, for the distribution of power among the three branches of government. It is a price that today may seem exorbitant to many. Today a kindly President uses the seizure power to effect a wage increase and to keep the steel furnaces in production. Yet tomorrow another President might use the same power to prevent a wage increase, to curb trade-unionists, to regiment labor as oppressively as industry thinks it has been regimented by this seizure.

MR. JUSTICE JACKSON, concurring in the judgment and opinion of the Court. . . .

The actual art of governing under our Constitution does not and cannot conform to judicial definitions of the power of any of its branches based on isolated clauses or even single Articles torn from context. While the Constitution diffuses power the better to secure liberty, it also contemplates that practice will integrate the dispersed powers into a workable government. It enjoins upon its branches separateness but interdependence, autonomy but reciprocity. Presidential powers are not fixed but fluctuate, depending upon their disjunction or conjunction with those of Congress. We may well begin by a somewhat over-simplified grouping of practical situations in which a President may doubt, or others may challenge, his powers, and by distinguishing roughly the legal consequences of this factor of relativity.

1. When the President acts pursuant to an express or implied authorization of Congress, his authority is at its maximum, for it includes all that he possesses in his own right plus all that Congress can delegate. In these circumstances, and in these only, may he be said (for what it may be worth) to personify the federal sover-

eignty. If his act is held unconstitutional under these circumstances, it usually means that the Federal Government as an undivided whole lacks power. A seizure executed by the President pursuant to an Act of Congress would be supported by the strongest of presumptions and the widest latitude of judicial interpretation, and the burden of persuasion would rest heavily upon any who might attack it.

2. When the President acts in absence of either a congressional grant or denial of authority, he can only rely upon his own independent powers, but there is a zone of twilight in which he and Congress may have concurrent authority, or in which its distribution is uncertain. Therefore, congressional inertia, indifference or quiescence may sometimes, at least as a practical matter, enable, if not invite, measures on independent presidential responsibility. In this area, any actual test of power is likely to depend on the imperatives of events and contemporary imponderables rather than on abstract theories of law.

3. When the President takes measures incompatible with the expressed or implied will of Congress, his power is at its lowest ebb, for then he can rely only upon his own constitutional powers minus any constitutional powers of Congress over the matter. Courts can sustain exclusive presidential control in such a case only by disabling the Congress from acting upon the subject. Presidential claim to a power at once so conclusive and preclusive must be scrutinized with caution, for what is at stake is the equilibrium established by our constitutional system. . . .

Assuming that we are in a war de facto, whether it is or is not a war de jure, does that empower the Commander in Chief to seize industries he thinks necessary to supply our army? The Constitution expressly places in Congress power "to raise and support Armies" and "to provide and maintain a Navy." This certainly lays upon Congress primary responsibility for supplying the armed forces. Congress alone controls the raising of revenues and their appropriation and may determine in what manner and by what means they shall be spent for military and naval procurement. I suppose no one would doubt that Congress can take over war supply as a Government enterprise. On the other hand, if Congress sees fit to rely on free private enterprise collectively bargaining with free labor for support and maintenance of our armed forces, can the Executive, because of lawful disagreements incidental to that process, seize the facility for operation upon Government-imposed terms?

There are indications that the Constitution did not contemplate that the title Commander in Chief of the Army and Navy will constitute him also Commander in Chief of the country, its industries and its inhabitants. He has no monopoly of "war powers," whatever they are. While Congress cannot deprive the President of the command of the army and navy, only Congress can provide him an army or navy to command. It is also empowered to make rules for the "Government and Regulation of land and naval Forces," by which it may to some unknown extent impinge upon even command functions.

That military powers of the Commander in Chief were not to supersede representative government of internal affairs seems obvious from the Constitution and from elementary American history. Time out of mind, and even now in many parts of the world, a military commander can seize private housing to shelter his troops. Not so, however, in the United States, for the Third Amendment says, "No Soldier shall, in time of peace be quartered in any house, without the consent of the Owner, nor in time of war, but in a manner to be prescribed by law." Thus, even in war time, his seizure of needed military housing must be authorized by Congress. It also was expressly left to Congress to "provide for calling forth the Militia to execute the Laws of the Union, suppress Insurrections and repel Invasions. . . ." Such a limitation on the command power, written at a time when the militia rather than a standing army was contemplated as the military weapon of the Republic, underscores the Constitution's policy that Congress, not the Executive, should control utilization of the war power as an instrument of domestic policy. Congress, fulfilling that function, has authorized the President to use the army to enforce certain civil rights. On the other hand. Congress has forbidden him to use the army for the purpose of executing general laws except when expressly authorized by the Constitution or by Act of Congress. . . .

We should not use this occasion to circumscribe, much less to contract, the lawful role of the President as Commander in Chief. I should indulge the widest latitude of interpretation to sustain his exclusive function to command the instruments of national force, at least when turned against the outside world for the security of our society. But, when it is turned inward, not because of rebellion but because of a lawful economic struggle between industry and labor, it should have no such indulgence. . . .

In view of the ease, expedition and safety with which Congress can grant and has granted large emergency powers, certainly ample to embrace this crisis, I am quite unimpressed with the argument that we should affirm possession of them without statute. Such power either has no beginning or it has no end. If it exists, it need submit to no legal restraint. I am not alarmed that it would plunge us straightway into dictatorship, but it is at least a step in that wrong direction.

As to whether there is imperative necessity for such powers, it is relevant to note the gap that exists between the President's paper powers and his real powers. The Constitution does not disclose the measure of the actual controls wielded by the modern presidential office. . . .

But I have no illusion that any decision by this Court can keep power in the hands of Congress if it is not wise and timely in meeting its problems. A crisis that challenges the President equally, or perhaps primarily, challenges Congress. If not good law, there was worldly wisdom in the maxim attributed to Napoleon that "The tools belong to the man who can use them." We may say that power to legislate for emergencies

belongs in the hands of Congress, but only Congress itself can prevent power from slipping through its fingers. . . .

MR. CHIEF JUSTICE VINSON, with whom MR. JUSTICE REED and MR. JUSTICE MINTON join, dissenting. . . .

The whole of the "executive Power" is vested in the President. Before entering office, the President swears that he "will faithfully execute the Office of President of the United States, and will to the best of [his] Ability, preserve, protect and defend the Constitution of the United States." . . .

A review of executive action demonstrates that our Presidents have on many occasions exhibited the leadership contemplated by the Framers when they made the President Commander in Chief, and imposed upon him the trust to "take Care that the Laws be faithfully executed." With or without explicit statutory authorization, Presidents have at such times dealt with national emergencies by acting promptly and resolutely to enforce legislative programs, at least to save those programs until Congress could act. Congress and the courts have responded to such executive initiative with consistent approval. . . .

History bears out the genius of the Founding Fathers, who created a Government subject to law but not left subject to inertia when vigor and initiative are required. . . .

Whatever the extent of Presidential power on more tranquil occasions, and whatever the right of the President to execute legislative programs as he sees fit without reporting the mode of execution to Congress, the single Presidential purpose disclosed on this record is to faithfully execute the laws by acting in an emergency to maintain the status quo, thereby preventing collapse of the legislative programs until Congress could act. The President's action served the same purposes as a judicial stay entered to maintain the status quo in order to preserve the jurisdiction of a court. In his Message to Congress immediately following the seizure, the President explained the necessity of his action in executing the military procurement and anti-inflation legislative programs and expressed his desire to cooperate with any legislative proposals approving, regulating or rejecting the seizure of the steel mills. Consequently, there is no evidence whatever of any Presidential purpose to defy Congress or act in any way inconsistent with the legislative will. . . .

The broad executive power granted by Article II to an officer on duty 365 days a year cannot, it is said, be invoked to avert disaster. Instead, the President must confine himself to sending a message to Congress recommending action. Under this messenger-boy concept of the Office, the President cannot even act to preserve legislative programs from destruction so that Congress will have something left to act upon.

. . . No basis for claims of arbitrary action, unlimited powers or dictatorial usurpation of congressional power appears from the facts of this case. On the contrary, judicial, legislative and executive precedents throughout our history demonstrate that in this case the President acted in full conformity with his duties under the Constitution. Accordingly, we would reverse the order of the District Court.

Source: 343 U.S. 579 (1952).

Document 50   *United States v. Nixon* (1974)

In 1972, when news broke that there had been a break-in at Democratic National Committee headquarters in the Watergate building in Washington, D.C., no one would have predicted that it would lead to the first resignation of a president from office. As investigation of the break-in expanded, it became clear that aides to President Richard Nixon and the president himself had engaged in a cover-up of their knowledge of the burglary. Following an indictment alleging violation of federal statutes by certain staff members of the White House and political supporters of the president, the special prosecutor who had been appointed to investigate the scandal filed a motion for a subpoena duces tecum *for the production before trial of certain tapes and documents relating to precisely identified conversations and meetings between the president and others. Nixon, claiming executive privilege, filed a motion to quash the subpoena. Finding that the special prosecutor had met the burden of proof for why the needs of the trial should override the claim of privilege, the court issued an order for an in camera examination of the subpoenaed material. The court stayed its order pending appellate review, which the president sought in the court of appeals. The special prosecutor then filed in the Supreme Court a request for an expedited review of the case. Within days of the Court's unanimous opinion ruling against Nixon, he resigned from office.* United States v. Nixon *is significant not only because it contributed to Nixon's resignation, but also because of its position on the constitutional status of executive privilege. Although the decision was a defeat for Nixon, it can be viewed as a victory for the presidency because of the Court's grant of constitutional legitimacy to the practice of executive privilege.*

MR. CHIEF JUSTICE BURGER delivered the opinion of the Court....

JUSTICIABILITY

... Our starting point is the nature of the proceeding for which the evidence is sought—here a pending criminal prosecution. It is a judicial proceeding in a federal court alleging violation of federal laws and is brought in the name of the United States as sovereign. Under the authority of Art. II, 2, Congress has vested in the Attorney General the power to conduct the criminal litigation of the United States Government. It has also vested in him the power to appoint subordinate officers to assist him in the discharge of his duties. Acting pursuant to those statutes, the Attorney General has delegated the authority to represent the United States in these particular matters to a Special Prosecutor with unique authority and tenure. The regulation gives the Special Prosecutor explicit power to contest the invocation of executive privilege in the process of seeking evidence deemed relevant to the performance of these specially delegated duties.

. . . . So long as this regulation remains in force the Executive Branch is bound by it, and indeed the United States as the sovereign composed of the three branches is bound to respect and to enforce it. Moreover, the delegation of authority to the Special Prosecutor in this case is not an ordinary delegation by the Attorney General to a subordinate officer: with the authorization of the President, the Acting Attorney General provided in the regulation that the Special Prosecutor was not to be removed without the "consensus" of eight designated leaders of Congress.

. . . In light of the uniqueness of the setting in which the conflict arises, the fact that both parties are officers of the Executive Branch cannot be viewed as a barrier to justiciability. It would be inconsistent with the applicable law and regulation, and the unique facts of this case to conclude other than that the Special Prosecutor has standing to bring this action and that a justiciable controversy is presented for decision.

THE CLAIM OF PRIVILEGE

... [W]e turn to the claim that the subpoena should be quashed because it demands "confidential conversations between a President and his close advisors that it would be inconsistent with the public interest to produce." The first contention is a broad claim that the separation of powers doctrine precludes judicial review of a President's claim of privilege. The second contention is that if he does not prevail on the claim of absolute privilege, the court should hold as a matter of constitutional law that the privilege prevails over the subpoena duces tecum.

In the performance of assigned constitutional duties each branch of the Government must initially interpret the Constitution, and the interpretation of its powers by any branch is due great respect from the others. The President's counsel, as we have noted, reads the Constitution as providing an absolute privilege of confidentiality for all Presidential communications. Many decisions of this Court, however, have unequivocally reaffirmed the holding of *Marbury v. Madison* (1803), that "[i]t is emphatically the province and duty of the judicial department to say what the law is."

No holding of the Court has defined the scope of judicial power specifically relating to the enforcement of a subpoena for confidential Presidential communications for use in a criminal prosecution, but other exercises of power by the Executive Branch and the Legislative Branch have been found invalid as in conflict with the Constitution. . . . Since this Court has consistently exercised the power to construe and delineate claims arising under express powers, it must follow that the Court has authority to interpret claims with respect to powers alleged to derive from enumerated powers.

Our system of government "requires that federal courts on occasion interpret the Constitution in a manner at variance with the construction given the document by another branch." . . .

Notwithstanding the deference each branch must accord the others, the "judicial Power of the United States" vested in the federal courts by Art. III, 1, of the Constitution can no more be shared with the Executive Branch than the Chief Executive, for example, can share with the Judiciary the veto power, or the Congress share with the Judiciary the power to override a Presidential veto. Any other conclusion would be contrary to the basic concept of separation of powers and the checks and balances that flow from the scheme of a tripartite government. We therefore reaffirm that it is the province and duty of this Court "to say what the law is" with respect to the claim of privilege presented in this case.

In support of his claim of absolute privilege, the President's counsel urges two grounds, one of which is common to all governments and one of which is peculiar to our system of separation of powers. The first ground is the valid need for protection of communications between high Government officials and those who advise and assist them in the performance of their manifold duties; the importance of this confidentiality is too plain to require further discussion. Human experience teaches that those who expect public dissemination of their remarks may well temper candor with a concern for appearances and for their own interests to the detriment of the decisionmaking process. Whatever the nature of the privilege of confidentiality of Presidential communications in the exercise of Art. II powers, the privilege can be said to derive from the supremacy of each branch within its own assigned area of constitutional duties. Certain powers and privileges flow from the nature of enumerated powers; the protection of the confidentiality of Presidential communications has similar constitutional underpinnings.

The second ground asserted by the President's counsel in support of the claim of absolute privilege rests on the doctrine of separation of powers. Here it is argued that the independence of the Executive Branch within its own sphere, in-

sulates a President from a judicial subpoena in an ongoing criminal prosecution, and thereby protects confidential Presidential communications.

However, neither the doctrine of separation of powers, nor the need for confidentiality of high-level communications, without more, can sustain an absolute, unqualified Presidential privilege of immunity from judicial process under all circumstances. The President's need for complete candor and objectivity from advisers calls for great deference from the courts. However, when the privilege depends solely on the broad, undifferentiated claim of public interest in the confidentiality of such conversations, a confrontation with other values arises. Absent a claim of need to protect military, diplomatic, or sensitive national security secrets, we find it difficult to accept the argument that even the very important interest in confidentiality of Presidential communications is significantly diminished by production of such material for in camera inspection with all the protection that a district court will be obliged to provide.

The impediment that an absolute, unqualified privilege would place in the way of the primary constitutional duty of the Judicial Branch to do justice in criminal prosecutions would plainly conflict with the function of the courts under Art. III. In designing the structure of our Government and dividing and allocating the sovereign power among three co-equal branches, the Framers of the Constitution sought to provide a comprehensive system, but the separate powers were not intended to operate with absolute independence. . . .

To read the Art. II powers of the President as providing an absolute privilege as against a subpoena essential to enforcement of criminal statutes on no more than a generalized claim of the public interest in confidentiality of nonmilitary and nondiplomatic discussions would upset the constitutional balance of "a workable government" and gravely impair the role of the courts under Art. III.

Since we conclude that the legitimate needs of the judicial process may outweigh Presidential privilege, it is necessary to resolve those competing interests in a manner that preserves the essential functions of each branch. The right and indeed the duty to resolve that question does not free the Judiciary from according high respect to the representations made on behalf of the President.

The expectation of a President to the confidentiality of his conversations and correspondence, like the claim of confidentiality of judicial deliberations, for example, has all the values to which we accord deference for the privacy of all citizens and, added to those values, is the necessity for protection of the public interest in candid, objective, and even blunt or harsh opinions in Presidential decision-making. A President and those who assist him must be free to explore alternatives in the process of shaping policies and making decisions and to do so in a way many would be unwilling to express except privately. These are the considerations justifying a presumptive privilege for Presidential communications. The privilege is fundamental to the operation of Government and inextricably rooted in the separation of powers under the Constitution. In *Nixon v. Sirica* (1973), the Court of Appeals held that such Presidential communications are "presumptively privileged," and this position is accepted by both parties in the present litigation. We agree with Mr. Chief Justice Marshall's observation, therefore, that "[i]n no case of this kind would a court be required to proceed against the president as against an ordinary individual."

But this presumptive privilege must be considered in light of our historic commitment to the rule of law. This is nowhere more profoundly manifest than in our view that "the twofold aim [of criminal justice] is that guilt shall not escape or innocence suffer." We have elected to employ an adversary system of criminal justice in which the parties contest all issues before a court of law. The need to develop all relevant facts in the adversary system is both fundamental and comprehensive. The ends of criminal justice would be defeated if judgments were to be founded on a partial or speculative presentation of the facts. The very integrity of the judicial system and public confidence in the system depend on full disclosure of all the facts, within the framework of the rules of evidence. To ensure that justice is done, it is imperative to the function of courts that compulsory process be available for the production of evidence needed either by the prosecution or by the defense. . . .

In this case the President challenges a subpoena served on him as a third party requiring the production of materials for use in a criminal prosecution; he does so on the claim that he has a privilege against disclosure of confidential communications. He does not place his claim of privilege on the ground they are military or diplomatic secrets. As to these areas of Art. II duties the courts have traditionally shown the utmost deference to Presidential responsibilities. . . .

No case of the Court . . . has extended this high degree of deference to a President's generalized interest in confidentiality. Nowhere in the Constitution, as we have noted earlier, is there any explicit reference to a privilege of confidentiality, yet to the extent this interest relates to the effective discharge of a President's powers, it is constitutionally based.

The right to the production of all evidence at a criminal trial similarly has constitutional dimensions. The Sixth Amendment explicitly confers upon every defendant in a criminal trial the right "to be confronted with the witnesses against him" and "to have compulsory process for obtaining witnesses in his favor." Moreover, the Fifth Amendment also guarantees that no person shall be deprived of liberty without due process of law. It is the manifest duty of the courts to vindicate those guarantees, and to accomplish that it is essential that all relevant and admissible evidence be produced.

In this case we must weigh the importance of the general privilege of confidentiality of Presidential communications in performance of the President's responsibilities against the inroads of such a privilege on the fair administration of criminal justice. The interest in preserving confidentiality is weighty indeed and entitled to great respect. However, we cannot conclude that advisers will be moved to temper the candor of their remarks by the infrequent occasions of disclosure because of the possibility that such conversations will be called for in the context of a criminal prosecution.

On the other hand, the allowance of the privilege to withhold evidence that is demonstrably relevant in a criminal trial would cut deeply into the guarantee of due process of law and gravely impair the basic function of the courts. A President's acknowledged need for confidentiality in the communications of his office is general in nature, whereas the constitutional need for production of relevant evidence in a criminal proceeding is specific and central to the fair adjudication of a particular criminal case in the administration of justice. Without access to specific facts a criminal prosecution may be totally frustrated. The President's broad interest in confidentiality of communications will not be vitiated by disclosure of a limited number of conversations preliminarily shown to have some bearing on the pending criminal cases.

We conclude that when the ground for asserting privilege as to subpoenaed materials sought for use in a criminal trial is based only on the generalized interest in confidentiality, it cannot prevail over the fundamental demands of due process of law in the fair administration of criminal justice. The generalized assertion of privilege must yield to the demonstrated, specific need for evidence in a pending criminal trial. . . .

Since this matter came before the Court during the pendency of a criminal prosecution, and on representations that time is of the essence, the mandate shall issue forthwith.

Affirmed.

Source: 418 U.S. 683 (1974).

Document 51   *INS v. Chadha* (1983)

The legislative veto is a by-product of the twentieth-century move toward delegating legislative power to executive and independent agencies. Not willing to relinquish complete authority over the output from these agencies, Congress began using the legislative veto as a way of maintaining some control over executive branch implementation of statutes. In its basic form, the legislative veto establishes a procedure by which Congress may review and reject regulations produced by government agencies. Over the course of the century, use of the veto increased dramatically, correlating no doubt with a similar increase in delegations. Between 1932 and 1983, the year the Supreme Court decided INS v. Chadha, 295 veto procedures had been adopted in 196 different pieces of legislation. The most significant increase occurred in the 1970s, a period of heightened conflict between Congress and the president brought on by divided government and fallout from the Vietnam War and Watergate.

The veto in question here, Sec. 244(c)(2) of an immigration statute, provided for review (by one house of Congress) attorney general decisions on deportation of aliens. In this case, Jagdish Chadha, an alien from Kenya, sought suspension of his deportation from the attorney general, who agreed to his request. The House of Representatives, however, reversed that judgment in exercising its authority under this procedure, ordering that Chadha's deportation be reinstated. Chadha sued, arguing that the legislative veto arrangement violated the separation of powers. Chadha *appeared to be an important victory for the executive branch in its struggles with Congress, but in subsequent practice an informal use of legislative vetoes continued and was acquiesced to by the executive in order to receive the authority it wished to have delegated to it by Congress.*

CHIEF JUSTICE BURGER delivered the opinion of the Court. . . .

We turn now to the question whether action of one House of Congress under 244(c)(2) violates strictures of the Constitution. We begin, of course, with the presumption that the challenged statute is valid. Its wisdom is not the concern of the courts; if a challenged action does not violate the Constitution, it must be sustained. . . . By the same token, the fact that a given law or procedure is efficient, convenient, and useful in facilitating functions of government, standing alone, will not save it if it is contrary to the Constitution. Convenience and efficiency are not the primary objectives—or the hallmarks—of democratic government and our inquiry is sharpened rather than blunted by the fact that congressional veto provisions are appearing with increasing frequency in statutes which delegate authority to executive and independent agencies:

. . . [P]olicy arguments supporting even useful "political inventions" are subject to the demands of the Constitution which defines powers and, with respect to this subject, sets out just how those powers are to be exercised.

Explicit and unambiguous provisions of the Constitution prescribe and define the respective functions of the Congress and of the Executive in the legislative process. Since the precise terms of those familiar provisions are critical to the resolution of these cases, we set them out verbatim. Article I provides:

"All legislative Powers herein granted be vested in a Congress of the United States, which shall consist of a Senate and House of Representatives."

"Every Bill which shall have passed the House of Representatives and the Senate, shall, before it becomes a law, be presented to the President of the United States. . . ."

"Every Order, Resolution, or Vote to which the Concurrence of the Senate and House of Representatives may be necessary (except on a question of Adjournment) shall be presented to the President of the United States; and before the Same shall take Effect, shall be approved by him, or being disapproved by him, shall be repassed by two thirds of the Senate and House of Representatives, according to the Rules and Limitations prescribed in the Case of a Bill."

These provisions of Art. I are integral parts of the constitutional design for the separation of powers. We have recently noted that "[t]he principle of separation of powers was not simply an abstract generalization in the minds of the Framers: it was woven into the document that they drafted in Philadelphia in the summer of 1787."

The Presentment Clauses

The records of the Constitutional Convention reveal that the requirement that all legislation be presented to the President before becoming law was uniformly accepted by the Framers. Presentment to the President and the Presidential veto were considered so imperative that the draftsmen took special pains to assure that these requirements could not be circumvented. . . .

The decision to provide the President with a limited and qualified power to nullify proposed legislation by veto was based on the profound conviction of the Framers that the powers conferred on Congress were the powers to be most carefully circumscribed. It is beyond doubt that lawmaking was a power to be shared by both Houses and the President.

The President's role in the lawmaking process also reflects the Framers' careful efforts to check whatever propensity a particular Congress might have to enact oppressive, improvident, or ill-considered measures. . . .

Bicameralism

The bicameral requirement of Art. I, 1, 7, was of scarcely less concern to the Framers than was the Presidential veto and indeed the two concepts are interdependent.

By providing that no law could take effect without the concurrence of the prescribed majority of the Members of both Houses, the Framers reemphasized their belief, already remarked upon in connection with the Presentment Clauses, that legislation should not be enacted unless it has been carefully and fully considered by the Nation's elected officials. . . .

We see therefore that the Framers were acutely conscious that the bicameral requirement and the Presentment Clauses would serve essential constitutional functions. The President's participation in the legislative process was to protect the Executive Branch from Congress and to protect the whole people from improvident laws. The division of the Congress into two distinctive bodies assures that the legislative power would be exercised only after opportunity for full study and debate in separate settings. The President's unilateral veto power, in turn, was limited by the power of two-thirds of both Houses of Congress to overrule a veto thereby precluding final arbitrary action of one person. It emerges clearly that the prescription for legislative action in Art. I, 1, 7, represents the Framers' decision that the legislative power of the Federal Government be exercised in accord with a single, finely wrought and exhaustively considered, procedure.

The Constitution sought to divide the delegated powers of the new Federal Government into three defined categories, Legislative, Executive, and Judicial, to assure, as nearly as possible, that each branch of government would confine itself to its assigned responsibility. The hydraulic pressure inherent within each of the separate Branches to exceed the outer limits of its power, even to accomplish desirable objectives, must be resisted.

Although not "hermetically" sealed from one another, the powers delegated to the three Branches are functionally identifiable. When any Branch acts, it is presumptively exercising the power the Constitution has delegated to it. When the Executive acts, he presumptively acts in an executive or administrative capacity as defined in Art. II. And when, as here, one House of Congress purports to act, it is presumptively acting within its assigned sphere.

. . . Not every action taken by either House is subject to the bicameralism and presentment requirements of Art. I. Whether actions taken by either House are, in law and fact, an exercise of legislative power depends not on their form but upon "whether they contain matter which is properly to be regarded as legislative in its character and effect."

Examination of the action taken here by one House pursuant to 244(c)(2) reveals that it was essentially legislative in purpose and effect. In purporting to exercise power defined in Art. I, 8, cl. 4, to "establish an uniform Rule of Naturalization," the House took action that had the purpose and effect of altering the legal rights, duties, and relations of persons, including the Attorney General, Executive Branch officials and Chadha, all outside the Legislative Branch. Section 244(c)(2) purports to authorize one House of Congress to require the Attorney General to deport an individual alien whose deportation otherwise would be canceled under 244. The one-House veto operated in these cases to overrule the Attorney General and mandate Chadha's deportation; absent the House action, Chadha would remain in the United States. Congress has acted and its action has altered Chadha's status.

The legislative character of the one-House veto in these cases is confirmed by the character of the congressional action it supplants. Neither the House of Representatives nor the Senate contends that, absent the veto provision in 244(c)(2), either of them, or both of them acting together, could effectively require the Attorney General to deport an alien once the Attorney General, in the exercise of legislatively delegated authority, had determined the alien should remain in the United States. . . .

The nature of the decision implemented by the one-House veto in these cases further manifests its legislative character. After long experience with the clumsy, time-consuming private bill procedure, Congress made a deliberate choice to delegate to the Executive Branch, and specifically to the Attorney General, the authority to allow deportable aliens to remain in this country in certain specified circumstances. It is not disputed that this choice to delegate authority is precisely the kind of decision that can be implemented only in accordance with the procedures set out in Art. I. Disagreement with the Attorney General's decision on Chadha's deportation—that is, Congress' decision to deport Chadha—no less than Congress' original choice to delegate to the Attorney General the authority to make that decision, involves determinations of policy that Congress can implement in only one way; bicameral passage followed by presentment to the President. Congress must abide by its delegation of authority until that delegation is legislatively altered or revoked.

Finally, we see that when the Framers intended to authorize either House of Congress to act alone and outside of its prescribed bicameral legislative role, they narrowly and precisely defined the procedure for such action. . . .

Clearly, when the Draftsmen sought to confer special powers on one House, independent of the other House, or of the President, they did so in explicit, unambiguous terms. . . .

Since it is clear that the action by the House under 244(c)(2) was not within any of the express constitutional exceptions authorizing one House to act alone, and equally clear that it was an exercise of legislative power, that action was subject to the standards prescribed in Art. I. The

bicameral requirement, the Presentment Clauses, the President's veto, and Congress' power to override a veto were intended to erect enduring checks on each Branch and to protect the people from the improvident exercise of power by mandating certain prescribed steps. To preserve those checks, and maintain the separation of powers, the carefully defined limits on the power of each Branch must not be eroded. To accomplish what has been attempted by one House of Congress in this case requires action in conformity with the express procedures of the Constitution's prescription for legislative action: passage by a majority of both Houses and presentment to the President.

The veto authorized by 244(c)(2) doubtless has been in many respects a convenient shortcut; the "sharing" with the Executive by Congress of its authority over aliens in this manner is, on its face, an appealing compromise. In purely practical terms, it is obviously easier for action to be taken by one House without submission to the President; but it is crystal clear from the records of the Convention, contemporaneous writings and debates, that the Framers ranked other values higher than efficiency. . . . There is unmistakable expression of a determination that legislation by the national Congress be a step-by-step, deliberate and deliberative process.

The choices we discern as having been made in the Constitutional Convention impose burdens on governmental processes that often seem clumsy, inefficient, even unworkable, but those hard choices were consciously made by men who had lived under a form of government that permitted arbitrary governmental acts to go unchecked. There is no support in the Constitution or decisions of this Court for the proposition that the cumbersomeness and delays often encountered in complying with explicit constitutional standards may be avoided, either by the Congress or by the President. With all the obvious flaws of delay, untidiness, and potential for abuse, we have not yet found a better way to preserve freedom than by making the exercise of power subject to the carefully crafted restraints spelled out in the Constitution. . . .

Affirmed.

JUSTICE POWELL, concurring in the judgment.

The Court's decision, based on the Presentment Clauses, Art. I, 7, cls. 2 and 3, apparently will invalidate every use of the legislative veto. The breadth of this holding gives one pause. Congress has included the veto in literally hundreds of statutes, dating back to the 1930's. Congress clearly views this procedure as essential to controlling the delegation of power to administrative agencies. One reasonably may disagree with Congress' assessment of the veto's utility, but the respect due its judgment as a coordinate branch of Government cautions that our holding should be no more extensive than necessary to decide these cases. In my view, the cases may be decided on a narrower ground. When Congress finds that a particular person does not satisfy the statutory criteria for permanent residence in this country it has assumed a judicial function in violation of the principle of separation of powers. . . .

JUSTICE WHITE, dissenting.

Today the Court . . . sounds the death knell for nearly 200 other statutory provisions in which Congress has reserved a "legislative veto." For this reason, the Court's decision is of surpassing importance. And it is for this reason that the Court would have been well advised to decide the cases, if possible, on the narrower grounds of separation of powers, leaving for full consideration the constitutionality of other congressional review statutes operating on such varied matters as war powers and agency rulemaking, some of which concern the independent regulatory agencies.

The prominence of the legislative veto mechanism in our contemporary political system and its importance to Congress can hardly be overstated. It has become a central means by which Congress secures the accountability of executive and independent agencies. Without the legislative veto, Congress is faced with a Hobson's choice: either to refrain from delegating the necessary authority, leaving itself with a hopeless task of writing laws with the requisite specificity to cover endless special circumstances across the entire policy landscape, or in the alternative, to abdicate its law-making function to the Executive Branch and independent agencies. To choose the former leaves major national problems unresolved; to opt for the latter risks unaccountable policymaking by those not elected to fill that role. Accordingly, over the past five decades, the legislative veto has been placed in nearly 200 statutes. The device is known in every field of governmental concern: reorganization, budgets, foreign affairs, war powers, and regulation of trade, safety, energy, the environment, and the economy. . . .

. . . [T]he legislative veto is more than "efficient, convenient, and useful." It is an important if not indispensable political invention that allows the President and Congress to resolve major constitutional and policy differences, assures the accountability of independent regulatory agencies, and preserves Congress' control over lawmaking. Perhaps there are other means of accommodation and accountability, but the increasing reliance of Congress upon the legislative veto suggests that the alternatives to which Congress must now turn are not entirely satisfactory.

The history of the legislative veto also makes clear that it has not been a sword with which Congress has struck out to aggrandize itself at the expense of the other branches—the concerns of Madison and Hamilton. Rather, the veto has been a means of defense, a reservation of ultimate authority necessary if Congress is to fulfill its designated role under Art. I as the Nation's lawmaker. While the President has often objected to particular legislative vetoes, generally those left in the hands of congressional Committees, the Executive has more often agreed to legislative review as the price for a broad delegation of authority. To be sure, the President may have preferred unrestricted power, but that could be precisely why Congress thought it essential to retain a check on the exercise of delegated authority.

For all these reasons, the apparent sweep of the Court's decision today is regrettable. The Court's Art. I analysis appears to invalidate all legislative vetoes irrespective of form or subject. Because the legislative veto is commonly found as a check upon rulemaking by administrative agencies and upon broad-based policy decisions of the Executive Branch, it is particularly unfortunate that the Court reaches its decision in cases involving the exercise of a veto over deportation decisions regarding particular individuals. Courts should always be wary of striking statutes as unconstitutional; to strike an entire class of statutes based on consideration of a somewhat atypical and more readily indictable exemplar of the class is irresponsible. . . .

. . . The Constitution does not directly authorize or prohibit the legislative veto. Thus, our task should be to determine whether the legislative veto is consistent with the purposes of Art. I and the principles of separation of powers which are reflected in that Article and throughout the Constitution. We should not find the lack of a specific constitutional authorization for the legislative veto surprising, and I would not infer disapproval of the mechanism from its absence. From the summer of 1787 to the present the Government of the United States has become an endeavor far beyond the contemplation of the Framers. Only within the last half century has the complexity and size of the Federal Government's responsibilities grown so greatly that the Congress must rely on the legislative veto as the most effective if not the only means to insure its role as the Nation's lawmaker. But the wisdom of the Framers was to anticipate that the Nation would grow and new problems of governance would require different solutions. Accordingly, our Federal Government was intentionally chartered with the flexibility to respond to contemporary needs without losing sight of fundamental democratic principles. . . .

This is the perspective from which we should approach the novel constitutional questions presented by the legislative veto. In my view, neither Art. I of the Constitution nor the doctrine of separation of powers is violated by this mechanism by which our elected Representatives preserve their voice in the governance of the Nation.

. . . The Court's holding today that all legislative-type action must be enacted through the lawmaking process ignores that legislative authority is routinely delegated to the Executive Branch, to the independent regulatory agencies, and to private individuals and groups. . . .

This Court's decisions sanctioning such delegations make clear that Art. I does not require all action with the effect of legislation to be passed as a law. . . .

If Congress may delegate lawmaking power to independent and Executive agencies, it is most difficult to understand Art. I as prohibiting Congress from also reserving a check on legislative power for itself. Absent the veto, the agencies receiving delegations of legislative or quasi-legislative power may issue regulations having the force of law without bicameral approval and without the President's signature. It is thus not apparent why the reservation of a veto over the exercise of that legislative power must be subject to a more exacting test. In both cases, it is enough that the initial statutory authorizations comply with the Art. I requirements.

Nor are there strict limits on the agents that may receive such delegations of legislative authority so that it might be said that the Legislature can delegate authority to others but not to itself. While most authority to issue rules and regulations is given to the Executive Branch and the independent regulatory agencies, statutory delegations to private persons have also passed this Court's scrutiny. . . . Perhaps this odd result could be justified on other constitutional grounds, such as the separation of powers, but certainly it cannot be defended as consistent with the Court's view of the Art. I presentment and bicameralism commands. . . .

More fundamentally, even if the Court correctly characterizes the Attorney General's authority under 244 as an Art. II Executive power, the Court concedes that certain administrative agency action, such as rulemaking, "may resemble lawmaking" and recognizes that "[t]his Court has referred to agency activity as being 'quasi-legislative' in character." Such rules and adjudications by the agencies meet the Court's own definition of legislative action for they "alte[r] the legal rights, duties, and relations of persons . . . outside the Legislative Branch," and involve "determinations of policy." Under the Court's analysis, the Executive Branch and the independent agencies may make rules with the effect of law while Congress, in whom the Framers confided the legislative power, Art. I, 1, may not exercise a veto which precludes such rules from having operative force. If the effective functioning of a complex modern government requires the delegation of vast authority which, by virtue of its breadth, is legislative or "quasi-legislative" in character, I cannot accept that Art. I . . . should forbid Congress to qualify that grant with a legislative veto.

. . . [T]he history of the separation-of-powers doctrine is also a history of accommodation and practicality. Apprehensions of an overly powerful branch have not led to undue prophylactic measures that handicap the effective working of the National Government as a whole. The Constitution does not contemplate total separation of the three branches of Government. "[A] hermetic sealing off of the three branches of Government from one another would preclude the establishment of a Nation capable of governing itself effectively."

Our decisions reflect this judgment. As already noted, the Court, recognizing that modern government must address a formidable agenda of complex policy issues, countenanced the delegation of extensive legislative authority to Executive and independent agencies. The separation-of-powers doctrine has heretofore led to the invalidation of Government action only when the challenged action violated some express provision in the Constitution. . . . Because we must have a workable efficient Government, this is as it should be. . . .

I do not suggest that all legislative vetoes are necessarily consistent with separation-of-powers principles. A legislative check on an inherently executive function, for example, that of initiating prosecutions, poses an entirely different question. But the legislative veto device here—and in many other settings—is far from an instance of legislative tyranny over the Executive. It is a necessary check on the unavoidably expanding power of the agencies, both Executive and independent, as they engage in exercising authority delegated by Congress. . . .

Source: 462 U.S. 919 (1983).

Document 52   *Bowsher v. Synar* (1986)

In order to eliminate the federal budget deficit, which had ballooned in the 1980s, Congress enacted the Balanced Budget and Emergency Deficit Control Act of 1985, which set a maximum amount for deficit spending from fiscal years 1986 to 1991. If in any fiscal year the budget deficit exceeded the allowed maximum by more than a specified sum, the act required across-the-board cuts in spending to reach the targeted level. These reductions were to be instated under the "reporting provisions" spelled out in Section 251 of the act, which required the directors of the Office of Management and Budget and the Congressional Budget Office to submit deficit estimates and program-by-program budget reduction calculations to the comptroller general who, after reviewing the directors' joint report, would deliver a conclusion to the president. The president in turn was required to issue a "sequestration" order mandating the spending reductions specified by the comptroller general. The sequestration order would become effective unless, within a specified time, Congress legislated reductions of its own.

Michael Synar (D-Okla.), other members of Congress, and the National Treasury Employees Union challenged the act's constitutionality. The Supreme Court's opinion striking down the automatic cuts provision was greeted with pleasure by the Reagan administration, as it interpreted the opinion as an endorsement of the unitary executive theory with regard to appointment powers. As the administration mounted a challenge to the limits on executive control over independent agencies, Bowsher v. Synar *appeared to provide valuable support for its position that those exercising executive power must be controlled by the president.*

Chief Justice BURGER delivered the opinion of the Court.

The question presented by these appeals is whether the assignment by Congress to the Comptroller General of the United States of certain functions under the Balanced Budget and Emergency Deficit Control Act of 1985 violates the doctrine of separation of powers. . . .

Even a cursory examination of the Constitution reveals the influence of Montesquieu's thesis that checks and balances were the foundation of a structure of government that would protect liberty. The Framers provided a vigorous Legislative Branch and a separate and wholly independent Executive Branch, with each branch responsible ultimately to the people. The Framers also provided for a Judicial Branch equally independent with "[t]he judicial Power ... extend[ing] to all Cases, in Law and Equity, aris-

ing under this Constitution, and the Laws of the United States."

Other, more subtle, examples of separated powers are evident as well. Unlike parliamentary systems such as that of Great Britain, no person who is an officer of the United States may serve as a Member of the Congress. Moreover, unlike parliamentary systems, the President, under Article II, is responsible not to the Congress but to the people, subject only to impeachment proceedings which are exercised by the two Houses as representatives of the people. And even in the impeachment of a President the presiding officer of the ultimate tribunal is not a member of the Legislative Branch, but the Chief Justice of the United States.

That this system of division and separation of powers produces conflicts, confusion, and discordance at times is inherent, but it was deliberately so structured to assure full, vigorous, and open debate on the great issues affecting the people and to provide avenues for the operation of checks on the exercise of governmental power.

The Constitution does not contemplate an active role for Congress in the supervision of officers charged with the execution of the laws it enacts. The President appoints "Officers of the United States" with the "Advice and Consent of the Senate. . . . " Once the appointment has been made and confirmed, however, the Constitution explicitly provides for removal of Officers of the United States by Congress only upon impeachment by the House of Representatives and conviction by the Senate. An impeachment by the House and trial by the Senate can rest only on "Treason, Bribery or other high Crimes and Misdemeanors." A direct congressional role in the removal of officers charged with the execution of the laws beyond this limited one is inconsistent with separation of powers. . . .

In light of . . . precedents, we conclude that Congress cannot reserve for itself the power of removal of an officer charged with the execution of the laws except by impeachment. To permit the execution of the laws to be vested in an officer answerable only to Congress would, in practical terms, reserve in Congress control over the execution of the laws. . . . The structure of the Constitution does not permit Congress to execute the laws; it follows that Congress cannot grant to an officer under its control what it does not possess. . . .

To permit an officer controlled by Congress to execute the laws would be, in essence, to permit a congressional veto. Congress could simply remove, or threaten to remove, an officer for executing the laws in any fashion found to be unsatisfactory to Congress. This kind of congressional control over the execution of the laws, *Chadha* makes clear, is constitutionally impermissible.

. . . With these principles in mind, we turn to consideration of whether the Comptroller General is controlled by Congress. Appellants urge that the Comptroller General performs his duties independently and is not subservient to Congress. . . .

We agree with the District Court that this contention does not bear close scrutiny.

The critical factor lies in the provisions of the statute defining the Comptroller General's office relating to removability. Although the Comptroller General is nominated by the President from a list of three individuals recommended by the Speaker of the House of Representatives and the President pro tempore of the Senate, and confirmed by the Senate, he is removable only at the initiative of Congress. He may be removed not only by impeachment but also by joint resolution of Congress "at any time" resting on any one of the following bases:

"(i) permanent disability;
"(ii) inefficiency;
"(iii) neglect of duty;
"(iv) malfeasance; or
"(v) a felony or conduct involving moral turpitude."

This provision was included . . . because Congress "felt that [the Comptroller General] should be brought under the sole control of Congress, so that Congress at any moment when it found he was inefficient and was not carrying on the duties of his office as he should and as the Congress expected, could remove him without the long, tedious process of a trial by impeachment." . . .

. . . The separated powers of our Government cannot be permitted to turn on judicial assessment of whether an officer exercising executive power is on good terms with Congress. . . . In constitutional terms, the removal powers over the Comptroller General's office dictate that he will be subservient to Congress.

This much said, we must also add that the dissent is simply in error to suggest that the political realities reveal that the Comptroller General is free from influence by Congress. The Comptroller General heads the General Accounting Office (GAO), "an instrumentality of the United States Government independent of the executive departments," which was created by Congress in 1921 as part of the Budget and

Accounting Act of 1921. Congress created the office because it believed that it "needed an officer, responsible to it alone, to check upon the application of public funds in accordance with appropriations." . . .

Against this background, we see no escape from the conclusion that, because Congress has retained removal authority over the Comptroller General, he may not be entrusted with executive powers. The remaining question is whether the Comptroller General has been assigned such powers in the Balanced Budget and Emergency Deficit Control Act of 1985.

The primary responsibility of the Comptroller General under the instant Act is the preparation of a "report." This report must contain detailed estimates of projected federal revenues and expenditures. The report must also specify the reductions, if any, necessary to reduce the deficit to the target for the appropriate fiscal year. The reductions must be set forth on a program-by-program basis.

In preparing the report, the Comptroller General is to have "due regard" for the estimates and reductions set forth in a joint report submitted to him by the Director of CBO and the Director of OMB, the President's fiscal and budgetary adviser. However, the Act plainly contemplates that the Comptroller General will exercise his independent judgment and evaluation with respect to those estimates. The Act also provides that the Comptroller General's report "shall explain fully any differences between the contents of such report and the report of the Directors."

Appellants suggest that the duties assigned to the Comptroller General in the Act are essentially ministerial and mechanical so that their performance does not constitute "execution of the law" in a meaningful sense. On the contrary, we view these functions as plainly entailing execution of the law in constitutional terms. Interpreting a law enacted by Congress to implement the legislative mandate is the very essence of "execution" of the law. Under 251, the Comptroller General must exercise judgment concerning facts that affect the application of the Act. He must also interpret the provisions of the Act to determine precisely what budgetary calculations are required. Decisions of that kind are typically made by officers charged with executing a statute.

The executive nature of the Comptroller General's functions under the Act is revealed in 252(a)(3) which gives the Comptroller General the ultimate authority to determine the budget cuts to be made. Indeed, the Comptroller General commands the President himself to carry out, without the slightest variation (with exceptions not relevant to the constitutional issues presented), the directive of the Comptroller General as to the budget reductions. . . .

Congress of course initially determined the content of the Balanced Budget and Emergency Deficit Control Act; and undoubtedly the content of the Act determines the nature of the executive duty. However, as *Chadha* makes clear, once Congress makes its choice in enacting legislation, its participation ends. Congress can thereafter control the execution of its enactment only indirectly—by passing new legislation. By placing the responsibility for execution of the Balanced Budget and Emergency Deficit Control Act in the hands of an officer who is subject to removal only by itself, Congress in effect has retained control over the execution of the Act and has intruded into the executive function. The Constitution does not permit such intrusion. . . .

No one can doubt that Congress and the President are confronted with fiscal and economic problems of unprecedented magnitude, but "the fact that a given law or procedure is efficient, convenient, and useful in facilitating functions of government, standing alone, will not save it if it is contrary to the Constitution. Convenience and efficiency are not the primary objectives—or the hallmarks—of democratic government." . . .

Accordingly, the judgment and order of the District Court are affirmed.

JUSTICE STEVENS, with whom JUSTICE MARSHALL joins, concurring in the judgment.

When this Court is asked to invalidate a statutory provision that has been approved by both Houses of the Congress and signed by the President, particularly an Act of Congress that confronts a deeply vexing national problem, it should only do so for the most compelling constitutional reasons. I agree with the Court that the "Gramm-Rudman-Hollings" Act contains a constitutional infirmity so severe that the flawed provision may not stand. I disagree with the Court, however, on the reasons why the Constitution prohibits the Comptroller General from exercising the powers assigned to him by 251(b) and 251(c)(2) of the Act. It is not the dormant, carefully circumscribed congressional removal power that represents the primary constitutional evil. Nor do I agree with the conclusion of both the majority and the dissent that the analysis depends on a labeling of the functions assigned to the Comptroller General as "executive powers." Rather, I am convinced that the Comptroller General must be characterized as an agent of Congress because of his longstanding statutory responsibilities; that the powers assigned to him under the Gramm-Rudman-Hollings Act require him to make policy that will bind the Nation; and that, when Congress, or a component or an agent of Congress, seeks to make policy that will bind the Nation, it must follow the procedures mandated by Article I of the Constitution— through passage by both Houses and presentment to the President. In short, Congress may not exercise its fundamental power to formulate national policy by delegating that power to one of its two Houses, to a legislative committee, or to an individual agent of the Congress such as the Speaker of the House of Representatives, the Sergeant at Arms of the Senate, or the Director of the Congressional Budget Office. That principle, I believe, is applicable to the Comptroller General. . . .

JUSTICE WHITE, dissenting.

The Court, acting in the name of separation of powers, takes upon itself to strike down the Gramm-Rudman-Hollings Act, one of the most novel and far-reaching legislative responses to a national crisis since the New Deal. The basis of the Court's action is a solitary provision of another statute that was passed over 60 years ago and has lain dormant since that time. I cannot concur in the Court's action. Like the Court, I will not purport to speak to the wisdom of the policies incorporated in the legislation the Court invalidates; that is a matter for the Congress and the Executive, both of which expressed their assent to the statute barely half a year ago. I will, however, address the wisdom of the Court's willingness to interpose its distressingly formalistic view of separation of powers as a bar to the attainment of governmental objectives through the means chosen by the Congress and the President in the legislative process established by the Constitution. Twice in the past four years I have expressed my view that the Court's recent efforts to police the separation of powers have rested on untenable constitutional propositions leading to regrettable results. Today's result is even more misguided. As I will explain, the Court's decision rests on a feature of the legislative scheme that is of minimal practical significance and that presents no substantial threat to the basic scheme of separation of powers. . . .

Before examining the merits of the Court's argument, I wish to emphasize what it is that the Court quite pointedly and correctly does not hold: namely, that "executive" powers of the sort granted the Comptroller by the Act may only be exercised by officers removable at will by the President. The Court's apparent unwillingness to accept this argument, which has been tendered in this Court by the Solicitor General, is fully consistent with the Court's longstanding recognition that it is within the power of Congress under the "Necessary and Proper" Clause, to vest authority that falls within the Court's definition of executive power in officers who are not subject to removal at will by the President and are therefore not under the President's direct control. In an earlier day, in which simpler notions of the role of government in society prevailed, it was perhaps plausible to insist that all "executive" officers be subject to an unqualified Presidential removal power, but with the advent and triumph of the administrative state and the accompanying multiplication of the tasks undertaken by the Federal Government, the Court has been virtually compelled to recognize that Congress may reasonably deem it "necessary and proper" to vest some among the broad new array of governmental functions in officers who are free from the partisanship that may be expected of agents wholly dependent upon the President. . . .

It is evident (and nothing in the Court's opinion is to the contrary) that the powers exercised by the Comptroller General under the Gramm-Rudman-Hollings Act are not such that vesting them in an officer not subject to removal at will by the President would in itself improperly interfere with Presidential powers. Determining the level of spending by the Federal Government is not by nature a function central either to the exercise of the President's enumerated powers or to his general duty to ensure execution of the laws; rather, appropriating funds is a peculiarly legislative function, and one expressly committed to Congress by Art. I, 9, which provides that "No Money shall be drawn from the Treasury, but in Consequence of Appropriations made by Law." In enacting Gramm-Rudman-Hollings, Congress has chosen to exercise this legislative power to establish the level of federal spending by providing a detailed set of criteria for reducing expenditures below the level of appropriations in the event that certain conditions are met. Delegating the execution of this legislation—that is, the power to apply the Act's criteria and make the required calculations—to an officer independent of the President's will does not deprive the President of any power that he would otherwise have or that is essential to the performance of the duties of his office. Rather, the result of such a delegation, from the standpoint of the President, is no different from the result of more traditional forms of appropriation: under either system, the level of funds available to the Executive Branch to carry out its duties is not within the President's

discretionary control. To be sure, if the budget-cutting mechanism required the responsible officer to exercise a great deal of policymaking discretion, one might argue that having created such broad discretion Congress had some obligation based upon Art. II to vest it in the Chief Executive or his agents. In Gramm-Rudman-Hollings, however, Congress has done no such thing; instead, it has created a precise and articulated set of criteria designed to minimize the degree of policy choice exercised by the officer executing the statute and to ensure that the relative spending priorities established by Congress in the appropriations it passes into law remain unaltered. Given that the exercise of policy choice by the officer executing the statute would be inimical to Congress' goal in enacting "automatic" budget-cutting measures, it is eminently reasonable and proper for Congress to vest the budget-cutting authority in an officer who is to the greatest degree possible nonpartisan and independent of the President and his political agenda and who therefore may be relied upon not to allow his calculations to be colored by political considerations. Such a delegation deprives the President of no authority that is rightfully his. . . .

The deficiencies in the Court's reasoning are apparent. First, the Court baldly mischaracterizes the removal provision when it suggests that it allows Congress to remove the Comptroller for "executing the laws in any fashion found to be unsatisfactory"; in fact, Congress may remove the Comptroller only for one or more of five specified reasons, which "although not so narrow as to deny Congress any leeway, circumscribe Congress' power to some extent by providing a basis for judicial review of congressional removal." Second, and more to the point, the Court overlooks or deliberately ignores the decisive difference between the congressional removal provision and the legislative veto struck down in *Chadha*: under the Budget and Accounting Act, Congress may remove the Comptroller only through a joint resolution, which by definition must be passed by both Houses and signed by the President. In other words, a removal of the Comptroller under the statute satisfies the requirements of bicameralism and presentment laid down in *Chadha*. The majority's citation of *Chadha* for the proposition that Congress may only control the acts of officers of the United States "by passing new legislation," in no sense casts doubt on the legitimacy of the removal provision, for that provision allows Congress to effect removal only through action that constitutes legislation as defined in *Chadha*. . . .

The practical result of the removal provision is not to render the Comptroller unduly dependent upon or subservient to Congress, but to render him one of the most independent officers in the entire federal establishment. Those who have studied the office agree that the procedural and substantive limits on the power of Congress and the President to remove the Comptroller make dislodging him against his will practically impossible.

Realistic consideration of the nature of the Comptroller General's relation to Congress thus reveals that the threat to separation of powers conjured up by the majority is wholly chimerical. The power over removal retained by the Congress is not a power that is exercised outside the legislative process as established by the Constitution, nor does it appear likely that it is a power that adds significantly to the influence Congress may exert over executive officers through other, undoubtedly constitutional exercises of legislative power and through the constitutionally guaranteed impeachment power. Indeed, the removal power is so constrained by its own substantive limits and by the requirement of Presidential approval "that, as a practical matter, Congress has not exercised, and probably will never exercise, such control over the Comptroller General that his non-legislative powers will threaten the goal of dispersion of power, and hence the goal of individual liberty, that separation of powers serves."

. . . Under such circumstances, the role of this Court should be limited to determining whether the Act so alters the balance of authority among the branches of government as to pose a genuine threat to the basic division between the lawmaking power and the power to execute the law. Because I see no such threat, I cannot join the Court in striking down the Act. . . .

Source: 478 U.S. 714 (1986).

Document 53   *Morrison v. Olson* (1988)

The Supreme Court's decisions in INS v. Chadha *(1983) (Doc. 51) and* Bowsher v. Synar *(1986) (Doc. 52) encouraged Reagan administration officials to believe that the Court was sympathetic to its concerns about the need for the executive to control the entities and people exercising executive power. The independent counsel arrangement—created with the support of President Jimmy Carter through the Ethics in Government Act of 1978—was subsequently reauthorized by Congress in 1982, 1987, and 1994. (In 1999 it was allowed to expire, the victim of the controversies surrounding the Iran-contra investigation during the Reagan and Bush administrations and the Whitewater and Lewinsky investigations during the Clinton administration.) Presidents disliked the statute, and the Reagan Department of Justice even testified against it during the 1982 and 1987 reauthorizations. While expressing reservations about the arrangement's constitutionality, President Ronald Reagan signed those bills nonetheless, citing the need to reassure the public that independent investigation was ongoing in cases involving high-ranking executive officials.*

The constitutionality of the independent counsel was finally tested in Morrison v. Olson, *a case that arose out of an interbranch dispute between Congress and Reagan over access to Environmental Protection Agency and Department of Justice documents and a claim of executive privilege. Theodore Olson, a Department of Justice official who had encouraged Reagan to make the claim of executive privilege, was investigated by independent counsel Alexia Morrison for allegedly making false and misleading statements to Congress during its original investigation of EPA decision making. Olson challenged Morrison's authority to investigate, claiming that the independent counsel statute under which she operated violated the separation of powers. The Morrison decision was important for two reasons. First, the majority upholding the constitutionality of the statute diminished the ability of opponents to claim that the statute should fail for constitutional reasons. Opponents would have to fight it on another front. Second, its endorsement of* Humphrey's Executor v. United States *(1935) (Doc. 45) made clear that the Court's earlier decisions in* Bowsher *and* Chadha *did not signal its willingness to reexamine the modern administrative state and adopt the administration argument that the unitary executive required the president's control over all executive officers.*

CHIEF JUSTICE REHNQUIST delivered the opinion of the Court.

This case presents us with a challenge to the independent counsel provisions of the Ethics in Government Act of 1978. We hold today that these provisions of the Act do not violate the Appointments Clause of the Constitution or the limitations of Article III, nor do they impermissibly interfere with the President's authority under Article II in violation of the constitutional principle of separation of powers. . . .

. . . The initial question is, accordingly, whether appellant is an "inferior" or a "principal" officer. If she is the latter, as the Court of Appeals concluded, then the Act is in violation of the Appointments Clause.

The line between "inferior" and "principal" officers is one that is far from clear, and the Framers provided little guidance into where it should be drawn. We need not attempt here to decide exactly where the line falls between the two types of officers, because in our view appellant clearly falls on the "inferior officer" side of that line. . . .

This does not, however, end our inquiry under the Appointments Clause. Appellees argue that even if appellant is an "inferior" officer, the Clause does not empower Congress to place the power to appoint such an officer outside the Executive Branch. They contend that the Clause does not contemplate congressional authorization of "interbranch appointments," in which an officer of one branch is appointed by officers of another branch. The relevant language of the Appointments Clause is worth repeating. It reads: " . . . but the Congress may by Law vest the Appointment of such inferior Officers, as they think proper, in the President alone, in the courts of Law, or in the Heads of Departments." On its face, the language of this "excepting clause" admits of no limitation on interbranch appointments. Indeed, the inclusion of "as they think proper" seems clearly to give Congress significant discretion to determine whether it is "proper" to vest the appointment of, for example, executive officials in the "courts of Law." . . .

. . . Congress, of course, was concerned when it created the office of independent counsel with the conflicts of interest that could arise in situations when the Executive Branch is called upon to investigate its own high-ranking officers. If it were to remove the appointing authority from the Executive Branch, the most logical place to put it was in the Judicial Branch. In the light of the Act's provision making the judges of the Special Division ineligible to participate in any matters relating to an independent counsel they have appointed, we do not think that appointment of the independent counsel by the court runs afoul of the constitutional limitation on "incongruous" interbranch appointments.

Appellees next contend that the powers vested in the Special Division by the Act conflict with Article III of the Constitution. We have long recognized that by the express provision of Article III, the judicial power of the United States is limited to "Cases" and "Controversies." As a general rule, we have broadly stated that "executive or administrative duties of a nonjudicial nature may not be imposed on judges holding office under Art. III of the Constitution." The purpose of this limitation is to help ensure the independence of the Judicial Branch and to prevent the Judiciary from encroaching into areas reserved for the other branches. With this in mind, we address in turn the various duties given to the Special Division by the Act.

Most importantly, the Act vests in the Special Division the power to choose who will serve as independent counsel and the power to define his or her jurisdiction. Clearly, once it is accepted that the Appointments Clause gives Congress the power to vest the appointment of officials such as the independent counsel in the "courts of Law," there can be no Article III objection to the Special Division's exercise of that power, as the power itself derives from the Appointments Clause, a source of authority for judicial action that is independent of Article III. . . . In our view, Congress' power under the Clause to vest the "Appointment" of inferior officers in the courts may, in certain circumstances, allow Congress to give the courts some discretion in defining the nature and scope of the appointed official's authority. Particularly when, as here, Congress creates a temporary "office" the nature and duties of which will by necessity vary with the factual circumstances giving rise to the need for an appointment in the first place, it may vest the power to define the scope of the office in the court as an incident to the appointment of the officer pursuant to the Appointments Clause. This said, we do not think that Congress may give the Division unlimited discretion to determine the independent counsel's jurisdiction. In order for the Division's definition of the counsel's jurisdiction to be truly "incidental" to its power to appoint, the jurisdiction that the court decides upon must be demonstrably related to the factual circumstances that gave rise to the Attorney General's investigation and request for the appointment of the independent counsel in the particular case. . . .

Unlike both *Bowsher* and *Myers,* this case does not involve an attempt by Congress itself to gain a role in the removal of executive officials other than its established powers of impeachment and conviction. The Act instead puts the removal power squarely in the hands of the Executive Branch; an independent counsel may be removed from office, "only by the personal action of the Attorney General, and only for good cause." There is no requirement of congressional approval of the Attorney General's removal decision, though the decision is subject to judicial review. In our view, the removal provisions of the Act make this case more analogous to *Humphrey's Executor v. United States* (1935), and *Wiener v. United States* (1958), than to *Myers* or *Bowsher.* . . .

We undoubtedly did rely on the terms "quasi-legislative" and "quasi-judicial" to distinguish the officials involved in *Humphrey's Executor* and *Wiener* from those in *Myers,* but our present considered view is that the determination of whether the Constitution allows Congress to impose a "good cause"-type restriction on the President's power to remove an official cannot be made to turn on whether or not that official is classified as "purely executive." The analysis contained in our removal cases is designed not to define rigid categories of those officials who may or may not be removed at will by the President, but to ensure that Congress does not interfere with the President's exercise of the "executive power" and his constitutionally appointed duty to "take care that the laws be faithfully executed" under Article II. *Myers* was undoubtedly correct in its holding, and in its broader suggestion that there are some "purely executive" officials who must be removable by the President at will if he is to be able to accomplish his constitutional role. . . .

At the other end of the spectrum from *Myers,* the characterization of the agencies in *Humphrey's Executor* and *Wiener* as "quasi-legislative" or "quasi-judicial" in large part re-flected our judgment that it was not essential to the President's proper execution of his Article II powers that these agencies be headed up by individuals who were removable at will. We do not mean to suggest that an analysis of the functions served by the officials at issue is irrelevant. But the real question is whether the removal restrictions are of such a nature that they impede the President's ability to perform his constitutional duty, and the functions of the officials in question must be analyzed in that light.

Considering for the moment the "good cause" removal provision in isolation from the other parts of the Act at issue in this case, we cannot say that the imposition of a "good cause" standard for removal by itself unduly trammels on executive authority. There is no real dispute that the functions performed by the independent counsel are "executive" in the sense that they are law enforcement functions that typically have been undertaken by officials within the Executive Branch. As we noted . . . however, the independent counsel is an inferior officer under the Appointments Clause, with limited jurisdiction and tenure and lacking policymaking or significant administrative authority. Although the counsel exercises no small amount of discretion and judgment in deciding how to carry out his or her duties under the Act, we simply do not see how the President's need to control the exercise of that discretion is so central to the functioning of the Executive Branch as to require as a matter of constitutional law that the counsel be terminable at will by the President.

Nor do we think that the "good cause" removal provision at issue here impermissibly burdens the President's power to control or supervise the independent counsel, as an executive official, in the execution of his or her duties under the Act. This is not a case in which the power to remove an executive official has been completely stripped from the President, thus providing no means for the President to ensure the "faithful execution" of the laws. Rather, because the independent counsel may be terminated for "good cause," the Executive, through the Attorney General, retains ample authority to assure that the counsel is competently performing his or her statutory responsibilities in a manner that comports with the provisions of the Act. Although we need not decide in this case exactly what is encompassed within the term "good cause" under the Act, the legislative history of the removal provision also makes clear that the Attorney General may remove an independent counsel for "misconduct." Here, as with the provision of the Act conferring the appointment authority of the independent counsel on the special court, the congressional determination to limit the removal power of the Attorney General was essential, in the view of Congress, to establish the necessary independence of the office. We do not think that this limitation as it presently stands sufficiently deprives the President of control over the independent counsel to interfere impermissibly with his constitutional obligation to ensure the faithful execution of the laws.

The final question to be addressed is whether the Act, taken as a whole, violates the principle of separation of powers by unduly interfering with the role of the Executive Branch. Time and again we have reaffirmed the importance in our constitutional scheme of the separation of governmental powers into the three coordinate branches. . . . We have not hesitated to invalidate provisions of law which violate this principle. On the other hand, we have never held that the Constitution requires that the three branches of Government "operate with absolute independence." . . .

We observe first that this case does not involve an attempt by Congress to increase its own powers at the expense of the Executive Branch. Unlike some of our previous cases . . . this case simply does not pose a "dange[r] of congressional usurpation of Executive Branch functions." Indeed, with the exception of the power of impeachment—which applies to all officers of the United States—Congress retained for itself no powers of control or supervision over an independent counsel. The Act does empower certain Members of Congress to request the Attorney General to apply for the appointment of an independent counsel, but the Attorney General has no duty to comply with the request, although he must respond within a certain time limit. Other than that, Congress' role under the Act is limited to receiving reports or other information and oversight of the independent counsel's activities, functions that we have recognized generally as being incidental to the legislative function of Congress.

Similarly, we do not think that the Act works any judicial usurpation of properly executive functions. As should be apparent from our discussion of the Appointments Clause above, the power to appoint inferior officers such as independent counsel is not in itself an "executive" function in the constitutional sense, at least when Congress has exercised its power to vest the appointment of an inferior office in the "courts of Law." We note nonetheless that under the Act the Special Division has no power to appoint an independent counsel sua sponte; it may only do so upon the specific request of the Attorney General, and the courts are specifically prevented from reviewing the Attorney General's decision not to seek appointment. In addition, once the court has appointed a counsel and defined his or her jurisdiction, it has no power to supervise or control the activities of the counsel. As we pointed out in our discussion of the Special Division in relation to Article III, the various powers delegated by the statute to the Division are not supervisory or administrative, nor are they functions that the Constitution requires be performed by officials within the Executive Branch. The Act does give a federal court the power to review the Attorney General's decision to remove an independent counsel, but in our view this is a function that is well within the traditional power of the Judiciary.

Finally, we do not think that the Act "impermissibly undermine[s]" the powers of the Executive Branch, "disrupts the proper balance between the coordinate branches [by] prevent[ing] the Executive Branch from accomplishing its constitutionally assigned functions." It is undeniable that the Act reduces the amount of control or supervision that the Attorney General and, through him, the President exercises over the investigation and prosecution of a certain class of alleged criminal activity. The Attorney General is not allowed to appoint the individual of his choice; he does not determine the counsel's jurisdiction; and his power to remove a counsel is limited. Nonetheless, the Act does give the Attorney General several means of supervising or controlling the prosecutorial powers that may be wielded by an independent counsel. Most importantly, the Attorney General retains the power to remove the counsel for "good cause," a power that we have already concluded provides the Executive with substantial ability to ensure that the laws are "faithfully executed" by an independent counsel. No independent counsel may be appointed without a specific request by the Attorney General, and the Attorney General's decision not to request appointment if he finds "no reasonable grounds to believe that further investigation is warranted" is committed to his unreviewable discretion. The Act thus gives the Executive a degree of control over the power to initiate an investigation by the independent counsel. In addition, the jurisdiction of the independent counsel is defined with reference to the facts submitted by the Attorney General, and once a counsel is appointed, the Act requires that the counsel abide by Justice Department policy unless it is not "possible" to do so. Notwithstanding the fact that the counsel is to some degree "independent" and free from executive supervision to a greater extent than other federal prosecutors, in our view these features of the Act give the Executive Branch sufficient control over the independent counsel to ensure that the President is able to perform his constitutionally assigned duties. . . .

Reversed.

JUSTICE SCALIA, dissenting. . . .

The principle of separation of powers is expressed in our Constitution in the first section of each of the first three Articles. Article I, 1, provides that "[a]ll legislative Powers herein granted shall be vested in a Congress of the United States, which shall consist of a Senate and House of Representatives." Article III, 1, provides that "[t]he judicial Power of the United States, shall be vested in one supreme Court, and in such inferior Courts as the Congress may from time to time ordain and establish." And the provision at issue here provides that "[t]he executive Power shall be vested in a President of the United States of America." . . .

That is what this suit is about. Power. The allocation of power among Congress, the President, and the courts in such fashion as to preserve the equilibrium the Constitution sought to establish—so that "a gradual concentration of the several powers in the same department," can effectively be resisted. Frequently an issue of this sort will come before the Court clad, so to speak, in sheep's clothing: the potential of the asserted principle to effect important change in the equilibrium of power is not immediately evident, and must be discerned by a careful and perceptive analysis. . . .

. . . Where, as here, a request for appointment of an independent counsel has come from the Judiciary Committee of either House of Congress, the Attorney General must, if he decides not to seek appointment, explain to that Committee why.

Thus, by the application of this statute in the present case, Congress has effectively compelled a criminal investigation of a high-level appointee of the President in connection with his actions arising out of a bitter power dispute between the President and the Legislative Branch. Mr. Olson may or may not be guilty of a crime; we do not know. But we do know that the investigation of him has been commenced, not necessarily because the President or his authorized subordinates believe it is in the interest of the United States, in the sense that it warrants the diversion of resources from other efforts, and is worth the cost in money and in possible damage to other governmental interests; and not even, leaving aside those normally considered factors, because the President or his authorized subordinates necessarily believe that an investigation is likely to unearth a violation worth prosecuting; but only because the Attorney General cannot affirm, as Congress demands, that there are no reasonable grounds to believe that further investigation is warranted. The decisions regarding the scope of that further investigation, its duration, and, finally, whether or not prosecution should ensue, are likewise beyond the control of the President and his subordinates. . . .

To repeat, Article II, 1, cl. 1, of the Constitution provides:

"The executive Power shall be vested in a President of the United States."

As I described at the outset of this opinion, this does not mean some of the executive power, but all of the executive power. It seems to me, therefore, that the decision of the Court of Appeals invalidating the present statute must be upheld on fundamental separation-of-powers principles if the following two questions are answered affirmatively: (1) Is the conduct of a criminal prosecution (and of an investigation to decide whether to prosecute) the exercise of purely executive power? (2) Does the statute deprive the President of the United States of exclusive control over the exercise of that power? Surprising to say, the Court appears to concede an affirmative answer to both questions, but seeks to avoid the inevitable conclusion that since the statute vests some purely executive power in a person who is not the President of the United States it is void.

The Court concedes that "[t]here is no real dispute that the functions performed by the independent counsel are 'executive'," though it qualifies that concession by adding "in the sense that they are law enforcement functions that typically have been undertaken by officials within the Executive Branch." The qualifier adds nothing but atmosphere. In what other sense can one identify "the executive Power" that is supposed to be vested in the President (unless it includes

everything the Executive Branch is given to do) except by reference to what has always and everywhere—if conducted by government at all—been conducted never by the legislature, never by the courts, and always by the executive. There is no possible doubt that the independent counsel's functions fit this description. She is vested with the "full power and independent authority to exercise all investigative and prosecutorial functions and powers of the Department of Justice [and] the Attorney General." Governmental investigation and prosecution of crimes is a quintessentially executive function.

As for the second question, whether the statute before us deprives the President of exclusive control over that quintessentially executive activity: The Court does not, and could not possibly, assert that it does not. That is indeed the whole object of the statute. Instead, the Court points out that the President, through his Attorney General, has at least some control. That concession is alone enough to invalidate the statute, but I cannot refrain from pointing out that the Court greatly exaggerates the extent of that "some" Presidential control. "Most importan[t]" among these controls, the Court asserts, is the Attorney General's "power to remove the counsel for 'good cause.'" This is somewhat like referring to shackles as an effective means of locomotion. As we recognized in *Humphrey's Executor v. United States*—indeed, what *Humphrey's Executor* was all about—limiting removal power to "good cause" is an impediment to, not an effective grant of, Presidential control. We said that limitation was necessary with respect to members of the Federal Trade Commission, which we found to be "an agency of the legislative and judicial departments," and "wholly disconnected from the executive department," because "it is quite evident that one who holds his office only during the pleasure of another, cannot be depended upon to maintain an attitude of independence against the latter's will." What we in *Humphrey's Executor* found to be a means of eliminating Presidential control, the Court today considers the "most important[t]" means of assuring Presidential control. Congress, of course, operated under no such illusion when it enacted this statute, describing the "good cause" limitation as "protecting the independent counsel's ability to act independently of the President's direct control" since it permits removal only for "misconduct." . . .

As I have said, however, it is ultimately irrelevant how much the statute reduces Presidential control. The case is over when the Court acknowledges, as it must, that "[i]t is undeniable that the Act reduces the amount of control or supervision that the Attorney General and, through him, the President exercises over the investigation and prosecution of a certain class of alleged criminal activity." It effects a revolution in our constitutional jurisprudence for the Court, once it has determined that (1) purely executive functions are at issue here, and (2) those functions have been given to a person whose actions are not fully within the supervision and control of the President, nonetheless to proceed further to sit in judgment of whether "the President's need to control the exercise of [the independent counsel's] discretion is so central to the functioning of the Executive Branch" as to require complete control, whether the conferral of his powers upon someone else "sufficiently deprives the President of control over the independent counsel to interfere impermissibly with [his] constitutional obligation to ensure the faithful execution of the laws," and whether "the Act give[s] the Executive Branch sufficient control over the independent counsel to ensure that the President is able to perform his constitutionally assigned duties." It is not for us to determine, and we have never presumed to determine, how much of the purely executive powers of government must be within the full control of the President. The Constitution prescribes that they all are. . . .

Is it unthinkable that the President should have such exclusive power, even when alleged crimes by him or his close associates are at issue? No more so than that Congress should have the exclusive power of legislation, even when what is at issue is its own exemption from the burdens of certain laws. No more so than that this Court should have the exclusive power to pronounce the final decision on justiciable cases and controversies, even those pertaining to the constitutionality of a statute reducing the salaries of the Justices. A system of separate and coordinate powers necessarily involves an acceptance of exclusive power that can theoretically be abused. . . . While the separation of powers may prevent us from righting every wrong, it does so in order to ensure that we do not lose liberty. The checks against any branch's abuse of its exclusive powers are twofold: First, retaliation by one of the other branch's use of its exclusive powers: Congress, for example, can impeach the executive who willfully fails to enforce the laws; the executive can decline to prosecute under unconstitutional statutes; and the courts can dismiss malicious prosecutions. Second, and ultimately, there is the political check that the people will replace those in the political branches (the branches more "dangerous to the political rights of the Constitution") who are guilty of abuse. Political pressures produced special prosecutors—for Teapot Dome and for Watergate, for example—long before this statute created the independent counsel.

The Court has, nonetheless, replaced the clear constitutional prescription that the executive power belongs to the President with a "balancing test." What are the standards to determine how the balance is to be struck, that is, how much removal of Presidential power is too much? Many countries of the world get along with an executive that is much weaker than ours—in fact, entirely dependent upon the continued support of the legislature. Once we depart from the text of the Constitution, just where short of that do we stop? The most amazing feature of the Court's opinion is that it does not even purport to give an answer. It simply announces, with no analysis, that the ability to control the decision whether to investigate and prosecute the President's closest advisers, and indeed the President himself, is not "so central to the functioning of the Executive Branch" as to be constitutionally required to be within the President's control. . . .

In my view, moreover, even as an ad hoc, standardless judgment the Court's conclusion must be wrong. Before this statute was passed, the President, in taking action disagreeable to the Congress, or an executive officer giving advice to the President or testifying before Congress concerning one of those many matters on which the two branches are from time to time at odds, could be assured that his acts and motives would be adjudged—insofar as the decision whether to conduct a criminal investigation and to prosecute is concerned—in the Executive Branch, that is, in a forum attuned to the interests and the policies of the Presidency. That was one of the natural advantages the Constitution gave to the Presidency, just as it gave members of Congress (and their staffs) the advantage of not being prosecutable for anything said or done in their legislative capacities. It is the very object of this legislation to eliminate that assurance of a sympathetic forum. Unless it can honestly be said that there are "no reasonable grounds to believe" that further investigation is warranted, further investigation must ensure; and the conduct of the investigation, and determination of whether to prosecute, will be given to a person neither selected by nor subject to the control of the President—who will in turn assemble a staff by finding out, presumably, who is willing to put aside whatever else they are doing, for an indeterminate period of time, in order to investigate and prosecute the President or a particular named individual in his administration. The prospect is frightening (as I will discuss at some greater length at the conclusion of this opinion) even outside the context of a bitter, inter-branch political dispute. Perhaps the boldness of the President himself will not be affected—though I am not even sure of that. (How much easier it is for Congress, instead of accepting the political damage attendant to the commencement of im-

peachment proceedings against the President on trivial grounds—or, for that matter, how easy it is for one of the President's political foes outside of Congress—simply to trigger a debilitating criminal investigation of the Chief Executive under this law.) But as for the President's high-level assistants, who typically have no political base of support, it is as utterly unrealistic to think that they will not be intimidated by this prospect, and that their advice to him and their advocacy of his interests before a hostile Congress will not be affected, as it would be to think that the Members of Congress and their staffs would be unaffected by replacing the Speech or Debate Clause with a similar provision. It deeply wounds the President, by substantially reducing the President's ability to protect himself and his staff. That is the whole object of the law, of course, and I cannot imagine why the Court believes it does not succeed.

Besides weakening the Presidency by reducing the zeal of his staff, it must also be obvious that the institution of the independent counsel enfeebles him more directly in his constant confrontations with Congress, by eroding his public support. Nothing is so politically effective as the ability to charge that one's opponent and his associates are not merely wrongheaded, naive, ineffective, but, in all probability, "crooks." And nothing so effectively gives an appearance of validity to such charges as a Justice Department investigation and, even better, prosecution. The present statute provides ample means for that sort of attack, assuring that massive and lengthy investigations will occur, not merely when the Justice Department in the application of its usual standards believes they are called for, but whenever it cannot be said that there are "no reasonable grounds to believe" they are called for. The statute's highly visible procedures assure, moreover, that unlike most investigations these will be widely known and prominently displayed. . . .

In sum, this statute does deprive the President of substantial control over the prosecutory functions performed by the independent counsel, and it does substantially affect the balance of powers.

That the Court could possibly conclude otherwise demonstrates both the wisdom of our former constitutional system, in which the degree of reduced control and political impairment were irrelevant, since all purely executive power had to be in the President; and the folly of the new system of standardless judicial allocation of powers we adopt today. . . .

The purpose of the separation and equilibration of powers in general, and of the unitary Executive in particular, was not merely to assure effective government but to preserve individual freedom. Those who hold or have held offices covered by the Ethics in Government Act are entitled to that protection as much as the rest of us, and I conclude my discussion by considering the effect of the Act upon the fairness of the process they receive. . . .

Under our system of government, the primary check against prosecutorial abuse is a political one. The prosecutors who exercise this awesome discretion are selected and can be removed by a President, whom the people have trusted enough to elect. Moreover, when crimes are not investigated and prosecuted fairly, nonselectively, with a reasonable sense of proportion, the President pays the cost in political damage to his administration. If federal prosecutors "pick people that [they] thin[k] [they] should get, rather than cases that need to be prosecuted," if they amass many more resources against a particular prominent individual, or against a particular class of political protesters, or against members of a particular political party, than the gravity of the alleged offenses or the record of successful prosecutions seems to warrant, the unfairness will come home to roost in the Oval Office. I leave it to the reader to recall the examples of this in recent years. That result, of course, was precisely what the Founders had in mind when they provided that all executive powers would be exercised by a single Chief Executive. . . . The President is directly dependent on the people, and since there is only one President, he is responsible. The people know whom to blame, whereas "one of the weightiest objections to a plurality in the executive . . . is that it tends to conceal faults and destroy responsibility." . . .

. . . How frightening it must be to have your own independent counsel and staff appointed, with nothing else to do but to investigate you until investigation is no longer worthwhile—with whether it is worthwhile not depending upon what such judgments usually hinge on, competing responsibilities. And to have that counsel and staff decide, with no basis for comparison, whether what you have done is bad enough, willful enough, and provable enough, to warrant an indictment. How admirable the constitutional system that provides the means to avoid such a distortion. And how unfortunate the judicial decision that has permitted it. . . .

Source: 487 U.S. 654 (1988). For additional information on independent counsels and special prosecutors, see Katy J. Harriger, *The Special Prosecutor in American Politics,* 2d rev. ed. (Lawrence: University Press of Kansas, 2000).

Document 54   *United States v. Lopez* (1995)

The Supreme Court's expansive view of the commerce powers of Congress and its deference to judgments made under that authority prevailed until the 1990s. As the Court's make-up changed with the appointments made by President Ronald Reagan, so too did its jurisprudence with regard to federalism. The Court became more suspicious of Congress's actions and less willing to defer to the legislative branch on matters that appeared to overstep the bounds of national power and intrude on state sovereignty. In United States v. Lopez, the Court did not overturn any past precedent, but instead insisted that there must be limits on the commerce power. In striking down the Gun-Free School Zones Act of 1990, the Court argued that the relationship between guns in schools and commerce was so tenuous as to be unjustified under the commerce power. The significance of the decision is not yet known, but it clearly marks the end of the great deference the Court had given Congress in this area after the constitutional crisis of 1937. The multiplicity of opinions demonstrate, however, that there is no clear consensus about where the Court should go from here. Justice Clarence Thomas wants to return to a pre-1937 understanding of the clause, while Justices Sandra Day O'Connor and Anthony Kennedy caution against such a move. In fact, Justice David Souter in his dissent warns that the Court, in abandoning this deferential stance, may be putting itself into the position of the pre-1937 Court and with similar disastrous results for the institution.

CHIEF JUSTICE REHNQUIST delivered the opinion of the Court.

In the Gun-Free School Zones Act of 1990, Congress made it a federal offense "for any individual knowingly to possess a firearm at a place that the individual knows, or has reasonable cause to believe, is a school zone." The Act neither regulates a commercial activity nor contains a requirement that the possession be connected in any way to interstate commerce. We hold that the Act exceeds the authority of Congress "[t]o regulate Commerce . . . among the several States. . . . "

On March 10, 1992, respondent, who was then a 12th-grade student, arrived at Edison High School in San Antonio, Texas, carrying a concealed .38 caliber handgun and five bullets. Acting upon an anonymous tip, school authorities confronted respondent, who admitted that he was carrying the weapon. He was arrested and charged under Texas law with firearm pos-

session on school premises. The next day, the state charges were dismissed after federal agents charged respondent by complaint with violating the Gun-Free School Zones Act of 1990. . . .

Section 922(q) is a criminal statute that by its terms has nothing to do with "commerce" or any sort of economic enterprise, however broadly one might define those terms. Section 922(q) is not an essential part of a larger regulation of economic activity, in which the regulatory scheme could be undercut unless the intrastate activity were regulated. It cannot, therefore, be sustained under our cases upholding regulations of activities that arise out of or are connected with a commercial transaction, which viewed in the aggregate, substantially affects interstate commerce. . . .

The Government's essential contention . . . is that we may determine here that 922(q) is valid because possession of a firearm in a local school zone does indeed substantially affect interstate commerce. The Government argues that possession of a firearm in a school zone may result in violent crime and that violent crime can be expected to affect the functioning of the national economy in two ways. First, the costs of violent crime are substantial, and, through the mechanism of insurance, those costs are spread throughout the population. Second, violent crime reduces the willingness of individuals to travel to areas within the country that are perceived to be unsafe. The Government also argues that the presence of guns in schools poses a substantial threat to the educational process by threatening the learning environment. A handicapped educational process, in turn, will result in a less productive citizenry. That, in turn, would have an adverse effect on the Nation's economic well-being. As a result, the Government argues that Congress could rationally have concluded that 922(q) substantially affects interstate commerce.

We pause to consider the implications of the Government's arguments. The Government admits, under its "costs of crime" reasoning, that Congress could regulate not only all violent crime, but all activities that might lead to violent crime, regardless of how tenuously they relate to interstate commerce. Similarly, under the Government's "national productivity" reasoning, Congress could regulate any activity that it found was related to the economic productivity of individual citizens: family law (including marriage, divorce, and child custody), for example. Under the theories that the Government presents in support of 922(q), it is difficult to perceive any limitation on federal power, even in areas such as criminal law enforcement or education where States historically have been sovereign. Thus, if we were to accept the Government's arguments, we are hard-pressed to posit any activity by an individual that Congress is without power to regulate. . . .

To uphold the Government's contentions here, we would have to pile inference upon inference in a manner that would bid fair to convert congressional authority under the Commerce Clause to a general police power of the sort retained by the States. Admittedly, some of our prior cases have taken long steps down that road, giving great deference to congressional action. The broad language in these opinions has suggested the possibility of additional expansion, but we decline here to proceed any further. To do so would require us to conclude that the Constitution's enumeration of powers does not presuppose something not enumerated, and that there never will be a distinction between what is truly national and what is truly local. This we are unwilling to do.

For the foregoing reasons the judgment of the Court of Appeals is

Affirmed.

JUSTICE KENNEDY, with whom JUSTICE O'CONNOR joins, concurring. . . .

. . . Stare decisis operates with great force in counseling us not to call in question the essential principles now in place respecting the congressional power to regulate transactions of a commercial nature. That fundamental restraint on our power forecloses us from reverting to an understanding of commerce that would serve only an 18th-century economy, dependent then upon production and trading practices that had changed but little over the preceding centuries; it also mandates against returning to the time when congressional authority to regulate undoubted commercial activities was limited by a judicial determination that those matters had an insufficient connection to an interstate system. Congress can regulate in the commercial sphere on the assumption that we have a single market and a unified purpose to build a stable national economy. . . .

It does not follow, however, that in every instance the Court lacks the authority and responsibility to review congressional attempts to alter the federal balance. This case requires us to consider our place in the design of the Government and to appreciate the significance of federalism in the whole structure of the Constitution.

Of the various structural elements in the Constitution, separation of powers, checks and balances, judicial review, and federalism, only concerning the last does there seem to be much uncertainty respecting the existence, and the content, of standards that allow the judiciary to play a significant role in maintaining the design contemplated by the Framers. Although the resolution of specific cases has proved difficult, we have derived from the Constitution workable standards to assist in preserving separation of powers and checks and balances. These standards are by now well accepted. Judicial review is also established beyond question, and though we may differ when applying its principles, its legitimacy is undoubted. Our role in preserving the federal balance seems more tenuous. . . .

The statute before us upsets the federal balance to a degree that renders it an unconstitutional assertion of the commerce power, and our intervention is required. As the Chief Justice explains, unlike the earlier cases to come before the Court here neither the actors nor their conduct have a commercial character, and neither the purposes nor the design of the statute have an evident commercial nexus. The statute makes the simple possession of a gun within 1,000 feet of the grounds of the school a criminal offense. In a sense any conduct in this interdependent world of ours has an ultimate commercial origin or consequence, but we have not yet said the commerce power may reach so far. If Congress attempts that extension, then at the least we must inquire whether the exercise of national power seeks to intrude upon an area of traditional state concern. . . .

JUSTICE STEVENS, dissenting. . . .

Guns are both articles of commerce and articles that can be used to restrain commerce. Their possession is the consequence, either directly or indirectly, of commercial activity. In my judgment, Congress' power to regulate commerce in firearms includes the power to prohibit possession of guns at any location because of their potentially harmful use; it necessarily follows that Congress may also prohibit their possession in particular markets. The market for the possession of handguns by school-age children is, distressingly, substantial. Whether or not the national interest in eliminating that market would have justified federal legislation in 1789, it surely does today.

JUSTICE SOUTER, dissenting.

In reviewing congressional legislation under the Commerce Clause, we defer to what is often a merely implicit congressional judgment that its regulation addresses a subject substantially affecting interstate commerce "if there is any rational basis for such a finding." If that congressional determination is within the realm of reason, "the only remaining question for judicial inquiry is whether 'the means chosen by Congress [are] reasonably adapted to the end permitted by the Constitution.' "

The practice of deferring to rationally based legislative judgments "is a paradigm of judicial restraint." In judicial review under the Commerce Clause, it reflects our respect for the institutional competence of the Congress on a subject expressly assigned to it by the Constitution and our appreciation of the legitimacy that comes from Congress's political accountability in dealing with matters open to a wide range of possible choices.

It was not ever thus, however, as even a brief overview of Commerce Clause history during the past century reminds us. The modern respect for the competence and primacy of Congress in matters affecting commerce developed only after one of this Court's most chastening experiences, when it perforce repudiated an earlier and untenably expansive conception of judicial review in derogation of congressional commerce power. . . .

Source: 514 U.S. 549 (1995).

Document 55   *Clinton v. Jones* (1997)

Paula Jones, a former Arkansas state employee, sued President Bill Clinton under federal and state law to recover damages for alleged "abhorrent" sexual advances he made toward her while he was governor of Arkansas. She claimed that her rejection of those advances led to punishment by her supervisors in the state job she held at the time. Clinton filed a motion to dismiss without prejudice, claiming that he was immune from such suits while serving as president. The district judge denied dismissal on immunity grounds, ruled that discovery could go forward, but ordered any trial stayed until after Clinton left office. The Eighth Circuit affirmed the denial of dismissal but reversed postponement of a trial as the "functional equivalent" of a grant of temporary immunity to which the petitioner was not constitutionally entitled. Although establishing a rule for all presidencies that they lack immunity from civil suits based on their private actions, the case's greatest significance rests elsewhere. It was Clinton's testimony in this case, in which he denied having a sexual relationship with a former White House intern, Monica Lewinsky, that led to the impeachment process in 1998 and 1999. When an investigation by a special prosecutor revealed that he had in fact had a relationship with Lewinsky, the stage was set for the House to charge him with "high crimes and misdemeanors" for his alleged perjury in the Jones *case and in the grand jury investigation by the special prosecutor (Doc. 24).*

JUSTICE STEVENS delivered the opinion of the Court.

This case raises a constitutional and a prudential question concerning the Office of the President of the United States. Respondent, a private citizen, seeks to recover damages from the current occupant of that office based on actions allegedly taken before his term began. The President submits that in all but the most exceptional cases the Constitution requires federal courts to defer such litigation until his term ends and that, in any event, respect for the office warrants such a stay. Despite the force of the arguments supporting the President's submissions, we conclude that they must be rejected. . . .

First, because the claim of immunity is asserted in a federal court and relies heavily on the doctrine of separation of powers that restrains each of the three branches of the Federal Government from encroaching on the domain of the other two, it is not necessary to consider or decide whether a comparable claim might succeed in a state tribunal. If this case were being heard in a state forum, instead of advancing a separation of powers argument, petitioner would presumably rely on federalism and comity concerns, as well as the interest in protecting federal officials from possible local prejudice that underlies the authority to remove certain cases brought against federal officers from a state to a federal court. Whether those concerns would present a more compelling case for immunity is a question that is not before us.

Second, our decision rejecting the immunity claim and allowing the case to proceed does not require us to confront the question whether a court may compel the attendance of the President at any specific time or place. We assume that the testimony of the President, both for discovery and for use at trial, may be taken at the White House at a time that will accommodate his busy schedule, and that, if a trial is held, there would be no necessity for the President to attend in person, though he could elect to do so.

Petitioner's principal submission—that "in all but the most exceptional cases," the Constitution affords the President temporary immunity from civil damages litigation arising out of events that occurred before he took office—cannot be sustained on the basis of precedent.

Only three sitting Presidents have been defendants in civil litigation involving their actions prior to taking office. Complaints against Theodore Roosevelt and Harry Truman had been dismissed before they took office; the dismissals were affirmed after their respective inaugurations. Two companion cases arising out of an automobile accident were filed against John F. Kennedy in 1960 during the Presidential campaign. After taking office, he unsuccessfully argued that his status as Commander in Chief gave him a right to a stay under the Soldiers' and Sailors' Civil Relief Act of 1940. . . . [N]one of those cases sheds any light on the constitutional issue before us. . . .

That rationale provided the principal basis for our holding that a former President of the United States was "entitled to absolute immunity from damages liability predicated on his official acts." Our central concern was to avoid rendering the President "unduly cautious in the discharge of his official duties."

This reasoning provides no support for an immunity for unofficial conduct. As we explained in Fitzgerald, "the sphere of protected action must be related closely to the immunity's justifying purposes." Because of the President's broad responsibilities, we recognized in that case an immunity from damages claims arising out of official acts extending to the "outer perimeter of his authority." But we have never suggested that the President, or any other official, has an immunity that extends beyond the scope of any action taken in an official capacity.

Moreover, when defining the scope of an immunity for acts clearly taken within an official capacity, we have applied a functional approach. "Frequently our decisions have held that an official's absolute immunity should extend only to acts in performance of particular functions of his office." Hence, for example, a judge's absolute immunity does not extend to actions performed in a purely administrative capacity. As our opinions have made clear, immunities are grounded in "the nature of the function performed, not the identity of the actor who performed it."

Petitioner's effort to construct an immunity from suit for unofficial acts grounded purely in the identity of his office is unsupported by precedent. . . .

Petitioner's strongest argument supporting his immunity claim is based on the text and structure of the Constitution. He does not contend that the occupant of the Office of the President is "above the law," in the sense that his conduct is entirely immune from judicial scrutiny. The President argues merely for a postponement of the judicial proceedings that will determine whether he violated any law. His argument is grounded in the character of the office that was created by Article II of the Constitution, and relies on separation of powers principles that have structured our constitutional arrangement since the founding.

As a starting premise, petitioner contends that he occupies a unique office with powers and responsibilities so vast and important that the public interest demands that he devote his undivided time and attention to his public duties. He submits that—given the nature of the office—the doctrine of separation of powers places limits on the authority of the Federal Judiciary to interfere with the Executive Branch that would be transgressed by allowing this action to proceed.

We have no dispute with the initial premise of the argument. . . . It does not follow, however, that separation of powers principles would be violated by allowing this action to proceed. The doctrine of separation of powers is concerned with the allocation of official power among the three co equal branches of our Government. The Framers "built into the tripartite Federal Government . . . a self executing safeguard against the encroachment or aggrandizement of one branch at the expense of the other." Thus, for example, the Congress may not exercise the judicial power to revise final judgments or the executive power to manage an airport. Similarly, the President may not exercise the legislative power to authorize the seizure of private property for public use. And, the judicial power to decide cases and controversies does not include the provision of purely advisory opinions to the Executive, or permit the federal courts to resolve nonjusticiable questions.

Of course the lines between the powers of the three branches are not always neatly defined. But in this case there is no suggestion that the Federal Judiciary is being asked to perform any function that might in some way be described as "executive." Respondent is merely asking the courts to exercise their core Article III jurisdiction to decide cases and controversies. Whatever the outcome of this case, there is no possibility that the decision will curtail the scope of the official powers of the Executive Branch. The litigation of questions that relate entirely to the unofficial conduct of the individual who happens to be the President poses no perceptible risk of misallocation of either judicial power or executive power.

Rather than arguing that the decision of the case will produce either an aggrandizement of judicial power or a narrowing of executive power, petitioner contends that—as a by product of an otherwise traditional exercise of judicial power—burdens will be placed on the President that will hamper the performance of his official duties. We have recognized that "[e]ven when a branch does not arrogate power to itself . . . the separation of powers doctrine requires that a branch not impair another in the performance of its constitutional duties." As a factual matter, petitioner contends that this particular case—as well as the potential additional litigation that an affirmance of the Court of Appeals judgment might spawn—may impose an unacceptable burden on the President's time and energy, and thereby impair the effective performance of his office.

. . . As for the case at hand, if properly managed by the District Court, it appears to us highly unlikely to occupy any substantial amount of petitioner's time.

Of greater significance, petitioner errs by presuming that interactions between the Judicial Branch and the Executive, even quite burdensome interactions, necessarily rise to the level of constitutionally forbidden impairment of the Executive's ability to perform its constitutionally mandated functions. . . . The fact that a federal court's exercise of its traditional Article III jurisdiction may significantly burden the time and attention of the Chief Executive is not sufficient to establish a violation of the Constitution. . . .

. . . [W]e have long held that when the President takes official action, the Court has the authority to determine whether he has acted within the law. Perhaps the most dramatic example of such a case is our holding that President Truman exceeded his constitutional authority when he issued an order directing the Secretary of Commerce to take possession of and operate most of the Nation's steel mills in order to avert a national catastrophe. Despite the serious impact of that decision on the ability of the Executive Branch to accomplish its assigned mission, and the substantial time that the President must necessarily have devoted to the matter as a result of judicial involvement, we exercised our Article III jurisdiction to decide whether his official conduct conformed to the law. Our holding was an application of the principle established in *Marbury v. Madison* (1803), that "[i]t is emphatically the province and duty of the judicial department to say what the law is."

. . . "[I]t is settled law that the separation of powers doctrine does not bar every exercise of jurisdiction over the President of the United States." If the Judiciary may severely burden the Executive Branch by reviewing the legality of the President's official conduct, and if it may direct appropriate process to the President himself, it must follow that the federal courts have power to determine the legality of his unofficial conduct. The burden on the President's time and energy that is a mere by product of such review surely cannot be considered as onerous as the direct burden imposed by judicial review and the occasional invalidation of his official actions. We therefore hold that the doctrine of separation of powers does not require federal courts to stay all private actions against the President until he leaves office.

The reasons for rejecting such a categorical rule apply as well to a rule that would require a stay "in all but the most exceptional cases." Indeed, if the Framers of the Constitution had thought it necessary to protect the President from the burdens of private litigation, we think it far more likely that they would have adopted a categorical rule than a rule that required the President to litigate the question whether a specific case belonged in the "exceptional case" subcategory. In all events, the question whether a specific case should receive exceptional treatment is more appropriately the subject of the exercise of judicial discretion than an interpretation of the Constitution. . . .

. . . We think the District Court may have given undue weight to the concern that a trial might generate unrelated civil actions that could conceivably hamper the President in conducting the duties of his office. If and when that should occur, the court's discretion would permit it to manage those actions in such fashion (including deferral of trial) that interference with the President's duties would not occur. But no such impingement upon the President's conduct of his office was shown here. . . .

Accordingly, the judgment of the Court of Appeals is affirmed.

Source: 520 U.S. 681 (1997).

Document 56   Clinton v. City of New York (1998)

The line-item veto is a device used in many state governments. It gives the governor the ability to veto particular lines in a budget bill without being required to reject the entire bill. Its proponents have long argued that the practice promotes fiscal responsibility because legislators cannot load a bill with "pork"—pet projects for their district—when they know individual budget lines can be eliminated. Without such a veto, the argument goes, legislators have incentives to pack a bill with pork because they know the executive is unlikely to veto the entire bill. In 1994, as part of its Contract With America, House Republicans promised to enact a line-item veto. They gained control of the House that year and eventually enacted a line-item bill in early 1996. President Bill Clinton, reelected in 1996, was the first president who had the opportunity to use it (Doc. 33). When he did, the veto was challenged by groups with grants that were eliminated.

The facts of the particular dispute are laid out in Clinton v. City of New York. *The significance of the decision was twofold. First, it made clear that the only way to instate a line-item veto is through constitutional amendment, a much more difficult and extended process than simply passing a bill. Second, it demonstrated that the Supreme Court's interest in separation of powers cases, which appeared to have increased in the 1980s and 1990s, was not necessarily biased in favor of the executive. Earlier decisions, such as* INS v. Chadha *(1983) and* Bowsher v. Synar *(1986) (Docs. 51 and 52, respectively) had appeared to favor the executive over the legislative. In* Clinton, *however, the Supreme Court stated that Congress could not pass off its essential lawmaking power in this manner, however expedient the arrangement might seem. (See also Doc. 22.)*

JUSTICE STEVENS delivered the opinion of the Court.

The Line Item Veto Act (Act), was enacted in April 1996 and became effective on January 1, 1997. . . . [T]he President exercised his authority to cancel one provision in the Balanced Budget Act of 1997 and two provisions in the Taxpayer Relief Act of 1997. Appellees, claiming that they had been injured by two of those cancellations, filed these cases in the District Court. That Court . . . held the statute invalid, and we again expedited our review. We now hold that these appellees have standing to challenge the constitutionality of the Act and, reaching the merits, we agree that the cancellation procedures set forth in the Act violate the Presentment Clause of the Constitution. . . .

Appellees filed two separate actions against the President and other federal officials challenging these two cancellations. The plaintiffs in the first case are the City of New York, two hospital associations, one hospital, and two unions representing health care employees. The plaintiffs in the second are a farmers' cooperative consisting of about 30 potato growers in Idaho and an individual farmer who is a member and officer of the cooperative. The District Court consolidated the two cases and determined that at least one of the plaintiffs in each had standing under Article III of the Constitution. . . .

The Line Item Veto Act gives the President the power to "cancel in whole" three types of provisions that have been signed into law: "(1) any dollar amount of discretionary budget authority; (2) any item of new direct spending; or (3) any limited tax benefit." It is undisputed that the New York case involves an "item of new direct spending" and that the Snake River case involves a "limited tax benefit" as those terms are defined in the Act. It is also undisputed that each of those provisions had been signed into law pursuant to Article I, § 7, of the Constitution before it was canceled.

The Act requires the President to adhere to precise procedures whenever he exercises his cancellation authority. In identifying items for cancellation he must consider the legislative history, the purposes, and other relevant information about the items. He must determine, with respect to each cancellation, that it will "(i) reduce the Federal budget deficit; (ii) not impair any essential Government functions; and (iii) not harm the national interest." Moreover, he must transmit a special message to Congress notifying it of each cancellation within five calendar days (excluding Sundays) after the enactment of the canceled provision. It is undisputed that the President meticulously followed these procedures in these cases.

A cancellation takes effect upon receipt by Congress of the special message from the President. If, however, a "disapproval bill" pertaining to a special message is enacted into law, the cancellations set forth in that message become "null and void." The Act sets forth a detailed expedited procedure for the consideration of a "disapproval bill," but no such bill was passed for either of the cancellations involved in these cases.

A majority vote of both Houses is sufficient to enact a disapproval bill. The Act does not grant the President the authority to cancel a disapproval bill, but he does, of course, retain his constitutional authority to veto such a bill.

The effect of a cancellation is plainly stated in § 691e, which defines the principal terms used in the Act. With respect to both an item of new direct spending and a limited tax benefit, the cancellation prevents the item "from having legal force or effect."

Thus, under the plain text of the statute, the two actions of the President that are challenged in these cases prevented one section of the Balanced Budget Act of 1997 and one section of the Taxpayer Relief Act of 1997 "from having legal force or effect." The remaining provisions of those statutes, with the exception of the second canceled item in the latter, continue to have the same force and effect as they had when signed into law.

In both legal and practical effect, the President has amended two Acts of Congress by repealing a portion of each. . . . There is no provision in the Constitution that authorizes the President to enact, to amend, or to repeal statutes. Both Article I and Article II assign responsibilities to the President that directly relate to the lawmaking process, but neither addresses the issue presented by these cases. The President "shall from time to time give to the Congress Information on the State of the Union, and recommend to their Consideration such Measures as he shall judge necessary and expedient. . . ." Thus, he may initiate and influence legislative proposals. Moreover, after a bill has passed both Houses of Congress, but "before it become[s] a Law," it must be presented to the President. If he approves it, "he shall sign it, but if not he shall return it, with his Objections to that House in which it shall have originated, who shall enter the Objections at large on their Journal, and proceed to reconsider it."

His "return" of a bill, which is usually described as a "veto," is subject to being overridden by a two-thirds vote in each House.

There are important differences between the President's "return" of a bill pursuant to Article I, §7, and the exercise of the President's cancellation authority pursuant to the Line Item Veto Act. The constitutional return takes place before the bill becomes law; the statutory cancellation occurs after the bill becomes law. The constitutional return is of the entire bill; the statutory cancellation is of only a part. Although the Constitution expressly authorizes the President to play a role in the process of enacting statutes, it is silent on the subject of unilateral Presidential action that either repeals or amends parts of duly enacted statutes.

There are powerful reasons for construing constitutional silence on this profoundly important issue as equivalent to an express prohibition. The procedures governing the enactment of statutes set forth in the text of Article I were the product of the great debates and compromises that produced the Constitution itself. Familiar historical materials provide abundant support for the conclusion that the power to enact statutes may only "be exercised in accord with a single, finely wrought and exhaustively considered, procedure." Our first President understood the text of the Presentment Clause as requiring that he either "approve all the parts of a Bill, or reject it in toto."

What has emerged in these cases from the President's exercise of his statutory cancellation powers, however, are truncated versions of two bills that passed both Houses of Congress. They are not the product of the "finely wrought" procedure that the Framers designed. . . .

The Line Item Veto Act authorizes the President himself to effect the repeal of laws, for his own policy reasons, without observing the procedures set out in Article I, §7. The fact that Congress intended such a result is of no moment. Although Congress presumably anticipated that the President might cancel some of the items in the Balanced Budget Act and in the Taxpayer Relief Act, Congress cannot alter the procedures set out in Article I, §7, without amending the Constitution.

Neither are we persuaded by the Government's contention that the President's authority to cancel new direct spending and tax benefit items is no greater than his traditional authority to decline to spend appropriated funds. The Government has reviewed in some detail the series of statutes in which Congress has given the Executive broad discretion over the expenditure of appropriated funds. In those statutes, as in later years, the President was given wide discretion with respect to both the amounts to be spent and how the money would be allocated among different functions. It is argued that the Line Item Veto Act merely confers comparable discretionary authority over the expenditure of appropriated funds. The critical difference between this statute and all of its predecessors, however, is that unlike any of them, this Act gives the President the unilateral power to change the text of duly enacted statutes. None of the Act's predecessors could even arguably have been construed to authorize such a change. . . .

If there is to be a new procedure in which the President will play a different role in determining the final text of what may "become a law," such change must come not by legislation but through the amendment procedures set forth in Article V of the Constitution.

The judgment of the District Court is affirmed.

JUSTICE KENNEDY, concurring. . . .

The principal object of the statute, it is true, was not to enhance the President's power to reward one group and punish another, to help one set of taxpayers and hurt another, to favor one State and ignore another. Yet these are its undeniable effects. The law establishes a new mechanism which gives the President the sole ability to hurt a group that is a visible target, in order to disfavor the group or to extract further concessions from Congress. The law is the functional equivalent of a line item veto and enhances the President's powers beyond what the Framers would have endorsed.

It is no answer, of course, to say that Congress surrendered its authority by its own hand; nor does it suffice to point out that a new statute, signed by the President or enacted over his veto, could restore to Congress the power it now seeks to relinquish. That a congressional cession of power is voluntary does not make it innocuous. The Constitution is a compact enduring for more than our time, and one Congress cannot yield up its own powers, much less those of other Congresses to follow. Abdication of responsibility is not part of the constitutional design.

Separation of powers helps to ensure the ability of each branch to be vigorous in asserting its proper authority. In this respect the device operates on a horizontal axis to secure a proper balance of legislative, executive, and judicial authority. Separation of powers operates on a vertical axis as well, between each branch and the citizens in whose interest powers must be exercised. The citizen has a vital interest in the regularity of the exercise of governmental power. If this point was not clear before *Chadha,* it should have been so afterwards. Though *Chadha* involved the deportation of a person, while the case before us involves the expenditure of money or the grant of a tax exemption, this circumstance does not mean that the vertical operation of the separation of powers is irrelevant here. By increasing the power of the President beyond what the Framers envisioned, the statute compromises the political liberty of our citizens, liberty which the separation of powers seeks to secure. . . .

JUSTICE SCALIA, with whom JUSTICE O'CONNOR joins, and with whom JUSTICE BREYER joins as to Part III, concurring in part and dissenting in part III. . . .

The Presentment Clause requires, in relevant part, that "[e]very Bill which shall have passed the House of Representatives and the Senate, shall, before it becomes a Law, be presented to the President of the United States; If he approve he shall sign it, but if not he shall return it." There is no question that enactment of the Balanced Budget Act complied with these requirements: the House and Senate passed the bill, and the President signed it into law. It was only after the requirements of the Presentment Clause had been satisfied that the President exercised his authority under the Line Item Veto Act to cancel the spending item. Thus, the Court's problem with the Act is not that it authorizes the President to veto parts of a bill and sign others into law, but rather that it authorizes him to "cancel"—prevent from "having legal force or effect"—certain parts of duly enacted statutes.

Article I, §7 of the Constitution obviously prevents the President from cancelling a law that Congress has not authorized him to cancel. Such action cannot possibly be considered part of his execution of the law, and if it is legislative action, as the Court observes, " 'repeal of statutes, no less than enactment, must conform with Art. I.' " But that is not this case. It was certainly arguable, as an original matter, that Art. I, §7 also prevents the President from cancelling a law which itself authorizes the President to cancel it. But as the Court acknowledges, that argument has long since been made and rejected. . . .

As much as the Court goes on about Art. I, §7, therefore, that provision does not demand the result the Court reaches. It no more categorically prohibits the Executive reduction of congressional dispositions in the course of implementing statutes that authorize such reduction, than it categorically prohibits the Executive augmentation of congressional dispositions in the course of implementing statutes that authorize such augmentation—generally known as substantive rulemaking. There are, to be sure, limits upon the former just as there are limits upon the latter—and I am prepared to acknowledge that the limits upon the former may be much more severe. Those limits are established, however, not by some categorical prohibition of Art. I, §7, which our cases conclusively disprove, but by what has come to be known as the doctrine of unconstitutional delegation of legislative authority: When authorized Executive reduction or augmentation is allowed to go too far, it usurps the nondelegable function of Congress and violates the separation of powers. It is this doctrine, and not the Presentment Clause, that was discussed in the *Field* opinion, and it is this doctrine, and not the Presentment Clause, that is the issue presented by the statute before us here. That is why the Court is correct to distinguish prior authorizations of Executive cancellation, such as the one involved in *Field,* on the ground that they were contingent upon an Executive finding of fact, and on the ground that they related to the field of foreign affairs, an area where the President has a special "degree of discretion and freedom." These distinctions have nothing to do with whether the details of Art. I, §7 have been complied with, but everything to do with whether the authorizations went too far by transferring to the Executive a degree of political, law-making power that our traditions demand be retained by the Legislative Branch.

I turn, then, to the crux of the matter: whether Congress's authorizing the President to cancel an item of spending gives him a power that our history and traditions show must reside exclusively in the Legislative Branch. I may note,

to begin with, that the Line Item Veto Act is not the first statute to authorize the President to "cancel" spending items. In *Bowsher v. Synar,* (1986), we addressed the constitutionality of the Balanced Budget and Emergency Deficit Control Act of 1985, which required the President, if the federal budget deficit exceeded a certain amount, to issue a "sequestration" order mandating spending reductions specified by the Comptroller General. The effect of sequestration was that "amounts sequestered . . . shall be permanently cancelled." We held that the Act was unconstitutional, not because it impermissibly gave the Executive legislative power, but because it gave the Comptroller General, an officer of the Legislative Branch over whom Congress retained removal power, "the ultimate authority to determine the budget cuts to be made," "functions . . . plainly entailing execution of the law in constitutional terms." The President's discretion under the Line Item Veto Act is certainly broader than the Comptroller General's discretion was under the 1985 Act, but it is no broader than the discretion traditionally granted the President in his execution of spending laws.

Insofar as the degree of political, "law-making" power conferred upon the Executive is concerned, there is not a dime's worth of difference between Congress's authorizing the President to cancel a spending item, and Congress's authorizing money to be spent on a particular item at the President's discretion. And the latter has been done since the Founding of the Nation. . . . From a very early date Congress also made permissive individual appropriations, leaving the decision whether to spend the money to the President's unfettered discretion. . . . Examples of appropriations committed to the discretion of the President abound in our history. . . . The constitutionality of such appropriations has never seriously been questioned. Rather, "[t]hat Congress has wide discretion in the matter of prescribing details of expenditures for which it appropriates must, of course, be plain. Appropriations and other acts of Congress are replete with instances of general appropriations of large amounts, to be allotted and expended as directed by designated government agencies." . . .

The short of the matter is this: Had the Line Item Veto Act authorized the President to "decline to spend" any item of spending contained in the Balanced Budget Act of 1997, there is not the slightest doubt that authorization would have been constitutional. What the Line Item Veto Act does instead—authorizing the President to "cancel" an item of spending—is technically different. But the technical difference does not relate to the technicalities of the Presentment Clause, which have been fully complied with;

and the doctrine of unconstitutional delegation, which is at issue here, is preeminently not a doctrine of technicalities. The title of the Line Item Veto Act, which was perhaps designed to simplify for public comprehension, or perhaps merely to comply with the terms of a campaign pledge, has succeeded in faking out the Supreme Court. The President's action it authorizes in fact is not a line-item veto and thus does not offend Art. I, §7; and insofar as the substance of that action is concerned, it is no different from what Congress has permitted the President to do since the formation of the Union. . . .

Source: 524 U.S. 417 (1998).

List of Cases

The following cases are cited in the chapter text, notes, and document section. An asterisk follows those that are reproduced as documents. See the index for their page numbers and cases referenced in the chapters.

Abrams v. United States, 250 U.S. 616 (1919)

Adair v. United States, 208 U.S. 161 (1908)

A. L. A. Schechter Poultry Corp. v. United States, 295 U.S. 495 (1935)*

Alden v. Maine, 527 U.S. 706 (1999)

American International Group v. Islamic Republic of Iran, 657 F. 2d 430 (D.C. Cir. 1981)

American Power and Light Co. v. SEC, 329 U.S. 90 (1946)

American Trucking Associations, Inc. v. EPA, 175 F. 3d 1027 (D.C. Cir. 1999)

Ashcroft v. Free Speech Coalition, 535 U.S. 234 (2002)

Ashton v. Cameron County Water Improvement District, 298 U.S. 513 (1936)

Atkins v. Virginia, 536 U.S. 304 (2002)

Bailey v. Drexel Furniture Co., 259 U.S. 20 (1922)

Baker v. Carr, 369 U.S. 186 (1962)

Barenblatt v. United States, 360 U.S. 109 (1959)

Bas v. Tingy, 4 Dallas (4 U.S.) 37 (1800)

Board of Trustees of University of Alabama v. Garrett, 531 U.S. 356 (2001)

Bowers v. Hardwick, 478 U.S. 186 (1986)

Bowsher v. Synar, 478 U.S. 717 (1986)*

Brown v. Allen, 344 U.S. 443 (1953)

Brown v. Board of Education, 347 U.S. 483 (1954)

Buckley v. Valeo, 424 U.S. 1 (1976)

Burke v. Barnes, 479 U.S. 361 (1987)

Bush v. Gore, 531 U.S. 98 (2000)

Carpenter v. Dane, 9 Wis. 249 (1859)

Carter v. Carter Coal Co., 298 U.S. 238 (1936)

Chevron U.S.A. Inc. v. Natural Resources Defense Council, Inc., 467 U.S. 837 (1984)

Cincinnati, New Orleans and Texas Pacific Railway Co. v. ICC, 162 U.S. 184 (1896)

City of Boerne v. Flores, 521 U.S. 507 (1997)

Civil Rights Cases, 109 U.S. 3 (1883)

Clinton v. City of New York, 524 U.S. 417 (1998)*

Clinton v. Jones, 520 U.S. 681 (1997)*

Cohens v. Virginia, 6 Wheat. (19 U.S.) 264 (1821)

College Savings Bank v. Florida Prepaid Postsecondary Education Expense Board, 527 U.S. 666 (1999)

Cooper v. Aaron, 358 U.S. 1 (1958)

Crockett v. Reagan, 558 F. Supp. 893 (D.D.C. 1982)

Debs v. United States, 249 U.S. 211 (1919)

Dellums v. Bush, 752 F. Supp. 1141 (D.D.C. 1990)

Dred Scott v. Sandford, 19 How. (60 U.S.) 383 (1857)

Duncan v. Kahanamoku, 327 U.S. 304 (1946)

Eastland v. United States Servicemen's Fund, 421 U.S. 491 (1975)

Index

Italic numbers indicate pages in the document section.